The Samuel Gompers Papers

THE
Samuel Gompers
PAPERS

VOLUME
9
The American Federation of Labor
at the Height of Progressivism, 1913–17

Editors
Peter J. Albert
Grace Palladino

Assistant Editors
Marla J. Hughes
Mary C. Jeske

UNIVERSITY OF ILLINOIS PRESS
Urbana and Chicago

A portion of the publication costs of this book was provided by
the National Historical Publications and Records Commission.

*The paper in this book meets the guidelines for permanence
and durability of the Committee on Production Guidelines for
Book Longevity of the Council on Library Resources.* ∞

Library of Congress Cataloging-in-Publication Data

The Samuel Gompers Papers

Includes bibliographies and indexes.
Contents: v. 1. The making of a union leader, 1850–86 —
v. 2. The early years of the American Federation of Labor, 1887–90 —
v. 3. Unrest and depression, 1891–94 — v. 4. A national labor movement
takes shape, 1895–98 — v. 5. An expanding movement at the turn of
the century, 1898–1902 — v. 6. The American Federation of Labor and
the rise of progressivism, 1902–6 — v. 7. The American Federation of
Labor under siege, 1906–9 — v. 8. Progress and reaction in the age of
reform, 1909–13 — v. 9. The American Federation of Labor at the height
of progressivism, 1913–17.
    1. Gompers, Samuel, 1850–1924—Archives. 2. Trade-unions—
United States—History—Sources. 3. Labor movement—United States—
History—Sources. I. Gompers, Samuel, 1850–1924.
HD6508.S218   2003   331.88'32'902   84-2469
ISBN 0-252-01138-4 (alk. paper : set)
ISBN 0-252-02755-8 (alk. paper : v. 9)

CONTENTS

INTRODUCTION

"The trade unions of America reached their highest development during the year 1913," Samuel Gompers announced in his annual report to the International Federation of Trade Unions. With two million members and the means to promote organizing and legislative campaigns, the American Federation of Labor was on the rise, exerting real influence, as Gompers put it, "in every sphere where human activity and human betterment can be obtained." Trade unionists were speaking out in government councils, educational forums, and federal courts, and their practical vision of industrial democracy was gaining support. Progressive politicians, reformers, and even some employers now echoed the AFL's call for unionization and trade agreements. Its influence was beginning to shape federal policy, too: William B. Wilson, a former union miner, served as the nation's first secretary of labor, and three AFL-approved trade unionists, Austin B. Garretson, John B. Lennon, and James O'Connell, represented labor on the newly organized U.S. Commission on Industrial Relations. Publicly acknowledging the value of the AFL's leadership—and its support—in industrial and labor affairs, President Woodrow Wilson not only met with the Executive Council during his administration but in the summer of 1916 delivered the main address at dedication ceremonies for the AFL's new headquarters.[1]

"It was not always thus," Gompers frankly admitted. "There was a time . . . when the doors of 'decent homes' were often shut in the faces of the men who dared think and dream and act and hope for the organization of the working people." As proud as he was of this "marvelous change," though, and the opportunities it offered, he was by no means satisfied. Respectability and acceptance were means, not ends, and as long as federal, state, and local judges continued to interfere with workers' rights to free speech, free press, and free assembly, the AFL would press on. The object was to attain "complete social justice," Gompers insisted, and that depended on economic strength and aggressive unionism, not political connections and persuasive testimony. "We, the workers, have never succeeded in obtaining any redress . . . by assuming a submissive attitude," the AFL Executive Council maintained in 1915. "We who have participated in the struggles of the labor movement during the last third of a century, know that only to the strong, well disciplined, well financed organization has success accrued."[2]

Charting the AFL's ongoing fight for social and economic power, this volume of the *Samuel Gompers Papers* covers the period from September 1913 through January 1917—a volatile time marked by economic uncertainty and industrial conflict, revolutionary upheavals in Mexico and cataclysmic war in Europe. For the AFL it was an era of significant growth and legislative triumphs: The Federation launched a wide-ranging campaign to organize women workers, expanded the Labor Forward Movement to organize the unorganized, tested new methods of reaching unskilled workers, and welcomed the American Federation of Teachers into the fold. During these years it also supported organizing efforts in Cuba, Mexico, and Puerto Rico and began the process of forming a Pan-American labor federation.[3] At the same time the AFL mounted an intensive legislative campaign that led to passage of the Clayton Antitrust Act in 1914, which declared that "the labor of a human being is not a commodity or article of commerce," and in 1915 the Seamen's Act, which "for the first time in the history of the world," as Gompers put it, "made the sailor a free man."[4] Other federal legislation included a child labor law, a workers' compensation law for federal employees, and an eight-hour law for railroad workers.

But AFL affiliates also suffered dramatic defeats during this period that not only checked the Federation's growth but aggravated tensions within the labor movement. In the course of the 1913–14 Calumet strike in northern Michigan, for instance, more than a thousand metal miners were arrested—and Western Federation of Miners president Charles Moyer was shot and run out of town—before the strike was lost. During the equally unsuccessful 1913–14 miners' strike in Colorado, strikers and their families at Ludlow were savagely attacked for refusing to return to work on their employers' terms.

Unfavorable judicial decisions compounded the impact of these losses. The U.S. Supreme Court continued to uphold the legality of anti-union "yellow dog" contracts, for example, and federal and state courts began to chip away at the Clayton Act's provisions limiting the use of injunctions.[5] While these defeats never altered Gompers' belief that the Clayton Act was a great victory, they led his opponents to condemn Federation leaders as "wormeaten fossilized booze fighters" and triggered a vigorous debate on alternative strategies such as industrial unionism, centralized strike funds, eight-hour legislation for non-government workers, and minimum wage laws for men as well as women.[6]

Gompers' leadership was tested during these years, especially as intellectuals, social reformers, and some employees of the Commission on Industrial Relations (and its privately funded successor, the Committee on Industrial Relations) championed new organizations, such as the Amalgamated Clothing Workers of America, or supported calls for government regulation of labor standards.[7] Frequently sparring with opponents such as Victor Berger, Adolph Germer, Morris Hillquit, Duncan McDonald, and Ellen Gates Starr, Gompers honed a theory of trade union self-help and solidarity that, he contended, was central to achieving working-class liberty on working-class terms. In the case of the Amalgamated, for instance, he believed that it was more valuable for disaffected unionists to fight for their beliefs on the convention floor than to drop out and form rival unions. In the case of government regulations, he urged wage earners to take responsibility for themselves: "Our movement has not asked and will not ask at the hands of government anything which the workers can and should do for themselves," Gompers reminded readers of the *American Federationist* in 1915. "The movement of labor is founded upon the principle that that which we do for ourselves, individually and collectively, is done best."[8] In Gompers' opinion, government protection only fostered a dangerous spirit of paternalism and dependence. On the other hand, the process of identifying interests and then fighting for rights promoted an "invaluable spirit of independence and self-responsibility . . . that really makes for progress and betterment."[9] "This is the spirit that has made the American labor movement the most aggressive labor organization in the world," Gompers wrote. "Unless the working people are organized to express their desires and needs, and organized to express their will, any other method tends to weaken initiative."[10]

Gompers and the AFL never underestimated the critical value of political power and support. But it was one thing to seek legislation protecting labor's right to organize and quite another to cede control of industrial relations to others, sympathetic or not. Gompers was willing to cooperate with outside agencies when it came to investigations and hearings, for instance, but he brooked no interference, "expert" or otherwise, on trade union matters. "Human betterment is not something that can be imposed from the outside or from above," he argued. "Industrial welfare and human development cannot be worked out like mathematical problems or settled by theories or academic demonstrations."[11] Consequently when the National Civic Federation sought his support for a congressional investigation of minimum wage legislation, he turned them down flat. "The workers will not delegate to any outsiders control over the labor movement," Gompers told Ralph Easley, "or the right to dictate terms and conditions of employment."[12]

Gompers' unshakable confidence in trade unionism may have angered his opponents, but it also helped elevate him to a position of trust both within and outside the movement. During these years he emerged as organized labor's national—and in some cases international—spokesman. If he took pride in this hard-won recognition, he also put it to good use: When Mexico's organized workers sought to present a case against American intervention to Woodrow Wilson, for instance, they turned to Gompers for help.[13] Throughout this period his considerable influence with—and access to—the Wilson administration also allowed him to raise a variety of important issues. "In my experience with United States Congresses of two score years I have not seen anything like the fine spirit toward labor . . . pervading all the branches of the Wilson administration," he wrote in 1916. It was evidence, he believed, of the administration's recognition "that labor should be made part of the national councils; that its patriotism should be conceded, and that its knowledge of its own needs should give it paramount voice in legislation directly and peculiarly affecting its own rights."[14]

The years of constant work and travel were beginning to catch up with Gompers, who was sixty-seven years old and a great grandfather by 1917. Still, his schedule was as busy as ever: In 1914 he completed an exhausting speaking tour of Puerto Rico, and in 1915 he not only learned how to drive but took on the responsibility of overseeing construction of the AFL's new headquarters building in downtown Washington, D.C. After war broke out in Europe in 1914, Gompers devoted more time to correspondence with international labor leaders, learning firsthand about the impact of war on wage earners and their families and advocating a world labor congress in conjunction with the peace conference at the war's end.

By January 1917 it had grown increasingly difficult to predict when the end of the war might come, and the threat of American involvement in the conflict became ever more real. Gompers took this turn of events quite seriously. He had lost a nephew in 1915 during military maneuvers in Haiti, and he was well aware that his grandsons were old enough to serve should the United States join the fight. Yet as he watched the internationalism of the working class give way to the intense nationalisms of the countries engaged in the war, and as he became suspicious of foreign influences that were allegedly encouraging labor conflict in some American cities, he lost his pacifist faith.[15] "I am not warlike—I am opposed to war," he told his good friend James Duncan in 1915, "but I believe it is the duty of the American people, the American democracy, to make it clear to the world that we shall, under all circumstances, be able to defend the republic in whose perpetuity we have pinned our faith and our hopes."[16]

In 1916 Gompers had an opportunity to put these words into action when he accepted an appointment to the Advisory Commission of the Council of National Defense, the government agency established to organize the nation's preparedness program. Proud of this opportunity to demonstrate what he—and the AFL—could do on the nation's behalf, he promised to be mindful of his responsibility, as he put it, "to give a spirit and a purpose to plans for national preparedness that shall make human welfare the paramount consideration."[17] This, after all, was Gompers' greatest goal as a trade unionist: "If we can understand the general concept of human justice and human freedom; if we can instill in the minds of all that the best and highest concepts and idealisms of freedom make for the utmost fraternity and unity of the peoples of our common country and of the whole civilized world," he maintained, "we shall have done something in the interest of labor, of the masses of humanity and for the perpetuation of our republic and the ideals and ideas . . . to which it aspires."[18]

ACKNOWLEDGMENTS

The Samuel Gompers Papers is indebted to many institutions and individuals who have provided ongoing, long-term support to our project or who have made specific contributions to this volume. Two federal agencies, the National Endowment for the Humanities (NEH) and the National Historical Publications and Records Commission (NHPRC), have provided the core of our funding over the years, and we deeply appreciate their support. In addition, NHPRC subventions to the University of Illinois Press have offset some of the publication costs of these volumes, and NEH matching grants have enabled us to raise additional funding for the project.

We are most grateful as well to the labor movement for its long-term support of the Samuel Gompers Papers. The AFL-CIO Executive Council and the George Meany Memorial Archives have made major financial contributions on an ongoing basis in response to the NEH matching grants. In addition, the AFL-CIO Executive Council, the Meany Archives, and many national and international unions have given us access to their Gompers-era records, granted us permission to copy and publish pertinent material, and followed the progress of our work with interest and encouragement.

We also want to acknowledge here the financial support given to the Samuel Gompers Papers in the crucial early years of the project by the Joseph Anthony Beirne Memorial Foundation of the Communications Workers of America; the Associated Actors and Artistes of America; the United Automobile, Aerospace, and Agricultural Implement Workers

of America International Union; the Bakery, Confectionery and Tobacco Workers' International Union; the International Brotherhood
of Boilermakers, Iron Ship Builders, Blacksmiths, Forgers, and Helpers; the International Union of Bricklayers and Allied Craftsmen; the
United Brotherhood of Carpenters and Joiners of America; the Amalgamated Clothing and Textile Workers' Union; the International
Brotherhood of Electrical Workers; the International Union of Elec-
tronic, Electrical, Salaried, Machine, and Furniture Workers; the International Union of Operating Engineers; the Association of Flight
Attendants; the United Food and Commercial Workers' International Union; the United Garment Workers of America; the International
Ladies' Garment Workers' Union; the Glass, Molders', Pottery, Plas-
tics, and Allied Workers' International Union; the American Flint Glass
Workers' Union; the American Federation of Government Employees;
the Graphic Communications International Union; the Laborers' International Union of North America; the National Association of Letter Carriers; the International Longshoremen's Association; the International Association of Machinists and Aerospace Workers; the
Mechanics' Educational Society of America; the United Mine Workers of America; the Newspaper Guild; the Office and Professional
Employees' International Union; the International Brotherhood of
Painters and Allied Trades of the United States and Canada; the United Paperworkers' International Union; the United Association of Journeymen and Apprentices of the Plumbing and Pipe Fitting Industry
of the United States and Canada; the American Postal Workers' Union;
the International Federation of Professional and Technical Engineers;
the Brotherhood of Railway Carmen of the United States and Canada; the Retail, Wholesale, and Department Store Union; the United
Rubber, Cork, Linoleum, and Plastic Workers of America; the Seafar-
ers' International Union of North America; the Service Employees'
International Union; the International Alliance of Theatrical Stage
Employes and Moving Picture Machine Operators of the United States
and Canada; the American Federation of State, County, and Municipal Employees; the United Steelworkers of America; the American
Federation of Teachers; the International Brotherhood of Teamsters,
Chauffeurs, Warehousemen, and Helpers of America; and the Amalgamated Transit Union.

We are deeply appreciative as well for the continuing support we
receive from the University of Maryland at College Park, acting in
partnership with the NHPRC, the NEH, and the labor movement. We
want to express our gratitude to John R. Lampe, chair of the Department of History, James F. Harris, dean of the College of Arts and Humanities, and Charles B. Lowry, director of the University of Maryland

Libraries, as well as to our colleagues in the history department, the members of the staff of the university's McKeldin Library, where our principal offices are located, and to Kathleen Russell and Jon K. Boone of the Academic Computing Services Office of the College of Arts and Humanities. The department, the library, and the university assist and encourage our work in countless ways, including giving us substantial financial support, office space, and computer and other technical assistance.

We have been helped by the staffs and have used the collections of many area libraries and research institutions in preparing this volume, particularly those of the Catholic University of America, the George Meany Memorial Archives, the Library of Congress, the Library of the U.S. Department of Labor, and the National Archives.

Many individuals gave us invaluable assistance in our work on this book, including, among others, Lynda A. DeLoach, the George Meany Memorial Archives; Christian Dupont, Special Collections, and Peter J. Lysy, Archives, University of Notre Dame, Notre Dame, Ind.; Gregory C. Harness and Donald A. Ritchie, U.S. Senate Historical Office, Washington, D.C.; and Diane Adams, Danette G. Kauffman, and Diane Lifsey. Diane Koch transcribed the documents in this volume with her usual skill and care. Janet F. Davidson worked with us for a year as an NHPRC Fellow, and we feel most fortunate to have had her as a colleague and fellow researcher.

Finally, we wish to acknowledge our debt to David Brody, Melvyn Dubofsky, and Irwin Yellowitz, members of our board of advisors, for their close reading of this volume and their invaluable suggestions for improving it.

As we were completing our work on the manuscript for this volume, we were saddened to learn of the death of Susan L. Patterson. A long-time friend and colleague, Susan had worked as the copy editor for the University of Illinois Press on the manuscripts of all our volumes, and we will deeply miss the skill, energy, good humor, and love of books that she brought to her work.

Notes

1. "President Gompers' Report to the International Federation of Trade Unions," *American Federationist* 22 (Mar. 1915): 198; Samuel Gompers sent this report to Carl Legien in July 1914. For the AFL's vision of industrial democracy, see Milton Derber, *The American Idea of Industrial Democracy, 1865–1965* (Urbana, Ill., 1970), pp. 123–28, and Joseph A. McCartin, *Labor's Great War: The Struggle for Industrial Democracy and the Origins of Modern American Labor Relations, 1912–1921* (Chapel Hill, N.C., 1997), pp. 9, 54–56.

2. AFL, *Proceedings,* 1913, pp. 6–7; "An Address at the Dedication of the AFL Office Building, Washington, D.C.," July 4, 1916, below; "Excerpts from Testimony before the U.S. Commission on Industrial Relations," May 21–22, 1914, below; AFL, *Proceedings,* 1915, p. 88.

3. Sinclair Snow, *The Pan-American Federation of Labor* (Durham, N.C., 1964).

4. U.S. *Statutes at Large,* 38: 731; AFL, *Proceedings,* 1916, p. 5.

5. Melvyn Dubofsky, *The State and Labor in Modern America* (Chapel Hill, N.C., 1994), pp. 47–48.

6. "From Daniel Tobin," Jan. 22, 1914, below.

7. For the Amalgamated Clothing Workers of America, see Steve Fraser, *Labor Will Rule: Sidney Hillman and the Rise of American Labor* (New York, 1991). For the U.S. Commission on Industrial Relations, see U.S. Congress, Senate, *Industrial Relations. Final Report and Testimony Submitted to Congress by the Commission on Industrial Relations . . . ,* 64th Cong., 1st sess., 1916, S.Doc. 415; and Graham Adams, Jr., *The Age of Industrial Violence, 1910–15: The Activities and Findings of the United States Commission on Industrial Relations* (New York, 1966).

8. Gompers, "Self-Help Is the Best Help," *American Federationist* 22 (Feb. 1915): 115. Gompers was quoting from the Executive Council's report to the 1908 AFL convention.

9. "To Harry Fulton," Aug. 31, 1915, below.

10. Gompers, "The Shorter Workday—Its Philosophy," *American Federationist* 22 (Mar. 1915): 169.

11. Gompers to J. Clarence Lukens, Jr., Apr. 3, 1916, reel 205, vol. 217, p. 811, SG Letterbooks, DLC.

12. "To Ralph Easley," Aug. 2, 1916, below.

13. For Gompers' and the AFL's relation to Mexican labor leaders, see Gregg Andrews, *Shoulder to Shoulder? The American Federation of Labor, the United States, and the Mexican Revolution, 1910–1924* (Berkeley, Calif., 1991).

14. "To Robert Woolley," Aug. 25, 1916, below.

15. There has always been a question about the influence of German spies in American ports and munitions factories (see, for example, "To Ernest Bohm," July 28, 1915, below). In fact, there is some evidence that in 1915 Ralph Easley set up a secret service agency through the National Civic Federation that documented subversive activities in the munitions industry. Because the records of the National Civic Federation, in the New York Public Library's Manuscript Division, were being microfilmed while this volume was in preparation, we were unable to fully investigate Gompers' role in this episode.

16. "To James Duncan," Dec. 31, 1915, below.

17. "To Newton Baker," Oct. 31, 1916, below.

18. AFL, *Proceedings,* 1916, p. 379.

SYMBOLS AND ABBREVIATIONS

AFL	American Federation of Labor
ALS	Autograph letter, signed or stamped with signature
CIO	Congress of Industrial Organizations
DLC	Library of Congress, Washington, D.C.
DNA	National Archives and Records Administration, Washington, D.C.
FOTLU	Federation of Organized Trades and Labor Unions of the United States and Canada
IWW	Industrial Workers of the World
KOL	Knights of Labor
NIC	Cornell University, Ithaca, N.Y.
NN	New York Public Library, Astor, Lenox, and Tilden Foundations
PLS	Printed letter, signed or stamped with signature
PLS and Sr	Printed letter, signed or stamped with signature, and signature representation other than stamp
SG	Samuel Gompers
T and ALpS	Typed and autograph letter, letterpress copy, signed or stamped with signature
TD	Typed document
TDc	Typed document, copy
TDpS	Typed document, letterpress copy, signed or stamped with signature
TDS	Typed document, signed
TLc	Typed letter, copy
TLcS	Typed letter, copy, signed or stamped with signature
TLpS	Typed letter, letterpress copy, signed or stamped with signature
TLS	Typed letter, signed or stamped with signature
TLtcSr	Typed letter, transcribed, copy, signature representation other than stamp
TLtpSr	Typed letter, transcribed, letterpress copy, signature representation other than stamp
TUC	Trades Union Congress of Great Britain
TWpSr	Typed wire (telegram), letterpress copy, signature representation other than stamp
TWSr	Typed wire (telegram), signature representation other than stamp
TWtcSr	Typed wire (telegram), transcribed, copy, signature representation other than stamp

AFL, *Proceedings*, 1908	AFL, *Report of Proceedings of the Twenty-eighth Annual Convention of the American Federation of Labor, Held at Denver, Colorado, November 9 to 21 Inclusive, 1908* (Washington, D.C., 1908)
AFL, *Proceedings*, 1912	AFL, *Report of Proceedings of the Thirty-second Annual Convention of the American Federation of Labor, Held at Rochester, New York, November 11 to 23, Inclusive, 1912* (Washington, D.C., 1912)
AFL, *Proceedings*, 1913	AFL, *Report of Proceedings of the Thirty-third Annual Convention of the American Federation of Labor, Held at Seattle, Washington, November 10 to 22, Inclusive, 1913* (Washington, D.C., 1913)
AFL, *Proceedings*, 1914	AFL, *Report of Proceedings of the Thirty-fourth Annual Convention of the American Federation of Labor, Held at Philadelphia, Pennsylvania, November 9 to 21, Inclusive, 1914* (Washington, D.C., 1914)
AFL, *Proceedings*, 1915	AFL, *Report of Proceedings of the Thirty-fifth Annual Convention of the American Federation of Labor, Held at San Francisco, California, November 8 to 22, Inclusive, 1915* (Washington, D.C., 1915)
AFL, *Proceedings*, 1916	AFL, *Report of the Proceedings of the Thirty-sixth Annual Convention of the American Federation of Labor, Held at Baltimore, Maryland, November 13 to 25, Inclusive, 1916* (Washington, D.C., 1916)
AFL and the Unions	Dolores E. Janiewski, ed., *The American Federation of Labor and the Unions: National and International Union Records from the Samuel Gompers Era,* microfilm (Sanford, N.C., 1982)
AFL Records	Peter J. Albert and Harold L. Miller, eds., *American Federation of Labor Records: The Samuel Gompers Era,* microfilm (Sanford, N.C., 1979)
AFL Weekly News Letter	*American Federation of Labor Weekly News Letter*
FOTLU, *Proceedings*, 1884	FOTLU, *Report of the Fourth Annual Session of the Federation of Organized Trades and Labor Unions of the United States and Canada, Held in Chicago, Illinois, October 7, 8, 9 and 10, 1884* (1884?; reprint ed., Bloomington, Ill., 1905)

SG Letterbooks   Records of the American Federation of Labor: Samuel Gompers Letterbooks, 1883–1924, Library of Congress, Washington, D.C.

The Samuel Gompers Papers, vol. 1   Stuart B. Kaufman et al., eds., *The Samuel Gompers Papers*, vol. 1, *The Making of a Union Leader, 1850–86* (Urbana, Ill., 1986)

The Samuel Gompers Papers, vol. 2   Stuart B. Kaufman et al., eds., *The Samuel Gompers Papers*, vol. 2, *The Early Years of the American Federation of Labor, 1887–90* (Urbana, Ill., 1987)

The Samuel Gompers Papers, vol. 4   Stuart B. Kaufman et al., eds., *The Samuel Gompers Papers*, vol. 4, *A National Labor Movement Takes Shape, 1895–98* (Urbana, Ill., 1991)

The Samuel Gompers Papers, vol. 5   Stuart B. Kaufman et al., eds., *The Samuel Gompers Papers*, vol. 5, *An Expanding Movement at the Turn of the Century, 1898–1902* (Urbana, Ill., 1996)

The Samuel Gompers Papers, vol. 6   Stuart B. Kaufman et al., eds., *The Samuel Gompers Papers*, vol. 6, *The American Federation of Labor and the Rise of Progressivism, 1902–6* (Urbana, Ill., 1997)

The Samuel Gompers Papers, vol. 7   Stuart B. Kaufman et al., eds., *The Samuel Gompers Papers*, vol. 7, *The American Federation of Labor under Siege, 1906–9* (Urbana, Ill., 1998)

The Samuel Gompers Papers, vol. 8   Peter J. Albert and Grace Palladino, eds., *The Samuel Gompers Papers*, vol. 8, *Progress and Reaction in the Age of Reform, 1909–13* (Urbana, Ill., 2001)

CHRONOLOGY

Documents

Excerpts from Testimony before the Select Committee on Lobby Investigation of the U.S. House of Representatives

Thursday, September 11, 1913.

. . .

Mr. Ralston. Mr. Gompers, you have put in evidence here itemized accounts of your political expenditures except for 1910.[1] I will ask you if this is a correct account of such expenditures as there were in 1910 (handing paper to witness).

Mr. Gompers (after examining paper). Yes, sir.

Mr. Ralston. Without taking up the time of the committee to read it, I will offer this in evidence.[2]

. . .

Mr. Gompers. We had no political expenditures for 1912, or expenditures in a political campaign. A word of explanation may be helpful. The American Federation of Labor entered into the campaign of 1906; was most active in the campaigns of 1908 and 1910. We had accomplished much that we desired, and that was publicity for our grievances and to arouse public attention to the relief which we sought. In the campaigns of 1906, 1908, and 1910 we found the representatives of the National Association of Manufacturers and the trail could be seen—the influences could be felt on every hand, of their activity and hostile attitude or hostile effort to anything we attempted to do. . . .

. . .

. . . The men of labor were never so active in any political campaign as they were in the campaign of 1908, but our very publicity, our very activity, was turned by the representatives of the National Association of Manufacturers and by the men of vested interests to their own account. In other words, men who were, say, opposed as a matter of party principle, probably, to the election of Mr. Taft, were driven into supporting Mr. Taft because as the National Association of Manufacturers declared every moment they had the opportunity, the country would go to the damnation bow-wows if Mr. Taft should be beaten and Mr. Bryan elected. It was said by them as a matter of fact that I had

3

written the platform, that I had dominated the campaign, that it was those labor-movement men who were dominating a political party.

This is probably a long way of getting at the point I want to make. In the 1910 campaign we too were active, but we believed we had made our point on the public mind and the public conscience and we could do better service in accomplishing our purpose of a change in the political complexion of this country—in the administration, in the legislation of this country—to change its political complexion in order to dislodge those who had been in power so long and imagined they were the dominating forces and the only expression of anything like the feeling and sentiment and conviction of the people of our country; and we had made up our mind that if we accomplished nothing further than that, it would clear the atmosphere and make things brighter and better in the country if the political parties were changed. In addition the Republican Party again neglected in 1912 the requests which labor submitted. The Democratic Party indorsed and adopted the requests which we made, requests in the interest of equal rights before the law and propositions seeking to maintain absolute equality before the law for all our people. Then we made up our mind that our campaign could be conducted much better without the publicity in 1912 than in 1908. So that our campaign was by a circular here and there, by a conference with some particular man, and the organizers, who understood the purpose for which we were contending.

. . .

Mr. Ralston. Now, Mr. Gompers, as a matter of historical interest at any rate, do you know of any political accounting, campaign accounting of receipts and expenses ever made prior to that made by the Federation of Labor, printed copies of which were submitted to the committee?

Mr. Gompers. We submitted the first—we printed our financial statement of that campaign before any other political party or political factor did so. . . .

. . .

Mr. Stafford.[3] You said you appeared before the respective party committees, and you refer to the Republican and Democratic Parties?

Mr. Gompers. Yes, sir.

Mr. Stafford. You never appeared before the Socialist Party convention to have any policies incorporated?

Mr. Gompers. No, sir.

Mr. Stafford. In fact, you are, as I understand your position, diametrically opposed to the Socialist Party movement?

Mr. Gompers. I do not think that that is my province at all, to be opposed to anyone. What I am opposed to is either that party or any other party attempting to interfere with the fullest normal and natural development of the organized labor movement of the workers of America. I can not undertake to dispute the theories of the Socialists any more than I can undertake to dispute the theories of the alchemists. I am busy enough in the work in which I am engaged, in trying to impress upon my fellow workers their duty to prevent deterioration in their condition. I am in entire discord and out of harmony, and in opposition, if you please, with the philosophy of socialism as it is expounded by the spokesmen for socialism. Of course, no one can tell who is really the spokesman, because there are 57 varieties of him, but I am speaking of those who are regarded as the spokesmen for the Socialists. I believe in the duty of man to make the life of himself and his fellows better to-day—to-day, not in the remote future, but to-day— and to make him better prepared, by reason of his improved conditions, to meet the human problems that confront him to-morrow.

Mr. Stafford. That policy is diametrically opposed to the principles enunciated by Carl Marx in his work on socialism—

Mr. Gompers (interposing). Des [*sic*] Capital?

Mr. Stafford. Yes, Des Capital.

Mr. Gompers. About 27 years ago I undertook to learn to read the German language for the purpose of reading Des Capita [*sic*] of Carl Marx in its original, and I have read the very best of what the philosophers and writers on socialism have had to say, as I have read and tried to digest that which the best economists of the past 300 years have had to say. Without egotism, and I hope little, if any, vanity, I will say I believe I have come to the conclusion many years ago that it is our duty to live our lives as workers in the society in which we live, and not to work for the downfall or the destruction or the overthrow of that society, but for the fuller development and evolution of the society in which we live; to make life the better worth the living; and if in the course of that effort some men are inconvenienced, then it is not to be ascribed to the detriment of that natural and evolutionary movement, but rather to the credit of that movement, because it is the great conservator of the peace and of the public welfare.

. . .

. . . I wish to say, Mr. Chairman,[4] a word in regard to two of our matters. One is the work in which the American labor movement is engaged. I shall not attempt to make any speech; I am admonished that I ought not, anyway; but I want to present to your consideration this fact, that in our country there is not any legend nor is there any tradition by which the employers of labor have any interest in the welfare of the workers, as such, except as they are workers and wealth producers. In other countries which have been in existence a thousand and more years, and which have emerged from a system of slavery and serf-dom and peonage and the ownership of workers, there has been some continuous interest which the owner of the slave or the master or the baron of the serf—there has been some continued interest of the patron, the father, the owner, in the well-being of his workers; and notwithstanding countries have broken through the shell of that condition, yet there is a manifest feeling in the conduct on the part of employers in Europe and in other countries to-day. In the United States we have just burst into a nation with conglomerate elements, no responsibility, no care for the workers, or of the workers, for their welfare, and in no country on the face of the globe is there such a relentless disregard of the human race by employers, of the workers of the country, than that which exists in our Nation. There is more regard for the horse owned by a man, more regard for the mule, more regard for any animal, for the loss of an animal would have to be replaced by purchase. It is costly.

Human life in our country has been so totally disregarded in relations of employers and employees that there must step in some power, some factor, which shall mitigate such a condition of affairs.

Mr. Stafford. May I just break in on you there for a moment. Take the State of Wisconsin, as to the legislation that our legislature has passed to protect the workingmen in their industrial employment. I would like to ask you, Mr. Gompers, if European nations are much further advanced in the protection of the life and the security of the workingmen than the legislation which we find in Wisconsin, and the resultant security that that legislation gives to the workingmen in the State of Wisconsin?

Mr. Gompers. We are, in the United States, not less than two decades behind many of the European countries in the protection of the life, health, and limb of the workers.

Here and there considerable improvement has been made, and even in Wisconsin the improvements have been made within the past 10 years.

Mr. Stafford. Yes.

Mr. Gompers. And to what without want of recognition and appreciation of the service rendered by public-spirited men, to what is attributable the protection which has come to the workers even in Wisconsin, except the agitation and the organization of the workers who have created the public sentiment and demand for the enactment of these laws? Without the associations of labor, without their activity before the legislatures and before the Congress they would be still working their 12 or more hours a day, and there would be no protection to life and limb and health in their work.

Workingmen's compensation—much progress has been made in the last two or three years in the United States upon that subject, but we are behind England 10 years; we are behind Germany 20 years.

Now, look how there still exists in our States, in some of the jurisdictions, the employer's defenses, the negligence of fellow employees, contributory negligence, the assumption of risks, or as the courts of the State of New York decided in the case of a woman who lost her arm in her work, that it was an assumption of risk when she took employment, and she was nonsuited, but she lost her arm.[5] Railroad accident cases might be cited. A man at a telegraph office at a way station fails to give the proper signal at the proper time. The railway engineer is killed by reason of it. Instead of compensation the plea is put forth that it was the fellow employee's negligence.

I mean to say this, that if there were not some power, some factor, to check this mad greed of employers, there would be no telling where the people of our country would drift industrially and commercially and politically, and particularly humanely.

The labor movement of America, crude as it is, poorly organized as it is, poorly officered as it is, is the only movement of a practical character which takes into consideration these conditions, and protests, and protests, and protests against the wrong and the slaughter of the humans, insists upon a better recognition and the safeguarding of the men and women who give their services that society may proceed and progress.

And that brings me to the second thought, and that is what I wanted particularly to emphasize, and it is this investigation by the House and the investigation by the Senate. I think that any man or association of men that use money corruptly, or corrupt means, or corrupt methods, ought to be hailed to the bar of the courts or the Congress and dealt with as they deserve. But to make a hue and cry about what is termed "lobbying."

Those who are in antagonism to our labor movement and who call themselves interested in the cause of labor—there are some who stigmatize us not only as labor conservatives, but who say that our movement is the barrier to their social revolution—it is they who charge us with begging and lobbying in Congress, and as one man has said, "He has worn out his knee pads in begging Congress to do justice to his fellow workers."[6] We have never called our representatives who have asked for legislation a lobby. We have given them the dignified name of a legislative committee, a committee seeking the furtherance of legislation in the interest of the common people of our country. There is not a piece of legislation that any man can charge us with advocating which is not in the interest of every man, woman, and child of the

United States. It is not confined to men of organized labor. It is the men of the organized-labor movement who stand sponsor for it and bear the brunt and expense of it, or who go down into their pockets in order to do it, or who give their efforts, many of them voluntary, many of them without payment and without hope of reward, many of them who devote their time and attention and talent to the work, and who, if they devoted the same time and attention and talent to business, might be made wealthy or might possibly figure in public office.

Why should we not have our labor representatives here as our legislative committee? Why should we not have representation in Congress? Why should we not have a representative in the Cabinet of the United States? In not less than eight countries in Europe, and in several countries in America, there is a department of labor, with a distinctively labor man, growing out of the ranks, or rather still in the ranks until selected for high office, at the head of the department. It is a recognition of the transition of society. It is an acknowledgment of the extending of this transition of society from the merely and purely political to the industrial and social. The men of labor were those who made the protest for the children; not me, not any of us who are living; but the men who have gone before. They made the first protest against the slaughter of innocents in industry, and we have simply taken up the work they did, and we are appearing here, appearing before Congress, appearing before the legislatures, purely as men and women who have this vital interest at heart, with the one dominating thought to make the life of the people better worth living; the exercise of our rights as men and citizens, our vote, our franchise, our judgment, our conscience, our power of speech, our power of thought, our power of association, in order to accomplish the best that can be accomplished in the interest of the entire American people.

· · ·

U.S. Congress, House, *Charges against Members of the House and Lobby Activities of the National Association of Manufacturers of the United States and Others. Hearings before the Select Committee of the House of Representatives Appointed under House Resolution 198,* 63d Cong., 1st sess., 1913, pp. 2465–66, 2472–74, 2531–33.

1. In his testimony before the committee on Sept. 10, 1913, SG had presented the AFL's published accounts of its receipts and expenditures in connection with the 1906 and 1908 political campaigns. The financial report for the 1906 campaign showed receipts of $8,226 and expenditures of $8,147; that for 1908 showed receipts of $8,532 and expenditures of $8,470 (U.S. Congress, House, *Charges against Members of the House and Lobby Activities of the National Association of Manufacturers of the United States and Others. Hearings before the Select Committee of the House of Representatives Appointed under House Resolution 198,* 63d Cong., 1st sess., 1913, pp. 2428–42, 2443–61).

2. The financial report for the 1910 campaign showed receipts of $3,609 and expenditures of $3,590 (*Hearings,* pp. 2466–69).

3. William Henry Stafford (1869–1957) was a Republican congressman from Wisconsin (1903–11, 1913–19, 1921–23, 1929–33).

4. The chairman of the committee, Finis James Garrett (1875–1956), was a Democratic congressman from Tennessee (1905–29). He later served as judge of the U.S. Court of Customs and Patent Appeals (1929–55).

5. A reference to the New York Court of Appeals decision in *Sarah Knisley* v. *Pascal P. Pratt et al.* (148 N.Y. 372 [1896]). The court ruled that Knisley, who lost her arm in a hardware factory accident, could not sue her employer for damages because she had knowingly assumed the risk of operating the machinery that injured her.

6. A reference to a statement apparently made by J. Mahlon Barnes at the 1904 AFL convention. See *The Samuel Gompers Papers,* vol. 6, p. 370.

An Excerpt from the Minutes of a Meeting of the Executive Council of the AFL[1]

Thursday, September 25, 1913.

AFTERNOON SESSION.

The members of the Executive Council with the exception of Vice-President Perham[2] met President Wilson, as per his appointment,[3] at 2 o'clock. President Gompers, speaking for the Executive Council, thanked President Wilson for the appointment of W. B. Wilson[4] as Secretary of the Department of Labor and for the appointment of Vice-President O'Connell[5] and Treasurer Lennon[6] on the Industrial Commission.

President Gompers then called the President's attention to the labor planks in the Democratic party platform in 1908 and 1912 and asked the President's cooperation, through his message to Congress[7] for the passage of the Bacon-Bartlett bill;[8] also called the President's attention to the Seamen's bill.[9] The President advised that he was very much interested in the Seamen's bill.

He urged the assistance of the President in the passage of legislation favorable to industrial education,[10] and then took up the matter of securing for the Department of Labor sufficient appropriations[11] to enable the Department to carry on the work for which it was created.

Secretary Wilson of the Department of Labor was also present.

At the close of the conference, 3:30, the members of the Executive Council returned to headquarters and reconvened in session there.

. . .

TDc, Executive Council Records, Minutes, reel 4, frame 1419, *AFL Records.*

1. The AFL Executive Council met in Washington, D.C., Sept. 22–27, 1913.

2. Henry Burdon PERHAM was president of the Order of Railroad Telegraphers of North America (1901–19) and an AFL vice-president (1909–19).

3. SG wrote President Woodrow Wilson on Sept. 22, 1913, asking him and Secretary of Labor William Wilson to meet with the AFL Executive Council, then in session. The president arranged the conference for Sept. 25.

4. William Bauchop WILSON served as U.S. secretary of labor from 1913 to 1921.

5. James O'CONNELL was an AFL vice-president (1896–1918), president of the AFL Metal Trades Department (1911–34), and a member of the U.S. Commission on Industrial Relations (1913–15).

6. John Brown LENNON was treasurer of the AFL (1891–1917) and a member of the U.S. Commission on Industrial Relations (1913–15).

7. In his annual message to Congress on Dec. 2, 1913, President Woodrow Wilson only briefly referred to antitrust legislation, deferring discussion of the subject to a later date. He subsequently addressed a joint session of Congress on the matter on Jan. 20, 1914, but he dealt only with business monopolies and mentioned neither the Bacon-Bartlett bills nor organized labor.

8. A reference to identical House and Senate bills endorsed by the AFL—H.R. 1873 (63d Cong., 1st sess.) introduced by Democratic congressman Charles Bartlett of Georgia on Apr. 7, 1913, and S. 927 (63d Cong., 1st sess.) introduced by Democratic senator Augustus Bacon of Georgia on Apr. 15—to limit the use of injunctions and to exempt labor organizations from the provisions of the Sherman Antitrust Act. The bills were not reported out of committee but were superseded by legislation introduced by Democratic congressman Henry Clayton (H.R. 15,657, 63d Cong., 2d sess.).

9. S. 4 (63d Cong., 1st sess.) was introduced by Republican senator Robert LaFollette of Wisconsin on Apr. 7, 1913. It was not reported out of committee but was later added as an amendment to S. 136 (63d Cong., 1st sess.), another seamen's bill introduced on Apr. 7 by Republican senator Knute Nelson of Minnesota, and was signed into law on Mar. 4, 1915 (U.S. *Statutes at Large*, 38: 1164–85). Known as the Seamen's Act, it included provisions regulating hours, payment of wages, shipboard conditions, and the punishment of seamen for specific offenses and imposed stringent safety requirements on all vessels trading at American ports. In addition, it abolished flogging and all other forms of corporal punishment of seamen. Finally, it prohibited the arrest and imprisonment of American seamen who deserted in foreign ports and foreign seamen who did so in American ports and called upon the president to terminate any treaties stipulating such action against seamen.

10. Three measures relating to industrial education were then before Congress. S. 3 (63d. Cong., 1st sess.), introduced on Apr. 7, 1913, by Republican senator Carroll Page of Vermont, did not become law. S.J. Res. 5 (63d Cong., 1st sess.), introduced on Apr. 7 by Democratic senator Hoke Smith of Georgia, provided for a commission to study the issue of federal aid for vocational education and became law on Jan. 20, 1914 (U.S. *Statutes at Large*, 38: 767–68). H.R. 7951 (63d Cong., 1st sess.), an agricultural extension bill introduced on Sept. 6, 1913, by Democratic congressman Asbury Lever of South Carolina, became law on May 8, 1914 (U.S. *Statutes at Large*, 38: 372–74).

11. Appropriations for the Department of Labor were included in a special appropriation bill (H.R. 2973, 63d Cong., 1st sess.) that became law on May 1, 1913 (U.S. *Statutes at Large*, 38: 1–3) and in two urgent deficiency bills that became law, respectively, on Oct. 22, 1913 (H.R. 7898, 63d Cong., 1st sess.; U.S. *Statutes at Large*, 38: 208–33), and Apr. 6, 1914 (H.R. 13,612, 63d Cong., 2d sess.; U.S. *Statutes at Large*, 38: 312–35). Appropriations for the department became part of the regular appropriation

process beginning with legislation for the fiscal year ending June 30, 1915, which became law on July 16, 1914 (H.R. 15,279, 63d Cong., 2d sess.; U.S. *Statutes at Large*, 38: 454–509).

A Circular

Washington, D.C., September 29, 1913.

To All Organized Labor:

Each new advance in human betterment leaves its furrows of pain and suffering across human hearts and lives. There is scarcely a worker in all America who does not know the meaning of a strike, during which the workers and their families have suffered and endured in order to obtain justice; or who has not felt the terrible fear for the physical safety of loved ones in the thick of the contest, or the heartbreaking pain because of inability to supply even the barest necessities of life for those dependent upon him. To you, members of organized labor, the brave struggle of the copper miners of Calumet, Michigan,[1] will appeal with greatest effect.

After exhausting all other means of securing the just demands which they made upon their employers, these miners laid aside their tools on July 23, and went out on a strike. They had been working a so-called ten-hour day, which in reality was an eleven-hour day, for wages that would not permit American standards of living. Miners have been forced to handle individually heavy drilling machines which had formerly been operated by two men. After considering all matters the men decided to demand an eight-hour day, three dollars as the minimum wage, and two men to handle drilling machines as formerly. All requests for conferences or consideration of these just demands were ignored and treated with contempt.

Despite the fact that the strike was inaugurated peacefully and has been conducted by the miners without even the slightest show of violence, seldom has there been such a display of arbitrary methods on the part of the mine operators and governmental authorities. The morning after the strike began hundreds of deputies were sworn in; the employers imported companies of Waddell-Mahon guards; finally State troops were sent to the mining district that the mine owners might be enabled to operate their mines and the voice of Labor in its appeal for justice might be silenced. All of this display of force was under the pretence of protecting property (when the miners did not attack it, nor contemplate attacking it); when the miners attempted to protect and promote human rights, they were ridden down in the streets, clubbed, fired upon!

Though there have been the usual efforts to foment strife and to stir up violence among the strikers, yet no property has been destroyed and the miners have remained steadfast in their determination to win their rights, and in their determination not to be forced into lawlessness.

The officials of the miners asked for an injunction restraining the appointment of additional deputies to serve the mine operators—their request was refused.[2] The mine operators asked for an injunction restraining the strikers from picketing, "molesting" men going to or from work and from parading in the vicinity of the mines—that order was granted.[3]

Such are the conditions under which these copper miners are waging their fight for justice and a life somewhat better worth living. With all the forces of capital and organized society working against them, they have maintained courage, determination and good spirit. There are 16,000 miners engaged in this struggle. A large number of miners and their families were evicted from their homes owned by the corporations. The lives, safety, and welfare of something like 50,000 men, women, and children are bound up with its fate. The strike has now been in progress for over two months and still the mine operators maintain stubborn resistance and unreasonable refusal to consider the demands of the men. The long, hard winter of northern Michigan is approaching, and these brave men, women, and children who are bearing the brunt of this fight for industrial justice for American workingmen are in need.

Two members of our Executive Council, John Mitchell[4] and John B. Lennon, have been among these strikers and presented to us unquestionable evidence of the conditions there.[5] After consideration of the conditions, the need and importance of the issues involved, the Executive Council makes this appeal to all the members of organized labor for prompt and generous financial assistance to aid these needy and suffering fellow-workers, their wives and children.[6]

We appeal in the name of all labor and common humanity that each local union at once make an appropriation from its funds of not less than five cents for each member; that each Central Labor Union select a committee to appeal to all workers and friends to contribute promptly and as generously as possible, and to use every other honorable means by which funds may be secured. The men and women and children of Calumet, Michigan, must not be starved into submission. They must and they will win, if the toilers of our country will but do their duty.

Remember that the splendid solidarity of the workers of America largely aided in securing the magnificent victory of the anthracite miners a few years ago. The newspapers have suppressed nearly all reference to the Calumet miners' strike. In this appeal we hope to reach the minds, hearts, and the consciences of our fellow-workers and friends, and thereby secure their ready response to the call for aid.

Send all contributions to Frank Morrison,[7] Secretary, American Federation of Labor, Ouray Building, Washington, D.C., who will return receipt for the same and promptly forward every dollar to the immediate aid of the struggling miners of Calumet.

Fraternally yours,   Saml Gompers.   President.

Attest: Frank Morrison   Secretary.

James Duncan,[8]   First Vice-President.

John Mitchell,   Second Vice-President

James O'Connell,   Third Vice-President

D. A. Hayes,[9]   Fourth Vice-President.

Wm. D. Huber,[10]   Fifth Vice-President.

Jos. F. Valentine,[11]   Sixth Vice-President.

John R. Alpine,[12]   Seventh Vice-President.

H. B. Perham,   Eighth Vice-President.

John B. Lennon,   Treasurer.

Executive Council,   American Federation of Labor

PLS and Sr, Executive Council Records, Minutes, reel 4, frame 1467, *AFL Records*.

1. For the Calumet, Mich., copper miners' strike, see *The Samuel Gompers Papers*, vol. 8, pp. 512–13, n. 2.

2. On Aug. 15, 1913, the Western Federation of Miners secured a temporary injunction restraining Houghton Co., Mich., sheriff James Cruse from hiring additional Waddell-Mahon detectives. The miners argued that the detectives had not fulfilled the three-month county residency requirement for sheriff's deputies that was stipulated by state law and that they were being used to break the strike rather than preserve the peace. On Aug. 23 state circuit court judge Patrick O'Brien refused to extend the injunction, ruling that the Waddell-Mahon men could be used to train deputies while not actually serving as such.

3. On Sept. 20, 1913, Judge O'Brien granted a preliminary injunction, on the request of the Calumet and Hecla Mining Co. and other firms involved in the northern Michigan copper strike, prohibiting the Western Federation of Miners from picketing, demonstrating, or any other activities interfering with employees of the companies. On the motion of the union, however, Judge O'Brien dissolved the injunction on Sept. 29. The companies appealed O'Brien's decision to the Michigan Supreme Court, which on Oct. 8 stayed dissolution of the injunction pending a hearing but ruled that peaceful parades and meetings by strikers were to be allowed. Finally, on Dec. 10, the state supreme court issued a writ of mandamus ordering O'Brien to reinstate the injunction (*Baltic Mining Co. et al.* v. *Houghton Circuit Judge,* 177 Michigan 632 [1913]).

4. John MITCHELL was an AFL vice-president (1899–1913), a member of the New York State Workmen's Compensation Commission (1914–15), and chair of the New York State Industrial Commission (1915–19).

5. Mitchell addressed mass meetings of striking copper miners in Calumet and Houghton in August 1913. An account of his visit is printed in the *AFL Weekly News Letter* of Aug. 30. John Lennon visited Calumet and addressed the strikers there in September; his report is printed in the *News Letter* of Sept. 20.

6. In addition to this one, the AFL issued appeals in behalf of the Calumet copper miners on Aug. 28, 1913, and Jan. 27, 1914. Together, the three raised a total of $55,174.

7. Frank MORRISON served as AFL secretary from 1897 to 1935 and as secretary-treasurer from 1936 to 1939.

8. James DUNCAN, of the Granite Cutters' International Association of America, was an officer of that union (1895–1923) and an AFL vice-president (1895–1928).

9. Denis A. HAYES was president of the Glass Bottle Blowers' Association of the United States and Canada (1896–1917) and an AFL vice-president (1901–17).

10. William D. HUBER served as president of the United Brotherhood of Carpenters and Joiners of America (1899–1913) and as an AFL vice-president (1906–13).

11. Joseph F. VALENTINE, of the International Molders' Union of North America, was president of the union (1903–24), an AFL vice-president (1906–24), and vice-president of the AFL Metal Trades Department (1908–24).

12. John R. ALPINE, of the United Association of Plumbers and Steam Fitters of the United States and Canada, was president of the union (1906–19) and an AFL vice-president (1909–19).

From James Kirby[1]

Office of James Kirby, Gen'l President
United Brotherhood of Carpenters and Joiners of America[2]
Indianapolis, Indiana Oct. 14, 1913.

Dear Sir and Brother:

While on my trip through Lower Canada I met up with conditions that were entirely new to me, and of which, it was hard to believe, could exist. We have seen chattel slavery abolished, also we are endeavoring to abolish wage-slavery, or, at least, some of its worst features but while in Canada I encountered a new proposition in the way of religious slavery. I found the Catholic clergymen bitterly arrayed against the International Trade Movement. They have an Organization formed termed the Workingmen's Federation.[3] Anybody is at liberty to join who is willing to contribute to the extent of 25 cts. per month. This includes the contractor, the lawyer, the physician as well as the working man.

The Parish of Three Rivers has erected a large brick building for the headquarters of this Organization[4] and the pulpit is used for the purpose of exhorting people to join.

In Montreal, they have not as yet gained any foothold. In Three Rivers the Carpenters have a fair Organization.[5] In Quebec there are three Central Bodies: the American Federation,[6] the Workingmen's

Federation[7] and some other institution. They are not, however, as strongly intrenched in Quebec as in Three Rivers. At Jonquieres we have a good working union of carpenters.[8] In Chicoutini, we have another organization,[9] but the fight is made very bitter against them.

We are fighting this proposition and continue to do so as we realize that if they are not beaten at home, they will spread and it is our intention to give them all the fight they want in the places mentioned.

We have two or three very good organizers speaking the French language, but it is very difficult for the Carpenters to carry this fight alone. If the other trades were organized it would be much easier for us.

My object in writing you is, as the Federation has a French-speaking organizer now at Montreal,[10] I would appreciate it a great favor if you would instruct[11] him to work in conjunction with our Organizer, N. Arcand,[12] of Montreal and assist him in starting a Federal Union in Jonquieres, Three Rivers and Chicoutini.[13] I believe this can be done, and as there are not enough of the other crafts to form one Organization, it will then interest everybody. I assure you I would appreciate this very much as it will not only materially strengthen our own Organization but assist the others as well, and have a tendency to keep the influences against our movement confined in Lower Canada.

Fraternally yours,   James Kirby
General President.

TLS, AFL Microfilm National and International Union File, Carpenters Records, reel 35, frames 2459–60, *AFL Records.*

1. James KIRBY was president of the United Brotherhood of Carpenters and Joiners of America (1913–15).

2. The United Brotherhood of CARPENTERS and Joiners of America.

3. Probably the Corporation Ouvrière Catholique des Trois-Rivières (Catholic Labor Corporation of Three Rivers), founded in January 1913 with the encouragement of Bishop Emile Cloutier. Although employers were not allowed to join, workers who did so agreed not to strike or join "foreign" unions and promised to accept binding arbitration of disputes.

4. Bishop Cloutier gave land to the Corporation Ouvrière Catholique for its headquarters in March 1913 and dedicated the building later that year.

5. Carpenters and Joiners' local 1793 of Trois-Rivières, Que.

6. The Quebec (City) Trades and Labor Council was chartered by the AFL in 1910.

7. Probably the National Trades and Labor Council of Quebec, the city's affiliate of the Canadian Federation of Labor.

8. Carpenters and Joiners' local 1338 of Jonquière, Que.

9. Carpenters and Joiners' local 1368 of Chicoutimi, Que.

10. G. R. Brunet, a member of International Printing Pressmen's and Assistants' Union of North America 52 of Montreal.

11. Frank Morrison wrote Brunet on Oct. 24, 1913, asking him to assist Carpenters and Joiners' organizer Narcisse Arcand in forming a federal labor union in Trois-Rivières, Chicoutimi, and Jonquière (vol. 366, p. 866, Morrison Letterbooks, George Meany

Memorial Archives, Silver Spring, Md.). Morrison informed Kirby of his action the same day (ibid., pp. 867–68).

12. Narcisse Arcand, a member of Carpenters and Joiners' local 134 of Montreal. For an undated circular addressed to Catholic workers in the province of Quebec, attacking Arcand as a socialist and a Mason, see Executive Council Records, Correspondence, reel 19, frame 800, *AFL Records*. Morrison sent a translation of the circular to the AFL Executive Council on Jan. 7, 1914.

13. The AFL chartered Federal Labor Union (FLU) 14,592 of Trois-Rivières on Nov. 22, 1913. Brunet submitted applications for FLUs in Jonquière and Chicoutimi in March 1914, but neither was chartered.

To Bruce Barton[1]

Oct. 22, 1913.

Mr. Bruce Barton,
416 West 13th Street, New York City.
Dear Sir:

The American Federation of Labor as you are aware is as the name implies a federation of nationals, internationals, central bodies, state federations and federal labor unions directly affiliated. The total membership of the affiliated organization is now over two million. This shows the impossibility of answering your questions in regard to church attendance.

In the other questions you use the terms "the Labor Union Man" evidently in the type sense in which some have used the terms the "economic man," the "political man," or the "average man" of statistics. In my opinion there is no such thing as a type of a class of men, what the term usually covers is something without reality or existence, of no use except for speculative purposes. There is no such thing as "the Labor Union Man." There are many men who belong to labor unions, and one man differs from another in nature, in convictions, in beliefs. As individuals but not as members of labor unions these men may have any relations that they desire with any church they may favor. If you go among the men who work you will find some individuals for whom the Christian church has comfort and aid; you will find others indifferent or skeptical; you will find others who regard the church as the embodiment of hypocritical cant.

Each man counts, but none too highly. It is therefore manifestly useless and misleading to formulate any generalization about "the Labor Union Man."

As to whether modern churches represent the teachings of Jesus of Nazareth, the carpenter, you find just as many opinions as you find thinking working men. What Jesus of Nazareth would think of modern churches is not a question of fact but of supposition. He is not physically living now and the church did not exist then. Any speculative question as to what would have taken place had history developed differently might be of dialectic interest to a few individuals but the labor movement finds its power and effectiveness must be devoted to the real present problems arising in the work of toil and practical affairs. There is so much to do for the misery and suffering in the world, that organized labor cannot afford to turn aside from these problems that only we can solve, to promote any other cause, however worthy, which might cause dissentions among our members and defeat our real purposes.

Very truly yours,   Saml Gompers.
President.   American Federation of Labor.

TLpS, reel 176, vol. 188, pp. 578–79, SG Letterbooks, DLC.

1. Bruce Barton (1886–1967) was at this time an assistant sales manager at the publishing firm of P. F. Collier and Son. In 1919 he was a founder of the advertising firm of Barton, Durstine, and Osborn (after 1928, Batten, Barton, Durstine, and Osborn), and in 1925 he published *The Man Nobody Knows*. Barton later served as a Republican congressman from New York (1937–41).

To J. Harada

Oct. 28, 1913.

Mr. J. Harada,
Editor, Middle-Western Japanese Year Book Pub. Dept.,
3850 Lake Avenue, Chicago, Ill.
Dear Sir:

Your favor of the 14th instant[1] is received and contents noted. To the question "What in your opinion are the main contributing causes that disturb the good feeling between Japan and the United States," no better reply can be made than that which Herbert Spencer made to the Premier of Japan, a letter which was kept confidential until after Spencer's death.[2] The gist of that reply is that the basic cause is not a question of sociology but a question of biology. When two races have such incompatible physical characteristics that mental, ethical, and social standards are conflicting, they do not readily or advantageously mingle socially or intermarry. This gives rise to "particularism" and results in a continual struggle for mastery. Such antagonistic rivalry can only terminate in extermination or subjugation.

The Japanese would deem a large immigration of the Caucasian race into their own country, undesirable and hurtful to their own nation. In any country the acquisition of land by aliens is something to be avoided, and, if necessary, resisted. National feeling, customs, and institutions cannot withstand the transmuting tendencies and influences emanating from aliens who cannot be assimilated. This is the reason why the Caucasian race of the United States is concerned for the preservation of its own identity.

Friendship and mutual good will between the United States and Japan will be best preserved and promoted when each of the two nations follows its natural line of development without interfering in the domestic affairs of the other, without attempting to acquire lands belonging to the other, and without disturbing the industrial and social condition of the other by intruding upon it. Each country has its individual sphere of development and world service for which it is best adapted. Mutual exchange and intercourse should exist where they will bring benefit, but should not be forced or allowed when they will bring dissension or restriction upon either nation.

If the United States should grant the privilege of naturalization to the Japanese, the act would constitute an invitation to future misunderstandings, grievances or possibly worse. The privilege would encourage immigration of a race which cannot be assimilated by the Caucasians. It is not a question of the superiority of one race over the other, it is only a question of a difference so great that the two races have not a common basis of similar traits and ideals which would make amalgamation possible. It is best and wisest to recognize this difference and to regulate relations with due regard to its existence. When founded upon a basis of recognized facts and conditions, nothing will interfere with the feeling of mutual respect and good-will between the United States and Japan.

Very truly yours,　Saml Gompers.
President,　American Federation of Labor.

TLpS, reel 176, vol. 188, pp. 741–42, SG Letterbooks, DLC.

1. In his letter of Oct. 14, 1913, Harada asked SG's opinion as to the causes of friction between the United States and Japan and the possibility of granting the right of naturalization to the Japanese under certain conditions (Files of the Office of the President, General Correspondence, reel 76, frames 498–99, *AFL Records*).

2. Herbert Spencer's letter, dated Aug. 26, 1892, was actually written to Baron Kentarō Kaneko (1853–1942), who in the 1880s had been the private secretary to Premier Hirobumi Itō (1841–1909) and who later served as a minister in Itō's government. Spencer encouraged Kaneko to communicate the contents of the letter to the premier.

Excerpts from Accounts of the 1913 Convention of the AFL in Seattle[1]

[November 10, 1913]

REPORT OF EXECUTIVE COUNCIL

. . .

Minimum Wage Legislation

Resolution No. 20, by delegate Henry Prinz,[2] of the New York State Federation of Labor, requested the Rochester Convention[3] to refer to the Executive Council of the American Federation of Labor the question of establishing by law a minimum wage for women. The convention referred "the subject and the principle involved" to the Executive Council "with instructions to make an investigation and submit a report to the next convention."

In compliance with the action of the Rochester Convention, we have secured and examined all available data from States where such laws are in existence, and we beg to report that the following States have enacted minimum wage laws for women during the legislative sessions of 1912 and 1913:

California, May 26, 1913.[4]
Colorado, May 14, 1913.[5]
Massachusetts, June 4, 1912.[6]
Minnesota, April 26, 1913.[7]
Nebraska, April 21, 1913.[8]
Oregon, February 17, 1913.[9]
Utah, March 18, 1913.[10]
Washington, March 24, 1913.[11]
Wisconsin, August, 1913.[12]

Bills introduced in Congress for the purpose of establishing a minimum wage for female workers are: S. 579,[13] by Senator Chilton of West Virginia; S. 1925,[14] by Senator Lewis[15] of Illinois; H.R. 1803,[16] by Representative Lafferty[17] of Oregon; H.R. 4901,[18] by Representative Vare[19] of Pennsylvania. The Lewis bill is possibly the most comprehensive of these measures, it calling for the appointment of a National Minimum Wage Commission.

Bills were introduced in several other State Legislatures during the legislative sessions of 1913, but information now at hand from such States is too meager to justify reference to them. We should add, however, that the bill introduced in the Legislature of Missouri[20] was strongly pressed by its advocates, but at the last moment failed of passage.

. . .[21]

Conclusions and Recommendations[22]

From the report we have given, it will be observed that the movement for a minimum wage for women and minors has gained considerable headway in our country, and that sentiment in favor of a living wage is rapidly crystallizing. That this growth of sentiment among the people is due to the activities of the organized wage-earners there can be no doubt. The organized labor movement has insisted from the beginning upon the establishment of a living wage as a minimum, and it has, through the force of organized effort, succeeded in establishing minimum wages and maximum hours of labor far superior to those prescribed by the wage boards of other countries.

There is a marked difference, however, between the laws of other countries and the laws enacted or proposed in various States in our country. In England and in Australia authority is vested in wage boards to fix minimum wages for men workers as well as for women and minors; whereas in America these laws relate exclusively to women workers and to minors. If it were proposed in this country to vest authority in any tribunal to fix by law wages for men, Labor would protest by every means in its power. Through organization the wages of men can and will be maintained at a higher minimum than they would be if fixed by legal enactment.

But there is a far more significant ground for opposing the establishment by law of a minimum wage for men. The principle that organization is the most potent means for a shorter workday, and for a higher standard of wages, applies to women workers equally as to men. But the fact must be recognized that the organization of women workers constitutes a separate and more difficult problem. Women do not organize as readily or as stably as men. They are, therefore, more easily exploited. They certainly are in a greater measure than are men entitled to the concern of society. A fair standard of wages—a living wage, for all employed in an industry, should be the first consideration in production. None are more entitled to that standard than are the women and minors. An industry which denies to all its workers and particularly denies to its women and minors who are toilers a living wage is unfit and should not be permitted to exist.

We recognize, of course, that in our time legislation of this character is experimental and that sufficient experience with it has not been had to enable us to secure comprehensive and accurate information as to its tendency and its effect upon wages and industrial conditions; therefore, we recommend that for the information of the labor movement the Executive Council be instructed to watch developments where such legislation is in force and to record carefully the activities, the decisions and the trend of minimum wage boards.

We recommend that in all minimum wage laws the organized workers should see to it that provision is made for the representation on minimum wage boards of the organized wage-earners, and that the laws are so changed or drawn and administered as to afford the largest measure of protection to women and minor workers—those they are designed to protect.[23]

. . .

AFL, *Proceedings,* 1913, pp. 12, 59, 63–64.

1. The 1913 AFL convention met in Seattle, Nov. 10–22.

2. Henry Prinz represented the New York State Federation of Labor at the 1912 AFL convention in Rochester, N.Y. At that time he was a member of Cigar Makers' International Union of America 74 of Poughkeepsie, N.Y., and president of the Poughkeepsie Central Trades and Labor Council.

3. The 1912 AFL convention met in Rochester, Nov. 11–23.

4. California, Laws of 1913, chap. 324, enacted May 26, 1913, established an industrial welfare commission with authority to investigate wages, hours, and working conditions of women and minors under age eighteen and to set minimum wages, maximum hours of work, and standard conditions of labor for women and minors employed in any occupation or trade in California. Failure to pay the minimum wage was punishable by a fine or imprisonment.

5. Colorado, Laws of 1913, chap. 110, enacted May 14, 1913, created for two years a state wage board to investigate the wages paid to women or minors under age eighteen in any specific mercantile, manufacturing, laundry, hotel, restaurant, telephone, or telegraph business in Colorado and set minimum wages in any such establishment. Failure to comply was punishable by fine or imprisonment.

6. Massachusetts, Laws of 1912, chap. 706, enacted June 4, 1912, and amended by Laws of 1913, chaps. 330 and 673, established a minimum wage commission with the power to investigate and set minimum wages for women and minors under age eighteen in any occupation in Massachusetts. The commission was authorized to publish the names of employers who did not comply with its rulings.

7. Minnesota, Laws of 1913, chap. 547, enacted Apr. 26, 1913, created a minimum wage commission with authority to investigate and set minimum wages for women or minors (males under age twenty-one or females under age eighteen) in any occupation in Minnesota where one-sixth or more of those employed were paid less than a living wage. The commission's decisions were enforceable by fine or imprisonment.

8. Nebraska, Laws of 1913, chap. 211, enacted Apr. 21, 1913, created a minimum wage commission to investigate and set minimum wages for women and minors under age eighteen in any occupation in Nebraska. The commission was directed to publish the names of noncomplying employers.

9. Oregon, Laws of 1913, chap. 62, enacted Feb. 17, 1913, established an industrial welfare commission empowered to investigate and set standards for minimum wages, maximum hours, and working conditions for women and minors under age eighteen in any occupation in Oregon. Its decisions were enforceable by fine or imprisonment.

10. Utah, Laws of 1913, chap. 63, enacted Mar. 18, 1913, set specific minimum wages for female employees in Utah.

11. Washington, Laws of 1913, chap. 174, enacted Mar. 24, 1913, created an industrial welfare commission to investigate and set minimum standards for wages and working conditions for women and minors under age eighteen employed in the state of Washington. Its decisions were enforceable by fine.

12. Wisconsin, Laws of 1913, chap. 712, enacted July 31, 1913, gave the state's industrial commission authority to determine minimum wages for women and minors in Wisconsin.

13. S. 579 (63d Cong., 1st sess.), introduced by Democratic senator William Chilton of West Virginia on Apr. 9, 1913, to provide for a minimum wage for female workers, did not become law.

14. S. 1925 (63d Cong., 1st sess.), introduced on May 14, 1913, to establish a national wage commission, did not become law.

15. James Hamilton Lewis (1863–1939) served as a Democratic congressman from Washington (1897–99) and as a Democratic senator from Illinois (1913–19, 1931–39).

16. H.R. 1803 (63d Cong., 1st sess.), introduced on Apr. 7, 1913, to create a minimum wage commission for Washington, D.C., did not become law.

17. Abraham Walter Lafferty (1875–1964) served as a Republican congressman from Oregon (1911–15).

18. H.R. 4901 (63d Cong., 1st sess.), introduced on May 8, 1913, to establish a minimum wage and a minimum age for all government employees, did not become law.

19. William Scott Vare (1867–1934) served as a Republican congressman from Pennsylvania (1912–23, 1923–27).

20. A bill to establish a minimum wage commission that could, in turn, create wage boards with authority to set minimum wages in various occupations in Missouri was introduced in the legislature in January 1913. It failed to pass. The Missouri Senate then set up an investigatory committee to look into the wages of women and minors and report back to the next legislature.

21. Omitted here are a lengthy summary of the 1912 report of the Massachusetts commission on the wages of women and minors, a comment on the Oregon minimum wage law, and a passage on the minimum wage from Margaret Dreier Robins's address before a convention of the National Women's Trade Union League of America.

22. For the division of opinion in the AFL Executive Council on the question of minimum wage legislation for women, see AFL Microfilm Convention File, reel 26, frames 1291–93, *AFL Records*. In his report on the matter to the Council on Sept. 26, 1913, SG stated: "We aim to secure minimum wage rates through and by the solidarity of the working people themselves, through the economic forces of their associated effort in trade unions. We then know that we not only possess, but control the power over our own well-being, and we do not under such control have to parcel out our rights by proxy to politicians, theorists, inexperienced investigators or wage commissions. . . . The question of regulating wages by law, except of course for government employes, is a most delicate one, and one that I have ever looked upon with grave apprehension. It is questionable whether lasting, beneficial results would accrue to the working people of our country, or any part of the working people of our country, if their wages were fixed by a commission or by a statute" (Executive Council Records, Minutes, reel 4, frame 1427, *AFL Records*).

23. The convention unanimously approved the AFL Executive Council's recommendations on Nov. 18, 1913. The previous day, however, it had endorsed a report from the Committee on the Shorter Workday, which urged state federations of labor "to work unceasingly for the enactment of laws limiting the working hours of women and children to eight per day and not more than 48 per week" and recommended that "where women's eight-hour laws already exist an agitation should immediately begin for the enactment of general eight-hour laws" (AFL, *Proceedings*, 1913, p. 285).

WOULD PUT PROBE TO COLORADO CONDITIONS

Action looking toward the inauguration of a congressional investigation of conditions existing in Colorado, where a strike[1] is now being carried on by the Western Federation of Miners,[2] was taken by the American Federation of Labor convention this morning, when the report of the resolutions committee recommending that the executive council and the officers of the federation cooperate with the miners in efforts to bring about such action was adopted.[3]

The recommendation of the committee was based upon a lengthy statement of conditions in Colorado, which was submitted by a delegate of the miners' organization[4] and referred to the resolutions committee for a report. Although, as the committee stated, the communication asked for no definite action on the part of the American Federation of Labor, in view of conditions known to exist in Colorado the recommendation of cooperation in the matter of a congressional inquiry was made.

The communication read by Secretary Frey,[5] of the resolutions committee, declared the state to be in the grip of those greedy for gold. The miners, it was claimed, were striking for the right to organize, and demanded better wages and hours and the right to have a check weighman at the mouth of the mine who would see that the coal taken from the mine was properly weighed. The miners also demand the right of free speech.

At the conclusion of the report of the committee and before the question came to a vote, J. S. Hall[6] of the Wallace Trades Council[7] recited at length the conditions in West Virginia and affirmed that the investigation there[8] had accomplished nothing in the interests of the miners. The only way, in Mr. Hall's opinion, to secure proper recognition of the rights of labor is to see that men from the ranks of labor are elected to Congress. Mr. Hall referred to Patrick Henry's famous declaration for liberty or death and declared that unless conditions received remedial attention, nothing less than a revolution was impending in the United States.

John D. Lennon,[9] treasurer of the A.F. of L., rose at the conclusion of Mr. Hall's speech, to enquire if the recommendation of the committee carried with it an endorsement of the "William J. Burns language of the communication."

James Duncan,[10] chairman of the resolutions committee, replied emphatically that it did not and declared further that the communication, in effect, was not a resolution, did not ask the American Federation of Labor to do anything and did not, on its face, show that the delegate presenting it had the authority of his organization to bring it before the convention. In view of the importance of the Colorado situation, Mr. Duncan explained, the passing of the matter to the executive council was recommended.

In reply to the remarks made by Mr. Hall relative to West Virginia, Delegate Walker[11] declared that the strike there had accomplished much for the miners. The right to organize had been recognized, it was claimed; a check weighman had been placed at the mouth of the mine and the privileges of free speech and right of assemblage increased. The big advantage, however, Mr. Walker stated, was that the miners had been enabled to establish their organization thoroughly. Mr. Walker also declared that but for the activity of Minority Leader Mann,[12] in the House of Representatives, a congressional investigation would already have been ordered and many of the mining companies bound by agreements.[13]

Seattle Daily Times, Nov. 15, 1913.

1. On Sept. 23, 1913, after mine operators refused to meet with union representatives, the United Mine Workers of America struck the southern Colorado coalfields. The miners' demands included union recognition, the eight-hour day, a 10-percent wage increase, the right to elect their own check weighmen, the right to choose their own stores, homes, and doctors, enforcement of the state's mining laws, and an end to the use of armed guards in the mines. Three major firms led the fight against the union: the Victor-American Fuel Co., the Rocky Mountain Fuel Co., and the largest coal producer, the Colorado Fuel and Iron Co., a Rockefeller concern. The mine owners began evicting the strikers, who then set up tent colonies on adjacent land. The owners also brought in hundreds of Baldwin-Felts guards, many of whom were sworn in as sheriff's deputies. After a number of strikers were killed, Gov. Elias Ammons declared martial law and sent in the national guard in late October, but under the command of Adj. Gen. John Chase the guard was used to protect strikebreakers and intimidate the strikers. Escalating violence culminated in the Ludlow massacre of Apr. 20, 1914, in which at least five miners, two women, and eleven children were killed. In the aftermath of the massacre state labor leaders called on workingmen to arm themselves and organize for self-defense, and a wave of retaliatory violence swept the mining district. On the request of Governor Ammons, President Woodrow Wilson ordered federal troops into Colorado on Apr. 29 to restore order. During the summer and fall of 1914 the mine owners rejected several efforts by Wilson to settle the dispute, and on Dec. 10 the United Mine Workers called off the strike.

2. Actually the United MINE Workers of America.

3. The recommendation of the Committee on Resolutions derived from resolution 20, a lengthy statement condemning the conditions in Colorado introduced on Nov. 11, 1913, by delegate Morris Brown of the Central Federated Union (CFU) of Greater New York and Vicinity. At its meeting on Nov. 23 the AFL Executive Council referred the matter to SG, who subsequently wrote United Mine Workers' president John White that he would cooperate in every way possible with that union's efforts to secure a congressional investigation. For the investigations of the strikes in Colorado and Michigan, see "To John Handley," Jan. 12, 1914, n. 6, below.

4. Actually resolution 20, introduced by delegate Brown of the CFU of Greater New York and Vicinity.

5. John Philip FREY represented the International Molders' Union of North America. He edited the union's official journal from 1903 to 1927.

6. John S. Hall was a Wallace, Idaho, carpenter.

7. The AFL chartered the Wallace Trades and Labor Council in 1907.

8. See *The Samuel Gompers Papers,* vol. 8, p. 519, n. 2.

9. Actually John B. Lennon, who represented the Journeymen Tailors' Union of America.

10. James Duncan represented the Granite Cutter's International Association of America.

11. John Hunter WALKER, a delegate of the United Mine Workers, served as president of the Illinois State Federation of Labor (1913–19, 1920–30) and of United Mine Workers District 12 (Illinois; 1905–8, 1909–13, 1931–33).

12. James Robert Mann (1856–1922) was a Republican congressman from Illinois (1897–1922).

13. On Nov. 7, 1913, Democratic congressman Edward Keating of Colorado asked the House of Representatives to discharge from the Committee on Rules and to consider immediately H.Res. 290 (63d Cong., 1st sess.), a resolution he had introduced on Oct. 21 calling for a congressional investigation of conditions in the Colorado coal mines. Mann spoke in opposition and made a point of order that a quorum was not present, after which the House voted to adjourn without taking action on Keating's request.

[November 18, 1913]

DESCRIBE CONDITIONS IN COPPER DISTRICTS

Shortly after the American Federation of Labor convention assembled yesterday afternoon, and following the reading of several communications[1] from Texas cities urging Fort Worth as the 1914 convention[2] city, the present strike and previous labor conditions at the Calumet & Hecla copper mines in Michigan were taken up. A number of impassioned speeches were made.

The question came up on a report of the committee on resolutions recommending the adoption of a resolution urging delegates, upon their return home, to arouse their local unions to an appreciation of conditions in Michigan with a view to rendering all possible aid to the strikers.[3]

Joseph D. Cannon, representing the United Mine Workers,[4] said he wanted the delegates to obtain an impression of the unspeakable conditions existing in the Calumet district.

"In Michigan," he said, "men are railroaded to the penitentiary on trumped-up charges, and the strike was not twenty-four hours old before 1,150 hired thugs and representatives of detective agencies invaded the district and the carnage started. There had not been an eye blacked up to the arrival of these thugs.

"One incident will be sufficient to illustrate conditions. Practically all of the miners' shacks are on company ground. Thirty-six hours after the strike started the militia was on the ground. The strikers were told they came in an impartial attitude and there would be no violence or martial law, and that their object was to protect life and property.

"Then an edict was issued that no one was to leave company property before 9 A.M. or to go in or out after 4 P.M. Two men who had been to a nearby village for their mail returned after 4 P.M. They were stopped by a shift boss, who forbade them to return to their homes. They disregarded him and then the shift boss, surrounded by six deputy sheriffs, followed them to the house where they lived, and while the fifteen occupants were at supper opened fire on them from the windows, killing one man and a youth. A babe in its mother's arms was badly burned by powder and the bullet plowed through the mother's clothing.["][5]

Blamed to "Act of God."

"Then the militia came, but not to arrest the murderers, but to prevent the friends and loved ones of the dead and injured from entering the house of the afflicted. Under the eyes of the militia, the deputy sheriffs gathered together sticks and bludgeons and bottles to manufacture them into evidence as the weapons of the strikers. At the inquest which followed we brought out the evidence that the shift boss was not an officer, not even a citizen; but the coroner's jury exonerated him and the deputies, blaming the deaths to 'an act of God.' Thus it was shown that even the law-executing bodies of the district were and are absolutely controlled by the corporations.

"Daily, the strikers held parades, always headed by the American flag, with sometimes a dozen American flags in the parade. The militia would ride through these parades, zigzagging on their horses, and deputies in automobiles would do the same thing, trying to incite the strikers to rioting so they could shoot them down.

"The men in the Calumet & Hecla mines worked under conditions words fail to describe. There are no similar conditions in this country and they would be a disgrace to a land of savages.["]

Demands of Strikers.

"All they demanded was a minimum wage of $3 a day for eight hours, recognition of the union and two men working on machines designed for two men. Such conditions exist in every other copper mine in the country, with the possible exception of one in Tennessee."

. . .

Speaker Overcome.

Delegate John H. Walker, representing the United Mine Workers, was so filled with emotion that his voice broke and tears filled his eyes as he described the conditions under which he declared men worked in the Calumet mines and the atrocities which he said were perpetrated by hired thugs.

"I was on the scene conferring with the men before the strike," said Walker. "Four of the mines are 8,000 feet deep and the heat at that depth is terrific. The men could wear only caps to hold their lights and shoes to protect their feet.

"Levels are run out hundreds of feet at a depth of 8,000 feet and there is absolutely no provision for fresh air except at the mine shaft. The men are required to breathe the exhaust from their machines, dynamite fumes and their own devitalized breath, while working in copper dust that eats out the system like acid.

"The average working life of the underground man there is less than three years and then he is thrown on the human scrap heap. In the least civilized countries in the world, such conditions do not exist and there are no precautions taken against accident or death.

"The state Legislature prevented the passage of a law[6] requiring the reporting of accidents and the man who reports them is required to leave the mines and the copper country. The history of the feudal ages shows no more abject slavery or more despotic tyranny than exists in the Calumet & Hecla mines.

"The corporation rules supreme. It absolutely controls the two newspapers[7] there and censors every article affecting the mines. It can drive any man in the district out of business.

"Its political dominance is supreme and even the churches are built upon company ground, and the salaries of the pastors guaranteed by the company. I cannot even express the truth and you cannot credit the things being done there. Thousands of men, women and children who know the truth regarding these conditions prefer death to returning to work under them. I can only add that I would do for them what I would do for you under like conditions."

. . .

Samuel Beattie,[8] of the Michigan State Federation of Labor, made an appeal for financial assistance for the strikers, as did Delegate Waterman[9] of the Kalamazoo Trades and Labor Council,[10] who said 50 per cent of the strikers would soon be evicted from their shacks for non-payment of rent to the company.

J. S. Hall, of the Wallace, Ida., Labor Council, recommends the levying of an assessment[11] on organized labor to enable the miners to win their strike and President Samuel Gompers added his word of appeal, telling what steps have been taken by the A.F. of L., and saying the miners cannot struggle without bread. He asked that all delegates, in all printed matter sent out by them at their homes, seek financial aid for the strikers, concluding with the couplet, "Sympathy, without relief, is like mustard without beef."

Seattle Daily Times, Nov. 18, 1913.

1. Printed in AFL, *Proceedings,* 1913, p. 279.

2. The 1914 AFL convention met in Philadelphia, Nov. 9–21.

3. Resolution 98 was introduced on Nov. 13, 1913, by delegates John Mitchell and Joseph Cannon on behalf of the AFL Mining Department. Adopted by the convention, the resolution demanded a congressional investigation of the Michigan copper miners' strike, endorsed the stand taken by the miners, and urged affiliated unions to contribute financially. For AFL financial assistance in behalf of the strike, see "A Circular," Sept. 29, 1913, n. 6, above.

4. Joseph D. Cannon actually represented the Western Federation of MINERS.

5. On the afternoon of Aug. 14, 1913, two striking copper miners, John Kalan and John Stimac, were stopped by shift boss Humphrey Quick as they took a shortcut to their boardinghouse across the property of the Copper Range Consolidated Mining Co. Quick brandished a club at them and ordered them off company property. The two ignored his demand and insults were exchanged. Quick then followed them to their boardinghouse, accompanied by two sheriff's deputies and four Waddell-Mahon guards. When the deputies caught up with Kalan they began attacking him with clubs. He ran into the building, whereupon the guards and one of the deputies opened fire. There were fifteen people in the house at the time, including two women and four children, and several of them were caught in the line of fire, including Alois Tijan, age eighteen, who was shot and died on the scene; Steve Putrich, the brother of the boardinghouse's owner, who was shot in the abdomen and died the following day; and Stimac and Stanko Stepic, who were wounded. The infant daughter of Antonia Putrich received powder burns. On Sept. 3 the coroner's jury ruled that Tijan had died as a result of gunshots fired by an unknown person; however, on Feb. 15, 1914, four of the deputies and guards were convicted of manslaughter in connection with the death of Steve Putrich and sentenced to imprisonment for periods of seven to fifteen years.

6. At its 1913 session the Michigan legislature passed a law requiring the operators of coal mines in the state to report to the state mining inspector all accidents resulting in injury (Michigan, Laws of 1913, chap. 177). At the same session the legislature blocked passage of a bill extending the state's inspection authority to other places of employment.

7. The English-language newspapers published in the Calumet region during this period included the *Calumet News,* the *Daily Mining Gazette* (published in Houghton, Mich.), and the *Evening Copper Journal* (published in Hancock, Mich.).

8. Samuel G. Beattie was a Grand Rapids, Mich., carpenter.

9. Homer F. WATERMAN of Kalamazoo, Mich., was secretary-treasurer (1911–15) of the Michigan State Federation of Labor.

10. The Kalamazoo Trades and Labor Council was organized in 1884 and received an AFL charter in 1901.

11. John Hall's recommendation did not come to a vote.

[November 18, 1913]

UTTER ROUT REBUKES RADICALS
WHO'D ALTER A.F.L. CONSTITUTION

In a struggle which sharply aligned the radical faction of the American Federation of Labor from that which believes the destinies of the movement are being ably guided by the present officials and executive council, an attempt to amend the constitution of the federation today at the convention in The Hippodrome was overwhelmingly defeated.

. . .

The resolution[1] which precipitated the battle was introduced by Delegate A. W. Bennett[2] of Chickasha, Okla., an organizer among the flour-mill workers of his state. In asking for the adoption of his resolution Bennett said that the A.F. of L. constitution now provides that a union must be in existence for a year and its members affiliated with the A.F. of L. for one year before being entitled to receive benefits.

Bennett pointed out that millers and other manufacturers took advantage of this fact to throttle unions in their incipiency and that in many instances the unions could not live without assistance from the A.F. of L. He cited an instance in which members of a new union were locked out within a few hours of their organization and before they had presented any demand whatever.

His resolution provided that laws of the A.F. of L. be so amended as to place within the power of the executive committee the right to go to the assistance of such union with the defense fund to prevent them from being at the mercy of the employers. The committee on laws recommended the passage of the resolution as they amended it. The amendment provided that the matter of such assistance should be placed at the discretion of the executive council.

WOULD WIPE OUT FUND.

Secretary Morrison[3] started the discussion on the question by stating that if the recommendation of the committee were adopted the executive council would be put in the position of paying strike benefits to some unions and compelled to turn down the applications of others. He said that the payment of strike benefits, even when there were few strikes, amounted to between $60,000 and $70,000 a year as the law now stands, and that the proposed change would obliterate the defense fund.

. . .

"Is it not true," asked President Gompers, "that the largest number of strikes occur in newly formed unions?" On being answered in the affirmative President Gompers said that most of such benefits would go to men on strike or locked out during their first year of organization.

"Where are you going to get the money?" asked the president. "The truth of the matter is that newly-organized unions go into strikes when the demands they present are refused."

Joseph Proebstle,[4] representing the Brewers' Union, said:

"Constantly we are confronted with the accusations of the I.W.W. that we are doing nothing for the benefit of labor. These men are entitled to strike benefits and let us meet these accusations by increasing the per capita tax and providing them with the protection they deserve. Let us give them protection even if we have to go to battle to do it.["]

Why Tie Hands?

"Our secretary seeks to give the impression that the change recommended makes it compulsory on the part of the executive council to give such aid when the resolution as amended distinctly makes it discretionary. Why tie the hands of this body from giving aid when necessary?"

S. E. Heberling[5] of the Switchmen, asked: "Would you see an infant die in a ditch, die of starvation? That is what some new unions do in the first year of organization. The employers know our law preventing assistance within a year and take advantage of it. Put some confidence in your executive board and give them the power to help within a year at their discretion."

Delegate J. B. Cannon of the Miners not only recommended the adoption of the report on the resolution, but urged the convention to go further and increase the per capita of federal unions, as well as their dues, to put them in financial shape for troubles which may arise. He declared the fault for unions being snuffed out in their incipiency by employers lies in the present law of the A.F. of L.

President Gompers said: "I agree with properly increasing the per capita tax. I have deep sentiment and strong sympathy with men who are striking and making a sacrifice to protest against wrong and injustice. As a matter of fact most of the strikes in the past twenty years in the United States which have attracted the attention and aroused the sympathy of the people were in the ranks of those unorganized before the strike.["]

Doing Best Possible.

"We have met these situations as fast as we could. We have appointed committees to call upon the generosity and sympathy of the people of the country to contribute to help those engaged in the struggle. That is one way of doing it. The proposition of special benefits from the A.F. of L. is another question.

"Some delegates say the resolution does not make such aid compulsory on the committee, but merely discretionary. Is that a fact? Would not all union workers locked out or on strike think they were entitled to the benefit of $4 a week if the executive council approved? If the executive council approved every application submitted to them it would mean bankruptcy, not protection.

"If the treasury of the United States were at the command of the A.F. of L. it could not meet the obligations which this provision would place upon it. You say the executive council has discretionary power. In words, yes. If the council said yes it would mean bankruptcy. If it said no it would be damned from one end to the other of the entire country. It is not feasible. It is impracticable and impossible.

"I have heard the I.W.W. charge against the A.F. of L. It would be a bad time if we would have to halt in our work to meet the frivolous, purposeless charges or insinuations made by that sort of people. Every time they have made a fuss or row we have had to pay the piper or fiddler.["]

Would Imperil Cause.

"If the executive council should approve these applications for aid from newly organized unions this body would soon be bankrupt and driven from the labor movement."

Delegates J. Goldstone[6] of the Bakers and Bennett, who introduced the resolution, spoke in its favor and the question came up on the original motion,[7] a change in the constitution requiring a two-thirds vote to carry. The committee recommendation was voted down, 113 to 69.[8]

Delegate Arnold[9] then moved the adoption of the original resolution and a second debate was precipitated, one of the principal speakers in favor of the resolution being W. D. Mahon,[10] of the Railway Clerks, who said his union made it a point to pay strike benefits within two weeks after a strike started and that he considered it a disgrace for the A.F. of L. to have a law on record withholding such support for one year.

T. W. Rowe,[11] of the American Flint Glass Workers, took the floor and spoke in opposition to the resolution. He declared that while his organization was able to pay benefits when trouble came between its members and their employers, the union was 97 per cent organized, with but few in the trade outside the union.

After Delegate Emil Arnold, of the paperhangers, painters and decorators,[12] had spoken briefly in support of the resolution, Secretary

Kelly[13] of the committee on law obtained the floor and declared he would just as soon see the executive council damned as the convention of the federation for failing to pass the law.

Delegate James Wilson,[14] of the patternmakers, pointed out that the real question before the convention was: Where will the money come from to pay these benefits? He said that if the resolution carried, he would introduce another which would raise the per capita tax from 10 cents per member to 25; and from 2 cents for those below the age of 18 to 12 cents.

John P. Frey, of the molders,[15] secretary of the resolutions committee, addressed the convention against the resolution, asserting that when organizers went out to get new locals for federal labor unions, extravagant promises were sometimes made.

"The newly organized," he said, "fail to get the proper idea of paddling their own canoe. They think that they will have behind them the central labor council, the state and the American Federation."

A. J. Kugler of the brewers made a brief speech favoring the resolution, after which President Gompers obtained recognition a second time and took the floor for his remarkable speech which turned the tide and resulted in the vindication of the executive council.

Resents Hint of Treachery.

"I ask your attention," he began, "to a plain statement of fact. I resent the idea that any of the officers or myself because we oppose this resolution must therefore be playing into the hands of the employers. I have tried to give the movement to organize the workers some support, and have contributed perhaps to considerable extent along that line.

"I realize that there are some who would fire off all their ammunition at once. Then there are some tacticians who believe that each in the army has his own particular function to perform at a particular time for the advancement of all.

"I ask you what is the real question at issue. Not that we cannot support striking men who go out for the privilege of organizing. I asked Delegate Mahon, generally speaking, if strikes of street car men are not concluded before two weeks has expired, when their strike benefits begin.

"He said they were; and you can readily see the wisdom of the policy of the street car men when they say strike benefits begin after the second week; because it is a comparatively small number that is involved after the second week, and they are able to finance it. But if it was made in their constitution that benefits should begin on the first day of strike, I think they would have some provision so that the organization would not become bankrupt at its first strike.["]

MINE WORKERS CITED.

"Take the case of the United Mine Workers. Suppose that in 1897 in their meeting they had declared for guaranteed weekly benefits to miners who were members of the organization and were locked out on strike. On July 4, 1897, they called a strike in the bituminous regions where 150,000 men went out. If they had attempted to pay these men, and they went out on strike as they did, the mere fact the organization had made promises which it could not keep would disintegrate the membership.

"You cannot pay benefits unless you have means with which to pay them. I, too, have been in strikes, and a number of them—large strikes, long-continued—and I know as you know that one of the first things people on strike ask is: 'How much benefits am I going to get?'

"We have the great mass of unorganized workers to organize, and you dare not hold out promises to them that you cannot fulfill. To what is due this wonderful growth of the Federation to more than 2,000,000 members? Of last year when we had a gain of a quarter of a million? This talk of never reaching the 3,000,000 mark makes me impatient.["]

BE WARNED BY EXAMPLE.

"I want to repeat to you the warning that Shakespeare wrote when he put in the mouth of Friar Lawrence, speaking to Romeo: 'There are many men who lost their race by attempting to overrun.'[16] Don't forget the dog that lost his bone because he jumped after the shadow.

"Organize, work along practical lines; and for goodness sake don't commit the federation to promises, I repeat, that the treasury of the United States could not supply."

Following President Gompers' address, the previous question was moved, and those who favored the resolution rose to their feet. Secretary Morrison declared that 74 favored it; and on the call for those who opposed, 142 arose. The motion was then declared lost.

Seattle Daily Times, Nov. 18, 1913.

1. Resolution 7, introduced on Nov. 10, 1913, by delegate Albert Bennett of the Chickasha (Okla.) Trades Council, would have amended Art. XIII, Sec. 4, of the AFL constitution to authorize the Executive Council to pay benefits to members of newly organized directly affiliated locals discharged for forming a union. The Committee on Laws, to which the resolution was referred, recommended that it be amended to give the Council discretionary power to pay such benefits, but neither the original resolution nor the amended version was adopted by the convention.

2. Albert W. Bennett represented the Chickasha Trades Council. He was recording or financial secretary of Brotherhood of Painters, Decorators, and Paperhangers of America 1005 of Chickasha from 1909 to at least 1923.

3. Frank Morrison represented the International Typographical Union.

4. Joseph PROEBSTLE, of the International Union of the United BREWERY Workmen of America, served as financial secretary of the union from 1904 to 1922.

5. Samuel E. HEBERLING served as president of the SWITCHMEN's Union of North America from 1911 to 1921.

6. Jacob Goldstone (variously Goldstein) was an organizer (1911–40) for the BAKERY and Confectionery Workers' International Union of America and a member of Bakery Workers' local 163 of Brooklyn.

7. That is, the amended version proposed by the Committee on Laws.

8. The *Proceedings* give the vote as 113 to 67 (AFL, *Proceedings,* 1913, p. 288).

9. Emil Arnold, a member of Painters and Decorators' local 275 of Chicago, represented the international union at this convention.

10. William D. MAHON, of the Amalgamated Association of STREET and Electric Railway Employes of America, served as the union's president from 1893 to 1946.

11. Thomas William ROWE was president of the American FLINT Glass Workers' Union (1903–16).

12. The Brotherhood of PAINTERS, Decorators, and Paperhangers of America.

13. William J. Kelly was a member of United Brotherhood of Carpenters and Joiners of America 164 of Pittsburgh and served as its secretary-treasurer in 1914 and 1915. He also served as secretary (1902–4) and president (1909–12) of the Iron City Trades Council and was editor of its journal (1909–17). Kelly represented the Carpenters at this convention.

14. James Adair WILSON was president of the PATTERN Makers' League of North America (1902–34).

15. The International MOLDERS' Union of North America.

16. The passage, which is from Shakespeare's *King Henry the Eighth,* act 1, scene 1, reads, ". . . We may outrun / By violent swiftness that which we run at, / And lose by over-running. . . ."

[November 20, 1913]

BERRY'S HOPE FOR POLITICAL PARTY IN LABOR REALM DIES

George L. Berry's[1] dream of an immediate political party to be composed of Socialists, trade unionists, farmers and woman's suffrage advocates received an effectual quietus last night, the closing hours of the American Federation of Labor's session, when, after Berry had spoken until his voice was husky in support of his measure,[2] it was snowed under by a vote of 193 to 15.

At times the debate which Berry aroused by his statements urging political activity drifted so far from the main question at issue that the forum resembled that of the national convention of some party, rather than an economic assembly. So political were some of its aspects that Vice-President James Duncan, chairman of the committee on resolutions, inquired after one speaker had concluded as to the attitude of the speaker on the question before the house.

The resolutions committee, to which both the Berry resolution and still another,[3] introduced by J. S. Hall, of the Wallace, Idaho, Labor Council, along the same line, had been referred, moved that both resolutions be dropped and that a new one be adopted, recommending a greater growth along economic lines before a definite political propaganda was taken up.

. . .

Immediately after the committee had finished, Delegate Berry sprang to his feet and urged that the federation decline to postpone further its entrance into politics. He declared that the victory of the Democratic party was not permanent, and that their supremacy was the result of the action of the minority.

"The time is now opportune," he claimed, "because women are coming into their own. As long as we permit the struggle to go on between the workers who belong to the Socialist party and those who are not affiliated with it, so long are we going to be divided on the political field and victory be with the other side.["]

SOCIALISM.

"I am not a Socialist; but so long as we stand apart from them, so long are we going to be divided."

When Berry completed his speech the galleries joined in the applause which followed. President Samuel Gompers rebuked the visitors, saying that while they were welcome, the business of the convention was to be conducted by its delegates, and he would have to ask them to refrain from expressions of approval or disapproval.

Max S. Hayes,[4] of the International Typographical Union,[5] took the floor in opposition to Berry's resolution, and during the course of his speech made a stirring argument on behalf of Socialist tenets and against capitalism. He asserted, however, that it would be impossible for all the different factions as proposed by Berry to blend into one party.

"In this country it is an absurdity for men to attempt to make believe that they are something else than what they are," he said. "My contention is that when a man votes the Democratic ticket, he is a Democrat. Suppose we adopted this resolution by Delegate Berry. I am not prepared to say that the Socialists would go in with us, or that the women's suffrage leagues would, either."

. . .

Daniel J. Tobin[6] of the Teamsters' Union spoke briefly against the resolution, after which Vice-President Duncan, chairman of the resolutions committee, made an extended address, pointing out the ultimate hopes of organized labor that such a party would be formed.

In opening, he read from the constitution of the A.F. of L. a clause declaring that party politics, whether Democratic, Republican, Socialist, Populist, Prohibition or any other have no place in the conventions of the federation.[7]

"In its early years the federation was greatly bothered by politics," Duncan asserted. "For a number of years we have not been coming to these conventions as political units, but as trade unionists. We have voted as we thought best, here and there picking out a man no matter what his ticket may have been and voting for him if he was favorable to organized labor.

"Woman suffrage understands that it has a friend in organized labor, and that it always has had a friend.

"No one would like to see a Labor party ushered in any better than I would. But when there is so much need of organization in the economic field it would be a mistake to fall into the trap that other labor organizations have fallen into, and disrupt on politics."

When Duncan had finished, the previous question was called, and on the vote 193 favored the report of the committee postponing political action, and fifteen upheld Berry.

Seattle Daily Times, Nov. 20, 1913.

1. George Leonard BERRY, a representative of the International Printing Pressmen's and Assistants' Union of North America, served as president of the union from 1907 to 1948.

2. Resolution 149, introduced by Berry on Nov. 13, 1913, directed the AFL Executive Council to develop a program and platform for a labor party and establish a working agreement with the Socialist Party of America, the Woman's Suffrage League, the various farmers' unions, and the railroad brotherhoods. The convention instead adopted a substitute resolution recommending that the AFL continue the nonpartisan political activity authorized by previous conventions.

3. Resolution 93, introduced by John Hall on Nov. 13, 1913, directed SG to select nine delegates to draft a platform, to be adopted by the convention, for an "American Labor Party" (AFL, *Proceedings,* 1913, p. 230). The Committee on Resolutions considered resolution 93 along with resolution 149, and the convention adopted the same substitute resolution for both.

4. Max Sebastian HAYES was editor of the *Cleveland Citizen* from 1894 to 1939.

5. The International TYPOGRAPHICAL Union.

6. Daniel Joseph TOBIN, of the International Brotherhood of TEAMSTERS, Chauffeurs, Stablemen, and Helpers of America, served as president of the union from 1907 until 1952.

7. Art. III, Sec. 8.

[November 23, 1913]

GOMPERS AGAIN NAMED TO LEAD HOSTS OF LABOR[1]

Bringing the thirty-third annual meeting of the American Federation of Labor to a close with words of faith and optimism, figuratively pronouncing a benediction on the organized labor movement as delegates sat in hushed silence in the fleeting moments of the two weeks' session here, President Samuel Gompers, re-elected yesterday as head of the federation, brought down the gavel on his flag-draped table in the Hippodrome pavilion, and the convention adjourned sine die with a record of constructive legislation for the worker and the intelligent solution of the problems brought to the labor body for consideration.

Dramatic incidents marked the convention as the requiem of the thirty-third meeting was sounded. John Mitchell,[2] a national figure in the labor movement in this country, who retired yesterday from the executive council of the federation, bade good-by for a year, at least, to the delegates as an official in the labor movement. . . .

. . .

The convention, after unanimously indorsing a motion offered by John P. Frey, calling upon the executive committee to present resolutions, suitably engraved, expressing the appreciation of the federation and the council for the work of John Mitchell, called upon the retiring official to speak, stamping and applauding until he stepped to the platform.

JOHN MITCHELL'S APPRECIATION.

"It is impossible for me to express my keen sense of appreciation of your action," said the former president of the United Mine Workers of America, seriously, as he faced the convention. "My relations with the delegates to this convention and all preceding conventions I have attended have always been pleasant and instructive. I have no intention of lessening my interest in the trade union movement and the advancement of the working people, although I am no longer an official.

"Of my future plans, I don't know more than this: I propose in the future, to the extent of my ability and opportunities, to further the cause in which I most devoutly believe. I express the hope that next year there will be an increase in membership comparable to that of the past year. I am not without hope that the time is not far distant when all the working men and women will be enrolled in trade unions, and that those who labor will work out a destiny that will result in greater and juster rewards for the wealth that they produce.["]

PLEA FOR WOMEN AND CHILDREN.

"May I express the hope that the men of organized labor will give more effort and energy than they have in the past in organizing those of our fellow-workers who may not be skilled, and especially the women and children. I belong to a craft that employs no women workers, and I hope you will do your part, as I intend to do mine, in shielding and protecting the weaker worker from hardship, injustice and oppression."

To the credit of John Mitchell and the convention, his resolution urging the federation to levy in 1914 an assessment of 1 cent on all organized workers as a fund to start a campaign to organize women workers was passed later in the afternoon by unanimous vote.[3]

. . .

REID FACTION LOSES FIGHT.

The bitterest fight of the two weeks' session of the American Federation of Labor occurred yesterday on the floor of the convention when the controversy of the McNulty[4] and Reid[5] electrical workers, in the form of resolutions[6] on the strike of the Light and Power Council of California against the Pacific Gas & Electric Company,[7] were presented. The McNulty faction won a complete victory. Not a single concession was granted to the Reid workers, and the San Francisco Central Labor Council and local unions who aided the Reid strikers by going out with them were severely criticised. So far as the Federation of Labor is concerned, the controversy is at an end, although the convention directed President Samuel Gompers and members of the executive council to proceed to San Francisco[8] to encourage harmony and make an effort to secure the affiliation of the seceders with the recognized electrical union.[9]

Seattle Post-Intelligencer, Nov. 23, 1913.

1. The officers elected by the convention to serve during 1914 were SG, president; James Duncan, James O'Connell, Denis Hayes, Joseph Valentine, John Alpine, Henry Perham, John White, and Frank Duffy, first through eighth vice-presidents; Frank Morrison, secretary; and John Lennon, treasurer.

2. John Mitchell represented the United Mine Workers of America.

3. Resolution 70, approved by the convention, was introduced by Mitchell, the other delegates of the United Mine Workers, and Van Amberg Bittner of the Pennsylvania State Federation of Labor on Nov. 12, 1913. On Feb. 28, 1914, the AFL Executive Council issued a circular levying the assessment, which raised a total of $20,050. The money was used to pay twenty individuals assigned to organize women workers in 1914 and 1915.

4. Frank Joseph McNULTY served as president of the International Brotherhood of ELECTRICAL Workers (1903–19) and represented the union at this convention.

5. James J. REID was elected president of the Electrical Workers by a special convention of the union—later ruled illegal—in 1908. After an unsuccessful struggle for recognition by the AFL, he resigned his position in 1913.

6. Resolution 55, introduced by delegate Paul Scharrenberg of the San Francisco Labor Council, resolution 57 by Patrick Flynn of the California State Federation of Labor, and resolution 75 by Flynn and Scharrenberg jointly were all introduced on Nov. 12, 1913. They condemned interference by various AFL affiliates with the strike of the Light and Power Council of California, which included members of the Reid-Murphy faction of the Electrical Workers, against the Pacific Gas and Electric Co. The Com-

mittee on Resolutions recommended nonconcurrence in the resolutions and proposed instead that the convention endorse the action of the Executive Council, which had advised directly affiliated locals, the Labor Council, and national and international affiliates involved in the matter not to support the seceding electrical workers. The committee further recommended that SG and other members of the Executive Council visit San Francisco after the convention to urge a resolution of the matter. The convention adopted the committee's proposals.

7. On May 8, 1913, members of the Light and Power Council of California—an industrial federation of utility workers in the San Francisco Bay area that had been formed earlier in the year—struck the Pacific Gas and Electric Co. At issue were the wages of the company's electrical workers, who were affiliated with the Reid-Murphy faction of the international union. When the company responded by signing a three-year agreement with McNulty faction electricians on May 21, the strikers turned to sabotage and violence, cutting transmission lines and dynamiting substations. Although the San Francisco Labor Council supported the strike, the San Francisco Building Trades Council did not, and in July the AFL Executive Council ordered the Labor Council and affiliated international unions to refrain from supporting the Reid-Murphy electrical workers. The 1913 AFL convention endorsed the Executive Council's action, and on Jan. 13, 1914, the Light and Power Council called off the strike.

8. On Nov. 25, 1913, SG left Seattle for San Francisco, where he and other members of the AFL Executive Council held conferences with the two factions of Electrical Workers and the Pacific Gas and Power Co. SG left San Francisco on Dec. 6 for New York City, where he addressed several conferences and met with labor representatives between Dec. 10 and 15 before returning to AFL headquarters.

9. SG participated in negotiating an agreement between the McNulty faction of electrical workers and the Pacific district council of the Reid-Murphy faction, the text of which was published in the January 1914 number of the *American Federationist* (21: 59–60).

To Frank Morrison

Overland Limited
Extra Fare Train
Chicago-San Francisco
Dec. 7. 1913.

To Mr Frank Morrison
Sec'y A.F. of L.
Dear Friend Frank:—

Inasmuch as President White,[1] Sec'y Greene[2] & other officers of the U.M. of A have been indicted[3] by a federal Grand Jury under the criminal provisions of the Sherman Anti trust law, just as I generally predicted it is necessary that extra efforts be made by the A.F. of L. officers to secure the enactment of laws which shall exclude the voluntary organizations of the wage workers from the provisions of that law, or any other bearing upon the subject matter.

The Seattle convention directed that this be done and the Bartlett-Bacon Bill was specifically determined to [be] the measure sought. In conformity with the above I urge that you, with the Legislative Committee and such other official representatives of organized labor being in Washington call upon the Com. of the House of Representatives (Judiciary Com. I believe) and respectfully and urgently request that an early day, preferably in December, for the purpose of having representatives of our movement appear before the com.,[4] not necessarily for an argument but for a presentation of the need that the bill be early reported & enacted.

I suggest this most because I want Prest. White present & I want to invite him to be present. Jan. is his convention[5] and suppose he will then be unable to come to Washington.

#

The agreement to unite the Electrical Workers was the hardest job I ever had in my long experience. But I stuck to it until the end.

#

Left S.F. yesterday at 4. P.M. Am now near Ogden. May stop a day or so on the trip. Am awfully fagged out. Will go to New York before coming to the office. There are important matters I must give attention there.

Hope you found the family well and all things are moving along O.K.

Friday evening attended meeting of S.F. Labor Council. Had a "hot time" for them. I visited them the week before also.[6] Will tell you of these matters when I get back.

Best wishes to you and office friends.

Sincerely Yours   Saml Gompers.

ALS, Files of the Office of the President, General Correspondence, reel 76, frames 578–83, *AFL Records*.

1. John Phillip WHITE served as president of the United Mine Workers of America from 1911 to 1917.

2. William GREEN was secretary-treasurer (1913–24) of the United Mine Workers.

3. On Dec. 1, 1913, a Pueblo, Colo., federal grand jury indicted president White, secretary-treasurer Green, vice-president Frank Hayes, and twenty-two other members of the United Mine Workers on charges of attempting to maintain a monopoly of labor and conspiracy in restraint of interstate commerce in connection with their actions in support of the striking Colorado miners. The indictments were eventually dropped.

4. On Dec. 16, 1913, SG testified before the House Committee on the Judiciary on the need for the Bacon-Bartlett bill.

5. The 1914 United Mine Workers' convention met in Indianapolis, Jan. 20–Feb. 2.

6. SG attended meetings of the San Francisco Labor Council on Nov. 28 and Dec. 5, 1913. In his speech on Dec. 5 he emphasized the need for unity and condemned factionalism, asserting that "when an international determines on a course of action it must be the law if we hope to progress" (*Labor Clarion* [San Francisco], Dec. 12, 1913).

From John White

Office of President
United Mine Workers of America
Albany Hotel, Denver, Colorado, December 18, 1913.

Dear Sir and Brother:

Your favor of the 24th ult.,[1] extending congratulations on my election to the Seventh Vice Presidency of the American Federation of Labor, duly received, and I note your reference to the meeting[2] of the Executive Council which will be held at headquarters, Washington, D.C., January 19, 1914.

I appreciate very much your cordial congratulations, but wish to announce that I have fully decided not to serve in that position.

This may appear rather strange to you, but I feel that I would not be doing justice to the United Mine Workers if I accepted the office of Seventh Vice President.

Had I been in a position to attend the Seattle Convention, I would not have permitted the use of my name for the Seventh Vice Presidency. When John Mitchell announced his retirement from the office of Second Vice President, a position that he might have held indefinitely so far as I was personally concerned, my associates urged me to become a candidate for the position made vacant by Mr. Mitchell. I consented, with the understanding that that was the office to which I would aspire.

In the light of what has transpired, and in view of the fact that the United Mine Workers' Organization was entitled, in my judgment, to the recognition it had long enjoyed on the Council of the A.F. of L., I feel that I should not accept the Seventh Vice Presidency.

In my opinion, the loyalty of our organization to the American Federation of Labor cannot be questioned, and time has demonstrated that it has had no selfish motive, and the marked distinction enjoyed by its representative on the Council of the A.F. of L. has been viewed with pride and satisfaction by its membership and the general labor movement.

Of course, I do not understand what the underlying motives were that prompted some to view my aspirations with suspicion and alarm and that caused my friends to withdraw my candidacy for the office of Second Vice President, or what would lead others to believe that if I were elected to that position it might cause a break in the Federation and be instrumental in promoting internal discord.

In the absence of detailed information, I can only conclude that the opposition that developed, to which there might have been attached political significance, does not seem to be consistent, and I am at a loss to harmonize the final results. If there were any well defined reasons why I could not serve in the capacity of Second Vice President without endangering the internal peace of the Federation, I cannot see how I can honorably accept the office of Seventh Vice President.

Of course, I have nothing but the kindest feelings for my colleagues and friends who sought to advance me in the labor movement, but my convictions are deep and my decision unalterable. I would have preferred defeat for the Second Vice Presidency rather than to be chosen unanimously to the Seventh Vice Presidency, all things being considered.

I have endeavored to strengthen the United Mine Workers' organization in every legitimate way, and the records of the Federation will show that fifty per cent of the increase in the membership of the Federation during the last year can be credited to the United Mine Workers.

I hope my friends who assisted in conferring the Seventh Vice Presidency upon me will not think that I am ungrateful in pursuing the course I have decided upon, and you may be assured that I shall do all in my power to promote the organized labor movement of our country.

Therefore, in the light of the circumstances I have referred to, I hope you will consider my decision final.[3]

With the Compliments of the Season, I am,

Yours very truly,   John P. White
President,   U.M.W. of A.

TLS, AFL Microfilm Convention File, reel 26, frames 2610–11, *AFL Records.*

1. SG to John White, Nov. 24, 1913, reel 177, vol. 189, p. 18, SG Letterbooks, DLC.

2. The AFL Executive Council met in Washington, D.C., Jan. 19–24, 1914.

3. SG wrote White on Dec. 25, 1913, to explain that the numerical designations of the AFL's vice-presidents simply reflected length of service and the sequence in which the officers were elected. All vice-presidents were "co-equal in every particular and every sense," SG wrote, and there was "not any seniority in their positions nor power nor influence direct or indirect which any one exerts or exercises over another" (reel 177, vol. 189, pp. 511–19, SG Letterbooks, DLC, quotations at p. 516). SG asked White to reconsider his decision, and the AFL Executive Council reiterated this request on Jan. 20, 1914, but White was adamant in his refusal. The Executive Council then offered the vice-presidency to United Mine Workers of America secretary-treasurer William Green, but he also declined. (A transcript of SG's telephone conversation with Green on Jan. 23, urging him to accept the position, can be found in the AFL Microfilm Convention File, reel 26, frame 2612, *AFL Records.*) The office remained vacant until the 1914 AFL convention elected Green vice-president with "the full approval of President White" (AFL, *Proceedings,* 1914, p. 459).

SG published the correspondence with White in the February 1914 number of the *American Federationist* (21: 152–56). It was also included as part of the Executive Council's report to the 1914 convention, which voted unanimously to endorse the actions of SG and the Council. See also AFL Microfilm Convention File, reel 26, frames 2610–14, *AFL Records,* for further correspondence on the matter.

To Nieves Morales

Dec. 19, 1913.

Mr. N. G. Morales,
Secretary, Federal Labor Union #14365,[1]
Big Springs, Texas.
Dear Sir and Brother:

Your two favors of the sixth instant have been duly received. I have carefully noted all that you say in regard to the organization of the men in Big Springs and Toyah, that is, into separate unions of Mexican and American workers. I am not unmindful of the reasons you advance for the opinion you maintain, but yet I am of the belief that in view of the small membership, and the small number of the unorganized of both Mexicans and Americans, that it would be to the best interests of both classes of workers if they should all become members of Local #14365.[2] I would like you to take this matter under careful consideration with your colleagues, and with the unorganized American, as well as Mexican workmen, and advise me as to what can be done in the premises.

Hoping to receive your early reply, and with kind regards, I am,

Fraternally yours, Saml Gompers.
President, American Federation of Labor.

TLpS, reel 177, vol. 189, p. 363, SG Letterbooks, DLC.

1. The AFL chartered Federal Labor Union 14,365 of Big Springs, Tex., in 1912. In January 1915 it had forty-six members.
2. The AFL did not charter separate federal labor unions in Big Springs.

From Ernest Mills[1]

Denver, Colo., Dec. 27-[19]13.

I rec'd the following telegram from Prest Moyer[2] stating that ["]Charles H. Tanner[3] and Myself were brutally assaulted in my room in the Scott Hotel, Hancock, Michigan, tonight.[4] I was shot in the back and dragged more than one and one half miles through the streets of Hancock by a mob of Waddell Mahon thugs and Citizens Alliance. Put aboard a

Milwaukee train and threatened with death if I dared to return, but you can say for me that the Cause I represent is well worth the suffering I have undergone. The cause of the striking miners is just and they will win. (Signed) Charles H. Moyer.["] Take matter up immediately with Secty. of Labor Wilson.

Ernest Mills,
Secy.-treasr., Western Federation of Miners.[5]

TWtcSr, AFL Microfilm National and International Union File, Western Federation of Miners, Mine, Mill, and Smelter Workers Records, reel 45, frame 1578, *AFL Records.* Typed notation: "*Copy.*" Enclosed in SG to William B. Wilson, Dec. 30, 1913, reel 177, vol. 189, p. 700, SG Letterbooks, DLC.

1. Ernest MILLS, of the Western Federation of Miners, was secretary-treasurer of that union from 1907 to 1926.

2. Charles H. MOYER, of the Western Federation of Miners, was president of that union from 1902 until 1926.

3. Charles H. Tanner was a traveling auditor and an organizer for the Western Federation of Miners.

4. That is, the evening of Dec. 26, 1913.

5. SG wired Mills on Dec. 29, 1913, that he had sent organizers M. Grant Hamilton and James Roach to Calumet, Mich., and had asked AFL vice-president John Mitchell to accompany them (reel 177, vol. 189, p. 684, SG Letterbooks, DLC). A week later he sent organizer James Short to Calumet in place of Hamilton. SG sent a copy of Mills's telegram to Secretary of Labor William Wilson on Dec. 30, asking that his department make a thorough investigation of Moyer's deportation and the situation in Calumet (ibid., p. 700).

To W. E. Waddell

January 8, 1914.

Mr. W. E. Waddell,
General Manager, The American Talking Picture Company,
1493 Broadway, New York City, New York.
Dear Sir:

Last spring, while I was very seriously ill, you wrote[1] to me relative to making an engagement for me to give a five-minute talk for the Kinetophone. I was ill for a long while, and absent from my office for six months. This is the first opportunity since my resuming the regular duties of my office that I have had to write you.

I beg to say that if you still desire the five minute talk from me I think I shall be able to arrange for it some time about the middle of this month. Please let me have a word from you in regard to the matter,[2] and oblige

Yours very truly, Saml Gompers.
President   American Federation of Labor.

TLpS, reel 177, vol. 189, p. 955, SG Letterbooks, DLC.

1. W. E. Waddell to SG, Apr. 14, 1913, Files of the Office of the President, General Correspondence, reel 76, frame 50, *AFL Records.*
2. In response to SG's inquiry, representatives of the Edison Kinetophone Co. invited him to record a brief talk when he was in New York City.

To the *New York World*

Washington, Jan. 10. [1914]

The attitude of Henry Ford[1] toward organized labor and toward his employees has always been fairer than usually obtains in the automobile establishments of the United States. The new plan[2] inaugurated by the company will demonstrate its justice as well as its economic success, and will give an impetus to the workers in the automobile industry to endeavor to secure higher wages, better conditions, and an eight-hour work day. In the mean time, one of the great advantages which will accrue to the Ford establishment will be to attract to it the best men the trades afford. I can see no reason for Mr. Ford's plan proving an obstacle to old age pensions, and it is certainly much preferable to the plan[3] of the United States Steel Corporation in making a part of its employees shareholders. The Ford general plan will tend to benefit and not demoralize industry, either in the automobile or other trades.

The organized labor movement has no criticism to make, but welcomes the payment of the highest possible wages, the establishment of a normal work day and the introduction of the very best possible conditions for the working people. It is an historic fact that the best paid and conditioned workers are those who are best organized, and it is they who bear the burden in making the effort to organize the poorly paid and conditioned workers, and that work will go on with greater energy and persistence than ever before.

Samuel Gompers,
President   American Federation of Labor.

New York World, Jan. 11, 1914.

1. The automobile manufacturer and industrialist Henry Ford (1863–1947) was president of the Ford Motor Co.
2. The Ford Plan, announced on Jan. 5, 1914, included an eight-hour workday, a

forty-eight-hour week, and a five-dollar daily minimum wage that combined wages and profit-sharing for eligible employees. These included "married men living with and taking good care of their families," "single men over 22 years of age who are of proved thrifty habits," and "young men under 22 years of age, and women the sole support of some next of kin" (*The Ford Plan: A Human Document* [New York, 1915], p. 1). By the end of the first year about 90 percent of the Ford Motor Co.'s workforce was enrolled in the plan.

3. U.S. Steel had initiated a profit-sharing plan for management personnel in December 1902, with payments in cash and stock, and an elective stock subscription program for all employees in January 1903. (See *The Samuel Gompers Papers*, vol. 8, pp. 23–24 and pp. 24–25, nn. 4–5).

To John Handley[1]

Jan. 12, 1914.

Mr. J. J. Handley,
Secretary-Treasurer, Wisconsin State Federation of Labor,
207 Brisbane Bldg., Milwaukee, Wis.
Dear Sir and Brother:

Your favor of the fourth instant[2] reached me on the afternoon of the tenth instant. It was then impossible to give the subject matter of your letter the attention it required. In the meantime the subject matter of your letter has received my very serious consideration and beg to reply as follows.

The American Federation of Labor has done and is doing everything within its power to be of practical assistance to the men on strike in the Calumet district and to endeavor to secure for them the justice and the protection to which they are entitled. We have sent organizers into the district[3] and have had representatives at a conference held in Lansing,[4] Michigan, to take into consideration the situation prevailing in Calumet and the matters of importance presented to the consideration of the authorities. In addition every effort has been and is being made to secure a thorough investigation by Congress or by some other federal authority, of the conditions prevailing in the Calumet District.

The action of the Executive Board of the W.S.F. of L. to call a conference of every State Federation of Labor,[5] does not seem to be consistent with the first declaration contained in the second paragraph of your letter where you say, "believing that the greatest forces for progress in the labor movement lies with the parent bodies, etc., etc." No thinking, earnest man in the labor movement underestimates the potency and influence and splendid work performed by the State Federations, yet notwithstanding that fact, no one can understandingly say that they are the parent bodies of the organized labor movement of America. They are brought into existence by the trade unions of the several states. Nor is the American Federation of Labor itself the parent body of the trade union movement, but the members of the Executive Council of the American Federation of Labor are elected by the representatives of the entire organized labor movement of America. And yet you would accord to the Executive Council the privilege of being represented by a member of the Executive Council in a conference of the representatives, such as you have outlined in your letter.

It may be interesting for you to know that the Executive Council of the A.F. of L. will begin its regular meeting at headquarters in Washington, D.C., Monday morning, January 19, 1914, when the entire subject matter to which your letter refers, as well as other important matters affecting the rights and interests of the working people of America will be given full and ample consideration and such action devised and taken as may best serve the toilers of the North American continent.[6] If you will make inquiry from those who know, you will learn that so far as the A.F. of L. and its officers are concerned, no one can truthfully insinuate that we have given "mere words of sympathy." For evidence of "mere words of sympathy" it will be necessary to look elsewhere.

With best wishes, I am,

Fraternally yours,   Saml Gompers.
President,   American Federation of Labor.

TLpS, reel 178, vol. 190, pp. 50–51, SG Letterbooks, DLC.

1. John J. HANDLEY was secretary-treasurer (1912–41) of the Wisconsin State Federation of Labor (FOL).

2. Handley to SG, Jan. 4, 1914, AFL Microfilm Convention File, reel 26, frame 2569, *AFL Records.*

3. Between September 1913 and January 1914, the AFL sent organizers Emmet Flood, M. Grant Hamilton, John L. Lewis, James Roach, and James Short as well as AFL vice-president John Mitchell and AFL treasurer John Lennon to Calumet, Mich.

4. On Dec. 31, 1913, in reaction to Charles Moyer's deportation on Dec. 26, a group of about eighty representatives from labor organizations in Michigan met in Lansing with Gov. Woodbridge Ferris to discuss ways of ending the northern Michigan copper strike. Heading the labor committee were W. D. Mahon, president of the Amalgamated Association of Street and Electric Railway Employes of America, and Homer Waterman, secretary-treasurer of the Michigan State FOL. John Mitchell and Clarence Darrow also attended. The labor men were unable to persuade Ferris either to bring the two sides together for a joint conference or to call a special legislative session to deal with the strike.

5. At its meeting on Jan. 10, 1914, the executive board of the Wisconsin State FOL proposed calling a conference of representatives from state federations of labor to meet in Houghton, Mich., to urge Congress to investigate the Calumet strike. The board subsequently decided that congressional action on the matter made the conference unnecessary.

6. At its January 1914 meeting the AFL Executive Council rejected requests from the Western Federation of Miners for an assessment and a loan in support of the striking Michigan copper miners. The Council instead voted in favor of an appeal, which was issued on Jan. 27. The Council also directed SG to arrange a conference with the labor representatives in Congress, to meet with House Speaker Champ Clark and Congressman Oscar Underwood regarding a congressional investigation of the strikes in Michigan and Colorado, and to write the Democratic members of Congress about the urgent need for such an inquiry. SG and Frank Morrison met with Clark and Underwood on Jan. 21, and the Council met with the labor group in Congress that evening. For SG's letter to the Democratic members of Congress, see "A Circular," Jan. 20, 1914, below.

On Jan. 27 the House of Representatives approved H.Res. 387 (63d Cong., 2d sess.), introduced by Edward Keating of Colorado on Jan. 23, directing the House Committee on Mines and Mining to investigate the strikes in Michigan and Colorado. Similar resolutions—H.Res. 290, introduced by Keating on Oct. 21, 1913, and H.Res. 313, introduced by William MacDonald of Michigan on Nov. 20—had died in the Rules Committee in the previous session of Congress. The Committee on Mines and Mining appointed two subcommittees to conduct the investigations, which were held in February and March 1914 and later published (U.S. Congress, House, *Conditions in the Copper Mines of Michigan. Hearings before a Subcommittee of the Committee on Mines and Mining . . . ,* 63d Cong., 2d sess., 1914, and idem, *Conditions in the Coal Mines of Colorado. Hearings before a Subcommittee of the Committee on Mines and Mining . . . ,* 63d Cong., 2d sess., 1914).

From Archibald Lowe[1]

Harrisburg, Penna. Jan. 12th. [19]14.

Dear Sir and Brother:—

I have just been to Harrisburg meeting our organizer[2] who has been on the Pennsylvania for some time, trying to organize the trackmen. The result is failure as the Company dismisses the men as soon as they learn they have joined the organization.

I have met along with Brother Planten our organizer Brother Pierce,[3] of the B. of L.F. and E.[4] The Company is organizing or trying to organize a sort of Federation,[5] controlled by Railway officials of the Penn. R.Y. They were making such an impression on the younger firemen, meaning those young in the service, that Bro. Pierce feared the result would be serious, so on the principal of beating the enemy at their own game, he held public meetings of all interested employees, especially the un-organized or partly organized, such as the trackmen, and shop employees. At these meetings where the need of organizing in some other method more effective in protecting men who might join, than the method of craft organization had proven, the idea of a Federation of all for the protection of each was strongly urged upon him, and he was induced finally to give it a trial.[6]

The results so far show that the men are eager to join an organization of this kind and in spite of the present depression and the laying off of men or putting them on shorter hours, he is succeeding remarkably. When the force is again put to full strength there seems little doubt that in this manner he will be able to get an effective organization strong enough to improve the conditions of all who are part of it.

I am quite willing and have so informed him to allow him to take in the trackmen, and will turn over to him those already in our organization, believing that in this way we can aid them better than in any other, and have assured him of any aid I can give him later. I would like very much indeed if you can see your way to endorse the plan, under the peculiar circumstances of which you are doubtless well aware, prevailing on the Penn. Ry., and would take counsel concerning it with the officials of the Shop Crafts Organizations,[7] Bros. Johnson,[8] Kline,[9] Ray,[10] Franklin,[11] etc., and also will Brothers Stone,[12] Garretson,[13] Carter[14] and Lee,[15] especially Brother Carter.

If you can see your way to do this I am sure it will help all concerned in the improvement of these Penn. Ry. employees. I have been here time and again since 1897 trying to get the trackmen lined up. I have not only seen the failure of my own efforts to do any thing for them, but think the shop crafts have been very much in the same position. If we can get them organized in this way, Bro. Pierce is quite willing when it is accomplished to let the Craft's officials take care of the negotiations to follow. I feel sure if you can give this method of organizing these employees your endorsation, it will certainly have the effect of bringing almost a solid organization to the Road and will give each Craft an organization that they can hardly expect to have by any other method of organizing. Thus the final result will be if each Craft wishes to take care of their own membership, when the organizing is complete, the different Crafts will have a larger membership than they can reasonably expect to have under the present conditions.

With best wishes, I am yours,

Fraternally   (Signed) A. B. Lowe
President   I.B.M.W.E.[16]

TLtpSr, reel 178, vol. 190, pp. 321–22, SG Letterbooks, DLC. Typed notation: "*Copy.*" Enclosed in SG to John Hynes and others, Jan. 19–20, 1914, ibid., pp. 306–20.

1. Archibald Brown Lowe was president of the International Brotherhood of Maintenance of Way Employes from 1908 to 1914.

2. G. H. Planten, an organizer for the Maintenance of Way Employes.

3. Willis H. Pierce served as an organizer (1910–14) for the Brotherhood of Locomotive Firemen and Enginemen and as president (1913–15?) of the Brotherhood of Federated Railway Employes, an industrial union for railroad workers on the Pennsylvania Railroad.

4. The Brotherhood of LOCOMOTIVE Firemen and Enginemen.

5. The Mutual Beneficial Association of Pennsylvania Railroad Employes was incorporated on Dec. 20, 1913. The stated purpose of the organization, which was open to all employees of the company and which provided low-cost benefits in cases of illness, injury, or death, was to foster friendly industrial relations and cooperation between employer and employee on the Pennsylvania Railroad. George W. Brown, a passenger conductor, served as the association's first president (1914–25).

6. The Brotherhood of Federated Railway Employes was organized in Harrisburg, Pa., on Oct. 22, 1913. The Pennsylvania Railroad opposed the new organization, using railroad police to monitor its activities, harassing workers who attended meetings, and laying off a number of those who joined the union. The Brotherhood struck the railroad on May 7, 1914, calling for layoffs based on seniority and an end to company pressure on workers to join the Mutual Beneficial Association. Estimates of the number involved in the strike ranged widely, with Pierce claiming five thousand participants and railroad officials less than seven hundred. The strike lasted for several weeks but ended without attaining its goals.

7. SG wrote Lowe on Jan. 20, 1914, that if his plan met with the approval of the various unions involved, the AFL would have no objection to it (reel 178, vol. 190, p. 283, SG Letterbooks, DLC). On Jan. 19 and 20 SG sent a copy of Lowe's letter to the president of the AFL Railroad Employes' Department and the officers of fourteen international unions.

8. William Hugh JOHNSTON served as president of the International Association of Machinists from 1912 to 1926.

9. James Waller KLINE, of the International Brotherhood of Blacksmiths and Helpers, served as president of the union from 1905 to 1926.

10. Probably Martin Francis RYAN, the president of the Brotherhood of Railway Carmen of America from 1909 to 1935.

11. Joseph Anthony FRANKLIN was president of the International Brotherhood of Boiler Makers, Iron Ship Builders, and Helpers of America (1908–44).

12. Warren Sanford STONE was grand chief engineer (after 1924, president) of the Brotherhood of Locomotive Engineers from 1903 to 1925.

13. Austin Bruce GARRETSON was president of the Order of Railway Conductors of America (1907–19).

14. William Samuel CARTER served as president of the Brotherhood of Locomotive Firemen and Enginemen (1909–22).

15. William Granville LEE was president of the Brotherhood of Railroad Trainmen from 1909 to 1928.

16. The International Brotherhood of MAINTENANCE of Way Employes.

To John Blermstrong

Jan. 19, 1914.

Mr. John Blermstrong,
163 West Ave., Buffalo, N.Y.
Dear Sir and Brother:

I have been absent[1] from the city and have just reached your letter of January 5. I do not recall having given an interview or written an article in criticism of the numerous charity organizations to which you refer. As I have not investigated them I would not feel warranted in making a criticism of them.

Upon the general principle of charity, however, I am free to say that the only practical and helpful charity is to help those in need to help themselves.

Very truly yours,   Saml Gompers.
President,   American Federation of Labor.

TLpS, reel 178, vol. 190, p. 277, SG Letterbooks, DLC.

1. SG attended a number of conferences in New York City between Jan. 14 and 17, 1914, including a meeting of the National Civic Federation Executive Council on Jan. 15.

A Circular

Washington, D.C. Jan. 20-1914.

Dear Sir:

As you are aware, there is to be a caucus held of the Democratic Members of the House of Representatives on Thursday evening, January 22, 1914, for the purpose of considering the subject matter of ordering a special rule for the consideration and adoption of a resolution calling for an inquiry by a committee of the House into the very serious conditions which exist in the Calumet District of Michigan, and the coal mining district of Colorado.

From information coming to my associates and myself, only fragments of which have reached the public attention through the press, there exists in both these districts a condition of affairs almost putting credulity to the severest test. We know that it has been urged against such an investigation that the matters proposed to be investigated are within the states named; but when it is known that great fundamental rights are ruthlessly trampled under foot, rights guaranteed by the Constitution of the United States; when the material things produced in the districts under consideration are necessarily the products which enter into interstate commerce, and when we know that the Congress undertook an investigation of the Homestead situation several years ago,[1] and the United States Senate recently investigated conditions in the State of West Virginia, and when, better than all, we know that the great case of justice, liberty and humanity will be served by a thorough investigation and report upon the conditions prevailing in the districts to which your attention will be invited at the caucus meeting o[n]

Thursday evening, it seems that all right thinking men should favor, authorize, and empower such an inquiry and report.

The Executive Council of the American Federation of Labor has for months had these matters brought to its attention, and at our meeting held in this city directed the undersigned to, and I kindly ask that you will give your favorable consideration and support to the proposition coming before the Democratic caucus on Thursday evening, so that the inquiry may be directed to be made.[2]

I have the honor to remain,

Yours very respectfully,   Saml Gompers.
President,   American Federation of Labor.

TLpS, reel 178, vol. 190, pp. 301–2, SG Letterbooks, DLC. Handwritten notation: "Sent to Democratic members of Congress."

1. A subcommittee of the House Committee on the Judiciary held hearings in 1892 on the Homestead strike (U.S. Congress, House, *Investigation of the Employment of Pinkerton Detectives in Connection with the Labor Troubles at Homestead, Pa.,* 52d Cong., 1st sess., 1892, H. Misc. Doc. 335).

2. On Jan. 22, 1914, a caucus of the Democratic members of the House of Representatives voted in favor of a congressional investigation of conditions in Michigan and Colorado and directed the Committee on Rules to report a resolution authorizing such an inquiry. (See "To John Handley," Jan. 12, 1914, n. 6, above.)

From Daniel Tobin

Indianapolis Ind Jan 22 [1914]

At yesterday afternoon session of United Mine Workers convention disgraceful attack was made on American Federation of Labor by delegate Duncan McDonald[1] and Executive Council was called nothing but wormeaten fossilized booze fighters[2] No delegate in convention refuted these statements I think some member of Executive Council should appear before Miners convention and resent this insult[3]

D J Tobin

TWSr, AFL Microfilm Convention File, reel 26, frame 2604, *AFL Records.*

1. Duncan McDONALD served as secretary-treasurer of United Mine Workers of America District 12 (Illinois) from 1910 to 1917.

2. McDonald made this charge during a discussion of industrial unionism at the convention of the United Mine Workers on Jan. 21, 1914.

3. On Jan. 26, 1914, Western Federation of Miners president Charles Moyer addressed the convention and accused the AFL Executive Council of not adequately supporting the striking Michigan copper miners. United Mine Workers' secretary William Green invited SG to respond to Moyer's charges, and SG addressed the convention on

Jan. 29 and 30. Transcripts of his remarks are printed in "President Gompers at the Miners' Convention," *American Federationist* 21 (Mar. 1914): 189–223.

To Henry Hilfers[1]

Jan. 23, 1914.

Mr. Henry F. Hilfers,
Secretary, New Jersey State Federation of Labor,
68 So. Orange Ave., Newark, N.J.
Dear Sir and Brother:

My attention has been called to the bill introduced in the State Legislature by Mr. Benton H. Fischer.[2] I am informed that the bill prohibits any employers and workmen from entering into an agreement for the purpose of regulating the subject of apprenticeship.

Of course you understand as well as every other thinking, observing man knows, that the improvement of machinery and the tools of labor, and the division and sub-division which has gone on, has largely rendered the high skilled worker almost superfluous. Therefore, the question of apprenticeship regulation has been largely eliminated, but we also see the dumping of hordes of men in these industries has depressed conditions to such an extent that it has made the conditions of the workers a burdensome, hard lot for them to bear; that only in a comparatively few industries is an attempt at regulation of apprenticeship made, and unless such regulations were held, the same conditions would bear upon the result in them.

You know that those who pretend to speak of what they call the opportunities for the "American Boy to earn a livelihood" being eliminated,[3] is really hypocritical and a piece of sophistry. There are now all too many of our fellow workers in the country unemployed, men upon whom families depend, and we hear little if anything of expression or action on the part of these same opponents of labor proposing remedial effective legislation for that terrible condition. The working people have no desire to crowd out any American man or American boy from the opportunity of learning the means of earning a livelihood. But some recognition must be had of existing conditions and the tendency to do great wrongs and injury, in the effort of the workmen and fair minded employers to reach an honorable solution of the difficulties with which they are confronted should be encouraged rather than endangered and made unlawful by specious legislation such as indicated in this letter.

Hoping to hear from you whenever convenient, and with kind regards, I am,

Fraternally yours,   Saml Gompers.
President,   American Federation of Labor.

TLpS, reel 178, vol. 190, pp. 408–9, SG Letterbooks, DLC.

1. Henry F. HILFERS was secretary (1909–26) of the New Jersey State Federation of
Labor.
2. Bill No. 368, introduced on Feb. 13, 1913, by Bennett Fishler, an Essex Co., N.J.,
Democrat who served in the New Jersey General Assembly from 1913 to 1915, would
have made it unlawful to prevent individuals from learning a trade or becoming apprentices, restrict the number of apprenticeships in a trade, or interfere with the en-
rollment or employment of apprentices. The bill was not reported out of committee
nor, apparently, was it reintroduced in 1914.
3. Probably a reference to Anthony Ittner, chairman of the National Association of
Manufacturers' Committee on Industrial Education, who argued that the decline of
the apprenticeship system was due to trade union opposition to industrial education
and represented an erosion of opportunity for the so-called American Boy.

To George Young[1]

January 24, 1914.

Mr. George B. Young,
Chairman, Mediation and Conciliation Commission,
Court House, Newport, Vermont.
My dear Mr. Young:

In reply to your further inquiry of January 21,[2] I send you under
separate cover copy of Bulletin #98[3] issued by the United States Bureau of Labor Statistics. This bulletin contains an accurate compilation
of the mediation, conciliation and arbitration laws of the United States,
the several States and all the civilized nations on earth, with considerable additional matter which will be of exceptional help to you in the
study you and your associates are making on this great question.

I particularly call to your attention the special articles contained
therein by Mr. Arthur E. Holder,[4] a representative of Labor, who reported an investigation[5] he made in England as to the workings of the
Industrial Conciliation Act of England of 1896,[6] giving in concise terms
the attitude of the English workingman towards peaceful settlement
of labor disputes.

Mr. Maurice Low[7] made a similar investigation[8] on or about the same
time among the employers of Great Britain.

I particularly refer you to the report[9] made by Mr. Charles H. Wins-

low,[10] a representative of Labor, who reports the mediation, conciliation and arbitration efforts and successes in the needle trades.

I also send you the *American Federationist* for the month of February,
1913, which contains an article by myself on this question, under the
caption "Tying Workers to Their Tasks through Compulsory Government 'Investigation.'"[11]

In order that you may be further prompted I send you the enclosed
copy of the last act of Congress on the subject, it being the Newlands'[12]
Mediation, Conciliation and Arbitration act[13] governing employes
operating railroad trains engaged in interstate commerce.

You say "It seems to me that the effect of your letter is that organized
labor would not favor any law which required the submission of labor
disputes to settlement by any means other than negotiation. Is this a
correct understanding of the position?"

Replying to this question I will try to make it clear that the organizations of labor prefer and persistently work to the end by which their
accredited representatives may meet upon an equal footing with employers, or their representatives, for the purpose of making collective
bargains on the specific matters under consideration at the time. This
is what we term direct negotiations between first parties—those directly
interested and affected. I may add that as intelligence develops among
employers, this plan is found to be preferable even to them, although
it is invariably the case that the first suggestion made to them to adopt
this course is generally resisted, sometimes most strenuously.

Our second alternative is that where the interested parties in the
dispute either will not meet, or having failed to arrive at any satisfactory conclusion, that mediation by a third party may be resorted to.
Such mediators are usually selected because of their tactfulness and
patience in presenting from one party to the other its propositions.

From the step of mediation or conciliation, when not conclusive, it
is not unusual to recommend submitting the questions under dispute
to voluntary arbitration, by which the principals to the dispute select
an equal number of arbiters and they in turn finding it necessary select an odd man, agreeable to both sides, to act as chairman. This is
as far as we can consistently go and I may safely say that as a rule employers and employes who have submitted their disputes to voluntary
arbitration boards, have usually kept faith on their honor with the
conclusions and decisions of such voluntary arbitration boards.

You ask again "Should not the state provide some method that can
be devised which would be suitable and satisfactory to the labor interests?"

Answering this query academically, I might tentatively say "yes," but
our experiences in this direction has not been satisfactory. The men

who have been selected by some states to serve in such an onerous capacity are more frequently selected because of their political proclivities, or because of some particular influence they have exerted to secure the appointment, or for some other reason more or less satisfactory to themselves, but impractical for the difficult positions they have to fill. We have rarely, if ever, found men serving upon state arbitration commissions who were practically qualified, either from a technical or philosophical standpoint, consequently I believe that you can see the grave difficulty of having any one board in any state that could be, under the very best circumstances, selected who would be qualified to handle the extremely difficult technical questions that would be ultimately brought before it. In this age of specialization very few men know much of any other business than the one they are particularly trained for. Their usual duties are so intense that they have but little time left to qualify themselves for omniscient comprehension of other activities outside of the ones they are immediately engaged in, either for ambitions' sake, or for the more practical sake of making a living, consequently any such board would be inefficient and incompetent to deal with one one-hundredth of the cases that might be brought to it.

It is, therefore, much preferable to have such boards selected locally, as occasion might warrant, from qualified persons engaged in the industry, or in the locality in which the dispute was being threatened, or had come to an issue.

Hoping that I have answered your latter questions in such a way that it may be helpful to you, I remain,

Very truly yours,   Saml Gompers.
President   American Federation of Labor.

p.s. I am sending you under separate cover six copies of the pamphlet "No Compulsory Arbitration."[14]

S. G.

TLpS, reel 178, vol. 190, pp. 476–79, SG Letterbooks, DLC.

1. George Brigham Young, a Newport, Vt., attorney, was secretary (1914–18) and later president (1925–27) of the National Conference of Commissioners on Uniform State Laws and chair of its committee to draft legislation for the settlement of industrial disputes.

2. Young had initially inquired as to SG's views of the causes and nature of labor disputes, the possibility of submitting such disputes to existing or specially created tribunals, and the efficacy of compulsory arbitration and permanent courts of arbitration.

3. *Bulletin of the Bureau of Labor,* no. 98 (1912).

4. Arthur E. Holder served as a member of the AFL Legislative Committee from 1907 to 1915.

5. Holder, "Attitude of Labor toward Conciliation and Arbitration in Great Britain," *Bulletin of the Bureau of Labor,* no. 98 (1912): 179–202.

6. The Conciliation Act of 1896 (59 and 60 Vict., chap. 30) was enacted on Aug. 7, 1896. It authorized the Board of Trade to look into the causes of industrial disputes, to take steps to bring the contending parties together, and to appoint mediators (on the application of one of the parties in a dispute) or arbitrators (on the application of both parties) to resolve such conflicts.

7. A. Maurice Low, chief American correspondent for the *London Morning Post,* conducted investigations of British labor legislation and trade unions for the U.S. Department of Labor.

8. Low, "Attitude of Employing Interests toward Conciliation and Arbitration in Great Britain," *Bulletin of the Bureau of Labor,* no. 98 (1912): 161–78.

9. Charles Winslow, "Conciliation, Arbitration, and Sanitation in the Cloak, Suit, and Skirt Industry in New York City," *Bulletin of the Bureau of Labor,* no. 98 (1912): 203–72.

10. Charles H. Winslow was an authority on industrial education and, later, an attorney in New York City.

11. *American Federationist* 20 (Feb. 1913): 115–25.

12. Francis Griffith Newlands (1848–1917) served as a Democratic congressman (1893–1903) and senator (1903–17) from Nevada.

13. The Newlands Mediation, Conciliation, and Arbitration Act, which created a board of mediation to adjust railway labor disputes, became law on July 15, 1913 (U.S. *Statutes at Large,* 38: 103–8).

14. Probably a reprint of SG's editorial "No Compulsory Investigation or Arbitration," *American Federationist* 15 (May 1908): 386–88.

An Address before
the Twenty-fifth Anniversary Banquet of
the United Hebrew Trades in New York City

January 25, 1914.

The person who leaves friends and the land which has been his home and that of his fathers, and journeys to foreign shores to begin life anew in a foreign land, among strange people with strange ways and customs is making a venture that will test to the utmost heart, mind and endurance. But when a Hebrew leaves the spot where he has lived to seek a new dwelling place, he goes as one who for years has trod familiar streets and mingled with the townspeople, yet as one different and apart, and finds on alien shores the same race prejudice, the same unreasoning unfriendliness. That prejudice has its origin in ancient wrongs to the Jewish people which made them victims of the strong and ruthless, compelled them to live in sections isolated from other people, fixed for them a peculiar distinctive garb, limited the occupations they might follow, removed them from the protection of the laws of the land and gave them to the king as the special regalia from which he might extract revenue without restriction. This prejudice has yielded slowly to the mellowing touch of wider thoughts and more sensitive consciences, and even yet prevails with tremendous effectiveness in many lands.

To America, known as the land of freedom and equal rights, have come many of the Hebrew race. Indeed they tell us that it was Jewish money and faith that even enabled Columbus to realize his dream of the western route, and that among his crew were many Jews who had been imprisoned for loyalty to their faith. Be that as it may, since the new world has held up its promise of hope and opportunity many who were mistreated, persecuted, even reviled, in the land of their birth have sought here a chance to work, achieve and live as free human beings.

Of late years many have come from Austria, Germany, Russia and all the Slavic lands, where most bitter and inhuman abuse has been their portion. Like hunted animals they have sought some haven of protection. Mistreated, hunted, stripped of material possessions, made mistrustful by past experiences, shrinking and dreading additional abuse and wrongs, they have come to a strange land—our land. Even here they have not always met with sympathy, understanding or even justice. They sought the opportunity to earn a livelihood and met with merciless exploitation at the hands of employers, ofttimes even of their own religion and race. The great majority had only sufficient funds to bring them to the United States, and settled here in the gateway city— most of them on the East Side of New York. Here not only did they have to struggle against inhuman conditions of work and the grinding greed of employers, but also among fellow-workers, even co-religionists, did they find that every man's hand was against their hand. Caught in the merciless clutches of cut-throat competition of employers and fellow-workers, they struggled on against insuperable odds until the union, the salvation of the exploited, became a possibility for them.

The little organizations of trade workers that were started among the Hebrews of East Side New York had hard fights for existence. Many workers were so poor they had no funds to fight for decent standards of life. The unions had a precarious existence—but they lived. Twenty-five years ago the Hebrew locals of New York united in an organization which was to secure the existence of each local and to strengthen each by the combined assistance of all the others. For twenty-five years the United Hebrew Trades has been growing in power and in effectiveness. When this central body was first organized it was hampered by the inexperience, the peculiar notions of the members, by isolation from other workers and organizations. It was viewed with mistrust by other labor organizations that feared it would foster a spirit of alienism and set the interests of one group of workers against those of other groups. But these fears have proved groundless. The United Hebrew Trades has dealt with the peculiar needs and problems of the Hebrew workers and has brought to them hope, courage and confidence. As the years have gone by the ideas and the concepts of these trade unionists have broadened and deepened, they have been mellowed by more of human sympathy and kindliness as they have created friendliness and the spirit of co-operation among the workers. The workers have gradually been losing their mistrust of each other; they have learned to bargain wisely and effectively with employers; they have caught the spirit of hope and freedom; they have learned that better conditions and better opportunities and lives are within their realization if they assert themselves in demands for rights. The organization has developed ability and self-reliance among the workers, it has taught them the benefits of co-operation and has worn away the isolation, the peculiar customs and ideals that kept many of the Hebrew workers from becoming American citizens in thought and reality.

The changes that have been wrought in these Hebrew trade unionists have transformed to a great degree not only the outward lives but the character of the workers. Many of them came to our city, outcasts, peasants, helpless, wounded in body, mind and soul; hopeless, they accepted the dogma that there would be nothing better for them except in the great beyond. They have been turned toward hope in the present and have been made to realize the possibility of securing better conditions now. This is the work of the American trade union movement.

Nor has this transformation been an easy one. The Hebrew race is one whose character has been scarred by cruelty, injustice and mental and physical persecution that have lasted for centuries. The blind unreasoning prejudice against the race has been of such a character and such a degree that its effects are part of the very fibre of the people. Yet such has been the resistance, the vital force and the ambitions of these workers that they have been able to achieve many things even in spite of such obstacles. Though they have been forced to walk in lonely paths, isolated from the ways and the interests of those among whom they have lived, ever regarded as foreign, yet the intellectual gifts, creative power, desire for knowledge have only been dormant in these people, awaiting an opportunity for gratification. With the opportunity for increased material well being which the industrial organization has brought has come an eager acceptance of the intellectual benefits which New York has offered to the Hebrew workers and their children. The struggle together has developed a spirit of love and a sense of fraternity that have done much to break down mistrust and race isolation.

Yet all of the old racial characteristics, the deep awareness of reality and the spirit of mystical understanding that have given the world its greatest religions, are still dominant in the Hebrew race. Their love for their national ideals and for race is what one of the race has called "fibre love," a feeling which Nature intertwines with every fibre of the being and which keeps its strength even between those who scarcely have one thought in common.

It is a feeling of this nature that has made the Zionist movement alluring to the Hebrews and enabled it to touch the deepest chords of their nature. Yet many have realized and more will learn from experience that Zion is not a place, but a condition, a relation that may be established in any land where the heart and the spirit are free. No matter what allurement Zionists may offer the Jewish workmen of America are here to live their full lives, to rear their children here, to cast in their lot and destiny with that of the countrymen they accept in adopting this land of America as the fatherland.

It is the duty of the Jewish workers of America to become citizens of this land, to adopt its customs and ways and with whatever effectiveness is within their power to help in the development and progress of higher ideals and institutions for this land which has helped them so much in the struggle for better things. Let the members of the United Hebrew Trades adopt this as their fatherland and give it the same fervent devoted loyalty that they have ever given to all that they have held dear. Let them turn their backs upon the old Zion and the old conceptions and turn their faces toward liberty and freedom, industrial and political, and in their united might fight for the realization of this new purpose, a new Zion that shall mean for them and all Jewish workers better lives in this world and better lives for their children and their children's children.

Put into the daily task and into the relations of fellow workers the same glorifying spirit of poetry and exaltation [that] has given the Jewish music and literature its rare inspiration and power, and by so doing make the United Hebrew Trades organization a power that shall sweep all injustice from the lives of all Hebrew workers, however humble, native born or strangers in our gateway city. Hebrews have been ever mighty men and women in the world's history, may you be like the great of the race.

TD, Files of the Office of the President, Speeches and Writings, reel 111, frames 403–10, *AFL Records*.

To Tony Costello[1]

Jan. 27, 1914.

Mr. Tony Costello,
Washington, D.C.
My dear Mr. Costello:

In addition to what I have orally said to you, I want to take advantage of this means to express to you my great appreciation and congratulations upon the completion of a most wonderful self-imposed task and feat of carrying a congratulatory message from the working people of Galveston, Texas, to me on the occasion of the anniversary of my sixty-fourth birthday. The fact that you bore this message afoot, covering a distance of 2300 miles, a fact attested by the public authorities as well as labor officials, throughout the whole route, demonstrates beyond question that your self-imposed task was faithfully performed. The courage requisite for such a herculean undertaking, the endurance and physical hardships incident to it, the fact that you started from Galveston October 1, 1913, with the rigors of winter confronting you; that you left Galveston penniless and declared that you would not and did not ask for assistance of any character other than that which anyone would voluntarily contribute, the dignity and ability with which you carried yourself in every city and town you visited, has demonstrated by the expressions of public officials and labor representatives, as well as the labor press and the public press, your spirit of devotion to the cause of labor and to humanity, the kindly expressions of good will and confidence manifested by you toward the cause of labor and myself, all prove the quality of heart and mind with which you are so richly endowed.

I was pleased to be apprised of the thoughtfulness and cordiality of our fellow workers in Galveston in sending the message, and as the time of your approach came near, my interest in the project became larger, and I was gratified at the culmination of your journey when you delivered to me that message.

It is now but five hours since that event occurred, and I have had the pleasure of your company until I write this letter, and the purpose of my mentioning this fact is to say that every moment your character and personality have grown upon me, and it is a genuine delight to find you in such excellent physical and mental condition, and in such buoyant spirit.

I wish for you the greatest possible happiness and success.

Sincerely and fraternally yours,   Saml Gompers.
President,   American Federation of Labor.

TLpS, reel 178, vol. 190, pp. 524–25, SG Letterbooks, DLC.

1. Tony Costello was commissioned by the Galveston (Tex.) Labor Council to deliver congratulations to SG on the occasion of his sixty-fourth birthday. Costello left Galveston on Oct. 1, 1913, accompanied by his dog Circus II, and arrived in Washington, D.C., on Jan. 27, 1914. For a photograph of Costello, see Files of the Office of the President, Reference Material, reel 127, frame 390, *AFL Records.*

From John Coughlin[1]

Forward Movement
Brooklyn Central Labor Union[2]
Brooklyn, N.Y. Feb. 3, 1914.

Dear Sir and Brother:

I have your favor with enclosure and am very thankful indeed for your courtesy in sending me the transcript of the speech.[3]

The material contained therein will be of immense value to us. As to your suggestion to our committee at the conference with the Executive Council on the 20th of January[4] to submit to you the organizations that are connected with the N.Y. Federation of Labor, and have made arrangements to get the complete list. I am further sending you the list of unions outside the Central Union, and a list of the Trades that need organizing[5] and if you can get the Internationals to send in their representatives[6] we can get good results. Fifty-three Churches have aggreed to preach a Forward Sermon on Sunday next, and the Press has agreed to give us one page at least for a symposium. I shall send a copy of one or all of the papers Tuesday 10th instant to your office. This will advertise the movement much. Many of the Protestant Churches have offered their buildings for meetings and in all we are able to stir up considerable interest. The idea occurred to us that we might get the weekly news letter of the Federation to take this matter up and give us considerable of a write up in order to get the International Organizations woke up.[7] I know you are doing your utmost to assist us, but there is something wrong somewhere with the International Machinery; and the most pathetic part of the whole business is that the unions with extreme tendencies are the greatest obstructionists. For example: The Painters will vote for Industrialism in A.F. of L. Conventions and refuse to organize their trade in this locality. The Machinists[8] and other unions are in the same boat. However we are doing the best we know how, and if you will again call attention to the Internationals of this work we shall feel indebted.

Permit me to offer at this time our congradulation on your defence of the unwarranted attack of that Nueristhenic[9] from Illinois. Every one who was present at the Rochester Convention knows that he is not capable of sound statements, and that instead of being a miner, should have been an actor. You are particularly fortunate in your enemies.

Yours fraternally,   J. P. Coughlin
Chairman

TLS, AFL Microfilm Convention File, reel 26, frame 2206, *AFL Records.*

1. John Patrick Coughlin, a member of International Association of Machinists 401 of Brooklyn, later served as president of the Brooklyn Central Labor Union (CLU; 1915–21) and as vice-president (1921–22) and secretary (1923–27) of the Central Trades and Labor Council of Greater New York and Vicinity.

2. The AFL chartered the Brooklyn CLU in 1903.

3. In response to a request from Coughlin, SG sent him a transcript of an address he had given before the New York University Forum on Dec. 12, 1913, entitled "Syndicalism or Trade Unionism—Relation to Workers" (Jan. 27, 1914, reel 178, vol. 190, p. 508, SG Letterbooks, DLC; for a copy of the speech and a transcript of the subsequent discussion at the forum, see Files of the Office of the President, Speeches and Writings, reel 111, frames 373–94, *AFL Records*).

4. Coughlin and Maurice de Young appeared before the AFL Executive Council with the request that the Council encourage international affiliates to send organizers to support the Labor Forward Movement in Brooklyn.

5. For Coughlin's list of the Brooklyn trades in need of organizing, see AFL Microfilm Convention File, reel 26, frame 2206, *AFL Records.*

6. For a copy of SG's letter encouraging participation in the Labor Forward Movement in Brooklyn, see AFL Microfilm Convention File, reel 26, frame 2206, *AFL Records.*

7. On Feb. 8, 1914, Brooklyn churches participated in "Labor Sunday," organized by the Brooklyn CLU to inaugurate the local Labor Forward Movement. The *AFL Weekly News Letter* reported on the event in the issue of Feb. 14.

8. The International Association of MACHINISTS.

9. A reference to Duncan McDonald's attack on the AFL at the 1914 convention of the United Mine Workers of America.

To the Executive Council of the AFL

Washington, D.C., Feb. 4, 1914.

No. 11.

Executive Council, American Federation of Labor.

Colleagues:

On Monday evening, January 26th, I received a telegram[1] from Secretary William Green, of the United Mine Workers of America as follows:

"Indianapolis, Ind., Jan. 26, 1914

["]Samuel Gompers, Pres.,
["]American Federation of Labor,
["]Washington, D.C.

["]Delegates by motion invite you to address Miners convention and to reply to statements[2] made that Executive Council has not properly supported the striking copper miners of Michigan.

["]Wm. Green,
["]Secretary of Convention."

I immediately sent the following telegram:[3]

"Washington, D.C., Jan. 26, 1914.
["]John P. White,
["]State Life Bldg.,
["]Indianapolis, Ind.
["]I was trying to get Secretary Green or you over long distance telephone and only succeeded at eleven thirty this evening. I send this to confirm the statement I made to you that I shall be on the train due at Indianapolis ten fifty-five Thursday morning.[4]

["]Samuel Gompers."

Because of the fact that it was late in the evening and the convention of the Miners would be adjourned for the day, I called up President White over long distance telephone, reaching him about midnight and informed him that I would leave Washington on Wednesday, and would reach Indianapolis about 10:55 Thursday morning. I reached there on schedule time. A committee of the Miners' convention was there to meet me, as were also several representative labor men, whose offices are located in that city. The convention had made a special order to hear me at 2:30 that afternoon. I went there and delivered an address of two hours and twenty minutes duration. The Indianapolis Evening News of Friday, January 30th,[5] published my speech in part. It occupied seven columns. I asked our friend Edgar Perkins,[6] and he promised, to send the page of the paper containing my address to each member of the Executive Council. Inasmuch as copy has reached Secretary Morrison, I assume that it has been received by each member of the Executive Council.

The hall was packed to the doors. A systematic effort had been made in the earlier part of my address to create a noise on the outskirts of the delegates, which was discontinued by reason of some of our friends threatening bodily chastisement to the disturbers unless they desisted. I was informed later that a number of spies and detectives were interspersed in the body of the hall for the purpose of creating some sort of "rumpus." However, despite it all, as I proceeded, the large body of delegates had been evidently impressed with the straight forward truthful presentation of the American Federation of Labor's position in regard to the subject matter which had been brought to the convention, and of which you know.

I took it that the most important subject was whether the Executive Council or the A.F. of L. was justified in not levying an assessment upon the members of affiliated organizations for the copper miners of Calumet, and that because of many of the affiliated organizations being themselves engaged in disputes requiring the exertion of every financial effort on their part to sustain their own membership and organizations, therefore they were not in a position to pay an assessment; that an assessment would be ineffective, particularly in view of the fact that President Moyer of the Western Federation of Miners had declared that it would take $30,000. a week to sustain the copper miners in their strike.

In detail I recounted the activities of the American Federation of Labor and the Executive Council, including myself, to be helpful in every way to the striking copper miners and their families at Calumet, the assistance of the then Vice-President Mitchell and Treasurer John B. Lennon, who proceeded to the district and helped in the investigation of the matter and who participated in a conference[7] with the Governor of Michigan,[8] the several organizers[9] sent by the Federation into the Calumet district, the issuance of and all expenses of three distinct circulars at different periods appealing to the working people of America and friends to come to the financial aid and to give moral support to the strikers and their families, the effort made late last summer[10] to have a Congressional investigation made of the situation in Michigan to expose all wrongs committed against the people in Calumet, the fact that a committee consisting of Mr. Mahoney of the Western Federation of Miners, Mr. John Walker, of United Mine Workers of America, Mr. W. D. Mahon of the Street Railwaymen, and Mr. Taylor,[11] Secretary of the Michigan State Federation of Labor, appeared before our Executive Council meeting[12] and urged that President Gompers call Speaker Clark, and Mr. Underwood,[13] Leader of the House, to persuade them to urge the adoption of the resolution before the House of Representatives for an investigation in the Calumet situation, and that I should issue a letter[14] to the members of the labor group of the House and another letter[15] to every Democratic member of the House to attend the caucus and support the passage of the resolution for an investigation, that the Executive Council had so directed and I had performed that duty. I called attention to the meeting of the labor group at which I delivered an address on behalf of labor and for which the gentlemen above named who appeared before the Executive Council congratulated me: that the caucus by an

overwhelming majority pledged itself in favor of the investigation resolution and that the resolution was passed by the House by an overwhelming majority; that every request which the Western Federation
of Miners and United Mine Workers of America made was fully complied with and success achieved, except that the Executive Council did
not believe that an assessment would be productive of good results in
the interest of the copper miners' strike but would entail injury upon
all. I called their attention to the fact that if the A.F. of L. had been in
a position to levy an assessment upon affiliated unions that it would
have been ordered at the convention at Seattle; in fact that every other request had been complied with and that the delegates to the Seattle convention believed an assessment wholly impractical, inadvisable
and injurious.

Of course I took up other phases of insinuations and reflections
made against the A.F. of L. and the Executive Council but I regard
them as of minor importance. I should prefer, however, that the members of the Executive Council would take the time to read the speech.
It was about fifteen minutes of five when I concluded my address to
the convention: it was then impossible to take up any other business
than announcements, and Mr. Duncan McDonald asked me whether
I would remain over until the following day, as there was no time for
him to reply to my address. I told him that I would stay as long as I
possibly could the following day, until the departure of my train; that
for the purpose of coming to the Miners' convention I had broken an
important engagement of the Building Trades in Boston,[16] ordered by
the Seattle convention; that I had another important engagement in
New York on Saturday and that I could not break that one.

The following morning I attended the Miners' convention and Mr.
McDonald entered into a tirade of abuse, misrepresentation and wilful and malicious charges and insinuations against the A.F. of L.,
against the Executive Council, against Vice-President James Duncan,
and particularly against me.[17] Of course there was no way by which
these charges could be answered at the time, but I could not restrain
myself from denouncing his statements as those of a wilful liar and
slanderer.

In no other deliberative body would any man be permitted to attack
the character and the motives and purposes and work of men as was
Mr. McDonald permitted to indulge himself, and I was perforce required to sit and listen. Prompted by my own feelings of indignation
at his outrageous course, I would have been justified in anything that
I might have done to stop it, but out of respect to the delegates to the
convention, out of respect to the great labor movement, and because
of the strangers present at the convention, the newspaper men ready

to jump at anything that would reflect to the discredit of our cause, I restrained myself. How I did it I cannot even now understand; but I did.

You can imagine better than I can describe a great crowd of men, some of them irresponsible, some of them present for evil purposes, trying to impress upon the delegates the hilarity, the frivolity, and the "fun," if you please, which they would enjoy at the fiendish deviltry of a diseased mind giving expression to insinuations that could only be uttered from a waspish, wagging tongue.

It was supposed that President Moyer would follow Mr. McDonald, but in view of the manner in which the latter indulged himself, I could not and would not permit anyone to speak prior to my effecting a reply, and undertook to leave the platform unless that right was accorded me. I finally succeeded in being permitted to address the convention. I did so, consuming about one hour and fifteen minutes, after which I left the hall, and am informed that President Moyer made an address in which he still held that if the copper miners' strike of Calumet is lost, he would charge it "to the inactivity of the Executive Council of the American Federation of Labor to do anything to aid the strikers of the Calumet district.["]

The members of the Executive Council will please inform me if they have received copies of my speech published in the Indianapolis Evening News Friday, January 30th.

I am endeavoring to secure transcript of the addresses of McDonald, Moyer, and President White, of the first day of the convention, and also of the addresses of Mr. McDonald and Mr. Moyer, as well as my own, and when received, I shall have them copied and forwarded to the members of the Executive Council for their information.

It may be interesting to know that a large number of the miners, delegates and officers, and quite a number of officials of international unions and many of the delegates, who had some experience in the organization and in the movement, heartily congratulated me upon the matter which I presented and the manner in which I conducted myself before the convention.

Enclosed you will find copy of the circular[18] issued January 27th appealing to all organized labor of America for assistance in support of the struggling copper miners of Calumet, Michigan.

With best wishes, I am,

Fraternally yours,   Saml Gompers.
President,   American Federation of Labor.[19]

TLcS, Executive Council Records, Vote Books, reel 13, frame 13 and reel 12, frames 652–57, *AFL Records*. The first page of this letter, as sent to the AFL Executive Council, contained several errors. SG sent a corrected page to the members of the Council on Feb. 17, 1914. The transcription printed here incorporates the corrected page.

1. William Green to SG, Jan. 26, 1914, AFL Microfilm Convention File, reel 26, frame 2604, *AFL Records.*

2. Speaking before the convention of the United Mine Workers of America on Jan. 26, 1914, Charles Moyer, president of the Western Federation of Miners, said that loss of the Michigan copper miners' strike would be directly attributable to the inaction of the AFL Executive Council. His charge was later reiterated by United Mine Workers' president John White.

3. Reel 178, vol. 190, p. 469, SG Letterbooks, DLC.

4. SG left the office on Jan. 28, 1914, and reached Indianapolis on Jan. 29; he addressed the United Mine Workers' convention that afternoon and the following morning. His appointment records indicate that he then attended meetings of the committee on organization of the International Congress on Social Insurance in New York City on Jan. 31 and Feb. 2 before returning to AFL headquarters.

5. "Reply of Gompers to Attacks on the A.F. of L.," *Indianapolis News,* Jan. 30, 1914.

6. Edgar A. PERKINS was chief inspector of the Indiana State Board of Inspection (1913–15) and subsequently chairman (1916–17) of the State Industrial Board of Indiana.

7. The conference in Lansing, Mich., on Dec. 31, 1913.

8. Woodbridge Nathan Ferris (1853–1928), a Democrat, served as governor of Michigan (1913–17) and later as a U.S. senator from that state (1923–28).

9. See "To John Handley," Jan. 12, 1914, n. 3, above.

10. In August 1913 SG directed the AFL Legislative Committee to urge the House Committee on Rules to initiate an investigation of the Calumet strike. The Rules Committee did not comply with the request.

11. Claude O. TAYLOR was actually president (1912–17) of the Michigan State Federation of Labor.

12. The AFL Executive Council's meeting in Washington, D.C., Jan. 19–24, 1914.

13. Oscar Wilder Underwood (1862–1929) served as a Democratic congressman (1895–96, 1897–1915) and senator (1915–27) from Alabama. He was Democratic floor leader in both the House (1911–15) and Senate (1921–23).

14. SG's letter to the trade union members of Congress asked them to meet with the AFL Executive Council on the evening of Jan. 21, 1914 (SG to My dear Sir, Jan. 20, 1914, reel 178, vol. 190, p. 304, SG Letterbooks, DLC).

15. See "A Circular," Jan. 20, 1914, above.

16. On Jan. 30, 1914, representatives of fifteen international unions met in Boston, in accordance with a resolution approved by the 1913 AFL convention, to reorganize the Boston building trades council. In the absence of SG, Frank Morrison and James Duncan represented the AFL at the meeting.

17. The text of Duncan McDonald's reply to SG's first address is printed in "President Gompers at the Miners' Convention" in the March 1914 number of the *American Federationist* (21: 208–15) under the heading "The Tragedy of a Slanderous Tongue."

18. AFL Microfilm Circular and Neostyle File, reel 57, frame 1046, *AFL Records.*

19. SG's edited draft of this letter is in the AFL Microfilm Convention File, reel 26, frames 2603–4, *AFL Records.*

To James Duncan

Feb. 11, 1914.

Mr. James Duncan,
Vice-president American Federation of Labor,
Hancock Building, Quincy, Mass.
Dear Sir and Brother:

Your letter of the seventh instant[1] reached me this morning and I read its contents dealing with a number of matters with a great deal of interest. Perhaps I better take up the subjects with which it deals separately and in the order you mention them.

Will you do me the kindness of sending me a copy of President Kirby of the Carpenters telegram to you in regard to me so far as it affects my presence and talk at the Miners' Convention?[2] I should appreciate it very much.

Not only by word of mouth, men whom I met, but in letters and the labor press, it is quite evident that Mr. McDonald's false and unwarrantable attack upon the Federation, upon you and upon me, have proved a boomerang and has inflicted damage upon himself rather than upon any of us. You will recall that in my letter[3] to the Executive Council, recounting as concisely as I could the Miners' convention incident, I called attention to the fact that reports of the trade union movement outside of the Miners who were present at the convention commended me for the matter and manner of my presentation of the case and the self-control I manifested upon those occasions. If that is indicated in the telegram President Kirby sent you, and I quote here a statement made by Secretary Conway[4] of the Retail Clerks International Protective Association,[5] who was also present. It is as follows:

"I trust that you arrived home safe and sound from your momentous trip to the Miners' convention in Indianapolis, and I do not know that I ever enjoyed an address by you more thoroughly, only you did not do enough.

["]I heartily congratulate the boy in the labor movement who has reached the ripe age of sixty-four years upon his magnificent physical condition, his active and alert mentality and wonderful voice, as well as his deportment under the trying conditions surrounding him in Indianapolis. You are some kid, Sam! and we all hope that you may be spared for many, many years, retaining all of the wonderful faculties you now possess to the pride and delight of your friends and the discomfiture of your enemies."

I have already written[6] to Mr. Edgar Perkins asking him to send copies of the Indianapolis Evening News of Friday, January 30 to each member of the Executive Council. By the way, I see the Pittsburg Iron City Trades Journal of Feb. 6, 1914 contains a reprint of the Indianapolis News account of the subject.[7] Perhaps you may have it in your office among the labor papers which you receive. However, I shall see to it that you and all other members of the Executive Council are furnished with a copy of the address.

Many of our friends have advised that I print it either in the *American Federationist* or in pamphlet form. The difficulty that I have to overcome is to whether or not I should also print *McDonald's attack upon everybody and everything* and thus give *his libels further circulation*. I wish you would give me *your opinion as to this latter point*.[8]

Yes, Secretary Morrison has given me an account of the meeting of the Building Trades Unions in Boston, and I have a report[9] of his upon the matter. I shall have a copy of the latter made so as to furnish each member of the Executive Council with it.[10]

By the way, I should say that I am just in receipt of a telegram[11] from the Secretary-Treasurer[12] of the affiliated Brotherhood of Electrical Workers stating that the State Supreme Court has affirmed the decision of the lower courts and thus giving the affiliated Brotherhood complete legal victory.[13] This, together with the agreement reached at the conference in San Francisco, will I think and hope finally bring about unity among the Electrical Workers of the country. I am sending copy of the telegram to the Executive Council.[14] I venture to insert it for your information in this letter.[15]

The information as to the outcome of proposition[16] to affiliate the Bricklayers[17] to the American Federation of Labor reached me and I am in entire accord with your view of the situation.[18] I was advised that the officers of the Bricklayers International opposed the resolution as it was presented to the convention which was mandatory upon them to have that organization become affiliated and what they wanted, or at any rate declared that they wanted, was authorizing the officers to bring about affiliation after "due investigation and conference."

When I was in Indianapolis, President Kirby informed me as to the vote of the Brotherhood of Carpenters upon the question of withdrawing from the Building Trades Department, he said that the votes were more than 3 to 1.[19] In conversation with him he declared that he would insist upon and have every officer and member conform to true allegiance to the A.F. of L. but that the rank and file of the Brotherhood simply rebelled against what they believed to be the unjust and unfair action of the Department, particularly in the refusal of the convention to accede to the Brotherhood's request for a conference in the endeavor to reach an adjustment of the differences[20] between the U.B. and the Sheet Metal Workers.[21]

My understanding is (and this I give you partly sub-rosa) that at the meeting of the executive board of the Machinists there were but four members present, that upon the question of the withdrawal of the I.A. of M. from the A.F. of L. the vote stood two to two and that President Johnston cast the vote to submit the question to the membership; that he is not a member of the Executive Council, except ex-officio; that the question of referring matters to the membership for a vote can only be employed twice a year, January and July, so that the question cannot be submitted before July, 1914, and my information (not obtained from any member of the Executive Board) is that the proposition is for the officers to recount all the "grievances against the A.F. of L.," as far as jurisdiction matters are concerned and then to ask the membership a question somewhat as follows: In view of all of these grievances, shall the I.A. of M. remain longer affiliated to the A.F. of L.?[22]

Let me say that I have the names and addresses of the vice-presidents and all the members of the Executive Board of the I.A. of M. and I am communicating with them direct and sending them copies of the report[23] of the Executive Council of the A.F. of L. to the Rochester convention upon the question of Industrial Unionism and I propose to continue sending them matter so as to have in their minds exactly the position of the A.F. of L. You can rest assured that everything that can be done to clear away any wrong impression or prejudice, I will do.

I note with interest what you say regarding the Soft Stone Cutters[24] and of President D'Alessandro[25] of the Hod Carriers[26] and they are both interesting and will be kept in mind.[27]

There is no question in my mind that what you say is accurate, back of the I.A. of M. officers and of the Journeymen Tailors.[28] There is the one particular purpose behind it, that is to attack their standing in the labor movement of Brothers Lennon and O'Connell.

In connection with the Tailors Garment Workers[29] matter,[30] I have several days ago communicated[31] with the officers of these organizations with a view of having a conference. Yesterday I dictated a letter[32] to you and it will go forward to you in today's mail, in which I am asking you on my own account, as well as upon the suggestion of Secretary Brais,[33] that you act as the representative of the A.F. of L. in this matter.

I have been in correspondence both by mail and telegraph with Secretary Cary of the Chicago Newspaper Publishers' Association with a view of having a conference there with them at as early a date as possible.[34] More than likely the conference will be held either February 24 or March 2.

As you know, there are two additional matters[35] which the Executive Council, at its last meeting, directed me to take up with the sub-committee of the E.C. upon the occasion of my visit[36] to Chicago and it seemed to me that I ought not to be required to go there two or three times when I might possibly be able to arrange to give them attention all at one visit. I suppose that there will be many other things that will come up that will require my attention at Chicago, hence the arrangement which was attempted to be affected.

Today I am to have a conference with Governor Yager[37] of Porto Rico and General McIntyre,[38] Commissioner of Federal Insular Affairs, regarding matters of interest affecting the people of Porto Rico.

Last Saturday I had a most interesting conference[39] with the representatives of the Printing Trades Unions in New York upon the subject of the Federal Investigation[40] now being conducted by the Grand Jury under the Sherman Antitrust Law. They reported to me that their entire attitude has been changed so that they will make a stand-up fight for their rights and there is no question but what the Printing Trades Unions have been aroused to action and that we can count upon their better cooperation in endeavoring to secure the enactment of the Bartlett-Bacon Bill and the trades involved therein.

There are so many important matters which have occurred and are transpiring every hour of every day and night that it is simply impossible to recount them. I tried to give you an outline of some of the most important things which have occurred.

With best wishes to you and hoping to hear from you often, I am,
Sincerely and Fraternally yours,   Saml Gompers
President   American Federation of Labor.

P.S. Just returned from the conference with the Governor of Porto Rico.

T and ALpS, reel 179, vol. 191, pp. 123–28, SG Letterbooks, DLC.

1. James Duncan to SG, Feb. 7, 1914, AFL Microfilm National and International Union File, Granite Cutters Records, reel 38, frame 1532, *AFL Records.*

2. In his letter to SG, Duncan had mentioned receiving a telegram from James Kirby, president of the United Brotherhood of Carpenters and Joiners of America, congratulating the members of the AFL Executive Council on SG's response to Duncan McDonald's attack at the convention of the United Mine Workers of America.

3. "To the Executive Council of the AFL," Feb. 4, 1914, above.

4. Henry J. CONWAY was secretary-treasurer of the Retail Clerks' International Protective Association from 1909 until his death in 1926. He made this statement in a letter to SG dated Feb. 5, 1914 (AFL Microfilm National and International Union File, Retail Clerks Records, reel 36, frames 2211–12, *AFL Records*).

5. The Retail CLERKS' International Protective Association.

6. SG to Edgar Perkins, Feb. 11, 1914, reel 179, vol. 191, p. 82, SG Letterbooks, DLC.

7. "Gompers Addresses Convention," *Iron City Trades Journal,* Feb. 6, 1914.

8. Duncan wrote SG on Feb. 18, 1914, advising against publication of McDonald's attack. SG received the letter after the March number of the *American Federationist,* which reprinted the text of McDonald's remarks, had already gone to press.

9. A copy of the report of the meeting of Jan. 30, 1914, which Frank Morrison forwarded to SG on Feb. 4, can be found in Executive Council Records, Vote Books, reel 12, frames 668–73, *AFL Records.*

10. SG sent the AFL Executive Council a copy of Morrison's report on Feb. 11, 1914 (Executive Council Records, Vote Books, reel 12, frame 666, *AFL Records*).

11. Charles Ford to SG, Feb. 11, 1914, reel 179, vol. 191, p. 129, SG Letterbooks, DLC.

12. Charles P. FORD was secretary of the International Brotherhood of Electrical Workers from 1912 to 1925.

13. A 1912 decision of the Cuyahoga Co., Ohio, Court of Common Pleas that International Brotherhood of Electrical Workers funds on deposit in several Ohio banks properly belonged to the McNulty faction was upheld by the Cuyahoga Co. Court of Appeals in January 1913 (*Louis Geib et al.* v. *The International Brotherhood of Electrical Workers et al.,* C.P. No. 109,146 [1913]). The case was appealed by the Reid-Murphy faction, and on Feb. 10, 1914, the Supreme Court of Ohio sustained the ruling of the court of appeals (*James J. Reid et al.* v. *Frank J. McNulty et al.,* 89 Ohio St. 464 [1914]).

14. SG transmitted the text of Ford's telegram to the AFL Executive Council on Feb. 11, 1914 (Executive Council Records, Vote Books, reel 12, frame 665, *AFL Records*).

15. AFL Microfilm National and International Union File, Granite Cutters Records, reel 38, frame 1534, *AFL Records.*

16. When the Bricklayers', Masons', and Plasterers' International Union of America conducted a referendum in 1913 on affiliating with the AFL, the proposal was rejected. The issue was reintroduced at the union's 1914 convention, held in Houston, Tex., Jan. 12–14, where it was again defeated.

17. The BRICKLAYERS', Masons', and Plasterers' International Union of America.

18. In his letter of Feb. 7, 1914, Duncan wrote that the Bricklayers' convention had rejected affiliation by a two-to-one vote and that the union's officers had later criticized the form of the resolution. Duncan remarked that if that was the case they should have prepared a proposal that they found suitable.

19. The Carpenters withdrew from the AFL Building Trades Department in early 1914, following a referendum vote of the union's membership. The union rejoined the Department in late 1915.

20. See *The Samuel Gompers Papers,* vol. 8, p. 151, n. 8.

21. The Amalgamated SHEET Metal Workers' International Alliance.

22. The International Association of Machinists did not disaffiliate from the AFL nor was such a referendum placed before the union's membership.

23. AFL, *Proceedings,* 1912, pp. 114–17. The document was later published as *Industrial Unionism in Its Relation to Trade Unionism* (Washington, D.C., [1912?]).

24. The Journeymen STONE Cutters' Association of North America.

25. Domenico D'ALESSANDRO, of the International Hod Carriers', Building and Common Laborers' Union of America, served as president of the union from 1908 to 1926.

26. The International HOD Carriers', Building and Common Laborers' Union of America.

27. In July 1913 the Stone Cutters and the Bricklayers reached an agreement intended to settle a long-standing jurisdictional dispute over stone setting and stone cutting. Differences over implementation of the agreement were resolved at a conference between officers of the two unions during the Bricklayers' convention in January 1914. Duncan's letter to SG of Feb. 7 mentioned the arrangement between the two unions and D'Alessandro's denial of a rumor that the Hod Carriers had allied themselves with the Bricklayers.

28. The TAILORS' Industrial Union.

29. The United GARMENT Workers of America.

30. Faced with dwindling membership and loss of work due to the decline of custom tailoring, the Journeymen Tailors' Union of America voted at its August 1913 convention to extend its jurisdiction to include all workers in the tailoring industry and to change its name, effective Jan. 1, 1914, to the Tailors' Industrial Union. The Garment Workers protested this action to the AFL Executive Council, which ruled in February 1914 that the Tailors' name change and new jurisdiction claim violated the AFL constitution. The Tailors refused to accept this decision and in December voted to join the newly created Amalgamated Clothing Workers of America, which had been formed by seceding members of the Garment Workers. The merger proved short-lived, however. Threatened with losing the AFL's endorsement of their union label, the Tailors voted in July 1915 to withdraw from the Clothing Workers and to resume their previous name and jurisdiction.

31. SG to Eugene Brais, Feb. 2, 1914, reel 178, vol. 190, pp. 657–58, SG Letterbooks, DLC; SG to Bernard Larger, Feb. 2, 1914, ibid., p. 660.

32. SG to Duncan, Feb. 11, 1914, reel 179, vol. 191, pp. 141–43, SG Letterbooks, DLC.

33. Eugene J. Brais served as secretary of the Tailors (1910–15) and of the Amalgamated Clothing Workers of America (1915).

34. Henry N. Cary was secretary of the Chicago branch of the American Newspaper Publishers' Association, a trade association founded in 1887, and general manager of the City Press Association of Chicago. SG wrote him on several occasions in January and February 1914 in an effort to arrange a conference between a subcommittee of the AFL Executive Council and representatives from Cary's organization and from the International Printing Pressmen's and Assistants' Union of North America regarding a lockout of Printing Pressman's local 7 (Chicago Web Pressmen), which had been in effect since May 1912. Despite SG's efforts, no meeting took place.

35. At its January 1914 meeting the AFL Executive Council appointed a subcommittee consisting of John Lennon, John Alpine, and SG to meet in Chicago. In addition to the Newspaper Publishers and Printing Pressmen's controversy, the Council directed the subcommittee to take up matters concerning the International Brick, Tile, and Terra Cotta Workers' Alliance and the International Brotherhood of Steam Shovel and Dredge Men.

36. SG left AFL headquarters on Feb. 28, 1914, and arrived in Chicago on Mar. 1, where he addressed the Chicago Federation of Labor and held several conferences. He returned to Washington, D.C., on Mar. 6.

37. Arthur Yager (1857–1941) served as governor of Puerto Rico from 1913 to 1921.

38. Brig. Gen. (from October 1917, Maj. Gen.) Frank McIntyre was chief of the U.S. Bureau of Insular Affairs (1912–18, 1920–29).

39. SG met with representatives of the printing trades of New York City on Feb. 7, 1914.

40. On Feb. 3, 1914, a federal grand jury in New York City began a three-week investigation of the New York Allied Printing Trades Council for alleged violations of the Sherman Antitrust Act. No indictments were returned, and the case was referred to the attorney general of the United States. On Mar. 13 U.S. Assistant Attorney General G. Carroll Todd wrote the U.S. attorney in New York City that none of the council's actions violated the antitrust law.

The Gill Engraving Co., a firm that may have been connected to the original complaint, then brought suit for $50,000 in damages against International Photo-Engravers' Union of North America 1 of New York City and asked for an injunction to prevent members of the union from striking or otherwise interfering with its business. On May 4 Judge D. J. Hough of the U.S. District Court for the Southern District of New York refused to issue the injunction (*Gill Engraving Co.* v. *William Doerr et al.*, 214 F. 111

[1914]). In July Photo-Engravers' local 1 and Gill Engraving signed a three-year contract, and Gill dropped its suit for damages.

To George Perkins[1]

February 20, 1914

Mr. G. W. Perkins,
International President, Cigar Makers' International Union,[2]
Monon Building, Chicago, Illinois.
Dear Sir:

Replying to your favor of February 12, it is my judgment that the best workmen's compensation laws are those of Washington,[3] Wisconsin,[4] Ohio[5] and New York.[6] The laws of Michigan,[7] New Jersey[8] and Massachusetts[9] are also good. Of course this legislation is in an experimental stage of development. Generally speaking, I believe that it is progressing along right lines and is being made more comprehensive and more liberal. It has been our aim to get the principles of automatic workmen's compensation established so as to avoid suspense, expense and anxiety. We always felt that the beneficial features would be according to the demands of the citizens of each state and in proportion as the strength of our organizations develops.

With best wishes, and hoping to hear from you whenever convenient, I am,

Fraternally yours,   Saml Gompers.
President,   American Federation of Labor.

P.S. The workmen's compensation act recently enacted by the State of New York[10] is also an excellent one.

TLpS, reel 179, vol. 191, p. 504, SG Letterbooks, DLC.

1. George William PERKINS served as president of the Cigar Makers' International Union of America from 1891 to 1926.
2. The CIGAR Makers' International Union of America.
3. Washington, Laws of 1911, chap. 74, enacted Mar. 14, 1911, and amended in 1913 (Laws of 1913, chap. 148) required all employers of workers engaged in "extrahazardous" employments, enumerated in the act, to contribute to a state-controlled accident fund. Other employers could elect to participate as well. Compensation was to be paid in the case of disability resulting in the loss of more than 5 percent of the worker's earning power or death.
4. Wisconsin, Laws of 1911, chap. 50, enacted May 3, 1911, and amended in 1913 (Laws of 1913, chap. 599) provided for voluntary participation by private employers and mandatory participation by the state and its municipalities. Compensation was to

be made in case of disability lasting a week or more or death, with the payments funded by employer contributions to approved insurance companies.

5. Ohio, Laws of 1911, pp. 524–33, enacted June 15, 1911, and amended in 1913 (Laws of 1913, pp. 72–92, 656–57) required all employers of five or more workers to contribute to a state insurance fund, initially run by a state liability board and, after Sept. 1, 1913, under the control of the industrial commission of Ohio. Compensation was to be paid in case of disability of more than one week or death.

6. New York, Laws of 1910, chap. 352, enacted May 24, 1910, provided for voluntary participation by private employers. Workers' compensation payments were to be made in the case of disability of more than two weeks or death if either was the result of negligence on the part of the employer.

7. Michigan, Laws of 1912, Act No. 10, enacted Mar. 20, 1912, and amended in 1913 (Laws of 1913, Acts No. 50, 79, 259) provided for voluntary participation by private employers and mandatory participation by the state and its municipalities. Employers were required to demonstrate their ability to make payments or to buy insurance, and compensation was to be provided in case of disability lasting more than two weeks or death.

8. New Jersey, Laws of 1911, chap. 95, enacted Apr. 4, 1911, and amended in 1911 (chap. 368), 1912 (Laws of 1912, chap. 316), and 1913 (Laws of 1913, chap. 145) was a voluntary worker's compensation law. Payments were to be made in the case of disability of more than two weeks or death.

9. Massachusetts, Laws of 1911, chap. 751, enacted July 28, 1911, and amended in 1912 (Laws of 1912, chaps. 571, 666) and 1913 (Laws of 1913, chaps. 48, 448, 696, 807) was a voluntary worker's compensation plan for private employees and mandatory for state workers. Employers electing to participate could join the Massachusetts employees' insurance association or take out insurance from a state-approved liability company; compensation was to be provided in the case of disability of more than two weeks or death.

10. New York, Laws of 1913, chap. 816, enacted Dec. 16, 1913, required all employers of workers in "hazardous employments" either to give proof of their financial ability to make payments or to take out insurance from a state fund or a private company. Compensation was to be paid in the case of disability of more than two weeks or death. The statute was passed after the New York Court of Appeals struck down the state's previous mandatory compensation act (Laws of 1910, chap. 674, enacted June 25, 1910; *Ives* v. *South Buffalo Railway Co.*, 201 N.Y. 271 [1911]) and then reenacted and slightly amended the following year (Laws of 1914, chap. 41, enacted Mar. 16, 1914, and chap. 316, enacted Apr. 14).

To the Editor of the *Washington Herald*

[February 21, 1914]

Editor The Washington Herald:

In your issue of today[1] on the editorial page, you published a statement under the caption, "A Problem for the President," which is so extremely misrepresentative of the facts that I am impelled to write you in reply. The statement (for I cannot bring myself to believe that it is an editorial utterance), is printed in the unusual form of a double column, and deals with a principle which the organized workers of our country are endeavoring to persuade Congress to enact as amendatory of the Sherman anti-trust law, which, if enacted, would restore to the organizations of the workers the rights to which they were entitled, prior to the interpretation of that law by the courts, perverting the law to apply to the normal activities of the workers. This is an interpretation which the Senators who passed the bill refuted and repudiated in advance.

Under that interpretation, the Sherman anti-trust law is now made to apply particularly to the working people and the personal and normal activities, which are exercised by every other citizen of our country without let or hindrance, are declared to be unlawful.

Is it conceivable that there should be placed in the same legal category men who deal in merchandise and the products of labor and who control and monopolize them, and the men and the women who toil, who own and control nothing but their labor power, which is part of their very being and which cannot be separated from their very lives? Surely, there must be some different legal and logical concept of the combinations and corporations dealing in material things, and the association of men and women, who for their own interest and for the public welfare, merely seek to control their own physical and mental power to produce wealth. Or, is it your concept that inanimate matter, material things, are in the same category as human hearts and human souls?

But quite apart from the natural, normal and constitutional rights involved in man's ownership of himself, where pray is the justification for your statement that "every decent citizen" in the United States will uphold the Executive in interposing his veto against the enactment of a law which shall secure the justifiable relief for which the working people contend? Upon what grounds can you justify the statement that if the President should sign such a bill, when passed by Congress that his act would "defy the sense of justice" of the people of this country?

Are you aware that in the last Presidential campaign, both the Democratic party and the Progressive party specifically declared in their platforms for the legislation which the workers of our country urge, that is, for the right of associated effort for the working people in order that the organizations of the workers should not be held as illegal combinations in restraint of trade, and for the limitation and regulation of the present abuse of the injunctive writ, and that together these parties received a vote for their Presidential candidates of 10,412,992, and that the Republican party, which embodied in its platform no such declaration, received for its candidate a vote of 3,484,980? When the citizenship of the United States had cast 75 per cent of the votes in favor of these declarations, surely you do not interpret their intelligence correctly when you say either that the enactment of a law in compliance with these declarations will "defy the sense of justice" of the American people or that such a law is repugnant to "every decent citizen" in the country.

A week ago today, that is, February 12, you published an advertisement[2] inserted by the president[3] of that discredited organization, the National Association of Manufacturers. There is such a similarity of expression and purpose in the advertisement and in the editorial statement to which this letter refers, that the question has arisen whether the advertisement and the statement did not emanate from the same source. The question has been asked of me whether it would not have been fairer to your readers had the statement contained the legal requirement, "advt."[4]

Will you have the fairness to publish this letter?

Samuel Gompers.
President   American Federation of Labor.

Washington Herald, Feb. 21, 1914.

1. That is, Feb. 19, 1914. The *Washington Herald* published SG's letter on Feb. 21.

2. "Business Men's Associations," *Washington Herald,* Feb. 12, 1914.

3. George Pope, a Hartford bicycle manufacturer, was president of the National Association of Manufacturers from 1913 to 1918.

4. Along with SG's letter, the *Washington Herald* published a denial that the article was an advertisement. The paper published a further editorial on the matter on Mar. 11, 1914, and printed a reply from SG on Mar. 13. For R. Lee Guard's memorandum of Mar. 11 regarding the composition of SG's replies, see Files of the Office of the President, General Correspondence, reel 77, frames 24–25, *AFL Records.*

To Santiago Iglesias[1]

Feb. 27, 1914.

Mr. Santiago Iglesias,
Organizer, American Federation of Labor,
San Juan, Porto Rico.
Dear Sir and Brother:

Your favor of the 18th instant with enclosures came duly to hand, and I assure you that I have perused them with great interest. I do not know what you had in mind when you prepared that itinerary[2] or how it will be possible to cover the ground and to perform the duties which you indicate will be laid upon me. Is it your idea that I am to speak at all the cities and towns you mention? Surely you can have no such notion. As a matter of fact there would be no time for anything else, not even the slightest investigation which I may desire to make regarding economic and social conditions and the situation of the people. Under the proposed itinerary, I shall be talking to the people all the time rather than having an opportunity of sometimes having them talk to me and tell me of what they know, and how they feel, and I shall come back from Porto Rico with scarcely an item of information obtained by myself and from my own observation.

You remember that on my visit to Porto Rico in 1904, I took the time to go among the people and held investigations which you attended, and it was upon these investigations I was enabled to base the reports which I made as to conditions prevailing among the people of Porto Rico, and which at the time you said helped materially in their welfare. Of course if you want me to come back from Porto Rico without any information obtained, that my visit there is to carry the message and good wishes of the working people and the citizenship of the United States to the people of Porto Rico, why then that may be all right.

And yet you will remember that when I wrote you[3] upon the subject of my visit to the Island, I asked you to bear in mind the fact that not so long ago I underwent a critical ordeal. It is true that I have recovered my health and strength, being perhaps in better condition than before the last year's severe illness. Surely, there is no consideration of that as shown in the itinerary.

Looking over the map of Porto Rico in which you have indicated by red ink the circle around which I am to travel, it means the touching of almost every point in that circle.

And then again, what can I see of San Juan? I am due to arrive there at five o'clock on the evening and to leave there at nine o'clock the following morning. The same thing is true of the last day, and what shall I be enabled to see? With whom will I be enabled to confer in either of the other cities or towns?

There will be time for you to reply to this letter so that some further information may be contained therein.

Now in regard to the reception and meetings, I would like to ask you whether you advise that I do as I did on the visit last time, that is, to have with me my evening clothes?

You will remember that in my former letter[4] to you I said that Governor Yager asked me to call upon him; that I said I would pay my respects.[5] There is not even a chance to do that if your itinerary is to be carried out. Surely there is no time for a conference with him there.

Of course you know that he leaves by the same boat by which I expect this letter will be carried.

With best wishes, and hoping to hear from you at your earliest convenience, I am,

Fraternally yours,   Saml Gompers.
President,   American Federation of Labor.

TLpS, reel 179, vol. 191, pp. 968–70, SG Letterbooks, DLC.

1. Santiago IGLESIAS Pantín served as an AFL salaried organizer for Puerto Rico and Cuba (1901–33), was president of the Federación Libre de los Trabajadores de Puerto Rico (Free Federation of the Workers of Puerto Rico; 1900–1933), and was also editor of the labor journal *Justicia* (1914–25).

2. A copy of the itinerary that Iglesias prepared for SG's 1914 trip to Puerto Rico can be found in Executive Council Records, Vote Books, reel 13, frame 52, *AFL Records.* SG left New York for Puerto Rico on Mar. 21, accompanied by George Perkins and William Strauss of the Cigar Makers' International Union of America, Daniel Harris of the New York State Federation of Labor, and John E. Fitzpatrick, a Chicago business-man. Arriving on Mar. 25, SG made a circuit of the island, visiting the principal coast-al towns and essentially following the itinerary laid out by Iglesias. SG left Puerto Rico on Apr. 1, reached New York City on Apr. 6, and returned to Washington, D.C., on Apr. 8. He published a report of his trip in the May 1914 number of the *American Federation-ist* (21: 377–89).

3. SG to Iglesias, Dec. 29, 1913, reel 177, vol. 189, pp. 691–92, SG Letterbooks, DLC; and Feb. 10, 1914, ibid., reel 179, vol. 191, pp. 137–38.

4. SG to Iglesias, Feb. 11, 1914, reel 179, vol. 191, pp. 178–80, SG Letterbooks, DLC.

5. SG met with Gov. Arthur Yager on Mar. 26, 1914.

To the Editor of the *Intermountain Worker*

March 17, 1914.

Editor, The Inter-Mountain Worker,
Room 234, Moose Bldg., Salt Lake City, Utah.
Dear Sir:

Someone did me the courtesy of sending a copy of the Inter-Moun-tain Worker of March 14, 1914, and in it is published a letter[1] signed by Victor L. Berger,[2] the former Socialist Member of the House of Representatives. I shall not stoop to Mr. Berger's level in any respect, particularly in his billingsgate and vilification, and only in two partic-ulars shall I take notice of his so-called reasons for having voted to sustain President Taft's veto of the Immigration Bill.[3]

One is that the bill itself provided for a literacy test for immigrants. The worst that can be said against such a provision would be that it would have a tendency to induce prospective immigrants from other countries to attain some degree of education in order that they might meet the test. Is there any good reason for objection upon that score? The fact that there have been and are a number of unemployed workers in the United States ought to prompt men engaged in the affairs of our country to take some consideration of the workmen already here and that they might be vouchsafed a better opportunity to find employment than to open up freely the channels of the U.S. Steel Corporation and other capitalistic concerns which make it a practice to have a free flow of induced immigrants come to the United States, in order that there shall be a constant army of unemployed.

And then again, the idea of a Socialist Member of Congress voting to sustain a Presidential veto of an enactment passed by the representatives of the people. But of this more hereafter.

I am particularly concerned in the reasons given by Mr. Berger for his voting to sustain President Taft's veto of the proviso in the appropriation bill. That proviso reads as follows:

"Provided, however, that no part of this money shall be spent in the prosecution of any organization or individual for entering into any combination or agreement having in view the increasing of wages, shortening of hours or bettering the conditions of labor, or for any act done in furtherance thereof, *not in itself unlawful.*["]

Now it is quite true that that proviso could prevail only for one year but will anyone dispute the fact that the adoption of it by the Congress of the United States meant more than a mere inhibition for the one year? Place the most insignificant construction upon it that one can, and it will be seen that it at least is declaratory of an idea, of a purpose, of a principle and that fact alone would be a sufficient warrant for any man who sympathizes with the cause and the struggle of labor to vote in its favor rather than voting against it, and particularly voting to sustain the veto of President Taft, whom "Comrade" Berger joined in the chorus in stigmatizing as the father of injunctions.

Just a word upon the subject of the veto power of either a governor, or of the President. Every student of history knows that the veto power is a relic of royal prerogative and it was and is intended to be a check upon the expression of the people's will, and how any man declaring himself for freedom as an advocate of the rights of the people can vote to sustain the veto of a President is something perhaps which Mr. "Comrade" Berger may be able to square with his own conscience.

When Mr. Berger was a Member of the House of Representatives he declared that the United States Senate should be abolished and that the House of Representatives more directly representing the people should have the full power to enact legislation, without the concurrence, the check, or the veto of the United States Senate, and yet, forsooth, when a measure declaratory in its purposes in the interests of labor passes both the House and the Senate, and is vetoed by the President, Mr. Berger voted to sustain the veto.

Mr. Berger says "The attacks under the Sherman Act upon the trade unions were made in the civil courts." How little he knows of the entire subject is disclosed when it is known that the Longshoremen, the Seamen, and workmen in kindred occupations at New Orleans, were criminally indicted several years ago under the provisions of the Sherman Anti-Trust Law; that about three years ago men of labor in Jacksonville, Florida, were criminally indicted[4] under the Sherman Antitrust Law, and when the American Window Glass Blowers' Union[5] was dissolved[6] under the criminal provisions in the Sherman Antitrust Law.

If Mr. Berger believes that the proviso (the rider) on the appropriation bill was meaningless and was "a snare," he ought to read the protests made by the National Association of Manufacturers and their members and their official journal, The American Industries, and such newspapers as the New York Times and the Los Angeles Times.

The truth in the matter is that "Comrade" Berger is so dead set against any measure of a constructive character the American trade unions and the American Federation of Labor proposed or proposes that he will work and vote against it just as consistently and persistently as the worst elements in the National Association of Manufacturers.

Today I have before me a copy of Mr. Berger's paper, the Milwaukee Leader of Sunday, March 15th, in which he publishes a dispatch from Washington. The headings are, "Demand of Labor Halts Wilson in Trusts Program," "Congressmen Tell President Failure to Exempt Unions under Antitrust Law Means Defeat in the Fall Election," and in the body of the dispatch this appears, "The unions, however, have still insisted that any attempt to amend the law must include a response to their demand."

There is much more that I could quote from the dispatch and there is much more that I could say in regard to Mr. Berger's course in Congress, but I desist. All I respectfully ask is that you will also publish this letter[7] in the Inter-Mountain Worker so that "All comrades and non-comrades in Salt Lake may understand."

> Very respectfully yours,   Samuel Gompers.
> President,   American Federation of Labor.

TLpS, reel 180, vol. 192, pp. 618–21, SG Letterbooks, DLC.

1. This controversy began in late February 1914 when M. Grant Hamilton criticized Victor Berger for voting in 1913 against overriding President William Howard Taft's vetoes of an immigration bill with a literacy test (see n. 3, below) and an appropriation bill with a rider stipulating that the money could not be used to prosecute labor organizations under the Sherman Antitrust Act (see *The Samuel Gompers Papers*, vol. 8, p. 461 and p. 468, n. 2). In his reply, Berger wrote that he had voted as a representa-

tive of the "American Socialist movement," not of the "reactionary, rotten and drunken Gompers clique" ("Berger Writes Letter in Reply to Hamilton," *Intermountain Worker* [Salt Lake City], Mar. 14, 1914).

2. Victor Luitpold BERGER was editor of the *Social Democratic Herald* (1901–13) and the *Milwaukee Leader* (1911–29) and served on the national executive committee of the Socialist Party of America (1901–23). He also served as a congressman from Wisconsin from 1911 to 1913.

3. S. 3175 (62d Cong., 1st sess.), an immigration bill providing for a literacy test, was introduced by Republican senator William P. Dillingham of Vermont on Aug. 7, 1911. An amended version of the bill passed both houses of Congress on Feb. 3, 1913, but was vetoed by President Taft. The Senate passed the bill over Taft's veto on Feb. 18, but the House failed to do so.

4. On Dec. 16, 1911, five officers of International Longshoremen's Association 652 of Jacksonville, Fla., a black union, were indicted in the Circuit Court of the United States for the Southern District of Florida for violating the Sherman Antitrust Act (*U.S. v. A. Haines et al.*). The action was brought against them by the head of the Mason Forwarding Co., a Jacksonville shipping firm, after the union complained of short pay and demanded that he fire two foremen before members of the local would return to work. Mason reportedly said he "did not intend to be dictated to by a lot of negroes" and wanted to "teach them a lesson" (William Terry to Frank Morrison, Feb. 24, 1912, AFL Microfilm Convention File, reel 25, frame 2535, *AFL Records*). At the request of Longshoremen's president T. V. O'Connor, AFL organizer William Terry went to Jacksonville to investigate the situation and arranged for the defendants to enter guilty pleas in exchange for suspended sentences. In May their union was combined with local 348 of Jacksonville to form local 797.

5. The National Window GLASS Workers.

6. On Jan. 24, 1908, Judge George Phillips of the Cuyahoga Co., Ohio, Court of Common Pleas ordered the dissolution of the Amalgamated Window Glass Workers of America, which was headquartered in Cleveland. The judge ruled that the union's purposes and methods tended against the public good and that it was, therefore, an illegal organization. He maintained that the union sought to prevent nonmembers from working at the trades of window glass blower, gatherer, flattener, and cutter, undertook to limit the number of glass workers in the country, and placed restrictions on the output and hours of labor of its members and their use of machinery (*John A. Kealey et al.* v. *A. L. Faulkner et al.* [18 Ohio Dec. 498 (1908)]). The officers of the union promptly reorganized it as the National Window Glass Workers.

7. SG's letter appeared in the Apr. 4, 1914, issue of the *Intermountain Worker* under the headline "Gompers Replies to Victor L. Berger's Letter."

Excerpts from Testimony before the
U.S. Commission on Industrial Relations

Washington, D.C., Thursday, April 9, 1914.

. . .

Mr. Thompson.[1] In reference to the exercise of governmental authority in industrial disputes, what opinion have you with reference to the establishment of a Government body that would have the right to investigate, the power to call for the production of documents, and the swearing of witnesses, in order that the truth may be ascertained in the dispute, where there was no suspension of the right to strike or the right to lockout?

Mr. Gompers. The question is of its practicability, rather than its effect. Always bear this in mind, that strikes, in the largest number of cases, consist of those unorganized or the newly organized. As workmen and workwomen remain organized for any considerable time, strikes diminish. They establish for themselves and with their employers means and methods of conciliation, of arbitration, and it is only when those absolutely fail that there is a stoppage and break in their relations. After all, that which we call a strike is nothing more nor less than an interruption of the former relations which exist between the workmen and the employers for the purpose of arriving at a new working agreement. In cases where the workers are well or fairly well organized, the facts are known to the employers and the employees. In the case of an unorganized or a newly organized body, they know nothing of each other's conditions, or very little, are no respecters of each other's rights, and the methods by which the workers could establish the facts are exceedingly meager. Investigations authorized by the State could establish but very little in so far as the relations between the employers and the employees are concerned.

Mr. Thompson. But would not it be possible for such a body—with that power of investigation—to ascertain the facts and probably be able to help both of the parties to arrive at a remedy where the dispute involved matters of fact?

Mr. Gompers. Generally, they are not matters of fact. They are matters of mental attitude, the mental attitude of the employers, who consider that the workmen have no rights that they as employers are bound to respect, and the failure on the part of the workmen to demonstrate that they have some power to diminish the profits of the employer by a cessation of their work. It is not a question of facts. The facts are these: When an employer has a mass of unorganized working people working for him he is master of all he surveys, and any attempt upon the part of the workmen to petition or request a change is looked upon by him as a rebellion. It is an insult to his position and to his dignity, because he, in his mind, has furnished them with work and with the means by which they live. He is perturbed at the idea that his position as their benefactor has been called into question. On the other hand, the workmen, who have been docile all this time, who have regarded the employer as omnipotent and all powerful, when they finally revolt in desperation against that one-sided arrangement, when they are for a while—possibly a short while—out, they imagine themselves all powerful, and the employer as having no power at all. It is a question of a struggle—that is, a struggle of the workers to still remain idle without doing anything and to subsist. If these working people remain organized at the end of the controversy—whether they return by agreement or return with a victory or return with a defeat—if they retain their organization thereafter it was not a defeat, it was simply a retreat, and it will impress itself upon the employer in the very near future thereafter to establish better relations between them, where each will have a better understanding of the position of the other, and it will lead to an arrangement of recognition, understanding, and collective bargaining.

As to the investigation conducted by the State, while I can not see why there would be any objection where there would be no factors connected with it that would be of a compulsory character on either, my apprehension is this, Mr. Thompson, that once you place in the hands of the State this one feature, then you will have laid the basis for a continual effort which leads to compulsory arbitration. . . .

Mr. Thompson. Mr. Gompers, does your objection to compulsory arbitration and to the establishment of an institution for the purpose of investigation even, extend also to the establishment of a State body that could be appealed to for the purpose of mediation and conciliation?

Mr. Gompers. I think not. The chief objection I may have is that of apprehension as to the future, not of its immediate effect. I know of but very few instances in which there were any large contests between employers and employees involving public comfort, public safety, public convenience, where some means was not devised immediately, improvised, by which the parties were brought together and some sort of agreement reached.

Mr. Thompson. With reference, Mr. Gompers, to the forms of arbitration and conciliation which are voluntarily entered into by the parties under their trade agreement, have you any choice as between those boards of arbitration which are evenly divided between the two contending parties, and those boards which provide for the selection, either immediately of an umpire or third party, or which make provision for his selection in the end in case the parties are unable to agree?

Mr. Gompers. My preference is for a board of arbitration, where arbitration is the last resort, where the representatives of both parties are evenly divided. As to the umpire or odd man, perhaps it would be just as well if the contending parties decided that after all they could not agree and they would toss up a coin.

. . .

Mr. King.[2] I would like to say, first of all, that I agree wholly with Mr. Gompers, and I think also with Mr. Emery, in saying that I am very strongly opposed to compulsory arbitration. I do not think that any group of men, either employers or employees, should be compelled under penalties to continue under a certain condition of employment against their own free will, and what they conceive to be their interests. On the other hand, I think that Mr. Gompers, in linking compulsory arbitration and compulsory investigation together, if he did so— I am not quite sure whether he did or not, but I infer from his remarks that he did—is not aware that such a linking may be misleading.

As I regard compulsory arbitration, it is a means of compelling people to continue employment under certain conditions whether they wish to or not. Compulsory investigation, as proposed by the Canadian act,[3] does not do anything of the kind, as far as I am able to see it. All that compulsory investigation does under the Canadian act is to substitute another means of obtaining justice than that of the strike. If I am right in the interpretation of the motive that working men have in striking, it is that they conceive that is the last resort left to them to obtain what they believe to be justice. Mr. Gompers says it is slavery for a man to have to give up certain rights. It seems to me it is slavery for any body of men to be compelled to give up the right of earning their own living in order to obtain justice if the State can find any means of affording them justice other than that extreme measure. I think that such a means has been found in compulsory investigation.

. . .

[Mr. Gompers.] What is justice? Talk about the court of arbitration or the court of investigation finding out justice and declaring it. What is justice? What was justice 10 years ago is regarded as a great injustice to-day. Justice is a concept, is an attitude of mind. The report of the Anthracite Coal Strike Commission was quoted here as having been ideal. Is there any man in all America who imagines that an award of the character made by the Anthracite Coal Strike Commission could have been rendered if the coal miners' strike had not occurred?

In 1897 the coal miners in the bituminous and the anthracite fields were simply impoverished and demoralized, and living in poverty and misery while working—not while idle. Their committees, committees from these districts, would come into the cities with credentials signed by the mayors of the town and the governor of the State, authenticating that these men were making a justified appeal for the poverty of miners and miners' families, and they came to the workingmen, to us, to appeal for contributions while they were working. It was the strike of 1897 of the miners in the bituminous fields that checked that downward tendency of more than 15 years. You will remember during the political campaign of 1884,[4] when the misery of the miners in the Hocking Valley was flaunted before the people, and it was only in the political campaign, as a political event, that it was used as political material; but when the campaign was over men had not the slightest advantage as the result of that campaign; not a thing. They were pitied but that is all.

But in 1897, when the remnant of the miners' organization declared for a strike, I think on July 4, 1897, and the men responded in their desperation, finally after about 16 or 17 weeks' strike an agreement was reached with the operators, and there was the establishment of a scale. Within a year afterwards they met again and established another scale with an increase in wages, and established for the 1st of April the eight-hour workday and in all the bituminous coal fields improved conditions, brought about the abolition of the "pluck-me" store, the company store, the right of the men to purchase their things and necessities wherever they desired. The contagion caught the miners in the anthracite region, and they went out on strike, with the result as we know. The second strike was ended by the coal strike commission and the award.

It is true that that commission made the declaration quoted by Mr. Emery;[5] but it is equally true that that commission reduced the hours of labor to nine per day, and it also granted an increase of wages of 10 per cent, and it accorded to the miners the right to purchase their powder wherever they chose, and to make their purchases free from the coercion of making their purchases in the companies' stores, which meant, all told, more than 30 per cent increase in their wages and a reduction of their working hours and the establishment of better conditions.

Since then have come still greater and better improvements in the conditions of these men. And now, instead of the Federal authorities hearing and investigating and adjusting conditions between the coal operators in the anthracite coal regions and the coal miners, representatives of the coal operators and the representatives of the union miners meet and adjust their differences and endeavor to reach an agreement.

And this is the point I want to make: Had the coal miners prior to 1897 in the bituminous region appealed to a commission, if it were in existence in the United States, such as obtains under the act in Canada, if they were to ask for an investigation, an investigation would have come.

What justice would the miners have gotten? They might have gotten a cent or two a ton. But the strike of the miners in the bituminous regions and the strike of the miners in the anthracite region abolished wrongs and abolished misery and poverty and dependence that a century of investigation of a commission and all the altruism of which its members could be possessed would not have abolished, and that strike established justice that could not have been established in any other way.

. . .

U.S. Congress, Senate, *Industrial Relations. Final Report and Testimony Submitted to Congress by the Commission on Industrial Relations . . .*, 64th Cong., 1st sess., 1916, S. Doc. 415, 1: 683, 721–23, 732–33, 742–43.

1. William Ormonde Thompson, a Chicago attorney and former law partner of Clarence Darrow, served as an arbitrator in the garment industry and as counsel to the U.S. Commission on Industrial Relations.

2. William Lyon Mackenzie King (1874–1950) served as Canadian deputy minister of labor (1900–1908), minister of labor (1909–11), and prime minister (1921–26, 1926–30, 1935–48). From 1914 to 1918 he was head of the industrial relations department at the Rockefeller Foundation.

3. The Industrial Disputes Investigation Act of 1907 (6–7 Edw. VII, chap. 20), amended in 1910 (9–10 Edw. VII, chap. 29) and known as the Lemieux Act, provided for boards of conciliation and investigation in labor disputes in industries involving mining, public utilities, transportation, and communication. Under its terms, either party in a dispute could apply to the minister of labor for the appointment of such a board, with one board member recommended by each of the disputants and a third named jointly by the two parties. After investigation, the board was empowered to recommend a settlement, which would become binding only if accepted by both parties. During the time of the board's investigation, strikes and lockouts relating to the dispute were prohibited.

4. The desperate condition of striking Hocking Valley, Ohio, coal miners was exploited during the 1884 campaign when Republican presidential nominee James G. Blaine was accused of owning a large share of the mines. Blaine denied the charge. For the Hocking Valley strike, see *The Samuel Gompers Papers*, vol. 1, p. 426, n. 2.

5. James Emery quoted the Anthracite Coal Commission's statement: "It is adjudged and awarded that no person shall be refused employment, or in anyway discriminated against on account of membership or nonmembership in any labor organization; that there shall be no discrimination against or interference with any employee who is not a member of any labor organization by members of such organization." He characterized it as a "most important" principle (U.S. Congress, Senate, *Industrial Relations. Final Report and Testimony Submitted to Congress by the Commission on Industrial Relations . . .*, 64th Cong., 1st sess., 1916, S. Doc. 415, 1: 728–29).

A Statement Dictated by Samuel Gompers

On the Pa. R.R., Washington to New York,[1]
April 16, 1914.

The apparent lack of energy or interest of the Members of Congress in the fundamental legislation which labor demands at the hands of Congress, particularly the exclusion of the labor organizations from the operations of the Sherman Antitrust Law, worried me very much.

Most of the members individually with whom I came in contact declared themselves as favorable to the legislation, but few seemed to be spurred to action, and rather general dissatisfaction was manifested with some of the provisions of the Bartlett-Bacon Bill.[2] They found fault with certain provisions of the Bartlett-Bacon Bill, with some it was the direct terms in which exclusion of the labor organizations was made, and with others it was that provision to do things in furtherance of the interests of labor organizations not in themselves unlawful.

But quite apart from these provisions of the bill, there seemed to be a lack of coherence on the part of the Democratic members on the bill. They were not quite certain as to the Administration's policy and did not care to act independent of the direct expressed will of the President.

It was at the meeting of the Executive Council in January, 1914, at Washington, when I gave some expression of views upon the state of legislation, and said that I might later on in the session, or if not then, by correspondence, communicate these suggestions affecting legislation. What I had in mind was the calling of a conference of all the representatives of the International Unions of America similar in character and purpose to the conferences which were held in 1906 and 1908, and to demand at the hands of Congress the enactment of the bill in full accordance with the purposes and principles enunciated in the Bartlett-Bacon Bill dealing with the Sherman Antitrust Law, injunctions and contempt proceedings. However, I did not make this suggestion although it was frequently in my mind.

The campaign inaugurated from headquarters was accentuated and more intense, and found ready response among the organized workers of the country. The indictment of the officers of the United Mine Workers and the Federal Grand Jury investigation of the printing trade unions at New York and the conference with the representatives of these unions, all tended to intensify the feeling and in conference with you I urged that the issues be made and that an aggressive campaign be conducted as my friend Matthew Woll[3] will testify. The Board of Governors of the printing trades unions took the matter in charge and began a systematic campaign of agitation and education upon the subject. All these efforts had their influence upon the Members of Congress. In the meantime I drafted a brief and address[4] to the Senate and House of Representatives, a copy of which is hereby attached. The American Federationist and the Weekly News Letter carried the matters regularly and they in turn had their excellent influence. The arguments contained in the brief and in addition citation of the exemption of labor and fraternal organizations in the tariff act of 1909 and the clause exempting labor, fraternal, and other such organizations from the provisions of the income tax and the tariff act of 1913, had each significance to the men of Congress. They showed the way out of the difficulty they encountered, or imagined they encountered, regarding the exemption of the labor organizations from the Sherman Antitrust Law.

At a conference last Thursday, April 9, after my testimony before the Industrial Relations Commission,[5] I walked from there to the A.F. of L. office with John P. Frey, of the International Molders' Union. In discussing many matters he expressed his dissatisfaction with the apparent failure on the part of the Democrats who are in control of the legislation of Congress to enact the bill relieving the organizations of labor from the operations of the Antitrust Law. He declared that he was satisfied that they would not do so.[6]

He expressed my own misgivings and I put the question to him as to whether he believed the holding of a conference of the officers of International Unions at Washington, similar to the conference held in 1906 and 1908 would be of practical advantage. He declared that in his opinion the calling of such a conference was imperative and that the same should be held at a very early date. I told him on that evening I expected to have a conference with the Chairman of the Committee on Labor of the House of Representatives, Mr. Lewis,[7] and some others upon the question of the prospects of our bill, and I asked him to regard our conference relative to the holding of the conference as confidential, at least until I could see him the following day.

That evening, April 9, the conference was held in the room with the Committee on Labor of the House, in which Mr. Lewis, Attorney Jackson H. Ralston, Secretary Frank Morrison, Grant Hamilton,[8] Arthur Holder and I participated. We went over the situation and had a draft of the section of the Antitrust Bill which the Judiciary Committee of the House was considering. The section is as follows:

"Section 10: That nothing contained in this Act shall apply to fraternal, labor, consumers, agricultural or horticultural organizations, orders or associations operating under the lodge system, instituted for mutual help and not having capital stock or conducted for profit, or to individual members engaged in carrying out the objects of such associations."

Mr. Lewis informed us that this section being suggested to Hon. Henry D. Clayton of the Judiciary Committee, he expressed himself as greatly relieved of a difficulty with which he and his Democratic associates found themselves confronted regarding the "crude manner in which some of the provisions of the Bartlett-Bacon bill were drafted" and which offered obstacles to the committee considering it favorably. We went over the section. He asked us if this provision became part of the Clayton Bill[9] and the bills introduced by Mr. Clayton in this the 63d Congress, which passed the House of Representatives of the 62d Congress[10] were also made part of the bill, whether that would be approved by us and would satisfy the American Federation of Labor that the Democratic Party would faithfully carry out its platform declarations. After further consultation with our counsel, I answered that it would be.

I then called a conference in which the following gentlemen participated: Frank Morrison, Arthur E. Holder, Grant Hamilton, James O'Connell, A. J. Berres,[11] Andrew J. Furuseth,[12] Mr. Olander,[13] Edw. Nockels, John P. Frey, and myself. The conference was held in the office of the A.F. of L. Saturday, April 11, and lasted three hours, when the propositions were approved.

On Monday evening, April 13, I received word from Mr. Lewis asking me to come to his committee room at eight o'clock that evening, and to have Mr. Morrison, Mr. Ralston, and our Legislative Committee present. They were present, and also Mr. Edw. Nockels of Chicago. Another draft of the section to exclude the labor organizations from the Antitrust Law was made. The section read as follows:

"That nothing contained in the Anti-Trust Laws shall be construed to forbid the existence and operation of fraternal, labor, consumers', agricultural and horticultural organizations, orders or associations, operating under the lodge system, instituted for the purpose of mutual help, and not having capital stock or conducted for profit, or to restrain individual members of such orders or associations from carrying out the legitimate objects of such associations."

At one of the conferences in the room of the Committee on Labor of the House of Representatives, Mr. Ralston called attention to the fact that the injunction feature of the bill as proposed would not include the District of Columbia, for the courts of the District are not district courts of the United States. I thereupon wrote Chairman Clayton a letter,[14] copy of which is attached hereto.

The proposition was thoroughly discussed and analyzed when I expressed doubt as to the effectiveness of the word "restrain" in the latter part of the section. I finally suggested that the two words preceding it should be added, that is, "to forbid," so that it would read "or to forbid or restrain individual members" etc.

Mr. Lewis asked us whether we insisted upon that going in or its entire rejection. He informed us confidentially that the draft as submitted by him was made by the President in consultation with Chairman Clayton, Mr. Carlin,[15] and another Democratic Member of the House Judiciary Committee.

We all agreed that we would like to see those two words added but that if the President insisted that they should not go in, we would not interpose objection to the enactment of the bill without those words. He was greatly pleased and then informed us also in confidence that the President had declared to Mr. Clayton and his associates that day that he would insist upon Congress enacting legislation dealing with the trusts, that the bill would be introduced the following day, that is, Tuesday, that in fact every feature of the bill had been gone fully into and well understood.

Mr. Holder and Mr. Hamilton the day after the introduction of the Clayton bill in the House, went to Senator Hughes of New Jersey, and asked him if he would introduce the Clayton bill in the Senate, at the same time suggesting to him the advisability of having it referred to the Interstate Commerce Committee, of which Senator Newlands was Chairman. This suggestion was made because of the fact that it was feared that if the bill went to the Judiciary Committee that Senators Nelson of Minn., and Dillingham[16] of Vermont, and Root of New York, would insist upon hearings before the Committee, which would mean great delay and possibly a complete failure in getting a report from this committee. Another reason why the suggestion was made was because the Senate Interstate Commerce Committee then had and now has what is known as the trade commerce bill, or in other words an amendment to the Sherman Antitrust Act. Further than this, also, the personnel of the Senate Interstate Commerce Committee is composed of Senators who are in our judgment much more favorable to the legislation which we desired than is the Senate Judiciary Committee. Senator Hughes was favorable to our suggestion, but with the idea of avoiding any conflict Mr. Holder and Mr. Hamilton waited on Congressman Lewis and related to him the substance of the conference with Senator Hughes, and he, Representative Lewis, in turn went to Mr. Clayton, Chairman of the House Judiciary Committee, and re-related the conference held with Senator Hughes. Chairman Clayton expressed his objection to the bill being referred when introduced in the Senate to the Senate Interstate Commerce Committee, assigning as his reason in substance that he did not desire Chairman Newlands of the Senate Interstate Committee to appropriate to himself any of the ideas which he, Mr. Clayton, had evolved in this particular bill. Using other language, however, that was not at all complimentary to the Chairman of the Senate Interstate Commerce Committee. Following this it was discovered that there was a defect in the Clayton bill, and further negotiations along this line ceased.

Upon April 16th I wrote a letter[17] to the Executive Council of the A.F. of L., copy of which is attached hereto.

There is also attached hereto copy of the A.F. of L. Weekly News Letter of April 18th, containing the bill which has just come from the press today.

I have dictated the above on the train from Washington to Baltimore, en route to New York this Thursday afternoon, April 16, 1914, in the presence and hearing of Mr. Matthew Woll, President of the International Photo Engravers' Union,[18] and Chairman of the Governing Board of the International Printing Trades Associations.

After dictating the above statement, Mr. Woll expressed his belief that the enactment of the bill into law would not prevent suits brought by individuals against labor organizations, or against their members for damages under the existing Sherman Antitrust Law. I replied:

"I made the exact same objection to this provision of the bill at the conference last Monday night, but a copy of the Sherman Antitrust Law was brought forward and section seven of the law was read. I am quoting from memory its provision—'that any individual who may be injured by reason of anything forbidden in this act may recover threefold damages to that which he has sustained'—when that was shown to me I withdrew my objection because the exemption section of the proposed Clayton bill declares that nothing contained in the Antitrust Law shall be construed to forbid the existence, operation of . . .[19] labor organizations, etc. So that removes that objection entirely."

. . .

TD, AFL Microfilm Convention File, reel 26, frames 2349–50, *AFL Records.* Typed notation: "*Dictated by President Gompers to Miss Guard.*" Appended to this document are notes dated Apr. 25, Apr. 28, and May 5, 1914, relating to further conferences on the amendment of the Clayton bill.

1. SG left Washington, D.C., on the afternoon of Apr. 16, 1914, for New York City, where he met with a number of labor, business, and civic leaders on a variety of matters. He left New York on Apr. 18 for New Haven, where he met with representatives of the railroad brotherhoods, and returned to Washington on the evening of Apr. 19.

2. In 1912 Senator Augustus Bacon and Congressman Charles Bartlett, Georgia Democrats, introduced identical measures—S. 6266 and H.R. 23,189 (62d Cong., 2d sess.)— to limit the use of injunctions and exempt labor unions from the provisions of the Sherman Antitrust Act. They reintroduced the bills in 1913 (see "An Excerpt from the Minutes of a Meeting of the Executive Council of the AFL," Sept. 25, 1913, n. 8, above).

3. Matthew WOLL was president of the International Photo-Engravers' Union of North America (1906–29).

4. SG derived the brief and address from his letters to President Woodrow Wilson of Mar. 14 and Apr. 30, 1913 (see *The Samuel Gompers Papers,* vol. 8, pp. 460–68, 477–92). The document was printed in the *AFL Weekly News Letter* of Mar. 28, 1914 ("Bartlett-Bacon Bills Restore to the Workers of America Ownership in Themselves: A Breve"), in the *Congressional Record* under the date of Apr. 11 ("A Brief and Appeal," 63d Cong., 2d sess., vol. 51, pt. 17, Appendix, pp. 344–50), and as a pamphlet (*Labor and Antitrust Legislation: The Facts, Theory, and Argument. A Brief and Appeal* [Washington, D.C., n.d.]).

5. See "Excerpts from Testimony before the U.S. Commission on Industrial Relations," Apr. 9, 1914, above.

6. John Frey summarized his views in a letter to SG dated Apr. 16, 1914 (AFL Microfilm Convention File, reel 26, frame 2358, *AFL Records*).

7. David John Lewis (1869–1952) served as a Democratic congressman from Maryland (1911–17, 1931–39).

8. M. Grant HAMILTON served as an AFL salaried organizer (1903–12, 1914–15, 1918–19) and as a member of the AFL Legislative Committee (1908, 1912–13, 1918).

9. H.R. 15,657 (63d Cong., 2d sess.) was introduced by Democratic congressman Henry Clayton of Alabama on Apr. 14, 1914, and approved with amendments by the House of Representatives on June 5. It was referred to the Senate Committee on the Judiciary on June 6, reported out of committee on July 22, and approved by the Senate with amendments on Sept. 2. The House and Senate appointed a conference committee to resolve their differences on Sept. 4. The Senate agreed to the conference committee's report on Oct. 5, the House did so on Oct. 8, and the bill was signed into law on Oct. 15.

Known as the Clayton Antitrust Act, the law strengthened and supplemented the Sherman Antitrust Act and included several labor provisions sought by the AFL. Section 6 of the act declared that "the labor of a human being is not a commodity or article of commerce" and that "nothing contained in the antitrust laws shall be construed to forbid the existence and operation of labor . . . organizations . . . or to forbid or restrain individual members of such organizations from lawfully carrying out the legitimate objects thereof." Section 20 prohibited the use of injunctions in labor disputes except to prevent irreparable injury to property, and it declared that strikes, peaceful picketing, and boycotts were not violations of the law. Section 22 provided for jury trials in criminal contempt cases (U.S. *Statutes at Large*, 38: 730–40, quotations at p. 731).

10. A reference to H.R. 23,635 (62d Cong., 2d sess.), introduced by Clayton in 1912, and H.R. 4659 and H.R. 5484 (63d Cong., 1st sess.), which he introduced, respectively, on May 5 and May 23, 1913.

11. Albert Julius BERRES was a member of the executive board of the Pattern Makers' League of North America (1909–14) and secretary-treasurer of the AFL Metal Trades Department (1908–27).

12. Andrew FURUSETH was president of the International Seamen's Union of America (1897–99, 1908–38) and secretary of the Sailors' Union of the Pacific (1891–92, 1892–1936).

13. Victor A. OLANDER served as secretary (1909–20) of the Lake Seamen's Union (from 1919, the Sailors' Union of the Great Lakes), vice-president (1902–25) of the International Seamen's Union of America, and secretary-treasurer (1914–49) of the Illinois State Federation of Labor.

14. Apr. 15, 1914, reel 181, vol. 193, SG Letterbooks, DLC. The bill was amended to correct this oversight.

15. Charles Creighton Carlin (1866–1938) served as a Democratic congressman from Virginia (1907–19).

16. William Paul Dillingham (1843–1923), a former governor of Vermont (1888–90), served as a Republican senator from that state from 1900 until his death.

17. SG to the AFL Executive Council, Apr. 16, 1914, Executive Council Records, Vote Books, reel 13, frames 167–68, *AFL Records*.

18. The International PHOTO-ENGRAVERS' Union of North America.

19. Ellipses in original.

From Edward Doyle[1]

Denver Colo April 21 1914

Ludlow tent colony which housed 1,200 Colorado striking coal miners burned to ground after four men three women and seven children were murdered[2] One hundred fifty gunmen in militiamen's uniform and with state equipment have with six machine guns kept up constant attack on men women and children since day break Monday morning Indications are that mine guards intend to murder all strikers who refuse to go to work at companys terms One boy eleven murdered when he ran to get drink water for mother who had lain in cellar Four other children seven to eleven driven back by bullets of uniformed gunmen into blazing tents burned to death Gunmen guard all roads Passengers on trains say fifteen to twenty men and women are lying on prairies in ruins of tent colony Society women offer to nurse injured men women and babes but are refused Score more women and children probably smothered or murdered in most terrible massacre in American industrial history Water supply cut off early Monday Women and babes forced to lie in ditches and cellars 24 hours without food or water Murderous guards are keeping up attack on men and all may be slaughtered Will you for Gods sake and in the name of humanity call upon all your citizenship to demand of the President of the United States and both Houses of Congress that they leave Mexico alone[3] and come into Colorado to relieve these miners their wives and children who are being slaughtered by the dozen by murderous mine guards.

E L Doyle
Secretary Treasurer
Dist. 15 United Mine Workers of America[4]

TWSr, AFL Microfilm Convention File, reel 26, frame 2615, *AFL Records.*

1. Between 1912 and 1917 Edward L. Doyle of Denver served as secretary and then secretary-treasurer of United Mine Workers of America District 15 (Colorado).

2. On the morning of Apr. 20, 1914, members of the Colorado national guard attacked a tent colony of striking mine workers at Ludlow, Colo. During the course of the day, at least five miners, two women, and eleven children were killed, and the encampment was looted and burned. The miners responded over the next several days by arming themselves, attacking a number of mines, driving off or killing the guards, and setting fire to the buildings. The governor called out additional national guardsmen, and federal troops sent by President Woodrow Wilson arrived on Apr. 30. In the fighting between Apr. 20 and 30, at least fifty people, including those killed during the massacre, lost their lives.

3. On Apr. 9, 1914, eight American sailors were arrested in Tampico, Mexico, when they entered a restricted area of the city, which was under siege by Venustiano Carran-

za's Constitutionalists and under martial law. The government of Victoriano Huerta promptly released the men, but the American naval commander in the area demanded a public apology. Huerta refused to comply. President Woodrow Wilson, who had refused to recognize Huerta and had sought his resignation because he had seized power and assassinated his predecessor, Francisco Madero, asked Congress on Apr. 20 for approval of the use of force in compelling Huerta to recognize "the rights and dignity of the United States" (Arthur S. Link et al., eds., *The Papers of Woodrow Wilson,* 69 vols. [Princeton, N.J., 1966–94], 29: 474). The House of Representatives complied the same day, and the Senate did so on Apr. 22. In the meantime, informed that a German steamer carrying munitions for Huerta was approaching Veracruz, Wilson on Apr. 21 ordered the commander of American naval units in the area to occupy the city. The subsequent bombardment of Veracruz and its occupation by nearly seven thousand American military personnel led the two nations to the brink of war. At the end of April, Wilson and Huerta accepted an offer of mediation from Argentina, Brazil, and Chile. Huerta, under military pressure from Carranza, abdicated on July 15, and the United States withdrew from Veracruz in November.

4. Doyle sent SG two telegrams on Apr. 21, 1914, reporting the events at Ludlow— a brief, initial account of the massacre and a second, longer report, which is printed here. SG forwarded both to Martin Foster, chairman of the Committee on Mines and Mining of the U.S. House of Representatives, which was conducting an investigation of the strikes in Colorado and in Calumet, Mich.

To Henry Clayton

Washington, D.C., April 22, 1914.

Hon. Henry D. Clayton,
House of Representatives,
Washington, D.C.
Dear Sir:

In view of your commendation of the manner of presenting the suggestion to amend sections of the bill introduced by you April 14, H.R. 15657, in regard to the courts of the District of Columbia, in my letter to you of April 15, 1914, my associates who had the pleasure of a conference with you this afternoon suggest that the subjects matter which we discussed should be presented to you in similarly formal way.[1] Hence this letter.

We urge that Section 6 of H.R. 15657 be amended by striking out the following words on line 18, page 5 of said bill, "be construed to forbid the existence and operation of," and that the following words be substituted, "apply to."

That Section 6 of H.R. 15657 be amended by adding the word "organizations," after the word "such" on line 23 of page 5 of said bill, so that Section 6 of said bill may read as follows:

"Sec. 6. That nothing contained in the antitrust laws shall apply to fraternal, labor, consumers, agricultural or horticultural organizations, orders or associations operating under the lodge system, instituted for the purposes of mutual help, and not having capital stock or conducted for profit, or to forbid or restrain individual members of such organizations, orders or associations from carrying out the legitimate objects of such associations."[2]

It is further urged that Section 17 of H.R. 15657 be amended by substituting "," for "." on line 2, page 16, after the word "thereto," and by adding the following: "nor shall any of the acts enumerated in this paragraph be considered unlawful in any court of the United States."[3]

With these suggestions the bill will have the entire approval of the American Federation of Labor.

I have the honor to remain,

Very respectfully yours,   Saml Gompers.
President,   American Federation of Labor.

TLpS, reel 181, vol. 193, pp. 331–32, SG Letterbooks, DLC.

1. Alton B. Parker reviewed the Clayton bill on Apr. 20–21, 1914, at SG's request and recommended the amendments proposed in this letter. SG presented them to Henry Clayton at a meeting on Apr. 22 that was also attended by Frank Morrison, Arthur Holder, and Charles Carlin, a member of the House Committee on the Judiciary.

2. This amendment was not incorporated in the version of the bill approved by the House of Representatives.

3. The House of Representatives substantially adopted this amendment.

To John White

Washington, D.C., April 23, 1914.

Mr. John P. White,
1111 State Life Bldg., Indianapolis, Ind.

Your telegram[1] conveying harrowing conditions prevailing in Ludlow, Colorado, received. Information of similar import received[2] from Secretary Doyle of District fifteen and matter laid before Chairman Foster[3] of Congressional Investigating Committee.[4] Will present your matter to the responsible men in Congress and if possible to the President for consideration and action.[5] I feel confident that notwithstanding the outrage you will use every influence within your power to dissuade the miners of the country from entering upon a general strike,[6] particularly at this time.

Samuel Gompers.
President,   American Federation of Labor.

TWpSr, reel 181, vol. 193, p. 371, SG Letterbooks, DLC.

1. John White, Frank Hayes, and William Green to SG, Apr. 23, 1914, AFL Microfilm Convention File, reel 26, frame 2616, *AFL Records*.

2. See "From Edward Doyle," Apr. 21, 1914, above.

3. Martin David Foster (1861–1919) was a Democratic congressman from Illinois (1907–19).

4. See "From Edward Doyle," Apr. 21, 1914, n. 4, above.

5. On Apr. 22 and 24, 1914, SG, Frank Morrison, M. Grant Hamilton, and Arthur Holder met with a number of congressmen, including House speaker Champ Clark, House majority leader Oscar Underwood, Victor Murdock (leader of the Progressive party in the House of Representatives), Martin Foster (chairman of the House Committee on Mines and Mining), and David Lewis (chairman of the House Committee on Labor). On Apr. 25 SG met with Secretary of the Navy Josephus Daniels, who promised to present the matter directly to President Woodrow Wilson. The AFL subsequently distributed a United Mine Workers of America circular, dated May 12, 1914, appealing for financial aid for the Colorado strikers (AFL Circular and Neostyle File, reel 57, frame 1047, *AFL Records*).

6. In their telegram of Apr. 23, 1914, White, Hayes, and Green warned that a nationwide coal miners' strike was imminent unless action was taken on the Colorado situation. Nonetheless, on May 7 the executive board of the United Mine Workers, meeting in Indianapolis, voted against calling a general strike.

From Josephine Casey[1]

International Ladies Garment Workers Union[2]
New York, April 30, 1914.

Dear Sir and Brother:

When organizers are appointed, I should like to call to your attention one who has been of the greatest value during the big shirt waist strike last year.[3] Mrs. Scully[4] reached more Gentile American women than any other person in our movement and I know of the work of other women organizers. It seems a great pity that one so valuable should not be serving the cause. It is difficult to interest American girls as you know. Last year one of the men organizers informed me that it was impossible to touch a certain shop as "it would cost the International Union about Fifty Thousand Dollars" to do it. Just thirty minutes later, Mrs. Scully telephoned me that she had succeeded in getting down half the shop and wanted me to address them. The next morning the rest of the shop came down and Mrs. Scully called on the Firm and got an agreement.

The whole trouble with the officials of our locals is lack of experience and refusing to label things correctly. They give Mrs. Scully credit for what she does in strike time, but will not give her the opportunity to assist them in time of peace. In other words few care to be military officials, but every pin head thinks he can be a successful civil official.

In going around the country, I cannot help seeing how badly a woman organizer is needed. Take for instance, the strike of Electrical Workers in Toledo.[5] Brother Moley[6] was excellent but he needed a woman to help him take care of those 500 girl strikers. I helped him when I could, but after all I had my own work to do and could not give all the time I would have liked.

Our suggestion about organizers is this. Don't appoint *gentle* creatures. A woman organizer has to have certain unpleasant qualities to be a success. Just [as] a dude could not organize strong men so the nice soft voiced little thing can't make good as a woman organizer. The trade union woods are full of "lady" organizers who have their place it is true in interpreting the cause to the public, but we have enough lecturers, what we need is organizers.

With sincere regards, I remain,

Fraternally yours,   (Signed) Josephine Casey

General Organizer   Intl. Ladies G.W. Union[7]

TLtpSr, reel 181, vol. 193, p. 922, SG Letterbooks, DLC. Typed notation: "*Copy.*" Enclosed in SG to Hugh Frayne, May 5, 1914, ibid., p. 921.

1. Josephine Casey of Chicago was an organizer for the International Ladies' Garment Workers' Union (1911?–14). She had previously worked as a ticket agent for the Chicago elevated railroad, was a member of Amalgamated Association of Street and Electric Railway Employes of America 308 of Chicago, which she helped organize around 1903, and was active in the National Women's Trade Union League of America. Casey later worked as an organizer for the Congressional Union for Woman Suffrage and the National Woman's party.

2. The International LADIES' Garment Workers' Union.

3. See *The Samuel Gompers Papers,* vol. 8, p. 442, n. 2.

4. Mary P. Scully, a member of Ladies' Garment Workers' local 25 (Ladies' Waist and Dress Makers) of New York City, served as an organizer for the Ladies' Garment Workers' and as an AFL salaried organizer (1914–21).

5. On Jan. 20, 1914, about five hundred women workers struck the General Electric incandescent bulb plant in Toledo because of successive wage reductions and poor working conditions. The International Brotherhood of Electrical Workers organized the women into a union, and the Toledo Central Labor Union (CLU) gave them financial assistance. The strikers demanded a restoration of wages, a nine-hour day, a fifty-hour week, better working conditions, a shop committee to handle grievances, and a company pledge not to discriminate against strikers or union members. General Electric refused to enter into negotiations with the strikers and instead closed its Toledo plant. The Toledo CLU suspended its financial support in May; by that time most of the women had found other jobs.

6. Daniel M. Moley was a member of Electrical Workers' local 38 of Cleveland and an organizer for the international union.

7. SG met with Scully in New York City in June 1914 and appointed her a salaried organizer in July.

To Ellison Smith[1]

May 1, 1914.

Honorable Ellison D. Smith,
Chairman of the Immigration Committee, United States Senate,
Washington, D.C.
Dear Sir:

During our recent conversation regarding the subject of immigration, you stated that you were aware of the attitude of the American Federation of Labor and its affiliated organizations, as well as the two and a quarter million membership thereof, upon the subject of restricting immigration, but in order to prevent any misunderstanding or misrepresentation of Labor's attitude upon this issue you desired that the policy be formulated in a letter.

The immigration policy of the American Federation of Labor has been evolved out of the practical experiences of the workers in industrial fields. They found that unrestricted influx of alien workers whose standards of living were lower than those of Americans not only constituted an obstacle to improving conditions for American workers but by their willingness to accept poorer conditions and lower wages drove America's workers from many industries. American workers have found that the poorer, the more ignorant immigrant laborers who have come, or rather, have been brought here in the last decade, exercise a more depressing effect upon wages and labor conditions and are more difficult to Americanize. They have also found that the immigration problems in the western states require a different policy from those of the eastern states.

In the western states the nature of the immigration menaces our racial integrity—Oriental immigrants are of a race whose social, intellectual, moral and religious customs are absolutely foreign to those obtaining in the United States. The Orientals do not assimilate with the white race, but they build up separate colonies and sections among Americans, remaining always foreign. Because of their lower standards and ideals these Oriental workers undermine, menace and would ultimately destroy the higher standards and ideals of American workers.

The protection of American workers against Oriental immigrant workers involved the larger question of race preservation. Therefore the workers of the United States inaugurated, endorsed and furthered the American policy of exclusion of Oriental immigration. Yet even after the Chinese exclusion act was enacted, lax enforcement has deprived the working people of the benefits that should have been theirs. Our struggle to prevent racial deterioration resulting from increasing numbers of Oriental immigrants is still being waged. In fact in some industries in the western states Orientals have driven the white workers out, have established conditions and wages that are incompatible with American standards of work and life.

Immigration to the eastern states did not constitute a racial menace. When the American Federation of Labor was first organized immigration had not grown to its present tremendous volume, and only occasionally interfered with the welfare and progress of the workers. This interference was most frequently connected with assisted immigration. Assisted immigration had its origin in the greed of employers and their desire for immediate profits regardless of the welfare of human beings involved as workers. Again this was not a matter that concerned the workers alone, but it involved national welfare, since the workers are a part of the very fiber of the nation. Accordingly they sought and secured the prohibition of admission of contract immigrant labor.

But the number of immigrants admitted to our country yearly increased, and the opportunities open to them became more restricted, and the nature of immigration changed to include more illiterates with lower standards of work and living. Simultaneously with this increase in immigration was taking place combination and centralization of industries. Induced immigration for the profit of shipping industries increased steadily. Competition for work became more keen. Not only the workers, but statesmen, economists, public-spirited men were convinced that the saturation point had been reached and that the nation could not continue to assimilate immigration of the volume and character of the recent past.

Artificial immigration has been stimulated by shipping companies with utter disregard of the welfare of the immigrants or the nation upon which they are unloaded. Shiploads of people have been brought within our portals who constitute a menace to the lives and the health of our people; the immigrants themselves have been subjected to conditions dangerous to them physically and morally, and have been left to the mercy of sharpers and exploiters.

Many of these so-called immigrants are brought to increase the available supply of workers so that greedy exploiters may refuse to increase wages, refuse to grant better conditions and enforce their demands by using these work seekers as a club over their employes. Many of these workers settle in groups or colonies, never mingle with America's workers, and in fact are intentionally kept isolated so that they will not become infected with American standards and ideals of freedom. This constitutes a serious national menace.

Then too, induced or even forced immigration has been used by those who represent the survival of feudal privileges and despotism to eliminate from their territories those who might reasonably be expected to revolt or protest against injustice, ancient wrongs and archaic conditions. Titled and privileged classes, effete rulers utilize a system of induced immigration to strengthen their weakening control upon their subjects. Societies exist for that purpose. They work in collusion with shipping agents who infest the places where the poor and the lowly live. They instill false hopes and arouse impossible expectations of what may be secured in the United States—through these hopes and expectations they lead the immigrants out into danger with which they are incompetent to cope.

Then, again, removing these people from foreign countries removes the source from which might arise a healthy discontent that would insist upon reforms in their own country, or at least would make the necessity for these reforms too obvious to be ignored.

Some way must be found to sift from the mass of those seeking admission to our doors the most assimilable. No ideal test has been formulated, but the most practical is that which the American Federation of Labor endorsed in 1897—the educational test.[2] Since then the organized workers have consistently and persistently sought to have enacted an immigration law containing a literacy clause.

The Seattle (1913) Convention of the American Federation of Labor adopted the following resolution:[3]

Resolved, That we favor a literacy test so that immigrants may be required to be able to read and write the language of the country from whence they come or in some language or tongue.

Our purpose is to protect the interests and well-being of America's workers and thereby to insure national progress and development, physically, materially and socially. We believe that each nation can best solve the problem of the development and the education of the masses of its population, and that as American workers our first concern must be for national welfare. The best world progress will result when each nation bears its own burdens and solves its own difficulties, takes care of its own unfit. Even at the prospect of the enactment of the literacy bill,[4] Italy, with its high percentage of illiteracy, has begun to consider ways and means of education. A similar movement would result in all countries if the United States should establish a literacy test, and thereby betterment would come into the lives of many who could never find their way to our country. This law would not be a barrier to the welfare of any individual but would compel better things for all.

Very truly yours,   Saml Gompers.
President   American Federation of Labor.

TLpS, reel 181, vol. 193, pp. 693–97, SG Letterbooks, DLC.

1. Ellison DuRant Smith (1864?–1944) was a Democratic senator from South Carolina (1909–44).

2. The 1897 AFL convention endorsed restricting immigration by means of an educational test. See *The Samuel Gompers Papers,* vol. 4, pp. 412–13 and p. 414, n. 7.

3. Resolution 28.

4. H.R. 6060 (63d Cong., 1st sess.), an immigration bill providing for a literacy test, was introduced by Democratic congressman John Burnett of Alabama on June 13, 1913. The bill passed both the House and the Senate but was vetoed by President Woodrow Wilson on Jan. 28, 1915, because of the literacy provision. The House failed to pass the bill over Wilson's veto by a vote of 261 to 136, just 4 votes shy of the necessary two-thirds majority.

To John Kean

May 6, 1914.

Mr. John Kean,
President, Pacific Coast District, International
   Longshoremen's Ass'n.,[1]
948 Market Street, San Francisco, Cal.
Dear Sir and Brother:

Your letter of April 27th[2] came duly to hand and contents noted. I read your letter with great interest and thank you for the compliments both stated and implied.

Replying to your query I should say that of course your District convention is not in a position to pass any resolution which would have any binding effect upon the International Longshoremen's Association as such, nor could it have any binding effect upon any other International Union. And yet, if the District convention desired to adopt a resolution expressive of its judgment that an "amalgamation of all unions engaged in marine transportation" would be advisable, it would have the legal right to pass it.[3]

However, the question of a right and the advantage of the adoption of such a resolution may be an entirely different thing, for just as you say that the Longshoremen and other kindred organizations have had experience of failure many years ago, in the effort to establish "one big union."

Somehow or other there are people who get peculiar notions and imagine that bigness is always the synonym of success. They leave out of consideration the human equation, the strength and weaknesses of men, their altruism and selfishness, the breadth and narrowness of vision, their wisdom, their mental shortcomings, the pride or lack of pride which men have in the trade or calling in which they have lived and worked and devoted many years of their lives. Of course there is a greater feeling of solidarity among the working people of our country now than at any time in the industrial history of the civilized world, and it is good that these be cultivated so that all may give the heartiest possible support to any of their fellow workers of any trade or occupation in which they may be engaged. But there is something not yet understood, how much advantage there is in the devotion of men to the organizations of the trades or occupations in which they are engaged.

I wish that I could indulge myself in a fuller discussion of this question in this letter, in all its phases and from all its angles, but time and paramount important immediate work forbids. I content myself in enclosing herein a copy of the report[4] which the Executive Council of the American Federation of Labor submitted to the Rochester convention of the A.F. of L. in 1912. In it you will find the expression of the highest and best judgment of which my associates and I were capable of forming and expressing.

Wishing the fullest measure of success to your convention, to you, and to your associates, and to the great labor movement we have the honor to represent, and asking to be kindly remembered to your delegates to the convention, and that I may hear from you at your convenience, I am,

Fraternally yours,   Saml Gompers.
President,   American Federation of Labor.

TLpS, reel 181, vol. 193, pp. 945–47, SG Letterbooks, DLC.

1. The International LONGSHOREMEN'S Association.

2. AFL Microfilm National and International Union File, Longshoremen Records, reel 39, frame 2104, *AFL Records.*

3. The May 1914 convention of the Longshoremen's Pacific Coast district approved a resolution calling for longshoremen in each port to merge into a single local, regardless of the type of work performed. The proposal was subsequently endorsed by a referendum of the district's membership. At the convention of the entire international, held in July, the union's executive council was called upon to revoke the charters of all locals in the Pacific Coast district and to grant only a single new one in each port. Union president T. V. O'Connor opposed the proposition and introduced a substitute stating that the organization supported the idea of one local per port but would not attempt to implement such a plan without the consent of all the locals involved. The convention approved O'Connor's substitute.

4. For the Executive Council's report on industrial unionism to the 1912 AFL convention, see "To James Duncan," Feb. 11, 1914, n. 23, above.

To Charles Bowerman[1]

May 12, 1914

Mr. C. W. Bowerman,
Secretary Trades Union Congress Parliamentary Committee
General Bldg. Aldwych, London, England.
Dear Sir and Brother:

I beg to enclose to you herein the first page of the Washington Evening Times[2] of yesterday, May 11, a clipping from the Washington Evening Star[3] of the same date, and clippings from the Washington Post[4] and Washington Herald,[5] of May 12, all of them giving the decision of the United States Supreme Court in our contempt case.

As you will note from the enclosed, the case was thrown out on the Statute of Limitations with but two dissenting opinions.

It is needless for me to say how deeply we regret that the principle for which we have been making this long fight has not been passed upon by the court. It is true that the whole question has thus been widely agitated and public sentiment has been created and we hope and believe that the present Congress will pass the legislation for which we have been so long struggling, amending the Sherman Antitrust law so that the voluntary organizations of labor, farmers organizations, and fraternal societies not organized or conducted for profit shall be exempted from the provisions of that law.

The long fought case is ended and now, as you will note, [from the enclosed,] Justice Wright who imposed the original sentences upon Mr. Mitchell, Mr. Morrison and me, is on trial before the Judiciary Committee of the House of Representatives of the United States, appointed to investigate the charges brought against him.[6]

I have no feeling in the matter other than that I want to see justice extended to him, even though he so lamentably failed to show justice to us.

With kind regards and hoping to hear from you whenever convenient, I remain,

Fraternally yours, Saml Gompers.
President American Federation of Labor.[7]

TLpS, reel 182, vol. 194, pp. 113–14, SG Letterbooks, DLC.

1. Charles William BOWERMAN was secretary (1911–23) of the TUC, a member of its Parliamentary Committee (1897–1923), and a Labour Member of Parliament (1906–31).

2. "Gompers Is Freed of Contempt in Decision by U.S. Supreme Court," *Washington Times,* May 11, 1914.

3. "Labor Heads Win in Supreme Court," *Washington Evening Star,* May 11, 1914.

4. "Gompers Case Ended," *Washington Post,* May 12, 1914.

5. "Gompers Freed by High Court," *Washington Herald,* May 12, 1914.

6. On Feb. 17, 1914, Wade Cooper, president of the Union Savings Bank in Washington, D.C., wrote President Woodrow Wilson to accuse Justice Daniel Wright of the Supreme Court of the District of Columbia of official misconduct and moral turpitude. Wilson turned the matter over to Attorney General J. C. McReynolds, who on Feb. 28 referred it to Henry Clayton, chairman of the House Committee on the Judiciary. The House of Representatives authorized an investigation of the charges (H.Res. 446, 63d Cong., 2d sess.), and a subcommittee of the Judiciary Committee held hearings between May 1 and Aug. 26. Joseph Darlington, who had represented the Buck's Stove and Range Co. in its injunction case against the AFL and who had been a prosecuting attorney in the contempt case against SG, John Mitchell, and Frank Morrison, served as Wright's counsel during the hearings. When Wright submitted his resignation to President Wilson on Oct. 6, the Judiciary Committee dropped the investigation on the grounds that no further action was necessary.

7. On May 12, 1914, SG sent similar letters to twenty-two other labor men in various European countries, Puerto Rico, Cuba, Hawaii, the Philippines, Australia, and New Zealand (reel 182, vol. 194, pp. 89–112, 115–34, SG Letterbooks, DLC).

To Carl Legien[1]

May 14, 1914.

Mr. Carl Legien,
President, International Federation of Trade Unions,
Berlin SO 15, Engelufer 15, Berlin, Germany.
Dear Sir and Brother:

The Executive Council of the American Federation of Labor is now in session[2] at headquarters. As I wrote[3] you some weeks ago would be done, the Council took under advisement the matter of the date for the meeting of the International Federation of Trade Unions in San Francisco in 1915. I am now writing to advise you that the Executive Council has designated the first Thursday of June, i.e. *June third, 1915,* as the date for holding the convention[4] of the International Federation of Trade Unions in San Francisco.

It was further decided by the Executive Council that we shall recommend[5] to the next convention of the A.F. of L. which will be held in Philadelphia in November 1914 that the convention of the A.F. of L. for 1915 be held in San Francisco beginning the first Monday after the first Thursday in June, that is, June 7, 1915.[6] If our recommendation be adopted by the Philadelphia convention, it will afford the delegates to the International Federation of Trade Unions the opportunity of attending at least part of the convention of the American Federation of Labor.

Asking to be most kindly remembered to Mr. Baumeister[7] and Mr. Sassenbach,[8] and all of our good friends, in which Mr. Duncan joins, and hoping to hear from you at your early convenience, I am,

Fraternally yours,   Saml Gompers.
President,   American Federation of Labor.

TLpS, reel 182, vol. 194, pp. 169–70, SG Letterbooks, DLC.

1. Carl LEGIEN was secretary of the Generalkommission der Gewerkschaften Deutschlands (General Commission of German Trade Unions) and the International Federation of Trade Unions (IFTU) and was a socialist deputy in the Reichstag.

2. The AFL Executive Council met in Washington, D.C., May 11–16, 1914.

3. SG to Legien, Mar. 18, 1914, reel 180, vol. 192, pp. 729–30, SG Letterbooks, DLC.

4. The IFTU did not meet in San Francisco in 1915 because of the war in Europe.

5. Because the war made it unlikely that the IFTU would actually meet in San Francisco, the AFL Executive Council did not make this recommendation to the 1914 AFL convention.

6. The 1915 AFL convention met in San Francisco, Nov. 8–22.

7. Albert BAUMEISTER served as secretary (1908–13) of the Internationale Union der gastwirtschaftlichen Angestellten (International Union of Restaurant Employees).

8. Johann SASSENBACH was secretary (1909–21) of the German saddlers' union and served on the municipal assembly of the city of Berlin (1905–15).

From Max Zuckerman[1]

United Cloth Hat & Cap Makers of North America[2]
New York, May 14, 1914.

Dear Sir and Brother:

On the 26th of June, 1913 I wrote[3] to you in reference to a controversy[4] which arose between our Local #5 of Chicago and the Federal Local #12675[5] of that city. In that communication I brought to your attention, among other points, the fact that the millinery and ladies' straw hat trade by force of natural and evolutionary development became a part of our cloth hat making industry, and that all those who are engaged in the making of sewed ladies' hats are members of our organization and our trade.

Since that time conditions and developments in that trade have reached such a chaotic state that we are obliged to again draw your attention to the same matter and to ask for your cooperation and assistance in establishing proper lines of legitimate and responsible jurisdiction in this industry.

On the 30th of December, 1913, a conference took place in the office of Brother Hugh Frayne[6] at which Secretary Morrison, Martin Lawlor[7] of the United Hatters,[8] representatives of the Ladies' and Panama Hat Blockers, an independent organization, and representatives of our organization were present. At that conference I explained at length that the millinery and straw hat making is an inseparable part of our trade and that our connection with that trade is a natural one, as the sewed millinery found its origin in our trade. However, Secretary Morrison advised the Ladies' and Panama Hat Blockers to make application for a charter to the United Hatters, stating that in case the Hatters would not take them in, the Executive Council of the American Federation of Labor would issue them a separate charter.

What prompted Secretary Morrison to render such a decision and thus officially encourage dual organization in one industry we cannot understand. Did he not realize the fact that even an official decision of an authority cannot force back the natural trend of a trade or change its course into a different direction? The law of natural development and evolution is stronger than any decision. The only thing accomplished by such a decision would be the encouragement of jurisdictional fights between the organizations involved and, as a consequence, the further demoralization of that unorganized industry.

At that conference we also learned that through the efforts of Miss Melinda Scott,[9] who is now the president of the Women's Trade Union League, a charter to a local of female workers composed of millinery trimmers and operators[10] was granted by the Executive Council. This fact greatly surprised us as our arrangements with the Women's Trade Union League, previous to that, did not warrant such action on their part. In recent strikes where in certain shops a number of women remained at work, the Women's Trade Union League, upon our request for assistance, assigned Miss Melinda Scott to help us take the women down from the strike shops. It was the understanding between our Millinery and Straw Sewers Local #24[11] and the Women's Trade Union League that a female local of our organization should be organized under the supervision of the Women's Trade Union League. We have also applied several times to the League to recommend to us an able woman organizer for the purpose of doing organizing work among the women workers in the millinery trade. However, while our request for an organizer has never been complied with by the Women's Trade Union League, Miss Melinda Scott, representing that body, in direct violation of our arrangements applied for a separate charter and established an opposition local to our organization.

We cannot understand how the Executive Council of the A.F. of L. could grant a charter to a new local in the millinery trade, knowing from our communication of the 26th of June that we were already engaged in a jurisdictional dispute. We claim that we were at least entitled to be notified by the Executive Council before such or any other charter was granted.

We control nearly all the shops where a majority of male operators are employed, but find it difficult to gain control over the shops where female operators are employed, owing, to a great extent, to the fact that the blockers are not organized. We are in a position when not interfered with to do successful organizing work among the blockers in such shops and thus pave the way for the organizing of the women. But here we are again confronted with the question of jurisdiction. The granting of separate charters to blockers and operators would actually mean the splitting of the working force in the shop and in the entire industry.

In the summer of 1913 the rank and file of the blockers at a special meeting unanimously voted in favor of joining our organization. How it came about that the will and the vote of the rank and file were ignored and that their leaders turned down the outspoken decision of the members we do not know. What we do know is, as a matter of fact, that while up to about two years ago the blockers had some form of organization with several hundred members, at present their organization exists only on record and they have a very small and gradually decreasing membership. The cause of all this is very obvious.

As far back as 1903, following the advice of the American Federation of Labor, we endeavored to make some kind of arrangement with the United Hatters to lay out the lines of jurisdiction in that industry but with no results.[12] That has hampered and is still hampering our work of organizing the trade. But we are now forced by economic pressure to do something in that direction. The conditions in that trade are constantly growing more chaotic, to the detriment of all the workers employed in it. The great mass of the women workers are and will remain unorganized so long as this apparently eternal question of jurisdiction will last and thus undermine the welfare of that portion of the workers who are organized and enjoy more or less union conditions under the control and protection of our organization. We are now making arrangements to put a woman organizer in the field but we realize that under the existing disorder we will be greatly hampered in our undertaking.

It is now high time for the Executive Council of the American Federation of Labor to take a hand in this matter and give us the opportunity to do something for the thousands of unorganized workers in the millinery and straw industry.

We earnestly hope that you will give this matter due consideration.[13]

Yours fraternally,   M. Zuckerman

General Secretary-Treasurer,

United Cloth Hat and Cap Makers of N.A.

TLS, AFL Microfilm National and International Union File, United Cloth Hat and Cap Makers Records, reel 43, frame 2692, *AFL Records.*

1. Max ZUCKERMAN was secretary of the United Cloth Hat and Cap Makers of North America from 1904 to 1913 and secretary-treasurer of the union from 1913 to 1927.

2. The United Cloth HAT and Cap Makers of North America.

3. Zuckerman to SG, June 26, 1913, AFL Microfilm National and International Union File, United Cloth Hat and Cap Makers Records, reel 43, frames 2686–87, *AFL Records.*

4. Hat and Cap Makers' local 5 of Chicago was engaged in a jurisdictional conflict with two directly affiliated AFL local unions in that city: Ladies' Straw and Felt Hat Workers' Union 12,675 and Ladies' Straw and Felt Hat Operators' Union 14,440.

5. The AFL chartered Ladies' Straw and Felt Hat Workers' Union 12,675 of Chicago in 1908.

6. Hugh FRAYNE was an AFL salaried organizer (1902–34) and beginning in 1910 was in charge of the AFL's New York City office.

7. Martin LAWLOR was secretary-treasurer (1911–34) of the United Hatters of North America.

8. The United HATTERS of North America.

9. Melinda Scott, an English-born hat trimmer, had organized and served as president of hat trimmers' unions in Newark, N.J., and New York City. She served as treasurer (1911–13) and vice-president (1913–19) of the National Women's Trade Union League of America and was an organizer and president (1914–18) of the New York Women's Trade Union League. Scott was later an AFL salaried organizer (1917–22) and an organizer for the United Textile Workers of America.

10. The AFL chartered United Felt, Panama, and Straw Hat Trimmers' and Operators' Union 14,569 of Greater New York in September 1913.

11. Hat and Cap Makers' local 24 of New York City.

12. In 1903 the AFL Executive Council agreed to an extension of the jurisdiction of the Hat and Cap Makers to include straw hats and ladies' felt hats. The Hat and Cap Makers again attempted to expand their jurisdiction in 1910, but this new effort was resisted by the Hatters. Conferences between the two unions failed to settle the dispute, and in 1916 the AFL Executive Council accorded jurisdiction over the making of straw, felt, and Panama hats to the Hatters. The Hat and Cap Makers refused to comply with this ruling, and their charter was suspended in 1918. The 1920 AFL convention granted jurisdiction over cloth hats and caps to the Hatters, but in April 1924 the two unions reached a working understanding giving most millinery work to the Hat and Cap Makers; in October of that year the Hat and Cap Makers were readmitted to the AFL. The jurisdictional conflict resumed in 1931 but was resolved in 1934 when the two unions merged to form the United Hatters, Cap, and Millinery Workers' International Union.

13. SG referred Zuckerman's letter to the AFL Executive Council, which directed him to arrange a conference with the officers of the Hat and Cap Makers. There is no evidence that such a meeting was held during 1914.

Excerpts from the Minutes of a Meeting of the Executive Council of the AFL

Friday, May 15, 1914.

EVENING SESSION.

. . .

It was decided that the following resolution be forwarded[1] to the members of the Senate Committees on Foreign Affairs, Merchant Marine and Fisheries, to the President of the Senate[2] and the Speaker of the House:[3]

Whereas, Recent events[4] have more clearly demonstrated the lack of precautionary measures for the protection of life and property at sea because of the fact that ships have not been properly equipped with life-boats and other life-saving devices in case of accident and have not been sufficiently provided with seamen for the manning of the same; and

Whereas, Both the Baltimore convention of the Democratic party and the Chicago convention of the Republican party of 1912 pledged the speedy enactment of laws to safeguard human life at sea and to abolish the involuntary servitude under which seamen suffer; and

Whereas, The House of Representatives of the Sixty-Second Congress, almost immediately after the close of the National conventions of all the political parties, August 3, 1912, passed a bill[5] in accord with the promises given; and,

Whereas, This bill, though it received favorable action by both houses of Congress, failed to become law in the Sixty-Second Congress because it did not receive the approval of the President of the United States, and was again passed with minor amendments by the Senate of the United States in the Sixty-third Congress, October 23, 1913; and

Whereas, The International Convention of Safety at Sea,[6] signed in London, January 20, 1914, differs from the seamen's bill in many fundamental particulars, and its ratification by the Senate of the United States would mean that the Seamen's bill will not be passed; therefore, leaving no reasonable assurance for safety of life at sea; and,

Whereas, The convention in several important instances reduces the existing standards of safety of life both in the United States and some European countries; therefore, be it

Resolved, That we, the Executive Council of the American Federation of Labor, protest against the ratification of said convention and urge the passage of the Seamen's bill, Senate 136, by the House of Representatives, before the close of this session of Congress.

. . .

TDc, Executive Council Records, Minutes, reel 4, frame 1528, *AFL Records.*

1. SG forwarded the resolution to the Senate Committee on Foreign Relations, the House Committee on Merchant Marine and Fisheries, the Speaker of the House of Representatives, and the President of the Senate on May 28, 1914 (reel 182, vol. 194, pp. 632–34, SG Letterbooks, DLC).

2. James Paul Clarke (1854–1916) was president pro tempore of the Senate. He had served as governor of Arkansas (1895–97) and was also a Democratic senator from that state (1903–16).

3. Champ Clark.

4. SG is referring to a number of recent shipping disasters. See his second letter to Woodrow Wilson, Oct. 16, 1914, nn. 1–3, below.

5. H.R. 23,673 (62d Cong., 2d sess.), a bill to abolish the involuntary servitude of merchant seamen, prevent the unskilled manning of American vessels, and protect life at sea, was introduced by Democratic congressman William B. Wilson of Pennsylvania on Apr. 23, 1912. The bill was passed by both houses of Congress, but President William Howard Taft refused to sign the measure and it did not become law.

6. The International Conference on Safety of Life at Sea, a gathering of representatives from the principal maritime nations, met in London from Nov. 12, 1913, to Jan. 20, 1914. The treaty adopted by the conference, the International Convention on the Safety of Life at Sea, imposed uniform safety requirements on the merchant vessels of the signatories sailing outside their home waters. The Senate ratified the treaty on Dec. 16, 1914, but with a proviso reserving to the United States the right to impose higher safety standards on American vessels and on foreign ships in American waters.

Excerpts from Testimony before the
U.S. Commission on Industrial Relations

New York City, Thursday, May 21, 1914—10 A.M.

. . .

Mr. Walsh.[1] Mr. Thompson, it is the conclusion of the commission that in this one particular case they would waive the ordinary rule and let Mr. Gompers examine Mr. Hillquit[2] and Mr. Hillquit examine Mr. Gompers.

Mr. Thompson. . . . . I am through with the direct examination.

Chairman Walsh. If it is convenient, then, Mr. Gompers, you may proceed.

Mr. Gompers. Mr. Hillquit, in your statement this morning you said that the purpose of the Socialist Party—to help the trade-union movement in the achievement of its purposes; that is, for the material improvement of the condition of the working people.

Mr. Hillquit. I did.

Mr. Gompers. Has that been the policy of the Socialist Party and with its immediate predecessor, the Socialist Labor Party, of which you are a member?

Mr. Hillquit. It has been the uniform policy of the Socialist Party. It has been, I understand, the policy in principle, of the Socialist-Labor Party, although I am inclined to think that the principle was not properly applied by the Socialist-Labor Party for a time.

. . .

Mr. Gompers. Who was the candidate of the Socialist Party for President of the United States in 1912?

Mr. Hillquit. Mr. Eugene V. Debs.[3]

Mr. Gompers. Who was in 1908?

Mr. Hillquit. Likewise.

Mr. Gompers. And in 1902?

Mr. Hillquit. 1902, likewise. That is, there was no presidential candidate when you think of it in 1902.

Mr. Gompers. 1904?

Mr. Hillquit. In 1904 it was Debs.

Mr. Gompers. Is it unfair to assume that the candidate of your party for the Presidency of the United States expresses the views of the party? Is he the party spokesman, the standard bearer?

Mr. Hillquit. It is entirely unfair to assume, in view of the expressed position of the party itself on the subject. In other words, Mr. Gompers, when the Socialist Party, in convention assembled, officially takes a stand on its relation to organized labor, no individual member of the party, no matter what his position, can nullify or modify that stand.

Mr. Gompers. Do you know that Mr. Eugene V. Debs was present at the first annual convention of the organization which formed the so-called Industrial Workers of the World?

Mr. Hillquit. I do.

Mr. Gompers. Have you read any of his speeches during that convention?

Mr. Hillquit. I have read some.

Mr. Gompers. Do you regard his expressions as being friendly or in favor of the trades-union move[ment], the American Federation of Labor?

Mr. Hillquit. As I understand his position, his attitude is not friendly toward the leaders of the American Federation of Labor. His attitude is more friendly toward the members of the American Federation of Labor. At the same time one and the other are his personal views to which he is entitled.

Mr. Gompers. When Mr. Debs says: "The American Federation of Labor has numbers, but the capitalist class do not fear the American Federation of Labor. Quite the contrary." Do you regard that utterance as a friendly expression for the American Federation of Labor?

Mr. Hillquit. I do not, nor do I regard it as an authorized utterance of the Socialist Party.

Mr. Gompers. Speaking of the American Federation of Labor, and some Socialist[s], he says: "There are those who believe that this form of unionism can be changed from within. They are very greatly mistaken." Do you agree with Mr. Debs on that utterance?

Mr. Hillquit. Do I agree? I do not agree. I think, on the contrary, the American Federation of Labor is being forced, and will be forced more and more, to gradually change its form of organization, to adjust itself to more modern industrial conditions.

Mr. Gompers. I read this as an obscure expression of opinion. Mr. Debs says in that speech: "There is but one way to effect this change, and that is for the working man to sever his relation with the American Federation."

Mr. Hillquit. Yes. I do not agree with that, nor does the Socialist Party agree with that. And, to make our position clear once for all, Mr. Gompers, I will say it will be quite useless to quote Mr. Debs in his attitude to the American Federation of Labor. Mr. Debs took part in the organization of the Industrial Workers of the World. I think he has now lived to regret it, but whether he does or not the fact of the matter is he acted entirely on his own accord and on his own responsibility; that the Socialist Party at no time approved, directly or indirectly, of that stand; and at no time have they indorsed the Industrial Workers of the World as against the American Federation of Labor. And I will say further that the Socialist Party at no time had any substantial criticism of the American Federation of Labor, although I am just as frank to add that the Socialist Party, at least in the majority of its members, do believe that the present leadership of the American Federation of Labor is somewhat archaic, somewhat antiquated, too conservative, and not efficient enough for the object and purposes of the American Federation of Labor. That is the position.

. . .

Mr. Gompers. You have said that it is his individual stand, yet the speech in which I refer and in which he asks and urges the workmen to leave the American Federation of Labor was made some time in June or July, 1908, and Mr. Debs was twice made the standard bearer of the Socialist Party as candidate for President of the United States since that time.

Mr. Hillquit. Yes, sir. He was. There was absolutely no reason why he should not be, in view of the fact that the party itself had at some time in 1904 very explicitly declared its stand on organized labor, and it did not have to apprehend that any of its representatives may misrepresent its attitude.

Mr. Gompers. Do you know that Mr. Debs has, within these past weeks, issued a document[4] in which he urges the secession of two of the largest organizations from the American Federation of Labor, for the purpose of destroying the American Federation of Labor?

Mr. Hillquit. I do. May I add, Mr. Gompers, that this likewise was wholly and fully his own initiative and on his own responsibility, and in no way approved of or condoned by the Socialist Party. We tolerate liberty of expression and speech and opinion within the Socialist Party, you know.

Mr. Gompers. Do you regard that as the individual expression of opinion, when a man thrice the candidate of a political party urges that a movement be inaugurated to dissolve the only general federation of organized workmen that ever existed for a period of time, such as the American Federation of Labor?

Mr. Hillquit. I regard it purely as the literal expression of a man of the Socialist Party who never places its program, its views, into the hands of any individual candidate. It speaks for itself in convention.

Mr. Gompers. And the candidate for the Presidency of your party does not express, then, the sentiments and the views of the party itself; is that the inference to be drawn from your answer?

Mr. Hillquit. You may draw this inference, that inasmuch as the candidate of the Socialist Party for the Presidency, or otherwise, deviates from the principles of the Socialist Party, he does not speak for the party, but speaks entirely on his own responsibility.

. . .

Mr. Gompers. In a work entitled "Industrial Union Movement"[5]—the preface of it is written by C. H. Kerr, a prominent American Socialist, a member of the party and a large publisher of socialist literature—in which he says: "As Marxian students of evolution, we (Socialists) recognize that economical concentration has made trade-unions obsolete, and that the principle of industrial unionism socialism must be adopted in the near future."

Mr. Hillquit. What do you want to know with reference to that, Mr. Gompers?

Mr. Gompers. Is that a Socialist expression in favor of the American labor movement, the American labor union movement?

Mr. Hillquit. Why, it might be. . . . It seems to me that the passage that you read may be crude, but it contains, to my mind, a good deal of sound truth. In other words, what it means is that the industrial evolution in this country has been such as to bring the industrial—larger—generally all-embracing organization of production to the front, and under such circumstances the trade unions evidently will have to adjust themselves and become organized on an industrial basis, and where the American Federation of Labor might not say it in so many words I think it has felt it, and I think it is undergoing a process of change in its organization now in just that very direction.

. . .

Mr. Gompers. Did you read the proceedings of the Rochester convention of the American Federation of Labor held in that city in 1912?

Mr. Hillquit. Yes; I did, Mr. Gompers.

Mr. Gompers. Did you read the declaration of the executive council of the American Federation of Labor on the subject of "Industrial unionism"?

Mr. Hillquit. I presume so; but I don't recall it.

Mr. Gompers. It didn't make any sufficient impression upon your mind that you can now recall it?

Mr. Hillquit. No; but if you will be kind enough to just bring my attention to the point you have in mind, I suppose I shall remember it.

Mr. Gompers. I hand you a copy of that report.

Mr. Hillquit. Thank you.

. . .

Mr. Gompers. Mr. Hillquit, you have seen that pamphlet which I handed you and which is a reprint of the report of the executive council to the Rochester American Federation of Labor convention. You will find also a reprint in that same pamphlet of the report of the committee to which this declaration was referred and the action of the convention thereon.

Mr. Hillquit. Yes.

Mr. Gompers. Now, as an advocate of industrial unionism, will you point out to the commission that from which you dissent?

Mr. Hillquit. Why, but Mr. Gompers, I don't dissent. I stated, on the contrary, that the American Federation of Labor is rapidly and irresistibly drafting an industrial organization, and I am very glad of the process.

. . .

Mr. Gompers. Then, sir, if you don't dissent from the declaration of the American Federation of Labor upon the subject of industrial unionism, will you please tell the commission how it comes that Mr. Debs and other Socialists, whose names, many of whom I can mention at this time, advocate the dissolution of the American Federation of Labor on the question of industrial unionism?

Mr. Hillquit. I can not answer for the operation of the mind of Mr. Debs or anybody else, but I may point out the following: First, that the first declaration on industrial unionism adopted by Mr. Debs and his colleagues when organizing the I.W.W. was adopted in 1905, and the declaration of the Federation of Labor was adopted in 1912, seven years later. That is, the American Federation of Labor once more followed in the wake of the Socialist agitation. The next point, Mr. Gompers, is that I understand the difference between the industrialism advocated by you and the industrialism advocated by the I.W.W., or particularly by Mr. Debs, is this, that the industrial form of organization which you advocate consists of a federation of similar crafts or trades within one industry not organically united to cooperate with each other in matters of common interest, and that the industrial form of organization advocated by Mr. Debs is an organic union of all crafts employed and embodied within one industry.

. . .

[Mr. Gompers.] Apart from the establishment of the cooperative commonwealth wherein does the purposes of your movement differ practically from the social reform movement which is carrying out corrections and improvements on the present social system, with the aim of complete social justice, and a maximum of possible liberty and happiness for mankind, such as the American labor movement? the American trade union movement, the American Federation of Labor?

Mr. Hillquit. Mr. Gompers, I have not been trying to establish any differences between the socialist movement and the labor movement. On the contrary, it seems to me, you have been trying to establish them and vainly. The Socialists see a difference in degree only, but they see absolutely no antagonism between the activities of the Socialist movement and the labor movement, or economic movement. On the contrary, I want you to understand they claim that they go very well hand in hand; that each of them can exist and thrive with the support of the other, and we are perfectly willing to lend our part of the support, Mr. Gompers. Whatever little criticism we have of leaders or methods are purely in the nature of friendly criticism, and we are not here, or anywhere else, to criticize the organized labor movement of this country, particularly as against the public at large. We consider them as part of the labor movement, and consider ourselves as a part of the labor movement.

. . .

U.S. Congress, Senate, *Industrial Relations. Final Report and Testimony Submitted to Congress by the Commission on Industrial Relations . . .* , 64th Cong., 1st sess., 1916, S. Doc. 415, 2: 1443, 1471, 1474–76, 1478–80, 1488.

1. Francis Patrick Walsh (1864–1939), a Kansas City, Mo., attorney, was chairman of the U.S. Commission on Industrial Relations (1913–15) and the Committee on Industrial Relations (1915–18). He served on the Kansas City Tenement Commission (1906–8), as attorney for the Kansas City Board of Public Welfare (1908–14), and as president of the Kansas City Board of Civil Service (1911–13). In 1918 he was cochairman, with former president William Howard Taft, of the National War Labor Board.

2. Morris HILLQUIT was a leading figure in the Socialist Party of America.

3. Eugene Victor DEBS participated in the creation of the Socialist Party of America in 1901 and was its candidate for president in 1904, 1908, 1912, and 1920.

4. A reference to "Industrial Organization," published in the May 7, 1914, issue of the *Miners' Magazine,* the journal of the Western Federation of Miners. Debs urged that union and the United Mine Workers of America to merge, leave the AFL, and launch a new organization, to be called the "American Industrial Union." This action, he said, "would mark the actual beginning of revolutionary industrial organization in the United States."

5. Probably *Industrial Unionism,* an address delivered by Debs in New York City in 1905 and later printed by Charles H. Kerr and Co., a socialist publishing house founded in Chicago in 1886 by Charles Hope Kerr.

New York City, May 22, 1914—10 A.M.

. . .

Chairman Walsh. Now, Mr. Hillquit, you may cross-examine Mr. Gompers.

. . .

Mr. Hillquit. . . . The American Federation of Labor is unequivocally in favor of a shorter workday, and a progressive decrease of working hours in keeping with the development of machinery and other productive forces, is it not?

. . .

Mr. Gompers. Yes; and in addition, the need, the recognized need in our day for greater rest opportunities and time for rest and leisure and cultivation.

Mr. Hillquit. Quite so. Then, the American Federation of Labor is also in favor of a rest of not less than a day and a half in each week?

Mr. Gompers. Yes.

. . .

Mr. Hillquit. . . . Are you, or is the American Federation of Labor, in favor of more efficient inspection of workshops, factories, and mines?

Mr. Gompers. It is, it has always been, and has worked to the accomplishment of the purposes which you have just now read as being declared.

Mr. Hillquit. And does the federation also favor forbidding the employment of children under 16 years of age?

Mr. Gompers. It has, is, and has worked toward the accomplishment of that purpose.

Mr. Hillquit. Does the federation favor forbidding the interstate transportation of the products of convict labor and the product of all uninspected factories and mines?

Mr. Gompers. Yes sir. . . .

. . .

Mr. Hillquit. And do you also favor direct employment of workers

by the United States Government, or State governments, or municipal governments, without the intervention of contractors?

Mr. Gompers. Yes, sir; and to a large degree have accomplished that.

Mr. Hillquit. Very well, sir. And does the federation also favor a minimum wage scale?

. . .

Mr. Gompers. The American Federation of Labor is not in favor of
such a proposition; but on the contrary is very much opposed to it, and
it is necessary to say—

Mr. Hillquit (interrupting). Can you state your reasons why, Mr.
Gompers?

Mr. Gompers. The attempts of Government to establish wages at
which workmen may work is the experience of history to be the beginning of an era, and a long era, of industrial slavery. There was a time
in history where governments and courts, at court sessions, established
wages, and during periods where there was a dearth of workmen to
perform the work required, and employers offered higher wages, the
workmen and employers were brought into court and both punished,
punished by imprisonment and physical mutilation, because the one
asked, received, or demanded and the other was willing to offer, or did
pay higher wages.

. . .

Mr. Hillquit. Then your idea is, Mr. Gompers, if the legislature once
fixed a minimum wage, that then the machinery of the State would be
set in motion to enforce work at that rate, whether the worker desires
to render such service or not?

Mr. Gompers. I am very suspicious of the activities of governmental
agencies.

Mr. Hillquit. And your apprehensions are, then, in that direction,
that once the State is allowed to fix a minimum rate the State would
also take the right to compel women or men to work at that rate. Is
that it?

Mr. Gompers. That is my apprehension.

. . .

Mr. Hillquit. Mr. Gompers, you were in favor of a maximum workday established by law, are you not?

Mr. Gompers. I am.

Mr. Hillquit. Wouldn't you, by analogy, say that there should be an
apprehension that if the legislature once is allowed to establish a maximum workday that it might, by putting its machinery in motion, compel workmen to work up to the maximum allowed?

Mr. Gompers. I think that my answer has not been sufficiently intelligent or comprehensive when I answer by the two monosyllables, "I

am." I ought to say I am in favor of the legal enactment for the maximum hours of labor for all workmen in direct Government employment, and for those who do work that the Government has substituted for Governmental authority. I am in favor of the—and the federation is in favor of the—speaking for the federation—is in favor of the maximum number of hours for children, for minors, and for women.

Mr. Hillquit. Then do I understand you to say, Mr. Gompers, that the federation does not favor a legal limitation of the workday for adult men workers?

Mr. Gompers. Not by law of the State. As a matter of fact, the unions have established very largely the shorter workday by their own initiative and power and influence; they have done it for themselves.

Mr. Hillquit. I know that, Mr. Gompers, but is the federation opposed to similar legal enactment?

Mr. Gompers. For adult workmen?

Mr. Hillquit. Exactly; limiting their hours of work?

Mr. Gompers. By legal statutory authority?

Mr. Hillquit. Yes.

Mr. Gompers. It is.

Mr. Hillquit. It is opposed?

Mr. Gompers. Yes, sir.

. . .

Mr. Hillquit. Then, Mr. Gompers, as I understand you, the American Federation of Labor is in favor of a uniform shorter workday and would enforce it by means, say, of collective bargaining, or other methods employed by labor unions?

Mr. Gompers. I may say, Mr. Hillquit, that you have evidently a misapprehension of the functions of the American Federation of Labor. As a matter of fact, the unions themselves undertake the work of accomplishing the shorter workday. Say, for instance, that the International Typographical Union undertook a movement, giving employers more than a years' notice in advance, that on a certain day they would no longer work more than eight hours in each day. Almost immediately a large number of employers acceded to the request. Others refused. The men struck. Covering a period of more than a year, employers in numbers and individual firms came to an agreement acceding to the eight-hour day, and enforcing it, and finally the eight-hour day has been accomplished, not only by the printers, the International Typographical Union, but the eight-hour day prevails now generally in the printing trades; and that is true in many others, in the building trades. It did not require any law for the printers; it did not require any law for the granite cutters;[1] it did not require any law for the Cigar Makers' International Union, of which I have the honor to be a member. There was not any requirement in the law in the building trades, and many others, to introduce the eight-hour workday.

Mr. Hillquit. I fully understand that, but you have stated before that the American Federation of Labor, as such, at its annual conventions, adopted a resolution as early as 1884 approving of the movement for an eight-hour day,[2] encouraging it, and that it has since cooperated with the various affiliated organizations for the attainment of the eight-hour day.

Mr. Gompers. Yes; but it was necessary for the organizations themselves to take the initiative.

. . .

Mr. Hillquit. Very well, Mr. Gompers. As far as you know, Mr. Gompers, the United Mine Workers, and the Western Federation of Miners, both affiliated with the American Federation of Labor, have been very active in establishing in the several States of their operation, a minimum workday of eight hours. Is that a fact?

Mr. Gompers. In the Western States, for workmen who are employed beneath the surface of the earth.

. . .

Mr. Hillquit. From your knowledge of the sentiment and position of the American Federation, as such, would you say that the federation approves or disapproves of such activity of its affiliated unions of obtaining a maximum legally established workday?

Mr. Gompers. I think that the federation, if called upon to approve the course, would say that the organization acted within its rights, and if it deemed that the best we would not oppose it but, rather, approve it.

Mr. Hillquit. Notwithstanding the apprehensions you express.

Mr. Gompers. The fact of the matter is that some men unconsciously and with the best of intentions get to rivet chains on their wrists.

Mr. Hillquit. Now, Mr. Gompers, the federation would encourage the practice of its various affiliated organizations in endeavoring to secure a shorter workday, by means of a collective agreement, of certain groups of employers in a certain industry, would it not?

Mr. Gompers. It would.

. . .

Mr. Hillquit. Now, if the same proposition should come by means of a law bringing upon all employers in a given State, or, for that matter, throughout the Union, then the federation, as I understand, would not approve it?

Mr. Gompers. It would oppose it.

Mr. Hillquit. It would oppose it?

Mr. Gompers. If I understand the views and interpret the views of the American Federation of Labor, men and all alike, it would oppose it.

Mr. Hillquit. Well, now, let's understand that well, Mr. Gompers, for the record. Your opinion is that if there were a movement and a possibility of establishing a shorter workday, say, an eight-hour workday, by legal enactment throughout the land, and a minimum wage in the same way, the federation would be opposed to such measures?

Mr. Gompers. It would; because it has in a large measure accomplished it and will accomplish it by the initiative of the association, the organization, and the grit and courage of the manhood and womanhood of the men and women in the American Federation of Labor.

Mr. Hillquit. And if that grit and courage should express itself by forcing the legislatures of the various States to enact such a law and if the execution and performance of the law were backed by a strong labor organization in each State, with the same grit and courage, you would not object to it?

Mr. Gompers. Well, your hypothesis is entirely groundless.

Mr. Hillquit. Why, Mr. Gompers?

Mr. Gompers. When the organizations of labor, as I have already said, have accomplished that to a large extent, and propose to accomplish it again, further, on their own initiative and by their own voluntary association, it precludes the question of having a legal enactment for that purpose.

Mr. Hillquit. I just wanted to know why it precludes it. You say that the unions affiliated with you propose to enforce such rules; that means they have not done so yet.

Mr. Gompers. Unfortunately, that is so.

Mr. Hillquit. Unfortunately, that is so. Now, Mr. Gompers, my question is this: In proposing to do so, assume that it had a chance to accomplish, then, by the methods of legal enactment through their influence and in such shape and surrounded by the precautions satisfactory to labor organizations, then I want you to say whether or not the American Federation of Labor would be opposed to such measures.

Mr. Gompers. It would, for the reason I have already stated, and for the additional reason that the giving of the jurisdiction to government and to governmental agencies is always dangerous, when it comes to the government of working people.

Mr. Hillquit. Yes; I understand you rightly. Now, Mr. Gompers, does the American Federation of Labor favor a system of noncontributing old-age pensions for workers—

Mr. Gompers (interrupting). Yes, sir.

Mr. Hillquit (continuing). Reaching a certain age?

Mr. Gompers. Yes, sir.

Mr. Hillquit. It does?

Mr. Gompers. Yes, sir.

Mr. Hillquit. And that, of course, by legal enactment and governmental machinery?

Mr. Gompers. Yes.

. . .

Mr. Hillquit. . . . Does the federation favor Government relief of unemployed by extension of useful public works?

Mr. Gompers. Yes, sir.

Mr. Hillquit. It does?

Mr. Gompers. It does.

Mr. Hillquit. And does it also favor a provision that the persons employed on such work—

Mr. Gompers (interrupting). What?

Mr. Hillquit. Does it favor a provision to the effect that all persons employed on such work shall be engaged directly by the Government and work not more than eight hours, and at not less than the prevailing union wages?

Mr. Gompers. Yes.

Mr. Hillquit. The federation favors that?

Mr. Gompers. Yes.

Mr. Hillquit. Does the Federation favor a plan by which the Government should establish employment bureaus and loan money to States and municipalities without interest for the purpose of carrying on useful public works?

Mr. Gompers. Will you please read the question?

(The question was read by the stenographer.)

Mr. Gompers. It has not declared itself upon that subject, except as I have already stated in the blanket answer; that is, it favors any tangible, rational proposition that would help to meet and solve the question of unemployment.

Mr. Hillquit. Then you individually, Mr. Gompers, would not object to such a plan?

Mr. Gompers. Oh, no; I think not.

Mr. Hillquit. Now, Mr. Gompers, you also mentioned that the American Federation of Labor tried to improve the political status of the workers; that is correct, is it not, among other things?

Mr. Gompers. I should like to be quoted accurately. To improve the condition of the working people in every human field of activity; to protect and promote and advance their rights and interests.

Mr. Hillquit. Exactly. Now, every field of human activity includes the political field?

Mr. Gompers. It does.

Mr. Hillquit. And every right of the worker includes his political rights?

Mr. Gompers. It does.

Mr. Hillquit. Now, then, Mr. Gompers, is your federation in favor of the absolute freedom of press, speech, and assemblage?

Mr. Gompers. It is. May I amplify that answer?

Mr. Hillquit. You may.

Mr. Gompers. By saying that the American Federation of Labor has, in the effort to stand for the freedom of speech, freedom of the press, and freedom of assemblage, undertaken great risks, and has asserted it and maintained it. In addition to this, the American Federation of Labor looks askance upon any effort to curb the inherent, as well as the constitutional rights of free press and free speech and free assemblage, and holds that, though these rights may be perverted, may be improperly exercised, exercised for an unlawful purpose, say, and yet these rights must not, in advance, be interfered with. The right of assemblage, the right of expression through speech or press, must be untrammeled if we are going to have a republican form of government with freedom. If anybody utters that which is libellous or seditious or treasonable, they must be made and may be made to answer for those transgressions, but the right to expression must be unimpaired, and the American Federation of Labor has and will stand unalterably and unequivocally in favor of free assemblage, free speech, and free press.

Mr. Hillquit. So with the Socialist Party. We are there at one.

Mr. Gompers. I did not know that the Socialist Party was to be injected into this.

Mr. Hillquit. Why, we have had the two injected all along.

Chairman Walsh. If you will leave out the comment or the assertion—

Mr. Hillquit. Very well. Mr. Gompers, is your federation [for] unrestricted and equal suffrage for men and women?

Mr. Gompers. It is, it has been, and has done much to advance that cause.

Mr. Hillquit. Does your federation favor the initiative, referendum, and recall?

Mr. Gompers. It not only advocates it, has advocated it, but one of the members of an affiliated organization is a member who was the author of the first book upon direct legislation, initiative, and referendum in the United States—Mr. James W. Sullivan.[3]

Mr. Hillquit. Mr. Gompers, does your federation also favor the system of proportional representation?

Mr. Gompers. It has not, as an organization, taken affirmative action on that subject.

Mr. Hillquit. But it practices it in its own conventions, practically? Your vote is by membership?

Mr. Gompers. The proportionate representation, as that term is usually expressed, is not the proportional representation to which you refer in the voting in the conventions of the American Federation of Labor. The proportional representation—that is, I want to know whether I am right?

Mr. Hillquit. I will define it, Mr. Gompers.

Mr. Gompers. Yes.

Mr. Hillquit. I use proportional representation as denoting a system by which votes are cast and rights are exercised by representatives in proportion to the numerical strength of the constituents.

Mr. Gompers. Yes; I favor that.

Mr. Hillquit. You do?

Mr. Gompers. Yes, sir. The American Federation of Labor does.

Mr. Hillquit. Yes. Then, does the federation favor the election of the President and Vice President of the United States by direct vote of the people without intervention of the electoral college?

Mr. Gompers. It does, and so declared.

Mr. Hillquit. Does your federation favor a restriction upon the powers of judges to nullify laws or set them aside as unconstitutional?

Mr. Gompers. It does, and it has.

Mr. Hillquit. Does your federation favor a measure to make the Constitution of the United States amendable by a majority vote of the people?

Mr. Gompers. Amendable by an easier method than at present prevails. As to the specific proposition that you have just asked, I am not so sure. I don't know. No expression has been given before.

Mr. Hillquit. Personally, Mr. Gompers, you would think a simpler method of amending the Constitution would be a step in advance?

Mr. Gompers. The method now is very cumbersome and slow, and, being a written Constitution to be a chart, while it ought not to be subject to changes at every ebb and flow of the tide, it ought to be much easier than it is now.

Mr. Hillquit. Now, Mr. Gompers, are you in favor of curbing the powers of the court to punish for contempt in labor disputes, or to regulate that power?

Mr. Gompers. If I may adopt the tactics of the Yankee, I might say, "Do you doubt it?" Yes, sir.

Mr. Hillquit. Are you in favor of an enactment of further measures for general education, and particularly for vocational education in useful pursuits?

Mr. Gompers. Read the question.

(The question was read.)

Mr. Gompers. Yes. . . .

. . .

Mr. Hillquit. Is your federation in favor of the free administration of justice?

Mr. Gompers. It is.

Mr. Hillquit. I have enumerated to you all [the] political and industrial demands in the platform of the Socialist Party, and you find that your federation adopts them, with the exception of two points on the question of a maximum workday and the minimum wage. You would accomplish that by pure economic action, and the Socialist Party advocated legal enactments; is that correct?

Mr. Gompers. It is not correct.

Mr. Hillquit. Why?

Mr. Gompers. As a matter of fact, the Socialist Party has purloined the demands and the vocabulary of the American labor movement, and has adopted it as its own, and now you ask the American Federation of Labor whether they favor it.

Mr. Hillquit. Then, Mr. Gompers, whether we have purloined, or no matter in what way we arrived at it, the demands and the program that I questioned you upon, the American Federation of Labor, either as the original inventor or otherwise, fully approves of it, with the exception of the small difference I mentioned; is that correct?

. . .

Mr. Gompers. I say that these demands which you have enumerated have been promulgated, declared for, and fought for, and in many instances accomplished by the American Federation of Labor and the organized-labor movement of the country, and your question would indicate that you would want the adhesion of the American labor movement to your original propositions when, as a matter of fact, they have been put into your platform simply as vote catchers.

Mr. Hillquit. Exactly. Then, you admit the identity, but you deny priority on our part?

Mr. Gompers. And purpose.

. . .

Mr. Hillquit. Now, Mr. Gompers, to take up another subject, is it your conception, Mr. Gompers, or that of the Federation, that workers in the United States to-day receive the full product of their labor?

Mr. Gompers. I think, but I am not quite so sure, that I know what you have in mind.

Mr. Hillquit. Do you understand my question?

Mr. Gompers. I think I do, but in the generally accepted sense of that term, no.

Mr. Hillquit. In any particular sense, yes?

Mr. Gompers. No.

Mr. Hillquit. Then the workers of this country do not receive the whole product of their labor? Can you hazard a guess as to what proportion of the product they do receive in the shape of wages?

Mr. Gompers. I am not a good guesser, and I doubt that there is any value in a guess.

Mr. Hillquit. You have no general idea, have you, on the subject?

Mr. Gompers. I have a most general idea, but I am not called upon to guess.

Mr. Hillquit. No; will you please give us your most general idea?

Mr. Gompers. As to what proportion?

Mr. Hillquit. As to approximately what proportion the workers, as a whole, get from their product?

Mr. Gompers. I will say that is impossible for anyone to definitely say what proportion the workers receive as the result of their labor; but it is the fact that due to the organized-labor movement they have received and are receiving a larger share of the product of their labor than they ever did in the history of modern society.

Mr. Hillquit. Then one of the functions of organized labor is to increase the share of the workers in the product of their labor, is that correct?

Mr. Gompers. Yes, sir; organized labor makes constantly increasing demand upon society for reward for the services which the workers give to society, and without which the civilized life would be impossible.

. . .

Mr. Hillquit. . . . In your experience with the labor movement and in its ever forward march toward greater and greater improvement, and a greater and greater share of social justice, can you point out any line where the labor movement will stop and rest contented so long as it may receive short of the full product of its work?

Mr. Gompers. I say that the workers, as human beings, will never stop in any effort, nor stop at any point in the effort to secure greater improvements in their condition, a better life in all its phases. And wherever that may lead, whatever that may be, so far in my time and my age I decline to permit my mind or my activities to be labeled by any particular ism.

Mr. Hillquit. Do not try to attach any ism to me, please; but the question I ask is whether you maintain—whether the American Federation of Labor, and its authorized spokesmen have a general social philosophy, or work blindly from day to day?

Mr. Gompers. I think your question—

Mr. Hillquit (interrupting). Inconvenient.

Mr. Gompers. No. I will tell you what it is, it is a question prompted to you, and is an insult.

Mr. Hillquit. It is not a question prompted to me.

Mr. Gompers. It is an insult.

Mr. Hillquit. Why? Why, Mr. Gompers?

Mr. Gompers. To insinuate that the men and women in the American Federation of Labor movement are acting blindly from day to day.

Mr. Hillquit. I have not insinuated—

Mr. Gompers (interrupting). Your question implies it.

Mr. Hillquit. I am giving you an opportunity to deny.

Mr. Gompers. If a man should ask me whether I still beat my wife, any answer I could make would incriminate me if I answered yes or no. If I answered that I did not, the intimation would be that I had stopped. If I answered that I did, that I was continuing to beat her.

Mr. Hillquit. But Mr. Gompers, this question bears no analogy to that story—

Mr. Gompers (interrupting). Your question is an insult and a studied one.

. . .

Mr. Hillquit. Then, inform me upon this matter: In your political work of the labor movement is the American Federation of Labor guided by a general social philosophy, or is it not?

Mr. Gompers. It is guided by the history of the past, drawing its lessons from history, to know of the conditions by which the working people are surrounded and confronted; to work along the lines of least resistance; to accomplish the best results in improving the condition of the working people, men and women and children, to-day and to-morrow and to-morrow—and to-morrow's to-morrow; and each day making it a better day than the one that had gone before. That is the guiding principle and philosophy and aim of the labor movement—in order to secure a better life for all.

Mr. Hillquit. But in these efforts to improve conditions from day to day you must have an underlying standard of what is better, don't you?

Mr. Gompers. No. You start out with a given program, and everything must conform to it; and if the facts do not conform to your theories, why, your declarations, or rather, your actions, betray the state of mind "so much the worse for the facts."

Mr. Hillquit. Mr. Gompers, what I ask you is this: You say you try to make the conditions of the workers better every day. In order to determine whether the conditions are better or worse you must have some standards by which you distinguish the bad from the good in the labor movement, do you not?

Mr. Gompers. Certainly. Well, is that—

Mr. Hillquit (interrupting). Now, just—

Mr. Gompers (interrupting). Well, one moment. Does it require much discernment to know that a wage of $3 a day and a workday of 8 hours a day in sanitary workshops are all better than $2.50 a day and 12 hours a day and under perilous conditions of labor? It does not require much conception of a social philosophy to understand that.

Mr. Hillquit. Then, Mr. Gompers, by the same parity of reasoning, $4 a day and seven hours a day of work and very attractive working conditions are still better?

Mr. Gompers. Unquestionably.

Mr. Hillquit. Therefore—

Mr. Gompers (interrupting). Just a moment. I have not stipulated $4 a day or $8 a day or any number of dollars a day or eight hours a day or seven hours a day or any number of hours a day, but the best possible conditions obtainable for the workers is the aim.

Mr. Hillquit. Yes; and when these conditions are obtained—

Mr. Gompers (interrupting). Why, then, we want better.

Mr. Hillquit (continuing). You will still strive for better?

Mr. Gompers. Yes.

Mr. Hillquit. Now, my question is, Will this effort on the part of organized labor ever stop until it has the full reward for its labor?

Mr. Gompers. It won't stop at all.

Mr. Hillquit. That is a question—

Mr. Gompers (interrupting). Not when any particular point is reached, whether it be that toward which you have just declared or anything else. The working people will never stop—

Mr. Hillquit. Exactly.

Mr. Gompers (continuing). In their effort to obtain a better life for themselves and for their wives and for their children and for humanity.

Mr. Hillquit. Then, the object of the labor union is to obtain complete social justice for themselves and for their wives and for their children?

Mr. Gompers. It is the effort to obtain a better life every day.

Mr. Hillquit. Every day and always—

Mr. Gompers. Every day. That does not limit it.

Mr. Hillquit. Until such time—

Mr. Gompers. Not until any time.

Mr. Hillquit. In other words—

Mr. Gompers (interrupting). In other words, we go further than you. (Laughter and applause in the audience.) You have an end; we have not.

. . .

. . . I say that the movement of the working people, whether under the American Federation, or not, will be simply following the human impulse for improvement in their condition, and wherever that may lead, they will go, without having a goal up to yours or surpassing yours, but it will lead them constantly to the material and physical and social and moral well-being of the people.

Mr. Hillquit. Then, Mr. Gompers, you would not say that the difference between the program of the American Federation of Labor, and that of the Socialist Party is a quantitative one—that the Socialist Party wants more than the American Federation of Labor. You would not say that, would you?

Mr. Gompers. I don't know that it is necessary that the comparison—that I should answer as to the comparison. It is not interesting at all, nor is it a contribution to the subject which the commission desires to ascertain.

Mr. Hillquit. You decline to answer that point?

Mr. Gompers. The question is not germane to the subject under inquiry, and is not necessary.

Chairman Walsh. I would like to hear it answered if possible, Mr. Gompers. If it is not possible for any reason, very well.

. . .

Mr. Gompers. The Socialist Party proposition—socialism is a proposition to place the working people of the country and of the world in a physical material strait-jacket.

Mr. Hillquit. Pardon me, Mr. Gompers, I have not asked your opinion about what you consider to be the tendencies of the cooperative commonwealth. I am speaking merely about the aim to abolish the wage system and the program to secure to the workers the full product of their labor; and I am asking you, in this respect, whether we demand more than the American Federation has ultimately in view.

Mr. Gompers. I think you demand something to which the American labor movement declines to give its adherence.

Mr. Hillquit. Then do I understand you to say that the American labor movement would countenance the abolition of the wage system and the return of the full reward of labor to the workers?

Mr. Gompers. Your question is an assumption and is unwarranted, for as a matter of fact we decline to commit our labor movement to your species of speculative philosophy.

. . .

Mr. Hillquit. Now, Mr. Gompers, the employers as a class, being interested in retaining their share of the products, general product, or increasing it, and the workers, as you say, being determined to demand an ever greater and greater share of it, would you say that the economic interests between those two are harmonious or not?

Mr. Gompers. If you had omitted the two words "or not" the question would have meant just the same.

Mr. Hillquit. Well, they are there, and it does not cause me any effort to leave them there, so answer the question.

Mr. Gompers. I say they are not, and I may say this and take this opportunity, I am under affirmation before this commission, and I may take this opportunity of saying that no man of my knowledge, within the range of my acquaintance, has ever been so thoroughly misrepresented upon that question as is implied in your question than I have.

. . .

Mr. Hillquit. Can you conceive of any scheme by which the interests of the employers and those of the employees could be harmonious and could lead to the same beneficent results as the independent struggles of the workers?

. . .

Mr. Gompers. I know of no means by which the interests of the employers and the workingmen can be harmonious in the full broad sense of that term.

Mr. Hillquit. And do you concede that the labor leader or labor representative is most useful to his organization and to his movement who devotes his time and his thought, single mindedly, to the interests of the labor organizations?

Mr. Gompers. And to the working people.

Mr. Hillquit. To the working people?

Mr. Gompers. Yes, sir.

Mr. Hillquit. And do you consider a labor leader who combines with a number of prominent employers in an alleged effort to improve the condition of the workers to be doing useful work for the labor movement?

Mr. Gompers. I concede this that it is the duty of such men you designate as labor leaders to carry the word, to preach the doctrine, to carry the message and the gospel of labor, of justice to labor, to any place on earth, and to any people on earth; to defend that doctrine; to promote a better understanding among any and all; it is the duty of every leader to make his cause best known wherever the opportunity may afford.

Mr. Hillquit. For the benefit and advantage of the working class, is it not?

Mr. Gompers. Absolutely and alone.

Mr. Hillquit. And is it not likewise in the interests of the large employers of labor to carry the gospel of their interests wherever they can, and particularly into the camp of labor?

Mr. Gompers. Whether it is [in] their interests I am not prepared to say, but I judge from my own experience that that is not the truth, and it is not the fact.

. . .

Mr. Hillquit. Admitting that the employing classes have certain economic interests opposed to the working classes, would you think it natural to expect that it would organize in defense of its interests and against the organized labor movement?

Mr. Gompers. If they organized at all for the consideration of that subject, that would be the purpose.

Mr. Hillquit. Mr. Gompers, do you know the history and origin of the American Civic Federation?[4]

Mr. Gompers. I do.

Mr. Hillquit. By whom was it organized?

Mr. Gompers. By Mr. Ralph M. Easley,[5] together with some business men and publicists and a few workmen in the city of Chicago.

Mr. Hillquit. When it became a national institution, was it not the late Mark Hanna who was its first leading spirit?

Mr. Gompers. No, sir; that is a Socialist misrepresentation of the facts.

Mr. Hillquit. Was Mr. Mark Hanna connected with the organization at all, so far as you know?

Mr. Gompers. Several—many years—after its first formation.

Mr. Hillquit. When it became an institution of national scope was Mr. Hanna connected with it?

Mr. Gompers. After it had become an institution of national scope, and a considerable time after.

Mr. Hillquit. And while he was so connected, was not he rather a leading figure in the federation?

Mr. Gompers. He was for two years its president—president of the American Civic Federation. May I suggest at the start that when you speak of the American Federation of Labor you designate its name, and when you speak of the Civic Federation you designate it by name, and not confuse the record by the indefinite or confusing word "federation" as applied equally to both.

Mr. Hillquit. You would not want to have the American Federation of Labor mistaken for the American Civic Federation?

Mr. Gompers. Oh, I would not want by your indirection and insinuation to make such—to confuse.

Mr. Hillquit. Mr. Gompers, were not and are not some of the leading members of the National Civic Federation very well known capitalists?

Mr. Gompers. Yes, sir.

. . .

Mr. Hillquit. And the object of the federation, among other things, was to adjust certain labor disputes, was it not?

Mr. Gompers. It was not.

Mr. Hillquit. Doesn't the Civic Federation maintain a department of mediation, arbitration, and other instrumentalities for the adjustment of labor disputes?

Mr. Gompers. It has a department of mediation. It undertakes no effort at arbitration, unless called upon to do so voluntarily by both sides. It has brought employers and workingmen together engaged in tremendously important disputes, who could—who it seemed could not be brought together for the purpose of meeting and discussing their diverse points of view and diverse interests; and the result has been that agreements have been reached between large bodies of workers and large employers, the terms and conditions of labor being improved, and to the mutual satisfaction—at least temporary mutual satisfaction of both parties to the dispute.

Mr. Hillquit. Mr. Gompers, has not the Civic Federation also taken stands on various practical problems of the labor movement and labor legislation?

Mr. Gompers. Never; unless it was adhered to by the representatives of the working people.

Mr. Hillquit. Yes, sir; but with such adherence the Civic Federation has undertaken such work, has it not?

Mr. Gompers. Not undertaken it, but aided in it.

Mr. Hillquit. Aided in it?

Mr. Gompers. Aided the working people in their organized capacity to accomplish it.

. . .

Mr. Hillquit. Then, Mr. Gompers, your belief is that a capitalists' union, which has come in the Civic Federation and have ordinarily led, have done so for the benefit of the working class?

Mr. Gompers. Your assumption is wrong when you say that they have led the National Civic Federation.

Mr. Hillquit. They have participated in its work, have they?

Mr. Gompers. Yes, sir.

Mr. Hillquit. Now, Mr. Gompers, have they done so, in your opinion, for the benefit of organized labor?

. . .

Mr. Gompers. I will say that I don't know their motives. I simply know their acts, and I say that there has never been an action taken by the National Civic Federation that was hostile to the interests of the working people.

Mr. Hillquit. You have stated before, Mr. Gompers, that you believe there was no harmony between the interests of the employing classes and those of the workers, and that you believe that the workers must depend upon their own efforts as workers, without the interventions of intellectuals, you say, or others, to secure the improvements. Now, I am asking you, do you believe that they can secure such improvements with the intervention of capitalists of the type that you have named in the Civic Federation?

Mr. Gompers. First, when you speak of the intellectuals to which I referred I say the intellectuals who undertake to dominate our movement. The National Civic Federation have never attempted to dominate the affairs of our movement. And, second, you said regardless of what motives they have. I simply know their acts. It is most difficult for anyone to determine even your motive or my motive. I only can judge of people's acts, and I know their acts have never been hostile in the Civic Federation to the interests of the working people.

Mr. Hillquit. Then, you would not think it is perfectly proper for an official representative of the American Federation of Labor to cooperate with well-known capitalist employers for common ends?

Mr. Gompers. There is no such thing as that upon which your question is predicated.

Mr. Hillquit. Answer the question, whether you think it proper or not.

Mr. Gompers. This is another one of those questions the answer to which will convict.

Mr. Hillquit. It might, Mr. Gompers.

Mr. Gompers. Yes; and it will.

Mr. Hillquit. You think so?

Mr. Gompers. I may not be quite so clever, but at least I shall try to be truthful and assume nothing upon which—unless I have basis for it. There is no such thing as cooperation between the leaders of the labor movement and the leaders of the National Civic Federation. What is done is to endeavor to impress upon all with whom I—and I know that your questions are directed toward me without regard to anyone else—I say, so far as I am concerned, I can go anywhere where men assemble and where they consider the questions affecting the working people; I can meet with them and bring the message of labor to them; to argue and contend as best I can with them for the rights of the working people; and if I can influence them to any act of helpfulness toward any one thing in which the working people are interested I have accomplished something. I have never felt that I have come away with my skirts besmirched or my character impaired or my determination to toil and struggle for the working people impeded or impaired in any way.

Mr. Hillquit. And you think it is perfectly feasible and possible for a labor leader to influence large employers and capitalists to join the American Civic Federation and National Civic Federation to take measures for the benefit of organized labor?

Mr. Gompers. That is not the question. I will appeal to the devil and his mother-in-law to help labor if labor can be aided in that way.

Mr. Hillquit. And will you cooperate?

Mr. Gompers. Let me say this: The question comes with ill grace when Socialists are butting in everywhere, no matter whether the employed or the capitalist class—

Mr. Hillquit. Let's not try to evade the question.

Mr. Gompers. That is not evasion. That is a supplemental statement of fact.

Mr. Hillquit. Very supplemental. Now, Mr. Gompers, you have drawn the parallel between the National Civic Federation and the devil and his grandmother. Now, I am asking you, will you go to the extent—will you expect the devil or his grandmother to aid the American labor movement, and would you cooperate with him?

Chairman Walsh. Please proceed to some other question.

Mr. Hillquit. Very well. Mr. Gompers, do you know that is a contradiction between your previous statement to the effect that there is a certain antagonism between the interests of employers and of employees, that the struggles of the workers are directed against the employers, and that those struggles must be conducted by themselves as workers and your activities in the National Civic Federation?

Mr. Gompers. No.

Mr. Hillquit. Hold on—

Mr. Gompers. One minute. No. As a matter of fact, the National Civic Federation is quite as emphatically damned by the National Association of Manufacturers as it is by you and your associates, because, as the National Association of Manufacturers have said—they say that it is dominated by the labor leaders.

Mr. Hillquit. Do you agree with them—the National Manufacturers' Associations?

Mr. Gompers. I should prefer not to say. I would not care to weaken such influence as I might have with the National Civic Federation by claiming that I do dominate it.

. . .

Commissioner Garretson. I would like to ask you one question in regard to the Civic Federation. Have you ever heard the opinion expressed by labor men who do sit in the same room and eat at the same table with the employing class that benefits had been gained for laboring men through the agencies of such organizations as the Civic Federation?

Mr. Gompers. There is no question about it, sir. As a matter of fact it has—I am not prepared to say as to the motives of any of the men—but simply as a matter of fact—the Civic Federation men have been instrumental in bringing together the representatives of employers and the representatives of workmen who meet for the first time where all other agencies have proved futile, in trying to bring them together.

Commissioner Garretson. Have you ever seen the time when the agencies exercised by the organization and which you are able to put in motion through its influence brought conference and settlement where no other means were available?

Mr. Gompers. Time and time and again.

. . .

U.S. Congress, Senate, *Industrial Relations. Final Report and Testimony Submitted to Congress by the Commission on Industrial Relations . . . ,* 64th Cong., 1st sess., 1916, S. Doc. 415, 2: 1492, 1497–1502, 1504–6, 1526–30, 1534, 1537–41, 1545–46.

1. The Granite Cutters' International Association of America.
2. The 1884 FOTLU convention adopted a motion declaring that "eight hours shall constitute a legal day's labor from and after May 1, 1886" (FOTLU, *Proceedings,* 1884, p. 14; see also *The Samuel Gompers Papers,* vol. 1, p. 276).
3. James William Sullivan published *Direct Legislation by the Citizenship through the Initiative and Referendum* in 1892. He was a member of the International Typographical Union.
4. The National Civic Federation (NCF).
5. Ralph Montgomery Easley was a founder of the NCF in 1900 and served as its secretary (1900–1903) and as chairman of its executive council (1904–39).

To Peter Hassenpflue[1]

May 25, 1914.

Mr. Peter Hassenpflue,
Secretary, Cleveland Federation of Labor,[2]
310 Prospect Ave., S.E., Cleveland, Ohio.
Dear Sir and Brother:

Your favor of the 21st instant is at hand and contents noted. You say that the Cleveland Federation of Labor will hold a protest meeting on

May 31st against the action of the Cleveland Board of Education in declaring that any teacher in a Cleveland public school who holds membership in a teachers' union affiliated with the American Federation of Labor or the Cleveland Federation of Labor, will not be reappointed at the end of the present school term.[3] You request that I should come to Cleveland for the 31st of May and deliver an address at the protest meeting, as you understand I am to be in Cleveland[4] for the opening of the convention[5] of the Ladies' Garment Workers. I am in full sympathy with the purposes of the protest meeting and should like to be in a position to accept your invitation to make an address but I regret to say that it will not be within my power to do so. I have only today just returned from a ten days absence on official business,[6] participating in important conferences as directed by the Executive Council, giving testimony before the Industrial Relations Commission at its hearings in New York City, as member of the New York State Factory Investigating Commission, attending the public hearings of that body, etc., etc. I have important engagements at headquarters all of this week, to which I must devote my attention, just allowing sufficient time for me to leave Washington so as to keep my engagement to address the Ladies' Garment Workers' Convention.

I already have had several requests for other public addresses and meetings in connection with my trip to Cleveland for the Ladies' Garment Workers' Convention. Much as I should like to do so I cannot undertake to accept them all.

Anticipating seeing you and the other good boys in Cleveland, and with best wishes for the success of the protest meeting, I am,

Fraternally yours,   Saml Gompers.
President,   American Federation of Labor.

P.S. Since the above was written, I have been enabled to make other arrangements regarding a date which I had, and therefore I shall take pleasure in being with you at the mass meeting Sunday, May 31st.[7] I have just sent you a telegram[8] to this effect.

S. G.

TLpS, reel 182, vol. 194, pp. 440–41, SG Letterbooks, DLC.

1. Peter Hassenpflue, a member of Brotherhood of Painters, Decorators, and Paperhangers of America 102 of Cleveland, was president (1910–11), corresponding secretary (1912, 1913–14), business agent (1913–14), and treasurer (1915–17, 1919–26) of the Cleveland Federation of Labor (FOL).

2. The Cleveland FOL was chartered by the AFL in October 1909 as the successor to the United Trades and Labor Council of Cuyahoga Co., Ohio (UTLC), which had lost its charter the previous month after seating delegates from the Reid-Murphy faction of the International Brotherhood of Electrical Workers.

3. On May 14, 1914, members of the Cleveland Grade Teachers' Club voted to form a union and affiliate with the Cleveland FOL. Five days later the Cleveland Board of

Education announced it would not hire or reappoint teachers who became union members. The Cleveland FOL filed suit on behalf of the teachers on May 27, and Judge William B. Neff of the Court of Common Pleas granted an injunction in June barring the school board from dismissing teachers who joined the proposed union or indicated their intention to do so (*John G. Owens* v. *Board of Education of Cleveland* [1914]). When Cleveland superintendent of schools J. M. H. Frederick refused to reappoint six women who had been at the forefront of the movement to unionize, Neff ruled he was in contempt of court and sentenced him to ten days' imprisonment and a $500 fine (*In re Frederick* [1914]). Neff's rulings were overturned by the Cuyahoga Co. Court of Appeals in June 1915, and the teachers were not rehired (*J. M. H. Frederick* v. *John G. Owens,* Ohio App. 8 Dist. [1915]).

4. SG left Washington, D.C., for Cleveland on May 30, 1914, and returned to AFL headquarters on June 4.

5. The International Ladies' Garment Workers' Union held its 1914 convention in Cleveland, June 1–13. SG addressed the convention on June 1.

6. SG left for New York City on the afternoon of May 16, 1914, and returned to AFL headquarters on May 25. While in New York he met with labor representatives and attended hearings of the New York State Factory Investigating Commission and the U.S. Commission on Industrial Relations.

7. SG spoke in Cleveland on May 31, 1914, before a crowd of five thousand people.

8. SG to Hassenpflue, May 26, 1914, reel 182, vol. 194, p. 421, SG Letterbooks, DLC.

From Ralph Easley

The National Civic Federation
New York City May 26, 1914.

Dear Brother Gompers:

I tried to get hold of you on Saturday evening to congratulate you on going through a very trying ordeal with as much glory as anybody could under some of the police court regulations of the Commission.

I have just gone very carefully over the testimony, (we had a verbatim copy made for the office) and I have marked a number of things about which I want to talk to you when I see you. We certainly all want to thank you for the courageous and manly defence you made of the Civic Federation and I cannot see any place where they "caught you asleep at the switch."

I had supposed that O'Connell and Lennon were keeping right after you in reference to this particular discussion. It turns out that they were practically paying no attention to it and that you had to make your own plans and program after you got here. I do not know how you "pulled out" as well as you did in dealing with a shifty, unscrupulous lawyer like Hillquit. Your closing speech was a gem.[1] I am sorry that the quotation from *The Metropolitan Magazine* which you used on the last day had not been given to you at first.[2] I gave it to both Mr. Gordon[3] and Mr. Sullivan[4] and laid great stress on what I considered its importance. While it came in all right where it did, it would have much more nonplussed Hillquit if it had been put to him immediately after his enumeration of his ameliorative program. Nothing could more clearly show the claptrap of his pretensions that they really regarded those things as of any importance.

In one place the record has you practically admitting that the unions' goal is to take "all," which is about what the socialists propose, as brought out by Ballard[5] in his question to Max Hayes.[6] Has not the reporter got that mixed up? I have never before heard you say anything like the socialist statement: "To the worker belongs the product of his toil," that could be construed in the same sense as that declaration is made by the socialists.[7] The way they have you in the record you are open to that criticism, it seems to me, on the surface. However, as I said, it does not make much difference. You certainly hammered Hillquit up all right.

I expect to be over to see you either on Friday of this week or the first of next week.

Sincerely yours,   Ralph Easley

P.S. Please look in your pockets and dig out the form letters which Dr. Falkner[8] gave you in Washington and send them to us with your directions.

TLS, Files of the Office of the President, General Correspondence, reel 77, frames 240–41, *AFL Records.*

1. SG made his closing remarks before the U.S. Commission on Industrial Relations on May 23, 1914 (U.S. Congress, Senate, *Industrial Relations. Final Report and Testimony Submitted to Congress by the Commission on Industrial Relations . . . ,* 64th Cong., 1st sess., 1916, S. Doc. 415, 2: 1573–79).

2. SG quoted from an article by Morris Hillquit published in the July 1912 issue of the *Metropolitan Magazine* (36: 12–13) entitled "Socialism Up to Date: The Aim of Socialism." The quotation reads: "Stated in more concrete terms, the Socialist program requires the public or collective ownership and operation of the principal instruments and agencies for the production and distribution of wealth. The land, mines, railroads, steamboats, telegraph and telephone lines, mills, factories, and modern machinery. This is the main program, and the ultimate aim of the whole Socialist movement, the political creed of all Socialists. It is the unfailing test of Socialist adherence, and admits of no limitation, extension, or variation. Whoever accepts this program is a Socialist; whoever does not, is not" (*Final Report and Testimony,* 2: 1574).

3. F. G. R. Gordon.

4. James W. Sullivan.

5. Samuel Thruston Ballard, a Louisville, Ky., flour manufacturer, was a member of the U.S. Commission on Industrial Relations.

6. During the commission's hearings on May 23, 1914, Ballard asked Max Hayes if the Socialist Party of America and the AFL did not have the same goal, that is, to se-

cure for workers the entire product of their labor. Hayes agreed, stating that workers were entitled to ownership of the wealth that they produced.

7. SG did not address this question in his subsequent correspondence with Ralph Easley.

8. Roland Post Falkner, a statistician who had taught at the Wharton School of Finance and Economy at the University of Pennsylvania and had served as an assistant director of the U.S. Census, was the director of a National Civic Federation survey of social and industrial conditions. Falkner had given SG the draft of a questionnaire intended for officials of labor organizations, and SG returned it to him with suggestions on May 28, 1914. For a copy of the questionnaire that was eventually distributed, see Files of the Office of the President, General Correspondence, reel 77, frames 312–14, *AFL Records.*

To the Executive Council of the AFL

Washington, D.C., May 27, 1914

No. 82
Executive Council American Federation of Labor
Colleagues:

This is to officially apprise you of what you have no doubt seen in the newspapers this morning, that an agreement has been reached between the President, the House Judiciary Committee, the representatives of the American Federation of Labor, together with those organizations cooperating with us in regard to Section 7 of the Clayton bill on antitrust legislation.

The labor section of the bill, referring to the subject taking the labor organizations from under the Sherman antitrust law, is as follows:

"Sec. 7. That nothing contained in the antitrust laws shall be construed to forbid the existence and operation of fraternal, labor, consumers, agricultural, or horticultural organizations, orders, or associations instituted for the purposes of mutual help, and not having capital stock or conducted for profit, or to forbid or restrain individual members of such organizations, orders, or associations from carrying out the legitimate objects thereof. Nor shall such organizations, orders, or associations, or the members thereof be held or construed to be illegal combinations or conspiracies in restraint of trade under the antitrust laws."

The sections of the bill dealing with injunctions and contempt proceedings are as agreed to by the Executive Council at our last meeting.[1] The entire story of the above quoted section, as well as the injunction sections and contempt sections, will be published in the A.F. of L. Weekly News Letter,[2] which will be issued tomorrow and I shall see to it that a copy is sent to each member of the E.C. in an envelope.

It is not possible to recount the terrible struggle that has gone on to secure this final agreement and this satisfying conclusion. Conferences have been had with all parties in interest and Judge Parker, as well as Mr. Ralston, were in attendance to aid. It is confidently expected that the sections of the Clayton bill quoted and referred to herein and published in the Weekly News Letter will pass intact in the House within the next few days. It will then go to the Senate, where we have every reason to believe, it will be passed before the close of this Congress and receive the approval of the President.

It has been impossible to consult with all the members of the Executive Council in the various stages of the development of the labor sections of the bill, but the officers of the A.F. of L. at headquarters and the Legislative Committee, together with our counsel, have acted upon the general authority given to us by the Executive Council at our last meeting.

It has been a long struggle and victory for labor in these particulars seems now to be in sight.

With best wishes, I am,

Fraternally yours, Saml Gompers.
President American Federation of Labor.

P.S. The members of the E.C. will please regard the above as confidential for a time.

S. G.

TLcS, Executive Council Records, Vote Books, reel 13, frame 193, *AFL Records*.

1. SG is referring to the amendment to Section 17 of the original Clayton bill, which he had outlined in his letter to Henry Clayton of Apr. 22, 1914, above. (See also SG et al. to Members of the House of Representatives, May 5, 1914, AFL Microfilm Convention File, reel 26, frame 2369, *AFL Records*.)

2. "Victory Is in Sight," *AFL Weekly News Letter,* May 30, 1914.

A Circular

Washington, D.C., May 28, 1914.

To A.F. of L. Organizers:
Dear Sirs and Brothers—

At no time in the history of our country has the duty devolved so keenly as now upon the men of labor to put forth their best efforts to help the more thorough organization of all of our fellow workers, men and women, skilled and unskilled, in every occupation in which they are employed; at no time have the forces of antagonism been more active to prevent organization or to crush out the spirit of organized associated effort among the toilers. It therefore all the more devolves upon all engaged in our great humane and uplift work to put forth every energy to bring the unorganized within the beneficent fold of the organized labor movement of America.

You will recall the fact that at the Seattle Convention of the A.F. of L. special emphasis was placed upon the determined effort which should be put forth by all to accomplish this result.[1] Our movement has been crowned with more success than can here be recorded, but they are simply achievements which whet our purposes to still greater efforts.

We must organize the unskilled workers as well as the skilled.

We must organize the worker permanently domiciled in his locality as well as the itinerant worker who travels from place to place in search of employment.

We must organize the women workers in all branches of industry in which they are engaged. We must organize the office employes in the various branches of their occupations.

We must concentrate our effort to achieve greater benefits in wages, hours, and conditions of employment of the toiling masses of America.

We must secure for the toilers the rights to which they are justly entitled on the economic, on the political, on the legislative field. There is no effort which must be left untried to organize our fellow workers everywhere, to place them in a position where they will be best able to help themselves, to help their already organized fellow workers, and in turn to receive the assistance and cooperation of those already with the ranks.

The unions affiliated to the A.F. of L. have already passed the two million mark. It is our bounden duty to see that at the earliest possible date we have reached and passed the three million mark. Let every man of labor, and particularly our organizers, do their share in the work and bring better conditions, comfort, hope and encouragement to the toilers of America, for their own advancement and for the betterment of the generations yet unborn.

Organizers will please report to the undersigned from time to time as to what has been accomplished upon this renewed field of activity.

Thanking you in advance, I am,

Fraternally yours Saml Gompers
President, American Federation of Labor.

TLS, United Brotherhood of Carpenters and Joiners of America Records, reel 2, frame 678, *AFL and the Unions.*

1. The 1913 AFL convention adopted a resolution directing the Executive Council to continue and expand its campaign of education and organization among migratory and unskilled workers.

To Daniel Tobin

May 29, 1914.

Mr. Daniel J. Tobin,
President, International Brotherhood of Teamsters,
 Chauffeurs, Stablemen and Helpers of America,
222 E. Michigan St., Indianapolis, Ind.
Dear Sir and Brother:

Your letter of May the 26th[1] is received, in which you make complaint against the Laundry Workers' International Union,[2] and Bakery and Confectionery Workers International Union[3] for transgression of your jurisdiction in organizing and accepting to membership the drivers in their several lines of trade who properly come under the jurisdiction of your Brotherhood. I have taken the matter up with them[4] in line with the declarations and decisions of the American Federation of Labor, and urged upon them a change of policy and action so as to conform to the principles, declarations and policies of the American Federation of Labor. As soon as I hear from them[5] I will write you further,[6] and in the meantime a report upon the entire subject will be made to the next meeting of the Executive Council.[7]

I enclose to you herein a copy of letter which I have written to the Bakery and Confectionery Workers' International Union, and also the Laundry Workers' International Union. The letters to the officers of these organizations are similar, of course except as to their respective names and titles of organizations, and I trust that they will be satisfactory to you, as well as accomplishing the desired result.

As to writing to the Brewery Workers, I take it that some cognizance must be taken of the action of the Executive Council at its meeting last year upon the subject of Brewery Drivers,[8] for as you know that action was approved by the Seattle convention.

I entirely agree with you in the theory, practice and principle that the best form of trade union or industrial union, if anybody cares to call it that, among Teamsters, Chauffeurs, Stablemen and Helpers, is under an international brotherhood such as yours, in which all workers in this class of labor are eligible. When a fact is established it is most difficult to turn it aside and in so far as the Brewery Drivers are concerned, regardless of what views may be held in this instance, it is an accomplished fact. They are generally organized in the Brewery Workers' International Union, and it is doubtful, aye, perhaps impossible to change that by any decision which the A.F. of L. might render. Is it not therefore best to devote our efforts to the accomplishment of the best results in protecting the rights and interests of your Brotherhood while the entire matter is in its present stage?

There is one thing that I desire to say in connection with that portion of your letter in which you say that unless certain jurisdictions and decisions are protected and enforced, that there is very little use for your Brotherhood to be a part of the A.F. of L. That does not sound good nor is it like you and you ought to dismiss that train of thought from your mind. Bear in mind that the A.F. of L. is a voluntary federation and the only power that it possesses is that which is conceded by the affiliated organizations which constitute and make up the Federation. If the A.F. of L. declares that which it believes to be right and just and in furtherance of the interests of the workers it must rest for its enforcement upon the sense, the honor and justice of our men in the trade union movement. It has done more to bring this fact to a nearly satisfactory situation, than has been accomplished by any other movement in the whole civilized world, and as it goes on the influence of the Federation's declarations become more and more recognized as moral obligations and accorded. This is true within our movement, as well as its important work in the affairs of our people and our country. If anyone belittles the efforts of the labor movement, so may all, and I would hate to give my mind a free rein and contemplate what the situation of America's workers would be should the A.F. of L. become weakened or dismembered.

Of course our Federation is not perfect. No more are our International Unions or our local unions, and for the very good reason that our members, that mankind, are not perfect. We are all of us doing the best we can and to give the very best that is in us to protect and promote the rights, interests of the workers, and to the attainment of the justice to which they are entitled is deserving of the highest commendation and is a great tribute to the work and the achievements of the A.F. of L. Mark me, I would not want to prevent if I could, just criticism, for just criticism is helpful to every faithful worker in our cause.

Now in regard to the Brewery Workers' International Union continuing to organize soft drinks, soda and mineral water drivers, that is in direct contravention to the American Federation of Labor declarations and decisions, and the attention of the officers of the organization will be directed to it[9] so that the men who perform this line of work may properly be organized, and come under the jurisdiction of your International Brotherhood.

With kindest regards and best wishes, and hoping to hear from you often, I am,

Fraternally yours, Saml Gompers.
President, American Federation of Labor.

TLpS, reel 182, vol. 194, pp. 748–51, SG Letterbooks, DLC.

1. AFL Microfilm National and International Union File, Teamsters Records, reel 36, frames 2685–86, *AFL Records.*

2. In his letter to SG of May 26, 1914, Daniel Tobin complained that the LAUNDRY Workers' International Union was organizing laundry drivers, who properly came under the jurisdiction of the International Brotherhood of Teamsters, Chauffeurs, Stablemen, and Helpers of America. The 1914 AFL convention reaffirmed the Teamsters' jurisdiction, and on Dec. 18 SG issued a circular informing national and international unions, state federations, city central bodies, and AFL organizers of this action (AFL Microfilm Jurisdiction File, Teamsters Records, reel 55, frames 1244–45, *AFL Records*). He also published a notice of the convention's decision in the March 1915 issue of the *American Federationist* (22: 212).

3. Acting under the direction of the 1910 and 1911 AFL conventions, SG arranged a conference, which met on Mar. 7, 1912, between members of the Teamsters and the Bakery and Confectionery Workers' International Union of America, with Frank Duffy acting as AFL representative. Duffy recommended that the Bakery Workers be instructed to turn over to the Teamsters all drivers who were members of their union, and the 1914 AFL convention reaffirmed the Teamsters' jurisdiction over bakery wagon drivers. SG notified affiliates of this decision in his circular of Dec. 18—which also encompassed the Teamsters–Laundry Workers dispute—and in the March 1915 issue of the *American Federationist* (see n. 2, above). When the Teamsters continued to complain of the Bakery Workers' infringement of their jurisdiction, the 1915 AFL convention reaffirmed the 1914 decision. SG issued a second circular on Feb. 16, 1916, directing state federations and city central bodies not to seat Bakery Workers' locals with members who fell under the jurisdiction of the Teamsters.

4. SG wrote the secretaries of the Laundry Workers and Bakery Workers on May 29, 1914, informing them of Tobin's complaints and urging them to comply with AFL decisions granting jurisdiction over drivers to the Teamsters (SG to Harry Morrison, reel 182, vol. 194, pp. 736–37, SG Letterbooks, DLC; and SG to Charles Iffland, ibid., pp. 738–39).

5. Harry Morrison replied for the Laundry Workers on May 30, 1914, that SG's letter had been referred to the union's executive board (AFL Microfilm Jurisdiction File, Teamsters Records, reel 55, frame 1234, *AFL Records*). A. A. Myrup, treasurer of the Bakery Workers, wrote on June 30 that while the international had transmitted Duffy's 1912 decision to its locals, the union could neither enforce compliance nor make bakery drivers join the Teamsters (ibid., frame 1239).

6. SG sent copies of the replies he received from the Laundry Workers and the Bakery Workers to the Teamsters on June 4 and July 8, 1914 (AFL Microfilm Jurisdiction File, Teamsters Records, reel 55, frames 1236, 1240, *AFL Records*).

7. At its next meeting, held in Washington, D.C., July 13–18, 1914, the AFL Executive Council referred the matter to SG, who subsequently attempted unsuccessfully to arrange conferences between the various organizations.

8. At its July 1913 meeting the AFL Executive Council ruled that brewery drivers came under the jurisdiction of the International Union of the United Brewery Workmen of America and drivers in distilleries and mineral water establishments came under the jurisdiction of the Teamsters. The 1913 AFL convention endorsed this decision (see *The Samuel Gompers Papers*, vol. 6, pp. 367–68, n. 1).

9. SG wrote Louis Kemper on June 4, 1914, informing him of Tobin's complaint and urging the Brewery Workmen to comply with the 1913 AFL convention's decision regarding the Teamsters' jurisdiction over drivers in distilleries and mineral water establishments (reel 182, vol. 194, pp. 793–94, SG Letterbooks, DLC).

From Frank Morrison

Washington DC June 1st 1914

Samuel Gompers
Hollenden Hotel Cleveland O
Our amendment to section seven adopted unanimously by rising vote two hundred and seven voting[1] Eureka

Morrison

TWSr, Files of the Office of the President, General Correspondence, reel 77, frame 261, *AFL Records.*

1. On June 1, 1914, the House of Representatives unanimously adopted an amendment to Section 7 (formerly Section 6) of the Clayton bill to add the words "nor shall such organizations, orders, or associations, or members thereof, be held or construed to be illegal combinations or conspiracies in restraint of trade under the antitrust laws" (*Congressional Record,* 63d Cong., 2d sess., vol. 51, pt. 10, p. 9538).

From Daniel Tobin

Office of Daniel J. Tobin, General President
International Brotherhood of Teamsters, Chauffeurs, Stablemen, &
Helpers of America
Indianapolis, Ind. June 1, 1914

Dear Sir and Brother:

Your letter[1] received this morning and I have carefully read same, and I note what you say, especially your reference to the statement contained in my previous communication, wherein I stated that unless the jurisdiction of our International Brotherhood was protected that I could see very little use in our affiliation with the American Federation of Labor. You say in your letter that you are sorry for this expression. Let me say, first, that I am not expressing my own opinion in this matter, but I am expressing the opinion of the General Executive Board of this International Union in its session recently held in this office, and that this feeling or sentiment is prevalent amongst our entire membership. I reiterate this statement, that if nothing is done for us; if the decisions of the conventions of the American Federation of Labor are not enforced by the Executive Council, that our affiliation with the American Federation of Labor is absolutely useless. It is pointed out to me by our membership, that as the President of this organization, it is my duty to fight for its just rights and jurisdiction under our charter. The membership in Chicago, New York, Boston and in every other district, say, and very truly, that we are paying per capita tax to the American Federation of Labor for the rights and privileges guaranteed to us by our charter and the Executive Council is negligent in its duty when it absolutely refuses, and has done so for years, to protect this jurisdiction. Bear in mind that a great many of our membership are just as intelligent as the officers of the general organization. Personally, I am, I think, as firm a believer in the principles of the Federation as any trade unionist on the American continent, but my personal opinion has nothing to do with the question. I think I have demonstrated in the past, as much as any other individual, my position towards the American Federation of Labor and its principles, but even I am getting tired of this milk and water policy.

I have read your letter addressed to the Bakery and Confectionery Workers. I do not consider it strong enough at all, if you will allow me to criticise this letter. I believe that this organization and all organizations that refuse to obey or abide by the decisions of the Executive Council, which are really the decisions of the convention of the American Federation of Labor, should be told very plainly that within a specified time, its charter would be suspended unless they would be governed by said decisions. Understand me thoroughly, I understand the seriousness of the suspension of charters, but I believe that an International Union that allows a local union to defy its laws, its rulings and its decisions, is not much of an International if it cannot make this local understand that it must obey its International and the local is not much good to the International, and so it is with an International Union holding a charter from the American Federation of Labor. I do not agree with you that the American Federation of Labor is a voluntary organization in every sense of the word. As far as affiliation is concerned it may be voluntary, but when an International or National organization becomes so affiliated it pledges itself to abide by the decisions and rulings of the said American Federation of Labor, and any

International Union that believes that it cannot so abide by the decisions of said organization should withdraw from the A.F. of L. Therefore, I take it that when the Bakery Workers International Union, or the Laundry Workers International Union, or the Brewery Workers International Union stand out and defiantly refuse to recognize the authority of the American Federation of Labor they should be told in plain language that they are of very little use to the American Federation of Labor and that unless they agree, within a stated time, to abide by the decisions of the conventions of the American Federation of Labor, that their charters will be suspended. I think that the convention of the American Federation of Labor, from what I know of it, would approve of the action of the officers of the American Federation of Labor under such conditions. Most of the criticism that I find on the outside against the Executive Council is because of its refusal to enforce decisions or policies of the convention.

The other day I had the president[2] of the Laundry Workers in this office and he told me deliberately that he cared nothing at all about the American Federation of Labor or its decisions; that the Laundry Workers International Union believed in industrialism and socialism. This is also true of the Bakery Workers and the Brewery Workers. Now, if we are going to have forced down our throats in the American Federation of Labor and with the consent of the Council, who refuse to insist on decisions of conventions being carried out, I say, if we are going to have forced down our throats industrialism and socialism, the membership of this International, at least, are going to protest, and are not going, in my judgment, after the next convention to pay per capita tax to such an institution.

You refer to the Brewery Workers and the drivers. To prove the loyalty of this International Union towards the American Federation of Labor, we have, like men, abided by the decision of the last convention, to eliminate the Brewery drivers, although we felt that it was cruel for that convention to reverse the decisions of all the former conventions and to place the stamp of approval on industrialism. But, that convention also decided that the Brewery Workers had no right, under any circumstances, to take in and hold in their membership soda water, mineral water or soft drink drivers; then, if this International Union has decided to be governed by the decision of the American Federation of Labor in this particular question, it is only fair to ask you, as President of the American Federation of Labor, to force the Brewery Workers International Union to also live [up] to the decision. If a handful of Laundry Workers, whose organization amounts to nothing in the labor movement, through its officers, openly defy the American

Federation of Labor, and tell us that they will trample on our jurisdiction, it is only fair to ask you also to notify those officers that our rights must be protected, and to do so in such a way that they will understand that the Federation means something when it speaks. If a decision has been rendered by the American Federation of Labor convention, after the report of an umpire in the person of Frank Duffy,[3] on the question of the jurisdiction between the Bakery Workers International Union and the International Brotherhood of Teamsters, then it is also only fair and square to ask you to enforce that decision and to tell our socialistic friends, the Bakery Workers, that they must abide by the decision, and to do so in such a way that they will understand that it is not a joke. The organizations referred to above, whether the Executive Council desire to believe it or not, not only violate the decisions of the American Federation of Labor and trample on our jurisdiction rights, but on every opportunity that presents itself, the officers of said organizations denounce and despise the officers of the American Federation of Labor and all International Unions, that are not believers in industrialism, and this not in a way of honest criticism, but in a spiteful, disrespectful manner, that can hardly be imagined by a real trade unionist.

In closing, I again request you to endeavor to enforce the jurisdiction decisions between the International Brotherhood of Teamsters and the other organizations mentioned herein and thereby protect this organization of Teamsters that has always proven loyal and faithful to the American Federation of Labor.

Fraternally yours,   Daniel J. Tobin
General President

TLS, AFL Microfilm National and International Union File, Teamsters Records, reel 36, frames 2680–81, *AFL Records.*

1. "To Daniel Tobin," May 29, 1914, above.

2. James F. Brock was president of the Laundry Workers' International Union (1912?–32).

3. Frank Duffy served as secretary of the United Brotherhood of Carpenters and Joiners of America from 1903 to 1948 and as an AFL vice-president from 1914 to 1939.

To Thomas Flynn

June 4, 1914.

Mr. Thomas H. Flynn,
General Organizer, American Federation of Labor,
Victory Hotel, Detroit, Michigan.
Dear Sir and Brother:

Thank you for your letter of May 29 enclosing the financial statement of the Chicago I.W.W.[1] I should very much like to see this information regularly if you can obtain it.

With kind regards, and hoping to hear from you often, I am

Fraternally yours,   Saml Gompers.
President   American Federation of Labor.

TLpS, reel 182, vol. 194, p. 784, SG Letterbooks, DLC.

1. In 1908 the IWW split into two factions. One group, known as the Chicago IWW and led by Vincent St. John, favored direct economic action and disclaimed alliances with political parties. The other—the Detroit IWW, led by Daniel DeLeon—was linked to the Socialist Labor party. The Detroit IWW reorganized as the Workers' International Industrial Union in 1915.

To John Walker

June 11, 1914.

Mr. J. H. Walker,
President, Illinois State Federation of Labor,
304 Pierik Bldg., Springfield, Ill.
Dear Sir and Brother:

I read with much interest your letter of May 19, and the suggestion you made for the republication in pamphlet form of my two editorials, being a review[1] of the decision of the Supreme Court in the Hatters case, published in the March, 1908, issue of the *American Federationist,* and the personal editorial[2] published in the same issue.

I can't begin to tell you how gratified I am that at last you have had the opportunity of reading the general and personal editorial. You can just imagine how hard the task is of trying to make the rank and file of labor understand the real issues when you as one of the big, intelligent, active men in the labor movement, have just come to give the time to the reading and the understanding of the fundamental and important facts with which the editorials dealt, and as a matter of fact the reports to the convention, the editorial utterances and articles in the *American Federationist* are nearly all of them of equal importance.

And in connection with these very subjects, I am looking forward to the early time when the American Federation of Labor will have the full benefit of your splendid attainments.

This is neither flattery nor cajolery. If anything, it is a criticism. Regardless of any differences of opinion between you and me,[3] you know, and I have often referred to the fact that I regard you with deepest interest and friendship. My hope for you is that you will discard preconceived notions or speculative theories and analyze every question to its foundation and to apply the best that is in them to the practical work, the struggle of the toilers, and the achievement of their rights and the protection and promotion of their interests. This you have done for the miners. This you are seeking to do for the toilers of Illinois and elsewhere. This you can eventually do for the entire working people of all America, but it requires strength of character. It may mean parting with old theories, and old notions, and perhaps old friends. It may mean the unlearning of error so that the true light and the development of intelligence may pursue their rightful course, and above all it is the fidelity and the unswerving persistency to help direct the course of labor aright, to save it from its avowed enemies as well as its mistaken or hypocritical friends. It may mean being misunderstood, but it does mean and will mean being of real service in the every day struggle of the toilers, to with them achieve something for them, to make the life better worth living for them and their dependents, and to make them the better capable of meeting the struggles and the problems of the future.

To help build a labor movement founded upon the best conception of freedom of action consistent with unity of thought and action, with the human equation of strength and weakness in mind, to make the trade union movement as distinct as the billows yet as one as the seas, to have lived and contributed something toward the perfection of the organization and the federation as well as the solidarity and fraternity of the toilers, is doing something with which any man might be gratified as his life's work, and it is because I have great confidence in your intelligence, your integrity, your courage and fidelity, to the cause of labor that I have learned to respect and to admire you and to entertain the hope that you will give your undivided effort mental and physical to the much misunderstood and misrepresented trade union movement.

Quite a number have coincided with your view and have made the same suggestion that the editorials should be republished in pamphlet form,[4] and I have had the subject under consideration for a considerable time but have reached no conclusion in regard to it, and now in view of the pending legislation before Congress, and the probability that the Clayton Bill H.R. #15657 will be enacted into law, I am not quite so sure whether it will be necessary to republish these editorials. As I say I have it in mind and may do so later. Then again, the question of republishing my editorials and articles other than these two, it is exceedingly difficult to determine which are worthy of republication in pamphlet form and which are not. But I wish you would write me regularly in regard to this or any other matter which you have in mind.

Like the man who urges upon an unwilling listener to read his "spring poems," may I possess myself of the vanity of asking you to read some of the matter which has appeared in the American Federationist from time to time. If you won't accept the philosophy with which these matters deal, well, it can only help you to strengthen your views against it.

With kind regards and hoping to hear from you often, I am,

Fraternally yours,   Saml Gompers.
President,   American Federation of Labor.

TLpS, reel 183, vol. 195, pp. 69–72, SG Letterbooks, DLC.

1. "Labor Organizations Must Not Be Outlawed—The Supreme Court's Decision in the Hatters' Case," *American Federationist* 15 (Mar. 1908): 180–92.

2. "To Organized Labor and Friends," *American Federationist* 15 (Mar. 1908): 192–94.

3. A reference to John Walker's ongoing participation in the Socialist Party of America.

4. SG did republish "Labor Organizations Must Not Be Outlawed" as a pamphlet (Washington, D.C., n.d.).

To Peter Brady[1]

June 19, 1914.

Mr. Peter J. Brady,
Secretary, Allied Printing Trades Council,
Room 924, Pulitzer Bldg., New York City.
Dear Sir and Brother:

Thank you for your letter of June the 18th[2] in which you enclose replies received by you from several United States Senators in answer to the resolutions adopted at the mass meeting in Cooper Union on June the tenth.[3] I also note what you say in reference to Senator Clapp's[4] letter[5] and the matter will be looked after.

As to Section 7 of the bill, we decided upon that amendment after the most careful consideration of the entire matter in conference with Judge Alton B. Parker, Attorney J. H. Ralston, our Legislative Committee, Secretary Morrison and the undersigned. Not only that but other eminent authorities have also been consulted in the matter, and if Labor at last is deceived as to the provisions of Section 7, there will be many others, some of high legal authority, who will be equally deceived.

With kind regards, and hoping to hear from you often, I am,

Fraternally yours,   Saml Gompers.
President,   American Federation of Labor.

TLpS, reel 183, vol. 195, p. 298, SG Letterbooks, DLC.

1. Peter J. Brady (1881–1931) served as president of International Photo-Engravers' Union of North America 1 of New York City (1911–15), vice-president of the Photo-Engravers (1908–18), secretary (1910–16) and later president of the New York City Allied Printing Trades Council (APTC), and president of the New York State APTC (1914–24).

2. Brady to SG, June 18, 1914, AFL Microfilm Convention File, reel 26, frame 2399, *AFL Records.*

3. The mass meeting at Cooper Union on June 10, 1914, was held under the auspices of the New York City APTC. After addresses by SG, Illinois congressman Frank Buchanan, and Photo-Engravers' president Matthew Woll, the meeting adopted resolutions, drafted by SG, calling upon the U.S. Senate to pass the Clayton bill. Copies of the resolutions were sent to all the members of the Senate as well as to the president and vice-president of the United States (AFL Microfilm Convention File, reel 26, frames 2363, 2411, *AFL Records*).

4. Moses Edwin Clapp (1851–1929) served as a Republican senator from Minnesota from 1901 to 1917.

5. In his letter to Brady of June 17, 1914, Clapp wrote that he believed the Sherman Antitrust Act should be amended to exclude labor and farmers' organizations. He approved aspects of the Clayton bill, he said, but felt that in some ways it aided monopoly and warned that he could not vote for a bill that "did more harm than good" (AFL Microfilm Convention File, reel 26, frame 2399, *AFL Records*).

A Circular[1]

Washington, D.C., June 20, 1914.

To Organizers of the A.F. of L.:

In view of the situation in which the bill vitally affecting Labor is placed, there is nothing so important for the organizers of the American Federation of Labor to do as to follow the course hereinafter urged.

The Clayton bill, H.R. 15657, containing the provisions taking voluntary associations from under the Sherman Antitrust law, and the other sections remedying injunction and contempt proceedings abuses, has passed the House of Representatives by practically a unanimous vote. These labor provisions in the bill are satisfactory.

Reports are being circulated that the United States Senate, either through committee or in the Senate itself, may or will modify and thereby minimize the purpose of the legislation so essential to achieve the rights to which the toilers of our country are entitled.

If this legislation is intended not only to fulfill party platform declarations, but also to accord the working people their just rights, nothing short of the provisions in the bill as it passed the House will be agreeable or satisfactory. And, therefore, it is urged let every organizer make an extra effort for a few evenings and such other time as he can spare to visit as many unions as possible, to visit labor men at their work and in their homes, to confer with business men and other friends of labor and urge upon each and all of them individually, as well as collectively, to write a letter to each of their United States Senators, addressing them at U.S. Senate, Washington, D.C., insisting upon the passage of the labor sections of the Clayton Bill, H.R. 15657 by the United States Senate as they passed the House of Representatives, and that the law be enacted before the adjournment of the present session of Congress.

Organizers will please give this matter their immediate attention and report to me the results of their effort.

Fraternally yours,   Saml Gompers.
President,   American Federation of Labor.

TLpS, reel 183, vol. 195, p. 344, SG Letterbooks, DLC.

1. This circular was sent to AFL volunteer organizers. SG sent similar circulars, also dated June 20, 1914, to AFL salaried organizers and to the executive officers of affiliated national and international unions (AFL Microfilm Convention File, reel 26, frames 2403, 2408, *AFL Records*).

From Frank Glenn[1]

Butte Mont June 23 1914

Labor situation in Butte critical[2] seceders in complete control Moyer and other Western Federation Officials as well as officials Montana State Federation[3] compelled to seek safety in flight. Miners union hall razed by dynamite three people shot and further trouble feared despite all denials to the contrary the I.W.W. element is behind seceders.[4]

F J Glenn

TWSr, AFL Microfilm Convention File, reel 26, frame 2625, *AFL Records*.

1. Frank J. Glenn was a member of International Typographical Union 126 of Butte, Mont.

2. Longstanding tensions within Western Federation of Miners 1, known as the Butte Miners' Union, came to a head after a union election on June 2, 1914, in which dissident miners refused to participate because they felt the votes would be counted fraudulently. Following a protest meeting on the evening of June 12, thousands of miners boycotted the Butte Miners' Day parade on June 13 and then ransacked the union's hall. Western Federation of Miners' president Charles Moyer appeared in Butte, offering to set aside the election results, appoint provisional officers, and hold a new election, but the insurgents rejected these gestures, repudiated the Butte Miners' Union, and set up the independent Butte Mine Workers' Union. When Moyer tried to address a meeting of the remnant of local 1 on June 23, shots were fired, a riot ensued, the Butte Miners' hall was destroyed with dynamite, and Moyer was forced to flee.

During the summer, the Butte Mine Workers' Union signed up new members, wrote a constitution, and held elections; and in late August it demanded that miners show union membership buttons as a condition of employment. After the insurgents deported members of the Butte Miners' Union and a mining company employment office was dynamited, Montana governor Samuel Stewart declared martial law and sent the militia to Butte. Shortly thereafter, warrants were issued for the arrest of leaders of the Butte Mine Workers' Union, copper mining companies operating in Butte instituted the open shop, and Butte's mayor and sheriff, who had maintained an even-handed policy toward the miners, were removed from office. In November the president and vice-president of the Butte Mine Workers' Union were convicted and sentenced to prison for their role in deporting members of the Butte Miner's Union.

3. The Montana Trades and Labor Council was founded in 1894 and renamed the Montana Federation of Labor (FOL) in 1904. The AFL chartered it as the Montana State FOL in 1908.

4. In response to earlier telegrams regarding the situation in Butte, SG wrote Mortimer Donoghue, president of the Montana State FOL, on June 22, 1914, asking him to represent the AFL in restoring order to the labor situation there. (For a copy of Donoghue's report, dated July 16, see AFL Microfilm Convention File, reel 26, frames 2632–34, *AFL Records.*) At Moyer's request, SG also sent a circular letter to the executive officers of affiliated national and international unions on June 23, requesting that they send representatives to Butte (reel 183, vol. 195, pp. 505–7, SG Letterbooks, DLC).

To George Gompers[1]

June 30, 1914.

Mr. George Gompers,
Romney, West Virginia.
My dear George:

I regretted so very much that I could not keep my engagement to address the convention of the Instructors of the Deaf at Staunton, Virginia, on Monday evening, June 29. I had been away from Washington for some days in Buffalo and New York,[2] fulfilling a number of important engagements. In New York City part of my work there was attending and presiding at the meeting of the New York State Factory Investigating Commission, of which I am a member. While in New York, I did not stop at the hotel where I usually stop, and hence my folks could not reach me when they got the news of the death of Henry's[3] boy, little Louis.[4] I knew nothing whatever of the little fellow's illness and death until I got back to Washington on Sunday afternoon. Then I remained here but a few hours, leaving for New York by the seven o'clock train, so as to be there in time to attend the funeral on Monday. I got back to Washington this morning, coming on the midnight train, and after my hard work in Buffalo and New York, the night travel and the strain of the whole circumstances of the child's death, I am very much fatigued and tired out. Of course, nothing else than death or extreme illness would have prevented my keeping my Staunton engagement.

Henry was here at the time the boy died, and he and his mother[5] immediately went to New York on Saturday morning. She is now there and will probably remain with them for some days. If Sadie[6] knew that I was writing, she would join me in love and good wishes.

Sincerely and affectionately your uncle,

Saml Gompers.

TLpS, reel 183, vol. 195, pp. 721–22, SG Letterbooks, DLC.

1. George Gompers, SG's nephew, was the son of Alexander and Rachel Gompers. He was employed as drill master, assistant supervisor in the domestic department, and assistant instructor in printing at the West Virginia School for the Deaf and Blind in Romney, W.Va.

2. SG attended conferences in Buffalo and New York City, June 24–27, 1914, before returning to Washington, D.C., on June 28. He went back to New York City on June 28 for the funeral of Louis Gompers and returned to Washington on June 30.

3. Henry Julian GOMPERS was the son of SG and Sophia Julian Gompers.

4. Louis Gompers, SG's grandson, was the son of Henry J. and Bessie Phillips Gompers.

5. Sophia Julian GOMPERS, SG's wife.

6. Sadie Julian GOMPERS was the daughter of SG and Sophia Julian Gompers.

From Edwin Weeks[1]

Brotherhood Railway Carmen of America[2]
Kansas City, Mo. July 17th. 1914.

Dear Sir and Brother:

I received a letter[3] from you in which reference is made to assessing the entire membership for the purpose of meeting any expenses of lock-outs, strikes, etc., and asking for information as to whether International Unions will agree to power being vested in the A.F. of L. of levying assessments, collecting the same and distributing them for the purpose of aiding, financially, strikes, lock-outs, etc.[4] All I can say is that my experience as General Secretary-Treasurer of this Brotherhood for seven years tells me that the members are paying about as much as they will pay, and while some may be in favor of assisting the members, I know from past experience that it would be a difficult job to collect an assessment from our members. Some would pay and pay cheerfully, but a large number, alas, would not.

I know all about attempting to collect assessments from the bitter experience I have had in the past and the information that I can give in reference to this matter is that I believe the members are taxed as much now as they will stand, but as stated above, it might go through with a Hurrah! at the convention to levy assessments, but a very different tale would be told when it came to collecting them.

I think, perhaps, it would be well to address a letter of this nature to our General Executive Board, because you see, I can only answer myself and give my views on the matter.

Yours fraternally,   E. Wm Weeks
General Secretary-Treasurer.

TLS, AFL Microfilm Convention File, reel 26, frame 2528, *AFL Records.*

1. Edwin William WEEKS of Kansas City, Kans., was secretary-treasurer of the Brotherhood of Railway Carmen of America (1907–26).

2. The Brotherhood of RAILWAY Carmen of America.

3. The letter, signed by SG, Frank Morrison, Thomas Williams, William Spencer, James O'Connell, Albert Berres, and Thomas Tracy, was dated July 13, 1914, and was sent to all affiliated international unions (reel 184, vol. 196, pp. 132–33, SG Letterbooks, DLC). SG sent a follow-up letter on Sept. 12 to unions that had not responded to the first one (AFL Microfilm Convention File, reel 26, frame 2515, *AFL Records*). For replies to these letters and additional correspondence on this subject, see ibid., frames 2510–42.

4. Resolution 111 introduced at the 1913 AFL convention called for the creation of a committee to prepare a plan under which the AFL could levy, collect, and disburse a tax on the members of affiliated unions to support strikes or lockouts "of a national character, or in cases involving the general interest of the labor movement" (AFL, *Proceedings,* 1913, p. 236). The convention referred the resolution to the Executive Council, which appointed a committee in January 1914 to look into the matter. On July 13 the committee sent a letter of inquiry to all affiliated international unions to determine if they would concede the necessary authority to the AFL (see n. 3, above). The Council reported to the 1914 AFL convention that nineteen of the unions responding favored the proposal, twenty-eight were opposed, and twenty-two were undecided. The Committee on the Report of the Executive Council recommended that no further efforts be made along these lines, and its recommendation was adopted by the convention.

To Rafael Zubarán Capmany[1]

July 25, 1914.

Mr. R. Zubaran,
United States Representative Mexican Constitutionalists,
Burlington Apartment, Washington.
Dear Sir:

From direct communication as well as from statements published in the newspapers within the past few days, the situation now existing in Mexico[2] has been fairly and accurately presented to my associates, the Executive Council of the American Federation of Labor, during our last week's session. We are prompted, and I was directed, to communicate to you and respectfully ask that you communicate in turn to General Carranza,[3] chief of the Constitutionalists of Mexico, the following statement of fact and expression of hope:

But first, let me say, that it is with much satisfaction that the Executive Council of the A.F. of L. extends felicitations to the Constitutionalist cause and expresses hopes for its early and successful consummation.

At the outset I should say that the working people of the United States are intensely interested in the affairs of the people of Mexico, as they are by their very position and organization vitally concerned in the affairs of the people the world over, and especially those conditions which effect the working people and their conditions of life and work.

Nor is it amiss to say that during the Mexican revolution against the autocratic and tyrannical administration of President Diaz, the American Federation of Labor aided, as best it could, and particularly in the field of information and the creation of public opinion in the United States in the movement to depose Diaz. We were greatly gratified when, as a result, the great Madero[4] was installed into office as President of the Republic and in the high purpose to which he was devoting his talents and ideals for the benefit of the Mexican people.

When General Huerta[5] and his coterie, by assassination and treachery, overturned the government of President Madero and General Huerta established himself as Provisional President and then dispersed the Mexican Congress and proclaimed himself dictator, there was no power, outside that of the government of the United States, which exerted so potential and international influence in the solution of the difficulty which confronted the Mexican people as the American Federation of Labor.

We helped in sustaining the attitude of the government of the United States in its refusal to recognize Huerta up to the present hour and for the success of the revolutionary movement headed by General Carranza.

Now the only difficulty which seems to be in the way of a complete settlement of the contest of the last several years is the avowed declaration on the part of those who speak or assume to speak in the name of General Carranza, that punishment and retribution of the most draconian character will be meted out by him and his government to the Huertists and those responsible for the overturning of the Madero government.

What I have in mind is, that since the American Federation of Labor, as no other American instrumentality outside of the government of the United States, has aided for the success of the prospective government, we have the right to suggest to those who represent General Carranza and the vict[oriou]s revolutionary army that the higher humanitarian consideration be given, aye, even to those who have been guilty. And that in our judgment, such a policy would have a tranquilizing effect, promoting the successful inauguration of the new constitutional government of Mexico and would tend to unite the people of Mexico in support of an orderly government of the country.

And it is also earnestly hoped and respectfully suggested that some definite declaration be made not only upon the lines indicated above, but should be coupled with an avowal of purpose that the constitutionalists will carry into effect a rightful and justifiable division of the lands of Mexico for the working people.

We feel confident that such a declaration faithfully carried into effect would institute and maintain a better economic condition and a more humanitarian policy than have heretofore prevailed in Mexico.

In our judgment such a declaration and policy would do more than aught else to bring peace, unity, and progress to the people of Mexico and the stability of their government, all of which is submitted to the respectful consideration of yourself and your Chief from [th]e sincere purpose of your well wishers and friends.

Very truly yours,
Executive Council,   American Federation of Labor,
Saml Gompers.   President.

TLpS, reel 184, vol. 196, pp. 513–16, SG Letterbooks, DLC.

1. Rafael Zubarán Capmany (1875–1948) was the confidential agent of the Mexican Constitutionalist party in Washington, D.C. He later served as minister of the Mexican Secretariat of Government (Nov. 1914–15) and minister of the Secretariat of Industry and Commerce (1920–21).

2. Victoriano Huerta resigned as president of Mexico on July 15, 1914, in the face of military defeat by Constitutionalist forces under Venustiano Carranza.

3. Venustiano Carranza (1859–1920) served as "First Chief" (1914), provisional president (1915–17), and president of Mexico (1917–20). His government was overthrown in 1920 by Alvaro Obregón.

4. Francisco Madero (1873–1913) headed a successful armed revolt against Porfirio Díaz and served as president of Mexico from 1911 to 1913. His government was overthrown by Huerta in February 1913.

5. After deposing Madero, Victoriano Huerta (1845–1916) served as president of Mexico from February 1913 to July 1914.

To Carl Legien

Washington, D.C., July 30, 1914.

Legien
Fifteen Engelufer Berlin
All wars deplorable Austrian Servian war[1] deserves condemnation Every honorable effort justifiable to end it

Gompers

TWpSr, reel 184, vol. 196, p. 750, SG Letterbooks, DLC.

1. Archduke Franz Ferdinand, the Austrian heir apparent, and his wife, Sophie, were assassinated at Sarajevo on June 28, 1914, by Serbian nationalist Gavrilo Princip. With the backing of Germany, Austria-Hungary declared war on Serbia on July 28. Russia responded by mobilizing forces on the border of Austria-Hungary, and both Russia and Austria-Hungary declared general mobilization on July 30.

From Fred Evans[1]

8-3-[19]14.

Dear Sir:

I have been referred to you by a young man whose name is Edgar Grey; he told me to consult you in regard to a union, for the colored elevator and hallmen, who work in the N.Y. City, apartment houses.

Now Mr. Gompers, I would like very much to enlist your indispensable services as without you, we, are as a ship without a rudder.

Will you, Mr. Gompers, as an effort to help the poor colored men, encourage and assist us to found a union?

We are married and most of us have families and you must know that we can just exist on $25.00 per month.

That tipping system is a bygone; a thing of the past; something you read of but, never see. Why $8.00 per month tips is not only excellent but it is also very, very rare.

Mr. Gompers, kind sir, I appeal to your noble nature. You are an illustrious man, a man of the world and if you will condescend to help us please, I know that we can be benefited more that way than any other.

I appreciate the "colorline" between the races and I know of the obstacles we must undergo, but, if you as a philanthropic act toward the negro race in particular and the Brotherhood of man in general, can only spare us some of your most valuable time and start us off, I feel as if we will prove ourselves worthy of it.

"Gentle and affable to us, has been thy condescension, and shall be honored ever with Grateful memory."

Thanking you in advance to manifest our response to whatever aid, no matter how small.

We want better wages Mr. Gompers, and of course we will give "A-1" service. $40.00 per month is our idea of a reasonable amount of salary and I hope and pray to God, Almighty, to move you please Sir, to act in our behalf.

I have 100 men to start with and I know that as we progress we can and will always recruit, and before 1 year I feel positive of over 5000 men in the Union. I call this a modest assertion (5,000).

Now kind Sir, please give this pathetic, almost tragic account of the deplorable condition of the willing, industrious, colored man some consideration.

We don't ask any quarter, all we hope for is a square deal and your powerful aid.

By this small act on your part, worth inestimable value to us (the poor, illiterate, colored man) why you can immortalize yourself to the negro, become a 2nd Abe Lincoln to the world and earn the gratitude of 10,000 souls.

Please, Mr. Gompers, hear and heed to the prayer I earnestly solicit for my people. Trusting to mercies of that all-seeing Power, and awaiting your pleasure,[2] I am,

Very respectfully,
(Signed) "colored" Fred D. Evans

TLtpSr, reel 185, vol. 197, pp. 4–5, SG Letterbooks, DLC. Typed notation: "*Copy.*" Enclosed in SG to Hugh Frayne, Aug. 6, 1914, ibid., p. 3.

1. Fred Evans was a New York City porter.

2. SG forwarded Evans's letter to Hugh Frayne, the AFL's representative in New York City, on Aug. 6, 1914, and informed Evans of his action the same day (reel 185, vol. 197, pp. 2–3, SG Letterbooks, DLC). The AFL did not charter a federal labor union of elevator operators in New York City at this time.

To Charles Bowerman

Aug. 4, 1914.

Mr. C. W. Bowerman,
Secretary, Parliamentary Committee, British
   Trades Union Congress,
General Buildings, Aldwych, W.C., London.
Dear Sir and Brother:

No doubt the question that has driven itself home among the people of the civilized world, as I feel confident it must in a more acute form in England and the rest of the European countries, is the terrible situation in which Europe now finds itself by reason of the wars declared and expected.[1] It is a situation which must distress every thinking, liberty loving man, he who has given his time and efforts for the betterment of the people's condition, who has been engaged in the constructive work for a larger and a better conception of justice and humanity, who has worked for the democratization of the institutions of the world.

I cannot begin to tell you the distressed feeling and depression which has come to the people of the United States by reason of the present European situation and outlook. Despite the fact that they are so fortunately so far removed from the immediate seat of contention and struggle, as well as the possible horrors of war. We were living in hopes that in the second decade of the twentieth century with the interests of the peoples of the world so closely allied, and the common impulses, ideas and ideals more closely interwoven, that a war of any kind, but particularly the war which is threatened, would be averted now and for all time to come. It is a rude awakening shock and calls for severest criticism and condemnation of those who are responsible. It is impossible that I should express to you the feelings which prevail among our people, nor could I begin to convey to you my own feelings of horror and indignation.

In connection with the situation, the question of the holding of the British Trades Union Congress in September has come up for consideration. If martial law is declared in England, as it has already been declared in so many of the European countries, is it likely to interfere with the holding of the British Trades Union Congress in September?[2] You know that one of the fraternal delegates from the American Federation of Labor to your Congress, Mr. W. D. Mahon, is in Europe now, more than likely marooned in Germany, Austria, Switzerland, or France, and if the Congress is to be held, why of course he will attend. The other fraternal delegate, Mr. Matthew Woll, is in my office now, and the question he has asked of me is as to whether he should make the trip from here to England to attend the Congress at Portsmouth. Will you do me the kindness to write me immediately upon receipt of this as to whether there is to be any interference with the holding of the Portsmouth Congress, or if there be not sufficient time to write, kindly cable a word.[3] Our cable address is "AFEL" Washington. Mr. Woll contemplated leaving New York August 22d or a day or two after. The International Union of which he is President holds convention[4] the week preceding, hence he cannot leave earlier.

Wishing you and the labor movement the very best of success, and earnestly hoping that the awful horrors of war may yet be averted, I am,

Sincerely and fraternally yours,   Saml Gompers.
President,   American Federation of Labor.

TLpS, reel 184, vol. 196, pp. 913–15, SG Letterbooks, DLC.

1. Following Austria-Hungary's declaration of war on Serbia on July 28, 1914, Germany declared war on Russia on Aug. 1 and on France on Aug. 3. Germany's invasion of neutral Belgium on the night of Aug. 3–4 led to a declaration of war by Great Britain at midnight, Aug. 4. Austria-Hungary declared war on Russia on Aug. 5.

2. The TUC did not hold its annual meeting in 1914.

3. Charles Bowerman replied on Aug. 11, 1914, that the annual meeting of the TUC had been postponed. SG informed Matthew Woll of his response on Aug. 13 (reel 185, vol. 197, p. 398, SG Letterbooks, DLC).

4. The 1914 convention of the International Photo-Engravers' Union of North America met in Indianapolis, Aug. 17–22.

To Ralph Easley

August 4, 1914.

Mr. Ralph M. Easley,
Chairman, Executive Council,
33 Floor, Metropolitan Tower, New York City.
Dear Sir:

Owing to pressing and important work incident to the meeting of the Executive Council of the American Federation of Labor and my absence from the city in connection therewith, it has been impossible for me to take up your letter of July 21[1] in which you request any suggestions or criticisms on the report[2] prepared by President Low and Mr. Willcox[3] on the model bill reported by the Executive Council of the Department of Regulation of Interstate and Municipal Utilities.

I have just returned to headquarters to-day and I see from your letter that you request a reply not later than August 5. It will be impossible for me to go through the report and let you have reply by to-morrow. I regret not being able to reach the matter earlier, but it has been utterly impossible for me to do so.

Though very tardy, yet I want to express my great appreciation for the courtesy you extended to me and the splendid time I had at your house the early part of last month,[4] and by the way you may have seen the tennis racquet which I left at your house. When convenient some day bring it to your office in New York, and I shall get it on the occasion of my call.

Kindly remember me to Mrs. Easley,[5] Ronald,[6] and Donna.[7]

Sincerely yours,　Saml Gompers.

TLpS, reel 184, vol. 196, pp. 905–6, SG Letterbooks, DLC.

1. Ralph Easley to SG, July 21, 1914, Files of the Office of the President, General Correspondence, reel 77, frame 500, *AFL Records.*

2. In 1914 a subcommittee of the National Civic Federation (NCF) Department on the Regulation of Interstate and Municipal Utilities drafted a model public utility bill. The NCF Executive Council approved the document in October, and it was published under the title *Draft Bill for the Regulation of Public Utilities, with Documents Relating Thereto* (New York, 1914).

3. William Russell Willcox, a New York City attorney, was a member of the NCF Executive Council (1909–20) and served as chairman of the NCF Welfare Department (1909–14) and Pension Department (1915–20). He was chairman of the Republican National Committee (1916–18) and managed the 1916 presidential campaign of Charles Evans Hughes.

4. SG left Washington, D.C., on July 2, 1914, and probably visited Easley over the weekend of July 3–5 before attending a number of conferences in New York City on July 6. He returned to AFL headquarters on July 7.

5. Minerva (variously Nerva) Cheney Easley was Ralph Easley's first wife.

6. Ronald Merl Easley, the Easleys' son.

7. Donna Rachel Easley, the Easleys' daughter.

To James Manning[1]

Aug. 7, 1914

Mr. James F. Manning,
Secretary, Central Labor Union,[2]
31 Oak street, Taunton, Mass.
Dear Sir and Brother:

Your favor of the 5th instant addressed to Secretary Morrison has been referred to me for attention.

You ask for information relative to political discussions in the central body, and state that some delegates claim that political matters should be discussed freely on the floor of the central body while others insist that no discussion of this character should proceed at all. I desire to state that the policy of the American Federation of Labor is that affiliated organizations should investigate the platforms of candidates whether they be for municipal, state or federal offices, with the object of informing the members of organized labor fully upon the attitude of these candidates toward organized labor and all measures affecting the interests of labor.

The constitution of the American Federation of Labor prohibits the discussion of party politics whether they be Democratic, Republican, Socialistic, Populistic, Prohibition or any other, in the conventions of the American Federation of Labor, and this likewise applies to affiliated bodies. When, after years of effort, Congress persistently turned a deaf ear to the appeals and demands of organized labor to enact the legislation that had been endorsed and urged by the American Federation of Labor looking to remedying existing wrongs and restoring to labor the exercise of her constitutional rights, a conference was called of the representatives of all affiliated international organizations for the purpose of considering what action should be taken in order that labor might get a better hearing in her legislative halls and in the Congress of the United States. That conference, which was held at Washington, D.C., March 1908,[3] as you are no doubt aware, drafted Labor's Bill of Grievances, which was presented to both Houses of Congress and to the President of the United States, and at the same time declared to the members of organized labor the political policy, to which as champions of the cause of labor they are in duty bound to adhere. This declaration did not deviate from the previous declarations of the American Federation of Labor upon its political policy, but was in the nature of a rallying call to labor, that our political declarations should not be regarded as mere sentiments, but must be actively enforced. The slogan adopted by that conference and which explains the political policy of the American Federation of Labor fully, is:

"Stand by our friends and elect them;

["]Oppose the indifferent and hostile to our cause and defeat them."

Therefore, the issue that your central body should take up in a political question is the record of every candidate and his attitude toward organized labor, as fully and as accurately as such a record can be secured, and for the members then to support by their votes the one to whom the interests of labor can be most reasonably and safely trusted. Members of organized labor can vote properly without the institution of a formal political party. If they will not do it as individual members of organized labor, which surely their good sense and judgment should point out to them as obviously their duty, then they would not do it by reason of a political party. The history of efforts of this character in the past has brought nothing but distress and defeat to the cause of the working people. It has divided them in political party camps, influencing and severing men from each other and in their loyalty to their organized labor bodies. By the political activity of the organized labor movement in being partisan to a principle and not partisan to any political party, regardless of its name, we have secured more beneficent legislation in the interests of the workers than could be obtained by any other known means. Our movement must stand united and our men must stand true to our labor movement, without permitting any political partisan domination of Labor's forces.

With best wishes and hoping to hear from you, I am,

Fraternally yours, Saml Gompers.
President, American Federation of Labor.

TLpS, reel 185, vol. 197, pp. 88–90, SG Letterbooks, DLC.

1. James F. Manning served as secretary of the Taunton (Mass.) Central Labor Union (CLU) in 1914 and 1915.

2. The AFL chartered the Taunton CLU in 1901.

3. Actually, the conference that adopted "Labor's Bill of Grievances" met in March 1906 (see *The Samuel Gompers Papers,* vol. 7, pp. 3–6 and p. 6, n. 1). The March 1908 conference drafted "Labor's Protest to Congress" (ibid., p. 320, n. 3 and pp. 323–29).

To Ed Nolte

August 8, 1914

Mr. Ed. Nolte,
The Mechanics National Bank of Trenton,
Trenton, N.J.
My dear Mr. Nolte:

I thank you very much for your letter of August 3rd.[1] I am gratified to know that my expressions in regard to the situation in Europe have met with your commendation. The situation is most deplorable and each day seems to add to the magnitude of what can almost be regarded as a tremendous catastrophe, certainly as a terrible calamity in Europe.

To-day I was asked to give an expression of opinion by telegraph, upon the European war, and I sent the following:

"For more than a quarter of a century the American Federation of Labor has pressed home upon the people of our country and the people of the world the atrocity and futility of international war. Few of the news agencies either heeded or helped.

"All wars are deplorable. The present European one is condemnable from every viewpoint. Since the first rumblings of this unholy and unjustifiable conflict I have gone on unsparing of myself in the effort to arouse the people of our country and of the civilized world and to compel a halt in this inhuman strife. I will gladly go to any length and associate myself with any movement to bring to an end the present European struggle and which will make for permanent international peace and the democratization of the institutions of the world."[2]

On Friday evening, July 31st, I delivered an address upon the war, before the delegates to the New York Central Federated Union. I am just in receipt of one copy of the abstract of the address[3] and I am writing[4] to New York requesting that a copy be sent to you.

Rest assured I should be glad to do anything within my power to be helpful in an early termination of this terrific struggle and if possible, to abolish international war for all time to come.

Very truly yours,   Saml Gompers
President   American Federation of Labor.

TLpS, reel 185, vol. 197, pp. 72–73, SG Letterbooks, DLC.

1. Ed Nolte to SG, Aug. 3, 1914, Files of the Office of the President, General Correspondence, reel 77, frames 582–83, *AFL Records.*

2. SG made this statement in a telegram sent to the *Chicago Examiner* dated Aug. 7, 1914 (reel 185, vol. 197, p. 21, SG Letterbooks, DLC).

3. For an abstract of SG's address before the Central Federated Union of Greater New York and Vicinity on July 31, 1914, see Files of the Office of the President, Speeches and Writings, reel 111, frames 487–88, *AFL Records.*

4. SG to Ernest Bohm, Aug. 7, 1914, reel 185, vol. 197, pp. 74–75, SG Letterbooks, DLC.

A Memorandum

Aug. 15, 1914.

MEMORANDUM FOR ANTITRUST FILE.

President Gompers addressed a meeting of the Central Federated Union on Friday, July 31st. He took the opportunity to suggest that resolutions should be adopted by the C.F.U. and sent to all U.S. Senators urging the passage of the Clayton Bill H.R. 15657 in the form in which it passed the House. This was done by the C.F.U.

On August 13th,[1] in a letter to Secretary Hilfers of the New Jersey

State Federation of Labor, he made the same suggestion for the convention[2] of that body.

August 12,[3] same suggestion was made to Secretary Hays[4] of the I.T.U. relative to the convention[5] of that organization at Providence, R.I., the week of August 17th.

August 14,[6] the same suggestion made to Present Matthew Woll of the Photo Engravers as to his convention in Indianapolis the week of August 17th.

TD, AFL Microfilm Convention File, reel 26, frame 2405, *AFL Records.*

1. SG to Henry Hilfers, Aug. 13, 1914, reel 185, vol. 197, pp. 314–15, SG Letterbooks, DLC. SG's letter recommended that the convention of the New Jersey State Federation of Labor (FOL) urge the Senate's passage of the Clayton bill and condemn the war in Europe.

2. The 1914 convention of the New Jersey State FOL met in Newark, Aug. 17–19.

3. SG's letter to John Hays of Aug. 12, 1914, also recommended statements on the Clayton bill and the war (reel 185, vol. 197, pp. 224–25, SG Letterbooks, DLC).

4. John W. HAYS served as secretary-treasurer (1909–28) of the International Typographical Union and as president of the AFL Union Label Trades Department (1916–28).

5. The 1914 convention of the Typographical Union met in Providence, Aug. 10–15.

6. SG's letter to Matthew Woll of Aug. 14, 1914, urged the same actions as his letters to Hilfers and Hays (reel 185, vol. 197, pp. 406–7, SG Letterbooks, DLC).

From Eugene Jones[1]

National League on Urban Conditions among Negroes.
New York City. August 18th, 1914.

Dear Mr. Gompers:

I am interested at present in the status of the colored musician in New York City, especially as it relates to the Musical Mutual Protective Union, which has "declared war" against the non-union colored musician,[2] who finds it expensive and not so pleasant to ally himself with the Musical Mutual Protective Union.

I have taken the matter up with Mr. Frayne, The National Organizer, and he promised to use his influence with Mr. Porter,[3] President of the local union. I have also spoken with President Carothers of the American Federation of Musicians.[4] The colored musicians with whom I have conferred have been almost unanimous in their desire to form a separate colored local, with a charter or sub-charter, subject to the supervision or control of the now existing local chapter. The colored men feel that they can maintain the "esprit de corps," give better control to their members and get better results on the whole in a separate organization, especially since orchestras made up of colored men are exclusively colored and orchestras made up of white men are exclusively white.

The local chapter has taken the position that Negroes must come into their union under the same condition as the white members and must be subject to the same regulations and control, which of course gives no opportunity for holding office or having any appreciable influence in the management of the local's affairs. From your wide knowledge of the different types of American citizens you understand the psychology of this desire on the part of the colored men.

I write to you explaining the condition because I remember that some time ago you and your colleagues at Atlantic City sent broadcast the statement that colored men who desire to become unionized would be treated fairly and would reap the benefits of the Federation's successes.[5] I feel that a word from you in the present situation would be of material assistance in my efforts to get a "square deal" for the colored musician of New York City.[6]

Sincerely yours,   (Signed) Eugene Kinckle Jones.

TLtpSr, reel 185, vol. 197, pp. 546–47, SG Letterbooks, DLC. Typed notation: "*Copy.*" Enclosed in SG to Hugh Frayne, Aug. 19, 1914, ibid., p. 545.

1. Eugene Kinckle Jones (1885–1954) served the National League on Urban Conditions among Negroes (from 1920, the National Urban League) as field secretary (1911), associate chief executive (1912–16), coexecutive secretary (with George Haynes, 1916–17), executive secretary (1917–41), and general secretary (1941–50).

2. In the spring of 1914, American Federation of Musicians 310 of New York City, the Musical Mutual Protective Union, began a campaign to organize black musicians who played in the city's theaters. The predominantly white local, which attempted to force employers to replace black nonunion musicians with union members, offered new black members up to four years in which to pay their initiation fee, reportedly $100.

3. D. Edward Porter served as secretary (1910–11) and president (1914, 1916–17) of Musicians' local 310.

4. Francis K. CAROTHERS served as president of the American Federation of Musicians from 1914 to 1915.

5. At the AFL Executive Council's July 1913 meeting, held in Atlantic City, George Haynes, director of the National League on Urban Conditions among Negroes, appeared before the Council to secure cooperation of the AFL and its affiliates in "educating the negro in union principles." The Council stated that the AFL was committed to "the thorough organization of all working people without regard to sex, religion, race, politics, or nationality" and would welcome the cooperation of the league in realizing this goal (*The Samuel Gompers Papers*, vol. 8, p. 504). The Council's statement was published in the *AFL Weekly News Letter* of Aug. 9, 1913, under the heading "Colored Workers."

6. SG wrote Jones on Aug. 19, 1914, that he should contact Hugh Frayne, the AFL's representative in New York City, regarding the matter but noted that each international affiliate had final jurisdiction over its own trade. SG sent Frayne a copy of Jones's let-

ter and his reply the same day (reel 185, vol. 197, pp. 545, 548, SG Letterbooks, DLC). No separate black musicians' local was chartered in New York City in 1914 or 1915.

From John Golden[1]

United Textile Workers of America[2]
Address Box 1454, Atlanta, Ga. Aug 22nd, 1914.

Dear Sir and Brother;—

In regard to the situation[3] in Atlanta, Ga, I found a pitiable situation among the strikers; They are fighting very game however. and in spite of evictions by Ne[. . .] other such disreputable tactics they are unable to break the ranks of the strikers. Since my arrival a number of foreigners, mostly Greeks have been imported into the mill, this is something unusual in this locality, and has aroused considerable indidnation among the community, whose sympathies have been with the strikers from the beginning. Just what will be the result of this latest move I am unable to say at this time, however doesnt appear to worry the strikers very much, but may have the result of creating a strike among the English speaking people who are at work in the mill.

What is most needed is funds to feed the strikers, just as long as we can fill their stomachs we can keep them in line, just as one of the women remarked the other day Mr Golden you find the eats, we will do the fighting, we are better off than we ever were in the mill, for all we ever got when we were in the mill was just enough to eat, with neither fresh air or any sunshine to pour in. My presence here has undoubtedly put new life into the strikers, also in the local labor men who have rendered such noble service in behalf of the strikers. I shall lay awake nights in the effort to secure the necessary funds to carry on this fight for the betterment of the damnable conditions of the textile workers both here and every other part of the South, conditions that are a disgrace to twentieth century civilization.

I am laying plans to carry on the work of organization in other parts of the South which from what I gather is now ripe for organization work. The I,W,Ws are at work in several parts of the South, and between you and I Brother Gompers and the lamp post, a taste of I,W,Wism in a few plants in the South wont do very much harm.

I am in touch with Mr L, F, Hollis[4] of the Parker Cotton Mills, Greenville S,C, whose letter to you dated Aug 11th[5] was forwarded to me, and will be prepared to start a couple of Organizers to work on these mills which are very extensive, providing the outlook warrants it after my coming talk with Mr Hollis.

Just while closing this I hear that one hundred and twenty Italians have arrived to start work in the mills next Monday morning, so I expect some lively doings next week. I shall stay on the ground for some time in order to help out all I can, should I leave at all it will be for the purpose of securing funds which is our greatest problem just now. I will keep you posted from time [to time] on the situation as I know your intense interest in the cause of these poor people down here. This strike must be won at all hazards, it means much for our future in the South.

With best regards,

> Fraternally Yours.   John Golden
> General President.   U,T,W of A.

TLS, AFL Microfilm National and International Union File, United Textile Workers Records, reel 42, frame 2630, *AFL Records*.

1. John GOLDEN served as president (1904–21) of the United Textile Workers of America and was editor (1915–21) of the union's official journal.

2. The United TEXTILE Workers of America.

3. Textile workers struck the Fulton Bag and Cotton Mills in Atlanta on May 20, 1914, demanding union recognition, reinstatement of those discharged for joining the union, a wage increase, a fifty-four-hour week for women and minors, the abolition of child labor, and consideration of other grievances. By May 25 some eight hundred fifty workers were out. When the company began evicting strikers from their homes, strike leaders erected a tent colony near the mill and established a commissary. The AFL supported the strike with a fund-raising circular (see "To Charles Moyer," Sept. 17, 1914, n. 6, below), but the strike was lost and the strikers were forced to look for jobs elsewhere.

4. Lawrence Peter Hollis was director of welfare activities for the Parker Cotton Mills Co., which was organized by Lewis Wardlow Parker in 1910.

5. Hollis to SG, Aug. 11, 1914, which SG referred to Golden on Aug. 14 (reel 185, vol. 197, pp. 448–49, SG Letterbooks, DLC).

From James O'Connell

> United States Commission on Industrial Relations
> Portland, Oregon, August 22, 1914.

My dear Sir and Brother:

I wrote you yesterday[1] regarding our hearings at Seattle,[2] but I forgot to mention that Brother Lennon and myself addressed a very large meeting of the Central Labor Union at Seattle, where there were more than 200 delegates in attendance. From the apparent enthusiasm created, I am sure that our addresses to the Central body were appreciated and will have a most beneficial effect, in renewing enthusiasm in the leading Washington labor men and their loyalty toward the A.F. of L., and the movement in general.

Last night we addressed the Central Labor Union of Portland[3] at a specially called meeting of the C.L.U., at which meeting there was an attendance of an exceptionally large representation of the leading labor men of this city and vicinity.

Professor Commons was also present and addressed the meeting in addition to Brother Lennon and myself, and I am sure that those who attended the meeting will have a new conception of the aims and purposes of our labor movement, and especially the A.F. of L.

Some things have come up in our hearings that would indicate that at least some of the professional men, in particular, some of our professors, do not thoroughly understand our movement, and I took advantage of the opportunity at the C.L.U. meeting last night to talk very plainly, and with as much force as I could bring to my assistance, as to the position of the A.F. of L. and some of the things it has accomplished, and pointed out that there was no progress made by this country or its people that the trade union was not the leader in the movement. In addition I pointed out the efforts that have been made by the A.F. of L. to organize the unskilled men and women of the country, which I am sure was fully appreciated by those present, and was a revelation to the Professors, and others present, who do not seem to fully appreciate what we have accomplished in this country.

Throughout the Northwest there is a general sentiment that the A.F. of L. is doing nothing at all to organize the unskilled workers, and that our movement is made up of skilled men and women only.

I have no desire, you understand, to throw bouquets at myself, but will simply state that Brother Lennon, after the meeting, said to me that my address as to the A.F. of L., what it has done and is doing, was the finest he ever heard.

With best wishes, I am,

Fraternally yours,　Jas. O'Connell

TLS, AFL Microfilm Convention File, reel 26, frame 2278, *AFL Records.*

1. James O'Connell to SG, Aug. 21, 1914, AFL Microfilm Convention File, reel 26, frame 2278, *AFL Records.*

2. Between July and September 1914 the U.S. Commission on Industrial Relations held hearings in Chicago, Lead, S.Dak., Butte, Mont., Seattle, Portland, Oreg., San Francisco, and Los Angeles. For O'Connell's reports to SG on these hearings see AFL Microfilm Convention File, reel 26, frames 2275–82, *AFL Records.*

3. The AFL chartered the Central Labor Council of Portland and Vicinity in 1908.

From Carl Legien and Albert Baumeister

International Secretariat of
National Trad[e Union Centres]
Berlin, August 27, 1914.

My dear Gompers,

I have endeavored, by wire and letter, to state a few facts of interest to you, in regard to the conditions now obtaining in Germany.[1] Not knowing, however, whether my communications reached you, I am handing this letter to Bro. Meyling,[2] an American who has been employed in our office for some time.

I mentioned the fact that the American press news about our conditions here are absolutely false, in my previous communications to you. You have no doubt, meanwhile, received further proof for this statement, for the truth must have been published by now even in your country. I therefore refrain from repeating previous statements.

You may rest assured that we have done everything possible to preserve peace and to prevent war, but unfortunately our power was too limited yet and we have not been able to make this terrible war impossible, in which almost all of the civilized nations of Europe are involved. Even Japan has declared war against us,[3] a fact to be proud [of in a certain sense, alth]ough I doubt whether this can also be s[aid for those who pushed the Japs on the wa]rpath.

[Time alone will judge this actio]n of a so-called [civilised nation of Western Europe, or wheth]er it behooves a civilised [people to cut German-American cables[4] for] the purpose of preventing [Germany to oppose the most abominable] lies that are being circulated [by British and French press agencie]s in regard to Germany. I am happy [to say that the British working] class, as far as they belong to the [organized labor movement, ha]ve nothing to do with these and similar shameful acts.[5] We learn from occasional news that have leaked through—no direct communication being possible—that the British workers too have fought bravely against the danger of war. This fact alone will doubtlessly facilitate the British and German workers joining hands again—as soon as this bloody struggle is ended—to fight for their common interests against the employing class. Our international movement must not and shall not die, although the workers of various lands are compelled to-day to use deadly weapons against their own brothers on the other side of the frontier.

The sacrifice necessary for this terrible war must be tremendous, but we hope this may be one more reason to end wars for ever. I firmly believe that such a cry of terror and shame will go round the civilised world as soon as the loss of human life is made known, that this must be the natural result. I think all the nations of Western Europe will have to unite then for the sake of humanity and of civilisation. Such a union would put a stop to the fearful influence exercised for more than 150 years by Russia over European politics, and perhaps make Russia a civilised nation. Russia has succeeded in getting the nations of Western Europe to fight each other, to spend senseless sums on war preparations and, the most terrible of all, to make the well advanced French and German workers cut each others' throats, who would otherwise continue their united efforts against their common enemy, the capitalist. It may sound utopian to utter any opinion as to the end but I think a British-French-German alliance after the war will be the only means by which to save the present state of civilisation of Western Europe.

Our trade unions are endeavouring hard to support the great army of unemployed. They are, in these endeavours, assisted by the government, which, although opposing us up to quite recently, appears to have learned now the importance and value of the trade union movement in such critical times as these. We may even some day be thanked for having developed our organizations in spite of a government entirely guided by the employing class. Things are being carried out for which we have been fighting many years—in vain. Unemployment benefit on the so-called "Ghent" scheme,[6] for instance. Berlin has started in this direction already and other cities are following the lead thus given. No doubt the state as such will have to do the same before long.

I am afraid we shall have to give up our long cherished plan of meeting in San Francisco next year. It will scarcely be possible to meet in Frisco even if we were to succeed in re-uniting the trade unions of all lands before that time. Our unions will not be able to afford the expense and I am afraid conditions will be worse in all other countries affected by the war. The presidents of our unions, furthermore, will be badly wanted over here for the next few years, for the difficult work of putting new life into the unions.

I am writing in haste, not knowing whether you will ever read this letter. As soon as I get a reply[7] from you, however, perhaps via Bro. Appleton,[8] I will write more fully and also send receipts for the money received[9] from Bro. Morrison.

Best wishes to all mutual friends

yours fraternally   C. Legien
President

More good wishes from yours sincerely

A Baumeister

TLS, AFL Microfilm Convention File, reel 27, frames 2069–70, *AFL Records*.

1. SG received a telegram from Carl Legien dated July 30, 1914, requesting an expression of opinion on the war (AFL Microfilm Convention File, reel 27, frame 1028, *AFL Records*). See SG's reply, "To Carl Legien," July 30, 1914, above. SG also received letters from Legien dated Aug. 25 and 27 and a telegram dated Aug. 26, all denying press reports of the repression of German unions (ibid., frames 2069, 2072, and reel 28, frame 1744; Legien's telegram of Aug. 26 was published in the *AFL Weekly News Letter* on Aug. 29).

2. Herman Meyling.

3. Japan declared war on Germany on Aug. 23, 1914.

4. On the morning of Aug. 5, 1914, the British cut the German transatlantic cables in the English Channel, thereby depriving Germany of direct cable communication with the Western Hemisphere for the duration of the war.

5. The text in brackets is supplied from a transcribed copy of this letter in the Executive Council Records, Vote Books, reel 13, frames 404–5, *AFL Records*.

6. In 1901 the Belgian commune of Ghent inaugurated an unemployment fund for those involuntarily unemployed but excluding the sick, the incapacitated, and those on strike as a short-term supplement to their income from such other sources as union benefits or savings. By 1913 nearly seventy communes in Belgium had adopted unemployment relief programs based on the Ghent model.

7. SG replied on Sept. 30, 1914, expressing horror at the war and disappointment that the 1915 meeting in San Francisco of the International Federation of Trade Unions would have to be canceled (reel 186, vol. 198, pp. 677–80, SG Letterbooks, DLC). In response to a query from Frank Morrison, SG directed him not to publish Legien's letter in the *AFL Weekly News Letter* because "it would arouse unfavorable comment and feeling and re-act injuriously to him and the movement in that country" (AFL Microfilm Convention File, reel 27, frame 2070, *AFL Records*).

8. William Archibald APPLETON was secretary of the General Federation of Trade Unions (1907–38).

9. On July 6, 1914, Frank Morrison sent Legien $1,948, the per capita tax owed the International Secretariat on 2,045,000 AFL members for the twelve months ending June 30, 1914 (vol. 389, p. 572, Frank Morrison Letterbooks, George Meany Memorial Archives, Silver Spring, Md.).

To the Executive Council of the AFL

Washington, D.C., Sept. 3[2], 1914.

No. 132.

Executive Council, American Federation of Labor.

Colleagues:

At 4:15 o'clock this afternoon the U.S. Senate passed the Clayton bill strengthening and improving the labor features of the bill as the bill passed the House of Representatives.

Section 7 removing the labor organizations from the operations of the Sherman Antitrust Law was improved in this particular. The section now as it passed the Senate starts out with this statement:

"The Labor of a human being is not a commodity and is not an article of commerce."

That declaration is the most important ever made by any legislative body in the history of the world. It is a recognition of the absolute right of man to the ownership of himself and his labor power. It is a new emancipation from legalism which has in any and every form in the past held that either directly or impliedly anyone could have a property right in the labor or the labor power of a workman.

The bill now goes to conference of the representatives of the House and the Senate, and I have little doubt but what the bill in its improved and strengthened form in so far as it applies to working people and organized labor will be agreed to by the conferees and enacted into law. The American Federation of Labor is to be congratulated upon the splendid achievement which has thus far attained and the almost absolute certainty of its final enactment into statute law.

With best wishes, I am,

Fraternally yours,   Saml Gompers.
President,   American Federation of Labor.

TLcS, Executive Council Records, Vote Books, reel 13, frame 347, *AFL Records.*

To Frank Farrington[1]

Sept. 3, 1914.

Mr. Frank Farrington,
Member, Committee of Executive Board,
    United Mine Workers of America,
Hydah Hotel, Seattle, Wash.
Dear Sir and Brother:

Owing to absence from the city on official business,[2] designated by the Executive Council of the A.F. of L., and since my return my attention to Labor's legislation, particularly the Clayton bill, which as you have noted by the press reports this morning passed the Senate yesterday, I have been unable to reach your letter[3] earlier.

In regard to the questions you ask, let me say that it appears that the Western Federation of Miners and the United Mine Workers of America have both expressed themselves as favorable to amalgamation.[4] At the January convention of the United Mine Workers of America, I gave expression to some satisfaction that progress had been made upon the line of amalgamation. After all, it must be a question of practicability and mutual advantage.

But in addition to this, I must express my opinion to you frankly, and by the way not confidentially, but freely and openly for such use as your information and influence in the interests of our movement may warrant.

It appears that owing to the policy and public declarations of the Western Federation of Miners, that organization has aroused the bitterest antagonism of employers generally and particularly in the metalliferous industry. The Western Federation of Miners may be on a somewhat friendly footing with some of their employers but I do not know of any one of them. Events in Minersville, New York,[5] and in Calumet, Michigan, demonstrate that to be a fact. Recent happenings in Butte[6] have accentuated differences in the ranks of the metalliferous miners themselves.

Though the Western Federation of Miners may change its policy and perhaps become one of the most conservative bodies of organized labor of America, there does not seem to be any hope for very many years, at least, that any kind of a friendly footing can be established between the organization and any considerable number of employers, so, even though as you say there does not seem to be "any industrial relations" between the two organizations, I believe that the only safety for the Western Federation of Miners not only to exist as an organization but to be of benefit to the metalliferous miners and to exert power in the interests of the workers, is by some form of agreement or perhaps amalgamation by which the identity of the organization may be changed or its present title lost by its joining with the United Mine Workers, perhaps in the form of a district, and thereby help to solve the present problem and the awful situation in which the organization finds itself.

Whether we agree with the Western Federation of Miners or disagree; whether we have disagreed or agreed with the organization's policy in the past, the facts are as they are, and any expedient which will rid the organization of that condition and situation already mentioned must have an influence for good.

It may be true as you say that amalgamation cannot result, but perhaps prove somewhat of a disadvantage to the United Mine Workers, but your organization is large in membership and powerful and influential. With amalgamation under the general laws of the United Mine Workers of America, with a well defined policy and the proper safeguards, the danger of injury can be minimized or perhaps entirely eliminated, and it would be no end of good to the metalliferous miners throughout America.

Trusting that I may hear from you further[7] at your convenience, and with kind regards, I am,

Fraternally yours, Saml Gompers
President, American Federation of Labor.

TLpS, reel 185, vol. 197, pp. 910–12, SG Letterbooks, DLC.

1. Frank Farrington, a member of United Mine Workers of America 800 of Streator, Ill., served on the executive board of the international union (1910–14) and as president of United Mine Workers' District 12 (Illinois; 1915–26).

2. SG left Washington, D.C., on Aug. 19, 1914, for Atlantic City, where he held several conferences with labor men between Aug. 19 and 24. He then traveled to Schenectady, where he attended the convention of the New York State Federation of Labor, Aug. 25–26, addressing the convention on Aug. 26. He returned to AFL headquarters on Aug. 29.

3. Farrington wrote SG on Aug. 24, 1914, asking his confidential views on the question of amalgamation between the United Mine Workers and the Western Federation of Miners (AFL Microfilm Convention File, reel 26, frame 2646, *AFL Records*). Farrington indicated that he opposed the merger.

4. The 1914 conventions of the United Mine Workers and the Western Federation of Miners authorized the appointment of committees to discuss the possibility of amalgamating the two organizations. Farrington was a member of the United Mine Workers' committee. After meeting in Butte, Mont., on Oct. 12–13, 1914, and again on July 27–28, 1915, the committees concluded that such a merger was impracticable.

5. On Jan. 23, 1913, about twelve hundred iron miners, under the leadership of the Western Federation of Miners, struck Witherbee, Sherman, and Co. and the Port Henry Iron Ore Co. in Mineville, N.Y. They demanded a wage increase, an eight-hour day, union recognition, and the reinstatement of several discharged miners. Although the mine operators agreed to the wage increase and a shorter workday, they refused to recognize the union and, on Jan. 27, began posting eviction notices at company housing. Within the next few days, most of the strikers returned to work.

6. See "From Frank Glenn," June 23, 1914, n. 2, above.

7. Farrington replied on Sept. 12, 1914, that his union was already under a tremendous financial burden and that he opposed undertaking an additional obligation out of a desire to aid the Western Federation of Miners (AFL Microfilm Convention File, reel 26, frame 2647, *AFL Records*).

To Richard Hobson

Sept. 3, 1914.

Hon. Richard P. Hobson,
House of Representatives,
Washington, D.C.
My dear Mr. Hobson:

Your favor of August 21st reached my office during my absence on official business, and this is the first opportunity I have had to reply thereto. I beg to assure you that I appreciate the honor of your selecting me as a member of the National Constitutional Prohibition Committee on Cooperation, but I must ask you to excuse me from accepting or serving upon the committee. I am frank enough to say to you that I am out of harmony with the prohibition movement by Constitutional provision or statute enactment. I know of a better way other than by legalized prohibition to secure temperance and temperate habits, not only in the liquor traffic but in any of the personal activities of men.

There is no movement in all the country so potent to make the people temperate as is the much misunderstood and misrepresented organized labor movement of the country. Increasing wages, establishing a shorter workday, affording the opportunities for the cultivation of better tastes, better aspirations, higher ideals, which the better standard of living and freedom of burden[some . . . o]f toil will bring, the opportunity for better homes and surroundings and better working conditions, all of these I repeat have been more potent and will prove to be more potent in establishing temperance and temperate habits than any attempt to regulate the personal habits or to inaugurate prohibition by law.

As you will observe, I am not in harmony with the purpose of your movement, and hence cannot consistently accept an appointment upon the committee. I therefore again respectfully request you to remove my name from the National Constitutional Prohibition Committee on Cooperation.

> Very truly yours,   Saml Gompers.
> President,   American Federation of Labor.

TLpS, reel 185, vol. 197, pp. 852–53, SG Letterbooks, DLC.

From Charles Moyer

Western Federation of Miners
Denver, Colo. September 10, 1914.

Dear Sir and Brother:—

I beg to acknowledge receipt of yours of the 5th,[1] and note the telegram[2] from Mr. Guy E. Millers,[3] member of our Executive Board, and your reply[4] to the same, and while I, of course, trust that your action will prove advantageous and that some good results will follow, yet I am fearful indeed that it is too late now to have any beneficial effect.

I say this because of the developments of the past few days,[5] which you are undoubtedly familiar with. The company having declared for the open shop, I take it that it will make but little difference to them whether one local recognizes the card of an other or not.

I am firmly convinced that, following the occurrences in Butte City on the 23rd of June, if all internationals had responded to my appeal and been represented in a conference in Helena, Montana, and have shown to the employing companies of Butte City that they meant business, that there would have been a different outcome in that camp, but regardless of the fact that I did everything in my power, sending telegrams and letters to all of the internationals at interest in Montana along the same lines that I wired you,[6] pleading with them that concerted action be had at that time, while I received an acknowledgment from most of the heads of the internationals, there were only two who took interest enough in the situation to send representatives, and as a result, no action was taken.

As to the causes leading up to the deplorable situation in Butte City, regardless of all that has been published as to the grievances of the men against their local unions and the general organization, I want to say that underlying it all can be traced the slimy trail of the so-called Industrial Workers of the World. The disruption of the Butte Miners' Union No. 1[7] is the consummation of a plan hatched seven years ago by the leaders of this so-called organization, which had for its purpose the poisoning of the minds of the member ship against myself to the end that I might be deposed as President of the organization, believing that by so doing they could again place it back into the Industrial Workers of the World, which organization had been repudiated by a referendum vote of the membership sent out by me after my release from prison in the state of Idaho, and that failing to do so, the organization was to be destroyed. How well they have done their work is evidenced in Butte, Montana, and while the blow is aimed at the miners' organization, it will fall as heavily on other internationals represented in that state and the effect be equally as disastrous, for the Butte Miners' Union has made possible the success of the different crafts in that state, and as it goes down, they are bound to go down with it. Not only will the effect be felt in that one state, but I am fearful that it will reach out to other states, especially throughout the West, where the same tactics are being pursued, and I submit that if the movement can be destroyed in the strongest organized state that it is not impossible in the weaker ones.

The lack of concerted action of the different craft organizations represented in Butte has not only been noticeable to the miners, but even the general manager of the Amalgamated Copper Company, Mr.

Kelly,[8] reminded our committee that waited on him September 8th that the craft organizations had absolutely lain down in this fight. More than two months ago, or at the time I first went to Butte, which was about the 18th of June, advice reached me from the same source that all internationals at interest in the mining industry in that camp, in fact, in the entire town, should come to Butte and show to the employing company that they were really sincere in their desire that bona fide unionism should be maintained, but this lack of interest has encouraged the companies to take advantage of the situation, and while they declare that the independent union[9] is impossible and will not be tolerated at the same time they declare that they will not discriminate against their employes should they belong to the same, neither will they discriminate against the Western Federation of Miners. In other words, when the question was put direct to him as to whether the attitude of the company meant an open shop, he answered yes.

As to the outlook for the future in Butte City, while there is little to encourage us, yet I am not free to say that the situation is not hopeless, but am inclined to believe that if the miners who have followed this disruptive element can be made to realize the position which confronts them because of the declaration of the company, and brought back into the bona fide movement so as to present a solid front, that by the time our wage contract expires, which is some time in the month of June, 1915, and the other crafts will become active so that the company may know that they will have a united movement to deal with, it is just possible that they may change their position at that time. Personally I have made the best fight that I know how, both against the enemy outside of the organization and on the inside, and shall continue to do so for the short time that I expect to yet occupy an official position in the organization.

Now, Mr. President, there is a matter of vital importance that I wish to bring to your attention with the hope that I may receive not only your advice but your hearty cooperation. It is unnecessary for me to go into the history of the Michigan strike, as you are fully familiar with it, suffice to say that after a nine month's struggle there we were compelled to surrender, and at a time when the possibilities for victory were of the very best. When the strike was declared off because of lack of funds, the striking miners and their dependent ones were in destitute circumstances, and the suffering would have been intense had it not been that we were able to secure credit with wholesale houses with which we were doing business in the amount of more than $25,000 for supplies. In addition to this there were many other bills contracted, and unpaid, outside of the loan from the United Mine Workers of Illinois for $100,000, and the $25,000 loan from the United Brewery

Workers, in round figures, the Federation came out of the Michigan strike with an approximate of $200,000 of indebtedness standing against them. Following this we have had the Butte situation to contend with, which has practically destroyed our largest local, and now we have an industrial depression, especially in the mining industry, that has thrown out of employment more than half of our membership, the other half only working part time because of the curtailment in production. We, therefore, as you can readily see, find ourselves with an exhausted treasury and while we are not discouraged, having faced as serious conditions in the past, yet we are facing an immediate emergency which must be met and we know of no place to turn unless it be the labor movement.

You will remember that during the Michigan strike, as has been the history in all conflicts of this kind, those involved in the conflict were charged with almost every crime in the calendar, 631 of our men and women having been placed under arrest charged with offenses ranging from making a noise on the street to that of murder. Fortunately we were able to follow all of these cases and out of those that were brought to trial, which were many, only two convictions were had, these for minor offenses, the defendants receiving a short sentence in the county jail. But when the strike was declared at an end, there was left in the county jail at Houghton three men, namely Nick Vrbanac, Joseph Juntenen and Hjalmer Jalonen, charged with murder.[10] These men have been confined in prison since the 4th of last March and their trial is now set for October 19th. I have absolute confidence in their innocence and know that we can prove beyond a question of doubt that imported gunmen employed by the Waddell-Mahon strike-breaking agency are guilty of the crime and not the striking miners, but how to furnish them with that necessary defense, is the problem which we must solve, and we want to ask you if you will come to our assistance, or rather, to the assistance of these persecuted men. There is a large number of witnesses who have left the state of Michigan that must be brought back to testify in their behalf; we must have able counsel to defend them, and while I am sending out an appeal to our local unions, yet owing to the conditions which I have above outlined, I feel that the response will not be sufficient to give these three men the defense to which they are justly entitled.

In addition to this, you will remember that the grand jury sitting in Houghton county indicted thirty-six of our members, including the officers of the Federation and the entire Executive Board, for conspiracy.[11] It is charged in the indictment that the defense did conspire, combine, confederate and agree together with other leaders, organizers, agitators, etc., to violently, unlawfully and riotously, and by other unlawful means, to-wit parades, picketing without the authority of law, to interfere with certain laborers of certain mining companies, and by striking, picketing, parading, etc., attempted to prevent said mining companies from doing business. You can readily see that the principle involved here strikes directly at the right of labor to organize and declare a strike. This case, we are advised, is to be tried either before, or directly following the case of the three men charged with murder. As far as the penalty is concerned, if found guilty, we are not at all concerned, as we are advised that a conviction would only carry with it a maximum sentence of one year in the county jail, but we feel that the principle is of vital importance not only to the miners' organization, but to the entire labor movement, and as the great mining interests in the state of Michigan, backed by the present governor of the state, who is a candidate for re-election, are determined to secure a conviction in this case, having named 300 witnesses, including James McNaughton,[12] and other mine operators, we feel that unless we can interest the labor movement to the end that they will come to our assistance financially that we will be unable to successfully cope with this powerful combination.

I trust that in this brief review I have furnished you with sufficient information as to the exact status of these cases and the condition of our organization, yet, should there be any thing further, I will be only too glad to forward the same at the earliest possible moment, and in conclusion I want to earnestly appeal to you to give these matters your most careful consideration, and I sincerely trust that you may find some way to assist us in giving these three innocent men that defense necessary to snatch them from the clutches of their corrupt and venomous persecutors.

Thanking you in advance for anything you may do in this matter,[13] with kindest regards, I am

Yours in the cause of Labor,   Chas H. Moyer
President   Western Federation of Miners.

TLS, AFL Microfilm Convention File, reel 26, frames 2644–45, *AFL Records*.

1. SG to Charles Moyer, Sept. 5, 1914, reel 185, vol. 197, pp. 994–95, SG Letterbooks, DLC.

2. Guy Miller wired SG on Sept. 4, 1914, that AFL Federal Labor Union (FLU) 12,985, the Butte (Mont.) Workingmen's Union, had voted to accept membership cards from the Butte Mine Workers' Union, and he asked SG to protect the jurisdiction rights of the Western Federation of Miners (AFL Microfilm Convention File, reel 26, frame 2643, *AFL Records*). See "From Frank Glenn," June 23, 1914, n. 2, above.

3. Guy E. Miller of Joplin, Mo., served as a member of the executive board of the Western Federation of Miners from 1912 to 1918.

4. SG wired Miller on Sept. 5, 1914, that he had directed Samuel Johnson, secretary of FLU 12,985, not to accept membership cards from the Butte Mine Workers' Union

(AFL Microfilm Convention File, reel 26, frame 2643, *AFL Records*). SG included copies of Miller's wire of Sept. 4 and his telegrams to Miller and Johnson of Sept. 5 in his letter to Moyer of Sept. 5.

5. See "From Frank Glenn," June 23, 1914, n. 2, above.

6. Moyer to SG, June 23, 1914, AFL Microfilm Convention File, reel 26, frame 2625, *AFL Records*.

7. Western Federation of Miners 1 (the Butte Miners' Union).

8. Cornelius F. Kelley was vice-president and managing director of the Anaconda Mining Co.

9. The Butte Mine Workers' Union.

10. On Feb. 27, 1914, John Huhta, a member of the Western Federation of Miners, confessed to the murder of Arthur Jane, Henry Jane, and Thomas Dally at a boardinghouse in Painesdale, Mich., during the early morning hours of Dec. 7, 1913. The Jane brothers had just arrived in the copper mining district to take jobs vacated by strikers; Dally's wife ran the boardinghouse. In his confession, Huhta named three other members of the union—John Juuntunen, Hjalmer Jallonen, and Nick Verbanac—as his accomplices. Huhta was convicted of first-degree murder on Nov. 21, 1914, but the cases against Juuntunen, Jallonen, and Verbanac were dismissed on Nov. 24 when Huhta refused to testify against them.

11. Thirty-eight officers and members of the Western Federation of Miners were indicted on Jan. 15, 1914, by the Houghton Co., Mich., grand jury on charges of conspiracy to shut down the copper mines in Houghton and Keweenaw counties and prevent nonstriking miners from working. Those indicted included Moyer, vice-president Charles Mahoney, members of the union's executive board, several organizers, and officers and members of local unions in the copper mining region. The cases never came to trial, however, and on May 17, 1915, the prosecution moved to have them dropped.

12. James MacNaughton of Calumet, Mich., was general manager of the Calumet and Hecla Mining Co.

13. For SG's response, see "To Charles Moyer," Sept. 17, 1914, below.

A Statement[1] by Samuel Gompers

September 11, 1914

The ballot is the symbol of political freedom. It gives its possessor political existence with the right to a voice in the determination of matters that vitally concern his daily life. The right of ballot means full membership in organized society, and brings a sense of superiority and of freedom. Men of many ages have struggled and fought for the right of the ballot. The denial of the ballot means exclusion and limited power, that those denied are somehow different from the others, and consciousness of that recognized difference becomes a part of the individuality of those excluded from the right. The ballot is the instrument for realizing democracy.

Democracy is an old word—it is an ideal that has fired the ardor of many. But the old term has stood for a constantly widening concept. Others early tried to establish a democracy. To the Athenians democracy was founded upon slavery; their ballot was given only to a privileged leisure class. But this early idea of government by the people was a conception linked with that of the city state. Later it was conceived as possible for national governments and larger territories. The conception of the purposes of government widened. Government was instituted to protect property, later to protect life. This second function has assumed increasing importance as society's appreciation of the value of human life has been perfected. This function and all of its ramifications have proved to be as manifold and as diverse as the interests of all the people. Since government does touch the people so closely there is no longer reason for denying them a voice in controlling government. The ballot is the means by which participation in the government is secured.

When government was concerned with property, property ownership was the qualification for the right of the ballot. When it was concerned with land, land was the logical qualification. When it was concerned with a state religion, religious affiliation was the qualification. When it concerned itself with group or racial welfare, membership in that class or that race was the qualification. When it concerns itself with sex welfare, membership in that sex is the logical ground for exclusion. But when it concerns itself with human welfare, existence as a rational human being is the only qualification.

Many familiar reasons have been urged for the denial of the ballot to women, who have participated in the government only through indirection, through influence. Instead of directly doing what they consider right, women must convince men and persuade them to do what they want done. It is waste of energy—it is humiliating to women who live and work shoulder to shoulder with men. It is sanction of a distinction not justified by the nature and functions of government.

Not only is the distinction unjustified under present conditions but it constitutes a menace to the welfare of the wage earning women. This classification as somehow different and not a member of the body politic has become embedded in the individuality of the masses of women and has silenced initiative. The theory handed down from the military ages that women are weaker than men and must be protected has had its effect upon the thought and the mental attitude of today. But democratic government is not founded upon force but upon consent. There is something greater than force, creative faith that is more essential to good government. That is not a matter of sex but of personality. The government needs the women as much as they need the ballot.

Women's life has been revolutionized during the past two hundred years. Their intellectual similarity to men has been recognized in equal and identical educational opportunities. Industrial changes have developed for them similar and identical industrial problems. Women have become wage earners. Work that formerly was done in the homes has been taken to factories, shops and stores. Women's work has always contributed to the family income, in former years the contribution was in the form of assistance in work or family comforts, now it is in the money form. The work takes women outside the protection of the home into the factories or the stores or the mills where they must rely upon their own efforts.

The training of centuries is reflected in the helplessness and the morale of many wage earning women. They have lived as individuals and now find themselves drawn into an industrial world organized on a social basis. They have not yet learned the lessons and the value of united action. Because they haven't learned these things they have been considered in theory at least as the special wards of the State. But is that protection adequate and is it the best sort of protection? Does this dependence upon outside help develop the highest type of character?

Women are for the time being at least a part of the industrial world. According to the last census more than eight million women are gainfully employed. The industrial world is no place for those who can not protect themselves. Women must learn to take their work seriously and to solve their own problems. Though their individual connection with employment may be temporary yet the employment of women is not temporary. Women must learn that work problems are concerned with life problems of tremendous importance to other women and the race. They must feel individual responsibility as members of society. To do this they must assume the dignity and the responsibility of determining the regulation of society.

Many of the regulations concern the relations with employers and conditions of work. It is imperative for personal freedom that control of these be retained by the workers. Control over the labor power of free women must be vested in those women. As individuals they are powerless to make terms of work with employers in large industries. But united in unions they are collectively strong enough to force employers to accept just terms. This has been done without the ballot, but it has been struggling against unnecessary difficulties and resistance. Women without the ballot have not the same potential reserve force as women with the ballot. Their protests, their demands, do not receive immediate consideration. "Influence" must be invoked. Nothing engenders respect like power to do things. Working women need power to do things.

The welfare and the interests of the working women cannot be entrusted entirely to legislation by men or by men and women. Matters of personal relations must be decided by the individuals concerned and must be subject to their direct regulation.

There are many things which touch the lives and the welfare of the workers which cannot be regulated by collective action. These interest working women directly or indirectly through their effect upon others.

The increasingly widening functions of the government make legislative and administrative problems of increasing concern to women—working women and the wives and daughters of working men. The organization of the markets, food prices, pure food laws, municipal sanitation, building regulations, school laws, child labor laws, and an almost endless list, bring politics very close into the common life. These things should and do concern women very vitally. For that reason women should participate in their consideration and determination directly.

Working women need the ballot for their protection at work, at home and in all the manifold relations of life.

They should have the ballot because they are human beings, members of society regulated through the use of the ballot.

TD, Files of the Office of the President, Speeches and Writings, reel 111, frames 489–94, *AFL Records*.

1. SG prepared this statement at the request of Harriot Stanton Blatch, president of the Women's Political League of New York City.

To Robert Hoxie[1]

Sept. 17, 1914.

Professor Robert F. Hoxie,
United States Commission on Industrial Relations,
Transportation Building, Chicago, Illinois.
My dear Mr. Hoxie:

It is most gratifying to know that you are to make the study of Scientific Management in its relations to Labor for the Industrial Relations Commission,[2] as your habitual fairness to organized labor makes me confident that your study will be of humanitarian value.

In regard to the information you desire[3] I am unable to give you the data you wish for the basis of your study. I have not here in this office information collected of the plants now under scientific management.

That information is probably most definitely given in the Washington hearings upon that subject before the Industrial Relations Commission.[4] No doubt the international presidents of those trades that have been the subjects of these experiments have specific information that would assist you. However, I wish to call your attention to the fact that there are very few plants where the system in its entirety has been installed to apply to the whole process of production. This was brought out in the Washington hearings by the repeated requests by the Commissioners that the "efficiency" experts name plants in which their systems were installed.

You can readily see that the American Federation of Labor with its limited means and the many demands for the solution of immediate concrete problems has not had the means or agents to make a thorough, scientific study of scientific management or to collect data for that purpose. We have to get our results as we can.

In regard to the second matter you present in your letter, I think Mr. John P. Frey is in every way fitted to assist you in the capacity as union expert upon scientific management.[5] He knows thoroughly the viewpoint of the workers and understands what would be a benefit to them and what would be a detriment.

The main objections which organized labor raises against scientific management are: The "system" operates not to develop the individual powers and creative faculties of the workers but produces mechanical workers who are to be treated as part of the machinery. That is to say, the system is dehumanizing—it degrades rather than elevates. The practical results of the operation of experience with scientific management indicate that it is a speeding-up device that increases the profits of the employers but benefits only a few individual workers.

Scientific management has been used as a union-destroying agency. Experiences of the workers prove that their welfare depends ultimately upon their own initiative and collective effort.

After all, whatever of value there may be in the so-called efficiency systems seems in the last analysis to resolve itself into an educational problem. True efficiency can result only from developing and stimulating the creative ability of each individual.

The working men feel that the practice of holding a stop-watch or any timing system over the individual workers has a tendency to make them strained and unnatural. They often feel this practice in connection with other devices to reduce them to a definite number of mechanical reactions and to check up their work by elaborate accounting systems makes of them mere automata and is correspondingly degrading.

Organized labor opposes no effort to secure the welfare of the workers. If a system of scientific management could be evolved that would benefit and not injure, organized labor would certainly do its part in co-operating to establish such a system. However, the great obstacle to any such conference and agreement by employers and employes upon scientific management has been the refusal of employers to recognize the union. No agreement is possible except through representatives of the workers and organizations of labor are the only agencies through which that can be accomplished.

Great press of work precludes my replying more in detail to your questions, but if in any way I can be of future assistance kindly let me know.

Hoping for your success in your study and confidently anticipating that the workers will be benefited thereby, I am

Very sincerely yours,   Saml Gompers.
President   American Federation of Labor.

TLpS, reel 186, vol. 198, pp. 355–57, SG Letterbooks, DLC.

1. Robert Franklin Hoxie, professor of political economy at the University of Chicago, was a special investigator (1914–15) for the U.S. Commission on Industrial Relations.

2. Hoxie's study was later published as *Scientific Management and Labor* (New York, 1916).

3. In a letter to SG on Aug. 31, 1914, indicating that the Commission on Industrial Relations had appointed him to study the relation of scientific management to labor, Hoxie asked SG to suggest which plants should be investigated and to summarize labor's objections to scientific management. He also asked SG's opinion of John Frey as a trade union representative to help with the investigation (AFL Microfilm Convention File, reel 26, frame 2279, *AFL Records*).

4. The Commission on Industrial Relations held hearings on "Efficiency Systems and Labor" in Washington, D.C., Apr. 13–16, 1914 (U.S. Congress, Senate, *Industrial Relations. Final Report and Testimony Submitted to Congress by the Commission on Industrial Relations . . .* , 64th Cong., 1st sess., 1916, S. Doc. 415, 1: 763–1024).

5. The Commission on Industrial Relations subsequently appointed Frey to assist Hoxie. Frey published an article on the subject, "Scientific Management and Labor," in the April and May 1916 numbers of the *American Federationist* (23: 257–68, 358–68).

To Charles Moyer

Sept. 17, 1914.

Mr. Charles H. Moyer,
President, Western Federation of Miners,
503–11 Denham Bldg., Denver, Colo.
Dear Sir and Brother:

It is with the deepest interest that I have received and perused the contents of your letter of the tenth instant.[1] Your narration of the circumstances and the deplorable conditions prevailing in Butte have been noted and re-read.

A few days ago President Donoghue[2] of the Montana State Federation of Labor, stopped in Washington on his way to attend the Dominion Trades and Labor Congress[3] as Fraternal Delegate from the American Federation of Labor, and I had a talk of nearly two hours with him in my office. He reviewed the situation and the conditions prevailing in Butte, and he knows just what they are. I was exceedingly glad to have the opportunity of going over the situation with him.

When I was first advised of the trouble in Butte, as you know I communicated promptly[4] with the officers of our International Unions, urging them strongly either to go to Butte or to send a competent representative of their respective organizations. Of course you understand that I have not the power to enforce compliance with such requests. It would have been better had there been at the conference[5] in Butte a full complement of men representatives of the various International Unions to devise ways and means to protect the rights and interests of the workingmen, that they should organize and be true to their locals and to their international unions, as well as to the general labor movement as represented by the American Federation of Labor. Our hopes must be that time and opportunity will demonstrate the utter illusory policy which the dissident element has pursued for some considerable time past.

You refer to the men and women involved in the Michigan strike and that 631 of them were placed under arrest, charged with offenses ranging from "making a noise on the street to that of murder"; that only two convictions were had and they for minor offenses, the punishment being a short sentence in the county jail, but when the strike was declared at an end there were left in the county jail at Houghton three men charged with murder and whom you say you know to be absolutely innocent of the charge. You further say that the trial of these men is set for October 19th, and the question now comes as to providing ways and means to adequately defend them. You then ask if I can come to their assistance. I should be very glad to do anything within my power but the question is after all the limitations of that power. When numbers of men are out of work, as you know they are at this time, by reason of the disarrangement of industry and commerce, due to the European war, it becomes a difficult question for the various organizations of labor to meet their own expenditures for their members who are unemployed, involved in strikes or lockouts in some section or other of the country, whereby the international union of the trade is required to pay strike benefits or to make donations or levy assessments, to be of general help.

All of these things make it practically impossible to raise money either by assessment or now even by an appeal for voluntary assistance. I am made heartsore at times by the fact that we cannot as frequently and generously as we would desire, come to the financial rescue of our fellow workers, and this too through no fault of either the Federation, its officers or any one person. The fact is that the men of labor are making the best fight that they can under adverse conditions and circumstances. That they are holding their own now or making some progress under the present adverse conditions is saying much for the much misunderstood and misrepresented trade union movement.

Reverting back to the three men who are under indictment, there certainly ought to be afforded the proper opportunity for defense in the courts, no matter how unpromising conditions seem. I have submitted copy of your letter to my colleagues of the Executive Council of the A.F. of L. from whom I hope to have an expression of opinion upon this subject[6] which will certainly receive the attention of the Executive Council at its forthcoming meeting October 12th.[7]

With kind regards, and hoping to hear from you further, I am,

Fraternally yours,   Saml Gompers.

President,   American Federation of Labor.

TLpS, reel 186, vol. 198, pp. 421–23, SG Letterbooks, DLC.

1. "From Charles Moyer," Sept. 10, 1914, above.

2. Mortimer M. DONOGHUE was president of the Montana State Federation of Labor (1909–19).

3. The 1914 convention of the Trades and Labor Congress of Canada met in St. John, N.B., Sept. 21–26.

4. For SG's circular of June 23, 1914, to international affiliates, see "From Frank Glenn," June 23, 1914, n. 4, above.

5. On July 10, 1914, representatives of the Bakery and Confectionery Workers' International Union of America, the International Association of Bridge and Structural Iron Workers, the International Association of Machinists, the Brotherhood of Painters, Decorators, and Paperhangers of America, and the Amalgamated Association of Street and Electric Railway Employes of America met in Butte, Mont., in response to SG's circular of June 23.

6. SG sent a copy of Moyer's letter to the AFL Executive Council on Sept. 17, 1914, but the Council took no action on Moyer's request at that time (Executive Council Records, Vote Books, reel 13, frame 374, *AFL Records*). The 1914 AFL convention adopted a resolution calling upon affiliated bodies to give financial assistance to the miners on trial for murder in connection with the Michigan copper miners' strike. The resolution was referred to the Executive Council for action, which on Dec. 3 issued a circular appealing for financial aid for the miners, the United Textile Workers of America strike in Atlanta, and the International Glove Workers' Union of America strike in New York, with contributions to be divided among the three unions. The appeal raised $6,372, of which $2,138 went to the Western Federation of Miners.

7. The AFL Executive Council met in Washington, D.C., Oct. 12–17, 1914.

From William Appleton

General Federation of Trade Unions.
London, W.C. 23rd September, 1914.

Dear Mr. Gompers,

I am enclosing the pamphlets and articles indicated in your letter of the 5th instant,[1] and I am also trying to obtain copies of the "Academy" containing articles which I wrote on the Insurance Act[2] some time since.

I gave Sullivan every possible facility for acquiring information while he was in London and he will be able to tell you many things. If you think my experience will be of any value please do not hesitate to write; I shall only be too happy to help you to avoid some of the mistakes we have made, particularly those mistakes which have led us to contravene business principles in our efforts to conciliate sentiment.

I understand that Sullivan will have many things to tell you concerning the war. The whole business is most deplorable and after you have read *Bernardi's book*[3] and the White papers[4] issued I am certain that your conclusions concerning the responsibility for the war will harmonise with ours here. You will be delighted to learn that there is *little real hostility towards the German* while, at the same time, you will expect to hear that there is the strongest possible antipathy to the *Prussian military* caste and a determination to do everything possible to break this up and leave the better part of German feeling and aspiration to develop itself more naturally.

The bitterness towards the Prussian military system has been intensified by the destruction of Louvain and other Belgian villages,[5] and by the wanton and foolish destruction of the Cathedral at Rheims.[6] In war one must always deduct greatly from the stories concerning outrage and atrocity but even after very liberal deduction it is obvious that Germany has *carried on this war,* particularly in Belgium, an inoffensive and neutral State, exactly on the *lines advocated by Treischki*[7] and Bernardi. They have acted as if the power to slay conferred the right to slay even the non-combatant. The counter-charges made against the Belgians[8] do not appear to be supported by a single shred of evidence. Up to the present the only affidavit in support of these countercharges appears to be one filed by a person claiming to be a Swiss but who is a German so well known to the Swiss Police that they expelled him from Switzerland just recently.[9] These same Swiss Police aver that Counstans was under their observation for some time and could not possibly have been an eye-witness of what he alleges has been perpetrated by Belgians upon the German Troops.

It is exceedingly sad that just when we appeared to have brought the International movement on to the plane of practicability all our efforts should have been nullified. It will take some years to restore the situation or *even to* convince large numbers of our people that the International *Secretariat is not a part of the German system of espionage*. Under such circumstances it will be our duty to maintain and develop, as far as possible, the *amicable relationships between the English speaking workers,* to draw closer the cords that bind their organizations together, and to hold ourselves in readiness for the time when the resuscitation of [the] International movement becomes possible.

You are often in my thought and I wonder many times how best to develop the relationships between the trade union movement of the two countries. Periodical speeches and interchange of delegates does much but the interlocking of practical relationships will do infinitely more. I know this is difficult but it is not impossible and I sometimes feel that the greatness of the task will appeal to you and set you on the move. If ever this happens you may count upon the loyal and plenary co-operation of,

Yours faithfully,   (Signed) W. A. Appleton.[10]

TLtcSr, Executive Council Records, Vote Books, reel 13, frame 406, *AFL Records.* Enclosed in SG to the AFL Executive Council, Oct. 12, 1914, ibid., frame 404.

1. SG wrote William Appleton on Sept. 5, 1914, asking him to send copies of publications on industrial insurance (reel 185, vol. 197, p. 968, SG Letterbooks, DLC).

2. The National Insurance Act of 1911 (1 and 2 Geo. V, chap. 55) created a system of compulsory contributory health insurance for British workers, with most of the cost being borne by workers and their employers and the balance being contributed by the state. The benefits included medical treatment and payments for sickness and disability. The act also provided short-term unemployment insurance for specified workers, including those involved in construction, shipbuilding, mechanical engineering, iron work, the building of vehicles, and woodworking.

3. Friedrich von Bernhardi (1849–1930), a German cavalry officer, was the author of *Germany and the Next War* (1912). The book maintained that war was both a pragmatic necessity and a moral good, essential for the development of German national character and the legitimation of German foreign policy.

4. In August and September 1914 the British Foreign Office published a selection of diplomatic correspondence bearing on the outbreak of the war, most notably the Blue Book, containing 159 documents, which was put before Parliament on Aug. 6.

5. Between Aug. 25 and 28, 1914, following a reversal at the hands of the Belgian army at Malines, the German army sacked and burned the Belgian city of Louvain, killing some 250 civilians, deporting another 1,500, and destroying the city's incomparable library, with its collection of medieval manuscripts and incunabula. The Germans also pillaged and burned a number of smaller Belgian villages and towns, with the destruction accompanied by mass executions and deportations of civilians.

6. The Cathedral of Rheims was destroyed during the German bombardment of the city in September 1914.

7. Heinrich von Treitschke (1834–96), a professor of history at the University of Berlin, was the author of *The History of Germany in the Nineteenth Century* (5 vols., 1879–94). He emphasized the fundamental importance of a powerful German state with an expanding empire maintained by force of arms.

8. The Germans maintained that the Belgians were responsible for their attacks on noncombatants because Belgian civilians had purportedly committed atrocities in resisting the German invasion.

9. The Germans claimed that their charges of Belgian atrocities were substantiated by the reports of a Swiss Red Cross worker in Liège named Hermann Consten. Press accounts published in Paris and London maintained that Consten was a German national with a criminal record who had been expelled from Switzerland.

10. SG replied to Appleton on Oct. 12, 1914: "The importance of your letter is tremendous and I can only express the hope that there is a mistake somewhere and that there is no basis in what you say that it will take some years 'even to convince large numbers of our (English) people that the International Secretariat is not a part of the German system of espionage'" (reel 187, vol. 199, pp. 43–45, SG Letterbooks, DLC, quotation at p. 43).

A Circular

Washington, D.C., Oct. 3, 1914.

Critical situation arisen regarding our bill that is the labor provisions of the Clayton bill. The labor provisions in the bill are entirely satisfactory, affording the proper relief which Labor has asked. There is opposition to some of the other provisions of the bill as presented by the conference committee of both houses. Unless the bill is passed within the next week, the bill, with our labor provisions, is in danger. Among the senators who are opposing the bill is Hon. John W. Kern,[1] from your state. Communicate at once by telegraph, day or night letter, with Senator Kern, at Washington, and urge him to avoid the calamity of the possible defeat of the labor provisions of the Clayton Antitrust bill by delay. Also ask your friends to do likewise. Act promptly.

Samuel Gompers
President   American Federation of Labor.

TWSr, reel 186, vol. 198, p. 818, SG Letterbooks, DLC. Typed notation: "This telegram was sent to the central bodies and organizers in Indiana, N.Y., Tenn., Colo., Okla., and Ill. in regard to Senators Kern, O'Gorman,[2] Shields,[3] Thomas,[4] Borah,[5] and Lewis.[6] 178 telegrams in all."[7]

1. John Worth Kern (1849–1917) served as a Democratic senator from Indiana (1911–17).

2. James Aloysius O'Gorman (1860–1943) served as a Democratic senator from New York (1911–17).

3. John Knight Shields (1858–1934) served as a Democratic senator from Tennessee (1913–25).

4. Charles Spalding Thomas (1849–1934) served as a Democratic senator from Colorado (1913–21).

5. Actually Thomas Pryor Gore (1870–1949), who served as a Democratic senator from Oklahoma (1907–21, 1931–37).

6. James Hamilton Lewis (1863–1939) served as a Democratic congressman from Washington (1897–99) and Democratic senator from Illinois (1913–19, 1931–39).

7. For SG's draft of this telegram, see AFL Microfilm Convention File, reel 26, frame 2418, *AFL Records*. SG sent a similar note to unions in New Jersey with reference to Senator James Martine of that state (ibid., frame 2419).

From Ben Tillett[1]

7-10-[19]14.

Dear Gompers:—

We are in the throes of a mighty war, and all that is good in us, is being exhausted in this armageddon. There never was a more horrible example of Military and Capitalist aggression. It is arrogant autocracy gone mad, and our people, the men and the women of the working classes of the nations involved who are paying the price of lives and bloodshed and sacrifice. I am still an Internationalist Gompers, but one must love one's country and we in Britain have well and truly for a greater democracy. Because our German Comrades have been copying and even improving on some of our best examples, the Prussian oppressors have been driven to panic fear.

Hence this war, a war for Trade, for political power, for military ascendancy: and all the horrors that ascendancy will mean to us. Our own attitude is more than ever justified when one sees the torture, the devastation and the blood and beast-lust let loose in fury and hatred: even of our class who are fighting against their Comrades of Belgium, France and ourselves, with unexampled energy.

I want the American Workers to see to it that all the liberties—political, social, religious, we have risked all to maintain: are not drawn into the vortex of Capitalist-International sordidness and riot.

The brutality shown to the Catholic Institutions, the rack of Louvain, Rheims, Brussels[2] on the top of the worst oppression and bullying, the vilest rule of nations has ever known—is proof that we had to take a hand and a big fist in this fight. We want our American German Comrades to realise this war must go on to the bitter end, but the people who will lose in life and liberties will be our own class—unless and in fact we make it manifest to our "Pastors and Masters," that we want in the settlement some say, and an assurance that war will not be undertaken in future for a set of sordid, bestial capitalists who are international financiers. The slaughter is dreadful and although we shall win, with the Allies; we shall be mauled until every home and every wife and mother, will be crucified with the agony of bereavement and loss. We had to fight, the war of aggression was long contemplated and the Prussian militarists, thought so contemptibly of Britain, that we were not considered, but was told by the Bully of Prussia to keep out of the fight until France was conquered and the German Capitalist ensconced opposite our Coast, with every outlet for further aggression in trade and in a military sense. The whole business has been ruthless, maybe we shall scotch the war monster for a generation or more. We shall soon have a million of men in the field, already all that means lethal weapons of war, practices for the further efficiency of the troops, and all the deadly preparation for a continuous war, are being forced apace. The Government have taken an appreciable interest in the wants of the army, the needs of the relatives, and we are hoping to press them to realise the value of the lives being sacrificed most cheerfully by our men—for the Country but unfortunately the rich classes for whom the War is being waged are so mean, that they have subscribed just a little over a million to the Prince of Wales's Fund, the most of the money coming from the pence of the poor and the contributions of the middle classes.

When you realise that our increase in profits, dividends and trade has been yearly on the up grade by the hundred millions of pounds, you can guess how miserly and sordid our richest classes are, with some notable exceptions. While we are demanding generous treatment for the Soldier at the front, a competence for the families of the men at the front as well, we are also asking for generous relief to the unemployed of the country. We have also in our own defence encouraged every fair means of enlisting, although we have found some of the panicky employers, forcing unemployment on the younger men, to save money and to take sordid advantage of the horrible meaning of war, some of the employers are acting generously with their employees, giving allowance, in some cases giving half wages to the families, but in the majority of cases the employers are shouting patriotism and sticking at home, while the fighting is being done for them, at the expense of other people's lives, and the Country's sacrifice.

Anyway, tell the American workers, that Britishers will not stand for Prussian bosses, we shall I hope be in the fight against the Militarism which has embroiled us in this war, against Kaiserism, either of the

Prussian or British order. All Europe is in turmoil, the war is wasteful and is torturing us all. Over a half million have rushed to join the colours, there is another half million ready, the standard of health, height and chest is raised which shows you the response being made to the call of Country. May the war soon terminate and bring us back the peace and goodwill, now violently and ruthlessly crushed. Our old Country is going to fight this to a finish, and the democracy will have a say in the settlement, we shall have a greater say, if the Democracy of Germany help us to smash the Prussian bullies and the military caste—for ever. Good luck,

Yours sincerely,   Ben Tillett.[3]

TLtcSr, Public Record Office. Published with the permission of the Transport and General Workers' Union. Typed notations: "Copy" and "Copy Letter to Gompers."

1. Benjamin TILLETT was general secretary of the Dock, Wharf, Riverside, and General Labourers' Union of Great Britain and Ireland (1889–1922).

2. Brussels was occupied by German forces on Aug. 20, 1914, and an indemnity of 50,000,000 francs (about $10,000,000) was imposed on the city.

3. In his reply to Tillett of Oct. 20, 1914, SG noted his regret that, due to the war, no fraternal delegates from the TUC would attend the 1914 AFL convention.

To the Executive Council of the AFL

Washington, D.C., Oct. 8, 1914.

No. 154.

Executive Council, American Federation of Labor.

Colleagues:

At 4:35 this afternoon the House of Representatives passed the Clayton bill with the labor provisions intact by a vote of 244 in favor to 54 against, and the bill now goes to the President. There is no doubt in the mind of anyone but that the President will sign the bill.

Thus, although the ultimate fact has not been accomplished, that is, its enactment, I am justified in saying that the principle for which the American Federation of Labor has been contending for twenty six years, that is the period of the consideration and enactment of the Sherman Antitrust law, and the twenty four years since its enactment to secure relief from its provisions, relief from the interpretation of that law applying it to the normal activities of organized labor, is a practically established fact. As Admiral Schley said after the naval battle at Santiago,[1] Cuba, "there is glory enough for us all," and it is a triumph to the practical policy and persistent and consistent effort and work of the American Federation of Labor.

I take this opportunity of not only officially informing the members of the Executive Council of the A.F. of L. of this wonderful victory but of tendering my felicitations to every man who has contributed in any way towards achieving it.

Fraternally yours,   Saml Gompers.
President,   American Federation of Labor.

TLcS, Executive Council Records, Vote Books, reel 13, frame 403, *AFL Records.*

1. On July 3, 1898, an American squadron destroyed the Spanish fleet as the Spanish were attempting to escape from the harbor of Santiago, Cuba.

To Frank Coffey[1]

Oct. 9, 1914.

Mr. Frank M. Coffey,
Secretary-Treasurer, The Nebraska State Federation of Labor,
Lincoln, Nebraska.
Dear Sir and Brother:

Your letters of October 3, addressed to myself and Mr. Frank Morrison, Secretary of the American Federation of Labor, to hand, and same has been turned over to me for reply.

I have read your letter carefully, but the time at my disposal will not permit me going minutely into the Workmen's Compensation Act[2] passed during the 1913 session of the Nebraska Legislature, and which you say has been held up for a referendum vote invoked by the personal injury lawyers of your State.

You ask me for my opinion concerning the principle of automatic compensation for injured workmen in industry.

Replying to same, permit me to say, that I personally, most emphatically favor the principles of an automatic Compensation Act, first, in order to avoid lawsuits; second, in order to avoid expense; third, removal of anxiety and suspense; fourth, the securing of immediate pecuniary benefits for afflicted workmen's families during the period of stress and trouble when such funds are the most needed by the injured workman's family.

Of course, the whole Compensation principle is new in the United States, and has to be worked out in order to find what is best and most practicable. Let me remind you that it is only six years ago since the

American Federation of Labor secured the enactment of the first Compensation Act in the United States.[3] Since that time, through the efforts of the members of our organizations, with such assistance as I have been able to render, twenty-two States have enacted legislation of this character, and I am pleased to say that in all of the States where such legislation has been enacted, there is a constant endeavor on the part of the organized employes and sympathetic public citizens to continue to try and improve the legislation enacted, in order to more equitably and comprehensively protect laborers in their employment and sustain them under affliction because of accidents in industry.

The American Federation of Labor is giving its time and attention to this subject to its fullest possible capacity, and I take great pleasure in sending you, under separate cover, copy of Senate Document #419,[4] published by the United States Senate, which contains the report of a special Commission of the American Federation of Labor, working in cooperation with the National Civic Federation, in which the whole subject matter is thoroughly dissected and dealt with. I am sure that this document will be of material value to you and your associates in the arguments that you may feel disposed to make in behalf of the Compensation Act passed by your State Legislature.

I hope that the trade unionists in Nebraska will vote for the Act on the referendum submitted during the November elections. Kindly say for me to all your associates and fellow citizens, that it is not the height of wisdom to wait for the time when a law of this kind can be thoroughly perfected in every detail. The good sense and alertness of the working people of Nebraska can be depended upon in future to perfect what weak spots may be found in the law or the administration thereof, and, as you say, can be attended to at subsequent sessions of the Legislature.

Let me add, that the Compensation laws of Germany[5] and England were not perfect at their first submission for enactment; neither of them are perfect yet, but the people of both countries, in their wisdom, accepted what in their best judgment was possible to secure at the time, and they have constantly improved upon their work. This is the same position that members of organizations affiliated to the American Federation of Labor have taken with the Federal Government Compensation Act and with the several Acts passed by the State Legislature, and I may add, that there is a keen sense of rivalry among our members in the several States to see which can produce the best results.

With much appreciation for the active interest and splendid service in behalf of this highly necessary legislation by the officers and members of the Nebraska State Federation of Labor and its local unions, and trusting that you may be completely successful in securing the ratification of this measure during the coming election, I remain,

Fraternally yours,   Saml Gompers.

President,   American Federation of Labor.

P.S. In my judgment the New York State Workmen's Compensation Law is the best thus far enacted.

S. G.

TLpS, reel 187, vol. 199, pp. 40–42, SG Letterbooks, DLC.

1. Frank M. COFFEY was a member of International Typographical Union 209 of Lincoln, Nebr., and secretary-treasurer of the Nebraska State Federation of Labor (1913–22?).

2. Nebraska, Laws of 1913, chap. 198, enacted Apr. 21, 1913, provided for voluntary participation by private employers and mandatory participation by all state agencies. Compensation was to be made in the case of disability lasting two weeks or longer or death as a result of negligence by the employer, with the payments funded by employer contributions to approved insurance companies. The measure was upheld in a referendum on Nov. 3, 1914.

3. H.R. 21,844 (60th Cong., 1st sess.), providing government employees with compensation for accidents, was introduced by Republican congressman DeAlva Alexander of New York on May 12, 1908, and became law on May 30 (U.S. *Statutes at Large,* 35: 556–58).

4. In 1913 a joint National Civic Federation–AFL commission consisting of Cyrus Phillips, J. Walter Lord, Otto Eidlitz, Louis Schram, and AFL vice-presidents James Duncan and John Mitchell undertook an investigation of state workmen's compensation laws. The commission visited several states, sent a questionnaire to some twenty-five thousand employers and workmen, and held conferences with employers, labor leaders, state commissioners, accident boards, and representatives of insurance companies. It drafted a model bill that was sent to state legislatures in 1914, and the commission's report was published as a Senate document (U.S. Congress, Senate, *Workmen's Compensation. Report upon Operation of State Laws. Investigation by Commission of the American Federation of Labor and the National Civic Federation* . . . , 63d Cong., 2d sess., 1914, S. Doc. 419).

5. The German law, enacted in 1911, provided compensation for accidental, employment-related injuries causing disability of more than three days or death.

To Woodrow Wilson

Washington, D.C., October 16, 1914.

Hon. Woodrow Wilson,
President of the United States,
Washington, D.C.
My dear Mr. President:

I deeply appreciate your thoughtfulness and courtesy in sending me one of the pens with which you signed the Clayton bill. It will be added to my collection of historic pens, among them being the pen with which President Cleveland signed the bill making Labor Day a legal holiday.

Permit me at the same time to take this opportunity of expressing to you my great appreciation of your approval of the Clayton Bill, the labor provisions of which are indeed a magnificent piece of legislation, according to the working people of our country the rational, constitutional and inherent rights of which they have too long been denied.

Very sincerely yours,   Saml Gompers.

TLS, Woodrow Wilson Papers, DLC.

To Woodrow Wilson

Washington, D.C., Oct. 16, 1914.

Hon. Woodrow Wilson,
President of the United States,
Executive Offices, Washington, D.C.
Sir:

This session of the 63rd Congress is drawing to a close; adjournment or recess in the very near future, is announced in public print. Several bills are mentioned as scheduled to be passed prior to such adjournment or recess, but the Seamen's bill is not among them. The promise made at the Baltimore Convention of the Democratic party two years ago was that a bill for the improvement of the condition of seamen and for better safety of life at sea was to be speedily enacted.

One bill has been passed by the Senate; a substitute has been passed by the House; the whole matter is back in the Committee on Commerce, where the House substitute was sent for comparison.

The hearings upon this legislation have run through years and have been most searching and exhaustive. Interest in the legislation has been stimulated from time to time by such great losses of human life as resulted from the sinking of the Titanic, the Volturno,[1] the Monroe[2] and the Empress of Ireland.[3] Each accident demonstrated the necessity for this legislation.

The hearings on this measure have shown that under existing laws and treaties it is not possible for the United States to build up a merchant marine, the differential in the cost of operation in favor of foreign vessels is too great.

It is generally conceded that the enactment of the Seamen's bill as it passed the Senate would wipe out this differential, and, so far as the cost of operation is concerned, would put American vessels on an equality with all other vessels.

It seems that since the bill has passed both houses and the question at issue is one of difference between the two Houses, the bill might well go into conference and be disposed of at this session.

The seamen are yet subject to imprisonment for violation of a civil contract of labor, and vessels are running under the same conditions that they were when the great losses above referred to occurred.

There is a promise in the Democratic campaign book that this bill will be enacted before adjournment. If Congress should adjourn without passing the bill there is no doubt but that this fact could be used to the serious detriment to the party's campaign and would place us in a position which we should find extremely difficult to explain or defend.

Your attention is called to the 12th paragraph on page 11 of the Democratic Text Book of 1914, just issued, in which it is stated that "at this writing the bill (the Seamen's bill), is in conference, but it is certain of becoming a completed 'achievement' before Congress adjourns."

Six years ago we submitted to the then President of the United States, to the Vice-President and to the Speaker of the House, our Bill of Grievances, in which we urged as strongly as we knew how, certain specific items of legislation for the well-being of the working people of our country. Some of these items of legislation are now law. Another your signature made law on October 15. The legislation for the liberation of seamen and the protection of the traveling public was included in that Bill of Grievances and placed at its head. It would mean much to us and might mean much to others if we were enabled through the passage of this bill, to say to the working people and to the citizenship of the country generally that the main items of the Bill of Grievances have been enacted into law, and that the others which were given less important places in the Bill of Grievances are before Congress with the prospect that they will become law before this Congress adjourns.

In freeing the seamen and guaranteeing to them a percentage of the wages earned in order that they may be able to defend their freedom and to make use of it, we are asking but for the enactment into law of a definite pledge given to the American people and the fulfillment of the hopes and expectation of all men who love liberty.

Is it not possible that you may be enabled to exert your great influence so that before this session of Congress shall have adjourned the Seamen's Bill may be enacted into law?[4]

Thanking you in advance for whatever assistance you may be able to render in this humanitarian piece of legislation, I have the honor to remain,

Very respectfully yours,   Saml Gompers.

President,   American Federation of Labor.

TLS, Woodrow Wilson Papers, DLC.

1. The steamship *Volturno,* en route from Rotterdam to New York, caught fire on the morning of Oct. 9, 1913, and burned at sea, with the loss of 136 lives.

2. After being struck in a dense fog by another vessel, the steamship *Monroe* sank off the coast of Virginia on Jan. 30, 1914, with the loss of forty-one lives.

3. After colliding with another ship, the Canadian liner *Empress of Ireland* sank in the St. Lawrence River on May 29, 1914, with the loss of over a thousand lives.

4. Woodrow Wilson asked his private secretary, Joseph Tumulty, to respond to this letter, explaining that he (the president) considered it "imperative" to give precedence to other legislative matters (Wilson to Tumulty, n.d., Woodrow Wilson Papers, DLC).

From John Fitzpatrick[1]

Headquarters
Chicago Federation of Labor
Chicago, Ill., October 22, 1914.

Dear Sir and Brother:—

When I wrote you recently[2] in regard to the Harness Makers Local #17[3] I made the statement that in ten years we had unseated some fifty Local Unions.

At our last meeting I had to gavel another Local out of the Labor Movement, one of the oldest and best Locals we had, Local No. 69 of the Steam Engineers. I dared not let the meeting act upon our Executive Committee's report which was to comply with the law of the A.F. of L. If I put that motion it would have been voted down. So I had to rule motions out of order and declare that the matter was one of the enforcement of the laws of the A.F. of L., and we would comply with the instructions contained in your letter.[4]

Now, we have under consideration or in abeyance the unseating of thirteen locals of Brick Makers[5] and in a short time the Harness Makers will be put on the rollers.[6]

The split in the Garment Workers[7] will affect us to the extent of sixteen Locals. I know of only one Local of Garment Workers in Chicago that will remain in Rickertts'[8] organization.

If we keep on we will soon have a fine aggregation of trades to form an Independent Central Body, which would be composed of locals who are held in the highest possible regard by their fellow trades Unionists, because in every instance the Trades Unionists of Chicago feel that this is a matter of persecution and they consider the ousted organizations the under dog, and I give you my word and I think I know something about the C.F. of L., that if the representative active Union men and women of Chicago were allowed to vote upon such expulsions they would vote "no" almost unanimously.

Now I consider this a most serious and dangerous situation and I can't tell the moment when they will sweep me off my feet and take matters in their own hands.

I have been President now some eight years and meet constantly with these delegates once every two weeks. It is not like meeting them only once every year and the old adage is: "familiarity breeds contempt." The delegates are showing increasing contempt of my continued effort to enforce the A.F. of L. laws and more especially when they feel that the enforcement of such law is a rank denial of justice. I find that in each instance where a Local is expelled by an International Union the delegates of other Unions always feel that sufficient consideration was not accorded the expelled Union and there is a common demand that a full, fair, disinterested, impartial hearing be had and when such a hearing is denied, the delegates doubt the democracy of the Labor Movement and are ready to rebel against what is now generally termed the "steam roller," (the International Unions).

It seems to me that the A.F. of L. has a duty to perform in the premises and that is, to declare and assure Local Unions of International Unions that they shall not be Steam Rolled.

The Local Unions, City Central Bodies and the State Federation of Illinois, at least hold the American Federation of Labor in the highest possible regard and they look to the A.F. of L. for sympathy and encouragement and they have an abiding faith and confidence in the American Labor Movement as represented by the A.F. of L., but if the A.F. of L. is going to be the pressure through which the International Unions are going to enforce their unfair, unreasonable and despotic decisions, the A.F. of L. will surely bring about its own undoing.

The A.F. of L. should be big enough to take itself out of the position where it is now used to crush the courage, independence and fighting spirit which pervades the rank and file because if you crush the spirit to resist when they believe a great injustice has been perpetrated by the International officers, you make the rank and file servile when it comes to resisting injustice upon the part of the employers.

I say the A.F. of L. is used to compel the Locals of the International Union to comply with decisions whether these decisions are right or wrong and without redress.

Now the A.F. of L. can at least declare that such procedure is against the best interests of the Organized Labor Movement and it surely has the power to amend its own laws so as to refuse to expel from Central Bodies or State Federations the old fighting Locals and install new Locals made up of strike breakers and scabs, because some deal exists between the International office and the employer, that the International will protect the employers' interests.

I feel it my duty to bring these matters to your attention and hoping they are received in the same spirit as they are sent, I am,

Sincerely,　John Fitzpatrick[9]

TLS, AFL Microfilm National and International Union File, Leather Workers Records, reel 39, frame 1268, *AFL Records.*

1. John J. FITZPATRICK was president of the Chicago Federation of Labor (FOL; 1900–1901, 1906–46) and an AFL salaried organizer (1903–23).

2. Fitzpatrick to SG, Sept. 24, 1914, AFL Microfilm National and International Union File, Leather Workers Records, reel 39, frames 1265–66, *AFL Records.*

3. United Brotherhood of Leather Workers on Horse Goods 17 of Chicago.

4. SG wrote Edward Nockels, secretary of the Chicago FOL, on Aug. 18, 1914, calling on him to unseat International Union of Steam and Operating Engineers 69 of Chicago in conformity with the AFL constitution (reel 185, vol. 197, pp. 499–500, SG Letterbooks, DLC). The international union had revoked the local's charter for making unauthorized agreements with contractors and had chartered local 569 in its place.

5. A reference to locals of the United Brick and Clay Workers of America, which seceded from the International BRICK, Tile, and Terra Cotta Workers' Alliance in 1913.

6. Leather Workers' local 17 faced suspension by the international union because it was unable to pay its per capita tax. SG took the matter up with the Leather Workers, and in February 1915 an agreement was reached whereby local 17 would remit 50 percent of its gross receipts to the international until it attained a membership of 150.

7. When the 1914 convention of the United Garment Workers of America met in Nashville on Oct. 12, the credential committee denied seats to 105 delegates, particularly those from tailors' locals in New York City, alleging that their payments of per capita tax were in arrears. The delegates from the union's Chicago locals protested, but Garment Workers' president Thomas Rickert, who was presiding, refused to permit a vote appealing the credential committee's decision. The protesting delegates and those who had been excluded then left the convention and met at another location in the city, declaring that they represented the majority of garment workers and were, therefore, the legitimate union. They elected officers and delegates to the 1914 AFL convention, but that meeting refused to seat them or give them a hearing. The seceding faction met in New York City on Dec. 26 and organized as the Amalgamated CLOTHING Workers of America.

8. Thomas Alfred RICKERT served as president of the Garment Workers from 1904 to 1941.

9. For SG's response, see "To John Fitzpatrick," Oct. 31, 1914, below.

To Paul Scharrenberg[1]

Washington, D.C., Oct. 28, 1914.

Mr. Paul Scharrenburg,
Underwood Bldg., 525 Market St., San Francisco, Cal.

To agitate the foreign land holding question[2] at present is most unfortunate and may cause great embarrassment or worse to the people of our country.[3] For over thirty years I have been and am still with the Pacific Coast on Asiatic questions but in the best interest of all our people I urge that the subject of new agitation be deferred until after the close of the terrible European war from which we are at present happily free.

Samuel Gompers.

TWpSr, reel 187, vol. 199, p. 553, SG Letterbooks, DLC.

1. Paul SCHARRENBERG, a member of the Sailors' Union of the Pacific and editor (1913–21, 1922–37) of the *Coast Seamen's Journal* (from 1918, the *Seamen's Journal*), was secretary-treasurer of the California State Federation of Labor (1909–36).

2. The Alien Land Act (California, Laws of 1913, chap. 113, enacted May 19, 1913) barred Asian immigrants from owning land in California but allowed them to lease it for agricultural purposes for up to three years. The California State Federation of Labor opposed the leasing provision, however, and its October 1914 convention proposed questioning candidates for the state legislature in the upcoming election about their position on the issue.

3. Japan's declaration of war on Germany led to speculation that, in exchange, it would ask Great Britain, France, and Russia to support its demand that Japanese in the United States be accorded the same rights and privileges as their citizens living in the United States.

From W. D. Mahon

Amalgamated Association of Street and Electric
Railway Employes of America
Detroit, Mich. Oct. 30, 1914.

Dear Sir and Brother:

On arriving at the office this morning I was handed your letter regarding the Mayors' Convention at Philadelphia.[1] Now, I don't imagine that it will be possible for me to reach Philadelphia at the opening of the Convention. We are now up against the hardest fight of our lives and possibly I may not get there at all. The Street Railway Company at Indianapolis sought an injunction against our Association through Federal-Judge Anderson.[2] The temporary injunction was granted and on Monday the hearings on the case opened. I have never met anything like it in my life. When we started in with the hearing, the Judge first announced that it was a case in equity and that all evidence would be heard. This made us feel rather good, for we felt that we had plenty of evidence on which to win the case. But as soon as we attempted to cross-question the witnesses, we were stopped. We were not allowed to do so. When our witnesses who were summoned by the Company were put on the stand, he denounced them as liars, and would not allow us to question on the points that we sought to bring out. The Company was allowed to ask any kind of a question they wanted to, but when we attempted the same we were denied and abused. Our lawyers were abused. Yesterday, in the arguments, one of our lawyers he would scarcely allow to say anything until he was interrupted. When the question of the Clayton law came up, he denounced that law as unconstitutional and took up the names of the different Senators who had promoted the law, such as Commons[3] and men of that character, and criticized them calling the law "punk" and saying that it was unconstitutional and that the Congress had no right to interfere with the power of the Federal Court. Now, he has taken 10 days in which to make his decision. We imagine that he is going to make a sweeping decision against the International Union. He denounced the outsiders for coming in and interfering and he said he was going to stop it. So we look for a sweeping injunction, and it being the first one under the Clayton law I presume will have to be fought to the end. I expect I will have to go back to Indianapolis and arranged for Bonds to get the case carried up and that will come just about the time of the opening of the A.F. of L. Convention and I question whether I will get there until late in the session, if I do at all. So if you want the Federation represented at the Mayors' Congress, or Convention, you had possibly better elect somebody else. I would suggest Jim Sullivan as a mighty good fellow, who knows the situation in Europe as well as anybody.

Now, I think it would be well for you to write to Duffy and some of the representatives of the Federation in Indianapolis, and get them interested in this matter. There are a number of things in connection with the case there that I would prefer to talk with you about and will make it a point if I get to Philadelphia, but I write this in explanation of my position.[4]

With best wishes, I remain,

Fraternally yours, W D Mahon
International President.

TLS, AFL Microfilm Convention File, reel 27, frames 1214–15, *AFL Records*.

1. SG's letter of Oct. 27, 1914, addressed to W. D. Mahon, John Lennon, and L. D. Bland, informed the three that he had named them AFL delegates to the upcoming conference of American mayors. The meeting, held Nov. 12–14 in Philadelphia, considered policies relating to municipal utilities (reel 187, vol. 199, p. 502, SG Letterbooks, DLC).

2. On Sept. 23, 1914, Judge Albert B. Anderson of the U.S. District Court, District of Indiana, issued a restraining order prohibiting the Amalgamated Association of Street and Electric Railway Employes of America from striking the Indianapolis Traction and Terminal Co. (*Guaranty Trust and Safe Deposit Co.* v. *Mahon et al.*). He reiterated this ruling in a temporary injunction on Oct. 30. The union denied it had intended to strike and appealed the injunction, which was overturned on Jan. 2, 1917, by the Circuit Court of Appeals, Seventh Circuit, on the grounds that a federal court had no jurisdiction in the case (*Mahon et al.* v. *Guaranty Trust and Safe Deposit Co.*, 239 F. 266 [1917]).

3. Albert Baird Cummins (1850–1926) served as Republican governor of Iowa (1902–8) and as a Republican senator from that state (1908–26). On Sept. 1, 1914, he offered an amendment to the Clayton antitrust bill that began with the phrase "the labor of a human being is not a commodity or article of commerce." This statement was subsequently incorporated into the version of the bill passed by Congress (*Congressional Record*, 63d Cong., 2d sess., vol. 51, pt. 14, p. 14546).

4. The 1914 AFL convention adopted a resolution instructing SG and the AFL Executive Council to assist the Street Railway Employes in the case. SG addressed a mass meeting in Indianapolis on the subject on Jan. 4, 1915, and his address was published in the *Union*, an Indianapolis labor paper, on Jan. 8.

To John Fitzpatrick

Oct. 31, 1914.

Mr. John Fitzpatrick,
President, Chicago Federation of Labor,
166 W. Washington St., Chicago, Ill.
Dear Sir and Brother:

Your letter of October 22d[1] received, and I have carefully noted all that you have said in regard to the Chicago Federation of Labor requiring certain local unions to withdraw therefrom.

Copy of your letter will be furnished to the Executive Council of the American Federation of Labor and you may rest assured that anything that can be done will be done.[2] The desire is to protect the rights and the interests of the working people.

There must be some orderly procedure in the American Labor movement if we hope to make it a general organized, crystallized sentiment to protest against wrong and insist upon the rights and the best protection for the labor unions, and particularly for the men employed at daily toil.

You will recall that when the Cigar Makers' International Union raised its dues for the purpose of better protecting the interest of its members in any contest with employers, and for the purpose of further mutual protection, there were a number of local unions which not only protested, but seceded from the International Union, forming what they termed an International Progressive Cigar Makers' Union. The fight lasted for four or five years, and finally the so-called Progressives became part of the International Union.[3] In a few small cities the Progressives held sway. Of course, everything had been done by the general organized labor movement with the encouragement of the A.F. of L. to bring to bear all the pressure possible in order that one international union of the trade be established and maintained, and this as you know has been successful.

If for instance a local union of the Horse Shoers[4] were to disregard and defy the laws of the international union, I take it for granted that as a member of the Horse Shoers International Union you would help to the fullest that the unity of the international union should be maintained; and also that the central body would help to enforce the law or refuse recognition.

I do not want you to imagine for a moment that I underestimate the importance of the statements that you make; on the contrary, I understand their gravity, but in spite of all that has come and gone, that has been done and left undone, we present the most comprehensive and concentrated effort of organized workers, nationally, internationally, and locally, of any movement on the face of the globe.

If we look at this question from a broad comprehensive view point, then I am sure you will agree with me that much as we have cause to regret certain incidents, we have great gratification in the glorious achievements, and a brighter outlook for the future.

Looking forward to meeting you in Philadelphia at the Convention, and with kind regards, I am,

Fraternally yours,   Saml Gompers
President,   American Federation of Labor.

TLpS, reel 187, vol. 199, pp. 580–81, SG Letterbooks, DLC.

1. "From John Fitzpatrick," Oct. 22, 1914, above.

2. On Nov. 7, 1914, SG sent the AFL Executive Council a copy of Fitzpatrick's letter of Oct. 22 (Executive Council Records, Vote Books, reel 13, frame 417, *AFL Records*). The Council considered the matter at its November meeting but decided no action was necessary.

3. For the controversy between the Cigar Makers' International Union and the Cigarmakers' Progressive Union of America, see *The Samuel Gompers Papers*, vol. 1, pp. 247–49, 365–66.

4. Fitzpatrick's union, the International Union of Journeymen HORSESHOERS of the United States and Canada.

Excerpts from Accounts of the 1914 Convention of the AFL in Philadelphia

[November 14, 1914]

. . .

MOTHER JONES'[1] SPEECH.

Horticultural Hall yesterday was the scene of the most remarkable demonstration of a convention which has been replete with demonstrations. "Mother" Jones, "the angel of the miners," who has been the storm center of every strike into which her "boys" have been precipitated for the last two decades made a blood and thunder speech that moved the delegates to tears and inspired an almost continuous acclamation.

Eighty-three years old, this small white-haired woman with a bit of a brogue, threw a power, an eloquence and a stirring appeal into her speech unequaled by any of the men who have addressed the convention.

She came unannounced from the coal fields of Colorado. When Gompers said she was in the rear of the hall, every one turned and as "Mother" came up the center aisle on the arm of Frank Hayes,[2] vice-president of the United Mine Workers of America, each row of delegates she passed stood upon its feet until the entire convention was standing and as she reached the platform a thunder of applause broke.

She reviewed the history of the Colorado, West Virginia and Michigan strikes and "the burning of the children and women at Ludlow." She said: "I could mediate in five days; the investigation has already taken a committee seven months.

"I would tell Rockefeller[3] that he had insulted every citizen in the United States by his treatment of the President's proposal to settle the Colorado strike.[4] I would give him five days to settle and then the United States flag would fly over the mines and the people would own them.

"I would say to Rockefeller," she screamed, "if you are President of the United States we are ready to make war with you. Come on. If I could send the screams of the burning children to Washington and let the President hear them I wonder if that would make him move.

"Are you building palaces on the quivering heap of their bodies? Don't you hear the voices of the children crying who were shot in the trenches by the 'uniformed murderers' and then the oil of John Rockefeller thrown over them to burn them to a crisp?"

DEMAND AID.

"Mother" Jones demanded aid for the men who were indicted in connection with the strike in Michigan and in Colorado.

"Those men in jail," she said, "are the foremost fighters of labor. We cannot permit the Shaws,[5] of Boston, to put our men behind the bars. We will win in Colorado and when I have cleaned the State up I am going out to organize the steel workers.

"I have heard that women are taking a part in the affairs of the nation. What did they do about this? I tell you there is no brutal act committed by a man, but there is a woman more or less responsible for it. If women would put in more time planting the human spirit in the breasts of the young we should not have so many savages as we have to-day."

The speaker said that when she refused to leave Colorado on the order of General Chase,[6] she was thrown into a cellar and spent twenty-six days and nights fighting rats with a beer bottle that had nothing in it.[7]

She charged that Rockefeller had an army of gunmen who were shipped from one part of the country to another as the necessity arose.

Mother Jones told of her interview with Villa.[8] "I had a talk with him," she said. "He's a fine boy. I had $65 that some one gave me for a present and I offered it to him.

"Villa," I said to him, "I want you to come over into our country to kill off some of those people who have crucified women and children—you're needed."

"I'll come," said Villa, "as soon as I am through with these murderers and crucifiers here."

. . .

Philadelphia Press, Nov. 14, 1914.

1. Mary Harris "Mother" JONES was an outspoken advocate in behalf of miners and other workers.

2. Frank HAYES served as vice-president (1910–17) and president (1917–20) of the United Mine Workers of America and represented the union at this convention.

3. At the time of the United Mine Workers' strike, John Davison Rockefeller, Jr. (1874–1960), was director and a major stockholder of the Colorado Fuel and Iron Co.

4. President Woodrow Wilson submitted a proposal for ending the Colorado coal strike to the United Mine Workers and the coal companies on Sept. 5, 1914. The union voted to accept the plan, but Rockefeller and the mine operators rebuffed the president.

5. A reference to the family of Quincy A. Shaw, Jr. Shaw's father was a founder of the Calumet and Hecla Mining Co., and Shaw himself was president of the firm at the time of the 1913–14 Calumet, Mich., copper miners' strike.

6. John Chase, a Denver physician, was adjutant general of the Colorado national guard during the 1913–14 Colorado miners' strike.

7. Mother Jones made at least three attempts in early 1914 to visit striking Colorado miners. On Jan. 4 she was stopped at Trinidad, Colo., and within a few hours deported to Denver. Returning to Trinidad on Jan. 12, she was arrested and held incommunicado until Mar. 15, when she was again deported to Denver. She was stopped a third time, on the morning of Mar. 23, en route to Trinidad and was held for twenty-six days in a cell in the basement of the jail at Walsenburg, Colo.

8. Francisco "Pancho" Villa (1878–1923), a Mexican bandit and revolutionary leader, fought with Francisco Madero to overthrow Porfirio Díaz and with Venustiano Carranza against Victoriano Huerta. Along with Emiliano Zapata he broke with Carranza in late 1914 and was defeated and driven into northern Mexico in 1915. He precipitated American intervention in Mexico—the Punitive Expedition under the command of Brig. Gen. John Pershing—with his raid into New Mexico in March 1916 but evaded the American forces, which withdrew in early 1917.

[November 19, 1914]

RADICAL WING OF LABOR BODY MEETS DEFEAT

The American Federation of Labor took no chances yesterday on indorsing amendments to the Newlands Federal arbitration act that would make the findings of Federal arbitration boards mandatory upon employers.

"We can't force compulsory arbitration upon the employers without tying our own hands," said T. W. McCullough,[1] chairman of the committee on the executive council's report, in a heated afternoon discussion over the arbitration question. Eventually almost the whole convention swung around to his way of thinking.

Mr. McCullough's committee had indorsed the Newlands act. Delegate O'Connor,[2] of the Switchmen's Union, agreed that the Newlands act was good so far as it went, but wanted the Federation to go on record as favoring an amendment which should make the findings of all arbitration boards mandatory upon employers. It took Mr. McCullough and Delegate Andrew Furuseth, of the Seamen's Union,[3] nearly half an hour to convince the O'Connor faction that mandatory legislation usually worked both ways.

"You had better think this over pretty well," cautioned Mr. Furuseth. "Look at what has happened in Canada, Australia, and New Zealand under compulsory arbitration;[4] and remember that the Newlands bill does not take from us the right to strike in extremity. There isn't an employers' association in Maine or California or the Caucasus Mountains that wouldn't jump at the chance to get the upper hand of labor by just such mandatory legislation."

In the end, the committee's indorsement was opposed by the faintest possible murmur of noes.

RADICAL WING DEFEATED

Yesterday's proceedings were chiefly noteworthy for the overwhelming defeat of the convention's radical wing. There was not a murmur of opposition when the "organization by industries" program[5] was smothered with a shout of "ayes," or when the resolution to exclude the fraternal delegates of religious organizations from the convention sessions[6] was over-ruled by President Gompers on technical grounds. The weakness of the radical wing has appeared so plainly in the actual business transactions of the convention, that the conservative delegates now utterly discredit all talk of Socialist opposition to President Gompers in the elections now scheduled for Friday.

. . .

In a brief address, but one of the most striking of the day, President Gompers opposed a proposition to raise his own salary from $5000 to $7500.[7] "When I went as a fraternal delegate to a European Labor Congress in Paris a few years ago,[8] do you know what the most embarrassing charge raised against me was?" he asked. "It was that I, the designated leader of the toilers, the oppressed, the poor of America, was drawing a salary of 25,000 francs. I do not wish to seem over-modest. With the demands that my position places upon me, the money will be welcome. But I can get along on what I have. I do not want any American man or woman to be alienated in sympathies from the American Federation of Labor through any suspicion that the officers of the Federation are receiving more than their due. I say to you in all candor—don't do it!"

SALARIES ARE RAISED.

In spite of the President's objection, the salary was raised by a vote of 150 to 33. Secretary Morrison's salary was raised on the same motion from $4000 to $5000.

. . .

Philadelphia Public Ledger, Nov. 19, 1914.

1. Theodore W. McCullough represented the International Typographical Union.

2. James Bartholomew Connors of Chicago served the Switchmen's Union of North America as national organizer (1902), vice-president (1903–15, 1924–33), and assistant president (1915–24). He also served as a vice-president of the Illinois State Federation of Labor (1919–20, 1922–39).

3. The International SEAMEN's Union of America.

4. The Australian Commonwealth Conciliation and Arbitration Act, enacted in 1904 and subsequently amended, created a court of conciliation and arbitration empowered to prevent or resolve industrial disputes. For the Canadian Industrial Disputes Investigation Act of 1907, see "Excerpts from Testimony before the U.S. Commission on Industrial Relations," Apr. 9, 1914, n. 3, above. For the New Zealand Industrial Conciliation and Arbitration Act of 1894, see *The Samuel Gompers Papers,* vol. 5, pp. 307–8, n. 5.

5. Resolution 28, introduced on Nov. 10, 1914, by delegates Edward Menge and William Mushet of the National Brotherhood of Operative Potters, called for the AFL to organize along industrial rather than craft lines.

6. Resolution 11, introduced on Nov. 10, 1914, by Frederick Wilson of the Milwaukee Federated Trades Council, contained the trades council's instruction to Wilson to oppose the seating of fraternal delegates from religious organizations. The Committee on Resolutions pointed out that such instructions to delegates on how they should

vote were not open to discussion or action by the convention, and SG ruled that Wilson's resolution should never have been accepted for consideration.

7. Resolution 67, introduced on Nov. 11, 1914, by Henry Nolda of the Washington, D.C., Central Labor Union, proposed increases in the salaries of SG and Frank Morrison to $7,500 and $5,000, respectively. After a debate, in which SG and Andrew Furuseth opposed the raises, the convention voted to approve the measure.

8. See *The Samuel Gompers Papers*, vol. 7, pp. 487–89.

[November 20, 1914]

ELEVENTH DAY—FRIDAY NIGHT SESSION

. . .

REPORT OF COMMITTEE ON RESOLUTIONS.

Delegate Frey,[1] secretary of the committee, reported as follows:

Resolutions No. 144 and No. 149 were acted upon together,[2] and the committee has endeavored in its report to announce the policy of the American Federation of Labor.

. . .

The committee offered the following as a substitute for the resolution:

The American Federation of Labor, as in the past, again declares that the question of the regulation of wages and the hours of labor should be undertaken through trade union activity, and not to be made subjects of laws through legislative enactment, excepting in so far as such regulations affect or govern the employment of women and minors, health and morals; and employment by Federal, State or municipal government.

A motion was made and seconded to adopt the recommendation of the committee.

Delegate Taylor,[3] of the Machinists: I am opposed to the recommendation of the committee. The American Federation of Labor went on record, regardless of the interpretation that has been placed upon the resolution passed in Seattle, in favor of and instructing State federations and men belonging to State federations and the labor movement in the different States where the women's eight-hour law had been passed by legislation to immediately enact laws for a general eight-hour day.

. . .

I believe where it is possible to reduce the hours of labor by our organization it is a very good thing to do. The machinists' organization, which I represent, has spent $800,000 in the Northwest since 1910 trying to reduce the hours of labor for the metal trades, and it has not been successful. When this law was placed upon the ballot, or before it was placed upon the ballot,[4] the machinists put an organizer in the field in Washington and paid him a salary to assist in having the law put upon the ballot. After getting 35,000 signatures upon the ballot, one of the main causes of the defeat of that eight-hour measure in Washington was the fact that the statement was circulated that the president of the American Federation of Labor was opposed to legislation for the enactment of an eight-hour law for men.[5] I leave it to this convention whether that is a fact.

This report . . . of the Seattle proceedings of the convention of 1913 will bear out the statement I make. This is the report of the Committee on Shorter Workday: . . . "Where women's eight-hour laws already exist an agitation should immediately begin for the enactment of general eight-hour laws."

The president of the American Federation of Labor, in speaking before the Resolutions Committee, stated that that meant Government employes, or State employes, or something of that kind. This is not a report of any Government committee, any Federal committee or State body committee; it is the report of a committee acting on the shorter workday in the industries of this country. As a result of the interpretation placed upon that law by the president of the American Federation of Labor, all of the manufacturers' associations, all of the leaders of the employers in the State of Washington, where they have thrown mud and dirt at all representatives of the American Federation of Labor and all representatives of any organization affiliated with this body—all leaders of this movement from the bottom up—used this statement to the detriment of the men and women in the State of Washington and other States on the Pacific coast to defeat that law.

I have here a poster that was put up all over the State of Washington. I wish to read it. . . . The poster got out by the Manufacturers' Association of the State of Washington and by the Metal Trades in the State of Washington, that the machinists' organization spent hundreds of thousands of dollars to force them to give the eight-hour day, said: "President Gompers, of the American Federation of Labor, denounces a compulsory eight-hour law, Initiative Measure No. 13. He says that if there were a movement to establish an eight-hour day and a minimum wage he would oppose such policies. Mr. Gompers ought to know, and he does know, and every intelligent laboring man knows, a compulsory eight-hour day will increase living expenses and hurt the laborer more than anything else. Mr. Laborer, do you want eight hours instead of ten, and maybe lose your job altogether? Do you want to quit having overtime? Your employer cannot give you overtime under this law." And there are thousands of unemployed men in the State of Washington and no one should be allowed to work one minute overtime. "Can you pay higher prices for all you eat and wear and still support your family on eight hours a day and no overtime?"

I want to show you the extent to which the manufacturers' and employers' associations went in the States on the Pacific coast to prevent the law from passing. If we are going out to work for the initiative and referendum law, if we are going to spend our time and money and energy going out and speaking for the initiative and referendum, then let us use that to get those laws that will benefit organized labor and unorganized labor as well. . . .

. . .

Delegate Frey, secretary of the committee: The question raised by the committee's report is not one of an eight-hour or of a shorter workday, but is instead the announcement of the policy of the American trade-union movement as to how we will endeavor to secure a shorter workday. There are but two methods of securing conditions that affect our lives as workers. One is through legislation, State and Federal, and the other through the activities of our trade-union organization. The policy of the American trade-union movement in the regulation of wages, in the regulation of the other terms of employment, has always been to endeavor to secure them through the strength of our unions and through negotiations with employers.

The experience of our movement and of trade-union organizations in Europe has led the American trade-union movement to believe that is the most effective and that it is the safest method of procedure. We have tried in this country, as workingmen have endeavored to do in others, to secure through legislation a guarantee that our rights to organization and to trade-union effort should not be interfered with. That has been one form of legislation which the trade-union movement has most heartily and effectively applied. We have endeavored through legislative enactment to have our rights as freemen guaranteed so that we could then apply our trade-union method to regulate the terms of employment.

There are workmen in this country and in other countries who do not believe the trade-union method is most effective and they have placed their reliance upon the legislative method; and it is the results that have followed their efforts to establish a regulation of wages and hours of labor that have convinced the trades unionists that it is not a safe method. . . .

. . .

Is there anywhere in the experience of our industry, in the experience of workmen organized into trade unions, where they have ever secured anything determining the terms of labor for themselves through legislative enactment that it did not return as a boomerang, that it did not establish the machinery that gave the courts an opportunity to render decisions that created an obstacle in the path of the movement it required years to overcome? Only eighteen years ago that wonderful system was adopted in Australia and New Zealand. The men there are about as well organized as in any of our countries. Although they control the Parliament at the present time, they have been unable to repeal any legislation they enacted and have since discovered [that they have] only put brass bands around their movement they could not burst, and have held them backward instead of allowing them to go forward.

It is not a question of an eight-hour day, a shorter workday, but the method our trade-union movement is going to sanction that will be used to regulate and determine the conditions under which we are going to work for our employers.

. . .

Delegate Germer,[6] of the United Mine Workers: . . . I am surprised to hear it said in a convention of the American Federation of Labor, which is supposed to be the cream of intelligence and enlightenment of the American labor movement, that it is unsafe to ask a maximum workday by legislation. If it is unsafe to get an eight-hour workday by legislation it is unsafe to get an anti-injunction law or have a law passed declaring that the working class really has become human. If it is safe and desirable that we pay lobbying committees at Washington, that we pay committees in our different State Legislatures to beg for laws in the interests of the common people, if it is safe to ask for legislation of that nature, I want to know why it is not safe to ask for legislation regulating the hours a human being shall work?

. . .

If it is really unsafe, if that is the truth, then there is something wrong with our Government, with our political authority, with our executive officials and with our judicial branch of the Government. And if there is something wrong with them, and they are elected, then there is something wrong with the working class in the use of the ballot. They elect the legislators, the executive officers, the legislative officers, the judicial officers, and if legislation is unsafe in their hands it is time the working people stop knifing the political party that uses its funds, its press and its efforts to elect proper representatives.

We come here representing the organized trade-union movement of America, and I want to say that if the real rank and file, the men in the shops, the mills, the factories and the mines, were here and witnessed this farce comedy that has been going on for the last several days, they would clear out the whole bunch and reorganize the American Federation of Labor. I have heard considerable of the conventions of the American Federation of Labor. I am not speaking for popular sentiment, but this fact remains undisputed—you can ridicule it, you can cast odium upon it if you will—but the fact, nevertheless, remains that the organized trade-union movement of the United States is not using its energy, is not using its power, in the interests of labor. We have become an adjunct to the capitalist political machines, and instead of electing working people, men of our own rank, we elect "our friends" and then take hat in hand and go and beg legislation from them, and say legislation is not safe in the hands of those we elect!

I am willing to leave the eight-hour day to the legislatures; I am willing to leave it to Congress. It is easier to be a friend of the workingman than to be a workingman, and "our friends," whom we endorse and put into the legislative departments of our government—I want the legislation left in their hands, that we may see what our friends are doing with the interests of the working people of this country. If it is wrong to legislate for an eight-hour day and say no one shall work more than that, I again say it is unsafe to ask for anti-injunction bills to be passed by our Congress and our State Legislature; they say it is unsafe. But to leave it to the economic organizations[—]we ought to join the I.W.W.s and the syndicalists, and say, "To the devil with the laws!" We ought to go to sabotage and take direct action. They have no confidence in the Legislatures; they say it is unsafe. . . .

. . .

You leave legislation alone and say it is dangerous. John D. Rockefeller thinks it is pretty safe, because he goes after legislation. The Vanderbilts and Goulds and Wall street think legislation is pretty safe because it is in their hands. If we get our men into office and use our political strength and political unity along with our economic unity we would not need to come here and say that eight hours by legislation is unsafe. I am not afraid of losing anything if Congress passes an eight-hour law; in fact, it will give us added strength and prestige; we can appeal to the public, and if the employers force us on strike to enforce a law, if that is necessary as a last resort, we can go before the public and prove that our enemy is a violator of the law.

But if we have no law on the statute books we have no basis except our economic strength, and probably the merits of our argument, and the merit of our logic does not appeal to "John the Baptist"; it does not appeal to the Goulds and the Vanderbilts; it is force you want, not only force on the economic field, but along with that the political force, the political unity of the working class along working class lines.

. . .

[Delegate Gallagher:][7] I hope this will be borne in mind—and it is not a threat in any sense, but in every sense is true—that the effort to keep your men within the fold, and you international officers ought to remember this, that the effort to keep a good many of your men in the fold in the Western States, is tremendously hard. Just why that is so some of us have never been able to ascertain, except that it is this: That a man living in a country not surfeited with things and not surrounded by so many things as in the Eastern cities likes to move in the most direct way to get what he wants. He lives in a country that has not removed very far from the direct stage of things, and he wants to move, and move as fast as he can, to the thing he wants.

I believe, and I believe it frankly, and I believe it as a result of having been up and down the coast and into the States of Arizona, New Mexico, Oregon and all those States in that part of the country, that there is growing a division—it may be only nebulous now; it may be only veiled—but there is growing a division between the views of the Western workers and the Eastern workers as represented in these conventions. And you want to send the delegates of the West back and say the American Federation of Labor has said in convention, "In so far as you try to enact a legal workday for other than Government employes or women and children you are wrong and your efforts must cease. . . ."

. . .

President Gompers: I realize the difficulty of the effort to burn gunpowder the second time. Yesterday I was before the Committee on Resolutions upon the resolution now before the convention and upon which the committee has made the report. Perhaps I would not have done that had it not been for the fact that, either directly or indirectly, intentionally or otherwise, the resolution reflected upon my conduct. I wish I could make the speech over again I made yesterday, because I am sure it was more persuasive than any one I can make now.

. . .

I want to use just an old doggerel, and it has no reflection upon any delegate to this convention, but it seems to me as an abstract proposition it is good—that "Fools rush in where angels fear to tread." We have been asked, or advised, to go for all the laws we can get. Save the workingmen of America from such a proposition! There are numbers of laws we can get, but prudence and defense of the rights and the liberties of the toilers are much more important than the effort to secure all the laws we can get. There are some men who fail to understand this one thing, that the labor movement of America is still in its infancy, and that in the cycle of time fifty or a hundred years count as but a minute.

The question of what was law and what was the interpretation of law, and what was the administration of law, so far as they governed labor— it is only within the past half century that there has been any effort to take the grip of tyrannical Government from the throat of labor. It is less than a month ago the Congress of the United States declared that the labor of a human being is not a commodity or article of commerce. It required a third of a century to work for the accomplishment of this one declaration, and in spite of that, one of the delegates said: "Why, pass such a law as the maximum eight-hour law and no court would dare to enforce anything like compelling men to work eight hours or more." Is that so? Since the passage of the labor provision in the Clayton bill, signed by the President of the United States, the ink upon that act scarcely dry, a Federal Judge, Judge Anderson, sitting in Indianapolis, has issued an injunction forbidding the men of labor to quit their work. . . .

. . .

One delegate said, "Why, if you are opposed to the eight-hour workday for men by law, did you ask for a law regulating and limiting injunctions?" And it discloses the gentleman's discernment of actual facts! In the law to limit and regulate injunctions we propose to clip the power of the court in so far as labor is concerned, and in an eight-hour law for men it is to give the courts still greater power than they now have. Is there no difference? It is a fact, admitted not only by lawyers, but by every thinking, earnest labor man, that once you give a court jurisdiction over any matter the court will find a way to exercise that jurisdiction. Place it in the power of the courts to take jurisdiction, to assume jurisdiction, to acquire jurisdiction, or to have jurisdiction accredited to them, and they will leave no stone unturned to exercise it to the detriment of the men and women of labor, who, after all, in all times have been compelled to suffer the tyranny and oppression of an oligarchy, under whatever name it might be known.

. . .

Let me say to you, friends, I think it is a safe thing to assume, and it is generally regarded as safe, that the idea which any one advocates is predicated on that which he sees in its favor. Now, I am not going to quote anybody who is against this proposition, but I am going to call your attention to what the advocates of this measure say in regard to it. I hold in my hand a pamphlet. I have it from the gentlemen who favor this legislation that the pamphlet was got out by the Eight-hour League, those who were the sponsors and those who are carrying on the campaign for the enactment of this measure.

Delegate Scharrenberg:[8] In one State only?

President Gompers: Yes, that is true—in the State of Washington. I am very glad that at least without so openly declaring, Brother Scharrenberg and I share the shame that any men calling themselves labor men would issue a pamphlet of this character.

Delegate Scharrenberg: I am not responsible for it, Brother Gompers.

President Gompers: I am glad you disavow it. I would be glad to hear the representatives from Washington disavow it.

Delegate Brown:[9] None of the labor people were primarily responsible for issuing that. They selected a committee from the Central Labor Council, put it in charge and the committee issued the pamphlet.

. . .

President Gompers: . . . Early last week these pamphlets were on the table in front of every delegate. They were distributed as part of an educational campaign among we benighted trade unionists, so that we might be convinced of the error of our ways. They did not put one on my desk, but passing along I happened to see this picture on the title page. You cannot all see it now, but I will pass it around so that you can. There are two pictures. One of them, below, is a ballot box, beautifully carved, with a padlock. On the top is what is described as a strike scene, and the strike scene is in an industrial town with factories and chimneys all in flames; workmen en masse engaged in conflict with the militia; some wounded lying around; some women and children on the side looking on and apparently bewailing the whole scene. That is the idea of the proposers of this measure as to what constitutes a strike and a strike scene!

Delegate Gallagher: Pardon me for interrupting, but when the president uses the term "proposers" I don't know whether he means the advocates of the eight-hour law. You can't tie me up with the Reds any way you try.

President Gompers: I am glad, because so long as that condition prevails you are safe. But I warn you as a friend that unless a man is well grounded in his understanding of the history and philosophy of the trade-union movement, the subtlety of the sophistry is very dangerous to honest men. I venture to say that not the worst enemy of labor, the National Association of Manufactures, the Erectors' Association, with Dan Davenport and Walter Drew, ever painted a picture of a strike scene more lurid and more untruthful than was published in this pamphlet.

Delegate Germer: Ludlow.

President Gompers: I will say a picture of Ludlow. The worst conditions that could be conceived are described by those who advocate a labor measure as a typical strike scene.

Delegate Germer: That is true, absolutely.

President Gompers: Of course, from a man who describes this convention of the American Federation of Labor as a farce, I should prefer to get some confirmation as to what he says is true. This pamphlet is: "An Eight-hour Day by Strike or Ballot—Which?" As if they were the only alternatives—strike or ballot. I venture to say that the eight-hour workday has been enforced and introduced in more trades and industries without strike than with strike, and even if it should be a strike, it ill becomes the men of labor to publish a picture of this character and say it is a typical strike scene, and urge the men to work for an eight-hour workday law rather than to go on strike. There are some people who don't know really that, after all, even in a strike, there is developed more character and more independence and more intelligence and more cogent solidarity among the working people in a short time than in any other movement of which you can conceive.

Delegate Germer: And more shot.

President Gompers: There are some people who can never stop their tongues wagging, though their minds stand still!

Delegate Germer: I perfectly agree with you.

Delegate Daly, of the Metal Polishers:[10] Can't we have a truce while we gather up the wounded?

President Gompers: I call your attention to what is stated in this pamphlet—"Which Way? Ballots or Strike?" I agree there is so much one can say in regard to this, because though superficially it may appear it is simply a matter of difference of judgment and difference of opinion, it is not a difference of opinion. If we can get an eight-hour law for the working people, then you will find that the working people themselves will fail to have any interest in your economic organization, which even the advocates declare is essential in order that such a law can be enforced.

Why, it is with considerable difficulty you can make non-union workingmen understand that it is only about twenty years ago that the old "pluck-me" stores were found generally; when you had to board with the employer or where the employer directed; when barbers had to live with their employers or they could get no jobs, and single life among them was the rule because they had to live with their employers. It is a difficult thing, I venture to say, for the officers and organizers of the barbers to get the young workmen in their trade to realize that that was a fact.

In the mining industry, I cannot for the life of me understand how and why the United Mine Workers' delegates can consistently advocate the doing by law that which they did themselves. In my own trade—I speak of my own experience and used the statement yesterday before the committee—in my own trade it is difficult to make the cigarmakers of to-day understand that at one time the tenement-house system prevailed to such an extent that the entire trade practically was operated under that system. It is difficult to make young men in my trade understand that at one time the men would work from early morning until late at night. And in 1886 we established the eight-hour day for every union cigarmaker on the North American continent. It is difficult to make these young men understand, these men to whom we shall have to at last yield this movement, and it is only by helping to keep our heads erect, to keep the movement going on, and on, and on, in a logical, sequential and naturally developed order, so that the ranks of organized labor may be augmented, moving forward and preaching the gospel of unity and self-help and mutual help, mutual responsibility to bear each others' burdens, and not to mimic and mock and repeat the abuses and the misrepresentation of what is underlying the great labor movement of our time.

If we keep our heads, if we move along the charted road, we will make progress and have no setbacks; we will continue to grow in numbers, in influence, in the confidence of our fellows, deserving as well as earning the respect of our fellow-citizens, and constantly as we grow make our impression upon the public conscience. It is not to-day so much political statesmanship which is required; it is the industrial, humanitarian statesmanship which the times demand of us.

Upon motion, debate was closed.

. . .

ROLLCALL ON REPORT OF COMMITTEE ON RESOLUTIONS 144 [AND] 149.

Ayes . . . 11,237 votes.
Nays . . . 8,107 votes.
Not Voting . . . 607 votes.

. . .

AFL, *Proceedings*, 1914, pp. 421–25, 427–28, 433–34, 439–44.

1. John Frey represented the Iron Molders' Union of North America at the convention.

2. Resolutions 144 and 149 were introduced on Nov. 12, 1914, the former by Paul Scharrenberg of the California State Federation of Labor (FOL) and the latter by James Taylor of the International Association of Machinists, J. G. Brown of the International Union of Timberworkers, and Harley Hughes of the Washington State FOL. Resolution 144 called for a reaffirmation of the Federation's 1913 declaration that state federations of labor should "work unceasingly" to enact laws limiting the hours of women and children to eight per day and no more than forty-eight per week and then "immediately" turn to "agitation . . . for the enactment of general eight-hour laws" (AFL, *Proceedings*, 1913, p. 285). The convention readopted the 1913 statement on Nov. 17, as part of the report of the Committee on the Shorter Workday (AFL, *Proceedings*, 1914, pp. 340–41). Resolution 149 endorsed "the direct-legislation method of shortening the workday" wherever state federations of labor thought the strategy "desirable and expedient" (AFL, *Proceedings*, 1914, p. 421).

3. James A. TAYLOR was a member of International Association of Machinists 79 of Seattle.

4. Initiative No. 13, which provided for an eight-hour workday in Washington State, was defeated at the polls on Nov. 3, 1914, by a two-to-one vote.

5. During his testimony before the U.S. Commission on Industrial Relations on May 22, 1914, SG stated that the AFL opposed establishing an eight-hour workday through legislation except for government workers, women, and minors (see "Excerpts from Testimony before the U.S. Commission on Industrial Relations," May 22, 1914, above). An abstract of SG's testimony was printed in the *American Federationist* in July and August 1914 under the title "The American Labor Movement: Its Makeup, Achievements, and Aspirations" (21: 537–48, 621–35) and was also published as a pamphlet under the same title (Washington, D.C., [1914]).

6. Adolph F. GERMER served as an organizer for the United Mine Workers of America (1913–14) and national secretary of the Socialist Party of America (1916–19).

7. Andrew Gallagher represented the San Francisco Labor Council at this convention.

8. Paul Scharrenberg represented the California State FOL.

9. J. G. BROWN of Seattle was president of and a delegate from the International Union of Timberworkers.

10. Timothy M. DALY was president of the METAL Polishers', Buffers', Platers', and Brass and Silver Workers' Union of North America and represented the union at this convention.

[November 21, 1914]

. . .

After spending the day in adjusting bitter jurisdiction quarrels between international unions, the convention of the American Federation of Labor yesterday rejected a plan submitted for eliminating these fights from future conventions.

James O'Connell,[1] chairman of the adjustment committee, proposed that a permanent board of mediation and conciliation be established by the American Federation to deal with jurisdiction disputes all through the year instead of having them unloaded by the score on every annual convention. He advocated a permanent board of three.

"As it is now," he said, "delegates come here with blood in their eyes and war in their hearts, some of them so bitter that it is impossible for them even to speak civilly to their fellow-delegates.

"The quicker we get at these grievances and sit down to reason with the contending parties the better. The longer you let these grievances drag along the more bitter and unreasonable both sides become. You may reject the idea submitted by the adjustment committee. But you will come back to it. Some day you will have to do something to wipe out these internal fights, to put a stop to the wire-pulling in the conventions by men who are out hunting for votes in favor of their sides in a quarrel.

"You can't settle disputes permanently in that way. We are wasting entirely too much of our strength in these jurisdiction quarrels which very often are inspired by employers who want to keep your power divided or by men paid by employers to go among you and create these never-ending dissensions."

PLAN VIGOROUSLY OPPOSED

Opposition to O'Connell's plan for ending the wasteful internal, factional disputes sprung up from all directions.

Andrew Furuseth, of the seamen's union, feared that the establishment of a permanent board of mediation and conciliation within the American Federation would furnish congress with a precedent for forcing compulsory arbitration on the unions.

Several other delegates expressed fears that a permanent commission might strip their organizations of some of their freedom of action, and it was finally decided to lay the matter over for a year, the executive council of the American Federation in the meantime to investigate the subject and report[2] to the next annual convention.

. . .

Philadelphia North American, Nov. 21, 1914.

1. James O'Connell represented the International Association of Machinists at the convention.

2. The AFL Executive Council reported to the Federation's 1915 convention that it considered such a board to be impractical and out of harmony with the voluntary spirit in which the AFL addressed jurisdictional disputes. The convention endorsed this position.

[November 22, 1914]

GOMPERS ELECTED HEAD OF A.F. OF L. WITHOUT CONTEST

By an almost unanimous vote Samuel Gompers was re-elected president of the American Federation of Labor in the last official session of the convention yesterday. The organized opposition of the socialistic element to his candidacy crumbled into a mere semblance of the force it had shown during the last week. They submitted without even attempting to nominate their own candidate.

The election, coming as it did upon the heels of the battle on Friday night over the enactment of an eight-hour law, in which Gompers triumphed in a brilliant fashion, indicated a complete surrender by the radicals. Only after Gompers took his seat again as president did a dozen Socialists who had kept silent during the nomination rise to place themselves on record as voting against Gompers.[1]

. . .

All of the officers representing the American Federation of Labor last year were re-elected. . . .[2]

The next convention will be held in San Francisco, beginning on the second Monday in November, 1915. There was no opposition to this, and the motion was carried unanimously.

. . .

At least two dozen resolutions were introduced condemning the war in Europe. All these were adopted by the convention. In this mass of resolutions only one urged the delegates to approve of the war. A member of the Seamen's Union, Andrew Furuseth, was responsible for this.[3] He defended it by saying that European nations had their problems to solve, problems which we in the United States could not understand, and that the best way to solve them was by war. His resolution was rejected.

Samuel Gompers offered a resolution in favor of calling an international meeting of the representatives of organized labor after the war to discuss action for permanent peace, which was unanimously accepted.[4] Mr. Gompers proposed that the convention meet in the United States.

. . .

Philadelphia Public Ledger, Nov. 22, 1914.

1. For those voting against SG, see AFL, *Proceedings,* 1914, p. 458.

2. The officers elected by the convention to serve during the following year were SG, president; James Duncan, James O'Connell, Denis Hayes, Joseph Valentine, John Alpine, Henry Perham, Frank Duffy, and William Green, first through eighth vice-presidents; Frank Morrison, secretary; and John Lennon, treasurer.

3. Resolution 97, introduced on Nov. 12, 1914, by Andrew Furuseth of the International Seamen's Union of America, argued that since the world war was caused primarily by the desire of the Balkan peoples for unification and self-determination and the aspiration of workers for a more equitable share of the fruits of their labor, the AFL should not take sides in the conflict or call prematurely for peace. It expressed hope for "new national boundaries, which shall be based on racial and lingual affinity, new opportunities for self-expression to those of the human family who feel themselves to be one and an improved social and industrial system that shall permit and foster a truer equality, a broader freedom, a higher justice and therefore a more lasting peace" (AFL, *Proceedings,* 1914, p. 287). The resolution was referred to the Committee on International Relations, which recommended nonconcurrence. After some debate, the convention voted against the resolution on Nov. 21.

4. Resolution 104, introduced by SG on Nov. 12, 1914, and adopted by the convention on Nov. 21, expressed sympathy to the organized labor movements in Europe, called for the continuation of fraternal relations with them, and authorized the AFL Executive Council to organize an international labor conference after the war in conjunction with the peace conference. On Dec. 10 SG sent copies of the resolution to the national trade union centers in Europe, Turkey, South Africa, Australia, New Zealand, Argentina, Brazil, and Japan (AFL Microfilm Convention File, reel 27, frame 2082, *AFL Records*). He reported to the 1915 AFL convention that he had received favorable replies from France, South Africa, and Melbourne and a negative response from Germany. For the German reply, see "From Carl Legien," Apr. 2, 1915, below.

Abraham Miller[1] to Samuel Gompers and Frank Morrison

[November 1914]

Dear Sirs & Bros:

We received yours of the 16th inst.,[2] telling us "that some misrepresentation has been made in regard to the personnel of the officers of The United Garment Workers of America," and directing us "that all communications and remittances for The United Garment Workers of America should be forwarded to Mr. B. A. Larger."[3]

In reply we beg to state that we fail to understand how you took it upon yourself to direct us to make remittances to Mr. B. A. Larger, when you refused to give our delegates a hearing at the Convention at Philadelphia, and denied them an opportunity to explain our case to the delegates. The convention also rejected a proposition to appoint a committee to make an investigation.[4]

Local No. 2[5] is one of the largest and best organized Locals in the United Garment Workers of America, paying its per capita regularly all the time, yet its delegates were physically driven out from the U.G.W. of A. convention at the Capitol, Nashville, Tennessee, under the direction of Rickert and Larger. The same treatment was accorded to delegates from many other tailor and cutter locals, representing an overwhelming majority of the membership, and all those delegates were forced to continue the Convention at another place.

This and a good many other matters we desired to put before the A.F. of L. convention, but you refused to hear our representatives. You chose to ignore the membership and stand by those who wrongfully claim to be our officers. We, however, stand by the membership and repudiate Rickert and Larger, as usurpers.

We recognize Sidney Hillman[6] as General President and Joseph Schlossberg[7] as General Secretary of The United Garment Workers of America, and will forward our communications and remittances to them.

Respectfully yours,

TLc, Amalgamated Clothing Workers of America Papers, Labor-Management Documentation Center, NIC.

1. Abraham Miller was a member of United Garment Workers of America 8 (Pants Makers) of New York City and, in December 1914, a founder of the Amalgamated Clothing Workers of America. He served as a member of the Clothing Workers' executive board (1920–63) and as secretary-treasurer of the union's New York joint board (1924–63).

2. SG to Locals of the United Garment Workers of America, Nov. 16, 1914, reel 187, vol. 199, p. 842, SG Letterbooks, DLC.

3. Bernard A. LARGER served as secretary of the Garment Workers from 1904 to 1928.

4. The 1914 AFL convention refused to seat delegates from the seceding faction of the Garment Workers or give them an opportunity to explain their position. It also rejected resolution 41, proposed by delegates of the International Ladies' Garment Workers' Union, to appoint a committee to investigate and attempt to resolve the dispute.

5. Garment Workers' local 2 (Basters) of New York City.

6. Sidney HILLMAN served as president of the Clothing Workers from 1914 until his death in 1946.

7. Joseph SCHLOSSBERG served as secretary (from 1920, secretary-treasurer) of the Clothing Workers from 1914 until 1940.

To Paul Mazur[1]

December 7, 1914.

Mr. Paul N. Mazur,
[c/o] Miner Chipman,
Problems of Management, Harvard Square, Cambridge, Mass.
Dear Sir:

Your favor of November 30 to hand, and contents noted. You ask—"What is the fundamental objection of Unionism (organized labor) to Scientific Management?"

Replying to same, I wish to say that organized labor stands, first, for men instead of for things. The labor of a human being is not a commodity, article of commerce, or a machine, to be geared up, oiled, speeded and driven at the pleasure of a master to accomplish a task. A machine is an inanimate thing, it has no life, no brain, no sentiment, no spirit, no place in the order of society. Profit mongers have tried to place the labor of a human being in the same order and under the same classification, but organized labor contends and insists upon society recognizing the fact that a working man or working woman is a living, moving, social being with high spiritual attainments, entitled to all the rights, all the privileges, all the opportunities, all the duties of responsible citizens, and entitled to and insistent upon receiving the same respectful consideration given to other elements of society. A working man would be less than a man if he did not resent the introduction of any bestial system which calculates to deal with him in the same way as a beast of burden or an inanimate cog in the wheel of a machine.

We intend to root the Taylor system out of the Watertown Arsenal and to stop its introduction in any other Federal department where men and women are engaged as employes. We will also do our best to prevent the spread of any form of stop watch, speeding up systems of labor, miscalled "Scientific Management," and wherever it is in operation we will do our best as rapidly as we can to remove its evil and degrading influences.

Yours very truly,   Saml Gompers.
President,   American Federation of Labor.

TLpS, reel 188, vol. 200, pp. 203–4, SG Letterbooks, DLC.

1. Paul Myer Mazur was employed at this time by efficiency engineer Miner Chipman. He later established himself as an authority on retailing and as an investment banker with Lehman Brothers.

To Tom Quelch[1]

December 15, 1914.

Mr. T. Quelch,
Hamilton House, Bidborough Street, London, W.C., England.
Dear Sir and Brother:

Your favor of November 18 to hand, asking me for literature concerning the various strike-breaking gunmen organizations in the United States, who employ the Labor Spy system.

There are several concerns in the United States operating various schemes, sometimes as detective agencies, others as employment agencies, and some that are bold enough to advertise among employers the exact purpose of their ventures. These concerns operate under the same name in various cities, and others operate under various names in various cities, but still under one centralized control. I enclose herewith a list of same.

The chief of all these institutions, however, is the National Association of Manufacturers. This concern was thoroughly exposed in a recent Congressional investigation[2] of it. I send you, under separate cover, copies of the House hearings,[3] also copy of statement[4] issued by the American Federation of Labor on that investigation, also copies of the *American Federationist* for the months of January, 1909, March, 1909, and May, 1909, which contain special articles[5] by myself upon the Turner and similar detective agencies—all of which will furnish you detailed information.

With regards to the so-called Industrial Workers of the World, I send you a copy of a report[6] containing a Federal investigation of a strike among the Textile Workers at Lawrence, Massachusetts, in which the I.W.W. obtained considerable notoriety.

The I.W.W. started in Chicago in 1905. There are now two "parties," each calling itself the simon pure, original I.W.W. Both parties combined have an officially declared membership of less than 17,000. Their career has been spectacular and injurious to the interests of the working people, and if the name of organized labor of America has not been brought into disrepute among the workers, as well as among the general public, it is due to no failure on the part of the so-called I.W.W. to make it so.

At times the I.W.W. has given our affiliated organizations some annoyance, but taking it as a whole, we have found the best policy to pursue was to ignore them. They thrive on the slightest recognition and make the greatest possible capital out of any overtures on the part of the bona fide organizations. To sum it up, it is a species of emotionalism which is bound to arise as a result of the relentless and unscrupulous hostility fostered by the Manufacturers' Association against the rational, normal, collective action on the part of the naturally developed organization of the working people—the trade union movement—with its adherence to the principle and the policy of unity, solidarity and fraternity as expressed by the American Federation of Labor.

I hope that this may be of service, and if there is any further information I can convey, I shall be glad to respond upon request.

With best wishes for you and your associates in this, your hour of extreme trials and difficulties, I remain, with much esteem,

Fraternally yours,   Saml Gompers.
President,   American Federation of Labor.

TLpS, reel 188, vol. 200, pp. 687–89, SG Letterbooks, DLC.

1. Tom Quelch was a leader of the British Socialist party (after 1920, the Communist Party of Great Britain).

2. In 1913 and 1914 committees of the U.S. Senate and House of Representatives held hearings on lobbying activities, particularly those of the National Association of Manufacturers. See "Excerpts from Testimony before the Select Committee on Lobby Investigation of the U.S. House of Representatives," Sept. 11, 1913, above.

3. U.S. Congress, House, *Charges against Members of the House and Lobby Activities of the National Association of Manufacturers of the United States and Others. Hearings before the Select Committee of the House of Representatives Appointed under House Resolution 198,* 63d Cong., 1st sess., 1913.

4. *National Association of Manufacturers Exposed . . .* (Washington, D.C., [1913?]).

5. SG is referring to three editorials published in the *American Federationist* in 1909: "Labor 'Secrets' Exposed," "Turner, Van Cleave's Detective, Exposed," and "Van Cleave Unmasked" (16: 49–52, 230–31, 457–59).

6. *Report on Strike of Textile Workers in Lawrence, Mass., in 1912* (Washington, D.C., 1912), prepared by the U.S. Bureau of Labor.

To Jane Addams[1]

Jan. 9, 1915

Miss Jane Addams,
New Willard Hotel, Washington, D.C.
My dear Miss Addams:

As I stated to you in my telegram of December 30th[2] I would do, I submitted[3] to my colleagues of the Executive Council of the American Federation of Labor, the request contained in your letter of December 23d,[4] for two women representatives of the American Federation of Labor to be appointed to participate in the meeting of representative women's organizations which will be held in this city next Sunday, January 10, "to consider the organization of a national peace committee of women."[5] I also submitted to my colleagues of the Executive Council copy of the printed tentative program which you sent to me.[6] I am now writing to advise you that the Executive Council is of the opinion that inasmuch as the propositions contained in your tentative plan are entirely out of harmony with the declaration upon the subject of international war and peace made by the last annual convention of the American Federation of Labor, held in Philadelphia, Pa., November 9–21, 1914, that compliance with your request would not be feasible or permissible.

The Executive Council in its report to the Philadelphia convention, dealt at length with the subject of international war and peace.[7] Copy of that portion of the report is enclosed herein. There is also enclosed copy of the report and recommendation of the committee to which this subject was referred and as adopted by the convention,[8] together with copies of three resolutions[9] upon the subject, submitted to the convention, and the action of the convention thereon.

You may rest assured that every action and effort will be exerted and every influence utilized for the purpose of bringing about peace among the contending European nations, with the hope of permanent peace founded upon justice, freedom and humanity.

Very truly yours, Saml Gompers.
President, American Federation of Labor.

TLpS, reel 189, vol. 201, pp. 177–78, SG Letterbooks, DLC.

1. Jane Addams (1860–1935), the founder of Hull-House in Chicago in 1889, was an advocate of a wide variety of social and labor reforms. She was a founder of the National Child Labor Committee (1904) and the National Association for the Advancement of Colored People (1909), president of the National Conference of Charities and Correction (1909), vice-president of the National American Woman Suffrage Association (1911–14), and president of the National Federation of Settlements (1911–35).

Devoted to the cause of peace, she helped organize and was elected chair of the Woman's Peace party in January 1915 and in April of that year was made president of the International Congress of Women at The Hague. Addams later served as president of the Women's International League for Peace and Freedom (1919–29), and in 1931 she was corecipient, with Nicholas Murray Butler, of the Nobel Peace Prize.

2. SG to Addams, Dec. 30, 1914, reel 188, vol. 200, p. 940, SG Letterbooks, DLC.

3. SG to the AFL Executive Council, Jan. 2, 1915, Executive Council Records, Vote Books, reel 13, frame 449, *AFL Records.*

4. Executive Council Records, Vote Books, reel 13, frame 450, *AFL Records.*

5. A two-day conference held in Washington, D.C., Jan. 10–11, 1915, organized the Woman's Peace party with Addams as chair.

6. Executive Council Records, Vote Books, reel 13, frames 451–53, *AFL Records.*

7. For the AFL Executive Council's report on the subject of "International War and Peace" and the action of the Committee on International Relations, to which it was referred, see AFL, *Proceedings,* 1914, pp. 48–49, 471. The convention approved the Council's report and ordered that it be printed as a pamphlet.

8. The report of the Committee on International Relations, which was approved by the convention, concluded: "We declare that war and its attendant horrors, want, privation, misery, suffering and death, fall most heavily upon the workers, and that in this present European war as well as in any which may follow, we hope for speedy peace— peace with honor and justice. While an expression of deep sympathy is extended to our fellow trade unionists embroiled in the present war with its awful carnage, for the making of which they are not responsible, let us not forget that sordid greed which profits by lack of proper safeguards, sanitation, low wages, etc., here as elsewhere on the industrial field and in transportation, takes more human lives, maims more human beings, causes more sickness, want and privation than have resulted from any previous war or may result from this war. The trade-union movement stands for honorable peace between nations and is the greatest force for the protection and the advancement of the best interests of the workers in the economic field of endeavor and must not be subordinated, neglected or forgotten. We stand for honorable peace on the economic field, but we demand justice as the fundamental condition for all progress. If denied we hold ourselves in readiness to fight for justice. When justice is established, peace will follow" (AFL, *Proceedings,* 1914, pp. 475–76).

9. Resolution 24, which was adopted, called for a prompt and just end to the conflict. For resolutions 97 and 104, see "Gompers Elected Head of A.F. of L. without Contest," Nov. 22, 1914, nn. 2–3, in "Excerpts from Accounts of the 1914 Convention of the AFL in Philadelphia," Nov. 14–22, 1914, above.

From John O'Hara[1]

Danbury, Conn. January 14, 1915.

Dear Sir & Brother:—

I am in receipt of your favor of the 11th. inst.[2] in reference to Mr. Burton, representing the Scripps-McRea Newspaper Service and would advise you that I received a call from Mr. Burton on January 13th.

He showed me letters from his employers and also told me that he was going to write up the situation[3] for the above syndicate.

I immediately secured the services of a speed conveyance and took him first to one of the most unsanitary factories here, after which I took him to one of the most destitute defendants—a widow, whose husband died during 1914. Also to some of the oldest and most incapacitated members, subjects under the decision.

I am also having photographs taken today of some of the defendants' houses with the children outside or the widow in one particular case. Also a photograph of an old house—the former residence of D. E. Loewe and a photo of his present mansion on Deer Hill Ave. Danbury.

All these, Mr. Burton assured me would be reproduced in the publications his company supply news papers to.

I am sorry to inform you that our local and only publication "The Danbury News" gave us very little account except the decision as handed down, and since then we read no more pertaining to the outrageous decision in the Danbury News.

Personally, I have accused the owners and editor—that all news relative to labor is censored by the Chamber of Commerce and the Manufacturers Association, but we are helpless in the matter.

Any items published in the local paper pertaining to the decision I will immediately mail to your office.

I wish to sincerely thank you on behalf of my constituents and myself for your assistance and consideration. Also for your great work in connection with the Clayton Bill.

I am with sincere wishes for good health and continued success,

Fraternally yours,   John O'Hara.
Sec'y Treas.   Local #10. U.H. of N.A.

TLS, AFL Microfilm Convention File, reel 27, frame 1301, *AFL Records.*

1. John J. O'Hara was secretary-treasurer of United Hatters of North America 10 of Danbury, Conn., from 1911 to 1922.

2. In his letter to O'Hara of Jan. 11, 1915, SG informed him that Harry P. Burton, who worked for the New York City office of the Scripps-McRae newspaper service, had been sent to Danbury to write a story on the Hatters' case and that Scripps-McRae had "always been friendly to Labor" (reel 189, vol. 201, p. 269, SG Letterbooks, DLC). SG asked O'Hara to send him clippings from any Danbury papers that carried Burton's story.

3. On Jan. 5, 1915, the U.S. Supreme Court upheld a lower court ruling that members of the Hatters were liable, along with the union's officers, to D. E. Loewe and Co. for the award of $252,131 in damages and costs in the case of *Loewe* v. *Lawlor* (235 U.S. 522). Loewe then began proceedings to take over the bank accounts and homes of nearly two hundred hatters in the Danbury area in an effort to compel the Hatters and the AFL to pay the award. The Federation eventually donated $214,911 to the union for this purpose.

To Margaret Dreier Robins[1]

January 22, 1915.

Mrs. Raymond Robins,
President, The National Women's Trade Union League,
Room 901 Unity Bldg., 127 North Dearborn St., Chicago, Ill.
My dear Mrs. Robbins:

The Executive Council of the American Federation of Labor met in regular session at headquarters the week of January 11–16.[2] I placed before my colleagues the report of Miss S. M. Franklin,[3] Secretary of the National Women's Trade Union League, which was submitted to me January 5th,[4] the report showing what has been done in training young women for organizing work, and the expenditure of the monthly appropriation made by the American Federation of Labor for the Women's Trade Union League.[5] The request was made not only for the continuation of the appropriation, but that an increased amount be allowed.[6]

I beg to advise you that the Executive Council deferred action until our next meeting, which will be held at headquarters April 19.[7] In the meantime I was instructed to communicate with you calling your attention to the action of the Executive Council at its meeting January, 1914.

The Executive Council directed that the monthly appropriation for the Women's Trade Union League be continued, that the expenditures of this appropriation by the League shall be made under the supervision of the President of the American Federation of Labor, and that organizers to whom the money appropriated by the American Federation of Labor would be applied should have the endorsement of the undersigned. It was further directed at the January, 1914 meeting that the reports of these organizers should be made at least monthly to the President of the American Federation of Labor.

What the Executive Council has in mind is, that if it be decided at our next meeting to continue the appropriation, it must be under the conditions as I have just indicated and as directed by the Executive Council at its January meeting in 1914.

I would therefore be pleased to hear from you in regard to the above at your convenience.[8]

I shall add that I anticipate being in Chicago February 3 and 4,[9] and though I have many important engagements and will be exceedingly busy while there, if we can possibly arrange it, I should like an opportunity of talking this matter over with you. As usual, I shall stop at the

Kaiserhof Hotel, and would suggest that you call me up by 'phone and we will endeavor to arrange an hour mutually convenient.[10]

With kind regards and anticipating seeing you in Chicago, I am,

Fraternally yours,   Saml Gompers.

President   American Federation of Labor.

TLpS, reel 189, vol. 201, pp. 816–17, SG Letterbooks, DLC.

1. Margaret Dreier Robins (1868–1945) was president of the National Women's Trade Union League of America (NWTUL; 1907–22). She had also served as president of the League's New York (1905) and Chicago (1907–13) branches and was a member of the executive board of the Chicago Federation of Labor (1908–17).

2. The AFL Executive Council met in Washington, D.C., Jan. 11–16, 1915.

3. Stella Miles Franklin (1879–1954), author of *My Brilliant Career* (1901), served as secretary (1911–13) and secretary-treasurer (1913–15) of the NWTUL and as assistant editor (1911–12), coeditor (1913–15), and editor (1915) of the League's journal, *Life and Labor*. She was a member of AFL Stenographers' and Typists' Union 12,755 of Chicago.

4. Franklin to SG, Jan. 5, 1914 [actually, 1915], AFL Microfilm Convention File, reel 27, frame 1422, *AFL Records*.

5. From June 1912 through December 1914, the AFL appropriated $150 a month to assist the NWTUL with organizing work.

6. Robins made this request in a letter to the AFL Executive Council dated Dec. 22, 1914 (AFL Microfilm Convention File, reel 27, frame 1422, *AFL Records*).

7. The AFL Executive Council met in Washington, D.C., Apr. 19–24, 1915.

8. Robins replied that the NWTUL would comply with the conditions outlined by the AFL Executive Council (Feb. 1, 1915, AFL Microfilm Convention File, reel 27, frame 1424, *AFL Records*).

9. SG left Washington, D.C., on Feb. 2, 1915, for Chicago, where he met with a number of labor representatives Feb. 3–4. From there he traveled to Cleveland, Jamestown, N.Y., Buffalo, and New York City. He returned to AFL headquarters on Feb. 8 or 9.

10. SG was unable to meet with Robins in Chicago so she appeared before the AFL Executive Council to discuss the matter on Apr. 21, 1915. After her presentation, the Council voted to expand the AFL's cooperation with the NWTUL by supporting a woman organizer, selected by SG and Robins, to organize women workers.

From George Mendelsohn[1]

Office of Local Union No. 2 of
San Francisco, Cal.
Tailors' Industrial Union (International)
Feb: 3rd 1915

Dear sir & Brother

as you are avare of the fact that our (International) *Union* has been instructed by the last convention of the american Federation Of Labor to go back to the old name of the *"Journeymen Tailors Union" of America*. by the first of April 1915. and now the G.S. of our union has amalgamated with the seceding faction of the U.G.W. of A. against the wishes of the entire membership of our organasation as only five thousand out of twelve thousand members voted on the question of amalgamation with the seceding faction of the U.G.W. of A. and in view of the fact that our local has voted by a unanimous vote against same amalgamation and as all the other locals that did vote in favor of the amalgamation are protesting and asking the G.S. to submit a nother vote to the entire membership and give (60) days time to consider same proposition over again. but the G.E.B. and the G.S. of our *Union* has turned a deaf ear to all those protests and claim that they will go ahead and amalgamate with the seceders. Now our local #2 refuses to stand by this action and propose to stand by the A.F. of L. but the General office has got a new sheme claiming that we will go back to the old name but the name will be (*The Journeymen Tailors Branch of the Amalgamated-Clothing Workers of America*) we would like that your honor give uss advice if the A.F. of L. will stand for this name and also what procedure shal we take to join the A.F. of L. and how can we protect our money as the constitution of our organasation says that if a local drops out from the International all moneys and property belongs to the General Office, and as we are a membership of (500) five hundreth, and all good members we would like that you give uss advice what to do in the matter as there is great unrest between our members against the proposed amalgamation.

P.S. Kindly answer uss as soon as posible as you will guide uss what to do and you will do uss a great favor which we will greatly apreciate trusting we will hear from you[2] [I] remain.

Fraternally-Yours,   Geo Mendelsohn.

Secy: Local #2

TLS, AFL Microfilm, National and International Union File, Tailors Records, reel 55, frame 1133, *AFL Records*.

1. George Mendelsohn was recording and corresponding secretary of Tailors' Industrial Union (from 1915, Journeymen Tailors' Union of America) 2 of San Francisco from 1914 to 1917 and was an organizer for the international union from 1917 to 1918.

2. In his reply of Feb. 13, 1915, SG sent Mendelsohn copies of a circular letter of that date that was sent to central and state labor bodies, AFL organizers, and the labor press. The circular reprinted a letter of Jan. 15, 1915, from the AFL Executive Council to Tailors' secretary Eugene Brais criticizing the international union for changing its name, extending its jurisdiction, and amalgamating with a seceding faction of the United Garment Workers of America; it also demanded that the union comply with the decisions of the 1914 AFL convention. A version of the circular was published in the *AFL Weekly News Letter* of Feb. 13, 1915, and in the March 1915 number of the *American Federationist* (22: 201–3).

To George Perkins

Feb. 12, 1915.

Mr. Geo. W. Perkins,
President, Cigarmakers' International Union,
Monon Building, Chicago, Ill.
My dear Mr. Perkins:

I am very much interested in the proceedings before the federal courts growing out of the baseball disputes.[1] I see that the cases are being brought under the Sherman Antitrust law, and some of the lawyers are quoting the provisions of the Clayton Antitrust bill. The purposes of my writing is to ask whether you could not at once get into touch with the lawyers for the men who contend that they cannot be held against their will, and call their attention to not only section 6 but to the second paragraph of section 20, and particularly the last sentence of section 20. You will no doubt have copy of the February issue of the American Federationist. You will find section 6 on page 107, and section 20 on pages 107–8, the last sentence appearing on page 108.[2] I am sure it will be helpful.

In so far as the internal dispute among the baseball clubs is concerned, I am not much interested, but with the principles involved I am very much so, for if a decision is rendered without the court's attention being called to the specific points, it may have a very damaging influence upon the situation in our own forces. But I am not quite so sure that the lawyers may not have entirely overlooked the provision of Section 20, because it seems almost hidden in the other language of the section.[3]

With best wishes, and hoping to hear from you whenever convenient, I am,

Fraternally yours,   Saml Gompers.
President,   American Federation of Labor.

TLpS, reel 190, vol. 202, pp. 915–16, SG Letterbooks, DLC.

1. In January 1915 the new Federal Baseball League sued the National and American leagues in the U.S. District Court of Northern Illinois for violations of the Sherman Antitrust Act. At issue was the reserve clause, which allowed National and American league team owners to unilaterally renew their players' contracts, thereby preventing them from moving to other teams. Federal League owners charged that this provision prevented them from hiring National and American league players. Judge Kenesaw Mountain Landis heard testimony in the case and then took it under advisement, but eventually a negotiated settlement was reached. Federal League owners received cash payments, and two of them were allowed to purchase major league teams; in exchange, the Federals dropped the lawsuit and dissolved their league.

Owners of the Baltimore Federals were not included in the settlement, however, and they subsequently brought their own suit under the Sherman Act. Successful at the trial level in the Supreme Court of the District of Columbia in 1919, they were awarded $80,000 in damages, which was tripled to $240,000 under the terms of the Sherman Act. This decision was reversed on appeal in 1920 by the Court of Appeals of the District of Columbia (*National League of Professional Baseball Clubs et al.* v. *Federal Baseball Club of Baltimore, Inc.*, 50 App. D.C. 165, 269 F. 681 [1920]), and the appeals court's decision was affirmed by the U.S. Supreme Court in 1922 (259 U.S. 200 [1922]).

2. The passages from the Clayton Antitrust Act were included in SG's editorial "Is Shylock Satisfied?" (*American Federationist* 22 [Feb. 1915]: 105–8).

3. For the text of section 20 of the Clayton Act, see "A Circular," Feb. 24, 1915, below.

From Léon Jouhaux[1] and William Appleton

Chief Office
General Federation of Trade Unions.
London, W.C., 16th February, 1915.

Dear Gompers,

You will see from the enclosed cutting, which is taken from the "Daily Chronicle" of February 15th, that a conference of representatives of the Socialist and Labour Parties of the allied nations was held in London on the 14th.[2] Neither the General Federation of Trade Unions nor the Confederation du Travail were in any sense responsible for convening the conference nor can they be held responsible for any opinions expressed. The Confederation du Travail and representatives of the Cooperative movement[3] of France were invited, but not the General Federation of Trade Unions nor the organised Co-operators of Britain.[4] When the Confederation du Travail realised the circumstances under which the conference had been convened they were averse to attending, but agreed to do so rather than give opportunity for public controversy.

The delegates from the Confederation were instructed to confer during their stay in London with the General Federation concerning the future of the International Secretariat. Yesterday afternoon (the 15th) long and serious discussion took place. There was no sign of personal animosity towards the German people, but all present agreed that racial bitterness had been engendered and would affect, amongst many other things, the position and usefulness of the international trade union movement. It was obvious to all that years must pass before British and Belgian and French could proceed to Berlin with the freedom and confidence which existed prior to the outbreak of the war; some new arrangement was therefore necessary if the international movement was to avoid disintegration and disaster.

All thought that the International Secretariat should, at least for a time, have its chief office in a country whose neutrality was guaranteed not only by treaty but by physiographical circumstances. America would have afforded an ideal solution but for her distance from other centres. Outside America Switzerland appeared to be the country best suited to the requirements of the Secretariat, and though the French preferred Geneva they waived the consideration of this city when it was pointed out that its Latin sympathies might make it objectionable to Germany. Ultimately it was agreed to epitomise and place before you the suggestions made and to ask you to assume the responsibility of forwarding them to Legien. All present felt that he would appreciate the situation. The representatives thought that the chief office of the Secretariat should be removed to a neutral country, preferably Switzerland; that the personnel of the Secretariat should be neutral and resident in Berne.[5]

We fully appreciate the gravity of these suggestions just as we appreciate the gravity of the situation and the desirability of avoiding any form of international trade union catastrophe.

There is not the slightest personal feeling against Legien and it is understood that the arrangement suggested may be only temporary.

Either Jouhaux or myself might have communicated with affiliated countries, but it seemed wiser to transmit our thoughts through non-belligerents, and we knew of no one who would so seriously consider what is suggested or who would more conscientiously act in the interests of international trade unionism than Samuel Gompers.

We send you the expression of our deepest regard and we know that you will try to understand our perplexities and difficulties, and our anxiety to maintain, irrespective of personalities, the solidarity of our movement.

Yours faithfully,
(Signed) For the French Federation of Labor,
Secretary L. Jouhaux.
For the General Federation of Trade Unions,
W. A. Appleton.

TLtcSr, Executive Council Records, Vote Books, reel 13, frame 631, *AFL Records*. Enclosed in SG to the AFL Executive Council, Mar. 4, 1915, ibid., frame 630. The second page of the original letter can be found in the AFL Microfilm Convention File, reel 28, frame 1745, *AFL Records*.

1. Léon JOUHAUX served as secretary of the Confédération Générale du Travail (General Confederation of Labor) from 1909 to 1940 and again from 1945 to 1947.

2. About forty socialists from Great Britain, France, Belgium, and Russia met at a conference in London on Feb. 14, 1915. The delegates passed resolutions condemning the war as a product of capitalism but maintaining that a German victory would mean the end of democracy and liberty. They demanded the liberation of Belgium,

self-determination by the people of Poland, the creation of a world federation at the end of the war, and an end to secret diplomacy and militarism.

3. Probably the Fédération Nationale des Coopératives de Consommation (National Federation of Consumers' Cooperatives), organized in 1912.

4. The Cooperative Union was organized in Great Britain in the nineteenth century. By 1914 it consisted of nearly fourteen hundred member societies with over three million members.

5. SG forwarded this suggestion to Carl Legien with his endorsement on Mar. 4, 1915, and on Apr. 28 informed him that the AFL Executive Council had considered and approved the proposal at its April meeting (reel 191, vol. 203, pp. 930–32 and reel 193, vol. 205, pp. 626–27, SG Letterbooks, DLC). Legien wrote SG on Apr. 12 that he opposed the proposition because he believed it would undermine future cooperation among the affiliated trade union centers, but he directed Jan Oudegeest to call a conference to consider the matter (see "From William Appleton," June 16, 1915, n. 2, below). The headquarters of the International Federation of Trade Unions (IFTU) remained in Berlin throughout the war, but Legien designated the national trade union center of the Netherlands, located in Amsterdam under the direction of Oudegeest, as an auxiliary office to deal with the trade unions of the Allied countries. Jouhaux, in turn, set up a separate correspondence bureau in Paris for communications among the trade unions of the Allied and neutral countries. The *American Federationist* published the correspondence relating to the IFTU in November 1915 (22: 925–64).

To Joseph Roebuck[1]

Feb. 17, 1915.

Mr. Joe Roebuck,
Secretary, Eldorado Trades Council,[2]
Eldorado, Illinois.
Dear Sir and Brother:

Your communication of January 29th, in which you acquaint me with the action of the Eldorado Trades Council, was duly received, but urgent stress of the manifold duties and the important work of helping to secure for the workers of the United States better conditions, higher wages, and the shorter workday has made it practically impossible for me to reply sooner.

You report that the central body of your city adopted a resolution condemning my position upon the policy of securing the eight-hour day by enactment of laws, and protesting against the action of the Philadelphia Convention upon a resolution endorsing legislation to regulate hours of work in private industry.[3]

Because I believe you have not fully considered all of the reasons and facts that have led to my decision and the decision of the representatives of the trade union movement as expressed in the Philadelphia

Convention, I shall briefly present them that they may be presented at the next meeting of the Eldorado central body.

The shorter workday movement is as old as the labor movement in the United States. Review briefly the history of the movement during the 19th century and you will find persistent efforts for first the ten-hour workday and then the eight-hour. Some labor unions or associations tried to secure their purpose by legislation and some by economic action. You will find that wherever the shorter workday has been established for men employed in private industries, it has been accomplished through strikes or trade agreements.

You will find that eight hours became the slogan after the Civil War. The National Labor Union endorsed the principle but shortly afterwards became a political institution and finally went to pieces. Eight-hour leagues and associations were formed in various cities and states. But the eight-hour workday became a reality in the lives of workers only when the great eight-hour movement was inaugurated by the American Federation of Labor.[4] The movement established, it proceeded upon the plan that each trade was to work toward securing the eight-hour day on or before May 1, 1886. Never has there been a movement of such spirit or greater enthusiasm or effectiveness. The eight-hour workday was established in many establishments and in three internationals before the Haymarket disaster temporarily checked the movement.

The organizations that have faithfully and wisely persisted in their efforts to secure eight hours have established it for the benefit of many workers. They have been secured it because they wanted it enough to fight for it and have vigilantly watched to protect this advantage. What they have done, all can do. The difficulties they have to overcome were as great as those that confront any trade today. The hardships and the sufferings they endured to achieve their purpose seared their very souls, but they were determined to better their conditions and they went at it in the most direct manner possible. They wasted neither time nor effort but made their fight directly with the men who controlled hours of labor in private industries.

Workers have tremendous power if they only unite to wield it wisely and effectively.

Whenever trades have established shorter hours and better conditions, it is because they have organized and used their power intelligently. The eight-hour workday as found today in private industry is the result of trade union activity.

Whenever the eight-hour workday is established by law for government work, that is the result of trade union activity which must be exerted indirectly through political representation of workers and of all the other people, and the enforcement of such laws results only from the persistence and vigilance of organized labor.

I assume, of course, from your communication that you are fully informed of the long struggle to obtain an effective federal eight-hour law in 1868. There have been continued efforts to secure amendments made necessary by interpretation of Attorney-Generals and other administrative officers; and that ceaseless vigilance by labor organizations alone secures the observance of the eight-hour day by those who have charge of government work. Not only is this true of federal legislation but for state legislation.

Everywhere the power that secures eight hours and enforces eight hours is the trade union. The indirect method of legislation is necessary on government work, but is neither necessary nor wise for private industries.

The workers in private industries who are organized will never secure an eight-hour day unless other workers who are organized have the legislation enacted and force its enactment. The economic organization is the power upon which all depends.

There have been attempts to secure the eight-hour workday in private industries through legislation. Consideration of the successfulness of some of these efforts is most suggestive.

There is on the statute books of Colorado an eight-hour day for miners but the mines of Colorado are not operated on an eight-hour basis. The miners' organizations are not sufficiently powerful to secure the enforcement of the law. The enforcement of that law was one of the causes of the last strike in Colorado, so you see enacting legislation does not necessarily secure the short workday nor "save strikes and the financial loss and the suffering caused by such methods of getting the 8-hour day" as you stated in your communication. Rarely has there been a strike that caused greater suffering than that of the Colorado miners.

The miners of Joplin, Mo., were organized and secured an eight-hour law.[5] Then, because of the law, they allowed their organization to dwindle away. Immediately progress and all improvement stopped for those miners.

The bakers of New York State secured a ten-hour law which was declared unconstitutional. Secretary Iffland[6] of that International (Journeymen Bakers) wrote me his opinion of the policy of regulating hours by legislation. It is as follows:

"The local unions of the state of New York through agitation spent considerable money and time to be successful in passing the law, in which we succeeded in 1896. At that time, we were of the opinion that by giving through our efforts to the bakery workers of that state the ten hour day by law, they would realize what the organization could do to that effect, and by that, would become members of our organization, but we had to find out very soon that we had made the mistake of our lives, as from that day on the members dropped from the organization and the unorganized threw up to those who tried to organize them, that they don't need an organization any more as they have the ten-hour work day by law.

["]Not alone this, but members who used all their energy to pass the law have been insulted as corrupt politicians, etc., and the radical labor papers of course, denounced at that time such action taken by organized labor as nothing could be expected from the political organizations under the present system of society. We very soon had to find out that we were confronted to regain our strength and make good the loss of membership as well as prestige in our organization in the state of New York, although the organization was weak, to institute agitation for a nine-hour work-day and it has proved that only through the effort of organized labor were we successful in gaining the shorter workday, and we welcomed the day when that law was declared unconstitutional."

Take any sort of legislation intended to protect the lives, health and safety of the workers, and you will find that the enforcement of such legislation corresponds exactly to the power of the economic organizations of the workers.

Many enemies, both open and secret, of organized labor, proposed legislative control of conditions of work in order to place that control in the hands of those outside the organizations of the workers, thereby expecting to exercise a dominating influence over the determination and regulation of those conditions. The enemies of labor know in what the power of labor consists and they are trying by every device to destroy that power. They purposely try to create the false impressions that organizations can no longer secure benefits for the workers and that these benefits must be secured by governmental agencies. They well know that the trade union is the heart of the effort to protect the workers and they seek to destroy and undermine that power.

Many of the workers fancy they see in proposals that are offered something that appears to be a benefit that can be secured quickly and easily. Blinded by the alluring vision, they forget to look beyond at the effects of that which appears to please, they forget to take thought for the future.

You organized workers of Eldorado—remember this one principle and apply it to all proposed methods: The Union is the motive power for all the benefits that come to the workers. Stick to your union, protect it against anything that may weaken it, retard its growth, or lessen its power. You desire your own welfare. Your welfare and that of your fellow workers has been the guiding purpose of the thirty-four years that I have been associated with the American Federation of Labor. Those years of study and work and practical experience with [the] labor movement of America and contact with the labor movements of all other countries, have convinced me that the policy which you favor, would not promote your immediate or future welfare. As a matter of principle, I must differ from you and I trust that further consideration and study will cause you to change your views and to withdraw the condemnation which you have expressed for me and my position in advising against the enactment of legislation to regulate hours of labor in private industries.

Because I am convinced that your condemnation was due to hasty and immature judgement, I ask you to read carefully my editorial in the January American Federationist, "Economic Organization and Eight-Hour Day,"[7] the article by August A. Bablitz,[8] in the February issue, "Historical Development of Trade Unions,"[9] noting especially the extract from Stephen's[10] History of Criminal Law of England,[11] quoted on page 99, which describes the results in England from governmental regulation of hours and wages in private industry, and also the editorials "The Danger of Shifting Duties,"[12] and "Self Help is the Best Help,"[13] and also an editorial which will be published in the March issue, "Trade Unionism, Progress and Liberty."[14] In these writings you will find presented at greater length the principles which in this letter are necessarily but briefly given.

Fraternally yours,   Saml Gompers.

President,   American Federation of Labor.

TLpS, reel 191, vol. 203, pp. 83–89, SG Letterbooks, DLC.

1. Joseph Roebuck was an Eldorado, Ill., coal miner and secretary of the Eldorado Trades Council (TC; 1914?–23).

2. The AFL chartered the Eldorado TC in 1909.

3. See "Eleventh Day—Friday Night Session," Nov. 20, 1914, in "Excerpts from Accounts of the 1914 Convention of the AFL in Philadelphia," Nov. 14–22, 1914, above.

4. See *The Samuel Gompers Papers*, vol. 1, pp. 276–77 and vol. 2, pp. 163–64.

5. Missouri House Bill 271, Laws of 1899, p. 312, enacted May 11, 1899, limited the hours of labor of certain types of miners to eight per day. An amendment (House Bill 13, Laws of 1901, p. 211), enacted Mar. 23, 1901, extended the law to include coal mining.

6. Charles IFFLAND was corresponding secretary (1912–22) of the Bakery and Confectionery Workers' International Union of America.

7. *American Federationist* 22 (Jan. 1915): 43–46.

8. August A. Bablitz was a Lexington, Ky., attorney. Previously a cooper, he had served as secretary of Coopers' International Union of North America 210 of Lexington (1904–12) and as secretary (1909) and president (1910) of the Lexington Central Labor Council.

9. The article was published in the February and May 1915 numbers of the *American Federationist* (22: 93–101, 340–46).

10. James Fitzjames Stephen (1829–94) was an English jurist and professor of common law.

11. Stephen, *A History of the Criminal Law of England,* 3 vols. (London, 1883), which was originally published as *A General View of the Criminal Law of England* (London, 1863).

12. *American Federationist* 22 (Feb. 1915): 108–10.

13. *American Federationist* 22 (Feb. 1915): 113–15.

14. *American Federationist* 22 (Mar. 1915): 174–76.

To Jere Sullivan[1]

Feb. 18, 1915.

Mr. Jere L. Sullivan,
Secretary, Hotel and Restaurant Employees' International Alliance,
    and Bartenders' International League of America,[2]
Commercial Tribune Bldg., Cincinnati, O.
Dear Sir and Brother:

Supplementary to my letter of the 16th instant,[3] in which I give you the information that the paper "Solidarity" is the official organ of the I.W.W., the information which you give regarding some of your local unions in which Socialists dominate, it seemed to me that your attention should be called to this fact of their so-called "consistency" in advocating separation of your International Union into two different branches, one of the culinary trade, the other of the bartenders. You know, as a matter of fact that it has been Socialist propaganda to demand so-called "Industrial Unionism" or "one big union" and attack the American Federation of Labor for proceeding in the orderly way as has been its history and as outlined by the Executive Council report to the Rochester A.F. of L. convention, under the caption of Industrial Unionism. I think it would be well to re-read that. Under separate cover I am sending you a copy of that part of the report, which was put into pamphlet form. A reproduction of that subject in the Mixer and Server[4] might be helpful, and the attention of the entire membership and of the world of Labor called to the conflicting and inconsistent attitude of the Socialists in their propaganda upon this subject. I know that it is simply a hollow mockery on their part and that they will jump from one species of attack to another. First it was the declaration for the Socialists demands or their political party being represented in the American trade union movement; then for the declaration of the co-operative commonwealth; then for industrial unionism, (and part separation) and now the regulation of the hours of labor of all working people by law rather than by trade union activity. When it has been demonstrated to all our fellow workers of the righteous position which the A.F. of L. has taken in the past issues and in the present, the Socialists will again shift their position to make some other ground of attack upon [the] trade union movement.

I simply desire to call your attention to a few of these matters to refresh your memory and which may be helpful to you.

With best wishes, I am,

Fraternally yours, Saml Gompers.
President, American Federation of Labor.

TLpS, reel 191, vol. 203, pp. 123–24, SG Letterbooks, DLC.

1. Jere L. SULLIVAN served as secretary-treasurer (1899–1928) of the Hotel and Restaurant Employees' International Alliance and Bartenders' International League of America and edited the union's official journal, *Mixer and Server* (1900–1928).

2. The HOTEL and Restaurant Employees' International Alliance and Bartenders' International League of America.

3. SG to Sullivan, Feb. 16, 1915, reel 191, vol. 203, p. 68, SG Letterbooks, DLC.

4. The AFL Executive Council's report on industrial unionism was published in the *Mixer and Server* of Apr. 15, 1915.

A Circular

Washington, D.C., February 24, 1915.

To the Organizers of the American Federation of Labor:[1]
Dear Sirs and Brothers:

There is an insidious and persistent attempt by the enemies of organized labor to minimize the importance of the labor sections of the Clayton Antitrust Act and to create the impression that the legislation has not secured for workers better protection in exercising their rights. Because the ultimate purpose of this attempt is to mislead the workers and to discourage efforts along the only lines from which progress can reasonably be expected and because many workers have not at hand sources of information by which they could inform themselves that the attacks upon the Clayton Antitrust Act are based upon untruths, I am putting in your hands this simple, concise statement. In your work among the rank and file of the workers you will find many opportunities to press home these truths and to counteract this attempt to mislead public opinion.

I urge upon you to let no misrepresentations go on unchallenged and unrefuted in regard to the great victory won by organized labor in the legislation embodied in the labor sections of the Clayton Act, which became law October 15, 1914.

The two sections of the act that are of greatest importance to labor are 6 and 20. Section 6 is as follows:

"Sec. 6. *That the labor of a human being is not a commodity or article of commerce.* Nothing contained in the antitrust laws shall be construed to forbid the existence and operation of labor, agricultural or horticultural organizations, instituted for the purposes of mutual help, and not having capital stock or conducted for profit, or to forbid or restrain individual members of such organizations from lawfully carrying out the legitimate objects thereof; nor shall such organizations, or the members thereof, be held or construed to be illegal combinations or conspiracies in restraint of trade under the antitrust laws."

The first sentence of this paragraph "that the labor of a human being is not a commodity or article of commerce" enacts into law the fundamental principle which is the basis of industrial liberty. That principle distinguishes between the labor power of a human being who produces an article and the thing which he produces.

In brief, the thing upon which that principle is justified is as follows: Men and women are not of the same nature as the things they make. *Labor power is not a product—it is ability to produce.* The *products* of labor may be bought and sold without affecting the freedom of the one who produced or who owns them—but the *labor power* of an individual *can not be separated* from his living body. Regulation of and conditions affecting relations under which labor power is used are a part of the lives and the bodies of men and women. Laws which apply the same regulation to workers, and to the products made by workers, are based upon the principle that there is no difference between men and things. That theory denies workers the consideration and the rights given to human beings. It denies the freedom and protection of free men and women.

All manual work was formerly done by slaves. Slaves were property. The law treated them as things. Legal theory was built upon that principle. The principle by which workers were branded with slavery runs through ancient legal precedents, procedure and judicial decisions.

The common law of England was tainted by this idea so degrading to human workers.

The law of the United States was built up on this legal and judicial heritage from Europe and chiefly from England. Although slavery as an institution never applied to white workers in this country, yet in the courts they have had to suffer from and combat this ancient injustice placed upon former workers. This injustice came by injunctions issued in industrial disputes and through perversion of the Sherman Antitrust law, its provisions were interpreted so as to apply to human beings. Both the injunction and the trust law are intended to apply to property, extension of their application to human labor power and normal human activities for human betterment reduces the workers to the same legal category as things.

This is a brief explanation why this statement *"the labor of a human being is not a commodity or article of commerce"* is epochal. It marks the end of the old period where workers were under the shadow of slavery and the beginning of a new period when workers nor their labor power are to be regarded as things—the property of another.

As all workers know that under present conditions they have benefits from industrial freedom only when they organize, as individuals they are unable to secure better conditions from employers or even to make agreements—otherwise they can only accept or decline whatever terms the employer chooses to offer. Immediate necessity may compel them to accept terms that are unfair. Judges have treated labor unions as organizations in illegal restraint of trade and have held that their normal activities were conspiracies.

One of the reasons assigned by the Supreme Court of the United States for holding that the Sherman Antitrust Act applied in the case of the Danbury Hatters was that the hatters' organization had succeeded in establishing the union shop in seventy out of eighty-two hat manufacturing establishments.

The second sentence of Section 6 secured to labor organizations recognition as legal organizations, the right to exist and to carry out the legitimate purposes of organization. It exempts labor organizations and their members from the provision of trust legislation, when they are performing the duties for which the unions were instituted.

The activities which are the legitimate purposes of organized labor are of vital importance. Courts through abuse of the writ of injunction and by judicial interpretation have denied workers the right to do that which is necessary in order to promote their welfare and secure their protection against employers' greed and injustice. Section 20 specifically enumerates certain rights formerly denied by courts which are now lawful. The text of Section 20 is:

"Sec. 20. That no restraining order or injunction shall be granted by any court of the United States, or a judge or the judges thereof, in any case between an employer and employes, or between employers and employes, or between employes, or between persons employed and persons seeking employment, involving, or growing out of, a dispute concerning terms or conditions of employment, unless necessary to prevent irreparable injury to property, or to property right, of the party making the application, for which injury there is no adequate remedy at law, and such property or property right must be described with particularity in the application, which must be in writing and sworn to by the applicant or by his agent or attorney.

"And no such restraining order or injunction shall prohibit any person or persons whether singly or in concert, from terminating any relation of employment, or from ceasing to perform any work or labor, or from recommending, advising or persuading others by peaceful means so to do, or from attending at any place where any such person or persons may lawfully be, for the purpose of peacefully obtaining or communicating information, or from peacefully persuading any person to work or to abstain from working; or from ceasing to patronize or to employ any party to such dispute, or from recommending, advising or persuading others by peaceful and lawful means so to do; or from paying or giving to, or withholding from, any person engaged in such dispute, any strike benefits or other moneys or things of value; or from peaceably assembling in a lawful manner, and for lawful purposes; or from doing any act or thing which might lawfully be done in the absence of such dispute by any party thereto; *nor shall any of the acts specified in this paragraph be considered or held to be violations of any law of the United States.*"

You will note that the second paragraph declares that workers have a right to quit work "singly or in concert"—that is, to strike. They have a right to ask others to join the strike movement. They have a right to "picket." They have a right to "withhold their patronage," or, in everyday English, to "boycott," and they have a right to recommend, advise or persuade others "to boycott." They have a right to pay strike benefits. They have the right of peaceful assemblage.

Then note particularly this significant clause:

"Nor shall any of the acts specified in this paragraph be considered or held to be violations of any law of the United States."

These rights enumerated here, now secured by the Clayton Act, have again and again been denied workers through the abuse of the injunctive writ. These injunctions were issued by the courts extending their jurisdiction and power, and then using this extended jurisdiction and power as precedents for further encroachment upon the workers' rights and liberties.

Now as to the decision in the Hatters' case, which occasioned the campaign of misrepresentation carried on through the daily press and organs of hostile employers. The Hatters' case was begun in 1903. That case and the decision of the Supreme Court in 1908 holding that the Sherman Antitrust law applied to organizations of labor, were what convinced the A.F. of L. that legislation to prevent such litigation was necessary to protect the very existence of organized labor. It was the effort to secure such legislation that finally succeeded in the enactment of the labor provisions of the Clayton Act, which became law October 15, 1914.

Law, of course, is not retroactive. A law enacted October 15, 1914, could have no application to any case pending in the courts prior to its enactment. The Clayton Act could not under any circumstances be held to apply to the Hatters' case. The Clayton law went into effect at once and is operative now and for the future.

Statements therefore intended to create the impression that the Hatters' decision demonstrates the inadequacy of the labor provision of the Clayton Act are mischievous and false, and have their origin in ignorance or deliberate intent to deceive the workers.

The courts have not yet interpreted the Clayton Act, but we have the avowed declarations of those who enacted the law as to its application.

Section 6 will prevent the institution of suits similar to that against the Danbury hatters for normal trade union activity since October 15, 1914.

Section 20 declares lawful the acts for which the Danbury Hatters were declared guilty and sentenced to pay threefold damages.

If any doubt the correctness of our contention, let them read the endorsement of former Attorney-General George W. Wickersham, who opposed the enactment of Labor's contentions into law and who surely can in no way be accused of an attitude of mind favorable to the workers. In regard to the Clayton Act, he stated:

"Had the Clayton law been then in force, it seems clear that the defendants' (Hatters) acts would not have been illegal.

"But by force of the Clayton law, whether any of the acts enumerated in the second paragraph of Section 20 be done singly, or in concert, henceforth they are equally legal in the eyes of the federal law. It is therefore apparent that the labor organizations have secured a statutory reversal of the principles of the decision in the Danbury Hatters' case and the legalization of the boycott as a lawful instrument to ensure the dominance of organized labor, thus substituting the Gompers conception of liberty for that of the Declaration of Independence, the Constitution of the United States and Abraham Lincoln."

In all the history of the working people of this or any other country, no such declaration has been enacted into law as was secured by the A.F. of L. in the enactment of the labor provisions of the Clayton Antitrust Act, which went into effect October 15, 1914. That law declares that *the labor of a human being is not a commodity or article of commerce.* It declares lawful the exercise of the normal activities of the labor movement of the United States. It gives freedom for the toilers of our country to work out their every-day problems of life, and to earnestly and persistently, as well as rationally, continue the struggle for a better and truer life for all.

Fraternally yours,   Saml Gompers.
President,   American Federation of Labor.

PLS, Executive Council Records, Vote Books, reel 13, frames 627–29, *AFL Records*. Enclosed in SG to the AFL Executive Council, Mar. 4, 1915, ibid., frames 626–27.

1. This circular was also sent to all AFL affiliated organizations and to the labor press.

To P. F. Evans

Feb. 24, 1915.

Mr. P. F. Evans,
Seminary Hill, Fort Worth, Texas.
My dear Sir:

Exhaustive replies to the questions you propound in your letter are of course, quite impossible but I shall endeavor to make brief replies that I trust will at least be suggestive.

I prefer to answer your second question first. The term "unskilled labor" is purely relative. There is no work that cannot be better performed by an alert, trained worker than by one who does not understand what he is doing, nor why he is doing it. Constant repetition of the same work, of course, brings a degree of facility if not skill. In any kind of labor the worker necessarily acquires a familiarity and a dexterity that enables him to perform that particular task better than someone else who has had no experience with it. However, a new worker with a trained mind may soon be able to surpass in skill others who have worked at the same task for years. By unskilled labor is generally meant those workers employed in occupations which require little or no previous training. Hence, the places of unskilled workers can be more readily filled than those of the so-called skilled workers. From this you readily understand that it is impossible to give the per cent of skilled workers in labor unions. There are in the American Federation of Labor organizations of the so-called unskilled workers such as hod carriers, building laborers, and street car men. Some of the local unions of these unskilled workers, particularly those of Chicago, contain more than 14,000 members. Although these members of organized labor may be regarded as belonging to the unskilled trades, yet they have developed a skill in organization that secures for them better wages and better hours than many so-called skilled workers or even members of the professions.

In regard to your third question,—Are the real wages of the Unskilled laborers on the increase or not?—of course, there is involved, as you know, the whole discussion hinging upon whether or not the purchasing value of money has increased or decreased. That is a discussion I scarcely care to take up at this time. However, you will find that the standards of living among the so-called unskilled laborers who have organized have been constantly raised. The standards of living among many unskilled workers, particularly among immigrant workers, are far below what should prevail among people living in America. The Federal Department of Labor has recently published several studies of prices during the past decade or two and you will find in them considerable information bearing upon the problem of real wages or the purchasing value of the wages paid. These no doubt, will help you in reaching your conclusions.

Fourth, undoubtedly the best way to increase wages and better conditions of work and to promote the welfare of the workers and to put them in a position so that they can make increasing progress is through the trade union movement.

Fifth, undoubtedly laborers who are not members of unions can become members. Of course, the difficulties confronting the extension of trade union organization are those confronting any other great living movement. It is confronted by all of the human characteristics that make for individual selfishness and failure to appreciate the duties and obligations to our fellow men. It is confronted by misunderstanding and perversions among the workers themselves. But in spite of all of these, and the infinite number of other difficulties, it has made great progress in promoting the industrial and social progress of all those who work for wages. It has also been a potent factor for justice and progress and the life of the nation.

In understanding the fundamental principles underlying the attitude of the American Federation of Labor towards regulation of hours of work and wages in private industry, you will find helpful my recent articles upon "Eight Hours by Law" published in the American *Federationist* for January, February, and March.[1] I trust that your study of this labor problem for your intercollegiate debate will lead you to further study of the labor problem and justice for workers, which are the great industrial and national problems of the day.

Very truly yours,   Saml Gompers.
President,   American Federation of Labor.

TLpS, reel 191, vol. 203, pp. 367–69, SG Letterbooks, DLC.

1. "Economic Organization and Eight-Hour Day," "Self-Help Is the Best Help," and "The Shorter Workday—Its Philosophy" were published in the January, February, and March 1915 issues, respectively, of the *American Federationist* (22: 43–46, 113–15, 165–70).

From George Perkins

Headquarters
Cigar Makers' International Union of America
Chicago, Ill. Feb. 24, 1915.

Dear Sir:

After reading Ex-President Taft's speech[1] recently delivered in New Jersey, concerning the war in Europe and its complications in so far as we are concerned, there is some apprehension in my mind on the question of the United States being drawn into the war.

A careful reading of Taft's speech leads me at least to understand that he means we should not only protect the rights of shippers on the high seas but the lives of American citizens regardless of where located. This all sounds very nice and very patriotic, but to my mind the lives of our citizens right here at home and what little property they may have are vastly more important than the alleged rights of profit mongers, who are doing business with the belligerents and with neutral governments, and where they are compelled to go thru the war zone to do so.

As I see it the great mass of the people of this country, who would have to do the fighting, are not in favor of becoming embroiled in this war, and the only ones who are ready to see us involved are the captains of big business, financiers, dealers in bonds, and those who hope to reap a rich harvest by trading with the nations of Europe and ultimately if war is declared, which will involve us.

My personal observations a little over a year ago in Europe[2] convince me that the workers over there did not want to see the war started between any of the nations, and that if they had had an opportunity they would have protested strenuously against the present war. The war however came so suddenly that no one had a chance to do so. If the workers here are opposed to becoming involved in the European war the time to protest is before the war starts; otherwise they would be in precisely the same position our fellow workers in Europe find themselves.

I have heard it promulgated that Jacob Schiff[3] of New York, who as you know is one of the big financiers of this country and who is said to be connected with nearly every peace movement or organization we have, is holding back any movement of a concrete or specific nature that would make for peace. I do not know whether or not there is any truth in this, but well-informed men have repeatedly asserted it in my presence and it is certain that they believe it to be true.

I have no suggestions to offer. I realize that you are in a position to get closer to the potential, underlying conditions, than I, and I have faith in your judgment concerning the time that labor is to speak in this matter. I repeat however that a careful reading of Taft's speech has created a feeling of apprehension that I seem unable to shake off.

Yours fraternally,   G. W. Perkins
Int. Pres.

TLS, AFL Microfilm Convention File, reel 27, frame 2088, *AFL Records.*

1. William Howard Taft had addressed the Washington Association of New Jersey in Morristown on Feb. 22, 1915, in the wake of a German announcement that proclaimed a war zone around the British Isles. The German government warned that beginning Feb. 18 all belligerent vessels found in the zone would be sunk and neutral shipping there would risk attack. Taft argued in favor of the principle of strict neutrality but defended the American sale of arms and ammunition to belligerents as consistent with this policy. He warned that German use of submarines and mines, resulting in the deaths of American citizens and the destruction of American property, would create a "grave issue" and would bring the country "face to face with a crisis" (*New York Times,* Feb. 23, 1915).

2. George Perkins was the fraternal delegate to the 1913 meeting of the International Secretariat of the National Centers of Trade Unions in Zurich.

3. Jacob Henry Schiff, a New York City financier and philanthropist, was the head of the investment firm of Kuhn, Loeb, and Co.

To R. W. Schloerb

Feb. 25, 1915.

Mr. R. W. Schloerb,
North-Western College, Naperville, Illinois.
My dear Sir:

Whether or not government ownership of the railroads and common carriers is the best policy is a question that for our country involves local conditions, local issues, and all the modifying elements that would determine the success or failure of the experiment. The same is true as to further centralization and consolidation of control over railroads. In some sections and upon some lines, the consolidation is expedient and beneficial. In other sections and under other conditions, short railroad lines have been very successful. In some sections it has been only possible to build and operate railroads as a monopoly. Whether or not such policies shall continue must be determined altogether by the immediate conditions surrounding those who must solve the problem and by all the influences and agencies concerned in carrying out the new policy. The progress that our nation has made in developing the resources of the country and arriving at its present degree of industrial development has been through private initiative and private ownership. No one will gainsay that the problems that we have overcome have been stupendous and that our achievements have been most gratifying. Of course mistakes have been made. There have been many unwise and unjust methods employed that must be corrected. That is characteristic of all life and all policies. Whether or not we might have followed a better policy is purely a speculative problem for which I have little time. Our problem is to solve and overcome existing difficulties rather than to speculate as to what might have been. Whether or not we are tending toward or away from government ownership of railroads is another very suggestive study for academic contemplation. A more vital problem is to scrutinize carefully the determinations and the policies of railroad control to the end that the railroads shall not be permitted to infringe upon the rights and liberties of railroad employes or all members of society. Whether or not government ownership would be expedient or practicable would depend entirely upon conditions under which it was undertaken and upon the agents concerned in carrying out the new policy. Government ownership in itself is neither good nor bad. It might under favorable conditions and with disinterested, progressive, qualified agents to carry out the plan, be productive of good results. Under reversed conditions, and operated by and influenced by the evils of partisan politics, it might result in nothing but evil. Since the expediency of inaugurating a policy of government ownership is qualified by so many conditions, and circumstances, I feel that categorical replies to your questions would only result in misunderstanding of the position of organized labor and the purposes it desires to attain.

Very truly yours,   Saml Gompers.
President,   A.F. of L.

[P.S.] Under separate cover I am [send]ing you the proceedings of the [1914] A.F. of L. Convention. It con[tains] an interesting report[1] by [Mess]rs. Mahon and Bland.[2]

TLpS, reel 191, vol. 203, pp. 396–97, SG Letterbooks, DLC.

1. "Labor Conditions on European Municipally Owned Railroads" (AFL, *Proceedings*, 1914, pp. 200–218).
2. Lawrence D. Bland (1872–1934) was a member of Amalgamated Association of Street and Electric Railway Employes of America 241 of Chicago and editor (1904?–

34) of the Street Railway Employes' journal in Chicago, the *Union Leader*. From 1917 until his death he served as treasurer of the international union.

To Walter Craig[1]

March 3, 1915.

Mr. Walter A. Craig,
University of Pennsylvania, Philadelphia, Pa.
Dear Sir:

Your favor of February 28th received and contents noted. You say that arrangements have been made for me to deliver my address at 3:15 at St. James Hall, 38th and Market Streets, as permission has again been refused the students to have the address delivered on the campus. I am indeed glad to have the opportunity of speaking to the students of your University. I expect to stop at the Walton Hotel, and will be glad to meet your committee there.[2]

Very truly yours,　Saml Gompers.
President,　American Federation of Labor.

TLpS, reel 191, vol. 203, pp. 687, SG Letterbooks, DLC.

1. Walter A. Craig was a student at the University of Pennsylvania.
2. Officials of the University of Pennsylvania had refused to allow SG to speak on campus. When students rented an off-campus site for his address, which he delivered to some five hundred students on Mar. 5, 1915, the university newspaper refused to publish notices of the meeting and posters advertising it were torn down. See "U. of P. Frowns on Free Speech," *American Federationist* 22 (April 1915): 277–80.

To John Lennon

March 12, 1915.

Re Document #36.
Mr. John B. Lennon,
Member, Industrial Relations Commission,
Bloomington, Ill.
Dear Sir and Brother:

Your favor of the 5th instant reached here the 8th, and contents noted. I have been so crowded with work requiring my immediate and constant attention that it was simply impossible to give even this important subject earlier attention. I do hope that the Commission will decide to make an investigation of the conditions in Porto Rico.[1] It would be possible for witnesses to leave Porto Rico March 17th or 18th, reach New York March 22, and be at Atlanta on the 24th or 25th. There are no witnesses in the United States proper who could give authentic testimony.

In my judgment you underestimate Mr. Santiago Iglesias' powers of thought and expression. His efforts in the conventions of the American Federation of Labor cannot be taken as a criterion. It is necessary to get into close touch with him, and he will easily persuade anyone with his intelligence, earnestness, and force of character, and he can express himself sufficiently well in English to be clearly understood, and to convey his meaning, and this is equally true of Rivera Martinez.[2] If the Commission will call these men by cablegram, I feel safe in saying that they will promptly respond and give such testimony as will not only throw light upon Porto Rican conditions, but will astound even the Commissioners, and which will be helpful to the Porto Rican people, particularly the working people of the Island, and be an act of justice exercised on behalf of the people of the United States. If Chairman Walsh will cable Santiago Iglesias, asking him to come to Atlanta, Georgia, and to have Rivera Martinez accompany him, I feel confident to say that they will respond and be in attendance.[3] A cablegram addressed as follows will be sure of delivery:

Mr. Santiago Iglesias,
60 Luna Street,
San Juan, Porto Rico.

Upon the conclusion of this letter I shall write Mr. Iglesias so that a letter may go in the mails tomorrow,[4] Saturday, and in all likelihood reach him by the time a cablegram will be sent to him, and that he may be enabled to leave Porto Rico on the steamer within a days notice, provided of course the cablegram is received advising him to come.

I believe that the entire expense to the Commission of the two men coming from Porto Rico to New York, to Atlanta, and return, would not be more than $500.00 in the aggregate, and as I say, it would be of inestimable value.

Now in regard to the statement that there is an element of labor people in Porto Rico which claims that Mr. Iglesias, or the Porto Rico Federation of Labor does not represent that element, let me say that that element to which you refer is very insignificant, and that whatever exists of it is made up of a few politicians who try to use the working men politically and as against the best interests of the working people themselves. It might be likened to the present remnant of the Knights of Labor now existing in the United States, as compared to the American Federation of Labor.

If the time can be made convenient, and I could appear before the Commission also to testify as to my own observations and investigations, I shall certainly do so,[5] but it would not have half the force and influence unless Mr. Iglesias and Mr. Martinez were also witnesses.

Trusting that the matter may commend itself to the favorable consideration of yourself and your associates on the Commission, I am, with best wishes,

Fraternally yours,   Saml Gompers.
President,   American Federation of Labor.

I may be in Chicago March 24.[6] It would be practically impossible for me to come to Atlanta during the week beginning March 22.

S. G.

T and ALpS, reel 192, vol. 204, pp. 95–97, SG Letterbooks, DLC.

1. The U.S. Commission on Industrial Relations held hearings in Washington, D.C., on labor conditions in Puerto Rico, May 26–27, 1915. These are printed in U.S. Congress, Senate, *Industrial Relations. Final Report and Testimony Submitted to Congress by the Commission on Industrial Relations . . .* , 64th Cong., 1st sess., 1916, S. Doc. 415, 11: 11027–224.

2. Prudencio Rivera Martínez, a San Juan cigarmaker, was a vice-president of the Federación Libre de los Trabajadores de Puerto Rico (Free Federation of the Workers of Puerto Rico) and a founder in 1915 of the Partido Socialista de Puerto Rico (Socialist Party of Puerto Rico).

3. Both Santiago Iglesias and Martínez testified before the commission.

4. SG to Iglesias, Mar. 12, 1915, reel 192, vol. 204, pp. 92–93, SG Letterbooks, DLC.

5. SG did not testify.

6. Between Mar. 23 and Apr. 3, 1915, SG met with labor representatives in Chicago and made a number of addresses. He returned to Washington, D.C., on Apr. 4.

To Melinda Scott

March 18, 1915.

Miss Melinda Scott,
President Women's Trade Union League,
43 East 22d Street, New York, N.Y.
Dear Madam:—

Your favor of recent date came duly to hand and contents noted. In connection with the subject matter about which you write, let me say that on January 27, 1915, I wrote a letter to Hon. Abram I. Elkus, Chief Counsel for the N.Y. State Factory Investigating Commission of which the enclosed is a copy.[1]

I was importuned not to resign my membership in the Commission, nor to make a minority report. It was urged that, unless there was unity in the Commission, particularly if I made any strong dissent upon the subject of minimum wage for women,[2] the whole effect of the other splendid constructive work of the Commission for the working people in the State of New York would be frustrated.

There was a hurried call for a meeting of the Commission in New York and I attended it.[3] There again I protested strongly against Compulsory Legal Minimum Wage for Women Workers, and then every other member of the Commission repeated with greater emphasizes the necessity of unity of action. Then again there was but a day within which the report could be submitted to the legislature. Upon my insistence several compulsory facts were cut out of the report. I could not get my fellow commissioners to modify the report further. Some of the commissioners who were not there, but who had signified their adherence to the report, had to be seen in order that they might sign the report. There was but one alternative, [not] to sign the report and destroy the entire work of the Commission for the year, or else sign a report which modified it in a way to my mind, and save the good work. I signed it, but I assure you that I am not proud of it.

Considering the matter in its entirety, I can say conscientiously to you that, if the same situation were again presented to me, I should withhold my approval and signature. These are the facts and you ought to know them.

I regret exceedingly that, owing to pressing important matters requiring my immediate and constant attention, I have been unable to reply to you earlier.

With best wishes, I am,

Sincerely yours,   Saml Gompers.
President   American Federation of Labor.

TLpS, reel 192, vol. 204, pp. 466–67, SG Letterbooks, DLC.

1. In his letter to Abram Elkus of Jan. 27, 1915, SG offered to resign as a member of the New York State Factory Investigating Commission because he had been unable to attend so many of its meetings. He went on to say that unless he were given the opportunity to review the commission's recommendations as to the recodification of the state's labor laws, he wished his name withheld from that document (reel 189, vol. 201, pp. 997–99, SG Letterbooks, DLC).

2. The final report of the New York State Factory Investigating Commission, submitted to the legislature on Feb. 15, 1915, proposed creating a wage commission that could make recommendations as to living wage levels for women and minors in various industries. Compliance with these recommendations was to be voluntary. The Factory Investigating Commission also called for amending the state constitution to authorize the establishment of a second, permanent wage commission that could mandate specific wages for women and minors, enforceable by law. SG endorsed the voluntary components of the proposal but opposed its compulsory features (see SG to Elkus, Jan. 30, 1915, reel 190, vol. 202, pp. 259–60, SG Letterbooks, DLC).

3. The meeting was held in Elkus's office in New York City on Feb. 13, 1915.

To Frank Morrison

Chicago, Ill. March 26. '15

To Mr. Frank Morrison
Sec'y. AF. of L.
Dear Frank:—

Just a word on one subject of importance. It is impossible to record the tremendous obligations of this trip.[1] Incidentally the Bldg. Tr. conference[2] don't look very hopeful. But to the matter I want to relate & you should know.

Last night I was informed that Mr. Bolander[3] of the Tailors (delegate to the Phila. convention) was in Chicago & wanted to see me. Indirectly he was told that would be O.K. Today, during the recess of the Bldg. Tr. conference, Mr. Bolander came to see me. He wanted to know what the E.C. of the A.F. of L. would do at the April 19 meeting. He said that a vote was being taken to reconsider the Amalgamated proposition, with the seceeding Garment Workers; that the vote would be counted May 1. 1915;[4] that he felt sure that things would be settled right, but that any drastic action would possibly place obstacles in the way of the Journeymen Tailors doing the right thing. He said many other things of some importance, but which I can't find the time to write out in long hand.

You may rest assured that I made the position of the A.F. of L. and the E.C. pretty plain. I stated that I could not positively state what action in the premises, the E.C. would take, but that the E.C. will beyond question do everything within its power to carry out to the fullest the rights & interests of the garment workers and tailors and due respect for the unanimous decision and declaration of the A.F. of L. convention. Then I stated that I felt sure that if the Executive Board of the Journeymen Tailors Union sent one or two officers or other authorized representatives to the April 19. E.C. meeting for the purpose of finding a solution of the present situation, the E.C. will be willing to listen, to advise and to be helpful.[5] He left, apparrantly, in a better frame of mind and gave assurances that things would come out all right.

Mr. Bolander, at the start rather too positively insisted that he came "unofficially" &c. Mr. G. W. Perkins Prest. C.M.I.U was present during the entire conference and he agrees with me that Mr. Bolander's visit was not quite so unofficial as he tried to impress on me.

I am writing this while in the conference with the Building Trade's conference. If I had the services of a stenographer and had the time, this statement could be made much more interesting. But I think you will agree that it is important as indicative of the fact that the Tailors may become a bit more amenable to a sense of justice & fair dealing.

Perhaps it might be a good thing to give the E.C. a copy of this for their information and (confidential for the time being) consideration.[6]

Am a bit tired by the constant grind but will stick.

Best wishes,

Yours Fraternally   Saml Gompers.

Prest   Am. Fed. of Labor

ALS, Files of the Office of the President, General Correspondence, reel 78, frames 711–14, *AFL Records.*

1. SG's trip to Chicago (see "To John Lennon," Mar. 12, 1915, n. 6, above).

2. In January 1915 the Chicago Building Trades Council ratified a controversial agreement with the Chicago Building Construction Employers' Association that lifted restrictions on output, machinery, tools, and the use of apprentices and established a joint arbitration board to set wages. A number of building trades locals objected to the agreement and urged the Chicago Federation of Labor to investigate, but Federation president John Fitzpatrick refused to do so, ruling that his organization had no authority in the matter. AFL Building Trades Department president Thomas Williams and SG then went to Chicago to meet with representatives of the building trades unions and the employers' association in an attempt to resolve the dispute. Some modifications were made in the agreement, but its essential features remained in force.

3. Carl N. Bolander was a member of Tailors' Industrial Union 49 of Louisville, Ky., and served as an organizer for the Tailors from 1913 to 1930.

4. Members of the Tailors voted 4,702 to 822 that the union should resume its former name, the Journeymen Tailors' Union of America. They also voted 3,897 to 1,385 to return to the union's previous, narrower jurisdiction and 3,961 to 1,339 to withdraw from the Amalgamated Clothing Workers of America.

5. No Tailors' representatives attended the AFL Executive Council's April 1915 meeting, but representatives of the United Garment Workers of America appeared in order to protest the Tailors' use of their union label on ready-made clothing and on clothing made by the seceding Clothing Workers. The Council then withdrew its endorsement of the Tailors' label until the union complied with the rulings of the 1914 AFL convention that the Tailors must resume their former name and suspend their support of the Clothing Workers.

6. SG informed the AFL Executive Council of his meeting with Bolander in his report to the Council's April 1915 meeting.

To John Golden

March 31, 1915.

Mr. John Golden,
President United Textile Workers of America,
86–87 Bible House, New York City.
Dear Sir and Brother:—

From your letter[1] it is evident that the New York Call did you an injustice in quoting your statement in regard to the value of the provisions of the Clayton Antitrust Law which regulate the issuance of injunctions.[2] The New York Call, of course, as you know, has pursued a policy of trying to disparage the value of the Clayton Act, and, from its quotation of your statement, the paper was evidently trying to establish additional evidence for continuing to disparage the Clayton law. In this policy the New York Call is but following the course pursued by Metropolitan papers which are the organs presenting the view points and interests of corporations and selfish employers. This policy has taken the form of efforts to create the impression that the Clayton Antitrust Act is of no value because states may still issue injunctions in industrial disputes coming wholly within state jurisdiction to prevent workers from doing those things which are necessary to accomplish the purposes of organized labor, acts which they may now legally perform when they come under the purview of federal legislation. In other words, these papers are endeavoring to deceive organized workers by confusing the jurisdiction of state courts with the jurisdiction of federal courts.

I recently issued a circular letter to the state federations of labor containing a proposed measure that should be enacted in all states in order to protect the workers of the states from the abuse of the injunctive processes of state courts and thus complete the protection secured through the enactment of the Clayton Antitrust Act.[3] I am enclosing a copy of this circular which will, no doubt, be of great interest, especially because of your work in connection with the passage of the Massachusetts Injunction Law.[4] Could you send me a copy of the injunction issued by Chancellor Kyle against the workers at Lenoir City,[5] and will you give me the date on which the injunction was issued against the Knitters' Union in Reading, Pa.?[6]

With best wishes, I am,

Fraternally yours,   Saml Gompers.
President   American Federation of Labor.

TLpS, reel 192, vol. 204, pp. 645–46, SG Letterbooks, DLC.

1. John Golden to SG, Mar. 22, 1915, AFL Microfilm National and International Union File, United Textile Workers Records, reel 42, frame 2634, *AFL Records.*

2. The *New York Call* claimed Golden had said granting a permanent injunction against strikers in Lenoir City, Tenn., would nullify the Clayton Act ("Clayton Law Endangered," Mar. 11, 1915). In his letter of Mar. 22, Golden told SG that the point of his statement, which was not reported by the paper, was that state legislation was necessary to extend the provisions of the Clayton Act to local jurisdictions.

3. The circular, issued at the direction of the 1914 AFL convention, was dated Mar. 15, 1915. For the text of the proposed model law see "Remedy State Injunction Abuse," *American Federationist* 22 (Apr. 1915): 275.

4. Massachusetts, Laws of 1914, chap. 778, enacted July 7, 1914, declared that labor was a personal not a property right, that it was not illegal for workers to organize for

better wages, conditions, and hours, and that injunctions were not to be issued by Massachusetts state courts except to prevent irreparable injury to property. The law was declared unconstitutional in 1916.

5. In March 1914 the United Textile Workers of America organized local 909 in Lenoir City. After the Holston Manufacturing Co. discharged the new local's leaders and lengthy negotiations failed to get them rehired, the union struck the firm on Feb. 8, 1915. On Feb. 19 Judge Hugh Graham Kyle of the Tennessee court of chancery issued a preliminary injunction that prohibited union members from picketing, congregating around the mill, or in any way interfering with employees of the company. The injunction, slightly modified, was made permanent in March.

6. On Mar. 13, 1914, members of United Textile Workers of America 900 (Full Fashioned Knitters) of Reading, Pa., struck the firm of Nolde and Horst, a local hosiery mill employing some fifteen hundred workers, to protest the discharge of union officers. On Apr. 25 Judge Endich of the Berks Co. Court of Common Pleas issued a temporary injunction against the striking knitters, enjoining them from picketing the firm. He made the injunction permanent on Feb. 20, 1915 (*Nolde and Horst Co.* v. *Kruger et al.,* Court of Common Pleas of Berks Co., No. 1,123 Equity Docket, 1914).

From Carl Legien

International Secretariat of
National Trade Union Centres
Berlin, April 2nd, 1915.

My dear Gompers,

When I wrote my last card on New Year's Eve I promised to write more fully as soon as possible. Hitherto, however, I have not been able to fulfil my promise, not because I had nothing to tell you but rather because I am so overburdened with work that everything remains undone which is not absolutely necessary.

Quite recently I read in American papers that you escaped a great danger on February 3, when you stayed at the Chicago Kaiserhof which went up in fire.[1] It is for this reason that I am writing to-day to tell you how glad I felt when I read the story of your lucky escape. I take it as good sign showing that your life will be spared many years yet for our great labour movement. I sincerely hope that we may once more be able to meet at that very Kaiserhof pursuing our common work.

Unfortunately, there is very little chance for such a meeting now. Who would have dreamt of such duration of this war or of its methods as practised between Great Britain and Germany to-day. We need not discuss whoever is responsible for these methods of warfare. By the way, my views on the matter would, of course, scarcely be without bias. The British government appears to try a starvation policy on the German people, but our submarine warfare against British commercial ships is a similar method. From our point of view we believe the one as dreadful as the other.

The object Great Britain had in view can not be achieved, however. At the very moment when the war commenced the possibility of our foodstuffs being insufficient had been taken into account. Every man and woman with some social feelings felt the necessity of safeguarding our women and children against hunger and privation. This is why the trade unions did not hesitate for one moment to do their share in this direction. The general organisation is in such working order to-day that the danger of famine is banished once for all. Our education along the lines of organisation has shown its full value during these days. I sincerely hope that the lessons learned now will not be forgotten after the war is over. It is quite possible that our capitalist society as well as our constitutionalistic and absolutistic state take the lesson to heart. In this case some progress on the social field would at least be one satisfactory outcome of the terrible calamity which has befallen the nations of Europe. Of course, all this would by no means be a compensation for the tremendous sacrifices this war demands from man and property.

I need not describe to you our feelings in reading the daily war bulletins or what our imagination shows us of modern warfare with modern weapons. It all is a fearful picture, although we in the middle of country do not witness any of these things ourselves. If it was not for the great number of active soldiers and of wounded in our streets, none of us would imagine what terrible tragedy is being played near the frontier, for our daily life appears so absolutely normal.

Many of us, and I among them, believed that the economic life of the country and, consequently, our unions, would break down immediately after the outbreak of war. After a few critical weeks, however, our unions have fully recovered, as you have certainly noticed from my reports in the "Correspondenzblatt." (I hope the paper reaches you regularly.) I am not too optimistic, however, as to the value of the present state of trade here. It is often said and rightly too "War nourishes war." This is true to-day as much as during the 30-years' war.[2] There is little doubt that as soon as millions of German workers return home to their work of peace, production will undergo a serious crisis and that many new difficulties will arise for our unions. We are already to-day preparing for that period, doing everything possible to keep our trade union and political organisations in perfect order.

We have indeed been able to maintain our unions in our own country and I sincerely trust that we will equally succeed to bring about our international organisation as soon as the war is terminated. I even hope that our international relations will become better and stronger than ever. I am not as pessimistic as Bro. Appleton appeared to be when he wrote his letter of November 11, 1914,[3] to you a copy of which he was good enough to send to my address. I maintain our old relations, as far as possible, with all national centres, ably assisted in this direction by Bro. Oudegeest[4] with whom I confer whenever anything of importance is at stake. I hope to meet him again to-morrow and hand this letter to him. In this way I think it will reach you safely and without undue loss of time.

Contrary to what I expected Sweden and Holland have sent their usual contribution to the I.F.T.U. and the German centre has also paid the usual quota. I believe this to be one of the best signs for the future of our international organisation. The International Federation of Trade Unions will not be able to offer much in exchange for these contributions at the present moment but I feel sure that this will be recovered soon after the war. The international feeling of solidarity of the workers has not been lost during this terrible crisis, as is shown by the action of these three centres.

The same ideas, by the way, are expressed in your peace resolution passed at the Philadelphia Convention of the A.F.o.L. Let me thank you and your friends heartily for this demonstration of international solidarity.[5] I have my doubts, however, whether it will be actually possible to hold a labour convention during the peace negotiations of the belligerent countries, because the state of war in these countries will not be withdrawn in time. [Our] direct influence on these negociations, moreover, will probably carry no weight. Indeed we all have permitted ourselves to be deceived as to the actual power of our labour organisations. We shall have to develop this power and make it sufficiently strong to avert a similar conflict in the future, as soon as our common work is started again at the end of this war.

These, briefly, are my ideas as to the next future. It would be better, however, if I were in a position to tell you of the end of the terrible slaughter and of the beginning of new international efforts on behalf of our common cause.

Please find enclosed, somewhat belated, a receipt for the contribution paid by the A.F.o.L. for our fiscal year 1913/14.

With best wishes and fraternal greetings to you and all our mutual friends, also to Mrs. and Miss Gompers, believe me to be

Yours sincerely   C. Legien
President   I.F.o.T.U.

TLS, AFL Microfilm Convention File, reel 28, frame 1748–49, *AFL Records*.

1. A small, easily contained rooftop fire broke out at the Kaiserhof Hotel in Chicago on Feb. 3, 1915, while SG was staying there.

2. The Thirty Years' War (1618–48) was a series of conflicts triggered by dynastic, religious, territorial, and commercial rivalries, fought primarily in German lands and involving most of the major powers of Europe.

3. William Appleton to SG, Nov. 11, 1914, AFL Microfilm Convention File, reel 27, frame 2084, *AFL Records*.

4. Jan OUDEGEEST was president of the Nederlandsch Verbond van Vakvereenigingen (Netherlands League of Trade Unions; 1908–18) and head of the auxiliary office of the International Federation of Trade Unions in Amsterdam.

5. Carl Legien was referring to SG's letter of Dec. 10, 1914 (see "Gompers Elected Head of A.F. of L. without Contest," Nov. 22, 1914, n. 3, in "Excerpts from Accounts of the 1914 Convention of the AFL in Philadelphia," Nov. 14–22, 1914, above).

To Timothy Neary[1]

April 7, 1915.

Mr. T. F. Neary,
Secretary, Joint Council #25, International Brotherhood of
    Teamsters, Chauffeurs, Stablemen and Helpers,
Room 506, 175 W. Washington St., Chicago, Ill.
Dear Sir and Brother:

Your favor of the 5th instant[2] just came to hand, the contents of which I have noted with interest, and regret, for it seemed to me before adopting a resolution of the character you name you would have asked me to make some word of defense, explanation or denial. As a matter of fact, I used no taxicab while in Chicago, other than those which were in front of the New Morrison Hotel, except on my arrival in Chicago, when I had a Parmalee taxicab at the Union Station, the driver of which wore his union button.

It may be interesting for you to know that some years ago the Chauffeurs of the Terminal Taxicab Company had a strike which was lost. From the time of the strike up to this present day I have not used the services of the Terminal Taxicab Company, and last Sunday morning when my train came into the Union Station at Washington, at 8:26 Sunday morning, I telephoned to the Barnett Brothers Taxicab Co., Main 5456, 209 11th Street, N.W. to send a taxicab to the station for me. I was waiting in front of the station more than half an hour in the snow and the slush resultant from the blizzard in Washington the day before. If you doubt this you can write or make other inquiry. It seems strange that union men should so easily and readily undertake to condemn me when I have all my life endeavored to consistently and persistently, in season and out of season, acted to protect and advance the interests of our fellow unionists, particularly our fellow union workers.

Fraternally yours,   Saml Gompers.
President,   American Federation of Labor.

TLpS, reel 192, vol. 204, pp. 910–11, SG Letterbooks, DLC.

1. Timothy F. Neary was secretary of International Brotherhood of Teamsters, Chauffeurs, Stablemen, and Helpers of America 727 (Auto Livery Chauffeurs) of Chicago.

2. In his letter of Apr. 5, 1915, Neary informed SG that Teamsters' Joint Council 25 had adopted a resolution protesting against SG's having patronized a nonunion cab while visiting Chicago in March (International Brotherhood of Teamsters, Chauffeurs, Stablemen, and Helpers of America Records, reel 4, frame 1432, *AFL and the Unions*). SG sent a copy of his reply to Neary to Daniel Tobin and Thomas Hughes, the president and the secretary of the Teamsters, as well as to W. J. Carrigan, the president of Teamsters' local 727, the union whose delegates had introduced the resolution at the Joint Council meeting.

To William Cannon

April 10, 1915.

Mr. W. P. Cannon,
Secretary, School Custodians and Janitors' Union No. 14596,[1]
408 12th St., S.E., Washington, D.C.
Dear Sir and Brother:

I received the proposed constitution and bylaws of your organization which you have submitted for approval, and on account of the demands made upon my time by other important business, I have been unable to give this matter my attention until the present moment.

In looking over the constitution and bylaws, I find that Section 2 of Article 1 reads as follows:

"It shall be composed of white Janitors, Assistant Janitors, Caretakers and Laborers of the Public Schools of the District of Columbia and such others as the Union may deem proper."

One of the principles for which the American Federation of Labor has declared is the organization of all wage earners irrespective of race, creed, sex, or color. However, realizing the importance of organizing the colored wage earners in every section of the country, not only for their own protection but for the protection of the white wage earners, and realizing still further the feeling which exists in many sections of the country regarding the organization of colored workmen with white workmen, and desirous of avoiding any unnecessary race antagonism, provision was made in the constitution of the A.F. of L. for the organization of unions of colored workmen exclusively wherever such a course might be found to the best interests of the workers themselves and of the movement in general. Not only that, but provision was also made in the A.F. of L. Constitution for the organization of Central Labor Unions composed of delegates from local unions of colored workers whenever that might be deemed necessary. Therefore, I would suggest that the word "white" in the above quoted section of your constitution should be omitted. If the question should afterwards arise as to the colored janitors, care takers, and laborers, then if it should be found advisable a separate union of these workers could be organized.

Another objection to Section 2 is contained in the words, "and such others as the union may deem proper." A charter was granted to your organization to cover only those who are engaged in the caretaking of school houses, but with the words as above quoted, it could be construed to mean any person no matter in what industry they may be engaged, and for these reasons section 2 of article 1 of your constitution does not meet with my approval.

Section 5 of article 15 which governs the amount of dues which should be paid by the members of your local union, that is, 50¢ per month, is at variance with section 12 of article 13 of the constitution of the American Federation of Labor. This article applies to the defense fund of the American Federation of Labor to which your organization would be a contributor. Section 1 of article 10 of the constitution provides that members of local trade unions or federal labor unions shall be required to pay a per capita tax of 15¢ per month per member, 5¢ of which must be placed in the defense fund. Section 12 of article 13 declares that no local union shall be entitled to any assistance from this defense fund unless it requires its members to pay not less than 60¢ per month, hence you will see that, though the members of your union would be contributing to the defense fund, they would not be entitled to any assistance from it in case of strike or lockout unless the constitutional·rate of dues, 60¢ per month, was paid by them into the treasury of their local union.

Let me suggest that your organization make the necessary changes as indicated above in your proposed constitution, and after having done so, return the same to this office for further consideration.

Fraternally yours,   Saml Gompers.
President   American Federation of Labor.

TLpS, reel 192, vol. 204, pp. 1030–32, SG Letterbooks, DLC.

1. The AFL chartered School Custodians' and Janitors' Union 14,596 of Washington, D.C., in 1913.

Samuel Gompers. (George Meany Memorial Archives)

SG relaxing with friends, including Max Morris (first row, second from right) and James O'Connell, James Duncan, and John Mitchell (second row, center, with SG). (George Meany Memorial Archives)

SG and friends out for a drive, 1911. (George Meany Memorial Archives)

SG and Paul Scharrenberg, 1911.
(George Meany Memorial Archives)

Miners' Hall, Butte, Montana, June 24, 1914, after dynamiting. (Montana
Historical Society, Helena)

Northern Michigan copper miners. (Michigan Technological University Archives and Copper Country Historical Collections)

Mother Jones leading a labor demonstration during the Colorado miners' strike, 1914. The flag on the right reads, "Ludlow." (Brown Brothers)

Joe Hill. (Special Collections,
J. Willard Marriott Library,
University of Utah)

Frank Walsh. (Brown Brothers)

SG at the ground-breaking ceremony for the AFL office building, October 28, 1915. (George Meany Memorial Archives)

SG and Woodrow Wilson at the dedication of the AFL office building, July 4, 1916. (George Meany Memorial Archives)

The AFL office building, Ninth Street and Massachusetts Avenue, N.W., Washington, D.C. (George Meany Memorial Archives)

Representatives of the Mexican labor movement and members of the AFL Executive Council after their conference in Washington, D.C., July 1916. First row, from left: Luis Morones, Carlos Loveira y Chirinos, Frank Morrison, SG, James Duncan, James O'Connell, Henry Perham, and John Alpine. Second row, from left: Baltasar Pages, Edmundo Martínez, Joseph Valentine, Frank Duffy, John Lennon, and William Green. Third row, from left: John Murray, Salvador González García, and William Spencer. (George Meany Memorial Archives)

Samuel and Sophia Julian Gompers, 1917. (George Meany Memorial Archives)

Excerpts from the Minutes of a
Meeting of the Executive Council of the AFL

Monday, April 19, 1915.

MORNING SESSION.

. . .

In connection with the war and the various efforts made by groups
of people for peace, and there are many of them, I have been invited
to participate in conferences, and mass meetings, for the purpose of
committing the American Federation of Labor to all sorts of movements. The one in project is proposed to be held in Cleveland in May,
at which will be advocated the establishment of an international court
based upon the idea of the Supreme Court of the United States.[1] I have
declined to participate in that conference, first, because of duties already devolving upon me and engagements already made, and secondly I do not believe that it is along the right lines.

On last Thursday night there was a mass meeting held in New York
City under the auspices of the Central Federated Union of New York,
to demand immediate peace, and the project was the advocacy of a
universal strike in the United States by all workers engaged in the
manufacture of all materials which could be utilized as war materials,
and also all the workers engaged in the production of food stuffs.[2] In
the first place, I was too busily engaged in work requiring my immediate attention at headquarters, and secondly, I could not give my approval of a movement that at this time meant a call for a universal
strike, which would be ineffective, because it would not be responded
to and because it would simply end in chaos and confusion to our
movement without accomplishing the result which the promoters
desired. There is not any doubt in my mind from the manner in which
the meeting was projected and by those who addressed the meeting
and the talk at the meeting, that it was just simply another movement
of the Socialist political partisans who tried to embarrass and injure
our movement.

Some weeks ago I was invited to participate in a Congress to be held
in Chicago for the purpose of laying out a plan for international peace.[3]
The meeting was to be primarily conducted by some prominent wom-
en of the country, particularly those located in Chicago. The date was
arbitrarily set without consultation, the program set forth without consultation, and I held that the convenience and time and opportunity
for representation of the American Federation of Labor should have

been consulted; the program before it was determined should have had the consideration of the Executive Council of the American Federation of Labor; that as the A.F. of L. was beyond question the most numerous and regarded as the most influential group of citizens of the United States, that if our cooperation was expected, we ought to be consulted both in the initial proceedings, as well as in the final determination of the program. The conference was held and it was decided to hold a Peace Congress at the Hague at which a number of women were to participate.[4] About ten days ago I received a letter from the representative[5] of the Women's Branch of this Congress, asking me whether I would not send a woman representative to The Hague. The date was so immediate, and I had no authority, and there was no time to consult the Executive Council, that I gave the information as I have just stated. I said that the Council will meet the week beginning the 19th, and if the Council believed that a delegate ought to go there, there would be time for the selection and a representative to go there. Before this, in the letter from this Boston lady, she suggested something along this line: that "there is a woman here belonging to the Telephone Operators' Union,[6] to whom I wish you would send a credential to attend the Congress as a representative of the American Federation of Labor." I answered that I could not do that; that the Executive Council in my judgment could not do that; that we were not acquainted with the lady, and we do not know of her qualifications. Then I added substantially this: that the request which she made, would if made public, disclose to the world that credentials were given to persons pro forma and that this was a type of the representatives of movements which they claim as constituents, and as a result the very purposes of the conference would prove its own undoing.[7]

. . .

Regarding the situation in Butte, the correspondence with Mr. Alpine who went there and his suggestions,[8] you have been informed.[9] I communicated that to the Council. The question as to time of my visit there accompanied by a few men is indefinite. We ought to hear something orally from Mr. Alpine when he arrives at the Council meeting. Mr. Alpine and I had a two hours conference with the President[10] and Vice-President[11] of the Amalgamated Copper Company at their offices in New York,[12] in which they showed themselves to be of a liberal open-minded disposition, desirous of doing business with the miners as an organized body. One of their statements was that the only reason they declared the mines an open shop was that they did not want to deal with the so-called independent or I.W.W. organization, and the bona fide old union had but a fragmentary membership. When the so-called I.W.W. union believed that the position of the company was for a union establishment, they held the membership intact. This organization charged 25 cents, and for the 25 cents each one got a button. They paid nothing more, the organization performed no other duty of unionism, and as soon as the company had declared for the open shop, the men who wore the buttons of this so-called I.W.W. organization, took off their buttons and no longer paid. He said that the rank and file of that organization are all right except that they were dissatisfied with the administration of the affairs of the old union; that the rank and file had no opportunity for participating in the proceedings of the organization; that funds were squandered and maladministered while the members could find no redress; and that about twenty of the active I.W.W. men came from different parts of the country to that city and fanned the discontent into the revolt and brutality which was manifested during the troublesome times there. The men believed that the suggestion of Mr. Alpine, that I ought to go there, was a good one, that to associate with myself some other labor men would be helpful, but the representatives of the company believed it would be unwise for me to go there within the immediate present, because the feeling now latent or dying out would be embittered again, and the antagonism which was manifested by the I.W.W. and the discontent of the rank and file would probably be fanned into life again, and that probably more injury would ensue than good. There is considerable correspondence from the active men in and around Butte, urging that I ought to go there and that the President[13] of the Mining Department, Vice-President Green, and one or two others whose names do not just occur to me ought to go with me. In the last few weeks I have heard little from Butte as to the situation there.

Mr. Lennon: I am still of the same opinion that if the Western Federation of Miners would consent to the formation of an independent union with a charter from the A.F. of L., say for a year or so, that we might go there and do business.

Mr. Morrison: There is only one solution for this thing, and that is, for the Miners to take the Western Federation of Miners.

Mr. Valentine: You made reference to the officers of the company, but no mention of their names was made.

Mr. Gompers: I referred to Mr. Ryan, President, and Mr. Kelly, General Manager. Both Mr. Kelly and Mr. Ryan of the Amalgamated Copper Co. expressed themselves as just suggested by Mr. Lennon, that if a union could be chartered by the American Federation of Labor direct—and there was no doubt in their minds but what such a union could be brought into existence—they would be glad to deal with it as an organized body.

Mr. Valentine: The statement made by these people was that they would not deal with the I.W.W. organization, but that too few of the others were left?

Mr. Lennon: Some of these men approaching the leadership said positively that their fight was on the Western Federation of Miners, and that they could not get the people away from it but if the union could be established locally they thought it should be done.

Mr. Morrison: Then immediately the cry would go forth that this was an employers' organization, and that the Federation was fostering it. It could not be done.

Mr. Valentine: Mr. Gompers made the statement that there were so few of the old union men left.

Mr. Gompers: Yes; because being but a few, to enter into an agreement with that small number would be in no way effective. They said that their dealings with the Butte local miners' union were always satisfactory.

Mr. O'Connell: And they would not deal with the I.W.W. crowd at all.

Mr. Gompers: The I.W.W. has declared that they do not regard agreements with employers as desirable or binding.

Mr. Valentine: That is the position of the Western Federation of Miners, too.

Mr. Morrison: They have changed from that, but changed too late.

Mr. Gompers: Referring to one feature of this, Mr. Morrison suggested that there was but one way out of this entire difficulty, and that was for the United Mine Workers to take over the Western Federation of Miners. In connection with that, let me say that I was asked my opinion by one of the members of the committee appointed by the United Mine Workers in regard to that subject, and I expressed my opinion pretty thoroughly to him on the same lines.[14] The answer[15] I received was that what the Western Federation of Miners wanted was that the United Mine Workers of America should bear all the financial obligations of the metal miners' organization, and that the Western Federation of Miners should have absolute autonomy and independence in the government of its own affairs.

Mr. Green: That is my understanding of their proposition.

The relations between the Western Federation of Miners and the United Mine Workers is much misunderstood. There is not a community of interests between the two organizations, but because of the term "mining" in both titles, it is naturally assumed that there is a good deal in common in both organizations. Now there is none other than the common interests of labor, just the same as there would be with the Machinists organization and our organization, because the metal mining is so much different from the coal mining. In the methods of mining there is no comparison. There is no similarity in the metal mining and the coal mining. For instance, the material produced by the metal miners has no influence on the production of coal. They are different altogether. Then as I just said, the method of mining coal and mining metal is entirely different. One man might be competent as a metal miner, but not as a coal miner, and vice versa. The only similarity between the two is that they go in the earth to mine. After that it is altogether different.

Mr. Gompers: Because that has been presented to either the Executive Council or to me, I want to ask you a question, so that all may hear the answer. Is there a close connection or interdependence between the metal miners and the coal miners? For instance in the matter of competition, or in cessation of work, a strike?

Mr. Green: There is none whatever, Mr. Gompers. There is not as much interdependence and community of interest between the metal miners and the coal miners, as there is between the machinists and the coal miners.

Mr. Morrison: Particularly between the coal miners and blast furnaces, etc.

Mr. Green: If the coal miners were involved in trouble, and the metal miners were to strike, that would not help at all, and vice versa. They stand out absolutely alone.

Mr. Gompers: A strike of the metal miners in sympathy with coal miners, would that not have any effect?

Mr. Green: None whatever, except the general effect that any body of laboring men would have, in calling attention to the situation, but so far as any substantial assistance is concerned, they could not give it, and the reverse situation is also true, except perhaps the coal miners could help the railroad men by withholding fuel, etc. In the coal mines there is lots of machinery used, and there is nothing so far as the metal miner is concerned. There is no relation. They would not help the coal miners a bit by shutting off the supply of metals that they mined. That would not help the coal miners in a fight. There are about a million coal miners in the United States. We have approximately four hundred thousand, so that we have got a lot of missionary work to do among the coal miners, without taking on an entirely new field, in which there is really no community of interest. We have got six hundred thousand coal miners that we want to organize.

Mr. Gompers: Then there is no interdependent community of interest.

Mr. Green: That is what I mean.

Mr. Valentine: In other words, if they changed that name, and called them metal miners, it would probably be a name more appropriate. The name Western Federation of Miners, is misleading.

Mr. Green: I am utterly opposed to any amalgamation between the two. It is assuming an obligation similar to say for instance taking over the machinists, or any other organization.

Mr. Morrison: The Western Federation of Miners would have come into the United Mine Workers at Rochester. And at that time they were not as much in favor of it as now, because I said to Moyer, "why don't you amalgamate with the coal miners?" He said, "We don't desire to lose our identity."

. . .

TDc, Executive Council Records, Minutes, reel 5, frames 1001, 1006–10, *AFL Records.*

1. The World Court Congress met in Cleveland, May 12–14, 1915, to discuss the establishment and jurisdiction of a world tribunal to adjudicate international disputes. William Howard Taft was one of the principal speakers at the meeting. SG declined an invitation to attend (to John Hays Hammond, Apr. 19, 1915, reel 193, vol. 205, p. 191, SG Letterbooks, DLC).

2. The meeting, held on the evening of Apr. 15, 1915, at Cooper Union in New York City under the auspices of the Central Federated Union of Greater New York and Vicinity, was attended by some three thousand people. Meyer London was the principal speaker. SG declined to attend the meeting (to Ernest Bohm, Apr. 7, 1915, reel 192, vol. 204, p. 916, SG Letterbooks, DLC).

3. The National Emergency Peace Conference was held in Chicago, Feb. 27–28, 1915, under the auspices of the Woman's Peace party, the Carnegie Endowment for International Peace, and other organizations. Jane Addams served as chair of the meeting, which was attended by some three hundred people. The conference endorsed the idea of continuous mediation between the belligerents, to begin at once rather than waiting for an armistice. SG declined invitations to attend the conference from Louis Lochner, secretary of the Emergency Federation of Peace Forces, and from Henry Haskell on behalf of the Carnegie Endowment (to Lochner, Feb. 10 and 11, 1915, reel 190, vol. 202, pp. 783, 794–95, SG Letterbooks, DLC; to Haskell, Feb. 11, 1915, ibid., p. 809).

4. The International Congress of Women met at The Hague, Apr. 28–May 1, 1915. Over one thousand voting delegates attending the meeting, representing more than one hundred fifty organizations from twelve countries. Jane Addams chaired the sessions. The conference voted to ask neutral nations to undertake continuous mediation between the belligerents and accept peace proposals, to send envoys to European nations and the United States, and to hold another international meeting of women in conjunction with the peace conference ending the war. The congress also established the International Committee of Women for Permanent Peace (from 1919, the Women's International League for Peace and Freedom).

5. Probably Sarah Wambaugh, secretary of the Massachusetts branch of the Woman's Peace party. She later became an internationally recognized authority on plebiscites and an adviser to the League of Nations and the United Nations.

6. Probably Annie E. Molloy, president of International Brotherhood of Electrical Workers 1A (Telephone Operators) of Boston from 1913 to 1916.

7. SG replied to this letter on Apr. 6, 1915 (to Wambaugh, reel 192, vol. 204, pp. 925–26, SG Letterbooks, DLC).

8. John Alpine recommended that SG visit Butte, Mont., with officials of the United Mine Workers of America and also suggested that he arrange a conference with John

Ryan, president of the Amalgamated Copper Co., in New York City (Alpine to SG, Feb. 14, 17, and 20, 1915, Executive Council Records, Vote Books, reel 13, frames 594–95, 599–600, *AFL Records*).

9. SG to the AFL Executive Council, Feb. 20 and 23, 1915, Executive Council Records, Vote Books, reel 13, frames 593, 598, *AFL Records*.

10. John D. Ryan served as president of the Amalgamated Copper Co. and its successor, the Anaconda Copper Mining Co., from 1909 until 1917. He stepped down from this position to assist in the war effort and in 1918 served as director of the Bureau of Aircraft Production and as assistant secretary of war. At the conclusion of World War I, Ryan became chairman of the board of Anaconda, holding that post until his death in 1933.

11. Cornelius F. Kelley was vice-president and managing director of the Amalgamated Copper Co. and the Anaconda Copper Mining Co. (1911–17) and later served as president (1918–40) and chairman of the board (1940–55) of Anaconda.

12. SG and Alpine met with Ryan and Kelley in New York City on Mar. 6, 1915.

13. James LORD served as president of the AFL Mining Department from 1914 until 1922.

14. See "To Frank Farrington," Sept. 3, 1914, above.

15. See "To Frank Farrington," Sept. 3, 1914, n. 7, above.

To Thomas McArdle

May 3, 1915.

Mr. Thomas E. McArdle,
Holmhurst Hotel, Atlantic City, N.J.
Dear Sir:

You are doubtless aware that the property corner 9th Street and Massachusetts Avenue, N.W., Washington, D.C., has been inspected by a committee representing the American Federation of Labor with a view of purchase of the site and the erection thereon of a building for the American Federation of Labor.[1] It is our intention not to have a structure erected for commercial or business purposes, but a dignified substantial building for the conduct of the office work of the American Federation of Labor. I mention this so that you may know that there is no speculative thought which prompts us in this matter. Nor is the ownership of a building by the American Federation of Labor either essential or necessary. It is a mere matter of convenience and pride.

We have had a number of different prices set for the sale of the site, and having been given your name and address, I write you direct to say that if you will accept Thirty Thousand Dollars, ($30,000.00) for the property, I shall recommend to my associates of the Executive Council that the property be purchased and I feel confident that any such recommendation will be approved by my associates, whereupon the sale may be made and the purchase price handed to you or your representative in cash.

Inasmuch as I may have to come to Atlantic City for Tuesday morning, May 11,[2] I shall be very glad to have a talk with you regarding the above offer. In all likelihood Mr. Frank Morrison, Secretary of the American Federation of Labor, will be in Atlantic City with me the early part of that day.

I hope to have a reply to the above at your early convenience,[3] and oblige,

Yours very truly,   Saml Gompers.
President,   American Federation of Labor.

TLpS, reel 193, vol. 205, pp. 782–83, SG Letterbooks, DLC.

1. The 1908 AFL convention authorized the Executive Council to spend $80,000 to purchase land and erect an office building for the Federation. The 1914 convention reiterated its authorization of a new building and approved raising additional funds. The lot for the new headquarters, at the corner of Ninth St. and Massachusetts Ave., N.W., was purchased in 1915 for $40,000 and groundbreaking took place on Oct. 28. The cornerstone was laid on Jan. 8, 1916, President Woodrow Wilson delivered the chief address at dedication ceremonies on July 4, and the Federation staff occupied its new seven-story, ninety-room headquarters on Aug. 26. The Executive Council reported the cost of erecting the building at $103,555.

2. SG met with Thomas McArdle in Atlantic City on May 11, 1915, on his return from a trip to New England and New York City. SG left Washington, D.C., on May 3 to deliver addresses in Amherst and Haverhill, Mass., and to hold conferences with labor representatives in Boston and New York City. He returned to AFL headquarters on May 13.

3. McArdle replied on May 4, 1915, that the asking price for the property was $41,000 and that he would not accept $30,000, but he agreed to meet with SG on May 11 (AFL Microfilm Convention File, reel 27, frame 1258, *AFL Records*).

To John Andrews[1]

May 14, 1915.

Mr. John B. Andrews,
Secretary, American Association for Labor Legislation,[2]
131 E. 23d Street, New York City.
Dear Sir:

Various experiences have given me an impression that the policies, the purposes and the spirit of the American Association for Labor Legislation are not in harmony with those of the wage-earners of America. This impression was made conviction by the course which the

American Association for Labor Legislation pursued with regard to the consolidation of the New York State Workmen's Compensation Law and the Department of Labor,[3] thus weakening the effectiveness of both Departments, thus using the influence of the A.A. for L.L. to fasten upon the workers policies which they had emphatically opposed, and assuming the responsibility of destroying legislation which they had approved and assisted to enact.

The wage-earners welcome counsel and aid but they deny the right of any one or any group of individuals to dictate measures which vitally concern the industrial welfare of the workers. They deny that the judgment of any group of men is more trustworthy than the consensus of opinion of those who have daily experience with industrial conditions and forces and therefore understand many tendencies that are not evident from the theoretical viewpoint.

As an official spokesman for this association you assumed responsibility for the enactment of the so-called Spring bill and made the statement that the measure was experimental. Contrary to the wishes and the judgment of the wage-earners, the American Association for Labor Legislation undertook a "scientific experimentation" which involved the welfare of those human beings.

The wage-earners of the United States deny the right of any man or any association to despotism whether political, industrial or intellectual. We are endeavoring to achieve our freedom and cannot co-operate with those whose aim is despotism even for a benevolent purpose.

For these reasons I hereby tender my resignation as a member of the American Association for Labor Legislation, to take effect immediately.

Very truly yours,   Saml Gompers.
President,   American Federation of Labor.[4]

TLpS, reel 193, vol. 205, pp. 946–47, SG Letterbooks, DLC.

1. John Bertram Andrews (1880–1943) served as executive secretary (1909–43) of the American Association for Labor Legislation and was founder and editor (1911–43) of its journal, the *American Labor Legislation Review*.

2. The American Association for Labor Legislation was founded in 1906 to encourage the investigation of industrial conditions and promote the passage of uniform labor legislation in the United States. It was particularly involved with the issues of workers' compensation and health insurance, unemployment, and workplace health and safety.

3. New York, Laws of 1915, chap. 674, enacted May 22, 1915, abolished the offices of the commissioner and the deputy commissioners of labor, the state industrial board, and the state workmen's compensation commission, transferring their functions to a five-member state industrial commission, which was also given direction of the state department of labor. The legislation, endorsed and in part drafted by the American Association for Labor Legislation, was introduced by New York state senator George F.

Spring, chair of the senate labor committee. It was approved by the state senate on Apr. 19 and by the assembly on Apr. 23. The measure was opposed by the New York State Federation of Labor and the Central Federated Union of Greater New York and Vicinity.

4. SG reprinted this letter in his editorial "Labor Must Decide Its Own Course," published in the June 1915 number of the *American Federationist* (22: 430–32).

To John Slaton[1]

May 22, 1915.

Hon. John M. Slaton,
Governor of the State of Georgia,
Atlanta, Georgia.
Sir:

May I not join with others in an appeal to you and those who may be officially associated with you, in exercising the great prerogative of commuting the sentence of Leo M. Frank[2] from death to imprisonment for life.

It is quite true that I am opposed to capital punishment, to the taking of human life, whether privately, in concert, or by the state. The American Federation of Labor has emphatically declared that position. But quite regardless of such a declaration, the case in point, that of Leo M. Frank, has been hedged about by so many peculiar situations, there rests in the minds of many of our people the opinion that after all Frank did not have a free, fair, impartial trial, and that somehow or other, other influences than judicial procedure aided in the jury reaching the verdict of guilty.

Surely, under the many circumstances to which I only refer rather than mention, may I not appeal that your great prerogative be exercised in commuting the sentence of Leo M. Frank from death to a life term of imprisonment? I make this appeal on the grounds of justice and humanity. I trust that it may commend itself to the favorable consideration and action of yourself and your associates entrusted with this great power.

Very respectfully yours,   Saml Gompers.
President,   American Federation of Labor.

TLpS, reel 194, vol. 206, pp. 178–79, SG Letterbooks, DLC.

1. John Marshall Slaton (1866–1955) served as Democratic governor of Georgia, 1911–12, 1913–15.

2. Leo Max Frank, a northern Jew who had moved to Atlanta to manage a pencil factory, was convicted in 1913 after a sensationalized trial and sentenced to death for

the brutal murder of Mary Phagan, a young employee whose body was found in the factory's basement. When Governor Slaton commuted Frank's sentence to life imprisonment on June 21, 1915, Georgia newspapers called on citizens of the state to take justice into their own hands. Frank survived an attack by another inmate in July, but on the night of Aug. 16 he was abducted from the jail and lynched.

To Frank Walsh

May 22, 1915.

Important. Please read.
Hon. Frank P. Walsh,
Chairman, Federal Commission on Industrial Relations,
Shoreham Hotel, Washington, D.C.
My dear Mr. Walsh:

It is greatly desirable and necessary that I should have an opportunity of appearing before the Commission on Industrial Relations for the purpose of presenting some answer to the charge and insinuation made by Mr. Walter Drew relative to the American Federation of Labor and myself relative to the arrest and kidnapping of the McNamaras, and the funds raised for their defense,[1] as I said when I publicly asked you for an opportunity to meet this matter in *all* its phases. I am not only desirous of doing this and submitting myself to such examination as may be necessary, but I am anxious to do so, and in justice to all concerned I ought to have that opportunity, and which you declared I should have.

In addition, I have opinions of learned counsel regarding the comprehensive effect of the Clayton law, taking the opposite view to that presented by Mr. Spelling and others before the Commission.[2]

Also I have some matters regarding the activities of detective agencies, strike breaking agencies, the activities of the U.S. Steel Corporation and the Standard Oil Company, showing their unlawful and brutal conduct toward citizens and toward working people engaged in an effort to improve their conditions. In all I think it would require not more than an hour of the Commission's time to present these matters, of course, subject to such cross examination by the Commission as they may desire.

I was requested by two committees of the New York State Constitutional Convention[3] to appear before these committees on last Wednesday, and because of the Industrial Relations Commission meeting here and expecting to be present to submit the above matters during this week, I asked for a postponement of the hearings at Albany, New York, until Wednesday, May 26th. The request was granted. On Monday the 17th, the New York State Federation of Labor will hold a conference at Albany in regard to the subject of Constitutional Convention, where the Constitutional changes which Labor is to recommend will be discussed. I mention this so that you will understand that my absence from Washington is actually forced, and the purpose of my writing is to inquire whether it will be possible for me to have the opportunity of appearing before the Commission Thursday or Friday, May 27th or 28th, preferably the latter date, for if it be Thursday it will necessitate my traveling five hours in the evening from Albany to New York, and then traveling by the midnight train to Washington.[4]

In addition you know that Mr. Iglesias and Mr. Martinez are here under summons from the Commission, and of course they too will be subject to the Commission's convenience.

Of course you will understand that I am not making any criticism of yourself or the Commission. On the contrary, I watched with interest and appreciation the testimony you have elicited during this past several days.

Will you kindly have someone communicate with my office, Ouray Building, Washington, D.C., and I will be advised as to your suggestion regarding the arrangements you can make for my appearance before the Commission.

Sincerely yours,   Saml Gompers.
President.   American Federation of Labor.

TLpS, reel 194, vol. 206, pp. 181–83, SG Letterbooks, DLC.

1. Walter Drew testified before the U.S. Commission on Industrial Relations in Washington, D.C., on May 17, 1915 (U.S. Congress, Senate, *Industrial Relations. Final Report and Testimony Submitted to Congress by the Commission on Industrial Relations . . .* , 64th Cong., 1st sess., 1916, S. Doc. 415, 11: 10731–69). His testimony included the assertion that organized labor knew the McNamaras were guilty even before the trial.

2. In his testimony before the commission on May 15, 1915, Thomas Spelling argued that the Clayton Act brought no advantage to workers but placed them at a greater disadvantage (*Final Report and Testimony,* 11: 10720–31).

3. The New York state constitutional convention met in Albany, Apr. 6–Sept. 10, 1915. The convention, dominated by Republicans, ignored the proposals submitted by the New York State Federation of Labor and approved a document that called for a sweeping consolidation of state government. The proposed constitution was overwhelmingly rejected by the electorate in a ratification vote on Nov. 2. SG, James Lynch, John Mitchell, and Homer Call all ran unsuccessfully for election as delegates to the convention.

4. SG testified before the commission in Washington, D.C., on the afternoon of May 27, 1915 (*Final Report and Testimony,* 11: 10852–61).

James Diggs to Frank Morrison

Washington, D.C. May 24 '15.

Mr. Morison,
Dear Sir:—

I call at your office this evening about 3:30 you was not in. I was sent there by the U.S. Attorney; he sent me there to see Mr. Gompers to see why the local union number 77 of steam hoisting engineers[1] could draw the color line against the colored engineers and at the same time hold one colored engineer in their union to prevent the colored engineers from getting a separate charter.

He sent me to see Mr. Gompers or you first before taking the matter up. Please answer at once, and, let me know, as he is waiting for an answer as we colored engineers have to live as well as the white ones.[2]

Yours truly, Jas. H. Diggs

I had to give my place of employment up on account of them (local union no. 77) not letting me join the union. I have tried several times for the last six or severn years and they (local union no. 77) have gave some excuse or other for not taking me in; such excuses as "We have more than we have work for," or "Come back in two or three months,["] and etc.

The first time I went to them (Local no. 77) I wanted to leave railroad construction work where I had been employed for five years or more. Local union no. 77 has nothing against me as they know I never tried to do them any harm in their trade or any other way.

They came in the months of February and April and had the bricklayers to join them to deprive me of my life as if I did not have a right to live as well as they leaving it for me to steal or starve. Then when a man gets in such circumstances where he has to steal or hold up and rob some one they and the rest of the public is shocked a great crime has been down claiming that the party or parties was or were a brute/s to do so.

When at the same time it is the oppression of grafters and conspirators who are the ones to blame and should be sentenced nine tenths of the time. If it was not for justice having to be purchased by money instead of by justice as it should be this world would be a better one and there would not be somany useful lives to-day being passed away in the silent city.

ALS, AFL Microfilm National and International Union File, Operating Engineers Records, reel 37, frame 2107, *AFL Records.*

1. International Union of Steam and Operating Engineers 77 of Washington, D.C.

2. Frank Morrison had received a similar complaint in February 1915 from Beverly Randall, another black engineer, and had been assured at that time by Steam Engineers' local 77 that the union did not draw the color line. Morrison forwarded Diggs's letter to James Hannahan, secretary-treasurer of the international union, on June 5 and informed Diggs of his action the same day (AFL Microfilm National and International Union File, Operating Engineers Records, reel 37, frame 2108, *AFL Records*).

To William Green

May 28, 1915.

Mr. William Green,
Secretary-Treasurer, United Mine Workers of America,
1102–1108 Merchants Bank Bldg., Indianapolis, Ind.
Dear Sir and Brother:

Your letter of May 20th[1] containing information as to the agreement secured by the miners of eastern Ohio, was read with great pleasure. The miners certainly fought a splendid fight and have earned the satisfactory agreement which was made with the mine operators.[2] It is more than gratifying to learn that the struggle has resulted in a greater degree of solidarity than was ever displayed before. The fact that they are able to secure the mine run method of payment by economic agreement, even when the legislature repeals the law providing for that method,[3] ought to be further proof to the miners that economic organization is the source of all of their power. I trust that they will not fail to see the importance of this matter.

I wish that it had been possible for you to have been in Washington during the past week to attend the hearings before the Commission on Industrial Relations. These would have been most intensely interesting to you, particularly the hearing of John D. Rockefeller, Jr.[4] The testimony of all the witnesses discloses the principle that no amount of legislation for the purpose of establishing democratic government or agencies for popular control is of any avail unless the people have economic independence. Economic independence can be achieved only by the workers themselves through organization.

Will you write me what the mine workers propose to do in order to secure a fair trial for John R. Lawson?[5] Lawson's fate is of great importance to the labor movement as it involves not only his own future life but the welfare of the miners already indicted and others who may be. I hope your organization has already taken steps to do something and you may rest assured that I will do all that lies in my power.

Write often. With best wishes, I remain,

Fraternally yours,   Saml Gompers

President   American Federation of Labor.

TLpS, reel 194, vol. 206, pp. 248–49, SG Letterbooks, DLC.

1. William Green to SG, May 20, 1915, AFL Microfilm National and International Union File, United Mine Workers Records, reel 40, frame 1390, *AFL Records*.

2. On the expiration of their contract with the United Mine Workers of America, mine operators in Ohio shut down nearly all the coal mines in the state on Apr. 1, 1914, rejecting miners' demands for a new contract stipulating payment by total weight of all coal mined (the run-of-mine method) at a uniform statewide rate per ton rather than payment only for screened, lump coal. Although mine owners in other sections of the state granted these concessions during the summer of 1914, operators in eastern Ohio continued to hold out, keeping over thirteen thousand miners out of work. The union finally achieved its demands at conferences mediated by Ohio governor Frank Willis and state mine inspector Jack Roan. The new agreement was signed on May 8, 1915, and ratified by the union's members on May 12.

3. Ohio Senate Bill 3, Laws of 1914, pp. 181–82, enacted Feb. 17, 1914, stipulated that miners in the state were to be paid on the run-of-mine basis and prohibited the use of screens. Senate Bill 72, Laws of 1915, pp. 350–52, enacted May 26, 1915, provided for run-of-mine payment unless otherwise agreed by employer and miner.

4. John D. Rockefeller, Jr., testified before the U.S. Commission on Industrial Relations on May 20–22, 1915, at hearings in Washington, D.C. (U.S. Congress, Senate, *Industrial Relations. Final Report and Testimony Submitted to Congress by the Commission on Industrial Relations . . .* , 64th Cong., 1st sess., 1916, S. Doc. 415, 9: 8592–715).

5. John R. Lawson, a member of United Mine Workers' local 1772 of Palisade, Colo., served on the executive board of the international union (1910–17) and was a leader of the 1913–14 miners' strike in Colorado. He was arrested, tried, and on May 3, 1915, convicted of first-degree murder in connection with the death of deputy sheriff John Nimmo at Ludlow, Colo., on Oct. 25, 1913. He was sentenced to life imprisonment. The judge at the trial, Granby Hillyer, had served as an attorney representing the Colorado Fuel and Iron Co. until he was appointed by the governor in the spring of 1915 to handle cases against the miners. On Aug. 17, 1915, the Colorado Supreme Court decided to review the case and stayed Lawson's sentence. It also ruled that Hillyer was biased and prohibited him from hearing any other cases arising from the miners' strike. In the spring of 1917 the state's attorney general filed a confession of error in the Lawson case and, shortly thereafter, the state supreme court overturned Lawson's conviction.

Green replied to SG's inquiry on June 4, 1915, that the attorneys in the case had moved for a new trial and that the union's locals had been asked to hold well-publicized protest meetings (AFL Microfilm National and International Union File, United Mine Workers Records, reel 40, frame 1611, *AFL Records*).

To Harris Weinstock[1]

May 29, 1915

Personal
Mr. H. Weinstock,
Commission on Industrial Relations,
c/o Samuel Gompers, Room 508 Ouray Bldg., Washington, D.C.
Dear Sir:

Of course you understand that I have been so extremely busy that I have been unable to write you in connection with your letter of May 5, 1915. You find fault with me because I used the following in my article in the May issue of the *American Federationist*.[2]

"From recent events it is fair to assume that Mr. W. has come under the influence of the Drews and the Merrits[3] of the National Association of Manufacturers."

I wonder whether you are still of the opinion that this statement of fact is unjustified. You ask any of your associates of the Industrial Relations Commission whether your whole course the last few months as a member of the Commission did not justify my statement.

When Mr. Drew at the New York hearing sent up his series of questions insinuating and diabolical, he sent them up to you to ask them and only upon my insistent demand did I extract the name of my real questioner.[4]

During the hearings here Mr. Drew's letters of an insulting and accusing character against laboring men; and in asking that they, together with other documents be made part of the record, were not addressed to the Commission but to you and you read them with all the airs and artifice of a finished elocutionist.[5] You think that Mr. Drew and the other Drews by other names, do not know their man?

Perhaps the article which the New York Evening Post is about to publish attacking, denouncing and insulting to the men in the labor movement of America, falsely charging them and misrepresenting them may have quite a familiar sound to you. Of course no one would insinuate that you had seen the article before publication.

I am writing this letter to you on this, the twenty-ninth day of May, 1915, but propose to defer mailing it to you until after the publication of the article in the New York Evening Post. I am mailing this letter to you in care of this office and shall hold it until after the publication of the article in the New York Evening Post, when I shall remail this letter to you with seal unbroken, the postmark on the letter indicating the date upon which it was written and mailed.

There was a time when labor men seemed to have hope for your helpfulness in their tremendous struggle for justice, right and humanity, but alas!

Very respectfully yours,   Saml Gompers.
President   American Federation of Labor.

TLpS, reel 194, vol. 206, pp. 377–78, SG Letterbooks, DLC.

1. Harris Weinstock, a member of the U.S. Commission on Industrial Relations from San Francisco, was involved in dry goods, banking, and real estate.

2. SG's editorial "Fixing Wages by Law or Unionism," published in the May 1915 number of the *American Federationist* (22: 363–67).

3. Walter Gordon Merritt, a New York City attorney, was associate counsel for the American Anti-Boycott Association. His father, Charles Hart Merritt, was chair of the association's executive board.

4. The questioning occurred during SG's testimony before the U.S. Commission on Industrial Relations in New York City on Jan. 22, 1915 (U.S. Congress, Senate, *Industrial Relations. Final Report and Testimony Submitted to Congress by the Commission on Industrial Relations . . .* , 64th Cong., 1st sess., 1916, S. Doc. 415, 8: 7638–57).

5. During the commission's hearings in Washington, D.C., May 10–27, 1915, letters from Walter Drew to Weinstock, dated May 18 and 20, were entered as evidence and made part of the official record (*Final Report and Testimony*, 11: 10834, 10920–21).

To Samuel Landers

June 10, 1915.

Mr. Samuel L. Landers,
Editor "The Labor News,"
48 Market St., Hamilton, Canada.
Dear Sir and Brother:

The clippings which you sent me in your letter of June 1st were read with great care. I know that your long experience in the labor movement has taught you that none of us are infallible; that we all make mistakes and sometimes those mistakes are caused by the best of intentions which have been misdirected because of failure to understand. However, your experience has also taught you that there is much good in all of us and somehow if that could be aroused and made to predominate over other things that the movement for human progress could be best promoted and quickened. I feel that this is particularly true with regard to the women's trade union movement. There has been of late years a tremendous awakening among the women of the world. There has been among them a growing appreciation of self-responsibility, not only for their own lives but for the effect of their lives upon those with whom they are associated in work and in the social relations of life. The Women's Trade Union League represents this awakening spirit among the wage earning women of the United States. It is a groping for something better, for greater justice and greater liberty. If those of us who understand the bigness and weakness of humanity could somehow direct this great woman movement we can be helpful in a cause that means much to the labor movement, and I think that we can be more helpful and helpful in a better way if we share with these women the fruits of our long experience and try to lead them rather than direct against them bitter criticism, whether it be merited or not. All of the traditions of woman's life and all of the conventionalities that have grown up around her life are a hindrance to her in the organized labor movement. Somehow or other wage earning women must break through these hindrances and work out their own salvation, and I am sure that if you will only allow that best vein of old time trade unionism that is within you to come to the surface, you will appreciate the value that the Women's Trade Union League can be to the organized labor movement and will join in the work of helping them.

Whenever anything comes to your attention in regard to this matter that you think is unwise and detrimental to the labor movement, I will be very glad if you would write them to me personally and then let us work out some plan to help them. Helpful criticism is constructive but there is a kind of criticism that drives away and embitters. Let us work together for the best interests of all of the wage earners.

Write me frequently. With best wishes, I remain,

Fraternally yours,   Saml Gompers.
President   American Federation of Labor.

TLpS, reel 194, vol. 206, pp. 785–86, SG Letterbooks, DLC.

An Article in the *New York Times*

Washington, June 10. [1915]

GOMPERS AGAINST WAR.

Samuel Gompers, President of the American Federation of Labor, tonight issued the following statement on the present international situation:[1]

"My opinion is that, regardless of what honorable position the United States may take, the effort will be made to drag us into the international conflict whether we like it or not. It is a great pity that there is not greater publicity regarding international relations and diplomatic communications, so that the people may be in a position to form their judgment, not after, but previous to definite action being taken. I suppose, however, that this thought can only find its acceptance when more normal conditions shall prevail. The influence of the American Federation of Labor, of the workers of our country, will be exerted for the maintenance of peace, and yet we cannot permit to be challenged the insistence that the lives of Americans shall not be unnecessarily and unwarrantably jeopardized."

New York Times, June 11, 1915.

1. On May 7, 1915, a German submarine sank the British passenger liner *Lusitania* with the loss of 1,198 lives. Among the dead were 128 Americans. In response, the United States addressed three diplomatic notes to the government of Germany, dated May 13, June 9, and July 21, demanding the abandonment of unrestricted submarine warfare, an apology, and reparations and warning that a repetition of the tragedy would be regarded as an unfriendly act. Secretary of State William Jennings Bryan resigned rather than sign the second note, which he feared would lead to war. Tensions eased after the German ambassador to the United States, Johann von Bernstorff, gave assurances on Sept. 1 that liners would not be sunk in the future without warning and provision for the safety of noncombatants (the *Arabic* pledge).

To Samuel Hughes

June 14, 1915.

Mr. S. T. Hughes,
Editor, The Newspaper Enterprise Association,
102 N. Fifth Ave., Chicago, Ill.
Dear Sir:

In your communication of June 7th you ask for information regarding my childhood ambitions. The information that you ask for has been completely crowded out of my mind by years of incessant activity and never-ceasing work for a great humanitarian movement. Indeed, if you knew that I became a workman at ten years of age you would understand that the grim necessities of life left me very few years for childhood's dreams. Those first ten years were spent in East Side London, and even into them the cares of life entered and I was denied an opportunity that society ought to accord to every human being,—the right to childhood and childhood's dreams.

I have no picture taken in childhood. We were poor people and there were many of us and we could not afford such luxuries.

There is so much work to be done in this world that I do not find time to decide whether I am disappointed or pleased because fancies have not been realized, and after all, it makes very little difference. We do what we have to do and do the best we can under the circumstances. That life is best which is fullest of good service, well and honestly rendered.

Yours very sincerely,   Saml Gompers.
President   American Federation of Labor.

TLpS, reel 194, vol. 206, p. 882, SG Letterbooks, DLC.

From William Appleton

Chief Office
The General Federation of Trade Unions
London, W.C. 16th June, 1915.

Dear Gompers,

I am enclosing you, under personal cover, a copy of our Annual Report. You will find reproduced therein the correspondence which has recently taken place in connection with the International Secretariat.[1] For the moment there is little further to add, but it is true that public opinion has hardened here and that any attempt to attend a conference, such as the one that has been called at Amsterdam,[2] would have increased our difficulties.

You are perhaps reading a lot of stuff about the drunkenness and delinquencies of the British workmen: don't believe one twentieth part. It is true that now, as always, there are a few here and there who play the fool and the rogue but, generally speaking, the whole working class community has borne itself with courage and quiet devotion to national interests and safety. My own candid opinion is that the outcry has been raised by the really responsible people to cover up their own shortcomings; experts were not expert enough. Government departments as usual were hide-bound, and contractors have cried out because having contracted to produce more than their machinery and appliances would permit they have had to find excuses somewhere.

You will have read of the deplorable anti-German outbreaks which followed the sinking of the "Lusitania." We were all very sorry for these outbreaks but they had been carefully prepared by the Northcliffe press;[3] for weeks and weeks it had been harping on the one string.

We all regret the fact of war but we are under no mis-apprehensions as to our position. Germany has definitely shown us that we must fight or die, and not only must we fight or die but all the other nations who dislike the idea of absorption into the German scheme must take up a similar attitude. We are not prepared as a nation to die just yet and we shall fight, and we expect to save ourselves and to help in the saving of other nations.

You will regret, for old associations' sake, to hear that one of the aeroplane raids[4] led to some damage being done in and around Shoreditch and to the loss of seven lives. There have been other raids in different parts of the country where the damage and loss of life has been sometimes more and sometimes less serious. Five times German aeroplanes or zeppelins have passed over the district in which my family live but fortunately no bomb has dropped nearer than three miles to the place. This district is entirely rural and, as far as we know, there are no fortifications within many miles.

We do not anticipate an early termination of the war because we recognise that it is a war in which endurance counts for much; we are not yet destitute of the capacity for enduring things.

With kindest regards,

Yours faithfully,   W A Appleton

TLS, AFL Microfilm Convention File, reel 28, frame 1759, *AFL Records.*

1. The General Federation of Trade Unions, *Sixteenth Annual Report and Balance Sheet, 1915* (London, 1915), pp. 16–34.

2. Acting on instructions from Carl Legien, Jan Oudegeest issued a call on May 31, 1915, for a conference to meet in Amsterdam in late August or early September to discuss the Anglo-French proposal to move the headquarters of the International Federation of Trade Unions (IFTU) to a neutral country. A majority of the trade union centers responded that a conference was unnecessary and that no change should be made in the IFTU, so the Amsterdam meeting was not held. Writing William Appleton on July 1, 1915, SG commented that "for several weeks the members of the Executive Council of the American Federation of Labor have had under consideration the advisability of either participating in the conference recommended by Mr. Legien and sent out by Mr. Oudegeest. We have also been thinking of possibly supplementing that call by an urgent appeal for the representatives of the labor movements of the various countries to take advantage of the opportunity and to meet, consult, and see whether some good could be brought out, some light be found to help in this awful, critical situation. The letters from yourself and from Mr. Jouhaux indicate quite clearly that such a conference at this time is out of the question: that the very fact that the representatives of the trade union centers of England and France not being represented would in advance make such a conference ineffective" (reel 195, vol. 207, pp. 836–38, SG Letterbooks, DLC, quotation at p. 836).

3. Alfred Charles William Harmsworth, Baron (later Viscount) Northcliffe (1865–1922), founded or acquired a number of major British newspapers. He established the *Daily Mail,* a popular tabloid, in 1896 and the *Daily Mirror* in 1903, and he took over the *Observer* in 1905 and the *Times* in 1908. Appleton is referring to the wave of anti-German violence that swept through Britain after the sinking of the *Lusitania* and the inflammatory coverage of the German submarine campaign in Northcliffe's newspapers. The *Daily Mail,* for example, called the Germans "pirates," "sea murderers," and

"baby killers," reported that there had been "unspeakable atrocities" against British prisoners, and labeled the sinking of the *Lusitania* "premeditated murder."

4. On the night of May 31–June 1, 1915, German zeppelins bombed the Ramsgate, Brentwood, and Shoreditch districts of London, killing seven and injuring thirty-five.

To Ernest Bohm[1]

June 18, 1915.

Mr. Ernest Bohm,
Secretary, Central Federated Union,
210 E. 5th St., New York City.
Dear Sir and Brother:

Your favor of the 15th instant[2] to hand today upon my return to the headquarters of the American Federation of Labor. In it you invite me to be present and address a meeting at Carnegie Hall, New York City, Saturday evening, June 19th.[3] It is simply impossible for me to leave the work which it is necessary for me to perform in Washington at the office of the A.F. of L. to attend the meeting. I was in New York the last two days,[4] and had the opportunity of speaking with Brother Robert Brindell[5] in regard to the meeting. Until then I had no knowledge that the meeting would even be held. My important and pressing duties made it impossible for me to stay over in New York, or as I have already said, to leave again tomorrow in order to be at the meeting.

But in addition there are other reasons, so many of them that they are too numerous to mention. I have not the time to communicate them to you if I entertain the hope that this may reach you tomorrow, Saturday morning. This much I may say, that you know that as far back as my young manhood I have always stood for peace: have had an abhorrence of war, with all the brutality which it entailed, but I have no hesitancy in saying to you that in my judgment there are some things that are even more abhorrent than war, that is, to be robbed of the birthright of freedom, justice, safety, and character. Against any attempt of any person or group of persons, or nation or nations, who may be engaged in an effort to undermine or destroy these fundamentals of normal, human existence and development, I would not only fight to defeat it, but prevail upon every red blooded, liberty and humanity loving man to resist to the last degree. Who deplores the struggle which resulted in the wringing from an unwilling king the Magna Carta? Who is there who has one harsh word to utter against the men who were engaged in the revolution to make the Declaration of Independence and the Republic of the United States actualities? Who now condemns

Abraham Lincoln in the fight which he and the men of his time contested for the abolition of human slavery and the maintenance of the union? How few are there who have a word of unkindness to say of the people of the United States in the struggle with Spain to secure justice, freedom, and independence for the Republic of Cuba.

The lessons which these struggles teach have their application also upon the industrial field where tyranny, wrong, injustice, and unfreedom are attempted to be imposed upon the workers, and who will deny to the toilers the right to enter upon the industrial struggle, with all of the sacrifices which they may entail, in order to maintain the degree of freedom and standards which we have already secured, and in the constant, ever pressing yearning hope and demand of the organized labor movement which the toilers make upon employers and society for a better return and reward for the services which the workers give to society.

The American Federation of Labor as a great group representing the workers of America, and I as an officer and a man, have done something for the maintenance of peace, and are willing to go to the fullest lengths for its maintenance. A reading of the cablegrams from Paris in this morning's newspapers[6] shows that one European nation has already declared its endorsement of the American Federation of Labor's proposition for peace and a constructive policy of permanent peace which the Philadelphia convention of the A.F. of L. by unanimous vote adopted.[7]

I am not willing to have either the labor movement or our men and women placed in a false position. The United States will not voluntarily enter into the present European war. Of that I am confident. We shall keep out of it if we possibly can with any degree of faithfulness to the fundamental principles of justice, freedom, and safety. If despite our reserve and self-control, we shall be dragged into it whether we like it or not, there will be but one position for us to take, and that is, to be true to ourselves, true to our fellows, true to the highest ideals of humanity for which our movement stands.

Fraternally yours,   Saml Gompers.
President,   American Federation of Labor.

TLpS, reel 195, vol. 207, pp. 48–50, SG Letterbooks, DLC.

1. Ernest Bohm was secretary of the Central Federated Union (CFU) of Greater New York and Vicinity (earlier, the CFU of New York City) from 1899 to 1921.

2. Bohm to SG, June 15, 1915, Files of the Office of the President, General Correspondence, reel 79, frame 122, *AFL Records*.

3. On June 19, 1915, over two thousand people attended a meeting sponsored by the New York CFU. According to Bohm, its object was "to propagate peace and to protest against the attempt to embroil the United States into the European killing, blood

letting and maiming" (Bohm to SG, June 15, 1915). The main speaker was William Jennings Bryan, who had just resigned as secretary of state. Other speakers included Frank Buchanan, Joseph D. Cannon, and Meyer London.

4. SG addressed the White Rats Actors' Union convention in New York City on June 17, 1915.

5. Robert P. Brindell (1879–1926) was born in Quebec, worked for a time in Providence, R.I., and in 1905 moved to New York City, where he found employment on the docks and joined the independent Dock Builders' Union, which later became AFL local union 12,429 (1907–9) and then United Brotherhood of Carpenters and Joiners of America 1456 (from 1915). Brindell became business agent of his union in 1912, president of the Carpenters' New York City district council in 1916, and president of the New York City Building Trades Council, which was chartered by the AFL, in 1919. Brindell enriched himself through payments of monthly "personal dues" from the members of his local and the extortion of "strike insurance" from contractors. An investigation by the Lockwood Committee led to his indictment for extortion in late 1920. Convicted in February 1921 and sent to prison, Brindell was released in December 1924 and died two years later.

6. On June 17, 1915, the French Confédération Générale du Travail endorsed an AFL proposal to hold a conference of labor representatives at the same time and place as the peace conference following the war.

7. A reference to resolution 104, adopted by the 1914 AFL convention, which authorized the Executive Council to call an international labor conference after the war (see "Gompers Elected Head of A.F. of L. without Contest," Nov. 22, 1914, n. 3, in "Excerpts from Accounts of the 1914 Convention of the AFL in Philadelphia," Nov. 14–22, 1914, above).

To George Wickersham

July 1, 1915.

Hon. George W. Wickersham,
40 Wall Street, New York City.
My dear Mr. Wickersham:

In reply to your inquiry in your letter of June 28th,[1] as to what I referred to in the article when I spoke of your "harsh and unjustifiable attacks"[2] on labor leaders and labor organizations, I will endeavor to make clear what I had in mind.

Your article assumes that organized labor and the leaders of labor organizations sought in the Clayton Act to secure special privilege and you so designated those attempts. The very term "special privilege" carries with it a criticism that is certainly harsh in view of the fact that we have explained over and over again and have demonstrated by giving practical illustrations that what we sought was merely opportunities for the wage-earners to protect themselves from the terrible grind of industrial competition and to secure for themselves opportunities for better living. I have repeatedly explained, and I know that you have read my explanations, why our demands for exemption from the provisions of trust legislation did not constitute "special privilege." Your familiarity with the law and with legal opinions make it unnecessary to explain to you that legislation must recognize distinctions between groups of people and between the needs and conditions which confront various groups and to give heed to these distinctions in legislation which shall effect these various groups. Legislation of this character usually termed "class legislation" has been repeatedly recognized as constitutional and necessary by judicial decisions and such legislation carries with it nothing of discredit to those who seek to obtain it. Yet your article at least reflects upon the motives of those who sought to "substitute the Gompers' conception of liberty for that of the Declaration of Independence and the Constitution of the United States and Abraham Lincoln." That conception of liberty which you have stigmatized you refer to as my dogma. Knowing as I do my own motives and knowing the actual conditions that confront the wage-earners, the injustices that have been heaped upon them in the industrial and in the legal fields, I can not but feel that the tone of your article as well as your phraseology is "harsh and unjustifiable." Of course, I know that you do not agree with me upon the fundamental principles involved, but I am convinced this is because you have not lived in the world of the wage-earners and do not know their lives, their problems and what is necessary to bring betterment and hope to them.

If you could understand the life of a man who works as a day laborer I am sure you would understand why organized labor insists that the wage-earners must be accorded the right to organize and the right to make organizations effective. If you could understand the feeling of those who have been denied their rights as free men, who have been denied justice because the law has held that the power of a man or woman to labor is the property of an employer, you would understand how deeply that one sentence reaches down into the heart of the labor problem.

In one part of your article you say that the wage workers in their propaganda for the immunity of such organizations from any liability for the consequences of acts which they may employ for the purpose of subjecting the conduct of American industries to regulations adopted by them for their own benefit *without regard to the interests of others,* and in your footnote to this you refer to an article by me in the New York World of August 2, 1914.[3] I venture to say that neither in that article or anywhere else will you find any statement by me that gives the warrant for the statement I have just quoted from your article.

The sentence in which you say: "They (liberty and law) prohibit contracts, combinations and conspiracies which unduly restrain the freedom of trade and commerce." Is that statement not based upon the concept that the labor of a human being is not a commodity and an article of commerce? And is it not a fact that the labor of a human being is inseparable from the human being himself? And hence the laborer must by your reasoning himself be a commodity and article of commerce. This principle that the labor power of a human being is not a commodity is recognized in the decision of the U.S. Supreme Court in the International Harvester Co. vs. the state of Missouri.[4] It is the basis of the following passage:

["]If this power of classification did not exist, to what straits legislation would be brought. We may illustrate by the examples furnished by plaintiff in error. In the enumeration of those who, it is contended, by combination are able to restrain trade are included, among others, 'persons engaged in domestic service' and 'nurses,' and because these are not embraced in the law, plaintiff in error, it is contended, although a combination of [companies uniting the power of $120,000,000 and able thereby to engross 85% or 90%][5] of the trade in agricultural implements, is nevertheless beyond the competency of the legislature to prohibit. As great as the contrast is, a greater one may be made. Under the principle applied a combination of all the great industrial enterprises (and why not railroads as well?) could not be condemned unless the law applied as well to a combination of maid-servants or to infants' nurses, whose humble functions preclude effective combination. Such contrasts and the considerations they suggest must be pushed aside by government, and rigid and universal classification applied, is the contention of the plaintiff in error; and to this the contention must come."

You say that the vast machinery of this organization (the A.F. of L.) was set to work to destroy the business of the Danbury Hat Manufacturers, and in this you are inaccurate in statement as others have been, for as a matter of fact, the American Federation of Labor was neither consulted nor asked to do, nor did anything, not even so much as to utter a word orally, in print or in writing, in connection with the dispute in any of its phases which the Hatters had with the Loewe Hat Manufacturers of Danbury, Conn., and not until after the suit was brought and the Hatters' organization almost depleted in its funds, did the American Federation of Labor undertake to have the merits of the controversy determined by the courts of the country.

In several parts of your article you discuss the law of conspiracy and the theory of conspiracy, but a man so learned in the law as you are, must know that in the last century nearly every government of civilized countries has modified the laws of conspiracy and particularly as they affect the associated efforts of working people to increase wages, lessen hours, and improve the conditions of employment.

You say: "They (Congress) made the interdiction (of the Sherman Antitrust Law) to include combinations of labor as well as of capital." You will look in vain either through the law or through the debates when the law was in the making in Congress for any justification of that assertion. Under separate cover I am mailing you a copy of the *American Federationist* for November 1914, containing an article under the caption "The Charter of Industrial Freedom."[6] In that article are quoted the salient points made upon this subject by Senators while the act was in the making, and nowhere will you find such a claim that the provisions of the law are intended to be "an interdiction including combinations of Labor as well as of Capital."

Your gratuitous statement that Labor's position "is on a par with jesuitical argument and action of the German government to justify a flagrant violation of its treaty to respect the neutrality of Belgium"[7] is not only unfounded, harsh and unwarranted, but is far from a parallel case and to say the least is wholly inaccurate.

And pray, when has "non-action, non-intercourse, essential non-resistance," become criminal and unlawful?

Of course it is needless to call your attention to the fact that when workers are unorganized and leave their employment—strike—to resist reduction, or to secure an increase in wages or other improved conditions, and take such normal action in furtherance of their interests, they are associated, that is, they are organized whether temporarily or permanently, but to all intents and purposes they are what is commonly known as a labor organization, and in the exercise of those normal rights now as you admit made lawful under the Clayton Act they secure choice and establish freedom.

I think that after a perusal of the above you will reach the conclusion that I have done you no injustice in the introduction I wrote to your article. Indeed, because of your opposition before the bill was enacted, the opinion of its provisions after it became law, makes your utterances all the more valued contribution to the discussion upon the subject, and I personally want to express the obligations I feel for the opinion you have written.

Yours sincerely,   Saml Gompers.
President   American Federation of Labor.

TLpS, reel 195, vol. 207, pp. 754–59, SG Letterbooks, DLC.

1. George Wickersham's letter of June 28, 1915, was printed in the September 1915 issue of the *American Federationist* under the heading "Justice Not Privilege" (22: 749). Also published in that issue of the *Federationist* were SG's letters to Wickersham of July 1 and 19 and Wickersham's to SG of July 12 (22: 749–55).

2. SG made this criticism in his introduction to Wickersham's article "Labor Legislation in the Clayton Act" (*American Federationist* 22 [July 1915]: 493–503).

3. "Mr. Gompers on Labor's Status under the Sherman Law; Reasons Why Labor Is Not a Trust and Should Be Exempt," *New York World*, Aug. 2, 1914.

4. In *International Harvester Co. of America* v. *State of Missouri* (234 U.S. 199 [1914]), the U.S. Supreme Court upheld the constitutionality of the Missouri antitrust acts of 1899 and 1909. The court ruled that the state legislature had exercised legitimate, not arbitrary, powers when targeting these laws at "persons and corporations dealing in commodities" and exempting "combinations of persons engaged in labor pursuits" (ibid., p. 200).

5. The text in brackets is supplied from *International Harvester Co. of America* v. *State of Missouri* (234 U.S. 213).

6. *American Federationist* 21 (Nov. 1914): 957–74.

7. A reference to an 1839 treaty signed by Austria, France, Great Britain, Prussia, and Russia guaranteeing the neutrality of Belgium. In their ultimatum to the Belgian government of Aug. 2, 1914, the Germans claimed self-defense to justify their invasion of that country, asserting that France intended to violate Belgian territory in order to attack Germany. In response to a British demand on Aug. 4 that the Germans observe Belgian neutrality, however, German chancellor Bethmann Hollweg dismissed the treaty as a "scrap of paper."

To William McAdoo[1]

July 2, 1915.

Hon. Wm. G. McAdoo,
Secretary of the Treasury,
Treasury Department, Washington, D.C.
My dear Mr. McAdoo:

The account which you wrote in your letter of June 29,[2] of the recent Pan-American Financial Conference,[3] was read with very great interest. From what you say, it is evident that the whole plan and purpose of the organization has followed the old conventional lines of thought and custom which are the outcome of that period of development when men's chief concern was to conquer the forces of environment and when slight concern was paid to the welfare and the lives of those human beings who were necessary agencies to accomplish this purpose.

However, there has been a widening in the thoughts of men and in the consciences of all, until now there is a growing recognition of the value of human personality and human ability. One of the most forceful and incontrovertible demonstrations of the present war that is embroiling all of Europe is, that no nation has anything of more vital and far-reaching importance than the welfare of its citizens and the conservation of their physical and mental powers. That nation will surely fail which permits its working people to deteriorate in any way. The best protection in industry, the most elevating conditions of work are of fundamental importance in conserving national vitality. No nation can be truly prosperous or truly great that is not made up of strong, healthy, wholesome men and women. As I have stated, human welfare is of fundamental consideration. There has been a growing recognition of this principle in the government of Australasia and Europe. In those countries men who represent solely and primarily human interests and human welfare occupy places of importance in the government on par with those who represent material interests and material welfare and prosperity. There can be no true civilization, no true progress, unless this principle is recognized in all governmental affairs. I do not for a moment disparage the importance of wealth and material prosperity, but these things are to be subordinated to human needs and human interests. They are to serve the people. The people are not to be held in service to these material things.

It is because human interests were not represented in this comparatively new activity of our government—an activity that is now seeking broader fields of usefulness, that I wrote you my previous letter.[4] Your explanation fails to show why plans for the Pan-American Conference did not include that which is of greatest value to our nation. You say that this Conference and the future work that shall grow out of the Conference should promote social intercourse between the peoples of the various countries and stimulate and strengthen their common ideas of justice, liberty and humanity. Indeed, that should be the result, but that result will only follow from careful and wise plans in order to achieve it. These plans have not been made. This purpose was ignored by the recent Conference.

Human welfare, liberty and justice do not result as accidental by-products. They are the result of careful planning and persistent [endeavors] to realize plans and [ideals.]

In formulating the various matters that were to come before the Conference for consideration, you name such things as "bills of exchange, protection of trade-marks, patent rights," etc. The list did not contain one institution that has been devised by the working people for their protection and for the protection of the best standards of work which are necessary to maintain helpfulness. I refer to "registered labels" of trade organizations. It is indeed a reactionary spirit that overlooks provisions for this important means by which wage-earners protect themselves, their lives and their welfare. Surely, the trade label, that represents higher standards of living for the wage-earners, better conditions of work, sanitary conditions of production, is of equal importance with "licenses for commercial travelers, warehouse receipts," etc. One represents a living, thinking, creative personality—the other represents the product of his hands and mind and will. In the history of the nation there can be no doubt as to which is the more important.

You say in your letter that you are profoundly convinced that whatever can be done to increase in the right way the material prosperity and happiness of all the good peoples of the Americas will promote human welfare. That is very true, but as I have pointed out, this recent Conference was not representative of all of the peoples of the Americas—it was representative of but few, necessarily those few are interested in their own material prosperity and happiness and only indirectly in the prosperity and happiness of the great masses of the people and there is no assurance that the deliberations of this Conference or of the future Conferences will be concerned with the welfare of all of the people.

The Commission that has been appointed to visit the countries of Central and South America,[5] you say is to be interested in the improvement of our commercial, financial and of "other relations." Presumably you include in this general statement "other relations" human welfare and human rights without even specifically naming them or deeming them worthy of special distinction. It is this attitude and this treatment of humanity and human beings that led me to call your attention to what I considered and still consider a grave and serious omission in planning the work of this new movement to unite the various people of Central and South America with our own country.

You say you will be glad to receive any suggestion from me as to anyone I think would be willing to make this trip under the existing conditions and contribute his time, talent and money to its objects. However, the invitation comes at rather a late day. You have already made your plans for the work of the committees and the whole has been inaugurated and whatever representatives I might designate would be merely additional members who had not been with the Commission from the start and who would necessarily feel themselves merely afterthoughts. Furthermore, it seems rather foreign to the democratic institutions and ideals of our country that this very grave matter should be arranged on such a basis that large masses of our people are necessarily precluded because of financial disability from representing in that Commission the greatest interests of our nation.

You say it is most difficult to get that kind of cooperation, when all pull together without partisan bias in a lofty spirit of patriotism and with a noble purpose to advance human rights and promote human welfare. That is especially true when the invitation is not extended to all of the citizens to unite in this work and they are not informed in regard to prospective undertakings of this nature.

Of course, I realize that under instructions from Congress[6] the invitations to participate in the conference were necessarily restricted because the purpose of the Conference was to improve the "financial relationships between Central and South American countries and the United States."

But you say that "as trade and transportation are essential elements in the creation and maintenance of financial relationships, the discussions of the conference naturally embraced those and other related subjects, and therefore, representative business men of the United States also participated in the conference." I submit, sir, that what you say in that quoted statement is founded upon a broad understanding of the purpose of such a conference, but will you hold that the human activities of the toilers of our country are not equally essential as trade and transportation, social relations and good will?

Again you say "we have reached the point in our economic development when it is essential to the happiness and welfare of our people that we shall secure a share of the world's markets, because we produce more than we can consume at home." Is that statement based upon careful investigation? There are many people in our country who are in need of the actual necessities of life. Have we really more than we *can* consume, or is it simply that many of our people are not able to obtain sufficient to enable them to share in the consumption of the products of our country?

I am very glad of your cordial invitation to write to you at any time that I may think I can suggest views and opinions that will be helpful to you and I shall consider it a duty as the representative of a great movement for human rights and human interest to place before you for your consideration such opinions and such views as shall correctly represent the ideas and interests of the masses of the citizens of America.

Very sincerely yours,   Saml Gompers.
President   American Federation of Labor.

TLpS, reel 195, vol. 207, pp. 823–28, SG Letterbooks, DLC.

1. William Gibbs McAdoo (1863–1941) served as secretary of the treasury (1913–18), director general of the U.S. Railroad Administration (1917–19), and Democratic senator from California (1933–38).

2. In his letter of June 29, 1915, McAdoo responded to SG's complaint of June 23 about McAdoo's appointments to the committees authorized by the Pan-American Financial Conference to visit Latin American countries. SG maintained that McAdoo's appointees were bankers and businessmen and included no notable figures in the areas of human rights and welfare. McAdoo replied that since the purpose of the conference was to improve financial relations, bankers and business leaders were the most appropriate committee members but that an expansion of trade and improvement of

financial relations would ultimately contribute to human welfare throughout the region (McAdoo to SG, June 29, 1915, RG 174, General Records of the Department of Labor, DNA).

3. The first Pan-American Financial Conference met May 24–29, 1915, in Washington, D.C. It was attended by finance ministers and bankers from eighteen Latin American countries and, from the United States, Secretary McAdoo, leading bankers and businessmen, and representatives of the Federal Reserve Board, the Federal Trade Commission, and Federal Reserve regional banks. The purpose of the conference was to develop trade and improve commercial relations between the United States and Latin American countries.

4. SG to McAdoo, June 23, 1915, reel 195, vol. 207, pp. 296–98, SG Letterbooks, DLC.

5. The Pan-American Financial Conference adopted a proposal that a group of leading U.S. bankers and business leaders should visit Central and South American countries to assist in developing closer commercial ties. On June 22, 1915, McAdoo announced the names of the committee members he had appointed to arrange the trip.

6. The Pan-American Financial Conference was authorized by the diplomatic and consular service appropriation act approved Mar. 4, 1915 (U.S. *Statutes at Large*, 38: 1116–28).

To George Shuster[1]

July 7, 1915

Mr. George Schuster,
Notre Dame University, Notre Dame, Indiana.
Dear Sir:

The most satisfactory way that I can answer your inquiry is by sending you a full report of my remarks before the Senate Judiciary Committee,[2] upon organized labor's attitude in regard to court proceedings against some members of the Structural Iron Workers Union.[3]

As you no doubt have learned in your studies and researches, it is not an easy matter to interpret or appreciate the motives that prompt any act. In order to pass judgment upon one's fellow-men, to judge whether or not they are justified in any course of action, one must be all-wise and all-knowing. There are few acts so simple and so clear cut that a person who has had much experience in the affairs of the world will venture to say or judge that the act was good or was bad. Any judgment at all must result from careful consideration of the conditions and the motives that prompted the act. The individual who assumes a right to judge or condemn the McNamaras and others who have used force, must be equally willing to condemn, ostracise and to punish the employers who have used their great wealth to prevent industrial justice, to make difficult if not impossible the purpose of organized labor and who have used all their resources to establish as an industrial principle that the workers are to be considered only as useful agencies of production, and not as human beings with rights and with the power for higher development.

A person who condemns the workers who revolt against the despotism of their employers must in all justice make a thorough study of the detective agencies and their methods that now put at the service of employers all the resources of organized violence.

The history of the recent coal miners strike of West Virginia, Michigan and Colorado is a most profitable field for investigation and study for the individual who condemns organized workers or unorganized workers because they attempt to protect themselves. Any such study and investigation will convince fair-minded people that workers must protect themselves in the industrial field.

When all of the resources of the Standard Oil Company are used to prevent a few thousand coal miners from securing the right to enjoy protection of laws and the right to live as American citizens, it is evident that these workers can expect no help outside of their own activities.

You will remember that John D. Rockefeller, Jr., made the assertion last year before the Committee of Congress, which investigated the Colorado situation,[4] that he would be willing to sacrifice every cent he had invested in Colorado rather than recognize the right of the miners to organize in order to promote their own welfare. You will also remember that five of the seven demands that the miners of Colorado made were for the enforcement of state laws. You will remember that the coal operators of Colorado fortified their mines, hired armed troops to protect their property, secured the services of the same strike breakers that had been used in West Virginia against the miners there, transported to Colorado quantities of ammunition and arms and had prepared a "death special" to be sent into the camps of unprotected women and children, and finally set fire to these camps. On the other hand neither society, nor the state, nor the federal government offered these coal miners protection or secured for them the justice that they demanded. There is inherent in every individual the right of civil protection, the right of revolt against wrongs and injustices that cannot be remedied through ordinary channels of organized society.

What I have mentioned is only a very faint glimpse into the heart of the fight that the workers are making for industrial justice. Before you or any one else ventures to pass judgment upon the workers, you ought to make a very thorough and exhaustive study of all the forces that create conditions, to overcome which the workers protest and organize.

Under present conditions when the interests and when the employers are using force and violence against the workers to deprive the workers of all means of self-defense—to organize—would be to condemn them to self-destruction.

Yours very truly,   Saml Gompers.
President   American Federation of Labor.

TLpS, reel 196, vol. 208, pp. 6–8, SG Letterbooks, DLC.

1. George Nauman Shuster graduated from Notre Dame in 1915. He later served as chair of the English department there (1920–24), managing editor of *Commonweal* (1925–38), president of Hunter College (1939–60), and director of the Center for the Study of Man in Contemporary Society and assistant to the president at Notre Dame (1961–69).

2. See *The Samuel Gompers Papers*, vol. 8, pp. 430–37.

3. The International Association of BRIDGE, Structural, and Ornamental Iron Workers and Pile Drivers.

4. John D. Rockefeller, Jr., testified on Apr. 6, 1914, before a subcommittee of the House Committee on Mines and Mining that was investigating conditions in the coal mines of Colorado (see "To John Handley," Jan. 12, 1914, n. 6, above).

From Margaret Dreier Robins

National Women's Trade Union League of America
Chicago July 9, 1915.

My dear Mr. Gompers:—

Your letter[1] calling my attention to "Coming Into Her Own"[2] reached me at Saranac Lake, New York, where I had gone to see my sister Dorothea[3] who has been ill there for nearly two years.

I only reached Chicago a day ago and at once turned to The Federationist to find "Coming Into Her Own." I wish I might tell you how very greatly I appreciate your large-minded understanding of the work of the National Women's Trade Union League and how heartily I thank you not only in my own name but in that of my associates for your generous statement in your editorial. You know how eager I have been that there should be mutual understanding and co-operation between the American Federation of Labor and the National Women's Trade Union League, and the reason I so greatly value your editorial is because it will make possible a far greater co-operation in the future.

It gives me great pleasure to inform you officially that Miss Emma Steghagen[4] of the Boot and Shoe Workers' Union, Local 96 Chicago,[5] for long years secretary of the Women's Trade Union League of Chicago, was elected Secretary-Treasurer of the National Women's Trade Union League at the convention in New York.[6] Miss S. M. Franklin was elected editor of *Life and Labor,* and Miss Alice Henry,[7] Lecturer for the

National Women's Trade Union League. Miss Steghagen takes office on July 12, 1915.

I am so very glad that we had the privilege of seeing you at the convention and that the rank and file of the trade union women of the American Federation of Labor had the opportunity of meeting and knowing you personally.[8]

Believe me with all possible good wishes,

Yours fraternally,   Margaret Dreier Robins.

P.S. May I ask you to have sent to me to my personal address, 1437 West Ohio Street, Chicago, one hundred copies of the July *Federationist?*

TLS, AFL Microfilm Convention File, reel 27, frame 1440, *AFL Records.*

1. SG to Mrs. Raymond Robins, June 28, 1915, reel 195, vol. 207, p. 526, SG Letterbooks, DLC.

2. SG's editorial "Coming into Her Own" was published in the July 1915 issue of the *American Federationist* (22: 517–19).

3. Dorothea Dreier had tuberculosis.

4. Emma Steghagen, a member of Boot and Shoe Workers' Union 94 of Chicago, served as secretary of the Chicago Women's Trade Union League (WTUL; 1907–15) and secretary-treasurer of the National Women's Trade Union League of America (NWTUL; 1915–21).

5. Actually Boot and Shoe Workers' local 94.

6. The 1915 NWTUL convention met in New York City, June 7–12.

7. Alice Henry (1857–1943) was born in Australia, where she worked as a journalist before coming to the United States in 1906. She became office secretary for the Chicago WTUL in 1907 and in 1908 became editor of the women's department of the *Union Labor Advocate.* She was editor (1911–12) and coeditor (1913–15) of *Life and Labor,* the official publication of the NWTUL, and later served the League as a lecturer, organizer, and head of the NWTUL education department.

8. SG addressed a mass meeting sponsored by the NWTUL at Cooper Union on June 7, 1915; he spoke before the convention itself on June 8. For a transcript of his June 8 speech, see Files of the Office of the President, Speeches and Writings, reel 111, frames 674–84, *AFL Records.*

To Ernest Bohm

July 28, 1915.

Mr. Ernest Bohm,
Secretary, Central Federated Union,
210 E. 5th St., New York City.
Dear Sir and Brother:

Your communication of the 24th instant[1] to hand and contents noted. In it you ask me to make a statement "relative to newspaper reports[2] in all of last week's papers alleging that officers of International Unions received 'German' money to pull off strikes in Bridgeport, Conn., and elsewhere in ammunition factories."[3]

In the first place in reply I would say that there are several misstatements in the question. I never mentioned officers of International Unions; nor did I use the word "German"; nor did I mention Bridgeport; nor did I refer to ammunition factories. What I did say was that authentic information[4] has come to me that efforts have been made to corrupt men for the purpose of having strikes inaugurated among seamen and longshoremen engaged in the handling of American products and manning ships containing American products consigned to certain European ports; that the corrupting influence was being conducted by agents of a foreign government, and that I had no doubt that the same agencies and influences were at work elsewhere with the same purpose in view.

In the effort to organize the yet un-organized workers of our country, in the effort to secure a reduction of the hours of labor, and higher wages, and better conditions for the toilers of our country, I am not only in entire sympathy but that has been my life's work and hope, and I shall continue to give every assistance to the fullest lengths of whatever ability I may have and opportunity which may present itself for their accomplishment, but such work must be done by the men and women in the trade union movement of America, but we should all enter a sympathetic protest and frown down upon any foreign interference, no matter by what motive actuated, particularly when that motive is ulterior and to the detriment of the good name, growth, and permanence of our great cause.

Already the enemies of the labor movement have bandied about and attacked the honor and good name of our movement, and the untruthful charge has been made that strikes have been inaugurated for a money consideration. That the effort has been made to corrupt some of our men for such a purpose is true, but that the strikes have been inaugurated is untrue, and it is untrue because the men who have given time and service to the workers of our country have interposed in time.

If men in the labor movement are to be criticized and condemned because they propose to stand true to its fundamental principles, to have it conducted from top to bottom honest and clean, that the labor movement shall be the guardian and the champion of the cause [o]f the workers when the toilers shall need it most, after this titanic struggle shall have come to an end, then earnest devotion to the struggle of labor and humanity will be in vain.

Fraternally yours, Saml Gompers.
President, American Federation of Labor.

TLpS, reel 196, vol. 208, pp. 632–33, SG Letterbooks, DLC.

1. Ernest Bohm to SG, July 24, 1915, Files of the Office of the President, General Correspondence, reel 79, frame 283, *AFL Records.*

2. For example, the *New York Times* reported on July 23, 1915, in an article entitled "Strike Fomenters from Abroad" that SG had left Washington, D.C., the previous evening for Bridgeport, Conn., to meet with leaders of unions involved in the munitions workers' strike in that city. The report went on to say that "Mr. Gompers has made no secret of his belief that emissaries of the Teutonic empires, or as he expressed it, persons interested in keeping the ammunition on this side of the water, have been diligent in encouraging the strike."

3. Bridgeport experienced a wave of strikes during the summer of 1915. The first began on July 12, when some three hundred members of the International Association of Bridge, Structural, and Ornamental Iron Workers and Pile Drivers struck the Remington Arms Co. because of a jurisdictional dispute. Within days the strike had spread to the Remington Cartridge Co., and on July 20, members of the International Association of Machinists employed by Remington seized the opportunity to demand an eight-hour day, union recognition, a minimum wage, and overtime pay. The company quickly conceded the eight-hour demand, and the machinists ended their strike on July 28. However, the demand for an eight-hour day continued to spread in Bridgeport, and by the end of the summer some fourteen thousand workers in a variety of trades had gained a shorter workday.

4. SG noted in a memo of July 14, 1915, that Andrew Furuseth had informed him that "the Seamen and Longshoremen of N.Y. and vicinity were approached by agents from the German Government to inaugurate strikes among the men and that large financial inducements were offered" (Files of the Office of the President, General Correspondence, reel 79, frame 239, *AFL Records*). New York City newspapers subsequently published reports that German agents had offered officials of the International Longshoremen's Association $1 million to foment strikes at Atlantic Coast ports during the course of the summer. Some fifteen hundred New York City dockworkers, led by the IWW Marine Transport Workers' Association, did strike on July 20, returning to work on July 26 after gaining a small wage increase.

In a memo of July 19 SG also reported that representatives of the International Union of Steam and Operating Engineers had told him that "rich Irish Glan [*sic*] na Gael men offered Pres't. Comerford large sums of money to inaugurate strikes among Engineers in Bridgeport, Conn.; that C. refused, although in entire sympathy with that movement" (ibid., frame 266).

From Edmundo Martínez[1]

Washington, August 5th, 1915.

Dear Sir:—

The Mexican Federation of Labor has in a special meeting at Veracruz, chosen me to come to the United States to present before the American workingmen our side of the Mexico case. They have taken this step, as the majority of the American Press, for one reason or another do not wish to publish facts as they really are, but in a very distorted manner; and also because we know that the time is ripe for an approachment between the two nations.

Now then, allow me to give our side of the question. The Mexican working people have chosen Mr. Venustiano Carranza as the leader of the people in its struggle for freedom and have appointed him the First Chief of its armies on the field. Owing to the desertion from the ranks of Generals Villa and Zapata[2] the struggle has been prolonged more than any Mexican desires. However, the whole nation responded to the call of the workingman and the goal is nearly reached.

You cannot look at the Rio Blanco,[3] where thousands of workingmen took up arms and went forward into battle, and deny that the Mexican laborer was willing to back up with his life what he was desirous of getting: Freedom and Liberty.

It is a well known fact that the laborer of Mexico never got any more than 18 cents or 25 cents a day for fifteen hours work or more. How much does he get today in the territory controlled by the Carranzistas? In the port of Veracruz itself you cannot get men to work for you for less than three or four pesos a day. We are anxious to have some representative of the American workmen go to Mexico, and we would give him all the facilities to look around and see for himself the true state of affairs.

We Mexicans are not ruled by Carranza against our will. On the contrary, we know he was the first man, who in company with Generals C. Aguilar,[4] A. Obregon[5] and other patriots took to the field against the tyrant Huerta, and after a terrible fight won. Now that the triumph of the Mexican workman is assured, somebody comes along in the U.S.A. and wants us to accept Tagle[6] or somebody else, as our leader. What has Tagle done for the country? Is it right that the army of a free people like the United States should be used against a people who is near freedom? After a terrible struggle, where even the women and children took part to secure their rights, when we consider that the enemy of mankind is vanquished, are we not entitled to have the sympathy of the American workman? I still have faith that the countrymen of Washington and Jefferson are with us in this our time of trouble. Still I think that they are our brothers.

Can the American Nation bear with us a little while longer, or is it possible that only powerful nations like Germany and England are entitled to her leniency?[7] Will the American people forget that ours is a Republic like herself and with the same laws and ideals? We have not been killing American citizens or sinking her ships.—On the contrary, every foreigner in Mexico has been and will be protected by Carranza and his followers.

The Mexican workingmen desire you to know that Villa and Zapata have followed the old tactics of pressing men against their will into their armies.—General Carranza, on the contrary, has only free men; or rather these volunteers have Carranza to lead them. If General Carranza's Government is recognised,[8] it will be the triumph of the people. Will you help us do it?

By the fact they are sending me here, we believe you will give us your moral aid.

With the greetings of the Mexican workingmen whom I represent, I beg of you to consider me your obedient servant.

Yours very respectfully,   Signed, Edmund E. Martinez.

TLtpSr, reel 196, vol. 208, pp. 775–77, SG Letterbooks, DLC. Typed notation: "*Copy.*" Enclosed in SG to Woodrow Wilson, Aug. 9, 1915, ibid., pp. 773–74.

1. Col. Edmundo E. Martínez, a representative of the government of Venustiano Carranza, had credentials from the Federación de Sindicatos Obreros de la República Mexicana (Federation of the Organized Workers of the Republic of Mexico), a labor organization in Veracruz.

2. Emiliano Zapata (1879–1919), an agrarian reformer and revolutionary leader, helped overthrow Porfirio Díaz in 1911. He pressed for the distribution of hacienda lands to the peasants, a reform embodied in his Plan of Ayala, and as a consequence was opposed by the regimes of Francisco Madero, Victoriano Huerta, and Carranza. He was assassinated in 1919.

3. In January 1907 textile workers in the state of Veracruz were locked out of their mills in an attempt to break their union, the Gran Círculo de Obreros Libres (Grand Circle of Free Workers), and force them to end their support of a strike in the town of Puebla. On Jan. 7, when mediation efforts failed, the hungry workers, denied credit at company stores, attacked the store in Río Blanco and set fire to the building. Federal troops were called in when violence began to spread, and over the next three days they killed between fifty and seventy of the workers.

4. Cándido Aguilar Vargas (1888–1960) was governor of the state of Veracruz (1914–17).

5. Alvaro Obregón Salido (1880–1928) was a commander of Carranza's forces, defeating Pancho Villa in 1915, and later served as president of Mexico (1920–24).

6. Manuel Vázquez Tagle, a Mexico City attorney, served as minister of the Secretariat of Justice in Madero's cabinet (1911–13). In the summer of 1915 Villa's consul general in the United States, Francisco Urquidi, proposed Tagle as provisional president of Mexico.

7. SG sent a copy of Martínez's letter to President Woodrow Wilson on Aug. 9, 1915, suggesting that he grant Martínez an interview (reel 196, vol. 208, pp. 773–74, SG Letterbooks, DLC). Wilson declined to do so but indicated he would consider the letter when reviewing the matter. The American government issued a statement on Aug. 12 that it would not intervene in the internal affairs of Mexico (see "To Edmundo Martínez," Dec. 30, 1915, n. 2, below). SG wrote Martínez on Aug. 23 that he was confident Wilson would "not feel obliged to in any way interfere with the internal affairs of Mexico except in an advisory and friendly capacity" (reel 197, vol. 209, pp. 372–73, SG Letterbooks, DLC, quotation at p. 373).

8. For SG's letter to Wilson urging recognition of the Carranza government, see "To Woodrow Wilson," Sept. 22, 1915, below. Wilson extended de facto recognition to Carranza on Oct. 19, 1915. In early 1917 the United States further regularized relations by sending an ambassador to Mexico, and later that year it gave full de jure recognition to the Carranza regime.

To Henry Julian Gompers

Aug. 16, 1915.

Mr. Henry J. Gompers,
17th & E. Streets, S.E., Washington, D.C.
Dear Son Henry:—

Your letter in which you made an offer to contribute the corner stone to the new building of the American Federation of Labor was submitted to the Building Committee yesterday. The committee, trustees of the A.F. of L. for the construction of the building, accepted your offer and extended to you the thanks of the committee on behalf of the membership of the A.F. of L. The members of the committee expressed appreciation of the peculiar fitness that the corner stone of the new building should be presented by the man who had been the first office boy of the A.F. of L.,[1] and who had always retained his connection with the organized labor movement.

Yours sincerely,　Saml Gompers.

TLpS, reel 197, vol. 209, p. 70, SG Letterbooks, DLC.

1. See *The Samuel Gompers Papers,* vol. 2, p. 26 and p. 26, n. 1.

To John Lawson

August 16, 1915.

Mr. John R. Lawson,
Las Animas County Jail, Trinidad, Colorado.
Dear Sir and Brother:—

As I read across the top of your letter[1] the words, "Las Animas County Jail," I felt more keenly than ever before intense indignation at those men who are trying to perpetrate such outrage and injustice on the workers of our country in order that they might enjoy their unjust privileges with impunity. The organized labor movement of our country must rally and do all in its power to prevent this great wrong or else they will find themselves in the clutches of a great economic power that will take away not only their industrial, but their political rights and ultimately their freedom.

As you know, I have been trying as best I can[2] to press home the facts involved in the miners' cases of Colorado and the significance of the principle in order that the protest against the condemnation of the courts of justice of Colorado might be most effective and the courts compelled to reverse their decisions. The people of the country, the workers and citizens generally are fully aroused to the fact that the political and industrial condition in Colorado is subversive to our free government and to the rights of the people.

On August 8th I spoke at a mass meeting[3] held in Philadelphia[4] in the City Hall Plaza which was a protest meeting in behalf of the miners of Colorado. Secretary Green of the Miners and Mr. Gifford Pinchot,[5] as well as Secretary Morrison and several others spoke. Every address delivered was a ringing protest against injustice and a warning to the people to protect their rights against all encroachments. This meeting, of course, was only one of many others, and I wish I could participate in many more of them. However, I am contributing somewhat, I hope, by advising and aiding those who are preparing for these meetings.

Of course, as you say in your letter, the general protest is not only for John R. Lawson, but it is for the United Mine Workers of America. However, it would not be fair to neglect to say that every member of our organized labor has a very deep and genuine admiration for the man, John R. Lawson. That manly statement[6] that you made to judge Hillyer when you denounced him as prejudiced and unfit to act in the capacity of judge, breathed the same spirit of patriotism that has maintained freedom in all of the countries. I am sure that all those who have read that statement were as greatly moved as I was. It is a statement that may well cause any man pride and gratification. Out of it all I hope that the suffering and burden of injustice that have been inflicted upon you and your fellow-miners who have been convicted by the courts of Colorado may cause such an effective protest that the power of the mine operators will be curbed and the workers of Colorado will be given an opportunity to live and work as free American citizens.

Mr. Doyle, whom you well know, has been most helpful to me in supplying me with invaluable information and literature upon the conditions prevailing in Colorado and keeping me in touch with the new developments. His own work in your behalf has been most effective. I sincerely hope that the decision of the Supreme Court of Colorado will be favorable to you, but whatever may happen you can rely upon the men and women of the organized labor movement to support you in the claim and the demand for justice.

With best wishes, I am,

Fraternally yours,   Saml Gompers.
President,   American Federation of Labor.

TLpS, reel 197, vol. 209, pp. 56–58, SG Letterbooks, DLC.

1. The first page of the letter, dated Aug. 8, 1915, can be found in the AFL Microfilm National and International Union File, United Mine Workers Records, reel 40, frame 1622, *AFL Records.*

2. SG published an article and two editorials about the Lawson case in the June, July, and August 1915 issues of the *American Federationist* ("Lawson a Convict—Rockefeller a Saint?," "Lawson's Trial—The Infamy of It," and "The Crime against Lawson" [22: 413–19, 507–8, 603–5]). The *Federationist* also published a letter from John Lawson in the November number under the heading "Organization Is the Thing: A Message from John R. Lawson" (22: 965).

3. On Aug. 8, 1915, some three thousand people attended a mass meeting in Philadelphia under the auspices of the Federal Council of the Churches of Christ. The meeting adopted resolutions denouncing the Colorado judiciary and calling for the removal of Granby Hillyer, the judge who presided at Lawson's trial.

4. SG attended the meeting as the last stop on a two-week trip. He left Washington, D.C., on July 28, 1915, for New York City, where he attended conferences on July 29 and 30. He spoke at a Labor Forward meeting in Meriden, Conn., on July 31 and at the convention of the Brotherhood of Locomotive Firemen and Enginemen in Cincinnati on Aug. 3 and attended conferences in Chicago on Aug. 4 before going to Philadelphia, where he addressed the Lawson protest meeting on Aug. 8. He returned to AFL headquarters on Aug. 9.

5. Gifford Pinchot (1865–1946), a prominent conservationist, was chief of the U.S. Division of Forestry (1898–1905) and of the U.S. Forest Service (1905–10) and later served as Republican governor of Pennsylvania (1923–27, 1931–35).

6. SG published an excerpt of Lawson's statement in "The Crime against Lawson," p. 604. Lawson made this statement during a hearing on July 11, 1915, at which Hillyer turned down his motion for a new trial, denied bail, and ordered him sent to prison.

From Jerome Klarsfeld[1]

The New York Times.
New York, August 16th, 1915.

Dear Brother Gompers:—

As per your request during our conversation of last evening, on the Roof Garden of the Elk's Club in New York,[2] I am herewith enclosing six copies of the picture showing the salute being fired over the body of your late nephew.[3]

This appeared in the New York Times picture Section of August 15th. You should be proud of the way in which he sacrificed his life for his country. It must have been a beautiful ritual; this naval burial with honors.

I trust you are in excellent health and that I will see you on your next trip to New York.

Yours fraternally,   Jerome R. Klarsfeld

TLS, Files of the Office of the President, General Correspondence, reel 79, frame 342, *AFL Records.*

1. Jerome R. Klarsfeld worked in the advertising department of the *New York Times*.

2. SG had gone to New York City to meet with Robert Brindell, AFL organizer Hugh Frayne, and president Joseph McClory of the International Association of Bridge, Structural, and Ornamental Iron Workers and Pile Drivers regarding the affiliation of independent New York City dock builders with United Brotherhood of Carpenters and Joiners of America 1456.

3. After a popular uprising led to the murder of Haitian president Vilbrun Guillaume Sam on July 28, 1915, U.S. sailors and marines under the command of Rear Adm. William Caperton landed at Port-au-Prince to restore order. Two American seamen—one of whom was SG's nephew William Gompers, the son of SG's brother Jacob and his wife, Sophia Spero Gompers—were accidentally shot and killed on the night of July 29 by other members of the occupation force. Press accounts at the time reported that they had been killed by sniper fire.

From Frank Walsh

Kansas City, Mo. August 22nd, 1915.

Dear Mr. Gompers:

Please pardon me for not answering your good letter of the 26th ult.,[1] which contained copy of letter and enclosures[2] from Mr. Santiago Iglesias. The same were made a part of our records at the time, but I was so completely absorbed at the time of receipt of your letter, trying to get our report in shape, that I was compelled to forego answering it until this time.

As you have probably noticed, we met with considerable opposition to getting out what we considered a truth-telling and fundamental report.[3] I am anxious for you to see it, and to receive your comment thereupon, if you will be good enough to give it.[4] I am very hopeful that the same will not prove altogether disappointing, even to those of you who are fighting in the trenches, as it were, and have the keenest possible understanding of conditions.

I cannot give grateful enough expression to you for all your kindness and cooperation. To have become acquainted with you the way I have, and to have arrived at the understanding which I think I have of your motives, plans and way of operation, has been a liberal education in itself.

Coming out of this fight as I have, I must express to you, in particular, as I wish I could to laboring men everywhere, the intelligent, persistent, loyal and aggressive service to the cause rendered by Messrs. John B. Lennon and James O'Connell upon this Commission. No words of mine are adequate to express my appreciation.

Of course, you will understand that it was up to us to condense our report sufficiently to have it read and easily understood. The labor representatives on the Commission, with what assistance I was able to render, placed the standard so high, and made the pace so hot, that I believe the report, as a whole, will present your cause. Even the employers' report, when properly analyzed, in my opinion, could be accepted as a basis of trade union propaganda.

In regard to the Porto Rican matter, will say that the report will contain the recommendations asked for by Mr. Iglesias and his fellow workers, in practically the language in which they submitted it to me.

Sincerely yours,

TLc, Frank P. Walsh Papers, Manuscripts and Archives Division, NN.

1. SG to Frank Walsh, July 26, 1915, reel 196, vol. 208, p. 571, SG Letterbooks, DLC.

2. Santiago Iglesias to SG, July 9, 1915, reel 196, vol. 208, pp. 572–73, SG Letterbooks, DLC. The enclosures may be found in ibid., pp. 574–79.

3. The U.S. Commission on Industrial Relations actually issued three reports. The first, known as the Major Report or as the Manly Report, after its author, Basil Manly, was signed by Walsh, John Lennon, James O'Connell, and Austin Garretson (U.S. Congress, Senate, *Industrial Relations. Final Report and Testimony Submitted to Congress by the Commission on Industrial Relations . . .* , 64th Cong., 1st sess., 1916, S. Doc. 415, 1: 11–167). The second, known as the Commons Report, was written by John Commons and Florence Harriman and was signed by Commons, Harriman, Harris Weinstock, S. Thruston Ballard, and Richard Aishton (ibid., pp. 169–230). The third, known as the Employers' Report, summarized the partial dissent of Weinstock, Ballard, and Aishton from the Commons Report (ibid., pp. 231–52).

4. See "To Frank Walsh," Sept. 15, 1915, below.

To Patrick Draper[1]

August 31, 1915

Mr. P. M. Draper,
Secretary, Canadian Trades and Labor Congress,
Lock Drawer 515, Ottawa, Ontario, Canada.
Dear Sir and Brother:

From several sources information has come to me that there is now in progress in Canada an effort to amend the Industrial Disputes Act, commonly called the Liemeux[2] Act. As you know I have repeatedly given warning of the dangers hidden in the Liemeux Act, or in every act that provides for compulsory labor in any degree or form or for any length of time. My position has been that the wage-earners can not guard too carefully their right to control their own labor power. That when they delegate to an outside authority the right to compel them to work for one moment longer than they desire, they have given up that right which makes them free workers. This is the same ground I have gone over so frequently in published and written statements, and I am sure my position is entirely clear to you.

And now there confronts the labor movement of Canada that serious menace against which I have warned you. From all that I can learn the present war conditions and needs are made the excuse for foisting upon the workers of Canada a regulation providing for compulsory labor.[3] Such a law would establish in Canada practically identical conditions that [. . .]tion.

Legislation of this kind means that a war has to be made an excuse to take away from the workers those rights which they have established through long years of trade union activity. Bad as the war is it ought not to be made the excuse to deprive the workers of that which they have secured through ages of toil and struggle. It is just another version of the old story that the workers are to bear the burdens of war; that their rights are to be sacrificed in the name of patriotism.

In the conference[4] that was held at the Philadelphia Convention upon the Liemeux Act, you will remember that the idea was presented that the organized labor movement of Canada could not effectively oppose the whole principle of that legislation but that the wiser course would be to secure such amendments to the Liemeux Act as would make it less burdensome upon the workers. From the accounts that have come to me, it appears that the amendments proposed will make the law even more drastic than before.

It seems to me that the organized workers of Canada must now take a firm stand in this matter. They must absolutely reject the principle of compulsory service and they must make their position known immediately and in such a way as to head off the attempt to extend the principle of compulsory labor at this time, which seems very propitious to the advocates of such legislation.

I hope you will give this matter your most earnest consideration and will confer with the other members of the organized labor movement of Canada for the purpose of deciding upon a policy and a plan for action in order to defeat the extension of the Industrial Disputes Act. Whatever you may do in this matter, I hope you will not fail to write me and keep me informed from time to time of the progress that is [made].

Of course you understand that while this is an official letter to you, more than likely if it were made public, the antagonists to the labor movement would utilize it to their own advantage and to the detriment of the workers of Canada and the plea would again be set up of "foreign" interference. Behind that cloak and under that insinuating plea in the name of so-called patriotism, crimes may be committed against the rights and the principles of the toilers of Canada with impunity.

With best wishes, and hoping to hear from you often, I am,

Fraternally yours,   Saml Gompers.

President,   American Federation of Labor.

TLpS, reel 197, vol. 209, pp. 705–7, SG Letterbooks, DLC.

1. Patrick Martin DRAPER was secretary-treasurer (1900–1935) of the Trades and Labor Congress of Canada.

2. The Canadian Industrial Disputes Investigation Act of 1907 was known as the Lemieux Act after Rodolphe Lemieux who, as minister of labor, had introduced it in the Canadian House of Commons.

3. In 1915 the Canadian minister of labor announced his intention of bringing all munitions work under the provisions of the Lemieux Act. This measure was implemented on Mar. 23, 1916, by means of an order-in-council, which extended the act's provisions to include disputes in the "construction, production, repairing, manufacture, transportation or delivery of ships, vessels, works, buildings, munitions, ordnance, guns, explosives and materials and supplies of every nature and description whatsoever, intended for the use of His Majesty's military or naval forces or militia, or for the forces of the nations allied with the United Kingdom in the present war" (P.C. 680, *Labour Gazette,* Apr. 1916, p. 1059).

4. A meeting to discuss amending the Industrial Disputes Investigation Act was held on Nov. 14, 1914, during the AFL convention in Philadelphia. The conferees included Canadian delegates to the convention and the executive officers of international unions with members in Canada.

To Harry Fulton[1]

August 31, 1915.

Mr. Harry W. Fulton,
Chairman, State of Idaho Minimum Wage Commission,
Boise, Idaho.
Dear Sir:—

Your letter of August 22nd. was read with great interest. You say that you have been made chairman of a commission to gather data and submit the same to the next state legislature upon the conditions of working girls and minors in this state. You say the purpose which your commission is to promote is the enactment of the Minimum Wage Law for women in the state of Idaho.

First of all I would like to call your attention to the several other grave matters involved in the work which you are undertaking. You state that you are investigating industrial conditions for women and for minors, and that you propose to recommend a minimum wage law for women but not for the minors. Now have you thought over very clearly just what reasons you will advance for recommending one policy for women and another for men?

You say you are a member of the Typographical Union, and that your union admits women to membership on equality with men. It was one of the first, if not the first, to recognize the fact that women who are men's competitors in industry, must be organized upon the same basis as men. How can you establish a principle for the regulation of wages of women throughout the state, and yet in the same shops apply an entirely different principle to men. Suppose the state law or the political agents of the state fix a minimum wage for women engaged in printing shops at a lower standard than that which the union has been able to establish, both for men and women. Do you not see the influence that that standard fixed by law will have upon the standards fixed by the unions? More and more it is being accepted as a recognized fact that women are now permanently a part of industry as workers. Since their relationship is not temporary, the wrong and injustice under which they are suffering become all the more serious. Some permanent method of remedying these wrongs and injustices must be adopted. It must be a method that will permit of every increasing improvement and development without retarding or hampering activities.

The point I want to get before you first of all is that there is no real fundamental difference in the industrial problems that confront women from the industrial problems that confront men. Whatever physical difference there may be between the two sexes of workers is not recognized by the employers except when they make that difference an additional means for exploiting women workers. Experience of all the wage earners has demonstrated that their hope and their safety lies in organization and in the trade union movement. Every other method of protection and advancement depends ultimately upon the economic organization, therefore, it is evident that in securing betterment of the wage earning women, our first consideration and endeavor must be to organize those women.

Organization will be a powerful means for educating the women, teaching them their rights, and showing them how to attain them through their own activities. Thus the trade union movement develops the women, as well as secures for them better working conditions.

On the other hand, the policy of protecting the women wage earners by establishing a Minimum Wage Law is based upon the opposite method for solving industrial problems; a method which is based upon a paternalistic idea and makes the women the wards of the state to be protected and safe-guarded by outside authorities. It is a policy that is subversive to the development of the initiative and resourcefulness and independence among the wage earning women.

Now all that I have said has no bearing whatever upon the fact that the wages of women ought to be raised, that the hours of work ought to be reduced, and that they ought to have better working conditions. Your investigation can reveal conditions that will substantiate these statements of mine, but the trade union movement holds that these conditions can be remedied only by according the wage earners, both men and women, the right to organize and to work out their own salvation.

In thinking over this problem some time ago, a thought occurred to me which I expressed first of all before the New York Factory Investigation Commission. I proposed that adult men and women workers should be accorded by legislation the right to organize and the right to make organization effective, but that in the case of minors, both boys and girls, it might be well to consider the enactment of legislation protecting them until they should reach such an age and such a development as to be able to manage their own affairs. Such a proposal would, of course, establish an industrial age of responsibility which would be the same for both boys and girls.

In connection with these thoughts which I have presented, I am sending you the following articles published in the *American Federationist:*

August 1913, Women's Work, Rights and Progress,[2]
March 1914, Working Women, Organize,[3]
January 1915, Economic Organization and Eight-Hour Day,
February 1915, Self-help is the Best Help,
    "   "   The Danger of Shifting Duties,
March 1915, The Shorter Workday—Its Philosophy,
April 1915, Australasian Labor Regulating Schemes,[4]
May 1915, And They Would Wish It On Us,[5]
    "   "   Fixing Wages By Law Or Unionism.

You will also find of interest in studying this problem the briefs submitted to the United States Supreme Court in the case of Stettler v. O'Hara, et al.[6] This is the case which involves the constitutionality of the Oregon Minimum Wage Law. Particularly interesting is the brief submitted by Rome G. Brown[7] of Minneapolis. Mr. Brown has also published a book entitled "Minimum Wage Law"[8] which is very suggestive. The book is published by the Review Publishing Company of Minneapolis, Minnesota.

All of the arguments in favor of minimum wage legislation present very serious indictments of present industrial conditions. I am in full accord with all of these indictments. They do not magnify the serious wrongs that exist, but I am not in accord with the remedy suggested in order to secure better industrial conditions. Indeed I fear that remedy very greatly. The remedy that ought to be proposed is the remedy that has always been endorsed by the trade union movement and has been recently approved by the Federal Commission on Industrial Relations, namely, that the wage earners ought to be allowed absolute freedom of organization and the right to work out their own salvation through trade unions.

In another place the Federal Commission on Industrial Relations modified that decision somewhat by favoring minimum wage legislation where the women did not have political equality with men, and had not been granted the ballot. However, that proviso would not hold good for Idaho.

It seems to me that you can best serve the working women of Idaho and the trade union movement by using your influence to see that the report of your commission recognize wider and greater opportunities for the trade union movement instead of binding down the workers by legislative ties which must be interpreted by judicial decisions and through court procedure in such a way that would ultimately deprive them of real industrial freedom, and would injure that invaluable spirit of independence and self-responsibility which recognizes one's rights and feels personally responsible for the realization and maintenance of those rights. That is the spirit that really makes for progress and betterment, and that is the spirit that is fostered by the trade union movement.

I hope you will study this problem over very seriously, for much may depend upon your decision. As you study, if any difficulties occur to you I hope you will write me very frankly and very fully, and I will do whatever is within my power to be of assistance.

With best wishes for this and all of your activities in the cause of labor, and hoping to hear from you frequently, I am,

Very truly yours, Saml Gompers.
President, American Federation of Labor.

TLpS, reel 197, vol. 209, pp. 560–63½, SG Letterbooks, DLC.

1. Harry W. Fulton, a member of International Typographical Union 271 of Boise, Idaho, worked as a printer for the *Boise Evening Capital News*.

2. "Woman's Work, Rights, and Progress," *American Federationist* 20 (Aug. 1913): 624–27.

3. *American Federationist* 21 (Mar. 1914): 231–34.

4. *American Federationist* 22 (Apr. 1915): 253–63.

5. "And Yet They Would 'Wish' It on Us," *American Federationist* 22 (May 1915): 333–37.

6. In 1913 Frank C. Stettler, a Portland, Oreg., paper box manufacturer, brought suit in state circuit court to vacate an order of the Oregon Industrial Welfare Commission stipulating maximum hours and minimum wages for women employed in Portland. The circuit court ruled against him in November, and the Oregon Supreme Court upheld this decision in March 1914 (*Stettler* v. *O'Hara et al.*, 69 Oreg. 519 [1914]). The case was then appealed to the U.S. Supreme Court, which affirmed the decision of the lower court in April 1917 in a four-to-four vote (243 U.S. 629 [1917]).

7. Rome G. Brown, a Minneapolis attorney, filed an amicus curiae brief in the appeal of *Stettler* v. *O'Hara et al.* to the Oregon Supreme Court and served as an attorney for the plaintiff in the appeal to the U.S. Supreme Court.

8. Brown, *The Minimum Wage Law, with Particular Reference to the Legislative Minimum Wage under the Minnesota Statute of 1913* (Minneapolis, 1913).

To Margaret Dreier Robins

August 31, 1915

Mrs. Margaret Drier [*sic*] Robins,
President, National Women's Trade Union of America,
166 W. Washington St., Chicago, Illinois.
Dear Madam:

You will remember that I wrote you[1] shortly after the Convention of the Women's Trade Union League of New York City, asking for correct information in regard to the report made by the Committee on Judicial Decisions.[2] It has only been quite recently that the report was received. Of course that section was one of the first to which I gave my attention.

My attention had been called to the report of the committee by a printed statement commenting on the fact that the Women's Trade Union League had endorsed a report expressing an opinion in opposition to that of the American trade union movement. This action of the Women's Trade Union League is greatly to be regretted because of the fact that organizations associated together in the trade union movement ought to present a united front against the attacks of all enemies. There is not an enemy of organized labor that does not delight to find some flaw in the achievements of the American Federation of Labor, to predict some shortcoming of legislation secured by it and to seek in every way to discredit or minimize what the movement has accomplished. For this reason it does seem as though the members of the organized labor movement ought not to officially endorse statements that only furnish ammunition to the [enemy]. Whatever of differences we may have among ourselves; whatever of doubt we may entertain—that ought to be a matter for our personal conferences in order that we may find ways to overcome the difficulties. Any weakness in our position ought not to be made public by an official statement which can not but fail to give comfort and aid to our enemies.

There are so many who are eagerly seeking and waiting for an opportunity to tear down the trade union movement that the burden of the work seems some times almost overwhelming. Yet the progress that we have purchased so dearly must not be lost through lack of courage or wisdom.

For these reasons I wish to discuss with you the report of the Committee on Judicial Decisions. The Committee pointed out what it termed a "joker" in section 5 of the Clayton "Bill," meaning, I presume, the Clayton Antitrust Act. That joker is supposed to be hidden in the phrase "Lawfully carrying out the legitimate objects thereof." The report further states that the committee felt that if the question of what constitutes legitimate objects and lawfully carrying out of same was left to the decision of the courts, it may be quite possible to have a repetition of the Danbury Hatters' case in the provisions of the Clayton Act. Since the committee presented no arguments substantiating their decisions, it is somewhat difficult to conjecture upon what they based their decision. Under our present system of government, it is impossible to prevent the courts from interpreting laws. In fact laws have to be interpreted in order to be administered. All we can do is to state our laws as clearly and succinctly as possible in order that there may be no difficulty in interpreting the law in accord with the purposes for which it was enacted.

I do not see how this phrase can be misinterpreted. The word "lawfully" of which some of our enemies have tried to make so much, does not effect the phrase one way or another. No court would sanction for a moment carrying out the purposes of organizations unlawfully. Trade union organizations have never asked to do that which is unlawful. It is true, we have asked to have laws changed in order to afford concepts of justice, but we have never sought special privilege nor desired to do that which is unlawful.

Section 6 was enacted for the purpose of distinguishing clearly between associations of wage-earners and organizations for profit. The distinction between human beings and property was necessary in order to exempt organizations of wage-earners from the provisions of trust legislation. That this section does accomplish this purpose is conceded even by the enemies of the organized labor movement. Frequently I have called attention to the opinion of Hon. George W. Wickersham, formerly Attorney General, in which he states that the Clayton Act makes impossible other legal proceedings like the Hatters' case. It can not be truly asserted that Mr. Wickersham is prejudiced in favor of organized labor or its contentions. This makes his opinion more valuable because it is so obviously free from bias.

In the September issue of the *American Federationist* you will find a series of articles dealing with this very question. I especially recommend to you for your careful consideration the article[3] by Senator Cummins of Iowa, Secretary of Labor Wilson, and Assistant Secretary of Labor Post.[4]

As to what the legitimate objects of organized labor are and how these may be carried out the Clayton Act makes further specifications in section 20. This section specifically enumerates certain acts which are legitimate activities of organized labor and which have been enjoined by injunctions and for doing which workers have been punished, and then ends with this very important clause: *"Nor shall any of the acts specified in this paragraph be considered or held to be violations of any law of the United States."* Section 6 must be considered in connection with section 20 and the rest of the act in order to appreciate its full meaning and its comprehensiveness. This is what I am sure your Committee will do.

Changes may be necessary in connection with the Clayton Act. In fact the American Federation of Labor at its Philadelphia Convention recommended that legislation be secured defining more clearly the difference between personal rights and rights resulting from the ownership of property. But the general consensus of opinion, not only of the friends of organized labor but of many of our most intelligent enemies is that section 6 accomplishes fully the purpose which the organized labor movement has so long sought to attain, namely: the exemption of the associations of workers from the application of trust legislation and the differentiation between living human workers and the products of their toil.

In your letter[5] to me in regard to this matter, you spoke with enthusiasm of the spirit of the girls who made this report and of the democratic spirit and ideals which were illustrated by their independent thinking and their expressed position to the decisions of the American Federation of Labor. Much as I admire independence in thought and action, I think that intelligence recognizes that we shall ourselves restrict our own independence to a statement of facts which we know. It seems to me that the women associated together in the Women's Trade Union League can enjoy the greatest independence and the greatest liberty when they are willing to cooperate with the trade union movement in order to further the cause of organized labor and when they take good care that nothing they say or do will contribute to the opposition against the workers of the labor movement.

I have been writing about this matter very freely to you because of its grave importance and because I appreciate how necessary is cooperation and singleness of purpose to the greatest progress of the labor movement.

While from some viewpoints a little opposition here and there, an official expression of difference of opinion, a clashing of interest may appear to be for the time being of little consequence, and in fact a manifestation of independence, my long experience in the labor movement has convinced me that these things are not of small importance but have a very great influence upon the solidarity and the unity of the whole movement.

May I hope that this letter will receive the most earnest consideration not only of yourself, but those associated with you in responsible positions in the Women's Trade Union League.[6]

With best wishes, I remain,

Yours very sincerely,   Saml Gompers.
President   American Federation of Labor.

TLpS, reel 197, vol. 209, pp. 948–52, SG Letterbooks, DLC.

1. SG to Mrs. Raymond Robins, July 9, 1915, reel 196, vol. 208, p. 98, SG Letterbooks, DLC.

2. The 1915 National Women's Trade Union League of America convention met June 7–12 in New York City. It adopted the report of its Committee on Judicial Decisions on June 12.

3. The articles by Albert Cummins ("The Clayton Act"), William Wilson ("The Clayton Antitrust Law"), and Louis Post ("Consistency of the Clayton Act") were published in the September 1915 issue of the *American Federationist* under the heading "Labor's Mission—The Achievement of Freedom" (22: 666–74).

4. Louis Freeland Post (1849–1928) served as assistant secretary of labor from 1913 to 1921.

5. Robins to SG, July 10, 1915, AFL Microfilm Convention File, reel 27, frame 1440, *AFL Records.*

6. In response, Robins asked SG to send her a brief statement on the importance of the Clayton Act; he complied on Sept. 22, 1915 (reel 198, vol. 210, pp. 550–54, SG Letterbooks, DLC).

To Frank Walsh

Washington, D.C., Sept. 15, 1915.

Hon. Frank P. Walsh,
Kansas City, Missouri.
My dear Mr. Walsh:

It is with regret that I find in reading the synopsis of the report of the Commission on Industrial Relations, the following statement in regard to the Clayton Antitrust Act:

"Important steps have been taken to deal with this situation by the enactment of the Clayton Act, applying to the Federal jurisdiction, and by the passage of laws in Massachusetts and New York[1] which define the rights of parties engaged in industrial disputes. The actual effect of the Clayton Act can not be ascertained until it has been tested in the courts, but *eminent legal authorities* have expressed grave doubts that it will accomplish the desired results. At any rate, it does not seem to remove the root of the existing injustice, and, furthermore, in all the states except New York and Massachusetts the grave and uncertain situation already described exists. This situation must be corrected."

This statement is so totally out of harmony with the splendid spirit of the report and the carefully considered decisions and recommendations that I am quite at a loss to explain it. From my recollections of the testimony before the Commission, the only doubts that were expressed as to the provisions of the Clayton Act were those expressed by the well-known enemies of the labor movement,—men whose names are associated with everything that is hostile to humanitarian effort and proposal. While I feel that the statement can not represent the spirit of those members of the Commission who were thoroughly sympathetic with the labor movement and its aims and purposes, yet that statement cannot fail to have its effect upon the minds of many. The organized labor movement has encountered so many obstacles and the fight for human welfare has been so difficult that it is doubly regrettable when even our friends increase the difficulties that we must encounter. You can appreciate what I mean when I say that we have to guard very carefully against furnishing ammunition to our enemies and against contributing to any misconception. For the protection of the workers, the organized labor movement must resist every attempt to foster the impression that the labor provisions of the Clayton Antitrust Act will not accomplish everything the legislators intended. We cannot afford to furnish the prepared basis for a decision for a hostile judiciary.

Of course, there is no doubt in my mind but that some day in some court, the protective labor provisions of the Clayton Antitrust Law will be attacked and legal authority, decisions and opinions of the present and the remote past will be quoted. Economists and official governmental reports will be quoted, and among them, I have no doubt that the statements contained in the report of the Commission on Industrial Relations and because the majority of its members who were known to be in entire sympathy with the cause of labor, great importance will be attached to this conclusion, and the doubt expressed in that report will be held as against the contentions of the labor movement. I know that the report of the Commission is not a legal document in the sense that it can be cited as a legal authority or a judicial opinion, nevertheless great stress will be laid upon it because you and Messrs. Lennon, O'Connell and Garretson, have manifested a sympathetic attitude toward labor and labor's contentions and this very sympathy will give your opinion additional weight against us.

Attention might be called to this fact that although the Anthracite

Coal Strike Commission appointed by President Roosevelt occupied perhaps less of an official position than the Industrial Relations Commission, because your Commission was created by law and the Anthracite Coal Commission was voluntary and appointed by the President without warrant of law, except in the exercise of his discretionary power, yet a recommendation[2] by that Commission regarding the so-called open shop has been more noted and emphasized and used by every enemy to the Trade Union against organized labor's cause than any other declaration contained in a document of similar character.

The attorneys who are quoted as urging the ineffectiveness of the labor provisions of the Clayton Antitrust Law, were Messrs. Davenport, Drew, Spelling, and I doubt that the labor movement regards them as "eminent counsel," on the other hand, former Attorney General Wickersham, an opponent of Labor and Labor's contentions in this legislation, wrote an extensive opinion in which he showed the effectiveness of the labor provisions of that law. At the closing hour of the session of your Commission in Washington, I took occasion to submit that opinion of Mr. Wickersham.[3] There has already been mailed to you a copy of the September issue of the American Federationist in which you will find opinions of Senator Albert E. Cummins of Iowa, Hon. Louis F. Post, Assistant Secretary of the Department of Labor, and Honorable Matthew Woll.[4] These three lawyers, I think, will compare with the so-called "eminent counsel" who adversely criticised the law. There are other men, among them, Hon. William B. Wilson, Secretary of the Department of Labor, who although not a lawyer, has given the subject as deep a consideration and as good an understanding as any other man, and though I very much dislike to inject my own personality into this question yet from more than thirty years of study of this subject, I think I have a fair notion of all that the labor provisions of the Clayton Law provide and the purposes Labor sought to accomplish and is succeeding in accomplishing, in securing its enactment. The feeling I have that you and our other three friends will be quoted against us by our enemies, makes me a bit apprehensive.

It seems to me that I ought to write you about this matter in order that you would be in a position to do what you can to help our cause, with which I know you are in such thorough sympathy.

With best wishes, and hoping to hear from you,[5] I remain,

Sincerely yours, Saml Gompers.
President American Federation of Labor.

TLS, Frank P. Walsh Papers, Manuscripts and Archives Division, NN.

1. Possibly a reference to Section 582 of the New York state penal code, which stated that "the orderly and peaceable assembling or co-operation of persons employed

in any calling, trade or handicraft for the purpose of obtaining an advance in the rate of wages or compensation, or of maintaining such rate, is not a conspiracy."

2. See "Excerpts from Testimony before the Commission on Industrial Relations," Apr. 9, 1914, n. 5, above.

3. During his testimony before the U.S. Commission on Industrial Relations in Washington, D.C., on May 27, 1915, SG submitted for the record a copy of an article by George Wickersham, "Labor Legislation in the Clayton Act," which was subsequently published in the July issue of the *American Federationist* (22: 493–503).

4. Matthew Woll, "Compulsory Labor a Thing of the Past—Free Labor Now Fully Established," *American Federationist* 22 (Sept. 1915): 685–87.

5. In his reply of Oct. 2, 1915, Frank Walsh wrote that while he should probably have given more attention to the paragraph on the Clayton Act in the commission's final report, he believed SG attached too much importance to it (Frank Walsh Papers, NN).

To Woodrow Wilson

Washington, D.C., Sept. 22, 1915.

Hon. Woodrow Wilson,
President of the United States,
White House, Washington, D.C.
Sir:

In accord with the direction[1] of the Executive Council of the American Federation of Labor, the following is respectfully submitted to you and which we hope will commend itself to your favorable consideration and action.

There has been going on just across our southern boundary a battle which is part of the world old struggle for freedom. Although that struggle may be associated with many things that are not in accord with our ideals, yet I am sure you recognize that these things are the first crude efforts of a people long accustomed to despotism and denial of the rights of free citizens to realize ideals of freedom. Nations, as well as individuals, as you well know, cannot at once assume wisdom in the exercise of freedom. They must learn to be free. They have the right to this freedom without unwarranted outside interference even from those who seek their welfare.

The revolt of the people under the leadership of Madero against the Diaz government was an effort to realize ideals. The support given to the ideals of Madero was a proof that national virility and resourcefulness had not been crushed out by the rule of despotism. It was a proof that there were yet ideals and yearnings for the opportunities that rightfully belonged to citizens under a free government.

Under the Madero government there were beginnings of a labor movement and an effort of the workers to organize for the realization of their ideals and for the betterment of themselves and their fellow workers. This hope was overshadowed by the barbarism of Huerta but again grew strong and steady when Carranza asserted himself as the leader of the people.

General Carranza is recognized as the friend of the working people and the real leader of the people generally of Mexico. He has granted to the wage-earners the right of organization and has secured them opportunities for carrying out the legitimate purposes of organization. He has been thoroughly in sympathy with the ideals of greater opportunity and freedom of the masses of the people. The working people have been supporting him. They have adjourned as lodges and trade unions to enlist in the Carranza army with their union officials serving as the officers of their regiments.

The workers of Mexico have tried as best they could with the resources available to present their request and their right to be allowed to work out their own problems. They asked you and our government for a little more patience and a little more time to prove that the Carranza government really represented the people of Mexico. You granted that request and time has proved that General Carranza is really the representative of Mexican democracy—that he represents their efforts to establish a government of the people and for the people. General Carranza has demonstrated his sympathy with the ideals for which Madero gave his life, and has refused to compromise these ideals with Mexican revolutionists who were seeking their own personal interests. He has endeavored to secure for the Mexican republic the dignity and the respect that ought to be accorded to any sovereign government.

The sympathies of the workers of the United States have been very deeply touched by the struggles of our fellow workers of Mexico. As recent events have drawn all of the countries of the two American continents more closely together, so the workers of these various countries have been more thoroughly aroused to the common interests and the common welfare of the wage-earners who are citizens of the countries.

It is with the desire that we Americans who have so much liberty and so much of opportunity should use our influence to aid those who are less fortunate, that as representatives of the labor movement of America we urge upon you recognition of General Carranza as the head of the Mexican government.

The matter we know is receiving your most earnest and most conscientious consideration, and we are sure that your sympathies are very strong for any genuine effort to secure larger liberty for the people, therefore, we wish you to have the assurance that the course we, as the representatives of the organized labor movement of America urge upon you, has, we are sure, the hearty approval and endorsement of the great rank and file of the citizenship of our country.

Very sincerely yours, Saml Gompers.
President, American Federation of Labor.[2]

TLS, Woodrow Wilson Papers, DLC.

1. At its September 1915 meeting the AFL Executive Council authorized SG to write President Woodrow Wilson urging him to recognize the government of Venustiano Carranza. Wilson acknowledged SG's letter on Sept. 24.

2. SG sent a copy of this letter to Edmundo Martínez on Sept. 24, 1915, with the suggestion that he forward it to Carranza.

To M. Grant Hamilton

Sept. 27, 1915.

Mr. Grant Hamilton,
Organizer, American Federation of Labor,
Apt. 59, Lucerne, 766 Sutter St., San Francisco, Cal.
Dear Sir and Brother:

A letter from John Burns of England contains the following request:

"Kindly ask the A.F. of L. representative to collect for me a parcel of literature from exhibit at San Francisco[1] relating to Industrial Hygiene, Accidents, etc., and send them to above address, (110 North Side Clapham Common, London, S.W.). Perhaps the Secretary to Exhibition may let me have anything relating to Public Health, Diseases, Crime, etc. of interest to one like myself who has studied these problems."

Will you please at your convenience comply with the request of Mr. Burns and send to him whatever literature you can gather together.

The Executive Council was in session here all of last week.[2] There were a great many matters that had to be considered owing to the fact that no meeting has been held since last April, and in addition, the E.C. report.

As you have probably seen by the papers, the Executive Council directed me to write a letter[3] to President Wilson urging upon him recognition of the existing question in Mexico with General Carranza at its head. A representative of the Mexican Federation of Labor, Mr. Edmund E. Martinez, has been in this country for several months. He came to see me when the probability of interference by our government in Mexico seemed most imminent, and came at the suggestion of Judge Douglas,[4] the representative of the Carranza government in Washington. Judge Douglas told him that he had given up hope, but if there was any agency that could exert any power in the crisis, it was the American Labor Movement. Mr. Martinez's statements, his credentials and his sincerity and earnestness impressed me greatly. I wrote[5] to the President asking him to give Mr. Martinez a conference. President Wilson found it impossible to comply with that request, but he afterwards sent word to both Mr. Martinez and me that he was greatly impressed with Mr. Martinez's statement, and that it would form a very considerable part of his thought in deciding the issue. As you know, intervention did not take place. Mr. Martinez represents the labor organization of Mexico which is organized on a trade union basis. The trade union movement began its real work when the Madero revolution attempted to secure for the Mexicans liberty and a real republican form of government. General Carranza is following the same ideals that Madero sought to establish. We feel that the action of the Executive Council, together with what has already been published for freedom in Mexico, will be the means of establishing closer fraternal relations between the labor movements of the two countries that are necessary in order to protect the wage-earners in our future industrial and commercial developments, such as were foreshadowed by the recent Pan-American conference.

Mr. B. Suzuki,[6] whom you have already met, appeared before the Executive Council and I later had a personal conference with him in my office. Mr. Suzuki told me that he brought greetings from the workers of Japan who wanted to learn about our organization, our methods and policies in order to utilize them in Japan. He said he was deeply impressed with the influence that the American Federation of Labor and its representatives could have upon the movements in Japan, and for the good of the workers generally. I urged upon him the necessity for avoiding entanglement with partisan political parties and explained to him the political policy that the A.F. of L. endorsed.

For your own information, I think you will be interested in knowing that I am now educating my feet. Under an instructor's directions I am now trying to use my right foot and my left foot, either separately or together, as well as turn the wheel. To be more specific, a friend of mine in New York whom I asked to look for a car for me succeeded in finding me a beautiful touring car that had been used comparatively little and at a greatly reduced price. It certainly is a great convenience, as well as enables me to get fresh air, rest and recreation that would otherwise be impossible. Several times last week I took the members of the Executive Council out for a drive.

I am sending you fifty additional copies of the September *American Federationist* thinking that you might desire more of that number for distribution in view of the matter it contains, and also one hundred copies of the October *American Federationist.*

With best wishes for your self and Marie,[7] I am,

> Fraternally yours,   Saml Gompers.
> President,   American Federation of Labor.

TLpS, reel 198, vol. 210, pp. 829–31, SG Letterbooks, DLC.

1. A reference to the AFL exhibit at the 1915 Panama-Pacific International Exposition in San Francisco, which was held to celebrate the completion of the Panama Canal. For descriptions of the exhibit, see M. Grant Hamilton, "The American Federation of Labor Exhibit at San Francisco," *American Federationist* 22 (Sept. 1915): 733–39, and *Panama-Pacific International Exposition, 1915: Exhibit of American Federation of Labor* (n.p., [1915]).

2. The AFL Executive Council met in Washington, D.C., Sept. 20–25, 1915.

3. "To Woodrow Wilson," Sept. 22, 1915, above.

4. Charles A. Douglas (1862–1939), a Washington, D.C., attorney, served as counsel to the government of Venustiano Carranza in its effort to secure recognition by the United States. He also served for many years as counsel to the governments of Nicaragua, Panama, and Cuba.

5. SG to Woodrow Wilson, Aug. 9, 1915, reel 196, vol. 208, pp. 773–74, SG Letterbooks, DLC.

6. Bunji SUZUKI was president (1912–30) of Yūaikai (Laborers' Friendly Society) and its successor organizations.

7. Hamilton's daughter.

An Excerpt from an Article in
the *Washington Post*

[October 5, 1915]

J.D., JR.'S, PLAN IS UNION

Samuel Gompers, president, and Frank Morrison, secretary, of the American Federation of Labor, issued statements today commenting unfavorably upon the Colorado Fuel and Iron Company's announced plan for dealing with its employes. Mr. Gompers said:

"So Mr. Rockefeller has formed a union[1]—a union of his employes of his Colorado Fuel and Iron Company—and perhaps imagines that he has solved the problem of just relations between himself and his employes. But with all his wealth and all his brains, and the brains that he could buy and suborn, he has missed his mark.

"Imagine an organisation of miners formed by the richest man in the world who employs its members. What influence can such a pseudo union have to insist upon the remedying of a grievous wrong or the attainment of a real right? And what about the representatives of the men sitting around the table with Mr. Rockefeller and his angelic representatives out in Colorado should the miners' spokesman have the temerity of insistence in the rightful demands of the miners?["]

GLAD THEY ARE ORGANIZED, ANY WAY.

"The miners employed by the Colorado Fuel and Iron Company, of which Mr. Rockefeller is the head, have been whipped by means of atrocious brutality and hunger into submission, back to the mines. And these miners have been formed into a union by Mr. Rockefeller's benevolent altruism. But he has organized them, and for that at any rate labor is truly grateful, for when men come together to discuss even in the most cursory way their rights and their interests and welfare, there is afforded a splendid field for development and opportunity.

"After what Mr. Rockefeller has done, that is, to organize a 'union' of miners in Colorado he should carry his benevolent and practical purposes into full execution in all his varied industries and not wait until another massacre, the like of which occurred at Ludlow, should break out at one of his other industrial institutions. Do not stop at Colorado, Organizer Rockefeller."

. . .

Washington Post, Oct. 5, 1915.

1. The Colorado Industrial Plan was adopted on Oct. 2, 1915, at a joint conference in Pueblo between officials of the Colorado Fuel and Iron Co. and representatives of the company's mining employees. It went into operation on Jan. 1, 1916. The plan, designed by former Canadian minister of labor Mackenzie King, sought to promote the voluntary adjustment of grievances through joint labor-management committees on industrial cooperation and conciliation, safety and accidents, sanitation and housing, and recreation and education.

To Leonard Wood[1]

Oct. 6, 1915.

Gen. Leonard Wood,
United States Army,
Governors Island, N.Y.
Dear Sir:—

There is much in your letter of September 20th[2] in which I heartily concur. Many indications mark a decline of national virility. To check this and conserve national strength, are the first steps in national protection. Something that would take men out into the open and bring them close to nature again, as were the pioneers of this country, will be very helpful in regaining that which has been lost through the changes in our ways of living.

One of the chief advantages of military training is to keep people physically fit. It follows then that the more general the outdoor life and physical training become, the better will be the physical and mental health of the people. This is one of the reasons why I urge that the opportunities to participate in such encampments as have been recently held in Plattsburgh[3] should become general.

In your letter you speak of certain educational qualifications as necessary for men who are to serve as officers in the army.[4] But after all, what does education mean? Education is not properly included in that rather narrow delimitation that refers only to book learning and academic instruction. All of life may be an education that develops personal powers and makes each master of himself a resourceful individual.

Let me call your attention to an instance which illustrates what I mean. It is not military but civil. An intimate personal acquaintance[5] of mine was deputy commissioner under the Workmen's Compensation Law of the state. The legislature reconstructed the Compensation Law and brought the commissioners under the civil service requiring commissioners to pass regular examinations. This man, who had been rendering splendid service and had been able to protect his fellow workers because of his intimate personal acquaintance with the conditions under which they were working, was unable to pass the examinations. His inability was due to the fact that he had been denied educational opportunities in his boyhood. Before he received more than a common school education, it was necessary for him to enter his trade as an apprentice, and all opportunities that are usually termed educational were denied him. However, the workshop and contact with men and the problems of life had given him a very liberal education in those things which are essential to the administration of compensation laws. Because of his lack of knowledge of the technique of education, he was debarred from service on the Workmen's Compensation Commission, although his associates realized that he was the most competent officer of those to whom the work was entrusted.

From my general observation and from your letter, I take it that in the army service men of education and high technical skill are generally deemed essential to the organization and to the determination of the executive work connected with the army. While this in general may secure the best results, yet I know men educated in the world of work who have developed unusual executive ability and skill in organization who intuitively pursue the right tactics and the right course in controlling men and situations, although they could not give a philosophical explanation of their actions. I know of no group of men that has more practice and ability in organizing and disciplining men than can be found in the organized labor movement of the country. But so far as I have been able to find out, the invitation to participate in the camp in Plattsburgh and the other camps would not include these men. They are men of great natural ability and of wide education in the particular sense of the term, but, of course, do not come under the head of professional men, business men, etc. They are men who would render invaluable service to the country, not only in the ranks of the army, but as officers.

It seems to me that if we are to plan for the best defense of our country, we must adopt policies that will enable us to secure the best men for each kind of service. One of the great difficulties in the way of securing the participation of workingmen in camps of the kind at Plattsburgh, is the fact that they are unable to pay their own expenses and give their services without compensation. However, that is a difficulty that our government ought and must take care of if we are to develop a plan for national defense founded upon the right basis. We must make plans for national defense if we are to maintain our rank as a nation and to provide opportunities for still greater progress.

The fact that we have a republican form of government and free governmental institutions does not mean that our political ideals are synonymous with weakness and that we should be unwilling or unprepared to maintain our ideals of justice. Because I know that some plan for national defense and protection must be worked out, it seems to me that in the very beginning the plan must be on a particular democratic basis and the purposes we have in mind must include the great mass of the citizenship and enable us to select those best adapted to each kind of service. There are many workmen who can and do take vacations, and who might under certain conditions avail themselves of opportunities for volunteer service and training. I urge, therefore, that plans for national defense ought to take into consideration all of the people of the country in order to best utilize our resources.

Very sincerely yours, Saml Gompers.
President, American Federation of Labor.

TLpS, reel 199, vol. 211, pp. 143–46, SG Letterbooks, DLC.

1. Leonard Wood (1860–1927) served as a military governor in Cuba (1899–1902) and the Philippines (1903–6), commander of U.S. forces in the Philippines (1906–8), and army chief of staff (1910–14). From 1914 to 1921 he was an army commander in the United States, and from 1921 to 1927 he was governor-general of the Philippines.

2. The letter is printed in Robert Cuff, ed., "Samuel Gompers, Leonard Wood, and Military Preparedness," *Labor History* 12 (1971): 283–86. The original is in the Wood Papers, DLC.

3. The first Plattsburgh Business Men's Camp, held Aug. 8–Sept. 6, 1915, was organized in response to concerns about military preparedness after the sinking of the *Lusitania*. Attended by some twelve hundred men—who were required to pay their own expenses—it was modeled on Wood's military training camps for college students. Similar camps were later organized in Illinois, San Francisco, and Washington, and in 1916, when the Military Training Camps Association of the U.S. was founded, over sixteen thousand men were trained using the Plattsburgh system.

4. In his letter of Sept. 20, 1915, Wood argued that since the men attending the Plattsburgh camp were being trained as a corps of reserve officers, educational qualifications were necessary. He maintained, however, that they were "a very typical American group" consisting of "college professors, college students, young men in the last year of high school, men from the New York Police Force, writers, doctors, lawyers, [and] business men" (Cuff, ed., "Gompers, Wood, and Preparedness," p. 283).

5. Probably Thomas Fitzgerald, who had served as deputy commissioner of the New York State Workmen's Compensation Commission (1914–April 1915).

From Emma Steghagen

National Women's Trade Union League of America
Chicago October 13, 1915.

My dear Mr. Gompers:—

I am enclosing copy of the September report[1] of Miss Myrtle Whitehead,[2] our apprentice organizer, and it seems to me she is improving in her work.

We have started the School[3] again this Fall with one pupil, whom we hope to get started as one of the active workers in the labor movement. Perhaps you know our School is now called the School for Active Workers in the Labor Movement.

I had the pleasure of going up to Oshkosh and attending the first meeting of the women who work at the carpenter trade and whom I think have now been chartered as a local union[4] of the Carpenters' International. They indeed need to be organized because their wages are about as low as could be paid, not enough to give them a decent livelihood. I hope much good will come from this organization.

With very best wishes, I am

Yours fraternally,   Emma Steghagen
Secretary-Treasurer

TLS, AFL Microfilm Convention File, reel 27, frame 1446, *AFL Records*.

1. Women's Trade Union League, New York City, Report for September 1915, AFL

Microfilm Convention File, reel 27, frame 1446, *AFL Records.* For reports from the earlier months of 1915, see ibid., frames 1428, 1434, 1440, 1444–45.

2. Myrtle Whitehead was a member of AFL Crown Cork and Seal Operatives' Union 14,204 of Baltimore until becoming an organizer for the National Women's Trade Union League of America (NWTUL). She served in that position in New York City and Philadelphia in 1915 and 1916.

3. The NWTUL Training School for Women Organizers, which offered a year-long program of academic training and field work, was established in January 1915 and reorganized later that year as the Training School for Active Workers in the Labor Movement. It was discontinued in 1926.

4. The Women Machine Wood Workers' Union of Oshkosh, Wis., applied to the AFL for a charter in November 1915. The application was forwarded to the United Brotherhood of Carpenters and Joiners of America for action, but the union was apparently not chartered.

To Max Hayes

Oct. 14, 1915.

Mr. Max S. Hayes,
The Andrews, 4th St. & Hennepin Ave., Minneapolis, Minnesota.
Dear Sir and Brother:—

Your letter of October 3 reveals how widely divergent are our viewpoints and perhaps discussion could bring us no closer together. However, there are one or two things that you say that I wish to consider briefly. Perhaps more to indicate that there is something more to be said on the subject rather than with the hope of bringing you around to my viewpoint.

You say that he who controls the economic power, the land and machinery of production, cuts the ground from under labor, so to speak, and holds labor in a condition of vassalage. It seems to me that you are wrong and that every day is revealing the impossibility of that contention. At least you must concede that there is arising a better and clearer conception of production and what constitutes productive power. This results in a rather clear cut distinction between those who do the creative work and those who do not. The human creative power has always been dependent upon mental ability, together with executive ability and the power to make coordination. From this it is apparent that the only distinction between all kinds of producers is quantitative rather than qualitative.

The value and the efficiency of the wage-earner who handles the tools or digs the ditches is conditioned by his mental ability and resourcefulness. It is the mind that makes the muscles effective. The same qualities make the business man and the entrepreneur efficient. Productive power is the power to handle the tools and the resources. The independence of the producer is in proportion with his power to stipulate the terms upon which he will give his services. This all leads up to the declaration that this power to control terms and conditions of work is the force that can be introduced into the industrial situation that will protect working men and all kinds of producers against a condition of vassalage dominated by those who own the land and machinery of production. The services of the working men in production are just as essential as any other factor. When the working men themselves realize this there will be a complete abolition of anything that has even the appearance of serfdom. The power to produce is just as much a part of the means of production as the materials used. The working men are independent, free, and they own their own labor power if they only realized the fact.

You are mistaken in asserting that I am embittered against everybody or anything that savors of socialism. What I resent and what I have persistently opposed is any effort that will mislead the wage-earners and delude them with vain hope. There have been so many burdens and so much suffering and so much misery heaped upon those who are called the wage-earners, that I resent with every particle of force within me anything that would perpetuate their suffering or lead them into greater depths. Because I am firmly convinced that socialism is founded upon principles that will not lead out into broader liberty, independence and opportunity, I have done what I could to show men the fallacies of the doctrine of socialism.

To my mind the trade union movement is the great agency that will bring betterment into the lives of the wage-earners, and I oppose anything that would minimize its power and effectiveness or would interfere with its progress. The effects of socialism would be to limit the development and activities of men and women. Trade unionism is the gospel of hope and betterment, and it is my most earnest desire that it may not be hindered in bringing this message to all mankind. My efforts are not to interfere with men's opportunities for freedom of thought and freedom of expression, but to defend the faith that is in me and to present forcefully and unmistakably what I think are the right concepts of freedom and betterment of the wage-earners.

With best wishes to you and yours, I am,

Fraternally yours,   Saml Gompers.
President,   American Federation of Labor.

TLpS, reel 199, vol. 211, pp. 374–76, SG Letterbooks, DLC.

To the Editor[1] of
the *United Mine Workers' Journal*

Washington, D.C., Oct. 28. [1915]

DANGERS OF EIGHT-HOUR DAY LEGISLATION

Editor, Mine Workers' Journal:

Dear Sir and Brother—

From the reply[2] that you make to my letter,[3] which you published in the September 30, 1915, issue of the United Mine Workers' Journal, it is evident that we differ very widely upon two fundamentals: First, the inference underlying the theory of your position is that a large number of workers are not organizable; second, the degree and extent of the economic power of the trade union movement.

And these two fundamental features, after all, form the differences existing between you and those who think with you on the one hand, and on the other the Philadelphia convention of the American Federation of Labor, upon the subject under discussion.[4]

The resolution introduced at Philadelphia declared for the enactment of a law providing for an eight-hour workday for all workers, whether in public or private employment. The convention adopted a declaration providing for the eight-hour workday upon all Government work, or work for the Government, and for the eight-hour day, or shorter workday, for all workers in private employment to be secured by the workers through their own united effort.[5] Inasmuch as in the first instance the Government is the employer, it follows that a law is necessary to secure the eight-hour workday for its employes. The question then arises as to whether it is to the advantage of the workers employed in private industry to have a law passed to secure for them the eight-hour workday, whether even though attainable it would prove advantageous to them, whether the influence of such a law would not really be baneful, and whether it would not encourage lethargy instead of energy, and whether it would not make for unfreedom and limitation of opportunity.

One need but read the history of the toilers to learn how potent has been the power vested in the constituted authorities of the time to twist laws intended to be of interest to the workers to their very undoing, even to the verge of tyranny and enslavement. In discussing a proposition of this character, can the human equation be left out of consideration? Can men be safely molded after one pattern, and particularly so by law? Has not the history of the human race demonstrated this fact clearly, that all voluntary effort to secure freedom must be the result of and be accompanied by the cultivation of character and ideals?

I grant you that upon the surface it seems plausible and reasonable to secure by one fell swoop the enactment of a law to secure the eight-hour workday, but the difference between appearances and fact is the difference between a mirage and the distant object reflected, or to use the more homely illustration, of the dog who plunged into the water for the shadow of the bone, and lost its substance.

If your premise were correct, that is, that the workers were unorganizable, then your position is safe. If they are organizable (and they are), every claim you make for an eight-hour workday by law for all workers in private industry is untenable.

And now for the last feature. Really, I admire the pride and satisfaction you manifest when you "deny the statement that the miners had to be aroused by any outside influence," and I am in no mood now, nor was I ever, to detract one iota from the credit, honor and pride claimed by any trade unionist in his organization or his craft, but truth is truth, and for the sake of truth it may not be amiss to our discussion to call attention to a few facts.

From 1873 fully until 1883 there was scarcely a season when delegations of coal miners were not sent throughout various industrial centers with credentials from mayors of coal mining towns and of Governors of States appealing to the union men for assistance to aid the miners in their deplorable condition, and I may add, not because they were on strike or engaged in any other labor dispute, but because of the impoverished condition of the miners.

For several years the late P. J. McGuire,[6] of the Brotherhood of Carpenters and Joiners, the late George Chance, of Typographical Union No. 2 of Philadelphia, and I undertook agitation in the anthracite coal mining districts of Pennsylvania and kept up the agitation for weeks at a time and covering a period of years, all for the purpose of arousing the miners to their own duties and responsibilities to organize. And what these men did in this district others did in the bituminous coal regions.

If you will search the records of the miners' National Headquarters, you will find that out of the $5,000 in the funds of the American Federation of Labor it was necessary, in June, 1894, for the A.F. of L. to donate the sum of $1,000 in order to help keep the United Mine Workers of America alive. That same month the secretary[7] of the United Mine Workers of America officially reported 4,871 organized miners.

In 1896 a conference was held at the Monongahela House in Pittsburgh, in which the following participated: Michael Ratchford[8] and

Chas. Pearce,[9] President and Secretary of the Miners; P. J. McGuire, Secretary of the United Brotherhood of Carpenters and Joiners; W. D. Mahon, President of the Amalgamated Street Railwaymen's Association; Michael Carrick,[10] then Secretary of the Brotherhood of Painters and Decorators of America, and myself. That conference was called as the result of Mr. Ratchford and Mr. Pearce coming to my office and laying before me the deplorable condition in which the organization was, and we there and then concluded to have the conference at Pittsburgh for the purpose of devising ways and means by which the miners could be aroused to some sort of united action. It was at the Pittsburgh conference when the entire situation was discussed and the plans laid for the call to all the bituminous miners, that unless the demands for a restoration of wages and conditions were conceded by the operators, the miners would be called upon to lay down their tools of labor and stop work on July 4, 1897.[11]

Of course you will recall the fact that during that strike officers of many International unions acted as organizers; that a conference[12] was held at Wheeling, W.Va., when nearly every executive officer of the American trade union movement responded, and participated, and laid plans by which every assistance could be rendered in order to bring about the successful culmination of that strike. And surely I need not dwell upon the assistance rendered by "outside influence" in both the anthracite coal strikes.[13]

I feel quite confident that the miners who read that part of your reply to my letter, and particularly those who have entered into the industry after your organization had been well established, felt a great pride that the miners never needed any outside help to start an effort to better their conditions, and they may feel chagrined that I have recounted the above. I would not have done so had you not challenged the point which I made in my first letter, and asserted that the miners "never needed any outside help to start an effort to better our (miners') conditions." I repeat as an absolute fact, which every trade unionist active in the movement at the time knows, that the miners of America were in as bad, if not worse, condition than the steel workers, laborers, etc., worked as long hours under as poor conditions, and under equal, if not more, tyranny and misery, and I further repeat and emphasize the fact that for years, and just prior to the July 4, 1897, strike of the bituminous miners, they seemed to many as unorganizable as do the iron and steel workers now.

Perhaps in all the realm of industry the civilized world over there were no workers so apparently unorganizable as were the dock laborers of England prior to 1883, and yet, through the efforts of John Burns, Ben Tillett, Tom Mann, Henry Broadhurst and other trade unionists, the dockers were organized by outside influence and aid and took and are taking their part in the labor movement of Great Britain. What is true of these workers is equally true of all others. Sometimes efforts are made to organize the apparently unorganizable without success, but in every industry the psychological time comes and the work of propaganda, agitation and education finds a lodgment and is given expression by a massed response of the workers.

Today the United Mine Workers of America has a membership of over three hundred thousand—a striking contrast to June, 1894, when they had less than five thousand. Today the coal miners of America, under the United Mine Workers of America, stands as a militant, aggressive, organized body of men in the general enjoyment of the eight-hour workday, with all the opportunities and advantages which it brings. Perhaps your observations differ from mine, but I am firmly convinced that there is no body of workers in this or any other country on the face of the globe which maintains its independence, its aggressiveness, in the determination to aspire and struggle for still higher achievements where the hours of labor in private industry[14] are regulated by law.

You say you do not believe "that there are many who hope or expect to bring about the eight-hour day through the mere passage of a law to the effect that eight hours shall constitute a day's work." Then, pray, what is the purpose in organized labor pinning its faith to the demand for an eight-hour law for all workers? Indeed, the statement I quote from your reply is an admission of the ineffectiveness and untenableness of your position. In all the realm of the activities of the labor movement there is no more potent slogan and watchword for agitation and education among the toilers than the demand for the eight-hour workday by economic effort, and what is best of all, is the success resulting from such a campaign.

There are two kinds of legislation which the workers demand at the hands of the government; one, the freedom to the exercise of the normal activities of the toilers in order that they may be free to do the things that they naturally and normally should do to protect and advance their rights and their interests; second, beneficial and reformatory laws with which the government alone can deal. In all else, that is, in everything which the workers can do for themselves, we should insist upon our right of doing them without governmental interference, particularly such interference with industrial relations. It is not yet generally understood how power has really gravitated from the political to the economic, and I commend to all real thinkers the meaning of this statement.

You do me a grave injustice when you say that you could not follow

Mr. Barnes[15] without also following me "as both seem opposed to leg-islation, looking toward better conditions for the workers." It is true that Mr. Barnes may be charged with being opposed to "better condi-tions for the workers," but where [in][16] all my connection with the labor movement or otherwise, can you point to one instance in which I have not given the very best that is in me to secure better conditions for the workers?

The contention which, with the American trade union movement, I have made, is that the effort to secure an eight-hour workday by law for all workers in private industry would not bring or promise to bring improved conditions for the workers, but that on the contrary, even if it could be secured it would lull them into fancied security; that it would instill lethargy where energy and activity are necessary; that it would stand as a hindrance to the fuller and broader activities in the exer-cise of their economic power, place in the hands of governmental agencies a weapon of potential power to inflict injury upon the toil-ers, and stand as a constant menace to block the "continuity of that divine discontent that moves the world forward."

The economic method operates through the economic organization and is the direct result of the volition of the workers and leaves abso-lutely within their own hands, power of regulation and control over industrial conditions. Once the wage-earners have an appreciation of the power that they wield through their part in production, you have given them an agency that is irresistible.

Once get the wage-earners to see that it is their own creative power, their intelligent personality that directs the muscles that use the tools of production, and you have given those wage-earners an appreciation of their own personalities and a respect for their individualities that will make them refuse to accept less than their rights. Only when there exist this spirit and determination and appreciation of their rights will the wage-earners maintain them.

You say in reply, "we place much importance in the agitation through which state and national legislators may finally be influenced to pass such laws; the arousing of public opinion, part of which public is the workers in the sweated industries whom we seek to benefit." The kind of agitation to which you refer is directed against those whose wills you wish to influence. They are the law makers and not the workers in the sweated industries. If you think the matter over again I am sure you must concede that not a large number of the workers in sweated in-dustries have a knowledge of pending legislation or efforts or argu-ments used in behalf of such humanitarian legislation. Agitation of this sort spends its force in indirection and does not come home to the wage-earners themselves, whose wills must be aroused before they can secure their industrial rights and establish and maintain better working conditions. And even after you have educated public conscience, after you have secured the legislation, you have not touched the vital problem in securing industrial betterment for the sweated workers.

And all through the years, the effort to secure legislation in the interests of men and women in the sweated needle industries fell upon their deaf ears. And yet within this past three years, through outside help and influence, the psychological moment was struck and the movement of all the workers in the sweated industries took form and shape, resulting in a great movement which has secured so great elimination of the evils of those industries that one can not look back without astonishment and gratification. It may not be amiss to also say that for many years the men and women in the needle trades were regarded as unorganizable.

What arouses and stimulates healthy discontent is appreciation of rights and recognition of existing wrongs and a determination to establish justice. These things are aroused best and most quickly by something [that is intimate and direct and not by something][17] that is so remote, so indirect, and usually so intangible as the law. Economic effort to secure economic betterment is a part of the lives of the workers. It grows out of their needs and out of their personal demands, out of their sufferings and out of their hardships, and it takes organized form as a result of the will and determination on the part of the workers. It enters into their innermost lives and becomes a part of their daily work. It is not associated with outside agents and with remote administrative officials. An eight-hour law on the statute books makes no appeal to the coal miner or any other worker until that coal miner feels that he has a right to the eight-hour day because he has worked out that consciousness as a result of his industrial experience, and feels that it can and ought to be his, and is ready to make it so.

The writing of this letter has been delayed owing to the fact of the work so essential to prepare for the forthcoming convention of the A.F. of L., which is to be held at San Francisco, and even now I have been unable to enter the discussion of the subject as fully as it merits. In any event, this is my present contribution to the discussion on this question.

I trust you will do me the courtesy to publish this letter as you did the one previous. It is necessary in order to make my position plain to the many readers of your Journal.

Fraternally yours,   Samuel Gompers,
President   American Federation of Labor.

United Mine Workers' Journal, Nov. 11, 1915.

1. Edgar Wallace served as editor of the *United Mine Workers' Journal* from 1912 to 1918.

2. "Reply to Mr. Gompers," *United Mine Workers' Journal,* Sept. 30, 1915.

3. SG's letter, dated Sept. 14, 1915, was published under the heading "Shorter Hours, Better Working Conditions through Economic Organization, Only" (*United Mine Workers' Journal,* Sept. 30, 1915). It was written in response to Wallace's editorial "Advancement by Every Means," published in the *Journal* on Aug. 19, 1915.

4. See "Eleventh Day—Friday Night Session," Nov. 20, 1914, in "Excerpts from Accounts of the 1914 Convention of the AFL in Philadelphia," Nov. 14–22, 1914, above.

5. For these resolutions, see "Eleventh Day—Friday Night Session," Nov. 20, 1914.

6. Peter James McGuire served as secretary (1881–95) and secretary-treasurer (1895–1901) of the Brotherhood (after 1888, the United Brotherhood) of Carpenters and Joiners of America.

7. Patrick McBryde served as secretary-treasurer of the United Mine Workers of America from 1891 to 1896.

8. Michael D. Ratchford served as president of the United Mine Workers from 1897 to 1898.

9. William Charles Pearce served as secretary-treasurer of the United Mine Workers from 1896 to 1900.

10. Michael Patrick Carrick served as president of the western faction of the Brotherhood of Painters and Decorators of America (1896–97) and as secretary-treasurer of the reunited international union (1901–4).

11. For the 1897 miners' strike, see *The Samuel Gompers Papers,* vol. 4, p. 345, n. 1.

12. See *The Samuel Gompers Papers,* vol. 4, pp. 355–59 and p. 359, n. 1.

13. For the anthracite coal strike of 1900, see *The Samuel Gompers Papers,* vol. 5, p. 263, n. 1; for the 1902 strike, see *The Samuel Gompers Papers,* vol. 6, pp. 13–14, n. 9.

14. The words "in private industry" are not included in the letterbook copy of SG's letter to Wallace (reel 199, vol. 211, p. 977, SG Letterbooks, DLC).

15. John Mahlon Barnes, a cigarmaker, had served as national secretary of the Socialist Party of America (1905–11) and as its campaign manager in 1912.

16. The text in brackets, omitted from the printed version, is supplied from the letterbook copy of this letter, p. 978.

17. The text in brackets, omitted from the printed version, is supplied from the letterbook copy of this letter, p. 980.

From G. B. Harris[1]

Office Local Chairman
The Order of Railroad Telegraphers[2] Division #3
Kankakee, Ill., November 5, 1915.

Dear Sir and Brother:

I have before me a copy of the constitution and bylaws of an organization incorporated at Indianapolis, Ind. Feb. 16th this year, with Mr. N. A. Zolezzi,[3] President, headquarters at 908 Fletcher Savings & Trust Building, Indianapolis, and going by the name of National Association of Railway Yardmen:

Their constitution in Par. 2 states as follows:

"An applicant for membership in this Association, must be a white male person—and shall have at least three months experience in the Railway Yards or on a steam railroad before the time of his admission."

Section 9 of the Bylaws states the same thing with the exception that it requires six months experience. They specify no craft, and I am given to understand that they are taking in Machinists, Switchmen, Car Repairmen, in fact any one from a general Yard Master down, just so he happens to work in a Yard Terminal. They promise to take in the Railway Clerks, which we are organizing on this System, and from what I can gather they are making progress rapidly, having issued thirty-two charters since their incorporation, and have five organizers in the field. I have received several invitations within the past month to attend their meetings, but as I am bust with other work, had supposed this was the local of the Maintenance of Way Employes which I have been encouraging in their organization work, looking forward to the time when we would be able to swing System Federation on the Big Four System. Yesterday I found that my M. of W. organization as well as the Electrical Workers have joined this Yardmen's Association. If I am any judge of the times, here is one of the nastiest jurisdictional fights in many moons. I believe they applied for admittance to the A.F. of L. and was rejected on account of their constitution taking in too much territory. This is to advise you that they are going right along, in this neck of the woods, and I am afraid they are going to make my dream for System Federation of the thirteen organizations of the System of the Big Four, harder to bring about than ever before. I would appreciate it very much if you would advise me[4] relative to this. I have instructed the Railway Clerks[5] to stay out of it, and am trying to hold off the Carpenters, who contemplate jumping into it also.

Thanking you for the favor,[6] and for the literature[7] just received, I have the honor to remain,

Fraternally yours,   (Signed) G. B. Harris,
Local Chairman.

TLtpSr, reel 200, vol. 212, p. 321, SG Letterbooks, DLC. Typed notation: "Copy." Enclosed in R. Lee Guard to Henry Perham and others, Nov. 15, 1915, ibid., pp. 301, 305, 318, 320, 335–36.

1. G. B. "Barney" Harris was the Chicago local chairman (1914–16) of division 3 of the Order of Railroad Telegraphers of North America. Division 3 covered the Cleveland, Cincinnati, Chicago, and St. Louis Railway, known as the "Big Four."

2. The Order of RAILROAD Telegraphers of North America.

3. Norman A. Zolezzi, an Indianapolis locomotive engineer, was the president in 1915 and 1916 of the National Association of Railway Yardmen.

4. R. Lee Guard acknowledged Harris's letter on Nov. 15, 1915, and informed him

that SG had sent a copy of it to several interested organizations (reel 200, vol. 212, p. 307, SG Letterbooks, DLC). Copies of the letter were sent to the International Brotherhood of Electrical Workers, the Brotherhood of Railway Carmen of America, the United Brotherhood of Carpenters and Joiners of America, the Brotherhood of Railway Clerks, the Railroad Telegraphers, and the AFL Railway Employes' Department (ibid., pp. 301, 305, 318, 320, 335–36).

5. The Brotherhood of RAILWAY Clerks.

6. SG to Harris, Nov. 1, 1915, reel 200, vol. 212, p. 34, SG Letterbooks, DLC.

7. At the request of Railroad Telegraphers' president Henry Perham, SG sent Harris and other members of the union copies of the AFL constitution and literature explaining the objects of the labor movement.

Excerpts from News Accounts of the 1915 Convention of the AFL in San Francisco

[November 16, 1915]

LABOR APPEALS FOR HILLSTROM[1]

Action was taken by the American Federation of Labor convention yesterday in the movement to obtain a new trial for Joseph Hillstrom, sentenced to be shot at sunrise Friday morning in Salt Lake City. Two speakers addressed the assemblage at the opening of the morning session. Thomas Mooney,[2] a non-delegate, was given the floor by unanimous consent and reviewed the case, declaring the Swedish agitator had not been given a fair trial. Delegate Camomile[3] of Salt Lake City also urged the convention to take action.

APPEAL TO PRESIDENT.

President Gompers referred the matter to the ways and means committee, which adopted a plan for appeal to President Wilson and the Governor of Utah[4] to prevent the execution.[5]

Hillstrom, a member of the Industrial Workers of the World, was convicted of the murder of Sergeant of Police[6] Morrisson in Salt Lake City January 10, 1914. He has twice been condemned to death by shooting.

. . .

San Francisco Examiner, Nov. 16, 1915.

1. Swedish-born Joel Hägglund (1879–1915), known as Joseph Hillstrom or Joe Hill, was an itinerant labor radical and IWW member, poet, and songwriter. Convicted of the murder of grocery store owner John Morrison in Salt Lake City on the night of Jan. 10, 1914, he was executed by a Utah firing squad on Nov. 19, 1915, and was subsequently memorialized as a labor martyr.

2. Thomas Joseph Mooney, a member of the International Molders' Union of North America, spoke as a representative of the International Workers' Defense League.

3. David A. Camomile, a member of International Brotherhood of Boilermakers, Iron Ship Builders, and Helpers of America 103 of Salt Lake City, represented the Salt Lake City Federation of Labor.

4. William Spry (1864–1929) served as Republican governor of Utah from 1909 to 1917.

5. On Nov. 16, 1915, the AFL convention unanimously adopted a resolution urging the governor of Utah to stop Hillstrom's execution so he could secure a new trial. The convention directed SG to send copies of the resolution to Governor Spry, the Utah Board of Pardons, the Swedish ambassador, and President Woodrow Wilson, and he complied the same day (reel 200, vol. 212, pp. 293–94, 304, 330, 338, SG Letterbooks, DLC).

6. Morrison had served as a patrolman in Salt Lake City around 1906.

[November 18, 1915]

LABOR TO PAY HATTERS' COSTS

Plans for refunding to the Danbury hatters the $252,000 taken from them by a court judgment, finally affirmed last January, were formed yesterday at the convention of the American Federation of Labor in Eagles' Hall.

Every member of organized labor in the United States will be asked to devote one hour's pay on January 27, the sixty-sixth anniversary of the birthday of President Samuel Gompers, for that purpose.[1]

. . .

San Francisco Examiner, Nov. 18, 1915.

1. The AFL Executive Council sent out this appeal on Dec. 18, 1915. The response was initially favorable but fell off after the press erroneously reported that contributions exceeded the amount needed by three or four times. A second appeal was issued on May 9, 1916, and the two together raised $216,025.

[November 19, 1915]

DEFENSE HOTLY DISCUSSED BY FEDERATION DELEGATES

Militarism and preparedness were productive of considerable oratorical fireworks, interspersed with some hissing which prompted the chairman to threaten to exclude visitors in the galleries, at the sessions of the American Federation of Labor in Eagles' Hall yesterday.

The national defense problems came up for consideration when a resolution[1] was introduced by Delegate Adolph Germer of the United Mine Workers, to the effect that the federation go on record as opposed to introducing military propaganda into the public schools. The resolution further resolved "that we call upon all workers to desist from affiliating with any branch of the military forces."

Threatens to Bar Visitors

Chairman McCullough[2] of the committee on executive council's report recommended non-concurrence in the resolution, and Vice-President James Duncan,[3] who was occupying the chair, put the question and secured a favorable vote on the recommendation, while Germer loudly called for permission to speak.

"I have tried to get the floor before that vote was cast," he called. "I think I talked loud enough to be heard on the stage."

"You were not heard," ruled Duncan. "I did not hear or see you."

Hisses broke out on the convention floor and from the visitors' galleries, and Duncan ruled that Germer might speak under the rule that the introducer of the resolution might discuss it before its final disposition.

Attacks Preparedness

Germer declared, amid frequent applause, that he refused to take a position where he might have to shoot some other workman with whom he had no quarrel or be shot by him in warfare. He declared that preparedness is backed by those who have grown fabulously rich in making war munitions, and advocated "spending money for preservation and not destruction." He objected strongly to teaching children "to snuff out human life."

"What, if any, action would you suggest," interrupted McCullough, "in case the United States were invaded or forced into war?"

"I am not fearful of a crippled Europe invading the United States for fifty years," was the response.

Plenty of Geese

Delegate Andrew Furuseth[4] was hissed by certain of the delegates when he declared that military training would be a good thing "if we wish to raise men instead of long-haired girls!"

"That's right. There's plenty of geese around here," he commented, when the demonstration arose.

Calls for a vote on the original motion led to balloting, which resulted in a continuation of the discussion by the close vote of 79 to 77. Chairman McCullough of the committee then took the floor and traced the history of America and Europe to show that preparedness to meet emergencies was the best thing, and training of the boys in schools insured proper defense in time of war.

Hisses Are Vigorous

The hisses against these sentiments were so loud and sustained, that Chairman Duncan rapped vigorously and called for a cessation of "such absurd methods of expressing negation." Delegate Walker[5] moved that if any delegate or visitor be caught hissing, he be expelled from the hall, but upon Duncan's suggestion that they be "given another chance," the motion was dropped.

Delegate Cannon[6] told the delegates that he opposed preparedness as it fostered trouble. He narrated experiences in gun-carrying communities and in striking miners' localities where possession of weapons by some led to conflict among all.

GOMPERS SEES NEED

"I am a pacifist," declared President Gompers, taking the floor, "and had hoped we would get away from the war idea. But when I saw the way the trade unionists of each European nation rallied to their colors in this war, I had to agree that the old Biblical sentiment, 'Love thy neighbor as thyself,['] has been shot to pieces. We want to see the people of the United States thoroughly trained so that they may control their military and naval forces in the interest of peace, democracy and humanity."

The report of the committee that the resolution be defeated was adopted by a considerable majority.

. . .

San Francisco Chronicle, Nov. 19, 1915.

1. Resolution 79, introduced by Adolph Germer on Nov. 10, 1915, was not adopted by the convention.

2. Theodore McCullough represented the International Typographical Union.

3. James Duncan represented the Granite Cutters' International Association of America.

4. Andrew Furuseth represented the International Seamen's Union of America.

5. John Walker represented the United Mine Workers of America.

6. Joseph Cannon represented the Western Federation of Miners.

[November 20, 1915]

A.F. OF L. MAY OUST 200,000 CARPENTERS

The most serious breach in organized labor that ever has threatened the order confronted the convention of the American Federation of Labor in Eagles' Hall last night.

The loss of 200,000 members was faced by the federation in the consideration of a resolution calling for the suspension of the United Brotherhood of Carpenters and Joiners, the second largest international union in America.

The motion to withdraw the charter of the carpenters' union was the result of the failure of the organization to refrain from encroach-

ing upon jurisdiction awarded to the machinists,[1] and a scornful attitude toward the federation's commands in this regard.

. . .

The carpenters' union was accused of repairing, dismantling and
setting up machinery in buildings in various cities, and with claiming
the right to do such work, in defiance of the express commands of the
federation convention in Philadelphia a year ago.

"I am against the revocation of charters of international unions," said
President Gompers. . . .

GOMPERS IS PUZZLED.

"This is the second recommendation in the last few hours for the
revocation of charters of international unions.[2] Where are you going
to stop? You seem to have entered upon a policy of mutual throat cutting.

"I think it would be better to let the carpenters understand that we
feel it has been guilty of unwarrantable extension of jurisdiction, and
that if it continues it will suffer the stigma of our disapproval."

. . .

George L. Berry, president of the printing pressmen's union,[3] offered a substitute for the resolution. He moved that a committee of
five representatives of international unions, with President Gompers,
be selected to attend the convention[4] of the carpenters and get them
to recede from the position they have taken if possible.[5]

Thomas Van Lear,[6] machinist, spoke with scorn of the proposal.

"Argue with them!" he cried. "Why not argue with burglars? Tell
them to be good or be gone. We can't settle this with a feast of reason."

The vote finally was put and Berry's substitute was carried by a considerable majority.

San Francisco Examiner, Nov. 20, 1915.

1. The jurisdictional dispute between the United Brotherhood of Carpenters and
Joiners of America and the International Association of Machinists began in 1912 when
the Machinists refused to install machinery made by the York Manufacturing Co. because the company did not recognize the union. The Carpenters installed the machinery instead and then went on to claim jurisdiction over all millwrights' work—the assembling, repair, and dismantling of machinery. The 1913 AFL Building Trades
Department convention and the 1914 AFL convention both supported the Machinists,
but the Carpenters ignored these decisions. The two unions finally reached an agreement on jurisdiction over millwrights' work in 1954.

2. On the afternoon of Nov. 19, 1915, the Committee on the Report of the Executive Council recommended that the charter of the Tunnel and Subway Constructors'
International Union be revoked if the union did not comply with the 1914 AFL con-

vention's decision regarding its jurisdictional dispute with the International Brotherhood of Blacksmiths and Helpers. The convention did not adopt the committee's recommendation.

3. The International Printing PRESSMEN's and Assistants' Union of North America.

4. The 1916 Carpenters' convention met in Ft. Worth, Tex., Sept. 18–28.

5. The AFL Executive Council directed that, instead, SG write a letter to the Carpenters' convention. He did so on Sept. 12, 1916.

6. Thomas Van Lear of Minneapolis represented the Machinists at this convention. He was the business agent of Machinists' District 32, which included machinists working on the major railroads operating in Minnesota, and in 1916 was elected mayor of Minneapolis on the Socialist ticket.

[November 21, 1915][1]

. . .

GOMPERS IS RE-ELECTED.

Samuel Gompers, for the twenty-second time, was elected president. All the other officers of the federation were re-elected, the president being the only candidate against whom any vote was cast.[2]

Baltimore was selected as the convention city for 1916[3] on the second roll call, defeating Providence, Buffalo and Fort Worth.

A resolution[4] calling for the adoption of the principle of the initiative, referendum and recall in all affairs of the American Federation of Labor, practically identical with resolutions offered at several previous conventions, was voted down with only a few dissenting votes after a tilt between President Gompers and Delegate J. Mahlon Barnes.[5]

Gompers read from the record of proceedings in Rochester in 1912, when an extended report condemning the principle in federation affairs was adopted,[6] in defense of his belief in its impracticability at this time. He accused Barnes of playing politics in the unions by the organization of a "correspondence club" of the cigarmakers. Barnes declared his belief in the principle and his honesty of purpose.

. . .

San Francisco Examiner, Nov. 21, 1915.

1. This article describes the convention proceedings of Nov. 20, 1915.

2. The officers elected by the convention to serve during the following year were SG, president; James Duncan, James O'Connell, Denis Hayes, Joseph Valentine, John Alpine, Henry Perham, Frank Duffy, and William Green, first through eighth vice-presidents; Frank Morrison, secretary; and John Lennon, treasurer. Adolph Germer was recorded as voting against SG.

3. The 1916 AFL convention met in Baltimore, Nov. 13–25.

4. Resolution 96, introduced by delegate John Fitzpatrick of the Illinois State Federation of Labor on Nov. 10, 1915, instructed AFL officers to employ the initiative, referendum, and recall in Federation business whenever practical. Fitzpatrick also introduced resolution 97, directing that the question of electing AFL officers by referendum vote be submitted to the members of all affiliated organizations. Neither resolution was adopted by the convention.

5. J. Mahlon Barnes represented the Cigar Makers' International Union of America.

6. For the discussion of the election of officers by initiative and referendum at the 1912 AFL convention, see AFL, *Proceedings,* 1912, pp. 162–79, 364–73. See also *The Samuel Gompers Papers,* vol. 8, pp. 282–85 and p. 286, n. 1.

[November 23, 1915]

STORMY TALK ENDS LABOR CONVENTION; GOMPERS ASSAILED

Culminating in a stormy outbreak of feelings between President Samuel Gompers and John Fitzpatrick, president of the Illinois State Federation of Labor,[1] which the repeated attempts at pacification by delegates failed to stop, the American Federation of Labor concluded its 1915 convention at Eagles' Hall yesterday.

The outbreak started slowly and was increased by the tired, hungry condition of the delegates who had met continuously from 10 A.M. until 8:30 P.M., with but a half-hour recess.

EIGHT-HOUR LAW DISCUSSED

The question of the eight-hour law was up for discussion. Fitzpatrick favored a resolution[2] which sought federation indorsement of legislative methods in securing a universal law. In speaking on the question, he referred to "the two million toilers in our country."

"Fitzpatrick has used the language of the enemies of labor" declared Gompers, who opposed legislative means in favor of the use of economic strength to gain ends. "They say we are only two million."

When a resolution was put later that the entire debate be printed,[3] Fitzpatrick arose and attacked Gompers in a speech.

CALLS GOMPERS UNFAIR

"If anything is to be published here, I want it clear as regards myself," he said. "I was speaking in a labor meeting and it was manifestly unfair that the president should say I am using the language of the enemies of labor."

"I believe I said that you 'innocently' used the language," interrupted Gompers.

"You did not. Don't try to twist it," retorted Fitzpatrick. "I think it unfair to adopt the trick of discrediting me in this way. I have a labor reputation to maintain, and I do not like those methods."

When Gompers tried to apologize by saying that he always considered Fitzpatrick honorable and fair, a motion was put by Delegate Barnes that Gompers' eulogy of Fitzpatrick be printed along with the discussion. Barnes made a remark which showed that he and Fitzpatrick had "talked things over."

"Between you two it looks like a case of 'a divinity which shapes our ends,'"[4] commented Gompers.

Thinks He Means "Affinity"

Fitzpatrick misunderstood that Gompers said something about an "affinity," and the laughter of the delegates at this mistake only inflamed him more. Delegate Berry arose and expressed the hope that the convention should not adjourn until the two leaders had been pacified, but Fitzpatrick contended that Gompers was only trying to make him look more ridiculous every time he spoke.

A vote was taken and Fitzpatrick's remarks were refused publication. He thereupon called upon Gompers to read a letter he had laid on his table.

Gompers quibbled for few moments and then ruled that though he had received a communication, he would not read it to the convention, on the ground that no delegate had the right to address letters to the convention.

The convention then adjourned. Fitzpatrick refused to disclose the contents and Gompers referred questions to Fitzpatrick, neither seeming to desire the burden to disclose its contents.

The debate on the eight-hour law was long and bitter. Certain delegates desired the federation to indorse a general legislative fight for a universal eight-hour working day; others believed that the present use of economic strength and power was the most advantageous method. The continuation of the present method was voted for by a delegation roll call vote with 8486 ayes and 6396 noes.[5]

Talks of Eight-Hour Law

"I know we don't get the eight-hour law as fast as we want it," said Gompers. "I am just as impatient as are you delegates. But the growth must come by natural means. Some are afraid of battle and believe that they can do things by dropping a ballot in the box. They forget that power is gravitating from the ballot box to the economic field more and more. We must fight not by pieces of paper, but by the scars of battle, the hunger of stomach. We must preserve our freedom to fight, the freedom to achieve. I shall never consent to anything else."

. . .

San Francisco Chronicle, Nov. 23, 1915.

1. Although John Fitzpatrick represented the Illinois State Federation of Labor (FOL) at the convention, John Walker was the president of that organization. Fitzpatrick was president of the Chicago FOL.

2. Resolution 152, introduced by Fitzpatrick on Nov. 10, 1915, and resolution 80, introduced the same day by Thomas Van Lear of the International Association of

Machinists, both endorsed establishing an eight-hour workday by legislative means. The proponents of these resolutions argued that they simply reiterated a position previously approved by the 1913 and 1914 AFL conventions. Neither measure was adopted by the 1915 convention.

3. AFL, *Proceedings*, 1915, pp. 485–503.

4. *Hamlet*, act 5, scene 2.

5. The vote was actually 8,500 in favor, 6,396 opposed, and 4,061 not voting (AFL, *Proceedings*, 1915, pp. 503–4).

From James Lord

Office of the President
Mining Department of the American Federation of Labor
En Route—Dec 1-[19]15

Dear sir & bro—

I have just come out of the Clifton-Morenci field,[1] and will try briefly to describe that unique situation to you.

There are between 3500 and 4000 miners and mechanical tradesmen on strike. Everything is closed up tight except light and water plants. The Mine Managers have all run away to El Paso. The Governor,[2] Sheriff,[3] deputies and public (what little there is outside of actual strikers) are absolutely with the strike. They have staked their reputations, money and everything in this strike which they say if won, will mean the complete unionizing of Arizona.

The situation is as quiet as a mill-pond, the Sheriff and his deputies allowing no one who might be a scab, detective or bad character of any kind to stay or loiter in the district.

One business man,[4] an ardent believer in unionism, has been the "angel" and has furnished provisions, to the strike committee and individuals to the extent of $25.000. The Copper Companies are putting forth every effort to destroy his credit with the wholesale houses, and he has reached the end of his string.

The W.F. of M. have not got a dollar, and the strike has been carried on so far by the trade unions of Arizona and Franz, the groceryman here.

This is the first time, to my knowledge, where an entire set of State Officials have got squarely behind a strike. Governor Hunt swears he will not allow anyone to interfere with rights of workingmen to organize, fight for better conditions, or otherwise exercise their constitutional rights in Arizona. The loss of the strike means the political annihilation of Governor Hunt and his crowd, the return of the old Republican ring to power, and possibly the "pen" for Sheriff Cash and his deputies.

This is not strictly a Western Federation strike, not having been officially called by them. The union already established in Arizona feel that they will surely go out of business if this strike is broken. The commissary is strictly flour & beans.

It is purely a question of "beans".

The Federal mediators have gathered some startling evidence here and feel that a conference can be brought about in a week or ten days, but fear the results if it becomes known to the crowd in El Paso that relief has failed to come in.

I am going to do everything in my power to raise some money, but it is hard to raise money quickly.

I hope you will be able to decipher this. This is the rockiest train I ever tried to write on.

I hope to see you at Washington in a few days,[5] and discuss the matter in detail. The significance of this strike, both politically and industrially, you can clearly see.

Sincerely your's   Lord.

(The militia is also engaged in keeping out strike breakers—queerest situation I ever saw.)

ALS, AFL Microfilm Convention File, reel 27, frames 2504–5, *AFL Records*.

1. On Sept. 11 and 12, 1915, mine and smelter workers employed by the Arizona Copper Co., the Detroit Copper Mining Co., and the Shannon Copper Co. in the Clifton, Morenci, and Metcalf district of Arizona went out on strike. Their chief demand was for wages on a sliding scale, used at other Arizona mines, that was tied to the price of copper. After mine managers left the strike region for El Paso, Tex., on Oct. 4, claiming they feared for their safety, Arizona governor George Hunt, who supported the workers, ordered the state militia into the area to keep the peace and prevent the importation of strikebreakers, and he later asked the U.S. Department of Labor to intervene. William B. Wilson sent Joseph S. Myers to look into the strike and serve as a commissioner of conciliation; he was later joined by Hywel Davies. The two mediators aided strikers and management in achieving a provisional settlement in early January 1916 under which the strikers agreed to a small pay raise and renounced their membership in the Western Federation of Miners, instead accepting a charter from the Arizona State Federation of Labor (FOL). After additional negotiations, the final settlement included a detailed wage scale based on the price of copper, a minimum wage, an end to discriminatory pay for Mexican workers, and grievance procedures.

2. George W. P. Hunt (1859–1934) was the Democratic governor of Arizona (1912–17, 1917–19, 1923–29, 1931–33).

3. James G. Cash, sheriff of Greenlee Co., Ariz.

4. Probably G. A. Franz of the Becker-Franz Mercantile Co.

5. The 1915 AFL convention adopted a resolution endorsing the strike and urging AFL affiliates to send assistance to the strike relief committee in Arizona. According to his appointment records, SG met with Lord on Dec. 18, 1915, and with him and George Powell, a representative of the Arizona State FOL, on Jan. 6, 1916. At the second meeting, SG agreed to write the companies involved in the strike, but he later decided against this because the strike was moving toward a conclusion.

From Alvin Dodd[1]

New York, Dec. 7, 1915.

President in his message[2] endorses Federal aid to Industrial Education National Society Promotion of Industrial Education[3] extends through me congratulations to you on culmination of your efforts.

(Signed) Alvin E. Dodd

TWtcSr, Executive Council Records, Vote Books, reel 14, frame 408, *AFL Records.* Typed notation: "*Copy.*" Enclosed in SG to the AFL Executive Council, Dec. 13, 1915, ibid., frame 407.

1. Alvin Dodd was secretary of the National Society for the Promotion of Industrial Education from 1915 to 1917.

2. President Woodrow Wilson's annual message to Congress of Dec. 7, 1915.

3. The National Society for the Promotion of Industrial Education (from 1917, the National Society for Vocational Education) was founded in 1906. It advocated the inclusion of industrial training in the public school curriculum and lobbied to secure federal support for vocational education. In 1926 it merged with the Vocational Association of the Middle West to form the American Vocational Association.

An Account by Samuel Gompers of a Trip[1] to Milwaukee and Chicago

[December 9, 1915]

MEMORANDUM.

The only paper that attacked us was Victor Berger's paper, and every paper said the meeting[2] was well attended. Berger's paper said that it was slimly attended, despite the boosts of the capitalistic press.[3]

I read the labor proviso in the Sundry Civil Service Bill.[4] I said that is the bill which President Taft vetoed and the only grounds he gave was that it contained that proviso, and Mr. Berger, Socialist Congressman, voted to sustain the President's veto. They were astounded, because the press generally did not mention it, and Mr. Berger's paper suppressed it. Bevins[5] and Ammon[6] both made socialist speeches. Bevins, notwithstanding, said that if any member of the Socialist Party in England voted as Mr. Berger did, he would have been expelled from the party.

When I got to Milwaukee, there was a dinner tendered me at which Governor Phillip,[7] ex-governor McGovern,[8] were present, and also about twenty judges of the state and federal courts, business men, public men, labor men, etc. After that, a mass meeting at the Auditorium, and then conferences with labor men. The following morning I spoke to the ladies at Downer College,[9] at 11 A.M., and they appreciated it very highly, and told me that it was a masterpiece. Some of the ladies told my daughter it was so different from the speeches usually made to the girls and ladies because they either spoke down to them, or they attempted to speak over their heads, and the girls resented it, and my speech appealed to their judgment and their conscience, and their sentiment.

Then immediately after I was driven to the City Club, where they had a luncheon which was the largest ever attended. Mr. Bryan and Mr. Wilson have both addressed the club members, and they did not attract the large crowd that I did. I addressed them for an hour and made what everybody said was a great speech. Right afterwards I went to see Col. Pabst,[10] with half a dozen of the labor men, and Mr. Rubin, and we had a very interesting seance, and right after that went to the Building Trades Council meeting, and had a conference with them. There were eight of us and we had a set to with some of the socialists, both local and foreign. We went in a closed automobile, and while on the way I made the statement that in Milwaukee, where they had the most fully formed political party, wages in all lines of work were the lowest of any city of the same size, and challenged the men with me to deny it. They said, "yes, but—" I said, "I don't want any excuses, that is the fact, is it not?"—and they could not deny it.

We went back to the hotel and packed, and returned to Chicago.

In Chicago, had conferences with Fitzpatrick, Nockels, Perkins, and Hillman of the seceding garment workers, and I denounced the brutality of the Chicago police in their onslaughts upon the striking garment workers,[11] in spite of the fact that they were not with us, I could not stand for the brutality exercised against them. Mr. Fitzpatrick seemed the same old Fitz. Mrs. Gompers tells me that when he saw her, he put his arms around her and said, "Hello, mother, how are you?" and she resented it. She said, you can't say anything like that to me after what you have said about my husband,[12] and he said, "mother, I am over it." I did not make any reference to it. I treated him just the same as of old.

Had a conference with Emmett Flood,[13] Organizer, and the other Chicago men, and Reardon,[14] the president of the Cleaners and Dye House Workers,[15] who have gone over to the Journeymen Tailors' Union. I learned that the Socialists are simply trying to drive out Mr. Reardon. Those who were with me said that my meetings at Los Angeles, and particularly at Milwaukee, were among the best pieces of work I had done on the trip.

Victor Berger in his paper projects this question into the luncheon, tendered me by the City Club, that the non-union men will be waiting on the table.[16] I did not know whether that is so, or not so. Nobody informed me when I went to the dinner, and I still do not know whether that was so. When I saw that statement in Mr. Berger's paper, the Milwaukee Leader, I asked someone about it. He said that no one had ever raised that question before, not any of the local labor men, or anyone. He simply injected that thing into it, and after the luncheon was had, his paper appeared later. I was informed, too, by an officer of the club, that Mr. Berger is a member of the City Club.

TD, Files of the Office of the President, General Correspondence, reel 79, frames 707–9, *AFL Records.* Typed notation: "Dictated by President Gompers upon his return to headquarters, Dec. 9, 1915. (regarding Milwaukee trip)."

1. SG's visits to Milwaukee and Chicago were the last stops on a much longer trip. He left Washington, D.C., on Oct. 30, 1915, for San Francisco, where he attended the conventions of the AFL (Nov. 8–22) and the AFL Building Trades Department (Nov. 23). He visited Los Angeles (Nov. 26–28), San Diego (Nov. 28–30), and the Grand Canyon (Dec. 1), and then stopped in Chicago and Milwaukee (Dec. 4–7) before returning to AFL headquarters on Dec. 9.

2. SG addressed a mass meeting, organized by the Milwaukee Federated Trades Council, on Dec. 5, 1915.

3. "Gompers Meeting Slimly Attended Despite Boast of Capitalist Press" was published in the *Milwaukee Leader* on Dec. 6, 1915.

4. The sundry civil appropriation bill for 1914 (H.R. 28,775, 62d Cong., 3d sess.). See *The Samuel Gompers Papers,* vol. 8, pp. 460–61 and p. 468, n. 2.

5. Ernest BEVIN, a national organizer for the Dock, Wharf, Riverside, and General Labourers' Union (1914–20), was a fraternal delegate from the TUC to the 1915 AFL convention.

6. Charles George AMMON, chairman of the Fawcett Association (1911–19), a precursor of the Union of Post Office Workers, was a fraternal delegate from the TUC to the 1915 AFL convention.

7. Emanuel Lorenz Philipp (1861–1925) served as Republican governor of Wisconsin from 1915 to 1921.

8. Francis Edward McGovern (1866–1946) was Republican governor of Wisconsin from 1911 to 1915.

9. Milwaukee-Downer College was a school for women established in 1895 through the merger of Milwaukee Female College and Downer College.

10. Col. Gustave G. Pabst was president of the Pabst Brewing Co. of Milwaukee (1904–21) and in 1916 was elected president of the U.S. Brewers' Association.

11. Chicago members of the Amalgamated Clothing Workers of America were on strike from Sept. 27 to Dec. 12, 1915, for a closed shop, a forty-eight-hour workweek, a pay increase, and arbitration provisions. From the outset the strikers complained of mistreatment at the hands of city police and men hired by the manufacturers, violence that reached its height on Oct. 26 when one striker was killed and two others were shot. Leaders of Chicago's civic, religious, and labor organizations denounced these attacks, as did SG, who condemned them as a "disgrace" and insisted that the strikers were "entitled to be treated by the police at least as human beings" ("Police Strike Acts Scored by Gompers," *Chicago Daily News,* Dec. 7, 1915). There was no general settlement of

the strike, but many individual shops signed contracts with the union providing for a forty-eight-hour week.

12. See "Stormy Talk Ends Labor Convention; Gompers Assailed," Nov. 23, 1915, in "Excerpts from News Accounts of the 1915 Convention of the AFL in San Francisco," Nov. 16–23, 1915, above.

13. Emmet T. FLOOD served as an AFL salaried organizer from 1904 to 1925.

14. William J. Riordan.

15. The AFL chartered Dye House Workers' Union 14,790 of Chicago in February 1915. The union affiliated with the Journeymen Tailor's Union of America in November to become local 161.

16. "Gompers Banquet to Be Served by Unorganized Men; Unionists Wrathy," *Milwaukee Leader*, Dec. 6, 1915.

To Daniel Tobin

Dec. 18, 1915.

Mr. Daniel J. Tobin,
Gen'l. Pres., International Brotherhood of Teamsters-
  Chauffeurs-Stablemen & Helpers of America,
222 E. Michigan Street, Indianapolis, Ind.
Dear Sir and Brother:

In reply to your letter of December 13, making inquiry as to whether or not I am responsible for certain statements and editorial comments of Chicago papers relative to violence in the Garment Workers Strike of that city,[1] let me assure you that I am in no degree responsible for any version or any interpretation put upon my statements by the Chicago papers. The public statement[2] that I made was concerned wholly with the question of police violence and brutality. It is a matter of common information that the attitude of the Chicago police toward the striking garment workers is in direct violation of all concepts of police authority or justice.

As the representative of the labor movement, which has for its purpose the promotion of justice and human welfare, it is certainly my right and my duty to protest against injustice wherever it occurs. Because the brutality of the Chicago police was directed against wage-earners who have been unable to maintain their rights, that brutality arises in me, as well as within every citizen who is a lover of justice, most intense indignation.

My protest was against the wrong done to human beings, against perversion of authority and disregard of fundamental principles of democratic government.

While I was in Chicago I had a conference with Sidney Hillman at which several representatives of the Chicago labor movement were present. At that conference, I told Mr. Hillman that the wrongs and the injustice that had been heaped upon the Chicago Garment Workers was due, in a large degree, to the fact that it was known that these Garment Workers constituted a secession movement. I told him that he was responsible for conditions and that upon him fell the responsibility for the broken heads and the broken hearts and the misery that had come upon the Chicago Garment Workers in this strike. I pointed out to him how incompatible secession movements were with the promotion and development to the labor movement and with protection for the best interests of the wage earners.

Of course, it is impossible to tell the world and the enemies of the labor movement the details of that conference, but it seems to me that the service that I have given to the labor movement—that the motives and the principles that you know have always guided my judgment, ought to have given you confidence that no matter what the papers might have stated in regard to my attitude, you would have felt that I was doing my utmost to promote the cause of Labor. Certainly, as a free man and as a representative of the cause of human justice, I must have the right to protest against injustice and brutality wherever they may occur.

Fraternally yours,   Saml Gompers.
President   American Federation of Labor.

TLpS, reel 200, vol. 212, pp. 904–5, SG Letterbooks, DLC.

1. According to Daniel Tobin, a circular on the Chicago clothing workers' strike quoted SG as saying that "honest organized workers may quarrel at times, may be split up through misunderstandings, but they are still brothers . . . their common cause still brings them together." It reported he had gone on to say the strikers were "fighting for the labor cause and . . . deserve the aid of all." In his letter of Dec. 13, 1915, Tobin, who was dealing with a secession movement in Chicago in his own union, asked SG if he had made these statements (International Brotherhood of Teamsters, Chauffeurs, Stablemen, and Helpers of America Records, reel 4, frame 1490, *AFL and the Unions*).

2. See "An Account by Samuel Gompers of a Trip to Milwaukee and Chicago," Dec. 9, 1915, n. 11, above.

To Robley Cramer[1]

Dec. 30, 1915.

Mr. R. D. Cramer,
Editor-Manager, *Labor Review,*
308 S. Sixth Street, Minneapolis, Minn.
Dear Sir and Brother:

The clipping you enclosed in your letter of December 16 refers to an interview[2] which I recently had with President Wilson, at which among other things I urged upon him consideration of the principle to which I have given considerable thought and which I have been urging wherever opportunity presented itself.

Last summer when Secretary of the Treasury McAdoo, as the authorized government official, had convened in this city a Pan-American Conference, and announced the appointment of a Commission to further closer and better relations between the countries of North and South America, I called his attention to the fact that the representatives in the Conference and on the Commission represented the great material interests of the country,—financial, banking institutions, railroads, steamboat transportation, great commercial, mercantile and industrial institutions, but that there was not a single individual who represented that which was of the greatest consequence in the development of all of the nations—that is, the human element.[3] The representatives named were connected with some institution which was to further the interests of people but there was no one who represented purely and simply human welfare and human interests. It is acknowledged that national development and national progress depends ultimately upon the increasing welfare, ability and progressiveness of those who constitute the nation. I called Secretary McAdoo's attention to the fact that there is but one organization that represented purely and simply human interests. That organization is the labor movement. This, I contended, ought to be recognized by the appointment on the Pan-American Commission of representatives of the organized labor movement of the various countries.

Not long ago Mayor Mitchell[4] of New York City appointed a committee of one thousand, with an executive committee of seven, to serve as his committee for national defense.[5] He appointed me to serve on the committee of one thousand. I wrote[6] him declining to accept the appointment and I called his attention to the same principle in connection with his Committee on National Defense. The executive committee of seven, (which, of course, all those familiar with the working of committees must know, is to be the real force and to determine everything of consequence) contained no representative of the people—only men associated with some industrial, financial or similar undertaking.

As the representative of the American labor movement I could not consent to serve where I could not be in a position to represent effectively and adequately the human interests whose chosen spokesman I am.

Mayor Mitchell has since acknowledged the force of my argument and has appointed two labor men[7] on the executive committee.

Since President Wilson has announced that he had under consideration plans for national defense and the appointment of committees, commissions, etc.,[8] I took advantage of the opportunity afforded by my interview with him, to urge upon him the fact that if plans for national defense did not truly represent the opinion and the will of the people, they could not be effective. True representativeness could not exist apart from consideration of the thought and the desires of America's workers. Therefore, I urged upon President Wilson that Labor should be given a voice in the determination of any plans or policies for national defense and in making preparations to carry out such plans.

From the foregoing you will see that the newspaper clipping you sent me contained but a very small portion of the facts about my interview with President Wilson. I am very glad that you wrote me about the matter and thus prevented further misunderstanding.

With best wishes and hoping to hear from you frequently, I remain,

Fraternally yours,   Saml Gompers.
President   American Federation of Labor.

TLpS, reel 201, vol. 213, pp. 383–85, SG Letterbooks, DLC.

1. Robley D. "Bob" Cramer (1884–1966) served as editor-manager of the *Labor Review,* published in Minneapolis, from 1915 until 1963.

2. SG, Andrew Furuseth, Frank Morrison, and William B. Wilson met with President Woodrow Wilson on Dec. 15, 1915.

3. SG to William McAdoo, June 23, 1915, reel 195, vol. 207, pp. 296–98, SG Letterbooks, DLC.

4. John Purroy Mitchel (1879–1918) served as mayor of New York City from 1914 through 1917. He was elected on a fusion alliance ticket.

5. Mitchel announced the members of the Committee of One Thousand on National Defense, also known as the Mayor's Committee on National Defense, on Nov. 14, 1915. That body held its organizational meeting on Dec. 16.

6. SG declined the appointment on Nov. 21, 1915 (to Theodore Rousseau, reel 200, vol. 212, p. 404, SG Letterbooks, DLC), and again on Dec. 9 (to John Mitchel, ibid., pp. 699–700).

7. The two men Mitchel added to the committee were John Mitchell and Alfred E. Smith.

8. In his annual address to Congress on Dec. 7, 1915, Wilson discussed the need to

create an advisory board of experts in transportation and manufacturing to coordinate the nation's mobilization efforts with army and navy leaders in the case of a national emergency. At his meeting with the president on Dec. 15, SG urged Wilson to name a labor representative to such a board.

To Edmundo Martínez

Dec. 30, 1915.

Mr. Edmund E. Martinez,
237 West 15th Street, New York City.
My dear Mr. Martinez:

Your favor of the 28th instant, replying to mine of Nov. sixth,[1] which by reason of your important visit to Mexico only reached you a few days ago, your letter dealing with other matters came duly to hand this morning, and I beg to assure you that I read the contents of your communication with interest and appreciation.

You say that there are some people in Mexico who are trying to so pervert the facts as to for themselves claim credit for the accomplishment of the results now existing in Mexico, who would ignore or perhaps deny the efforts put forth by the American Federation of Labor, as well as myself as its representative to help tide over the dark times in Mexico's recent history, and to refuse to recognize the valuable aid which it was the privilege of our movement to give. But what of that? Some men, some groups of men, will never lose their narrow, selfish point of view. There are men who will for their own self aggrandizement or vain glory claim for themselves deeds and achievements to which they are only remotely related, and perhaps not related at all. The American Federation of Labor, not only in sympathy for Mexico, [o]r mere sympathy for the Mexican people, but in conformity with the well grounded principle of fundamental right, stand for every nation's independence, for the exercise of the fullest freedom and democracy of the people of these respective countries. Mexico and the Mexican people are so closely related to the people and the nation of the Republic of the United States that of necessity the rights of Mexico and of the Mexican people were and are to us of paramount importance, and it has been the constant policy and activity of the A.F. of L. to help the masses of the people of Mexico to the attainment of at least some degree of freedom, autonomy, and independence. It was with that purpose in mind that I had the great pleasure in urging my fellow workers in the American labor movement to encourage the overthrow of the autocrat Diaz, and to stand by the people under the leadership of Madero; to help encourage in the overthrow of the bloodstained traitor Huerta, and to give every encouragement and aid in making the cause of constitutional government in Mexico under the leadership of General Carranza a living, actual fact.

You know as well as anyone does of my efforts as the representative of the A.F. of L. to prevail upon the President of the United States not to intervene in Mexico, not to send the United States troops into Mexico, to ask him to give General Carranza further time and opportunity as the leader under whom the white Mexican organized workers volunteered to serve in the cause of freedom. Then the entire existing situation was changed by President Wilson's declaration that intervention would not take place;[2] that the United States troops would not be sent into Mexico; and how that act changed the course of events in Mexico; and then later my letter[3] to President Wilson urging the recognition of General Carranza as the de facto government of Mexico, and that within a few days thereafter the President did so recognize the Carranza government as the de facto government, and that from that moment practically the revolutionary or rebellious effort against the Carranza government dwindled and died.

Whether the action of the American Federation of Labor and myself may be counted as cause and effect with the action of the President and of the Government of the United States, is not a question with which we can concern ourselves. The facts are as they are, and each must draw his own inference as his judgment and conscience may direct.

But whether there are some people in Mexico who wish to ignore that which we have done and tried to do in the interests of the Mexican people, and claim for themselves the entire credit and glory for what has been accomplished, is of lesser consequence for the present at least. That the Mexican working people have the appreciation of what the American labor movement has done and tried to do is of greater consequence, not only for the present, but portends much for the future, for if the Mexican working people will but remain organized, and still further extend the field of their activity in organizing the yet unorganized, in making the movement practical, to hold that movement well within their own hands, to press home upon the government the justice to which the toilers of Mexico are entitled, to realize their rights and their duties, to go no further than time, opportunity, and circumstances will permit, and yet hold themselves in readiness to defend the fundamental principles of right and justice and democracy, they will be the most potent factor in seeing that the government of Mexico shall be run right, and make for permanent internal peace, with a constructive policy in the interests of all.

There is one thing which you intimate, and which gives me considerable concern, and that is that due to the mental suffering through which you are passing, owing to the indifference of some of the Mexican people, you intimate your purpose to become a citizen of the United States. May I put it bluntly to you, and to say that in my judgment such a course on your part would be extremely hurtful to the cause of the people of Mexico. As an American citizen of course I would welcome any good, upright, honorable man as a fellow citizen of the United States, but in my judgment the people and the Republic of Mexico need you more than do the people of the United States as a citizen, and if you were to renounce your Mexican citizenship to become a citizen of the United States, your position not only in the future but in the past might be called into question. Placed in the same position as you now are, if I can place myself in it, I would rather remain a citizen of Mexico, even though in retirement for a while in the United States, than to renounce the country to which you have given so valuable services.

I cannot begin to tell you how deeply I am impressed with the action of the organized workers of Mexico in authorizing the making and the presentation of a medal to the American Federation of Labor in appreciation of what we have done or have tried to do.[4] The design is certainly beautiful as shown by the photographic reproduction of both sides of the medal. Of course I shall be very glad not only to receive the medal, for it will be one of the many expressions of good will, affection, and fraternity, now in the possession of the A.F. of L., but far more for what it expresses than for its intrinsic value will it form a part of the outward manifestations of what the American Federation of Labor stands for and tries to do.

And by the way, can you not secure for me as soon as possible the cut of the medal from which the photographs were made, for I desire to reproduce it in the American Federationist, the official magazine of the American Federation of Labor.

In all likelihood I may be in New York[5] on Monday or Tuesday, and if I am I shall let you know in advance, and ask you to come and see me, even for a short time. In any event, I shall want to arrange so that we may exchange views on the existing situation, and for the outlook for the future, either here or in New York.

Reciprocating your kind expressions, and wishing you and yours, and for the people of Mexico, a Happy and Prosperous New Year, and for the years to come, I am,

Sincerely and fraternally yours,   Saml Gompers.
President,   American Federation of Labor.

TLpS, reel 201, vol. 213, pp. 376½–80, SG Letterbooks, DLC.

1. SG to Edmundo Martínez, Nov. 6, 1915, reel 200, vol. 212, pp. 100–101, SG Letterbooks, DLC.

2. In August 1915 the United States invited representatives of Argentina, Bolivia, Brazil, Chile, Guatemala, and Uruguay to participate in a conference to find a peaceful solution to Mexico's civil war. When the Latin American nations agreed to attend but insisted that they would oppose military intervention, the American government assured them on Aug. 12 that its objective was "to obtain peace without resort to measures of force or interference in the internal affairs of Mexico" (*New York Times,* Aug. 13, 1915).

3. "To Woodrow Wilson," Sept. 22, 1915, above.

4. Martínez presented the medal to the AFL Executive Council in June 1916 on behalf of the Federación de Sindicatos Obreros de la República Mexicana. It was inscribed with the words, "To the American Federation of Labor as a loving token from the Mexican Workingmen to the Workers of America."

5. SG's appointment records indicate he met with Gen. Leonard Wood in New York City on Monday, Jan. 3, 1916, but there is no mention of a meeting with Martínez.

To James Duncan

Dec. 31, 1915

Mr. James Duncan,
First Vice President, American Federation of Labor,
Hancock Building, Quincy, Mass.,
Dear Sir and Brother:

Your several letters of the 20th[1] and 22nd inst. came duly to hand, contents of which are carefully noted. I can not begin to tell you how much I regret to learn that you have suffered so much and that you are not in your good old form even now.[2] I can fully sympathize with you, for the work and preparation for the San Francisco Convention, the Convention work, committees, addresses in public meetings and in union meetings, the many addresses at Los Angeles, San Diego and at Milwaukee, and then, with the accumulated work upon my return here where it was necessary to work on my nerves and nerves alone, put me on the broad of my back when I was in New York[3] the early part of last week.

While in New York it was necessary to have a trained nurse and the attendance of a doctor eight times in two days. For several days I was not permitted to have any nourishment of any kind and for nearly a week I lived upon liquids. Last night I ate the first solid piece of food. Both of us having suffered physically, it is not difficult for each of us to understand the conditions of the other. I know you will be glad to learn that I have mended greatly and feel now in fairly good fettle for the year's work.

To two matters about which you write I want to refer briefly. One—regarding the Germer resolution;[4] the other, the tariff commission resolution.[5] You know how absolutely you and I have been in unison in belief on international peace and how far I have gone in my stand upon that subject. Some years ago in Faneuil Hall in Boston[6] at a noonday meeting I declared my belief that the time would not be distant when if there would be no other way to prevent international war, then the working men of the different countries would not only refuse to fight each other but would refuse to make munitions of war.

How much attack and criticism were directed against me for those utterances I do not like now to even refer, much less enumerate, but it did not shake my faith and I kept battering for that thought. At the International Meeting in Paris in 1908,[7] I reiterated that statement, and believed firmly in it. Declarations of a similar import were made by the representatives of the various trade union centers of the other countries, and I was more firmly ensconced in the conviction that the labor movement and the pretentious declarations of the Socialists of the different countries and the international socialist movement, we had definitely reached the achievement of my hopes and faith. But when, at the bidding of the German government, the workmen—the socialists of that country—rallied to their colors and invaded Belgium, and undertook the conquest of other countries—when Belgian workmen and socialists responded to their colors, resisted and fought—when the Socialists and other workmen of France responded to their colors and took up arms and fought, and the trade unionists and socialists of England responded to their country and all this conflagration was in full force, and the men who had pledged their faith and honor to prevent a catastrophe which they permitted to occur—when it is a well-known fact that if in the beginning the men of Germany had kept faith and taken the chance of whatever would be involved, many might have lost their lives, but the international conflagration which has ruptured the tendrils of human hearts would have been prevented—are all these occurrences to have no lesson for us?

I am as much opposed to international war today as I have ever been in my life, but I also realize this fact—that peoples of other nations have not yet reached that step of development, and I am not sure that they will for many, many years to come, when they may take an aggressive movement not only against each other, but against the integrity, the entity and democracy of the people of the republic of the United States.

I am not warlike—I am opposed to war, but I believe it is the duty of the American people, the American democracy, to make it clear to the world that we shall, under all circumstances, be able to defend the republic in whose perpetuity we have pinned our faith and our hopes. A democracy must not spell or be synonymous with weakness or poltroonery. Unless we are physically and mentally able and fit to defend our liberties, we are not able to maintain our liberties or even be worthy of them.

A few days ago I received a copy of a brochure entitled "The Dangers of Peace."[8] It is a mighty interesting document, and I shall try to get a copy of it for you. If I do, I will send it to you[9] and ask you to read it with the care you always give to matters coming under your observation. After I have fully digested it myself, if I can not get another copy, I shall loan you mine, with the request, of course, that it shall be returned. But, as you say, we can discuss this as well as other matters when we meet.

In regard to the tariff commission subject, let me say that I quite agree with much of what you say. Fundamentally in the United States the entire subject of tariff legislation must be determined by the representatives of the people in Congress, but as you know, that for the past thirty five years the presidential campaigns have been determined upon an appeal to the direct fears and the ignorance, rather than the intelligence of the citizenship. During these campaigns catch phrases were employed, and "dinner pails," empty or filled, were insultingly flung into the faces of the citizens of our country. The appeal was to the stomachs rather than to the fundamentals of the well being and the democracy of our republic.

My idea as to the tariff commission is that it should be made up of representative men such as, for instance, the Interstate Commerce Commission, the Federal Trade Commission—a permanent body not subject to the political bias of either one or the other party, and that upon that tariff commission representatives of the labor movement—organized labor—shall be among its members. This commission should not decree what the tariffs shall be but ascertain scientifically and practically the facts, make recommendations to Congress of a character commanding the respect and the confidence of the people of the United States and having a great influence with the Congress of the United States in regard to tariff legislation, and so that tariff rates shall not be subject to the swinging of a pendulum from a "Republican Protective Tariff" or a "Democratic Free Trade Tariff for Revenue Only," but based upon the needs of labor, industry and commerce. However, this too we can discuss when we meet.

There is some literature which I have seen upon the subject which I shall have placed in your hands so that you can give it further consideration before finally determining your own course.

In regard to the meeting[10] of the Executive Council set for February 21st, will say that I, as you know, was not present when that date was decided. I regretted it very much, for I too desired to have the meeting in January and then again some time in May when we could not only transact our business but formally and officially participate in the dedication of the American Federation of Labor office building. I shall regret more than I can tell you if you cannot be present[11] at our meeting on February 21st—I want your presence—I want your advice and your counsel. Some times we may disagree (although we generally do agree) but in those points in which we disagree at least we can have each other's points of view and reach the best conclusions. I should have no hesitancy in consulting the members of the Executive Council as to holding a meeting of the E.C. some time in April or May.[12]

I wish you would write me[13] in regard to this as well as the other matters to which reference is made in this letter. Don't fail to write me fully and frankly upon the subject of the E.C. meeting, for I want you to be present.

Reciprocating your kind wishes for the holidays and trusting that you will already have fully regained your health and strength, and hoping for a prosperous New Year for you and yours and our great cause, I am,

Sincerely and fraternally yours,   Saml Gompers

President,   American Federation of Labor.

TLpS, reel 201, vol. 213, pp. 487–91, SG Letterbooks, DLC.

1. James Duncan wrote two letters to SG on Dec. 20, 1915. Both may be found in the AFL Microfilm National and International Union File, Granite Cutters Records, reel 38, frame 1542, *AFL Records*.

2. Duncan had collapsed in Los Angeles after the 1915 AFL convention in San Francisco while on an extensive and strenuous trip on the West Coast. He canceled the balance of his engagements and returned home to recuperate.

3. SG was subpoenaed to testify before a federal grand jury in New York City about an antiwar organization known as Labor's National Peace Council and the efforts of German agents to foment strikes in the United States. He went to New York on Dec. 19, 1915, appeared before the grand jury on Dec. 20 and 21, and returned to Washington, D.C., by Dec. 28.

4. Resolution 79 (see "Defense Hotly Discussed by Federation Delegates," Nov. 19, 1915, n. 1, in "Excerpts from News Accounts of the 1915 Convention of the AFL in San Francisco," Nov. 16–23, 1914, above).

5. Resolution 105, adopted by the 1915 AFL convention, endorsed the concept of a nonpartisan tariff commission.

6. A reference to a speech SG made on the subject of organized labor and international peace at Tremont Temple in Boston, Mar. 20, 1899.

7. The International Secretariat of the National Centers of Trade Unions met in Paris, Aug. 30–Sept. 1, 1909.

8. John William Allen, *The Danger of Peace* (London, 1915).

9. SG to Duncan, Jan. 6, 1916, reel 201, vol. 213, p. 689, SG Letterbooks, DLC.

10. The AFL Executive Council met in Washington, D.C., Feb. 21–26, 1916.

11. Duncan did not attend the Council's February 1916 meeting.

12. The next meeting of the AFL Executive Council was held on June 26–July 3, 1916, in Washington, D.C.

13. Duncan to SG, Jan. 5, 1916, AFL Microfilm National and International Union File, Granite Cutters Records, reel 38, frames 1542–43, *AFL Records.*

To Solomon Gompers[1]

Washington, D.C., Jan. 7, 1916.

Mr. S. Gompers,
159 Talbot Ave., Dorchester, Mass.
Have just been informed that you have been made great great grandfather by the advent of a boy[2] to Sophia[3] my Henry's daughter. Congratulations to you and all and for you long years of health and happiness. Tomorrow, Saturday, we lay the cornerstone for the American Federation of Labor office building. All the family join me in love to you and all of the folks.

Samuel Gompers.

TWpSr, reel 201, vol. 213, p. 695, SG Letterbooks, DLC.

1. Solomon GOMPERS was SG's father.
2. Charles E. Knight.
3. Sophia Gompers Knight, daughter of SG's son Henry Julian Gompers, lived in Oneida, N.Y., with her husband, Andrew E. Knight, a clerk in a steel works.

An Address at the Ceremony of Laying the Cornerstone of the AFL Office Building, Washington, D.C.

[January 8, 1916]

CORNERSTONE LAID

. . .

PRESIDENT GOMPERS' ADDRESS

Mr. Gompers: Ladies and Gentlemen, In the performance of this ceremony of the cornerstone laying, I am impressed so much, I am thrilled to such an extent, that it is exceedingly difficult for me to express what I have in my mind to say or what my heart prompts me to say.

It was my privilege in 1881 to be present at the convention[1] when the cornerstone was laid for the A.F. of L. Now, after thirty-five years, to have the great honor and privilege to lay the cornerstone for the structure that is to be erected here, an office devoted to service, to still greater service, in the cause of Labor, in the cause of justice, in the cause of freedom, in the cause of humanity—is to me so important a function that I fail to command myself and to give adequate expression to what all this portends, not only in our day, but for all time. This structure erected for service will mean to all those who read as they run, that there is still burning in the hearts of the people of America that flame which can not and must not be extinguished, the torch and the flame of liberty, the justice which must be kept burning, and to which men and women of our time and of the future must devote themselves, if liberty and justice and freedom and humanity shall have their fullest understanding and obligation.

The men of the organized labor movement of our time realize the mission resting upon them—the heritage of all of the struggles and the sacrifices of the past which made it possible that in this year of grace nineteen hundred and sixteen, we may enjoy the liberties secured for us by our fathers. The progress, the rights and the opportunities of today are the achievements of the long, hard struggle of those who have gone before. The labor movement is a world-old struggle for freedom. That progress has been made; that the lives of men are better and happier are due to those who had the courage to make the fight and who had an idea of what should be. Today our hearts are very tender toward the men and the women of the labor movement of past years. They made a fight against the forces of greed and inhumanity—they fought in the days when to belong to the labor movement meant actual physical danger and marked men for social ostracism and for persecution by all the agencies of organized society. The heritage we receive from them is a sacred trust—to be maintained and handed on to coming generations with enhanced potentiality.

As in physical life those members of our body which fail to exercise their proper natural and normal functions, so in political and our economic life, the man or the woman who fails to exercise the liberties which are theirs, the men and the women who flinch from the responsibilities and the consequences which the exercise of liberty entails, are unworthy of liberty—unworthy of liberty, unworthy of freedom, untrue to the traditions and the struggles and the heroism of the past—are cowardly and false to all future time.

Men of today must be willing to do their share of the world's work. Men of today must be willing to hazard the risk inevitably consequent to the determination to fight for the maintenance of freedom and the enlargement of the concepts of freedom and justice to struggle, or to give their all in order that liberty may live and our republic endure.

Our movement, the trade union movement, as understood and represented and expressed by the A.F. of L., has maintained and advanced the high standards it raised for the toilers, for the masses, for all the people. Our achievements are a great tribute to all that is good, and true, and noble.

We aim to bring more light and life in the homes and the work of the toilers of our country, and of the world. We have aimed to bring increasing opportunity into the lives of all who toil. Our primary demand is for a shorter workday.

A reduction of one hour per day in the labor of the workers of America affords twenty million golden opportunities for thought, for action, for human betterment every day.

Our demands have been effective in securing the eight-hour day for many workers—a gain which has had an incalculable influence in the lives of those workers. For the short-hour workers are workers with different standards of life, concepts, greater demands, than those who are deadened by fatigue and long hours of grinding toil.

We aim to develop higher standards of character and of duty with the understanding that rights and privileges carry with them duties and obligations.

Men and women of toil, we know not how long this structure when completed shall last. In the cornerstone of this structure is contained a copper box in which are enclosed a number of important documents[2]—the thought of today conveyed and expressed to those who shall come after us, and who may read and learn of what we have tried to do in our time. They are a message into the future. When with time this structure shall be crumbled into dust, when the men and the women of that time shall see an accounting of our work in our day, let us hope that they may realize that we have tried in the light that is given us to do our duty, to keep the faith with the past, and our duty for today, as well as our obligation for the future.

Men and women assembled here, thousands and thousands would have been only too glad to be here if they could. Let us express their thoughts and their hopes and their aspirations as we look upon this cornerstone and this uncompleted structure, that we may always be true to ourselves, true to our fellows, true to the duties devolving upon us, and that this structure of labor, typifying all that is good and true and noble, shall stand as an enduring monument—and better still that the movement of organized labor living in the hearts and the conscience of our fellow-workers shall be carried on, and on and on, time without day and shall ever encourage us now to do our duty by our fellows, to be willing to do, to consecrate anew our lives and our hopes in the attainment of the highest standards of life, of progress, of civilization, for the workers now, for the workers of the future, and for all mankind, and for all time.

. . .

American Federationist 23 (Feb. 1916): 111, 114–15.

1. The 1881 FOTLU convention, which met in Pittsburgh, Nov. 15–18.

2. For a list of the photographs and documents placed in the cornerstone, see SG to the AFL Executive Council, Jan. 8, 1916, Executive Council Records, Vote Books, reel 14, frames 432–33, *AFL Records.*

From Ellen Gates Starr[1]

Hull-House
Chicago January 8, 1916.

Dear Sir;—

I am sending you a copy of the January issue of the New Republic, containing a marked article entitled "Cheap Clothes and Nasty."[2] I would especially call your attention to the paragraphs marked on page 218, "So heavily lies the hand of Gompers on the trade union world of Chicago, etc." The hand which should have been the strongest and readiest to aid those brave and oppressed people was the one which shut off from them the most powerful sources of aid. Confused, indeed the public mind has naturally been, at the sight of this gallant army, fighting, not unlike the Belgians single handed against their oppressors except as a few individuals, independent or fearless or both, chose to take their own risks in aiding them;—the great force of organised labor, meanwhile, constrained by fear of the "heavy hand" to stand by, inactive onlookers.

And why? Because a spirited body of people unable to rid themselves, otherwise, of corrupt officials, had dared to secede in overwhelming majority and form a new and clean organization under honest and able leadership.

Naturally the "bosses" made the utmost use of the circumstance of the American Federation of Labor's attitude to confuse the public mind in their own interest, and to set it against the strikers. After all the harm that could have been done had been done—near the end of the strike, Mr. Gompers decided that he "sympathized" with the striking clothing workers. That sympathy at the beginning, or even at the time of the National convention, might have won the strike, outright, releasing as it would have done, the Chicago Federation and Woman's Trade Union League. The A.C.W. put up a magnificent fight, one which the Chicago manufacturers will not soon forget.

Some of us who had the courage of our convictions are proud to have been able to help in it. It should have won and it might have won,—but for the "heavy hand of Mr. Gompers."

Yours for the truth   Ellen Gates Starr—

TLcS, Amalgamated Clothing Workers of America Papers, Labor-Management Documentation Center, NIC. Handwritten notations: "Copy. Please return" and "Gompers sent his answer[3] to this to the New Republic,[4] & did *not* send my letter—a quite unheard of proceeding. The N.R. apologises for printing one without the other."[5]

1. Ellen Gates Starr (1859–1940) was a founder of Hull-House in 1889 and of the Chicago Women's Trade Union League in 1904. The Amalgamated Clothing Workers of America recognized her support of its 1915 strike in Chicago by making her an honorary member of the union for life. In 1916 she ran unsuccessfully for city alderman on the ticket of the Socialist Party of America.

2. The unsigned article "Cheap Clothes and Nasty" was published in the *New Republic* on Jan. 1, 1916, pp. 217–19.

3. "To Ellen Gates Starr," Jan. 28, 1916, below.

4. SG to the Editor of the *New Republic*, Jan. 28, 1916, reel 202, vol. 214, p. 734, SG Letterbooks, DLC.

5. The *New Republic* published SG's Jan. 28, 1916, letter to Starr on Feb. 19 (pp. 73–74) and Starr's Feb. 4 (misdated Feb. 12) reply to him on Mar. 4 (p. 130), with an apology for not printing it earlier with SG's letter. SG published this correspondence, together with Starr's to him of Jan. 8 and his to Starr of Feb. 10, under the headline "Here's Another One of 'Em" in the June 1916 issue of the *American Federationist* (23: 470–74).

To Frank Morrison

New York NY Jan 15 [1916]

Frank Morrison
AF of L Blg WDC
Am advised Porto Rican bill[1] is up Wish you would devote some time today to the matter Insist upon citizenship and oppose disfranchisement

Samuel Gompers

TWSr, Files of the Office of the President, General Correspondence, reel 80, frame 62, *AFL Records*. Handwritten notation: "Senator Lane[2] will introduce amendments to-morrow the committee to meet in E.C. session to consider amendments. Holder."

1. H.R. 9533 (64th Cong., 1st sess.), providing for civil government in Puerto Rico,

was introduced by Democratic congressman William Jones of Virginia on Jan. 20, 1916, and became law on Mar. 2, 1917 (U.S. *Statutes at Large*, 39: 951–68). Known as the Jones Act, it made Puerto Rico a U.S. territory, conferred U.S. citizenship on the people of Puerto Rico, and instituted male suffrage for the election of both houses of the Puerto Rican legislature. It did not, however, grant the islanders the right to vote for U.S. president or vice-president, and the elective resident commissioner who represented them in Congress had a voice but no vote. The original bill set property and educational qualifications for service in the Puerto Rican legislature, but the AFL opposed these requirements and they were stricken from the bill.

2. Harry Lane (1855–1917) served as a Democratic senator from Oregon (1913–17).

An Address before the Annual Meeting of the National Civic Federation in Washington, D.C.[1]

Washington, D.C., Jan. 18, 1916.

For seventeen months war such as has never been known in the history of man has been devouring life and consuming the handiwork of man. Such a stupendous horror has compelled men to think deeply of the principles underlying our institutions and the spirit that makes for human progress and liberty.

Before the outbreak of the present war, many believed that a great war involving many nations was no longer possible, that men had developed ideals of justice and of humanity that would prevent the possibility of their taking the lives of fellow-men even in the name of legitimate warfare. They hoped much—their ideals were untested.

With the declaration of war the men of each country rushed to their flags. Soon there were mobilized thousands of men fighting for conflicting ideals. When it was necessary to decide whether they proposed to stand by and see another nation invade their fatherland, trample upon their national ideals, ruthlessly disregard solemn pledges given in treaties, they found that there were some things of higher value than peace. They found that there are dangers of peace more far-reaching than the dangers of war. They realized that it is better to fight and die for a cause than to maintain peace and their physical safety at the sacrifice of their manhood and of the ideals that ennoble life.

And yet it is not an unbeautiful theory that has been dissipated by the shot and the smoke of the European war. There were many who held that an organized society was possible upon a basis of the brotherhood of men, in which all had regard for the rights of others and would subordinate their selfish interests to the welfare of others. This ideal made paramount the sanctity of human life and regarded war as a relic of barbarism possible only because institutions of justice had not been sufficiently developed. Wage-earners generally of all civilized countries proclaimed and endorsed this ideal and declared that they would use every means within their power to prevent war even to the extent of stopping all of the industries of the nations through a general strike. There were many extreme pacifists who could find no justification for war or the use of force in international affairs.

And I too found this ideal attractive. In a speech that I made in April 1899 in Tremont Temple, Boston,[2] I said:

"The organized wage-worker learns from his craft association the value of humanity and of the brotherhood of man, hence it is not strange that we should believe in peace, not only nationally, but internationally.

"It is often our custom to send organizers from one country to another for the purpose of showing to our fellows in other countries the value of our association in the labor movement. If international peace can not be secured by the intelligence of those in authority, then I look forward to the time when the workers will settle this question, by the dock laborers refusing to handle goods that are to be used to destroy their fellow-men, and the seamen of the world, united in one organization, while willing to risk their lives in conducting the commerce of nations, absolutely refuse to strike down their fellow-men."

My belief that war was no longer possible was based upon what I desired rather than upon realities because I felt so keenly the brutality, the destruction and the waste of war. It seemed to me that war and conditions of war cut through the veneer of civilization and disclosed the brute in man. The consequence and the purpose of war accustom man to treat human life lightly. They make men callous to human suffering and they idealize force. No one can hear of the atrocities, of the terrible carnage of the present war, of the destruction on the battle fields and on the high seas without a feeling of horror that civilized men can plan such methods, can use the skill of their minds and bodies and the wisdom of past generations to such terrible purpose. But what if these horrors done to the bodies of men shall prevent greater horrors to the minds—the souls of men?

The pacifists and those who hold to policies of non-resistance have failed as I had failed, to understand and to evaluate that quality in the human race which makes men willing to risk their all for an ideal. Men worthy of the name will fight even for a "scrap of paper" when that paper represents ideals of human justice and freedom. The man who would not fight for such a scrap of paper is a poor craven who dares not assert his rights against the opposition and the demands of others. There is little progress made in the affairs of the world in which resistance of others is not involved. Not only must man have a keen sense of his own rights, but the will and the ability to maintain those rights with effective insistence. Resistance to injustice and tyranny and low ideals is inseparable from a virile fighting quality that has given purpose and force to ennobling causes, to all nations.

Though we may realize the brutality of war, though we may know the value of life, yet we know equally well what would be the effects upon the lives and the minds of men who would lose their rights, who would accept denial of justice rather than hazard their physical safety. The progress of all the ages has come as the result of protests against wrongs and existing conditions and through assertion of rights and effective demands for justice. Our own freedom and republican form of government have been achieved by resistance to tyranny and insistence upon rights. Freedom and democracy dare not be synonymous with weakness. They exist only because there is a vision of the possibilities of human life, faith in human nature and the will to make these things realities even against the opposition of those who see and understand less deeply. The people who are willing to maintain their rights and to defend their freedom are worthy of those privileges. Rights carry with them obligation—duty. It is the duty of those who live under free institutions at least to maintain them unimpaired.

As the result of the European war there is hardly a citizen who has not in some degree modified his opinions upon preparedness and national defense. The belief prevails that there must be some policy of preparedness and national defense although there is wide diversion as to what policies ought to be adopted.

Preparedness and defense are practically the reverse and obverse sides of the same problem. There are two lines of approach to this problem—one indirect, involving consideration of the development, health and conservation of the citizens, and the other direct, involving the weapons of defense and specific plans for the use of power.

In the past we have trusted much to the rugged physiques, muscles and nerves trained and under control and ability to coordinate powers quickly to meet emergencies which belong to the outdoor life of a pioneer people. Life on the frontier developed physical strength and virile manhood. Mental and physical weakness could not survive in the dangers of that life. But the frontier has vanished. The majority of our citizens no longer live in the open and they show in their physical development the effect of the restricted life of the city. They have not the physical strength or endurance that would fit them without further preparation to be called into service in a citizens' army.

Since opportunities for physical training are not freely and readily available to all, some definite national policy must be devised for physical training and physical preparedness of all citizens. Such a training could be readily given through our public school system and other auxiliary agencies.

Physical training is properly a part of educational work and therefore should be under the control and direction of public agencies. We are constantly coming to a better appreciation of what proper physical development and good health mean in the life and for the working ability of each individual. Physical training and good health are just as important and just as necessary to all other interests of life as they are to national defense. The chief problem is that training of this nature should be in furtherance of broad general usefulness and ideals and not be narrowly specialized or dominated by the purpose of militarism.

Physical training must fit citizens for industry, for commerce, for service in the work of the nation, as well as for service in defense of the nation. But physical training and preparedness are insufficient. There must be a spirit among the people that makes them loyal to country and willing to give themselves to its service and protection. That spirit can not exist unless the citizens feel that the nation will assure to all equal opportunities and equal justice. They must feel that they are a part of the nation, with a voice in determining its destinies. This spirit of loyalty depends not only upon political rights, but upon justice and right on the industrial field, aye, in all relations of life.

National preparedness involves also power to coordinate and to utilize national forces and national resources. War as it is being waged today is not determined merely by the men on the battle field, but also by the mobilization of the national resources, national industries and commerce. The real problem is the organization of the material forces and resources of the country, the coordination of these in the furtherance of a definite defensive military policy. All of the power and resources of the belligerent countries are concentrated to sustain the armies in the field and to equip them with the necessary weapons of war. The contest between industries, the question of commercial control, of superiority of economic organization are fully as important as the contest between the soldiers on the battle field. Whatever then is the necessary part of the organization of industrial and commercial life is an important factor in national preparedness.

Our industrial and commercial development has been of a haphazard nature rather than in accord with any definite, constructive, statesmanlike plan. Because of the vast natural resources of our country and the variety of untouched opportunities, it has been possible for us as a nation to achieve tremendous results without definite plans, without much wisdom, and without the use of the best judgment. Considering our opportunities and the vast wealth of our country, to have failed would have been much more marvelous than the degree of success to which we have attained. As our population has increased, as free lands have disappeared, as there is no longer the former wide range of opportunity, success in the future will be more directly the result of the best use of available opportunities and of the best coordination of existing forces. As frontier opportunities have disappeared so frontier business policies will no long succeed. Commercial or industrial policies that aimed at immediate results with extravagant disregard for conservation or for economical utilization of materials will be replaced by better policies of developing commerce and industry upon a basis that means constructive development instead of exploitation. The economic highwayman must disappear as did the frontier highwayman.

Constructive development must have consideration for every factor concerned in production and must secure to each equal opportunities that will result in the best service and in the conservation of the future service. Such a policy will involve thorough organization of all the factors of production. This organization must extend to the human element in production in order that there may be accorded to the workers proper consideration of their needs and proper conservation of their labor power.

Preparedness as viewed from this standpoint is a part of the larger problems of national development—physical, mental, economic. It is a civic, an economic as well as a military problem. National development can be in accord with the highest ideals only when all citizens have the right to voluntary association to promote their own welfare and to activities necessary to carry out the purpose of such organizations. This broad general policy includes associations of wage-earners—trade unions. These associations of the workers must be recognized by all agencies, whether private or governmental, that are concerned with the life and the work of the workers.

Great Britain in dealing with immediate problems of national defense, has found that the labor movement must be recognized as the natural and official representative of the wage-earners. She has found that she can deal with national problems only when she considers the ideals and the demands of the chosen representatives of the workers.

But the principles of human welfare cannot be ignored in military matters or in plans for national defense just as they cannot be ignored in industry or commerce. That infinitely valuable and sacred thing—human creative power and the safeguarding of human rights and freedom are of fundamental importance and are correlated with national defense and must not be sacrificed to any false concept of national defense. For to what end will a nation be saved, if the citizens are denied that which gives life value and purpose?

The labor power of workers is to them their all. The deep significance of the protection and conservation of their labor—their very lives—is what the British government of today has failed to understand. The deep significance of this declaration made a few days ago in England by an important labor organization has a meaning for us:

"Unless the government is prepared to confiscate the wealth of the privileged classes for the more successful prosecution of the war, the railroad workers will resist to the uttermost the confiscation of men whose only wealth is their labor power."[3]

Some employers of our country and some government officials have refused to recognize organizations of wage-earners, but organizations of wage-earners are a necessary and an important part of the organization of industry and society and any national policy that refuses to recognize and take into account such an important force must prove ineffective.

National policies, whether political or military, must be in accord with broad democratic ideals that recognize all factors and value each according to the service that it performs. There is a human side to all of our national problems, whether industrial, commercial, political or military. It has been the general practice of governments to accord only to employers, the owners of capital, of the managerial side of commerce and industry, real participation in government and in deciding upon governmental policies. According to this custom the wage-earners belong to the class of the governed, never to the governing class. This policy is a reflection of conditions existing in the industrial and commercial world. However, a change has been coming. The wage-earners, through their economic associations, have been making the demand that those who supply the creative labor power of industry and commerce are surely as important to the processes of production as those who supply the materials necessary for production. They have, therefore, made demand that the human side of production shall at least be given as much consideration and as much importance as the material side. They demand that industries and commerce shall be conducted not only in the interests of production but with consideration for the welfare and the conservation of the human beings employed in production. They have asserted the right that every policy affecting industry, commerce, financial institutions and everything that is involved in the organization of society in some way affects the lives of those concerned in the industries or occupations and the welfare of those who are the consumers. Therefore, they demand that those who are concerned in the conduct of the industry or occupation must be given the same consideration as those who are to make profits by the industry. They have declared that there are principles of human welfare and have demanded that these must be considered in determining national policies. This is a democratic ideal and one which will promote the welfare of all of the people. Hence, it has an important bearing upon national preparedness, for it means that the great masses of the people will be better fitted physically and mentally to be intelligent, able protectors of the nation.

In addition to policies of general preparedness, which are a part of the larger problem of national development and conservation, there must be some specific plan and agency for national defense. Even the Socialists agree upon the necessity for wars of defense and for agencies of national defense. When war was declared the Socialists of Germany, of France and of England flocked to the national standard to defend the flag. There is not a national socialist organization in Europe that is not defending its participation in the war upon the plea of the necessity for national defense. The old international idealism of Human Brotherhood has, at least for this war, been shot to pieces on the battlefields of Europe. They forgot their theories of pacifism and flew to arms to defend their homes, their families and their governments.

And the Socialists of the United States have not escaped dissensions as the result of the war and are now in a bitter wrangle upon the degree of military preparedness that ought to be adopted by this country. Some of the more violent pacifists are trying to forcefully eject from the party those who declare a policy of non-resistance as incompatible with the conditions that confront our nation. Other Socialists, such as Charles Edward Russell,[4] renounce their old dreams and acknowledge that human nature makes it necessary for us to be ready for national defense. Prominent members of the Socialist Party—Joshua Wanhope[5] and W. J. Ghent[6]—declare that socialism is a revolutionary movement and hence Socialists cannot renounce the use of force. Both declare that the Socialist parties of the world have never taken the position of advocating Tolstoian non-resistance. Morris Hillquit has admitted that preparedness seems doomed to become the issue in the National convention and a plank in the Socialist Party platform. Henry L. Slobodin[7] has said:

"The Socialists had many occasions, during the last fifty years, to deliberate upon this problem and declare the Socialist attitude on military preparedness. And not once did the Socialists declare against preparedness. On every occasion they declared that the Socialists were, in their own way, in favor of military preparedness. The Socialists always were against standing armies and huge military establishments. But they always were and now stand committed in favor of *universal military training and a citizens' army.*"

Recent dispatches from Berlin say that the Executive Committee of the Socialist party has by a vote of twenty-eight to eleven adopted a resolution censuring twenty Socialist members of the *Reichstag* for attempting to thwart the party's policy by declining to vote in favor of the war credits.

Quite in contrast to this vacillation is the consistent attitude of the American Federation of Labor. The following declaration made years ago has stood the tests of the experiences of years. It embodies the wisdom Labor has gained in the struggle of life and work.

"A man who is a wage earner and honorably working at his trade or calling to support himself and those dependent upon him, has not only the right to become a citizen soldier, but that right must be unquestioned.

"The militia, i.e., the citizen soldiery of the several states in our country, supplies what otherwise might take its place—a large standing army.

"The difference between the citizen soldiery of the United States and the large standing armies of the many European countries is the difference between a republic and monarchy—it is the difference between the conceptions of liberty and of tyranny.

"While organized labor stands against the arbitrament of international or internal disputes by force of arms, yet we must realize we have not yet reached the millennium; that in the age in which we live we have not the choice between armed force and absolute disarmament, but the alternative of a large standing army and a small one supplemented by a volunteer citizen soldiery—the militia of our several states."

The 1915 San Francisco Convention of the A.F. of L. reaffirmed this position by refusing to adopt resolutions which called upon all workers to desist from affiliating with any branch of the military forces.[8]

A great majority of our nation are agreed upon the necessity for adopting a definite policy for necessary national defense. Of course there is not unity upon any one policy. Whatever plan may be adopted the organized labor movement of America, which is directly representative of millions of organized wage-earners and indirectly representative of millions of more unorganized workers, demands that certain fundamental principles must be regarded.

All policies and plans for national defense must be determined by representatives of all of the people. The organized labor movement which is the only means for expressing the will and the desires of the great masses of our citizenship, asserts its right to representation in all committees, commissions or bodies that decide upon military defense. The working people of all nations are always those most vitally affected by military service in time of peace or war. Upon them falls the burden of the fighting in the ranks and they have ever been expected to act as shock absorbers for the evil consequences of war. They have been the chief sufferers from evils of militarism wherever that malicious system has fastened itself upon a nation. Since they have been the victims of the hurtful policies of military defense, they will be the most interested in safeguarding our own national plans from dangers and from evils of militarism that have been disclosed by the experiences of other countries.

Preparedness is something very different from militarism or navalism. Both leave an indelible impression upon the nation, one for freedom and the other for repression. Militarism and navalism are a perversion of preparedness—instead of serving the interests of the people, the people are ammunition for these machines. They are destructive to freedom and democracy.

An understanding of human nature and of conditions is convincing proof that every nation must have some means of self-defense. The agencies and policies for this purpose must be carefully chosen.

The labor movement has always been a leader in the cause of democracy. The labor movement demands democracy in all things, including military organizations and institutions of the country. It holds that policies and methods of self-defense are best safeguarded when there is equal opportunity for all to become members of whatever organizations and institutions, whether military or otherwise, exist throughout the country. Not only must entrance to all institutions be freely and equally accorded to all but the military must be democratically organized, democratically officered and under the control of heads who are responsible to the citizens of the land.

In addition to the regular army there must be a citizenship physically fit, ready and able to serve. Equal opportunity for military training must be provided for the citizenship generally—opportunity attended by provisions that make it equal in reality and truly democratic.

All agree that physical training with knowledge and the ability to bear and use arms will have a wholesome effect upon the health, strength and preparedness of the people of the United States. If that training is given through voluntary institutions, organized upon a democratic basis, it will have a wholesome effect upon the civic life of the nation also.

Democratic spirit is essential. Any place that recognizes professions or other distinctions will tend toward military castes, a condition incompatible with the freedom, the spirit and the genius of our republic.

Absolute democracy in voluntary service for national defense will have an effect upon all other relations of life. It will make for better understanding. It will bind all together in unselfish service and broaden and deepen that which constitutes the common life of our nation. Man cannot resist the appeal of human nature.

The labor movement is militant. The workers understand the necessity for power and its uses. They fully appreciate the important function that power exercises in the affairs of the world. Power does not have to be used in order to be potential. The very existence of power and ability to use that power constitutes a defense against unreasonable and unwarranted attack. Ability and readiness for self-defense constitute a potential instrumentality against unnecessary and useless wars or the denial of rights and justice.

The labor movement has never advocated the abolition of agencies for the enforcement of right and justice, or for the abolition of the military arm of government, but it does demand that these shall be so organized as to prevent their misuse and abuse as a means of tyranny against the workers, and to prevent the development of pernicious results that have grown out of militarism, the building up of a separate military caste and the subversion of civic life to military government and military standards. When military institutions and military service are separated from the general life of the people they become subversive to the ideals of civic life, they become dangerous to the best development and the best interests of the nation.

The rights and privileges of citizenship impose a duty upon all who enjoy them. That duty involves service to the nation in all relations of the common life including its defense against attack and the maintenance of national institutions and ideals.

There are no citizens of our country who are more truly patriotic than the organized wage-earners—or all of the wage-earners, and we have done our share in the civic life of the nation as well as in the nation's wars. We have done our share to protect the nation against insidious attacks from within that were directed at the very heart of our national life and would have inevitably involved us in foreign complications. The wage-earners stood unfalteringly for ideals of honor, freedom and loyalty. Their wisdom and their patriotism served our country in a time of great need. No one can question that the wage-earners of the United States are patriotic in the truest sense. No one can question their willingness to fight for the cause of liberty, freedom and justice. No one can question the value of the ideals that direct the labor movement.

The labor movement takes the position that plans and policies for national defense and preparedness must be in accord with the educated conscience which can discern values and is able and alert to distinguish the vital from the less important and willing to insist upon the ideals and standards of justice, equality and freedom.

Every observer knows that there is no peace—all of life is a struggle, physical and mental. Progress results only from the domination of the forces making for freedom and opportunity over the forces of repression.

I may summarize the situation into these few concrete suggestions:

1. The recognition of and cooperation with the organized labor movement in all fields of activity, industrial, commercial, political, social, moral defense.

2. Establishment and extension of the citizen soldiery, democratically organized, officered, administered and controlled.

3. Prohibition of the use of the militia for strike duty.

4. Education of wage earners upon an equality with all other citizens in manual training, physical and mental development, in organizing, officering, administering and leading in the operations of a military character for the defense of our country.

5. Industrial education and vocational training as part of the educational system of the states, with financial aid of the Federal Government.

6. Education of the young, physical and mental; including the art and the duty of defense, the ability to bear arms, the inculcation of the ideals of democracy, civic rights, duties and obligations.

7. Inculcate in all our people a social conscience for a better concept of industrial justice.

The thoughts and suggestions, I have submitted, should commend themselves to the serious and favorable consideration and action of all of our people—all their groups and associations. Put into actual operation they will make, not only for immediate effective preparedness for defense, but will prove the potential means for permanent preparedness and defense, while at the same time make all our people more efficient in their every endeavor, and, in addition safeguard the spirit of justice, freedom, democracy and humanity.

TD, Files of the Office of the President, Speeches and Writings, reel 112, frames 16–40, *AFL Records.*

1. The 1916 convention of the National Civic Federation met in Washington, D.C., Jan. 17–18.

2. See "To James Duncan," Dec. 31, 1915, n. 6, above.

3. The resolution was adopted by the executive committee of the National Union of Railwaymen in opposition to the British government's first Military Service Act, enacted in January 1916, which provided for conscription of unmarried men between the ages of eighteen and forty-one.

4. Charles Edward Russell ran unsuccessfully on the Socialist Party of America (SPA) ticket for governor of New York (1910, 1912), mayor of New York City (1913), and

senator from that state (1914) and declined nomination as the socialist candidate for president in 1916. He supported the preparedness campaign and opposed the SPA call for an end to the manufacture of arms and munitions, which led to his expulsion from the party. He was a member of the U.S. diplomatic mission to Russia in 1917.

5. Joshua (variously Joseph) Wanhope was a socialist New York City journalist.

6. William James Ghent served as secretary (1906–9) and director (1909–11) of the Rand School of Social Science in New York City and as secretary to Victor Berger (1911–12). He resigned from the SPA in 1917 because of its opposition to American entry into World War I. From 1917 to 1919 he served as a member of the executive committee of the American Alliance for Labor and Democracy.

7. Henry L. Slobodin, a New York City attorney, wrote for the *New York Call* before breaking with the SPA over the war.

8. See "Defense Hotly Discussed by Federation Delegates," Nov. 19, 1915, in "Excerpts from News Accounts of the 1915 Convention of the AFL in San Francisco," Nov. 16–23, 1915, above.

A Statement by Samuel Gompers

[January 24, 1916]

The negro race was given the opportunity for freedom by the immortal Lincoln's Emancipation Proclamation of 1863. They have been achieving their freedom by the slow process of education and development. Booker T. Washington has been one of the great leaders in that struggle for freedom—with clear insight he understood that freedom for the negroes meant ability to render service to society that would assure their value and independence. His influence was to show his fellows that the things of every day life and work are the materials for building characters and for achieving that attitude toward life which is freedom.

The great things of life are simple—elemental. It was because Booker T. Washington taught his fellows the simple elemental things necessary to their betterment that he became a great leader of the negro race.

Though born in slavery, he made himself free and showed the pathway of freedom to others. He gave service and taught others the nobility of voluntary service.

His was a leadership of deeds as well as words. He was a great man. He will live on in the lives of many generations.

Saml Gompers.

TDpS, reel 202, vol. 214, p. 729, SG Letterbooks, DLC. Typed notation: "Statement sent to A. Robert White, 633 Plymouth Court, Chicago, Ill., to be published in book to perpetuate memory of Booker T. Washington. January 24, 1916."

To Charles Bowerman

Jan. 25, 1916.

Mr. C. W. Bowerman,
Secretary, Parliamentary Committee, British Trades Union
  Congress,
General Buildings, Aldwych, W.C., London.
Dear Sir and Brother:

No doubt you are aware of the fact that considerable information is published in the United States, not only regarding the war, but also many important events in connection with it, and among them are features of the law affecting the personnel, wages, hours and conditions of employment between trade unions and employers. It is stated that some of the trade union rules and regulations have been suspended during the war with the proviso that at the end of the war the trade union rules shall ipso facto be revived and come into full force and effect.[1] It is also stated that the Board of Trade for the Government of England, has underwritten and guaranteed these conditions. Many other points of interest are recounted.

Now the particular purpose of my writing is to see whether I cannot get from you authentically and officially the fullest information upon this subject. Could you not furnish me with a copy of the law or the laws upon this subject, or copies of the agreements or guarantees given by the Board of Trade?[2]

From all the information I have, and my own knowledge, I am quite sure that the people of the United States, through their government will undertake a greater measure of preparedness for national defense than has heretofore been the case. It is neither necessary nor practical to state from which angle the people of the United States feel that they will in time have to defend themselves. Suffice it to know the fact, that with all this preparedness I know of no one who has brought out, or even holds in reserve, the idea of militarism. Every loyal American citizen and every liberty loving citizen, holds as strongly against militarism but realizes that a republican form of government must not necessarily mean pusillanimity or inability to defend the republic and the people against attack.

So when any program of the character I have indicated is to be discussed and plans proposed, we want to be in possession of the best information and experience obtainable, and therefore I am writing to you and count upon you to help me to the fullest, furnishing me the information and data, and copies of laws and regulations and agreements already mentioned.

With assurances of best wishes, and asking to be remembered to all our good friends, I am,

Sincerely and fraternally yours,   Saml Gompers.
President,   American Federation of Labor.

N.B. I am also writing to Mr. W. A. Appleton, Secretary, General Federation of Trade Unions, a letter identical with this,[3] and I beg to suggest that you and he could cooperate in having the information furnished me as requested.

S. G.[4]

TLpS, reel 202, vol. 214, pp. 576–77, SG Letterbooks, DLC.

1. On Mar. 19, 1915, representatives of the British government and many of the principal British trade unions involved in war-related industries signed the Treasury Agreement, which provided that during the war there would be no work stoppages, that disagreements over wages or working conditions would be subject to binding arbitration, and that less-skilled male workers and women could be employed to increase production. On Mar. 25 the Amalgamated Society of Engineers signed a similar agreement, confirming that these provisions would only remain in effect during the war and clarifying the government's commitment to limit profits arising from the unions' concessions. These voluntary agreements by the unions were replaced by the Munitions of War Act of July 2, 1915 (5 & 6 Geo. V, chap. 54) and the Munitions of War (Amendment) Act of Jan. 27, 1916 (5 & 6 Geo. V, chap. 99).

2. Charles Bowerman replied on Feb. 9, 1916, that under the Munitions of War Act British labor unions had agreed for the duration of the war to accept the introduction of piecework and the use of unskilled and female labor.

3. SG to William Appleton, Jan. 25, 1916, reel 202, vol. 214, pp. 578–79, SG Letterbooks, DLC.

4. According to a memo dictated by SG on Jan. 24, 1916, he wrote to Bowerman and Appleton at the suggestion of Ralph Easley (AFL Microfilm Convention File, reel 27, frame 2060, *AFL Records*). SG sent similar letters to Léon Jouhaux and Carl Legien on Jan. 27.

To Ellen Gates Starr

Washington, D.C., Jan. 28, 1916.

Miss Ellen Gates Starr,
Hull-House, 800 South Halstead Street, Chicago, Illinois.
Dear Madam:

Your letter of January 8th[1] was received in due time, but there have been such pressing and constant demands upon my time and attention that I could not reply to you sooner.

It was indeed a surprise that one with your long and varied experience at Hull-House and intimacy with the lives of the toilers who live around South Halstead Street, Chicago, should have so little real understanding of that comprehensive force in the lives of the workers—the trade union movement.

However, I can understand your keen sympathy with the suffering and the hunger and the struggle of the garment workers in their recent strike. Undoubtedly it was that emotional sympathy that made you condemn so severely the trade union movement and me. The abuse and the injustice that have been inflicted upon these garment workers of Chicago, aroused me to protest against the unwarranted abuse, brutality and violence of the police of Chicago. Those who are in the labor movement, who have made the labor movement what it is by their sacrifices and their struggles understand that its power and effectiveness depend upon solidarity and united action, yet the labor movement is a voluntary association. It is subject to all the short-comings of democracy. Its progress and its continued existence depend upon the wisdom and understanding of its members. Years of experience have taught them their common interest and that they must stand together and fight out their differences within the organization.

Secession or any other disruptionary movement is fatal to the very existence of the labor movement. Secession means to the labor movement just what the secession of the southern states in 1860 meant to the union. It is the act of those who are willing to destroy the whole and jeopardize the welfare of all others in order that they may secure their own objects. Whatever the purpose of seceders may be, their act is that of those who are unwilling to present their demands and to abide by the decision of the majority. Secession is fatal to democratic organization. If the cause of the seceders is just, they ought to be willing to contend for their demands under the laws and regulations of their voluntary organizations and thus seek to establish justice without jeopardizing the welfare of themselves or their fellow-workers. But since the labor movement is a democratic organization, there is no authority or force that can compel them to remain within it. When they choose to secede they incur all of the dangers and all of the consequences that attend a secession movement. This is what the garment workers of Chicago brought upon themselves when they left the United Garment Workers.[2] Although we may regret their act and deplore the fact that they have been victimized, yet we cannot protect them from the consequences of their own acts, for to endorse and approve a secession movement would be to establish a standard that would endanger the existence of a united labor movement which would jeopardize the welfare not only of the organized workers but of the unorganized who benefit in some degree by the struggle and the success of the organized labor movement.

Since the progress and the very existence of the labor movement depend upon united action, there is no more insidious danger that can threaten the movement than contention within and secession movements.

There are innumerable enemies of the organized labor movement and oppressors of wage-earners who seek to disrupt the labor movement and to get the wage-earners within their power. If we do not unite solidly against the foes without, the cause of human welfare and freedom will suffer.

What the toilers need to learn and to have grounded deep into their consciousness is the advice that Spartacus[3] gave to his fellow-slaves whom he was leading in an effort to secure some rights from a despotic Roman government. His words to them were "If you must fight, fight your masters."

The fight of the wage-earners of America against their employers to establish better conditions of life and work is so tremendous that they ought not to waste a moment of time or a bit of their energy or resources in fighting each other. Is there no lesson for the wage-earners in that oft repeated axiom "Divided we cannot Stand." This declaration applies to the labor movement as well as to every other kind of human activity. Friction within and secession movements defeat the purposes of the movement.

Undoubtedly it was because you did not understand the fundamental principles of the trade union movement that you were so severe in your condemnation. It was not "the heavy hand of Mr. Gompers" that shut off sources of aid from the striking garment workers of Chicago, but it was their own voluntary act in dissociating themselves from the labor movement as well as the necessity and the duty of those who are in the labor movement to defend its existence from menace and attack both from without and within. The labor movement is a struggle against industrial and social wrongs and injustice. It must maintain organization and discipline, although of a voluntary nature, if it is to secure its purposes and secure better and greater opportunities for an increasing number of wage-earners.

Yours very truly,   Saml Gompers.
President   American Federation of Labor.

TLS, Amalgamated Clothing Workers of America Papers, Labor-Management Documentation Center, NIC.

1. "From Ellen Gates Starr," Jan. 8, 1916, above.

2. See "From John Fitzpatrick," Oct. 22, 1914, n. 7, above.

3. Spartacus, a slave and gladiator, led an insurrection against the Romans between 73 and 71 B.C.E.

From W. D. Mahon

Amalgamated Association of Street and Electric
Railway Employes of America
Detroit, Mich. Jan. 31, 1916.

Dear Sir and Brother:

In your communication[1] calling my attention to the complaints of the Metal Trades Department against our Association, you requested me to inform you of the results of any conferences that might take place between the representatives of our Association and the representatives of the Metal Trades.

You are no doubt aware that the main complaint against our organization from the Metal Trades was based upon our agreement[2] with the Elevated Railway Companies of Chicago, the Metal Trades Department claiming that we had an agreement covering their membership. By arrangement this matter was taken up by President O'Connell of the Metal Trades Department, and myself on January 18th.[3] We had the parties from both our organization and that of the different organizations belonging to the Metal Trades, meet with us and listened to their complaints. Our officers showed that our agreements in no way covered or affected the members of these trades and that these trades were at liberty to take up their questions with the Elevated Railway Company and deal for their own members. In order that these agreements might be clearly understood, a conference was arranged with Mr. Budd,[4] the President of the Elevated Railway Company. On the day this conference was held, I was sick with the grippe, and had Brother McMorrow[5] of our General Executive Board, accompany President O'Connell to this conference. President Budd assured Mr. O'Connell and those present that our agreement did not cover the skilled mechanics who belonged to the Metal Trades, and he pointed out how he was dealing with those members. Now, the result of this conference clearly shows that the Amalgamated Association of Street and Electric Railway Employes of America, so far as the Elevated men were concerned, were not interfering with the members of these trades and that it was up to these members themselves to take up their questions and make such arrangements, or agreements, as they desired to cover their membership working for this company.

I don't know as to what report Brother O'Connell will make to you upon this matter, but I am giving you the facts, and I feel that in justice to our Association these facts should be reported to the American Federation of Labor and that its Executive Council should know the facts. There was a great deal of charges made before the Committee at the A.F. of L.[6] upon this subject, of which I knew was not true. I prevented them from coming on the floor because I would not oppose the resolution which was unfair to our Association. There is some friction yet at Boston,[7] but that is a matter that will straighten itself out, I feel, in the near future.

I have always assured you and the Executive Council that it was not the intention of this Association to infringe upon the rights of any other organization. We are in a peculiar situation. We have to battle hard to establish conditions for the membership that we represent, and in connection with the trainmen there is the barn men, the car washers and cleaners, track greasers, watchmen, latch tenders, and a great army of poor men who receive a ridiculously low wage, which reflects of course upon our conditions, and it has always been our policy to take these men into our Association and to demand and establish a wage for them, and the records of our Association will show that we have done a great amount of good for this class of men. Here and there one of them might be classed as a mechanic by stretching your imaginations some, but even if he were, he would remain in the condition that he was, were we not to protect him and establish wages for him. Take for instance the women that work in the Elevated stations of Chicago. We took them into our organization at a time when they worked 12 hours a day for from $1.15 to $1.25 a day. Now we have these women on a 10-hour work day, receiving considerably over $2.00 a day for their work,—and this is a sample of what we have done on the Elevated in Chicago for this class of labor, that had we not considered and taken them into our organization would have yet been in a demoralized condition, and I appeal to you and to the Executive Council of the American Federation of Labor, to consider these matters in the light that they should be considered and to give to us the credit and consideration that is due to us for the work that we have been doing. It is discouraging to go into Convention and be assailed by every little whipper-snapper that comes along, and charged with stealing their membership, when they never would have attempted to do anything for these men had we not taken up the fight and established the conditions for them, and I appeal to you in behalf of this organization and the men and women who compose it, to give them justice in the reports of the American Federation of Labor and show them up in their true character. They are not pirates, neither are they thieves. They are earnest trade union men and women working to improve the conditions of themselves and their fellow workers, and there should be some report put out in such a manner as would stop these charges and insinuations and resolutions that are detrimental and discouraging to an organization of this kind.

I know that you know the struggle that we have put forth to build this organization,—what it has cost us in the way of work and money and efforts, and I appeal to you at this time that you will consider this thoroughly by your Executive Council and say something that will place us in the true light,[8] and counteract the effect of the resolutions and attitude that some people are assuming towards our organization, for it is not only discouraging to our membership, but these things are at once picked up by our employers and used against us.

With best wishes, I remain,

Fraternally yours,   W D Mahon
International President.

TLS, AFL Microfilm Convention File, reel 27, frame 2271, *AFL Records.*

1. SG to W. D. Mahon, Dec. 24, 1915, and Jan. 5, 1916, reel 201, vol. 213, pp. 20–22, 590, SG Letterbooks, DLC.

2. Amalgamated Association of Street and Electric Railway Employes of America division 308 of Chicago negotiated an agreement with the Chicago Elevated Railways in October 1915 to settle a strike that had begun in June.

3. On Jan. 18, 1916, Mahon and AFL Metal Trades Department president James O'Connell met in Chicago to investigate complaints that the agreement of Street Railway Employes' division 308 included metal mechanics, who properly belonged under the jurisdiction of Chicago metal trades unions. Both the president of division 308 and the head of the Chicago Elevated Railways met with Mahon and O'Connell and demonstrated that metal mechanics were not covered by the contract.

4. Britton I. Budd was president and director of the Chicago Elevated Railways.

5. Edward McMorrow, a member of Street Railway Employes' division 241 of Chicago, served the international union as a member of the executive board (1905–35) and as vice-president (1935–45).

6. Resolution 55, introduced by O'Connell at the 1915 AFL convention, complained that the Street Railway Employes included members who came under the jurisdiction of various metal trades organizations. The resolution, endorsed by the committee on adjustment and adopted by the convention, instructed the union to turn these workers over to their proper unions.

7. On May 1, 1916, Street Railway Employes' division 589 of Boston signed a contract with the Boston Elevated Railway Co. that included metal workers. After Mahon, John Reardon, and a committee of division 589 met with O'Connell in Boston on May 24, the local agreed to revise the contract so it would not cover machinists, blacksmiths, and other metal mechanics.

8. The AFL Executive Council considered the matter at its February 1916 meeting but decided that, as it was in the hands of the Metal Trades Department, no action was necessary. The Council reported to the 1916 AFL convention that the Street Railway Employes had consented to drop machinists, blacksmiths, and other metal workers from their agreements, thus resolving the dispute.

From Ellen Gates Starr

Chicago, Ill., Feb. 12th [4],[1] 1916.

Dear Sir:—

Thank you very much for your long letter,[2] stating your position. I realize that your time is occupied and I do not mean to trespass upon it far; but I cannot leave you with the impression that I think as I do and acted as I did (and should again) in regard to the strike of the Amalgamated Clothing Workers of America because I had no knowledge of the situation or had not thought about it at all, or was prompted by emotional sympathy alone. I simply differ from you in the assumption that one "secession" must be just like another. I do not accept your parallel example in the secession of the southern States from the Union, which was a secession of a minority to perpetuate a wrong; whereas, the secession of the Amalgamated Clothing Workers from the United Garment Workers was the secession of a majority and to do away with a wrong. I do not know why one should not refer as well to the example of the secession of the colonies or, if you please, of the American Federation of Labor from the Knights of Labor.

I respectfully offer these substitute examples for your consideration. The "power to discriminate between things which are different" (somebody has said that it is ["]next to the Grace of God") seems to me to be as much needed in a great labor leader as in other great leaders of men. Exactly cut out patterns and phrases will not cover all human situations, and from time to time a great human crisis will develop beyond the bounds of formula. The power to discern and utilize greatness in others,—is it not a very important factor in greatness?

Begging your indulgence for this second trespass upon your time,

Yours for the fuller rights of Organized Labor,

Ellen Gates Starr

P.S. Somebody to whom I have read this correspondence has suggested, the usefulness of publishing it. I assume that you would not object as it is not private in its nature.

TLcS, Amalgamated Clothing Workers of America Papers, Labor-Management Documentation Center, NIC. Handwritten notation: "Published in New Republic Mar 4, 1916—."

1. The correct date is supplied from the copy of the letter printed in the June 1916 *American Federationist* (23: 472).

2. "To Ellen Gates Starr," Jan. 28, 1916, above.

To Ellen Gates Starr

Washington, D.C., Feb. 10, 1916.

Miss Ellen Gates Starr,
Hull-House, 800 South Halstead Street, Chicago, Illinois
Dear Madam:

Your letter of February 4th[1] gives me additional grounds for believing that personal experience with the lives and problems of the workers and with the trade union movement is necessary for leadership in the movement and for determining its policies.

There are many who have information about the movement, who perhaps have observed it closely and have had some relations with the movement or with the members of the movement. Such individuals may be very helpful to the workers in attaining their purposes, but they are not competent to direct the workers' movement or to be final judges of the value of labor policies or to be final judges of the correctness or incorrectness of what the workers may determine in regard to their own problems.

The labor movement is founded upon principles of democracy. It is a movement of the workers, for the workers and by the workers. The workers welcome counsel and cooperation, but they refuse all efforts at domination in whatever guise they may come.

Just as you deem yourself mistress of your own soul and life so the workers know that they are also the masters of their own lives and their own organizations. The praise or the blame of outsiders matters but little. The workers must judge their own course in the light of the knowledge acquired by the experiences of life and work, and they cannot honestly accept the ideals and standards of others when these are not in accord with their own experiences.

The trade unions are doing a very important work for our country. They are the schools that are training men and women for citizenship as well as enabling them to participate in the commerce and industry of our country as free citizens.

There exists in the members of trade unions an appreciation of their rights and insistence upon rights and liberties, together with the knowledge and ability to make their insistence upon rights and liberties effective.

The trade unions develop a virile manhood and womanhood that are able to assert itself against wrongs and injustice. At the same time they develop a sense of discipline and an appreciation of the necessity for united action.

One who has not been in the labor movement, to whom the trade union movement is not a living human force operating directly in their lives for betterment, cannot grasp completely the conviction and understanding that sinks so deeply into the minds of the organized workers—that their well being, that their future opportunities depend entirely upon the organized labor movement, upon the solidarity and unity with which that functions. The workers united means better living, better opportunities. The workers divided means oppression, deterioration of present standards, loss of opportunities and freedom. Even though the labor movement may make mistakes, the workers have more to gain by remaining within the organization and somehow working out their differences together than when any part of the organization withdraws and attempts to deal with labor problems with diminished strength.

The rules of all labor organizations insure democracy in government. If the members of the organizations do not see to it that their interests and rights are maintained, that is their fault. They are jeopardizing their own interests and the interests of their fellow-workers if they refuse to stay within the organization, battle for the right, with the hope that the right and wise methods will finally prevail. When a majority is finally in favor of any measure or policy and is determined to secure their demands, they will control the situation, but until there is a majority for any demand, the advocates of that demand must submit to the will of the existing majority. This is a fundamental principle of democratic government.

You assert that the seceding members of the United Garment Workers constituted a majority, but you are merely asserting your opinion, which is in opposition to the statement made by authorized officials who are in possession of facts and figures. If the seceders of the United Garment Workers had been in the majority, they had the same rights to representation under the rules of the organization as the non-seceders. They could have legally and readily controlled the action of the Nashville Convention, and could have remedied any wrong which you assert to be the cause of their secession.

From your letter, I conclude that you are not entirely familiar with the reasons connected with the secession of the delegates who formed the dual organization of Garment Workers. Let me suggest that you talk over the conditions that resulted in the secession movement with President Thomas A. Rickert, whose address is 175 West Washington Street, Chicago, Illinois.

Then as to the exceptions you take to the parallel cases of secession which I cited in my letter to you. You object to my comparing the secession of the Garment Workers to the secession of the Southern States from the Union because "that was the secession of a minority to perpetuate a wrong."

Of course, you must recognize the fact that all do not agree with you in your interpretation of the cause of the secession of the Southern States. There were many high-minded, patriotic Southern men who went with the South because they were convinced that the cause of the South was right. They were convinced that under the constitution states rights were paramount to the Federal Government. These people were firmly convinced in their own minds of the justice of their cause, stood for the older ideals and the older interpretation of the Federal constitution and Federal powers. They had not kept in touch with the new concept of national government that had been developing. However, the fact remains that the withdrawal of the Southern States was an act of secession whatever anyone's opinion may be of the justice or injustice of the purpose of the secession, and if that secession movement had been successful, the effect upon the union and upon our American nation would have been equally harmful, whether the purpose of the secession had been right or wrong. What I had in mind in using the comparison was to show the nature of secession.

After all, secession is not the act of brave men who are willing to fight for their concepts of right or wrong, but it is the act of those who think they are taking an easier way and sometimes it is inspired by those who are misguided or who do not have at heart the best interests of those affected.

You say you prefer to use as examples of secession the secession of the Colonies or the Thirteen Original States from Great Britain or the American Federation of Labor from the Knights of Labor. Now, as a matter of fact, neither of these illustrations that you suggest constitute real acts of secession. The Thirteen Colonies rebelled against Great Britain but they did not secede. Secession implies withdrawal from an organization or union within which all are members on an equality, with equal enjoyment of all rights and privileges. The Colonies were not constituent members of Great Britain. They were subjects without a voice in determining the laws that governed them or a voice in fixing taxation. Their act of uprising must be differentiated from an act of secession.

Then as to the second illustration you propose. In that case also I think we must discriminate between the founding and organization of the American Federation of Labor and a secession movement from the Knights of Labor.

There would be point in your second illustration, that is, "secession of the A.F. of L. from the Knights of Labor" if it were founded upon fact. The American Federation of Labor, or under its former title, the Federation of Organized Trades and Labor Unions of the United States and Canada, was never part of the Knights of Labor.

The trade unions, which afterwards organized the Federation, had a separate and independent existence from the Knights of Labor. Many of them were organized decades before the organization of the Knights of Labor. The international trade unions maintained autonomy in their trades and had no connection whatever with the Knights of Labor. Many individual wage-earners who were members of trade unions were also members of lodges which were part of the Knights of Labor, but there was no connection between the trade union organizations as such and the Knights of Labor. Hence, of course, the organization of the American Federation of Labor could not be regarded in any sense as secession from the Knights of Labor. In fact, the movement for the better organization and for the federation of the international trade union organizations was given impetus by the policy pursued by the Knights of Labor, which was destructive to the very existence of trade unions, but it was a destructive policy directed against outside organizations which had no connection with the Knights of Labor.

I quite agree with you that my letter was "lengthy," but I think you will realize the fact that it is possible for one to make charges and insinuations and unfair criticism, condensed into one sentence, when it may be necessary for defense or explanation to occupy a volume.

After I wrote my previous letter to you, it occurred to me that the New Republic, which published the article you quoted and which you so heartily endorsed, would be willing to publish my reply to you, which was in part a reply to the article published in their journal. I, therefore, wrote to the editor of the magazine and asked him to publish my letter. I received a reply that my letter would be published as soon as possible. This, I judge from your letter, is in accord with your desire, and let me suggest that it would not be fair to the New Republic to give the correspondence to any other publication before the New Republic has had the opportunity of publishing it, and then the entire subject matter should be published, including your letter of the fourth, and this one.

Yours for the full rights and the self-government of the workers,

Very truly yours,   Saml Gompers.
President   American Federation of Labor.

TLS, Amalgamated Clothing Workers of America Papers, Labor-Management Documentation Center, NIC. Handwritten notation: "not published."

1. "From Ellen Gates Starr," Feb. 12 [4], 1916, above.

To James Duncan

Feb. 19, 1916.

Mr. James Duncan,
Vice-President, American Federation of Labor,
Hancock Bldg., Quincy, Mass.
Dear Sir and Brother:

I am prompted to write you by a most important event. Just now I was called up over the phone and Honorable William B. Wilson, Secretary of the Department of Labor, asked me when the Executive Council would be in session. Upon my informing him that the session will begin on Monday, February 21, and last during the entire week, he expressed a desire to have the Executive Council meet with all the members of the President's Cabinet and that the most convenient time would be during the day at a luncheon upon any day during the week of the Executive Council's session.[1]

I think it is not unfair to assume that Secretary Wilson has discussed this matter with the other members of the Cabinet and the President before inviting and making the arrangements for the members of the Executive Council and the members of the Cabinet to meet jointly. As a matter of fact, my assumption is not entirely imaginary or deduction.

Now in my opinion it is of the utmost importance to our movement that you should be present at that session. Of course you know how I feel, that your presence is important at our Executive Council meeting during the coming week, but this event is of such great importance for what it may mean in the future, or I may say paramount importance, so if you can come to our meeting by straining the situation with which you have to deal, please come, but if you cannot do that, I urge upon you the absolute necessity of your presence so that we can accept the luncheon invitation and you be present at this first joint meeting of the members of the Executive Council and the Cabinet of the President of the United States.

Secretary Wilson is to consult me Monday or Tuesday as to the best time for the luncheon and meeting, and I would like to have a telegram[2] from you stating that you will be present, or better still, if you can only come on immediately upon receipt of this letter. The importance of the occasion warrants the expenditure of time, effort and cost.

Sincerely and fraternally yours,   Saml Gompers.
President,   American Federation of Labor.

TLpS, reel 203, vol. 215, pp. 609–10, SG Letterbooks, DLC.

1. The AFL Executive Council met with Secretary of Labor William B. Wilson and other members of the cabinet on Feb. 23, 1916.

2. James Duncan wrote SG that he would be unable to attend the meeting (Feb. 21, 1916, Executive Council Records, Minutes, reel 5, frame 1144, *AFL Records*).

To Samuel Hughes

Feb. 21, 1916.

Mr. S. T. Hughes,
The Newspaper Enterprise Association,
1279 West Third St., Cleveland, Ohio.
Dear Sir:

Your local representative[1] of The Newspaper Enterprise Association left with me copy of a report upon "Profit Sharing," which was made for your Association.

After reading over the manuscript and considering the viewpoints presented, in accord with your request, I make the following suggestions in regard to the report:

The recent recrudescence of profit sharing as an employing-class labor-reform is not without a sinister significance. The question is being brought forward at employers' meetings, in the daily newspapers and the professional periodical press. Organized labor, with its accumulations of experience, is prompted in the presence of this movement to ask questions.

Would the topic of profit sharing be a live one were the market for labor over-stocked as it was but two short years ago?

What proportion of the establishments employing union labor are profit sharers or contemplate profit sharing?

To what extent can the movement be simply anti-unionist or increasingly exploitative, or otherwise a confession of [a] conscious weakness in the presence of today's uprising of labor?

In looking over notes and clippings concerning the moves and opinions of the new profit sharers, or proposed profit sharers, the expressions of altruism and philanthropy seem to be "lugged" into the discussion, while the language of calculating business comes to the front frequently and forcibly. The profit sharers are considering "the various methods by which employers may bind their employees closer to them"; they are seeking in an annual dividend to labor "a sound business move"; they wish "the employee to be governed by the same motives that animate the employer"; they invariably "seek efficiency." This language has a purely business-like sound. But wherein it indicates an increased happiness for the masses of labor is not, on first presentation, clear.

Not only on behalf of organized labor but on the part of the general public, one test of its social efficacy may at the outset be offered to the advocates of profit sharing. It is this: Will the employing profit sharer take as a basis the union scale of wages and hours in his occupation and the working conditions deemed fair by law and union custom, and proceeding from that level offer in addition any of the forms of profits which have been recommended by the professed upholders of profit sharing? How many names this question would eliminate from the list of its advocates is an estimate which any observer of the movement may make for himself.

Union wages and conditions form convincing evidence to the masses of wage-workers that the employer is fair and square. He stands before the community simply as a man, not bidding for the doubtful commendatory appellation of philanthropist or apostle of a new society. His actions are above suspicion. He is also a man of business sense; he has all the wage-workers in his line to choose from as employees. His "labor troubles" are, if not at an end, at least plainly confined to a well known area.

The nomenclature of profit sharing is singularly rich in equivocal terms. "Loyalty." Is the employee to be wholly loyal to his employer and not first of all loyal to himself? How loyal is an employer to his furnishers of raw material? He is loyal to them only so long as they sell him what he wants at the lowest market rate. "Efficiency." Never to be missed in any letter or discourse on profit sharing, this term points to push, grind, and hurry to the exhaustion of the employee, despite its admitted legitimacy up to the point of average physical abilities. "Profits." Is the withholding of five or ten per cent from an employee's wages during the year and returning it to him at an appointed annual date a sharing of profits or a mere restitution of withheld earnings?

An exhaustive analysis of profit sharing can, of course, be made only after a complete collection of testimony from the diverse groups of profit sharers. The movement is not so simple as its indefinite collective name—profit sharing. Its possibilities run from a general grabbing and grasping to an occasional generous giving.

Looking at the subject practically, the trade unionist might suggest that the employer wishing to demonstrate beyond cavil his desire to share his profits with his wage-workers, might initiate his proceedings by conference with union representatives to clarify his mind as to his own intentions and the benefits he would confer on his fellow-workers. In doing so, he would set himself apart from those employers who are using profit sharing as a cloak for hypocrisy and false pretense.

Very truly yours,   Saml Gompers.
President   American Federation of Labor.

TLpS, reel 203, vol. 215, pp. 672–75, SG Letterbooks, DLC.

1. Frederick M. Kerby, who met with SG on Feb. 15, 1916.

To Claude Travis[1]

Feb. 28, 1916.

Mr. C. C. Travis,
Secretary, Shreveport State Federation of Labor,[2]
P.O. Box 291, Shreveport, La.
Dear Sir and Brother:

The editorial[3] you sent me from the Shreveport Journal, which deals with the policy of John D. Rockefeller toward the Colorado miners, seems to be a part of a general campaign that is being carried on to explain away the responsibility, for the industrial warfare and injustice, that has been placed upon Mr. Rockefeller as a result of the publicity given to all the facts in the case.

The Rockefellers have employed publicity agent, Ivy Lee,[4] and are systematically attempting to refute all statements and charges that are brought against them. As a part of this program, Mr. Rockefeller published in the January Atlantic Monthly[5] an explanation of the organizations of miners that he recently instituted for his Colorado miners.

The insidious policy which Ivy Lee terms publicity is described in my editorial in the September, 1915, *American Federationist* entitled "An American Bernhardi."

I have written numerous editorials and articles dealing with the conditions confronting the miners of Colorado. By consulting these articles I think you will gain a general idea of the situation and the forces that operated against the miners in their fight for justice there:[6]

Rockefeller, Industrial Dictator by Divine Right, Editorial, June, 1914, page 474.

Organizing Despite the Grim Spectre. Editorial, June, 1914, page 478.

Executive Council on Colorado Outrages, June, 1914, page 489.

Colorado—A Call to Duty, July, 1914, page 559.

A Protest Against Tyranny, August, 1914, page 636.

Again Imperator Rockefeller, November, 1914, page 987.

Colorado Miners Strike Commission, January, 1915, page 46.

Rockefeller Responsible, April, 1915, page 280.

Lawson A Convict—Rockefeller a Saint, June, 1915, page 413.

The Crime Against Lawson, August, 1915, page 603.

I am glad that you have determined to make a reply to the article in the Shreveport Journal, for if we allow the Rockefellers to beguile the people into believing whatever story they publish by means of various agents of publicity, there will be less and less opportunity to get the facts in regard to the position of workers understood and believed by the citizens of the country.

If there should be any further assistance you need in preparing your reply to the editorial, I shall be glad to help you in any way possible.

Very truly yours,   Saml Gompers.

President   American Federation of Labor.

TLpS, reel 204, vol. 216, pp. 199–200, SG Letterbooks, DLC.

1. Claude (variously Claud) C. Travis (b. 1891?), a member of International Typographical Union 155 of Shreveport, La., served as secretary-treasurer (1915–16) and vice-president (1916–17) of the Louisiana State Federation of Labor (FOL).

2. Actually the Louisiana State FOL, which was organized in 1912 and chartered that year by the AFL.

3. The editorial "Capital and Labor" was published in the *Shreveport Journal* on Feb. 23, 1916, in reference to a pamphlet by John D. Rockefeller, Jr., on the 1913–14 miners' strike in Colorado. The editorial maintained that the pamphlet presented capital's side of the conflict "ably, forcefully and convincingly" and blamed the violence of the strike on "incendiarists" and "conscienceless agitators who . . . imbue peaceful workers with the idea that they are being wronged."

4. Ivy Ledbetter Lee (1877–1934), a journalist and pioneer in the field of public relations, was employed by Rockefeller between 1914 and 1916 to counter the negative publicity generated by the 1913–14 Colorado miners' strike. In April 1916 he opened his own public relations firm, Lee, Harris, and Lee (from 1919, Ivy Lee and Associates).

5. Rockefeller, "Labor and Capital—Partners," *Atlantic Monthly,* Jan. 1916, pp. 12–21.

6. These articles and editorials were published in the *American Federationist.*

To Thomas Fitzgerald

March 1, 1916.

Mr. Thomas D. Fitzgerald,

Chairman, Legislative Committee, New York State Federation of Labor,

210 Jay St., or 223 Arkay Bldg., Albany, N.Y.

Dear Sir and Brother:

While compensation legislation is still in the experimental stage, it seems to me that the wage-earners would be inviting grave dangers should they endorse the enactment of the system of insurance provided for under the proposed Health Insurance Act.[1]

As you probably know, the question of social insurance has been under consideration by the Executive Council of the American Federation of Labor for several years. Our report to the Philadelphia Convention contained a report[2] upon our investigations, which were not as thorough and as conclusive as we deemed necessary before deciding upon so important a policy, therefore, we recommended to that convention that the subject be given additional consideration before final action should be taken. At our recent meeting, held during the week of February 21, social insurance was given further consideration.

The system proposed by the bill introduced in the New York State Legislature called attention to what would be the inevitable consequences of adopting such legislation. It would build up a bureaucracy that would have some degree of control or authority over all of the workers of the state. It is in the nature of government that when even a slight degree of power is delegated, the tendency is to increase that power and authority so that the purposes of the law in question may be achieved more completely.

That the state should provide sickness insurance for workers is fundamentally based upon the theory that these workers are not able to look after their own interests and the state must interpose its authority and wisdom and assume the relation of parent or guardian. There is something in the very suggestion of this relationship and this policy that is repugnant to a free born citizen. It seems to be at variance with our concepts of voluntary institutions and of freedom for individuals.

There must necessarily be a weakening of independence of spirit and virility when compulsory insurance is provided for so large a number of citizens of the state. Dangers to wage-earners might readily arise under the machinery for the administration of this social insurance that would establish compulsory physical examinations. The purpose of such examinations has been perverted in many places and made to result to the detriment of workers. The discretionary power lodged in the administrative board could readily be used in efforts to coerce organizations of wage-earners for the administrative body has the power to approve societies and also to withdraw approval at any time.

The enactment of this proposed bill would be another step in the tendency to regulate everything by law and commissions. Several of our statesmen have been calling attention to the dangers lurking in this government by commission. It would inevitably build up a bureaucratic system which would be under the control and perhaps domination of agents not directly responsible to the people. This becomes especially serious when it has to do with such intimate matters as health. When once a political agent is authorized to take care of the health of citizens, there is no limit to the scope of his activities or his right to interfere in all of the relations of life. Even homes would not be sacred from his intrusions.

It is inevitable that if employers are to have financial interests at stake in the sickness or disease or death that may come upon their employes, their interests will be soon manifested in preventive as well as curative measures. Sickness prevention, as you know, is associated very intimately with the personal life of the individual. Is it wise to open up opportunities for government agents to interfere lawfully with the privacy of the lives of wage-earners? Would such authority be tolerated by employers, by professional men or those directing our financial, industrial and commercial institutions? Is it not a better way to undertake the problem of assuring to workers health by providing them with the information and the education that will enable them to take intelligent care of themselves and assuring to them such conditions of work and standards of wages as will enable them to give their information reality in directing and managing their own lives? Should the individual worker not be able to accomplish all desirable results, is it not better for him to augment his own efforts by voluntary associated effort, cooperating with his friends and fellow-workers?

Trade organizations are not unmindful of the health problem, in fact, they have done more to secure conditions of sanitation in places of work and to enable workers to have decent healthful homes than any other agency. As the information of the workers increases, they give more thought to problems of health and sanitation.

In connection with this, you will find of particular interest the work being done by the Garment Workers of New York City.[3] Through the efforts of their organizations, the Garment industry of New York City has been organized and standards of sanitation and health established and maintained. Already they are beginning upon the problem of personal health and personal hygiene. If you will get some of the reports and literature of the Sanitary Board of the Garment Workers, you will see the possibilities of efforts through economic organizations. In many international unions there is established the systems of social insurance in cases of illness, unemployment, and several other features. Even in international unions where these benefits have not been instituted, nearly every local union has established it, but quite apart from these benefits paid, or rather in addition to them, the trade union movement has secured a reduction in the hours of daily labor and better standards of wages and conditions of employment which have improved the physical and mental health of the workers, so much so that nearly every trade union can record the increased length of life of its membership, and one of them, that of my own craft, the Cigarmakers International Union, has increased the average length of life of the membership in that organization nearly fifteen years in the past two decades.[4] What is true of this organization is true more or less of every other organization of labor in America, that is, real social insurance and its tangible benefits, and will continue to progress and improve without surrendering authority and opportunity to government and governmental agencies to exercise tyranny and unfreedom.

I am suggesting these thoughts to you for your consideration in connection with the Health Insurance Act, and I wish to emphasize the far reaching effects that such a law will have.

With best wishes, and hoping to hear from you whenever convenient, I am,

Fraternally yours, Saml Gompers
President, American Federation of Labor.

TLpS, reel 204, vol. 216, pp. 254–57, SG Letterbooks, DLC.

1. On Jan. 24, 1916, New York state senator Ogden Mills introduced a bill providing health insurance to all manual laborers in the state and any other workers earning less than $100 a month. The legislation proposed coverage of medical expenses for up to twenty-six weeks and payments to help workers counter the loss of wages due to illness, with employers and employees each paying 40 percent of the cost and the state picking up the rest. The bill was not reported out of committee.

2. "Social Insurance," AFL, *Proceedings*, 1914, pp. 66–68.

3. The Protocol of Peace that ended the 1910 New York City cloakmakers' strike established a joint board of sanitary control with the authority to set standards of sanitation that both manufacturers and unions were obliged to maintain. After surveying the cloak and suit trade, the joint board identified the significant problems, formulated a code of sanitary standards, and then issued certificates to employers who complied, eventually grading shops according to sanitary conditions. In 1913 the joint board extended its jurisdiction to dress and waist shops and added a fire drill division.

4. These statistics are from the report of George Perkins, president of the Cigar Makers' International Union of America, to the union's 1912 convention.

To Nathan Alpert[1]

March 9, 1916.

Dr. N. Alpert,
The Warheit Bureau,
Alabama Apartment, Washington, D.C.
Dear Sir:

In accord with the understanding reached in our interview, I have your letter relative to the movement[2] to provide a home in Palestine for the Jews. You correctly state in your letter that the American Federation of Labor favors the enactment of the Burnett Immigration Bill[3] containing the literacy test. But you are in error in arriving at the deduction which you have apparently made in asserting that the doors of the nations of the whole world will be closed to the persecuted Jews of Russia and Poland. Section 3 of the Burnett Bill contains the following clause:

"That the following classes of persons shall be exempt from the operation of the illiteracy test, to wit: All aliens who shall prove [to] the satisfaction of the proper immigration officer or to the Secretary of Labor that they are seeking admission to the United States to avoid religious persecution in the country of their last permanent residence, whether such persecution be evidenced by overt acts or by laws or governmental regulations that discriminate against the alien or the race to which he belongs because of his religious faith."

The text of the proposed bill proves conclusively that it will not constitute a barrier to the admission of Russian or Polish Jews who are seeking a refuge from persecution because of their religion. The enactment of the Burnett Bill therefore, would not create any new reason for special efforts to protect the Jews or to set aside a special country for their home. I am entirely in accord and in sympathy with all efforts to secure for the Jews, or any other nation or group of people, equal rights and equal privileges with all of the citizens of any land of which they may be residents or citizens. The Jewish race is now widely distributed throughout all the countries of the world. The welfare of the Jews in any one country is inseparably identified with the general welfare of the rest of that nation. The idea that the Jewish race constitutes a peculiar people, set aside from all the other nations of the earth, belongs to the past. The welfare of the Jews of today depends upon their identifying themselves with the people among whom they live and upon the breaking down of the barriers that have kept them isolated and different.

At the San Francisco convention of the A.F. of L., the following resolution[4] was adopted:

Whereas, In some of the countries of Europe the Jewish people are still deprived of elementary political and civic rights; and

Whereas, Every form of religious oppression and discrimination is contrary to the spirit of the American people; therefore, be it

Resolved, That the American Federation of Labor requests the Government of the United States to urge upon the governments of the nations of other countries to cease discriminations wherever it exists and now practiced against the Jewish people; and be it further

Resolved, That the same appeal be made by the American Federation of Labor to the organized workers of all nations.[5]

This resolution is practically identical with a resolution adopted by the British Trade Union Congress at its last session in Bristol.[6] The members of the organized labor movement resent as injustice, all practices and customs that deny the Jews the rights and privileges that are granted to other citizens of the countries in which they reside. But they do not favor any plan or proposition to provide an exclusive territory or system of protection for the Jews, either in this country or elsewhere. Should the Jews adopt and work out such a plan for themselves we can have no objection, but it would not receive our sanction.

You ask whether or not I believe that the Jews should call a congress to attend the peace conferences of the warring nations when they shall be held in order that they may demand for the Jews political and religious rights in all civilized countries of the world, and also the right to emigrate freely to Palestine. I see no reason at all why the Jews or any other oppressed people, or any group of people having common interests, should not be represented and present their demands for the consideration of the world's peace congress which will undoubtedly be held at the close of the war. But I do not believe that the Jews or any other group of persons should demand special privileges or special concessions that would not be accorded to other citizens placed in the same situation in which the Jews find themselves. In other words, I think that Jewish demands will find favor only when they are confined to demands for the same rights and privileges that are accorded to other citizens of the country in which they reside and that no discrimination shall be made against their entrance into any country as immigrants. I do not see why any fair-minded person should oppose a demand of the Jews that they be entitled to admission into Palestine under the same regulations as affect immigrants of all other races. I am heartily in sympathy with any movement for equality and justice for the Jews and will do my utmost to further such an effort, but I am opposed to any policy or any effort to perpetuate the isolation of the race.

Fraternally yours,   Saml Gompers.

President   American Federation of Labor.

TLpS, reel 204, vol. 216, pp. 677–80, SG Letterbooks, DLC.

1. Nathan Alpert was a correspondent for the *Warheit* (Truth), an independent socialist paper published in New York City in Yiddish and English.

2. Under the leadership of Theodor Herzl, the first Zionist congress met in Basel, Switzerland, in 1897 with the aim of assuring for the Jewish people a publicly recognized and legally secured homeland in Palestine. In March 1915 American Zionists, among others, founded the Jewish Congress Organization Committee (JCOC) in hopes of establishing a democratically elected body in the United States to express the aspirations of the American Jewish community for such a homeland and to demand protection for the minority rights of the Jewish people in eastern Europe. The JCOC held its first conference in Philadelphia, Mar. 26–27, 1916. Alpert wrote SG and also met with him in an unsuccessful attempt to secure his endorsement of this meeting.

3. H.R. 10,384 (64th Cong., 1st sess.), an immigration bill that included a literacy test, was introduced by Democratic congressman John Burnett of Alabama on Jan. 29, 1916. It was passed over President Woodrow Wilson's veto to become law on Feb. 5, 1917 (U.S. *Statutes at Large*, 39: 874–98).

4. Resolution 113, adopted by the 1915 AFL convention on Nov. 22, 1916.

5. The AFL Executive Council adopted a resolution to this effect at its February 1916 meeting. It was printed in the *AFL Weekly News Letter* on Mar. 4, 1916.

6. The 1915 meeting of the TUC was held in Bristol, Sept. 6–11. The text of the resolution can be found on p. 306 of the convention's proceedings (*Report of Proceedings at the Forty-Seventh Annual Trades Union Congress . . .* [London, 1915]).

To Thomas Rickert

Washington, D.C., March 16, 1916.

Mr. Thos. Rickert,
Morrison Hotel, Chicago, Ill.

Can you direct your Organizer Adamsky[1] go at once to Buffalo for a few days and report to Stuart Hayward,[2] Seven Hundred eighty eight Seventh Street, Buffalo, New York. There are several thousand Polish workmen at Buffalo ready to be organized and a good agreement will no doubt result.[3] I.W.W. agents are on the ground and creating confusion. We shall be glad to pay Adamsky's expenses and salary. Your kindness will be greatly helpful and be appreciated. Wire answer.

Samuel Gompers.

TWpSr, reel 204, vol. 216, p. 904, SG Letterbooks, DLC.

1. Albert Adamski, a Buffalo tailor, served as an organizer for the United Garment Workers of America from 1916 to 1921.

2. Stuart (variously Stewart) A. Hayward, a member of Brotherhood of Painters, Decorators, and Paperhangers of America 161 of Buffalo, was president of the Buffalo Central Labor Council (CLC; 1915–17).

3. Some fifteen hundred laborers struck the Buffalo Copper and Brass Rolling Mill on Mar. 14, 1916, calling for an eight-hour day and a wage increase. Company management blamed IWW organizers for the trouble, and the Buffalo CLC sought the AFL's help in organizing the strikers. By Mar. 16 Buffalo Copper and Brass had agreed to the wage increase, and most of the strikers had returned to work.

To Carl Laurrell[1]

March 18, 1916.

Mr. Carl Ferdinand Malcolm Laurrell,
298 St. Nicholas Ave., Ridgewood, Brooklyn, N.Y.

Dear Sir and Brother:

A few days ago I went to Albany, New York, to appear before a committee of the state legislature in behalf of personal freedom and against proposed legislation to regulate personal habits in private life.[2]

There is also under consideration by the New York State legislature, as well as several other state legislatures, what is called the "Health Insurance Act." The medical provisions of this legislation constitute a serious menace to personal liberty and open the way for invasions of the privacy and sanctity of home life.

In thinking over these tendencies, there came back to me very vividly the old days in the shop and the many talks we had together, the debates, during which you made such unanswerable arguments for liberty and against efforts to regulate and reform by law. The advice you gave me, to test everything by the union card and your epigrammatic statement of the principle, have stayed by me all these years and have been a never failing guide.

I thought perhaps you might be interested in reading some of the editorials and articles that I have written recently dealing with fundamental principles. I am sending you a copy of the March, 1916, issue of the *American Federationist,* which contains two editorials I wish you would read, namely, "Regulation by Law! Law!! Law!!!" and "Intellectuals, Take Note."[3] In the March, 1915, issue of the *American Federationist,* copy of which I am also sending you, there is an article[4] dealing with the philosophy of the eight-hour workday.

As you, of course, are aware, there has been a persistent effort during the past two years to secure a declaration from the American Federation of Labor in favor of regulating hours of work in private industry by law. It has been a hard fight to make the wage-earners understand their own interests. There are so few who have a thorough comprehension of human freedom and the value and opportunities of freedom, that they are willing to subordinate everything to that one ideal. But you know me, and know that I am fighting for my own freedom, and I am sure that that cause will ultimately prevail.

It has been a long time since I have seen and talked with you. Couldn't you find time to come over to Washington or meet me in New York sometime when I am there? Write me about it. It would be so good to have one of the old time talks—just friends and comrades together—heart friends and mind friends.

With best wishes to you and yours, and hoping to hear from you soon, I am,

Fraternally yours,   Saml Gompers.
President   American Federation of Labor.

Please send me your address. Am delaying sending the *American Federationist* until I have your address.

Sam.

T and ALpS, reel 205, vol. 217, pp. 78–79, SG Letterbooks, DLC.

1. Carl Ferdinand LAURRELL was SG's mentor during the 1870s.

2. SG left Washington, D.C., on Mar. 14, 1916, for New York City, where he met with labor representatives before proceeding to Albany later that evening. On Mar. 15, at the request of the New York State Federation of Labor, he addressed the judiciary committee of the legislature in opposition to assembly bill 143, the Wilson-Fullagar bill, which prohibited the manufacture or sale of intoxicating liquors in New York State. SG returned to AFL headquarters on Mar. 16. The Wilson-Fullagar bill did not become law.

3. *American Federationist* 23 (Mar. 1916): 191–94, 198–99. The second editorial was entitled "'Intellectuals,' Please Note."

4. "The Shorter Workday—Its Philosophy," *American Federationist* 22 (Mar. 1915): 165–70.

To John Flett[1]

April 4th, 1916.

Mr. John A. Flett,
Organizer, American Federation of Labor,
135 Sherman Avenue South, Hamilton, Canada.
Dear Sir and Brother:

Your letters of recent date and enclosures have been received and read with great interest. I sincerely appreciate the valuable information that you have furnished me.

What you write me of the present proposals of the Government to place the trades manufacturing munitions and war supplies under the Industrial Disputes Act as a war measure, confirms the suspicion that made me very apprehensive when I first wrote you[2] about this matter. It is a well-known tendency of government to constantly extend its jurisdiction and its field of activity; it takes advantage of emergencies and crises to extend its authority to exercise arbitrary control, but it is never willing to give up those extensions and invasions of freedom when the emergency or danger has passed. The time to oppose aggression by the government, and to oppose policies and institutions that deprive the workers of freedom is when the measures are under consideration. It is easier to prevent the enactment of a law than to secure its amendment or its repeal, therefore, I feel very intensely that the workers of Canada ought to be aroused to their danger, and to be made to appreciate its fullest extent. Evidently they are awakened, judging from the accounts of a meeting at which they called their representative to account for his failure to protect their interests and to give them the necessary information and hearing.[3]

As the whole matter is of such great importance, I shall appreciate your keeping me in touch with further development, and supplying me with any information you think will be helpful.[4]

With best wishes, I am,

Fraternally yours.   Saml Gompers
President,   American Federation of Labor.

TLpS, reel 205, vol. 217, pp. 905–6, SG Letterbooks, DLC.

1. John Alexander FLETT served as an AFL salaried organizer in Canada (1900–1925).

2. SG to Flett, Oct. 5, 1915, reel 199, vol. 211, pp. 61–63, SG Letterbooks, DLC.

3. In January 1916 Thomas Crothers, the Canadian minister of labor, indicated to a delegation from the Trades and Labor Congress of Canada—including its president, James Watters, and its secretary, Patrick Draper—that the Industrial Disputes Investigation Act would be extended to cover workers in munitions and other war-related industries. When this extension was formally announced on Mar. 23, Watters and Draper received angry letters from several affiliated bodies, including the Hamilton Trades and Labor Council and the Toronto District Labor Council, complaining that they had not exercised proper vigilance regarding labor legislation.

4. For additional letters on this subject, see Flett to SG, Aug. 25, Sept. 30, Oct. 3, and Oct. 8, 1916 (Files of the Office of the President, General Correspondence, reel 81, frames 318–19, 450, 456–57, 482–83, *AFL Records*).

To George Berry

Washington, D.C., April 21. 1916.

Confidential
To Geo L. Berry Esq.
Rogersville Tenn.
Dear Friend:—

There is a matter about which I feel that I must write you, the circumstances demand it.

You know that the President has nominated Hon. Louis D. Brandies for Associate Justice of the U.S. Supreme Court.[1] The nomination has shocked the nerves of "the interests"—the grafters of all sorts. They realize that with Mr. Brandies as a member of that court his whole life work will make for the peoples rights and interests, and without doing violence to just rights and interests of any man, group or corporation. But despite this the latter aim to encompass the defeat of his nomination.

From information coming to me, it appears that Senator Shields of Tenn. holds the key to the situation; that is that the Com. will or will not favorably report Mr. Brandies' confirmation to the Senate.

Of course I know the influential position you occupy in the affairs of your State; that all know that you when you speak and ask upon any matter, you do so from deep convictions, high motives and for the best interests of labor—of all the people. Therefore I ask whether you could not at once commu[nic]ate with Senator Shields and urge him to do all in his power to have Mr. Brandies' nomination reported favorably by his Committee and to work for early confirmation.[2]

You know that I have no interest to serve other than that of right and justice.

Miss Kelly,[3] I am informed contemplates visiting her Brothers in your State and I have asked her to be the bearer of this letter to you, which for obvious reasons you will of course regard as confidential

Wishing for you the best of everything good, I am

Sinc[ere]ly yours   Signed Saml Gompers

ALS, Files of the Office of the President, General Correspondence, reel 80, frames 539–40, *AFL Records.*

1. President Woodrow Wilson nominated Louis Brandeis for the U.S. Supreme Court in January 1916, and the Senate confirmed the appointment on June 1.

2. George Berry replied on Apr. 24, 1916, that he had wired Sen. John Shields as SG requested and had obtained assurances from over a hundred prominent Tennesseeans that they would do so as well (Files of the Office of the President, General Correspondence, reel 80, frame 547, *AFL Records*). Shields voted in favor of the nomination.

3. Josephine T. Kelly was a clerk in the AFL office.

To Woodrow Wilson

Washington, D.C., April 29, 1916.

Hon. Woodrow Wilson,
President of the United States,
Washington, D.C.
Sir:

In a letter[1] from the representative of the American Federation of Labor in Porto Rico I received a copy of a report[2] made to the Chairman of the House of Delegates of Porto Rico by a commission that had been authorized to investigate charges that the government had suspended the constitutional rights of citizens in Arecibo.[3]

This statement of the commission contains an explanation of its failure to make a full, comprehensive report, but the workers of Porto Rico, those whose rights were denied, feel that the real explanation of the failure to make a comprehensive report is political rather than mere lack of time.

The statement made by the commission is of such significance that I wish to bring it to your personal attention. It is an official confirmation of the claims of the workers that they have been denied constitutional rights. A copy of the report is enclosed.

It has fallen to me as my duty on several occasions to call to your attention unwarranted acts of several of the officers of the government of Porto Rico—denial of justice to the workers, denial to them of rights guaranteed by the constitution of the United States, guaranteed to them by every law of honor, justice and decency.

It may not be amiss to say that when on March 6, 1916,[4] I submitted a complaint as to the action of government agents which denied the workers the fundamental rights of free citizens, you stated in your reply of March 20th[5] that you were referring my letter to the Governor of Porto Rico, in whom you had great confidence.

I have long been under the impression, as a result of my own observation, that in so far as the Governor's policy and course affect the interests, the welfare and the rights of the people of Porto Rico, Governor Yager is not deserving of the confidence that you feel toward him.

I am fully appreciative of the great duties and responsibilities that devolve upon you particularly at the present time, but I hope that this matter which I now bring to your attention will also receive your sympathetic and favorable action.[6]

Very respectfully,   Saml Gompers.
President   American Federation of Labor.

TLS, Woodrow Wilson Papers, DLC.

1. Santiago Iglesias to SG, Apr. 19, 1916, AFL Microfilm Convention File, reel 27, frame 2642, *AFL Records.*

2. A copy of the report, dated Apr. 13, 1916, and signed by Hermogenes Vargas, can be found in the AFL Microfilm Convention File, reel 27, frame 2642, *AFL Records.*

3. In early 1916 some forty thousand agricultural workers in the sugarcane fields of northern and eastern Puerto Rico launched a series of strikes for higher wages and shorter hours. Although agreements were soon reached in some localities, other areas, particularly the region around Arecibo, experienced a prolonged and violent conflict. Police beat and arrested many strikers, and a number of strikers were killed. The strikes ended in May, with the agricultural workers in the Arecibo area gaining a small wage increase.

4. Actually SG to Woodrow Wilson, Mar. 16, 1916, reel 204, vol. 216, pp. 1020–21, SG Letterbooks, DLC.

5. Wilson to SG, Mar. 20, 1916, Woodrow Wilson Papers, DLC.

6. Wilson replied on June 8, 1916, that while Arthur Yager might have made mistakes or been misled, Wilson was convinced the governor was just, fair, and patriotic (Woodrow Wilson Papers, DLC).

An Article by Samuel Gompers in
the *American Federationist*

[April 1916]

REASONS FOR IMMIGRATION RESTRICTION

As a people we have barely begun to appreciate the value of those qualities which make for real progress, the necessity to insist and persist in formulating sound policies to redound to the interests of the people of our nation. Indeed, for years we have delayed in even formulating a national policy that would protect us against such elements and conditions which act as a barrier to the development of American character and national unity. We have excused this delay on the ground that we were a young nation; that we had vast public lands and national resources that must be developed, and that we could afford to open our doors to a practically unrestricted immigration in order to increase our population.

But conditions have changed. We are no longer a young nation. We have wasted much of our national heritage and the frontier has practically disappeared. Recent events that have tested national institutions and men's faith to the uttermost, proved conclusively that we can not hope to be the ideal which America represents, we can not maintain a place of influence in the affairs of the world, if we do not plan to carry out those purposes. Haphazard development may do well enough for the ordinary activities from day to day but will not endure the tests of a great crisis or the slower test of time.

To achieve the best that is possible for our nation, and for our citizens generally, we can not escape the duty devolving upon us of thinking out a national policy that will develop out of the many peoples within our boundaries a homogeneous nation bound together by common ideals, common customs, common language and a common culture.

America has not yet become a nation. It is still a conglomerated mass of various and diverse ethnic groups. Hordes of immigrants have crowded into our ports, and have, for the most part, settled in the nearest industrial center. In some cases they have in masses moved further inland to industrial centers where the nature of the work required comparatively little skill. In many of these cases, the coming of the immigrants was due to the activities of managers of industries, who arranged to secure the financial advantages by employing foreign workers who still retained the standards and prejudices of other countries. So we find in many industrial centers sections that are known as

"Little Hungary," "Little Italy," etc. The inhabitants of these little nations transplant to American soil the institutions and the standards of their fatherlands. They gain nothing by coming. These communities speak a foreign language, read foreign papers, dress in accord with foreign customs and bring up their families in accord with foreign standards. There is practically no sustained effort on the part of society or the nation to assimilate these foreign groups and to make of them Americans. Nor is this condition confined only to the poorer immigrants. There are foreign communities in the resident districts of the large cities. These remain even more exclusively foreign because their wealth enables them to have foreign schools and foreign instruction for their children. Thus the foreign group and alien influence become rooted in the life of the community.

The workers of America have felt most keenly the pernicious results of the establishment of foreign standards of work, wages and conduct in American industries and commerce. Foreign standards of wages do not permit American standards of life. Foreign labor has driven American workers out of many trades, callings, and communities, and the influence of these lower standards has permeated widely.

For years the organized labor movement has called attention to these vicious tendencies which affect not only the workers but the whole nation, for national unity is weakened when the nation is honeycombed with "foreign groups" living a foreign life.

The labor movement has urged the adoption of a national policy that would enable us to select as future citizens of our country those who can be assimilated and made truly American. The American Federation of Labor has urged a literacy test, which shall be applied to all immigrants. Our nation has accepted as a fundamental principle that education enables the girl and boy to attain better development and to have better control over their own personal ability and powers. It has been our national purpose to eliminate from our country all illiteracy. It is, therefore, in accord with this general plan that we should establish the same requirements for foreign-born persons who desire to come and live in our country. It has been urged that this is not a perfect standard. Of course no standard is perfect but the literacy test is the most effective and practical. It has been claimed that our greatest criminals are often educated persons. These are, however, only conspicuous failures of education to achieve its desired ideal. Educated criminality is not the fault of education, but is the inherent fault or defect in the nature or the physical make-up of the individual. If it is urged that education tends to criminality it would seem the wisest course to remain in ignorance, a fallacy so patent that its mere statement carries with it its own repudiation. Education can not remedy all the inherent faults of human nature, but it is the greatest instrumentality for human development and betterment.

It has been urged against the literacy test that this standard would make many suffer because they had been denied opportunities. That may be true, but it is equally true that our nation can not work out all of the problems of all other nations. We can not undertake to educate all of those to whom other countries deny educational opportunities. Each nation must undertake and solve its own educational problems. The adoption of the literacy test by our own country would have a tendency to force nations to establish more general educational opportunities for all of their people. It is only a half truth to say that the literacy test would close the gates of opportunity to illiterate foreigners. As a matter of fact there is very little real opportunity for these people in our industrial centers. Usually they have been brought over here either by steamship and railroad companies and other greedy corporations, by employers, or as a result of collusion between these groups. They have been brought over here for the purpose of exploitation, and until they develop powers of resistance and determination to secure things for themselves they have little opportunity here. These same qualities would secure for them within their own countries many of the advantages that later come to them here.

The section of the Burnett Immigration Bill which establishes the literacy test provides for no unfair requirements. It says:

"All aliens over sixteen years of age, physically capable of reading, who can not read the English language, or some other language or dialect, including Hebrew or Yiddish; Provided, That any admissible alien, or any alien heretofore or hereafter legally admitted, or any citizen of the United States, may bring in or send for his father or grandfather over fifty-five years of age, his wife, his mother, his grandmother, or his unmarried or widowed daughter, if otherwise admissible, whether such relative can read or not, and such relative shall be permitted to enter. That for the purpose of ascertaining whether aliens can read, the immigrant inspectors shall be furnished with slips of uniform size, prepared under the direction of the Secretary of Labor, each containing not less that thirty nor more than forty words in ordinary use, printed in plainly legible type in some one of the various languages or dialects of immigrants. Each alien may designate the particular language or dialect in which he desires the examination to be made, and shall be required to read the words printed on the slip in such language or dialect."

An attempt has been made to create the impression that the literacy test will close America as a haven of refuge to political refugees and those persecuted because of religious faith. That this is wholly unwarranted in fact is evident from the following portion of the proposed act:

"That the following classes of persons shall be exempt from the operation of the illiteracy test, to wit: All aliens who shall prove to the satisfaction of the proper immigration officer or to the Secretary of Labor, that they are seeking admission to the United States to avoid religious persecution in the country of their last permanent residence, whether such persecution be evidenced by overt acts or by laws or by governmental regulations that discriminate against the alien or the race to which he belongs because of his religious faith. Provided, That nothing in this act shall exclude, if otherwise admissible, persons convicted, or who admit the commission, or who teach and advocate the commission, of an offense purely political."

The proposed legislation does not represent a radical change in the policy of our nation. It is an extension of our educational policy, and is in harmony with the conviction that has been growing recently that we, as a nation, must leave our haphazard methods of development behind, and inaugurate a definite sustained national policy that shall promote our best development, and shall coordinate and organize all of the resources of our country and plan for their best utilization.

Opposition to the literacy test and to any proposition to restrict immigration has come from steamship companies, steel corporations, coal operators and other employers whose financial interests were associated with the maintenance of large numbers of workers forced by their helplessness to work for low wages. The activities of these interests have been given a cloak of respectability by many who, for sentimental reasons, were unwilling to endorse any form of restriction of immigration. But selfish interest or sentiment that is contrary to the fundamental principles of national welfare can not frustrate efforts to promote the best interests of our nation.

The meaning of America lies in the ideal she represents. That ideal is liberty and opportunity. But beautiful as any ideal may be, it becomes of practical value when it has effectiveness in the daily lives of men and women.

Real liberty and opportunity mean a certain mental attitude toward life, certain standards of life and work, and possession of that which secures the enjoyment of opportunities.

America the ideal—the land of the free—exists only when her people are Americans in all things.

Ours has been a most perilous task—to weld together those from other lands who have sought our shores and to make of them homogeneous people—a nation with common ideals, common standards of living, a national language and an ideal national patriotism.

The building of a nation is not a thing of chance—it is the result of statesmanship, knowledge of tendencies, a discernment of cause and effect, ability to distinguish the good from the evil.

Too long our national policies have been determined by sentimental emotions, business profits and political expediency. But there must come a change. These months of terrible warfare have compelled a testing of things that have passed over. "The world is afire"—and we must put our own house in order lest we, too, be caught unawares. We must search out each weakness and strengthen every danger point.

The workers of America make the demand that there shall be restriction of immigration to such as can be readily identified and assimilated with Americans and can become truly American.

American Federationist 23 (Apr. 1916): 253–56.

From David Gibson

Male Nurses' Association of Massachusetts
Cambridge, Massachusetts May 5th, 1916.

Dear Sir:—

For sometime I have been contemplating writing you for information relative to certain conditions and situations which arise in the relation of my work with labor. First of all, let me be frank, I am heartily the friend of the laborer, so you may have no distrust of my writing or inquiries.

The past week one of our members accepted a position with the Standard Steel Car Co., Butler, Pa. to do "first aid" work in their factory. Now I note in the papers there is some difficulties over labor problems in this section, and it may be—this member will be placed in a position, where he will have to care for both union and non-union laborers. The nurse—ethically should know no distinction—but economically he should. I fear this member may be taken advantage of.

As you know, we nurses are under no definite laws of labor—by many ours is called a profession—in this state we are regulated by no definite laws as to hours of employment—minimum or maximum wage—protection by compensation—or protection in the pursuit of our living—skilled and unskilled are alike free to do as they please, and in other states it is practically the same. I believe the time is coming when we shall find our only protection in organization, but such organization must be substantiated by similar organizations, or such organizations, whose problems are those of the employers.

The fact we have no protection permits gross violation of what are now called for a better name is possibly subterfuge "ethics." As director of our associations, which is the first of its kind in the United States, I am daily meeting situations, which tax my knowledge, etc.

Many of our members are employed to care for laborers, who have been injured—we know not the attitude of labor unions etc. on workmen's compensation. We wish we did, we might help many poor unfortunates, who are ignorant of laws and conditions. Advantages are taken of these men and we, who, if we were injured even in the performance of our work in institutions municipal, or state, or private,— do not receive any compensation whatever do feel for these people.

In industrial life there is a growing demand for nurses to take care of "first aid" rooms in isolated places, where factories and industries are far away from hospitals—here the nurses are expected to perform nursing duties, do clerical work, write reports on insurance, etc. There is no definite training anywhere in the United States for the kind of a nurse—all must experience for themselves—still before our members start we would like to hear from you the labor union's view towards us— possibly we can help the laborer,—and by doing so also help ourselves.

I do not know whether you come to Boston, but if so, and it were convenient for you, I should at any time be glad to discuss some situations with you—as I know my influence is becoming national and I do not want to take missteps. I try, if possible, to acquaint myself with all phases of our work. It is impossible for me to leave Boston, as I am actively engaged in nursing and directing our new association, which is developing and [needs my atten]tion. Again I am going to enter the School for Health Officers, Harvard-Technology next Fall, so desire some information before entering here. My few discussions with the board of administration of this school would indicate caution. A strong influence is being brought to bear here, to crush if possible our new organization—medical politics is opposed to men in nursing and the sign of a first organization of such in Massachusetts is distressing them. They do not want us—yet the public wants us—I talk before the public—I am known to the public—Boston's blue-blooded clique have nothing on me (to use the vernacular). A great fear is felt lest we shall set a precedent or break some established ethical laws—and a greater one, lest we should at any time call ourselves laborers, become unionized and defeat some of their methods, as established for our welfare by them.

However, while I direct our association, I am in no fear of them— perhaps yet we may become the forerunners of something radical in nursing.—

Personally, I believe the days of sentimental nursing are gone—nursing is economic—and it can be powerful. Let us but know more of social civic and industrial life and we shall know where we can help. I should be glad for any information you may give us in labor's attitude towards "industrial nursing" or the care of union laborers under workmen's compensation. Perhaps some day the labor unions will supply their own nurses on the laborer who has been injured and thereby help him to square deal. Again they can help the nurse too!

Thanking you for a consideration of this letter,[1] I am,

Very sincerely yours,   (Signed) David H. Gibson R.N.,
Director,   Male Nurses' Asso. of Mass.

TLtpSr, reel 207, vol. 219, pp. 836–38, SG Letterbooks, DLC. Typed notation: "*Copy.*" Enclosed in SG to Frank McCarthy, May 10, 1916, ibid., p. 835.

1. SG wrote David Gibson on May 10, 1916, that he was forwarding his letter to Frank McCarthy, the AFL's representative in Boston (reel 207, vol. 219, p. 870, SG Letterbooks, DLC). SG sent McCarthy a copy of Gibson's letter the same day (ibid., p. 835).

To the Executive Council of the AFL

Washington, D.C., May 11, 1916.

No. 69

Executive Council, American Federation of Labor,
Colleagues:

I know that for years there has been agitation for the organization of the teachers into unions for the purpose of their mutual benefit and protection. The attempt on the part of the Cleveland school authorities and later by the school board in ordering the dismissal of teachers who favored unions was successfully fought in the courts[1] until now in Illinois it is practically an established fact that the teachers have the right to organize for the purposes above enumerated.[2] The agitation had gone on for years and found its reflex in the revived spirit for organization among the teachers of several states throughout the country.

I had a number of conferences with the teachers in Chicago, New York, Cleveland, Washington and other places. The matter has culminated into a conference of the representatives of several of the local teachers' unions, and they applied for a charter from the A.F. of L. On May 9th charter was issued to that national organization under the title of "American Federation of Teachers."[3] The headquarters for the time being are to be at Chicago, Illinois and the name of the President is Charles B. Stillman.[4]

It is contemplated that a lively campaign will be conducted pending vacation period and good results are expected.

It may be also interesting to say that the tentative draft of the Constitution was submitted to me. I went through it thoroughly, made several suggestions, and later some others which finally were accepted as the temporary organic law of the organization.[5]

I am sure that the members of the Executive Council will be gratified to learn of this new link in our international organization of workers and this is therefore written for the information and files of the members of the E.C.

With best wishes, I am,

Fraternally yours,   Saml Gompers.
President.   American Federation of Labor.

TLcS, Executive Council Records, Vote Books, reel 14, frames 645–46, *AFL Records.*

1. See "To Peter Hassenpflue," May 25, 1914, n. 3, above.

2. In September 1915 the Chicago board of education ruled that "membership by teachers in labor unions, or in organizations of teachers affiliated with a trade union, or a federation or association of trade unions, is inimical to proper discipline, prejudicial to the efficiency of the teaching force, and detrimental to the welfare of the public school system." It prohibited Chicago teachers from joining unions, demanded that union members relinquish their membership within three months, and required teachers to sign statements affirming they were not union members in order to be eligible for promotion, raises, or transfers. Opponents obtained a temporary injunction blocking enforcement of the board's ruling, and the injunction was upheld in the Superior Court of Cook County on Nov. 29 and in the Court of Appeals of Illinois, Chicago, First District, on May 1, 1916 (*The People ex rel. Fursman* v. *The City of Chicago et al.,* 199 Ill. App. 356 [1916], quotation at pp. 357–58). On Apr. 19, 1917, the Supreme Court of Illinois reversed the superior court and directed it to dissolve the injunction on the grounds that the board of education had "the absolute right to decline to employ or to re-employ any applicant for any reason whatever or for no reason at all" (278 Ill. 318 [1917], quotation at pp. 325–26).

3. The American Federation of TEACHERS.

4. Charles B. STILLMAN served as president of the Teachers from 1916 to 1923.

5. SG to Stillman, Apr. 21, 1916, reel 206, vol. 218, pp. 1020–23, and May 3, 1916, reel 207, vol. 219, pp. 521–23, SG Letterbooks, DLC.

To James Mathews[1]

May 11, 1916

Mr. J. W. Mathews,
Chairman Committee on By-Laws, Central Labor Union[2]
Municipal Building, Portsmouth, Virginia.
Dear Sir and Brother:

Your communication of May 5, enclosing copy of constitution, bylaws and rules of order of the Central Labor Union of Portsmouth, Virginia, has been received for approval.

Section 35 of the constitution provides: "Industrial Relations Committee—The duties of this Committee shall be to work in cooperation with the National Committee on Industrial Relations,[3] to aid in giving publicity on such matters of interest to the Labor movement from time to time by having public meetings and through the press, or in such other ways as may be suggested by the National Committee."

In Section 1 of your constitution, under the sub-head "Name and Objects" it is provided: "That the Central Labor Union shall be composed of trades and labor unions of the city of Portsmouth and vicinity and is affiliated with the American Federation of Labor; its jurisdiction shall be co-extensive with that of several branches composing the same and working under a charter from the American Federation of Labor . . .[4] so that a brotherhood may be formed for the defense of the rights and the protection of the interests of the laboring masses."

Let me call your attention to the fact that the Industrial Relations Committee is a self-constituted one and cannot speak with authority upon questions which concern and affect the general labor movement of our country. Whatever may be the action of the Industrial Relations Committee constitutes only the opinion of a group of individuals who cannot, from the very nature of the committee, speak with authority upon the policy nor practice of the labor movement as expressed by the American Federation of Labor. The highest tribunal in the labor movement is considered by 108 national and international unions to be the American Federation of Labor and all questions affecting the interests of the wage earners of the country are not only dealt with by the Federation but its conclusions and decisions are accepted by the great body of wage earners as the concrete and official expression of the general labor movement of our country. The American Federation of Labor is composed exclusively of wage earners, while in contradistinction the Industrial Relations Committee is not composed entirely of wage earners.

The trade unionists of our country have no means by which to direct the activities of the Industrial Relations Committee while they do guide and control the activities, the conclusions and policies of the American Federation of Labor. In my judgment it is against the best policy of our movement for any national union, state federation, central body, or local union to pledge its support to any other organization, committee or what not, [save][5] the American Federation of Labor.

The American Federation [of Labor is not averse to accepting][6] the assistance of those who are sympathetically inclined and it is opposed to the organizations of labor placing their destiny and having their activities guided by any group or combination of men outside of the general and recognized labor movement which means the American Federation of Labor. I, therefore, suggest for your earnest consideration the entire elimination of Section 35 of your constitution.

Under Section 38 it is provided that: "Any member of a union that is not connected with a national or international organization, who may feel aggrieved at the action of this union against him, shall have the right to appeal to this body for redress," etc.

According to the first section of your constitution which limits the membership to those organizations affiliated with the American Federation of Labor, the organizations referred to in the portion of Section 38 quoted must refer to those organizations directly chartered by the American Federation of Labor.

Permit me to call your attention to the fact that in cases covered by the section, the proper method for any union man to pursue, where he has either a real or a fancied grievance against his union is appeal to the parent body, the American Federation of Labor and not your central body. Dealing with questions of this character is not within the province of a central body. It is, therefore, suggested that in order to conform to the general trade union practice in the conduct of central labor unions that Section 38 be eliminated in its entirety.

Under Section 10 of the by-laws it is provided that: "Any delegate who shall use disrespectful or violent personal language, or refuse to obey the President when called to order," etc. This section presumes that such a case might occur. The constitution and by-laws of central bodies are generally speaking public property and it does not bespeak for the best interests of our movement to have incorporated such provisions because of the assumption that laws of this character are necessary for the proper conduct of our central bodies. The meetings of our central bodies can [b]e conducted with order and decorum without the incorporation of such a provision. Under Section 16 of your constitution it is provided: "That the President shall preside at all meetings and preserve order during the deliberations of the body; etc." The delegates to your central body, I am sure, will support the president of your central body in carrying out the provisions of Section 16 hereby quoted. Therefore, for the purpose of contributing to the dignity of your organization, it is suggested that the suggestion made with reference to the section under consideration be accepted and complied with. The other sections of your constitution and by-laws are in conformity with the laws of the American Federation of Labor and are hereby approved.

Let me hear from you at your earliest convenience relative to the disposition made by your central body of the suggestions herein incorporated.

With kind regards and best wishes, I am,

Yours fraternally,   Saml Gompers.

President   American Federation of Labor.

TLpS, reel 207, vol. 219, pp. 984–87, SG Letterbooks, DLC.

1. James W. Mathews served as president of United Association of Plumbers and Steam Fitters of the United States and Canada 272 of Portsmouth, Va., from 1913 to 1915.

2. The AFL chartered the Portsmouth Central Labor Union in 1901.

3. In late 1915 Frank Walsh organized the Committee on Industrial Relations, a private, voluntary organization designed to facilitate cooperation between organized labor and reformers wishing to implement the recommendations of the U.S. Commission on Industrial Relations. Chaired by Walsh, the committee included former commission members John Lennon, James O'Connell, and Austin Garretson, as well as John White of the United Mine Workers of America, Agnes Nestor of the International Glove Workers' Union of America, and Helen Marot of the National Women's Trade Union League of America, as well as Amos Pinchot, journalist Dante Barton, U.S. immigration commissioner Frederic Howe, and Episcopal bishop Charles Williams.

4. Ellipses in original.

5. The text in brackets is supplied from a copy of the letter in the AFL Microfilm Convention File, reel 27, frame 2223, *AFL Records.*

6. The text in brackets is supplied from a copy of the letter in the AFL Microfilm Convention File, reel 27, frame 2223, *AFL Records.*

To S. A. Olsen

May 15, 1916.

Mr. S. Olsan,
Secretary, Fargo Trades and Labor Assembly,[1]
515 Avenue N., Fargo, North Dakota.
Dear Sir and Brother:

Your favor of May 8 to hand, in which you ask me for information concerning an affiliation or relation between organized labor and organized farmers regarding political and law making bodies. You also say there is a farmers' organization, known as the Non-Partisan League[2] in your state with a membership of thirty-eight thousand farmers and that they have extended their hands to organized labor for cooperation and help.

This is cheerful information, coming from your state, because of the fact that we have so few industries and consequently so few purely industrial trade unions in North Dakota. I hope that the members of our organizations may see their way clear to cooperate with the organized farmers on a non-partisan basis and work for the common good. In many states such cooperation has been of great value, and before the United States Congress we cooperate gladly with the organized farmers and help each other to the fullest possible extent.

I am enclosing herewith copy of a model injunction limitation antitrust bill which is modeled after the law which we secured during the Sixty-third Congress, and in behalf of which the farmers' organizations cooperated with our organizations with the greatest unanimity.

I hope that you will exert yourself in North Dakota to secure the enactment of this much needed law in your State on the earliest possible occasion.

The attitude of the American Federation of Labor on a political program was declared at the Twenty-eighth Annual Convention held at Denver, Colorado, November, 1908.[3] That declaration has been reaffirmed at our conventions since and I do not think that I can add anything additional to the program therein outlined. The Denver convention declared as follows:

"The American Labor movement is not partisan to a political party; it is partisan to a principle, the principle of equal rights and human freedom.

["]We call especial attention to this statement, in order that we may emphasize its soundness and because it has to some extent been disputed. We appeal to public opinion, we do our best to so cultivate it, so that it may become on subjects which we urge sufficiently extensive and strong to be crystallized into law. One political party deals with our policies and rejects them; another deals with them and adopts them; that is, it expresses itself as being in agreement with us on these policies, and if we are to remain true to the principles and policies which we have urged upon the public, we necessarily must work with such party for the accomplishment of our object. If an endorsement of our contentions, by a political party is to compel us to abandon those contentions, then it needs but such endorsement of our very existence to compel us to disband. The thought needs but to be stated in order that it may be repudiated. Partisanship is exhibited by adherence to a party which refuses its endorsement, and non-partisanship consists in continued work for our principles regardless of what any political party may do. The President makes the following statement:

["]'Our conventions have frequently declared that our movement has neither the right nor the desire to dictate how a member shall cast his vote. It has been my privilege and honor always so to insist. I have not departed, and can not now depart, from that true trade union course. At the Minneapolis Convention[4] the following declaration was adopted:

["]'We must have with us in our economic movement men of all parties as well as of all creeds, and the minority rights of the humblest man to vote where he pleases and to worship where his conscience dictates must be sacredly guarded.'

["]Your committee are in full accord with this expression, and desire to reiterate the Minneapolis declaration . . . .[5]

["]We recommend that the policy be continued and that every effort be made to bring the principles for which we contended and for which we shall continue to contend, not only to all members of the labor movement, but to all friends and adherents of popular government."

I hope that our organizations in your State will be governed by the principles above announced and that you will cooperate with your friends, the farmers, in every way possible, keeping the non-partisan point always in view.

Keep me advised as to the progress you make in behalf of remedying the grievances of the workers on the farm, in the mill, in the factory, in the shop and on the railroad, and endeavor to your utmost to select tried and true representatives of your organizations to be elected to positions of public trust, as well as economic affairs. We always trust our own members and associates to serve us in our economic organisms. Let us learn to train and depend upon our own immediate associates in all of the responsible positions of life. By so doing, we will make rapid progress in behalf of genuine social welfare legislation; we will prevent interference by purely political speculators with our economic and political rights and we will gain for ourselves that respect which always comes to those who zealously protect their own interests.

With best wishes for your every success, I remain,

Fraternally yours,   Saml Gompers.
President   American Federation of Labor.

TLpS, reel 208, vol. 220, pp. 141–44, SG Letterbooks, DLC.

1. The AFL chartered the Trades and Labor Assembly of Fargo, N.Dak., in 1906.

2. The North Dakota Non-Partisan League was founded in early 1915 under the leadership of Arthur Townley. It criticized commercial practices that undercut farmers, sought public ownership of grain elevators, mills, packing houses, and cold storage plants, and advocated a rural credit system and higher prices for farm products.

3. AFL, *Proceedings*, 1908, pp. 222–23.

4. The 1906 AFL convention met in Minneapolis, Nov. 12–24.

5. Ellipses in original.

To the Secretary[1] of
the Casa del Obrero Mundial[2]

May 23, 1916.

Secretary Casa del Obrero Mundial,
City of Mexico.
Dear Sir and Brother:

Permit me on behalf of the American Federation of Labor to send fraternal greetings to the Casa del Obrero Mundial, to the entire labor movement of Mexico.

The labor movement of North America has seen with what splendid courage organized labor in Mexico has, from the time of the presidency of the late Francisco I. Madero, demanded and obtained recognition for the cause of labor and justice in our sister republic.

From time to time the American Federation of Labor has received confidential reports from delegates duly accredited by your organization and others who came to Washington in behalf of the Mexican labor movement and the Mexican cause. From these delegates the Executive Council of the American Federation of Labor has learned how deeply the spirit of international brotherhood has guided all your struggles in Mexico. We learned with intense interest of the historic agreement[3] between the Casa del Obrero Mundial and the Constitutionalist Government and signed on behalf of that government by Rafael Zubaran Capmany.

We have learned with what bravery and determination the Mexican miners in the state of Arizona organized and struck work with their brother Americans of the North and won advancement for themselves and the cause of international solidarity.

All these facts point to the necessity of a still closer understanding between the workers of all the Americas, particularly in this crisis[4] in the world's history. To this end and to propose a practical method of mutual cooperation between organized labor in Mexico and in the United States, I suggest that, at a date to be agreed upon, representatives from the Casa del Obrero Mundial and as many other of the labor organizations in Mexico as possible meet for a conference in El Paso, Texas, with representatives of the American Federation of Labor.[5] Matters for the mutual welfare of the sister republics could then be discussed and a future cooperative policy outlined.

With you I agree that the future peace of the world rests in the hands of the wage-earners, and this is most cogently expressed by the organized labor movement of each and all countries.

426 *May 1916*

I hope to hear from you as soon as possible as to the actual conditions of the Mexican labor movement at the present time, and a reply to the suggestion I have made herein.[6]

Fraternally yours,   Saml Gompers.
President   American Federation of Labor.[7]

TLpS, reel 208, vol. 220, pp. 417–18, SG Letterbooks, DLC.

1. Possibly Samuel O. Yudico, a Mexico City machinist.

2. The Casa del Obrero (House of the Worker; from 1913, the Casa del Obrero Mundial [House of the World Worker]) was organized in 1912 by anarcho-syndicalists in Mexico City and later established branches in other cities. The government of Venustiano Carranza shut down the Casa in August 1916 after it initiated a general strike in Mexico City.

3. The Casa del Obrero Mundial committed itself to support the Carranza government after Carranza issued a decree on Dec. 12, 1914, calling for social, political, and economic reforms. Representatives of the Casa signed a pact with the government on Feb. 17, 1915, promising to propagandize for the Constitutionalists, enlist for military service, and defend territories conquered by Constitutionalist forces. For its part, the Carranza government reaffirmed the decree of December 1914 and recognized the right of workers to organize.

4. Probably a reference both to the intensification of the European war and a crisis in U.S.-Mexican relations. The battle at Verdun, a major German offensive on the Western Front, began on Feb. 21, 1916, and ended on Dec. 18. The French suffered some 540,000 casualties during the battle and the Germans, 430,000. At the same time, military forces under the command of Francisco "Pancho" Villa in northern Mexico precipitated a confrontation with the United States. On Jan. 10 they murdered a group of American mining engineers at Santa Ysabel, Chihuahua, and on Mar. 9 they attacked the town of Columbus, N.Mex., killing nearly twenty American civilians and soldiers. In response, a punitive expedition under the command of Gen. John Pershing crossed the Rio Grande on Mar. 15 in pursuit of Villa. The Mexican government objected, and, following the clash of American forces with Carranza's troops and Mexican civilians at Parral, Chihuahua, on Apr. 12, Carranza demanded Pershing's withdrawal. When Mexican bandits—ostensibly members of Villa's forces—raided Glen Springs, Tex., on May 5, additional American troops entered Mexico and Carranza again demanded that the United States withdraw its forces, threatening to expel them by force if necessary. Small raids—some apparently by members of Carranza's forces—continued into June along the lower Rio Grande, and on June 21 American soldiers fought with Carranza's troops at Carrizal, Chihuahua. Nearly a hundred of the men engaged in the action were killed or wounded and two dozen Americans were taken prisoner, but war was averted when the American prisoners, held in the Chihuahua jail, were freed on the afternoon of June 28. Tensions eased thereafter, and a joint U.S.-Mexican commission was subsequently established to investigate relations between the two countries. President Woodrow Wilson ordered the withdrawal of Pershing's expedition in late January 1917, and the last American soldiers left Mexico on Feb. 5.

5. The Mexican labor movement sent representatives to the border town of Eagle Pass, Tex., but without first informing the AFL Executive Council, which consequently did not send its own delegation to meet them. The Mexican representatives at Eagle Pass then sent Luis Morones and Salvador González García to meet with the Executive Council in Washington, D.C., at the Council's regular meeting during the week of June 26. Carlos Loveira y Chirinos, Baltasar Pages, and Edmundo Martínez also participated in the meeting with the Executive Council. For an account of that confer-

ence, see "Excerpts of a Meeting of the Executive Council of the AFL," June 30–July 3, 1916, below.

6. The Casa del Obrero Mundial and the Federación de Sindicatos Obreros de la República Mexicana replied on June 11, 1916, accepting SG's invitation but without setting a date for the conference (Files of the Office of the President, General Correspondence, reel 80, frame 829, *AFL Records*).

7. SG sent copies of this letter to Carranza, Alvaro Obregón Salido, the governors of Chihuahua, Sonora, and Yucatán, and three other individuals (reel 208, vol. 220, pp. 415–16, 460–69, 493–94, SG Letterbooks, DLC).

From Frank Duffy

May 26th, 1916.

Dear Sir and Brother:—

I learned from *"The New York Call"* under date of Thursday May 25th, 1916,[1] a paper for which I have very little use on account of its socialistic tendencies, that you have called for an International Labor Conference to be held at El Paso, Texas, in the near future between the representatives of the Mexican Labor Movement and the representatives of the American Federation of Labor to consider and act upon certain matters, which to me are indefinite at the present time, but which I suppose relates to the well-being and betterment of the organized wage workers of Mexico.

I think no man in the labor movement understands me better than you do and you know what I have to say will be said plainly and, as has been said often, bluntly. I cannot imagine that the labor movement of Mexico amounts to anything. To me it is an organization on paper.

Knowing that the people of Mexico have been at war with one another for several years I cannot conceive how a remnant of organized labor still remains in that Country. In fact I have never known that even in the best times Mexico ever had, that the organized labor movement of that Country amounted to much. I do know, however, through literature received at this office, especially from Southern California and Southern Arizona that the socialistic element has been very busy in attempting, or trying to attempt to solicit our support in their behalf in Mexican affairs. I am also informed that the Obrero-Mundial is nothing more nor less than the Industrial Workers of the World. I therefore again say I cannot conceive how the American Labor Movement can hitch up with such parties. I have read your letters in *"The New York Call,"* under date already mentioned addressed to the secretary of the Obrero-Mundial and General Carranza and it makes me feel that so far in this transaction I, as a member of the Executive Council of the American Federation of Labor, have been ignored, especially so that when propositions of a similar nature were made by the chief officials of the labor organizations of Belgium, Germany, France and England, the members of the Executive Council were considered and copies of communications received by you from these officials supplied us and our advice sought. I admit you have the right, as President of the American Federation of Labor, to call conferences, to settle disputes, difficulties and misunderstandings but when these conferences are to be held with other nations then I think the members of the Executive Council of the A.F. of L., should be considered. Up to the present time I have not had a word from you relative to this conference.

"The Chicago Daily Tribune" of Thursday May 25th, 1916, says,

> *"Gompers Urges Labor Take Up Mexican Issues"*
> WASHINGTON AMAZED AT LETTER.
> SEE CARRANZA EFFORT TO
> BAR INTERVENTION.

For your information I herewith quote a few lines from the article referred to, "Officials in Washington were astounded when they heard of the Gompers letter. None of them would discuss it openly, but several expressed their private opinion that it was one of the most startling moves yet made by the forces back of Carranza in the United States to prevent an adjustment of affairs in Mexico." Is it possible that we would lend our support to such a proposition as just quoted? I would like to hear from you on this matter, as to how far we propose to go in Mexican affairs.

The United Brotherhood of Carpenters and Joiners of America claims Mexico under its jurisdiction, but so far we have not a single Local Union in that Country and you know we spend more money for organizing purposes than any other organization affiliated with the American Federation of Labor.

I feel you will willingly give me the information desired.[2]

With best wishes and kindest regards, I am,

Fraternally yours,
General Secretary.

TLc, United Brotherhood of Carpenters and Joiners of America Records, reel 2, frames 602–3, *AFL and the Unions.*

1. "International Labor Conference Is Called to Meet at El Paso," *New York Call,* May 25, 1916. The text of SG's letter of May 23 to the secretary of the Casa del Obrero Mundial was included in the article, together with the names of the other Mexican officials to whom it had been sent.

2. R. Lee Guard acknowledged Frank Duffy's letter on May 29, 1916, and forward-

ed a copy to SG, who was in Chicago (reel 208, vol. 220, p. 716, SG Letterbooks, DLC). In a letter to Duffy on July 20, SG reported he had been informed that over 250,000 trade unionists were organized in the Federación de Sindicatos Obreros de la República Mexicana (reel 210, vol. 222, pp. 535–38, SG Letterbooks, DLC). See also SG to the AFL Executive Council, July 22, 1916; Guillermo Carvallo, Domingo Ramos, and José Alonso to SG, July 15, 1916; and Lista de las uniónes pertenecientes a la Confederación de Sindicatos Obreros de la República Mexicana, July 15, 1916, all in Executive Council Records, Vote Books, reel 15, frames 70–76, *AFL Records.*

To John Dewey[1]

June 13, 1916.

Professor John Dewey,
University of Columbia, New York City.
Dear Sir:

While in conference with Chicago teachers,[2] to whom a charter has recently been issued under title of American Federation of Teachers, someone made the assertion that you had approved the effort for the organization of teachers in unions affiliated with the American Federation of Labor.

Because of your high standing as an educator and as an American citizen, I was very glad indeed of the information, and because of that assurance, I venture to write you in regard to the recently formed organization of university professors.[3]

Can you, without violating any confidence, tell me the sentiment in that organization toward affiliation with the American Federation of Labor, and whether there is any likelihood of such action?

There is another matter upon which I would like the benefit of your opinion—the so-called Gary system[4] and its adaptation to the schools of New York City.[5] As you probably know, the organized labor movement has been very much interested in the schools established under Mr. Wirts' direction and, of course, judges the results of such schools from the viewpoint of wage-earners and citizens. It would be of great value to the labor movement if we could have the benefit of your opinion from the viewpoint of an educator and a psychologist.

Because the matter is of such fundamental importance to the masses of America's citizenship we desire the opinion and the advice of your long experience and well established ability.

Very sincerely yours,   Saml Gompers.
President   American Federation of Labor.

TLpS, reel 209, vol. 221, pp. 160–61, SG Letterbooks, DLC.

1. John Dewey (1859–1952) was a principal theorist of the philosophy of pragmatism and a leading exponent of progressive education. A professor at Columbia University, he was a founder of the Teachers' League (1913), the American Association of University Professors (1915), and the American Civil Liberties Union (1920).

2. SG met with the officers and executive board of the American Federation of Teachers in Chicago on May 26, 1916, while on a lengthy trip through Illinois, Indiana, Ohio, and Michigan that extended from May 24 to June 21. During this trip SG also attended the Republican and Progressive party conventions in Chicago and the Democratic party convention in St. Louis.

3. The American Association of University Professors, organized in 1915 to ensure the academic freedom of faculty members.

4. The Gary Plan was developed by William Albert Wirt (1874–1938), the superintendent of schools in Gary, Ind., from 1907 until his death. Intended as a way of making more efficient use of school facilities, the plan called for dividing the students in a school into two groups or platoons, with one using classrooms for traditional instruction during the first part of the day and the other breaking into smaller groups to go on field trips or utilize libraries, gyms, and athletic fields, music and art rooms, or vocational training shops and science laboratories. The groups then switched during the second part of the day, making it possible to accommodate more students without building more schools or hiring more teachers.

5. New York City mayor John Mitchel attempted to introduce the Gary Plan in the city's schools between 1914 and 1917 and hired Wirt as a consultant. Critics—including parents, teachers, and the local labor movement—opposed the plan because it lengthened the schoolday, offered released time for religious instruction, and put working-class students in a track leading to factory jobs. Opposition peaked in 1917 when students began picketing schools to prevent implementation of the plan. After Mitchel was defeated for reelection that fall, the new mayor, John Hylan, ordered an end to the experiment.

A Memorandum by Florence Thorne[1]

June 22, 1916.

MEMORANDUM.

Mr. Gompers telephoned down to have a conference arranged for him, Judge Douglas, Mr. Murray,[2] Mr. Pages[3] and Mr. Loveiro.[4] This was arranged for 11:30. At the conference Mr. Gompers stated that last evening, while he was here at the office, someone called up who said he was Mr. George West,[5] and that he wished to get Mr. Gompers' position upon the following matter. A peace society, I think the anti-preparedness organization,[6] stated that they had most heartily endorsed the holding of a conference on the border line, and that if such a conference was to be held, they wished to send representatives, have Mr. Bryan present, and bring all of the anti-war forces in the country in a concentrated effort to prevent war. Mr. Gompers replied that if he was to have anything to do with the proposition, all outside people would have to keep their hands off; that there was too much at stake, he represented not himself alone but about three million organized workers, their families and sympathizers, and that he was not going to have the labor movement used by any outside organization to further their purposes and schemes. All fanatics would have to keep their hands off, and give him a chance to do. Mr. Gompers said that he left no mistaken idea in Mr. West's mind as to his attitude. He further said that the incident confirmed him all the more that Mr. Bryan ought not to be brought into the effort.

Then both Mr. Murray and Judge Douglas stated that Mr. West had also called them up in regard to the same matter. Judge Douglas said that he heartily approved of what Mr. Gompers had said, and also his manner of stating it. Mr. Murray said that he thought that Mr. West's own judgment was in hearty accord with Mr. Gompers' position, that he knew him personally and he knew what his views were in the matter. He was merely representing the peace organization and transmitting a message. Then Mr. Douglas said that in view of the events of the past night[7] he must modify the suggestions he made to Mr. Gompers the day before.[8] The proposition to withdraw the army after the attack on the army was entirely different from what it had been the previous day, and he knew that Mr. Gompers was a man of too much sense to make a proposition that the President could not accept. He thought that the only proposition that could be made was to call attention to Section 21 of the treaty of 1848 of Guadalupe Hildalgo.[9] He stated that in the last note[10] from the Carranza government there had been a section that was omitted from the quotation which Secretary Lansing[11] made in the end of his reply.[12] The part omitted referred to this section 21, and in the opinion of Judge Douglas it was a very serious omission, for evidently the idea in the mind of Carranza was that perhaps some suggestion would be made whereby the whole matter could be arbitrated, either by representatives of a neutral country or by a commission. He said that immediately upon leaving this office he intended to send a telegram to Carranza urging him to consider this section of the treaty and saying that he thought it was his duty as the aggrieved party to ask for mediation.[13]

The conference broke up with the understanding that they were to hold themselves in readiness for communication from Mr. Gompers on his return from the White House.

Mr. Gompers then went to the office of Secretary Wilson, where the Secretary showed him a letter that he had written the President embodying Mr. Gompers' expressed wish that if a commission were appointed, labor should be represented on that commission. He also showed him the President's reply, in which the President said that he had no information of such a commission, but if such a method should be adopted he would be glad to have in mind Mr. Gompers' suggestion. Secretary Wilson and President Gompers then went into conference with President Wilson at 12:30. Mr. Gompers related in his statement various incidents in which the American labor movement had tried to help the workers of Mexico in their struggles for freedom. He referred to the efforts during the rule of Diaz and Madero, and to prevent the recognition of Huerta, and later under the Carranza-Villa administration. He briefly told the President of the efforts the workers of Mexico were making to organize and that their movement had not yet taken form and shape; that it was crude, but it represented their opportunities and their efforts to take advantage of them. He said that the revolution in Mexico was identified with the Constitutionalist party and closely associated with the labor movement. He presented to him briefly the two suggestions that Judge Douglas put before him on the previous day stating that one was no longer possible, but he would leave with him the suggestion in writing if the President would care to look over it, or if later developments should make that suggestion possible, he would like him to consider it. He then called his attention to Section 21 of the treaty and left a copy of that section with the President. He called his attention to the failure of Secretary Lansing to include in his quotation one of the important statements of Carranza, namely, his reference to arbitration. The President seemed intensely interested in this. The President said that he had no information as to the cause of the battle of the previous night; that all he could do was to wait for information and advice. Mr. Gompers told him of the two delegates from the Yucatan labor movement;[14] that they were present at the conference this morning, and their position in the matter. He also particularly told him of Judge Douglas, emphasizing the fact that Judge Douglas was an American first of all; that he wished to do his duty by Mexico, but he was a citizen of the United States first. The purposes of all of the conferences[15] in the A.F. of L. office and all that had been done was to avoid a break. He told him that Judge Douglas had sent telegram to Carranza, and the President responded "that is very good" and that we might rest assured that if such a message is received it will be given ["]most serious consideration." Mr. Gompers replied that he hoped that direct information would disclose that the fault was not all with Mexico. From this opinion the President did not dissent. Mr. Gompers urged upon him the view-point that the present situation in Mexico represents the groping of those people for something better, for a realization of their ideals. Perhaps their expression of what they had in mind was not the highest or the best form, but it represented an ideal. As he said to the President, after all we can have no experience but our own, and each must learn for himself. Judge Douglas then told Mr. Gompers that in his telegram to Carranza in the morning, he had told him that he hoped later in the day to have some positive information as to how the administration would regard a proposition for arbitration. He asked Mr. Gompers whether in his opinion it would be a right statement to say that as the result of his conference with the President he was of the opinion that such a suggestion would be received with favor. Mr. Gompers said that were he sending the telegram he would use that expression. He asked Judge Douglas not to use his name in the telegram but that he might use his discretion about a private letter. Judge Douglas said that he would not use his name in the telegram, but unless he positively forbade it, he wished to use his name in the letter, because he thought that a plain statement of facts would be of incalculable value in the situation. Mr. Gompers said that the conference with the President was one of the most impressive in which he had ever been present, and he felt that it was momentous.

Florence C. Thorne

TDS, Files of the Office of the President, General Correspondence, reel 80, frames 864–68, *AFL Records.*

1. Florence Calvert THORNE was a research assistant to SG and an editor of the *American Federationist.*

2. John Murray (1865–1919), a socialist and a member of International Typographical Union 174 of Los Angeles, had served as editor of the *Los Angeles Socialist,* the *Union Labor News* (Los Angeles), and the *Los Angeles Citizen.* Active in Mexican causes since 1907, he traveled to Veracruz and Mexico City in 1915 with credentials as a journalist from the *New York Call* and established relations with the Casa del Obrero Mundial, becoming a member of its Comité Revolucionario.

3. Baltasar Pages was the editor of *La Voz de la Revolución,* the organ of the Partido Socialista de Yucatán.

4. Carlos Loveira y Chirinos (1882–1928), a novelist and labor organizer born in Cuba, was head of the Department of Labor of the state of Yucatán.

5. George Parsons West, formerly a San Francisco journalist, investigated the 1913–14 Colorado miners' strike for the U.S. Commission on Industrial Relations and served on the staff of the commission and its successor, the Committee on Industrial Relations.

6. The American Union against Militarism grew out of a pacifist group organized in New York City in 1915 known as the Anti-Militarism Committee or the Anti-Preparedness Committee. In June 1916 this group asked William Jennings Bryan, Frank Walsh, and David Starr Jordan, the chancellor of Leland Stanford University, to meet with three Mexican representatives—Dr. Atl (Gerardo Murillo), editor of *Acción Mundial,* Luis Manuel Rojas, director of the Biblioteca Nacional de México, and Modesto Rolland, an engineer from Yucatán—at El Paso, Tex., in an attempt to avert war between the United States and Mexico. Only Jordan and Rolland went to El Paso, however, meeting there on June 26. They subsequently adjourned to Albuquerque, N.Mex., where they issued a statement calling on the United States to support the government of Venustiano Carranza and refrain from armed intervention in Mexico. On July 5 and 6, Atl, Rojas, and Rolland met in Washington, D.C., with Jordan, Amos Pinchot, and

Boston attorney Moorfield Storey to establish the Inter-American Peace Conference and issue another statement condemning U.S. intervention.

7. The clash between American and Mexican forces at Carrizal (see "To the Secretary of the Casa del Obrero Mundial," May 23, 1916, n. 4, above).

8. In a meeting with SG on June 21, 1916, Charles Douglas encouraged SG both to call President Woodrow Wilson's attention to the arbitration provisions in the Treaty of Guadalupe Hidalgo and to recommend that the president withdraw American troops from Mexico.

9. Article 21 of the Treaty of Guadalupe Hidalgo, which ended the Mexican-American War in 1848, stipulated that Mexico and the United States would attempt to resolve any future political or commercial disagreements through negotiation or arbitration.

10. In its note to Secretary of State Robert Lansing on May 22, 1916, the Carranza government insisted that the United States withdraw its troops from Mexican territory. In case of refusal, the note said, the Mexican government would have "no further recourse than to defend its territory by appeal to arms, yet at the same time it understands its duty to avoid, as far as possible, an armed conflict between both countries, and relying on Article 21 of the Treaty of February 2, 1848, it considers it its duty to resort to every pacific method to solve the international conflict pending between the two countries" (*Papers Relating to the Foreign Relations of the United States, 1916* [Washington, D.C., 1925], pp. 552–63, quotation at p. 557).

11. Robert Lansing (1864–1928) served as secretary of state from 1915 to 1920.

12. In his reply of June 20, 1916, Lansing warned that the Mexican government's use of force would "lead to the gravest consequences" but made no mention of the reference to Article 21 in the Mexican note of May 22 (*Papers Relating to the Foreign Relations of the United States, 1916,* pp. 581–92, quotation at p. 591).

13. On July 4, 1916, the Carranza government suggested direct negotiations between the United States and Mexico or mediation by a third party. When Lansing endorsed the idea of direct negotiations, the Mexican government proposed on July 12 a joint commission with three members from each country, and the American government accepted this proposal on July 28. The joint commission met from Sept. 6, 1916, to Jan. 15, 1917, but was unable to reach an agreement.

14. Loveira and Pages.

15. In addition to the conferences on June 22, 1916, described in this memo, SG's appointment records indicate that on June 21 he met with Murray, then with Murray, Pages, and Loveira, and finally with Murray and Douglas.

To Venustiano Carranza

Washington, D.C., June 28, 1916.

General Venustiano Carranza,
First Chief, Constitutionalist Government,
Mexico City, Mexico.

In the name of common justice and humanity, in the interest of a better understanding between the peoples and the governments of the United States and Mexico, for the purpose of giving the opportunity to maintain peace and avoid the horrors of war, upon the grounds of highest patriotism and love, I appeal to you to release the American soldiers held by your officers in Chihuahua.[1]

Samuel Gompers
President   American Federation of Labor.

TWpSr, reel 209, vol. 221, p. 644, SG Letterbooks, DLC.

1. Venustiano Carranza replied on June 29, 1916, that his government had ordered the release of the American soldiers taken prisoner at Carrizal (Executive Council Records, Minutes, reel 5, frame 1200, *AFL Records*).

Excerpts from the Minutes of a Meeting of the Executive Council of the AFL

Friday, June 30, 1916.

AFTERNOON SESSION

. . .

President Gompers advised the Executive Council that Secretary Wilson of the Department of Labor had informed him that in all likelihood a bill will be enacted by Congress within a few days creating an Economic Board for the conservation of industries for the United States and to take such steps for industrial preparedness of the country as to meet any emergency which may arise.[1] The bill if enacted into law provides that the Secretaries of War, Navy, Interior, Agriculture, Commerce and Labor shall constitute that Board and that the President shall be empowered to appoint an Advisory Committee consisting of seven persons who are to represent labor, industry, commerce, agriculture and the public, and that President Wilson has asked Secretary Wilson to furnish him the name of a representative of Labor. Secretary Wilson desires to submit President Gompers' name to the President.

It was decided that President Gompers be advised to accept the appointment.

President Gompers stated that if there is any salary attached to the position that he will turn same over to the American Federation of Labor for the furtherance of the work of the Federation.

President Gompers stated that Secretary Wilson will meet with the members of the Executive Council at 9:30 Tuesday morning, July 4, to proceed to the office building of the A.F. of L. for the dedication ceremony.

. . .

Saturday, July 1, 1916.

Afternoon Session

Meeting called to order at 2:00 P.M., President Gompers in the chair. Present on roll call: Gompers, Duncan, O'Connell, Valentine, Alpine, Perham, Duffy, Green, Lennon and Morrison. Absent: Hayes.

In accordance with the special order the conference of the Executive Council with the following Mexican representatives was convened:

Luis N. Morones,[2] Salvador Gonzalo Garcia,[3] Representatives from Yucatan;

Carlos Loveira, Chief, Department of Labor, Baltazar Pages, Editor of Voice of the Revolution;

Representing Mexican Federation of Labor, Edmundo E. Martinez;

Credentials from Comite Revolucionario de la Casa del Obrero Mundial and I.T.U. of Los Angeles, John Murray.

. . .

President Gompers made a statement in which he outlined the principal developments of the revolution in Mexico, and the efforts of the American Federation of Labor to be helpful to the people of Mexico in their struggle for justice. His remarks are outlined briefly in the following:

The American Federation of Labor and its Executive Council have interested themselves in the struggles of the workers in all countries for a better concept of freedom, and it is our desire to be helpful. The American Federation of Labor has felt very keenly the condition of the people of Mexico during the past 25 years under the Diaz regime. So long as the Mexican people were docile they could not do anything but as soon as unrest against conditions was manifested among the Mexicans the A.F. of L. initiated action to be helpful.

We were informed that there would be both political and economic changes; that when Madero came into power the people were to be given greater opportunity of ownership of land. When Madero was installed as President, all seemed well. The United Mine Workers of America being interested in the welfare of the coal miners appointed a committee to see Madero for the purpose of having Madero agree to unionize the coal mines.[4] Madero declared for the right of the workers to freely assemble and unite and to exercise their normal activities of associated effort for general betterment of the lives of the workers. The coup d'etat of General Huerta, the imprisonment and assassination of President Madero, the assumption of dictatorship by Huerta brought on the fullest reaction to old conditions with the added tyranny exercised by the dictator and his representatives. Thus the Madero policy was reversed.

It was with great satisfaction when we learned that the Governor of one of the Mexican states, Carranza, questioned Huerta's authority and started a revolution to drive out Huerta. When Carranza and Villa were near success Villa broke away from Carranza and started a counter-revolution; we regarded Villa's act as questionable. When the situation became exceedingly critical we were helpful in prevailing upon the President not to intervene in that conflict. Col. Martinez called upon me and I placed what he had to say before President Wilson; about six weeks later Col. Martinez held an informal conference with the Executive Council.[5] The Executive Council decided to ask the President to recognize the Carranza government, and he did so, much to the surprise of many people.

A little later we saw in the papers the statement that Villa would prey upon the United States to compel the United States to enter and intervene in Mexico. I am not going to discuss the right of the United States to send soldiers into Mexico to capture the chief marauder, Villa. I suppose American history will say Mexico is responsible for the situation, and Mexican history will say the United States was responsible. Members of the United States army were killed at Carrizal and prisoners were taken. Soldiers can only be taken prisoners when a state of war exists. We were asked to communicate with General Carranza to release the soldiers. We wired in the afternoon[6] and in the evening extra editions of the newspapers announced that the prisoners had been released.

One of the chief reasons why we endorsed the constitutionalist government was that it not only stood for great reforms, but Carranza entered into an agreement with the representatives of labor of Mexico recognizing the right of freedom of association, freedom of the press and freedom of speech. The officers of the American Federation of Labor had assurances that such an agreement was entered into and carried out.

Arrangements were made for conferences between the representatives of the governments of the United States and the South American Republics for the purpose of considering and conserving their joint financial, industrial and commercial interests. Protest[7] was filed with Secretary of the Treasury McAdoo, because labor had been ignored in this conference. Reply was received from Secretary McAdoo that our position was right and that labor should be recognized. It was in the interests of labor that arrangements were made for a conference to be held at El Paso.

President Gompers read the following telegram:

"Chicago, Ill. July 1, 1916.

["]Sam'l. Gompers,
["]801 G Street, Washington, D.C.
["]Your letter[8] relative to the Mexican situation received. There are about fifty Mexican strike breakers employed in the Ills. Malleable Iron Works where the workers have been on strike for two months.[9] I am informed that the leader of these strike breakers has been arrested and is now under bond for carrying concealed weapons.

["]E. T. Flood."

President Gompers called attention to the fact that he had a copy of a circular issued by the president of one of the great coal and railroad corporations in which he announced he was going to import miners and railroad workers from Mexico for the purpose of Mexicanizing the mines of Virginia, West Virginia and Western Pennsylvania, and that there was a fairly well-defined movement to accomplish that purpose by the managers of several great industrial corporations. To counteract such a movement as well as to take into consideration the economic relations between the workers of the United States and Mexico and in addition the political crisis which existed in the relations between the two countries, that he extended the invitation for the conference between the representatives of the workers of the United States and Mexico.

It is our purpose to be helpful to the organized labor movement of Mexico so that the workers of that country may attain a better life, a better living condition. In all our efforts in the past two years Col. Martinez and Mr. John Murray have been very helpful to us.

Treasurer Lennon stated that we might emphasize the proposition to get in a position to be helpful to prevent war. We want their views as to what they can do to maintain peace in both countries.

Vice-President Duncan said that we are hopeful of seeing the land owned by the people, the establishment of an industrial democracy. A thorough organization of the workers will be necessary to safeguard their rights and interests.

The representatives of Mexico stated that when their representatives arrived at the border for the purpose of a conference the first thing they did was to send a message back to their people, that they should do nothing to incite the minds of their people to war. They said up until now their government was doing everything that was agreed upon. They said if the Carranza government was crushed by intervention, it would crush labor and it would take 25 or 30 years to get what they now have secured. As a matter of fact the labor movement of Mexico is one and the same as the revolutionary movement as expressed in the constitutionalist government of which Carranza is the First Chief. The coming of the Mexicans into this country as strike breakers is the result of conditions existing in Mexico at the present time. What they regard as the most important thing now is to prevent war.

Vice-President Duncan asked what definite understanding have the representatives of the people had with Carranza in regard to opening up the land and making real citizens of peons. The representatives of the Mexican workers expressed confidence that the question is safe in the hands of the constitutionalist government. The agrarian question was one of the chief matters touched upon. The representatives of the Mexican workers said that they would take care of that question. In Yucatan they are making their first distribution of land. Carranza wants a Federal Law for the whole country. He would make a national agrarian law. The land has been distributed in many states;[10] during the past six months they have had an eight-hour law and a compulsory arbitration law.

The following are the principal trades organized: Bricklayers and Masons, Railroad Workers, Longshoremen, Machinists, Printers, and Smelters. They are endeavoring to organize the agricultural workers.

The question was asked, "What is the cause of the feeling against the Americans?["]

Representatives of the Mexican workers replied that the children were taught in school and those who are unable to read were told by their parents and their fellow-workers that in 1848 the American Government had despoiled Mexico of a large part of her territory; that the American corporations had gone into Mexico and had exploited the workers and tyrannized over them to such a degree that they were treated worse than under the Mexican employers and that this had not tended to lessen the feeling of anger against Americans; that in the railroads as well as in other establishments while owned by American capital, opportunities for holding preferred positions in industrial, commercial and transportation concerns were withheld from Mexicans notwithstanding they had equal ability with the Americans to perform the services.

The question was asked as to what increase in wages had been secured during the past year. Reply was given that in the Federal District of Mexico City the increase had amounted to 200 per cent. They are endeavoring to form a national labor movement; it has not assumed any special line of direction; there is no one line of thought; socialism, syndicalism and trade unionism are all represented in the labor movement.

Question. Has there been any religious persecution?[11]

Answer. No.

Question. Has there been any denial of the right of freedom of worship?

Answer. No.

Vice-President Duncan expressed the opinion that it would be well for the representatives to return to Mexico and when the war cloud has passed that a conference be held that would bring about some substantial results.

Vice-President Green thought that a meeting under such conditions would bring about the best results and that in the meantime the labor movement of both countries endeavor to bring about peace.

It was decided that the representatives of the Mexican workers remain in the city until Monday, when they would reconvene in conference with the Executive Council, and a joint statement could then be prepared and issued in the interests of peace.

It was decided that the conference reconvene at 4 o'clock on Monday afternoon.

For convenience the proceedings of the conference of the Executive Council with the representatives of the organized labor movement of Mexico which was reconvened on Monday afternoon, July 3d at four P.M., is transferred from the latter position in the record and inserted here for continuity.

In accordance with previous action the conference between the Executive Council and the representatives of the Mexican Workers was convened at 4:00 P.M. The following was adopted as a joint statement to be issued by the representatives of the Workers of Mexico and the American Federation of Labor:

Washington, D.C. July 3, 1916.

The undersigned, the Executive Council of the American Federation of Labor and the representatives of the organized labor movement of Mexico express our deep gratification in the consummation of this conference which we hope and believe has laid the basis for better understanding and has welded ties that shall bind together the workers of our respective countries.

We are confident that personal conferences of the workers of the United States and of Mexico will be a constructive force in bringing about understanding necessary for better relations between our countries and for maintaining peace founded upon a proper regard for the rights of all. It is our opinion that this conference should be followed by another in which the workers of both countries shall be more generally represented for the purpose of agreeing upon plans for maintaining permanent relations and for the federation of the labor movements of all of the countries of the two Americas.[12]

In view of present relations between the United States and Mexico we are of the opinion that such a general conference is for the present untimely and we express the judgment that the holding of such a conference should be deferred until later in the year. However, in the event of an emergency which would make a general conference of advantage in averting an international crisis, such a conference could and should be called for the earliest time mutually agreeable. To carry this plan into effect a joint commission shall be chosen to consist of two members from both labor movements to remain in Washington until the present crisis is passed, the said joint commission to have the power of calling a general conference if necessary.[13]

We hold this to be fundamental—no relations between our countries can be permanent that are not based upon the will of the masses of the people and in accord with their concepts of justice.

We deem it an essential step toward democracy and justice that there shall be established for the masses who have hitherto been without regular agencies for expressing their views and desires, opportunities that will enable them to have a voice in helping to determine international affairs.

The labor movements of the various countries constitute the instrumentalities that can best accomplish this purpose and give expression to national ideas and convictions that have been too long inarticulate and impotent.

We direct that the President of the American Federation of Labor and the official representatives of organized labor of Mexico should keep in touch through correspondence and that they be authorized to carry out the purposes specified in this declaration.

In joint conference as the representatives of the workers, the masses of our respective countries, we urge upon our governments to adjust existing differences without war and to establish conditions conducive to permanent peace with justice.

We appeal to the workers and all of the people of the United States and of Mexico to do everything within their power to promote correct understanding of purposes and actions, to prevent friction, to encourage good will, and to promote an intelligent national opinion that ultimately shall direct relations between our countries and shall be a potent humanitarian force in promoting world progress.

It is an unavoidable conclusion that present differences between our countries are the result of misunderstanding growing out of inadequate or incorrect information; that the unfortunate consequences of past relations between the United States and Mexico have formulated a national attitude that questions the good faith of our governments; that existing agencies and methods of reaching an adjustment of these differences are unsuitable for dealing with these problems which are fundamentally human problems; and that the relations between our countries ought not to be directed in accord with abstract standards of justice but ought to be keenly sensitive and responsive to the human interests and moral forces. Therefore, we, the representatives of the organized workers, having the right to speak for all of the workers and in the interests of all of the people, urge upon our governments the appointment of a commission to be composed of high-minded citizens, fully representative of our nations, to consider differences that have brought our nations to the verge of war and to make such recommendations for adjustment as shall fitly express the highest ideals of the great rank and file of the citizenship of our two countries.

We direct that copies of this declaration shall be presented to the President of the United States, Honorable Woodrow Wilson, and to the First Chief of the Constitutionalist government of Mexico, General Venustiano Carranza, and that it be given widest publicity among the workers of our respective countries.

For the organized workers of the United States:

Sam'l. Gompers   President.

James Duncan   1st Vice-President.

James O'Connell,   2nd Vice-President.

D. A. Hayes   3rd Vice-President.

Jos. F. Valentine   4th Vice-President.

John R. Alpine   5th Vice-President.

H. B. Perham   6th Vice-President.

Frank Duffy   7th Vice-President.

Wm. Green   8th Vice-President.

John B. Lennon   Treasurer.

Frank Morrison   Secretary.

For the organized workers of Mexico:

C. Loveira.

Baltasar Pages.

L. N. Morones.

S. Gonzalo Garcia.

Edmundo E. Martinez.

. . .

TDc, Executive Council Records, Minutes, reel 5, frames 1201–2, 1204–9, *AFL Records.*

1. Legislation creating the Council of National Defense was included as a provision of the army appropriations act for the fiscal year ending June 30, 1917, and became law on Aug. 29, 1916 (U.S. *Statutes at Large,* 39: 619–70).

2. Luis N. MORONES Negrete was a founder of the Confederación del Trabajo de la Región Mexicana (Confederation of Labor of the Mexican Region) in 1916.

3. Salvador González García.

4. In October 1911 Mother Jones, Frank Hayes of the United Mine Workers of America, and Joseph Cannon of the Western Federation of Miners met with Francisco Madero and obtained his assurances that they would be allowed to organize Mexican miners.

5. Edmundo Martínez addressed the AFL Executive Council during its September 1915 meeting in Washington, D.C.

6. "To Venustiano Carranza," June 28, 1916, above.

7. See "To William McAdoo," July 2, 1915, above.

8. SG wrote AFL organizer Emmet Flood on June 28, 1916, to tell him of the upcoming conference between Mexican labor representatives and the AFL. SG asked Flood to disseminate this information and report to him about Mexican workers in his area of the country (reel 209, vol. 221, pp. 651–53, SG Letterbooks, DLC). SG sent a similar letter to a number of other AFL organizers the same day (ibid., pp. 654–62, 671–73).

9. On May 1, 1916, foundry workers and molders employed by the Illinois Malleable Iron Co. in Chicago struck for a wage increase; estimates of the number of strikers involved ranged from eight hundred to over two thousand. The strike was unsuccessful.

10. A decree of Jan. 6, 1915, authorized state governors or military commanders to return illegally taken hacienda lands to their respective villages.

11. Frank Duffy raised this issue at the February 1916 meeting of the AFL Executive Council, quoting a statement made by Bishop Emile Cloutier of Trois-Rivières, Que., that Carranza and his followers were "terrorizing Mexico, pursuing the Priests and martyrizing the Sisters, and causing death everywhere" (Executive Council Records, Minutes, reel 5, frame 1179, *AFL Records*). Acting at the direction of the Council, SG met on Apr. 5 with Secretary of State Robert Lansing and the chief of the division of Mexican affairs, Leon Joseph Canova, to investigate the matter and was assured that such accusations were without foundation. For Carranza's denial of the charges, see Martínez to SG, June 27, 1916, Files of the Office of the President, General Correspondence, reel 80, frames 887–91, *AFL Records*.

12. SG met with Santiago Iglesias, Carlos Loveira y Chirinos, and John Murray at AFL headquarters in Washington, D.C., on Jan. 31, 1917, and established a Pan-American Federation of Labor Conference Committee to lay the groundwork for the Pan-American Federation of Labor.

13. On July 6, 1916, the Mexican delegates decided that because the immediate crisis had passed it was unnecessary for a delegation to remain in Washington, D.C.

An Address at the Dedication of the AFL Office Building, Washington, D.C.

[July 4, 1916]

· · ·

Fellow workingmen and women, fellow citizens and friends: In the name of the great labor movement of our country I greet you and bid you welcome on this day and on this occasion when we are assembled to perform a double duty—the one which primarily brings us together here, to dedicate this splendid Temple of Labor and the day, the celebration of our independence as the Republic of the United States.

Several of our friends have asked me whether the day was not illy chosen and whether we might not have more fittingly celebrated or dedicated this structure on Labor Day. My answer was in substance that in the capital of our nation the American Federation of Labor building could be dedicated on no day quite so fitting as the Fourth of July, when we hoped, as we have realized, that the President of the United States would address this assemblage.[1]

My friends, it is a most difficult task for me to know just how to address you and what to say, and yet I take it you would not have me deal in a few generalities and thank you for your attention. May I then not say that this occasion affords the opportunity for the deepest reflection. Bear in mind that in the cycle of time, it has been only a few short years since the formation of the A.F. of L.—thirty-five or six years count but little. If, however, we take a retrospective view of the conditions of the toiling masses even of our country and compare the physical conditions, the economic situation and standards, the political contrasts and the wonderful changes which have come about in the life and the work and the rights and the hopes and the aspirations and the ideals of the toilers of our country, it is sufficient to cause us not only to pause but to give credit to those who have gone before, to renew the confidence we have in the men and the women of our time, and to look forward with an eye and a vision for the future that promises a world of happiness, of justice, of freedom, and the best concepts of humanity for all our people.

In the early days of the American labor movement it happened that through inexperience, coupled with high-mindedness, altruism, selfishness, sordidness, our movement could not have any cohesive existence nor a long continued career, and thus the organizations of labor sprung up over night and died in the morn. It has been to the credit of the A.F. of L. that for the first time in the history of the organized movement of the workers of our country, there has been a steadfast growth and development, a continuity and expansion of thought and hope and activity, always maintaining as one star in our mind to lead on and on and on. Though you and you and you and I have all been impatient with the apparent slow growth, the superficially slow growth in the achievement of the rights to which we claim the toilers are entitled, all too slow in the abolition and the remedying of the wrongs to which the toilers have too long been compelled to endure, yet our progress onward and upward has been sure and steady. I am as impatient as the most impatient among you, but when I take a retrospective view of the material, of the political, and of the social conditions at the time when the A.F. of L. was given to the world, and compare them with the conditions on this Independence Day, July 4, 1916, there is cause for gratification and jubilation, which gives us the incentive and whets our appetites and desires to the determination to go on and on and on in the attainment of every right to which the toilers are entitled, and the abolition of all wrongs which they have too long endured.

If those of you who are of mature years will bring your minds back, and, if you of more recent times, who may have read or heard of conditions prevailing in the olden time, will imagine the contrast when the doors of men and women in decent homes were closed in the faces of the men who dared preach the gospel of the rights of labor, and contrast that situation with now, this glorious era in which we live, when at the dedication of this magnificent structure erected for the service in the cause of labor, justice, freedom, and humanity, we find the President of this great Republic of ours adorning this occasion, with not only his presence, but the presence of members of his Cabinet, you will find a marvelous change. From the time of slavery, when all the workers, not only the blacks but the whites were slaves, when the owner, the master, was the lord of all, when there were none to say to him nay against his overlordship over those men and women workers whom he owned, from the time of serfdom to our institutions of industry of today, there has been a growth that dazzles the mind. This is a wonderful age in which we are privileged to live. There has been running through the course of history the struggle of the masses of the people, the hewers of wood and the drawers of water. Wherever injustice and tyranny were exercised, it was the masses, it was the people, the workers, who suffered. It was and is the mission of the masses of the people, it is the mission of the workers of our time, it is the mission of the much misunderstood and misrepresented organized labor movement, to carry on the work to its fulfillment so that the wonderful sentiment and view and rights declared in our Declaration of Independence, that man is endowed with certain inalienable rights, and that among these are the right to life, liberty and the pursuit of happiness, shall not only be a declaration that was given to the world but shall establish a new status and a new concept of new rights of man.

That declaration gave to us this Republic of ours with all its opportunities and it is the purpose of the organized labor movement of America to make these declarations a charter of human rights, the living actual rules of our every-day life. Men are not necessarily free because declarations of independence so declare. Men are not necessarily free because the Constitution guarantees freedom. Men are given the opportunities for freedom and they must, if they aim to be free, exercise the activities that come with the intelligent free men.

Through a long series of years there have come to the workers influences and activities that place them in a different category and occupying a different status from the rest of the citizenship of our country. This is not the time nor the occasion for criticism. All that is required or appropriate is to mention or to refer to facts that under interpretation of laws and extension of jurisdiction, the men and women of labor were placed in the category of products, inanimate products of labor. It was not conceded or understood in such concepts that in contrast to attributes of property and products the worker had a heart and a mind and a soul and that his labor could be separated from his very being, his very life. To place human labor in the same category with wood and coal and beef, cloth and wool and iron is to declare at the same time that the man who purchased that labor power is the master and owner of the worker.

It was because of the recognition of this unjustice, this unjust status into which we were temporarily forced, that the American labor movement resolved that come what may, every effort must be bent toward securing a legislative declaration solemnly enacted into law, that the labor power, the labor of human beings is not a commodity or article of commerce. Due to the campaign of organization and agitation and education and the driving force of our cause in the political arena, we finally prevailed upon our Congress to pass the labor provisions of the Clayton Antitrust law. The Honorable Woodrow Wilson was afforded the grand opportunity to affix his signature to the law.

My friends, there is not an overabundance of our own people who understand what is really contained in that declaration in section 6 of the Clayton Antitrust law. It solemnly enacts this declaration into law, that the labor of a human being is not a commodity or article of commerce, and for the first time in the history of the struggles of the human race, for the first time a high legislative body, or for that, any legislative body, in the world, repudiated the old doctrine that the labor of a human being is property, that the labor of a human being is a commodity, that the labor of a human being is an article of commerce.

In addition to that, supplementary to it, the enactment of the seamen's law gave greater security to life and to property at sea, and at the same time gave the opportunity to the seamen of the United States to be free in the ownership of themselves and their labor power when their vessels were in safe harbor. Quite apart from the other constructive legislation enacted by the Congress of the United States and by the legislatures of our several states if they were entirely barren of any results, the enactment of these two laws, the labor provisions of the Clayton Antitrust law and the Seamen's law, are themselves a monument to our civilization, larger vision, broader humanitarianism and highest concepts of human liberty. These two acts in themselves stand out as such a monument.

Just a word and I shall have done. The labor movement of our time is concerned in securing a larger share, a better reward as the result of the services that the workers give to society, but quite apart from a demand for a higher wage, for a shorter workday, for relief from burdensome toil, for the securement of safety, sanitation, workmen's compensation, old-age pensions, the labor movement of our country and our time, demands the right and opportunity to take part in all the affairs and in all the activities of our public life. The demand is justified by the service rendered, without which even civilization itself could not endure.

The toilers, the sovereign citizenship, together with the sovereign citizens of all other groups, make a demand that there shall be but one purpose, one hope, one struggle, and one ideal, the perpetuation of this republic, improved, handed down to those who follow us, that they may in their time say, well done, thou good and faithful servants.

There is not any act on the part of our government, there is no activity in any group of our people, in which the wage-workers, the toiling masses, are not concerned. Let us do all that we can do to help the man at the head of the affairs of our country who is weighted down with great responsibilities, the President of the United States, to see to it that we are kept out of actual war with any nation. We know how seriously and earnestly he is striving to achieve peace, but in order that his wise and humane purposes may be carried into effect it will require the loyal and intelligent support of the masses of the people of our country. We, his fellow-citizens who want peace, have a duty to perform. No man in all the world can stand alone. A man may become a hermit and try to free himself from his former environment but he is not alone and can not be alone. There are new conditions which confront and surround him. So I say, my friends, it is not only to believe in peace, it is not only the desire for peace, but let us give out the clarion call to our people that we by every honorable means at our command are going to see to it that the policy of trying to maintain peace shall be sustained. And yet I say that if after every honorable effort has been made and peace is no longer possible and the horrors of war shall come to us or be forced upon us, let me say this not only for myself, but for all the workers, for I believe I express the spirit and the purpose of the men in the labor movement of America, that they may be counted upon to give a good account of themselves.

Men and women, friends, and those of you who are wage-earners, I doubt the necessity and yet I can not close without abjuring you to see to it that those who are not members of organized labor join that movement at once. We may not always be right—we are human and are liable to err. If you know better than we, come in and make the contribution of your intelligence to the sum total and leaven it up. If you are honest and earnest and patriotic, come into the organizations and help us in the great work of upbuilding and to spread the gospel of the rights of Labor, and the duties and the obligations of the workers.

And you business men and public men and professional men, may I not appeal to you to take a broader view of this labor movement of ours than many of you have taken in the past? See to it that you endeavor to conduct your affairs in accord with the ideas and the purposes of the labor movement. Help us in this great, rational, natural constructive work to bring light and hope into the life and the work of the toilers of our country, and to help build up character and manhood and womanhood in the life and the hearts and the minds of the toilers. Help us that the children may have a broader and a better day than the men and the women of our time had during their child life. See to it that the citizenship shall have the opportunity of growth and development and to become one homogeneous citizenship, the manhood and the womanhood of today and the children of our time that they may take up the work where we were compelled to lay it down and carry on the good work to carry the good word on and on and on until the time shall come when man to man shall be a brother for a' that and a' that. So that time may come I plead with you on this sanctified holy day to be true to yourselves, true to each other, true to the organized labor movement, true to the institutions and the flag of our country, when we shall uphold in all times and against all obstacles no matter from which quarter they may come.

. . .

American Federationist 23 (Aug. 1916): 660–62.

1. President Woodrow Wilson's address at the ceremony dedicating the AFL office building is printed in the August 1916 issue of the *American Federationist* (23: 662–64).

To Warren Stone

July 7, 1916.

Personal and Confidential.
Mr. Warren S. Stone,
President, Brotherhood of Locomotive Engineers,[1]
B. of L.E. Bldg., Cleveland, Ohio.
Dear Sir and Brother:

Information comes to me from such high sources that its authenticity cannot be questioned, which is of utmost importance to the railroad brotherhoods.

Agents of the railroad companies are active in creating a mental attitude in Congress favorable to the enactment of a law authorizing the Federal Trade Commission to investigate the demands[2] of the railroad brotherhoods and to render a decision in regard to them which shall be enforced by the government.

In view of the declarations of the representatives of the railroad brotherhoods in regard to arbitration of a voluntary nature, I felt that this information ought to be in your possession as your organization would desire to defeat such legislation.

Should the railroad interests succeed in the enactment of a compulsory arbitration law, providing for compulsory investigation and arbitration and enforcement of award by the government, it would be a catastrophe that would react upon all of the workers of the country. Compulsory arbitration for the men of the railroad brotherhoods would deprive them of the protection and the advantages that they have secured through long years of effort and struggle backed by the power of their economic organizations.

This proposed procedure would take out of the hands of the railroad brotherhoods control over hours of work, wages and conditions of work. In a word, it would nullify all that has been secured through economic organization and finally would nullify economic organization itself.

Ever since economic organization was first proposed in this country, I have vigorously and unreservedly opposed the principle upon which it is based. The principle is subversive to industrial freedom.

In my writings, editorials and public utterances I have repeatedly taken issue with advocates of compulsory arbitration as well as the proposals of all other theorists who would establish a substitute for economic organization.

In order to defeat this danger that is impending to the railroad brotherhoods, you ought to have your legislative representatives on the ground to make active, insistent opposition and prevent the enactment of a law that would endanger the welfare of the members of your organization and which would be a precedent subversive to the best interests of all the workers of the country.

Let me assure you that efforts to prevent this catastrophe will have my hearty cooperation and assistance.

Fraternally yours,   Saml Gompers.
President   American Federation of Labor.[3]

TLpS, reel 209, vol. 221, pp. 951–52, SG Letterbooks, DLC.

1. The Brotherhood of LOCOMOTIVE Engineers.

2. On Mar. 30, 1916, the railroad brotherhoods, representing more than three hundred thousand workers, presented a demand for an eight-hour workday to the representatives of over four hundred fifty of the nation's railroads. The railroads rejected the proposal, and when negotiations in June were unproductive they called for federal arbitration. The railroad workers then voted to strike and set Sept. 4, Labor Day, for the walkout. After mediation efforts and an attempt by President Woodrow Wilson to broker an agreement proved fruitless, Wilson appealed to Congress on Aug. 29 to prevent a national railroad strike. He called for legislation giving an eight-hour day to railroad workers and amending the Newlands Mediation, Conciliation, and Arbitration Act of 1913 (see "To George Young," Jan. 24, 1914, n. 13, above) to bar a strike or lockout until a full public investigation could be held. Democratic congressman William Adamson of Georgia introduced an eight-hour bill in the House of Representatives (H.R. 17,700, 64th Cong., 1st sess.) on the afternoon of Aug. 31. Republican congressman John Sterling of Illinois offered a compulsory investigation provision as an amendment to Adamson's bill, but it was ruled out of order and was not included in the final version of the legislation passed by Congress (U.S. *Statutes at Large*, 39: 721–22). President Wilson signed the Adamson Act into law on Sept. 3, a Sunday, and then signed it again on Sept. 5 to avoid a challenge on that account. Several railroads secured injunctions against enforcement of the act, which established an eight-hour day for railroad workers as of Jan. 1, 1917, and in November they initiated a test case to challenge its constitutionality. The case was argued before the U.S. Supreme Court in early January 1917, and that court handed down a five-to-four decision on Mar. 19 upholding the Adamson Act (*Wilson* v. *New et al.,* 243 U.S. 332 [1917]).

3. On July 7, 1916, SG also sent this letter to William Carter, president of the Brotherhood of Locomotive Firemen and Enginemen, A. E. King, secretary of the Brotherhood of Railroad Trainmen, and C. E. Whitney, secretary of the Order of Railway Conductors of America (reel 209, vol. 221, pp. 945–46, 949–50, 953–54, SG Letterbooks, DLC).

To Samuel Young[1]

July 7, 1916.

Mr. S. B. M. Young,
President, Association for National Service, Inc.,[2]
Metropolitan Bank Bldg., Washington, D.C.
Dear Sir:

Your letter of June 21st is received.

While there is much in your letter with which I am in hearty accord, there is one expression from which I must dissent. Your statement is that "the youth of our nation would receive an education in physical hygiene, discipline and respect for authority."

My experience has been that we cannot respect authority simply because it is authority, but authority must earn our respect because it is right. Constituted authority has in many instances been guilty of gross wrong and injustice. Against such conditions the ideals of liberty require that the right of revolution must be retained. Revolution, of course, is not to be undertaken lightly but when other courses have failed—it must be retained as a reserve protection for men and women who wish to exercise their rights as free citizens.

I do not think that we would be promoting the best interests of our Republic or the best development of our nation if we taught our youth merely to respect constituted authority. Such a policy would result in subservience and facile obedience and would be subversive to initiative and independence.

I have already done something to contribute to the thought of our country upon the subject of national preparedness and the ideals that ought to direct all our policies for that purpose. I have written several articles, and would be glad to write others when that can be done consistent with my other duties, but I am writing you rather fully because I do not wish to be misunderstood upon this one point which I have amplified.

Very sincerely yours,   Saml Gompers.
President   American Federation of Labor.

TLpS, reel 209, vol. 221, pp. 947–48, SG Letterbooks, DLC.

1. Lt. Gen. Samuel Baldwin Marks Young was a veteran of the Civil and Spanish-American wars, the governor of the U.S. Soldiers Home (1910–20), and an advocate of universal military training.

2. The Association for National Service (from 1918, the National Association for Universal Military Training) was organized by Col. Henry Sheets in 1916 to promote equal and universal military service.

From Emma Steghagen

National Women's Trade Union League of America
Chicago July 10, 1916.

Dear Mr. Gompers:—

Enclosed you will find our regular News Letter. Thank you for taking the time to read it. I know how busy you are, and appreciate the favor.

In your acknowledgment[1] of our last number you said that you would urge me to keep in mind the fact that trade unionism must be made paramount because the trade union movement is that from which the workers must expect protection and betterment. I agree absolutely with you in that. The policy of the Boot and Shoe Workers Union,[2] of which I am a member, is based upon "Organization First." We even go so far as to grant the union stamp to manufacturers upon complete organization of their factories at the existing rate of wages no matter how low they are—confident that wages and conditions invariably improve through organization.

I was one of the thirty delegates who at our Convention in 1899 in Rochester, N.Y. adopted the program of "Organization First," and "High Dues" which has been so successful in our trade. Legislation and all the other activities of the Trade Union Movement in my opinion is only a means to an end—Organization. And while I am on this matter of "Organization First" I want to let you know also how keen I am about reaching the wives of union men and bringing to them the trade union idea. Last week the Chicago Women's Trade Union League held a meeting for the wives and children of the Illinois Malleable Iron Workers who are on strike. The meeting was a great success. There were about 400 women and children present. The women—most of whom are Polish—were very much impressed, and as one of the men told me a few days after the meeting they are not so eager to "chase" their husbands back to work, for they understand now what trade unionism means.

I want to thank you again for giving your valuable time to the perusal of our News Letter.

With best wishes,

Fraternally yours,   Emma Steghagen
Secretary-Treasurer.

TLS, AFL Microfilm Convention File, reel 27, frame 2195, *AFL Records*.

1. SG to Emma Steghagen, May 22, 1916, reel 208, vol. 220, p. 475, SG Letterbooks, DLC.

2. The Boot and Shoe Workers' Union.

To William Foster[1]

July 11, 1916.

Mr. William Z. Foster,
2205 N. Kimball Avenue, Chicago, Ill.
Dear Sir and Brother:

Your favor of the 7th instant reached here today and I have read the contents of your letter with interest. Yes, it is true that I desired to talk with you and when we had not the chance, I asked you to write me as a reminder. I had heard that in recent times you have taken an active part as an advocate and defender of true trade unionism. I had read some of your letters or articles[2] in the Lumbermen's Union[3] Official Journal and all these interested me, and it occurred to me that you might render a valuable service to the toiling masses of our country to a clearer understanding of their duty as workers and as trade unionists than prevails in the minds of many. Your past experiences and associations, together with your mental development should certainly prove an advantageous lesson to those who have not yet seen the true light of all that true trade unionism portends. Perhaps you might care to write a letter or an article upon this phase of the movement and should be glad if you consent to publish the same in the *American Federationist.*

The position you took upon the subject of Labor Day demonstration in Chicago was founded upon the best concept of the activities of the labor movement in the city. Now in many cities Labor Day is passed off as a pleasurable occasion without any significance whatever, and as a matter of fact, Labor Day is distinctively Labor's Day, and all the newspapers, weeks before each Labor Day and on Labor Day and the day after, give space to labor's cause which it would be impossible for labor to purchase in the form of advertisement. We spend large sums of money for agitation and education and yet when we can obtain it at the small cost of a Labor Day parade and without the expenditure of more than a few dollars, many central bodies will surrender the advantage and, as I say, lose the distinctive character and significance of Labor Day. I was astonished to hear Mr. Neary say that the only advantage of Labor Day was for the musicians. Of course, the musicians receive pay when they perform service. That is their work. If they were asked to parade with other labor bodies without performing their work, that is, without giving music, they would parade and would ask no compensation, but when they are expected to give their services and perform their work on Labor Day, they are entitled to compensation.

Is it too late to have a Labor Day parade for Chicago 1916?[4] I think not, and hope not.

Kindly let me hear from you in regard to these matters or any others.

With best wishes, I am,

Fraternally yours,　Saml Gompers.
President　American Federation of Labor.

TLpS, reel 210, vol. 222, pp. 84–85, SG Letterbooks, DLC.

1. In 1915 and 1916 William Z. FOSTER served as the business agent of the Chicago district council of the Brotherhood of Railway Carmen of America.

2. While working as an organizer for the International Union of Timberworkers in Seattle, Foster wrote several articles for the union's journal, the *Timber Worker*, in support of trade unionism, including "Too Many Unions" and "Are Trade Unions Revolutionary?"

3. The International Union of TIMBERWORKERS.

4. Chicago did not have a citywide Labor Day parade in 1916, but celebrations were held in South Chicago and nearby Joliet.

To John Frey

July 13, 1916.

Mr. John P. Frey,
Editor, International Molders' Journal,
Room 707, Commercial-Tribune Bldg., Cincinnati, Ohio.
Dear Sir and Brother:—

In your letter of July 7[1] you ask what policy I intend to follow in regard to the decision of the Massachusetts Supreme Court declaring the Massachusetts Injunction Law unconstitutional.[2]

You no doubt have noted in the decision of the Massachusetts Supreme Court that it holds that labor is property and by a species of sophistry, evidently for the purpose of smoothing over the court's own misinterpretation, states that it is the property of the human being, and it is only upon that basis that it can even make some apparent impression that the labor of a human being is property.

I should say that I have already written[3] to the attorneys[4] who had charge of the case for further information and as to what is contemplated to be done in the near future upon the subject, whether an appeal or rehearing can be had. I have also written[5] to the representative of labor[6] of Massachusetts upon the same subject.

In the next issue of the *American Federationist* I intend to publish an article[7] which Andrew Furuseth wrote and I also intend to comment upon the decision editorially.[8] The position that I shall take is that the court is mistaken in declaring against the fundamental principle that the labor of a human being is not a commodity or article of commerce. The court could only reach its decision by ignoring all the facts that throw light upon industrial and social conditions and by making a fetish out of legal precedence. In other words, as Junius says some place, "The court has had more regard for authority than for information."[9] This is due of course to the training that is given to all law students and the emphasis that is laid upon authority and precedent. This training is usually reinforced by the natural disposition of the jurist to withdraw himself from the rough struggle of everyday life and to maintain a sort of judicial isolation.

The point I expect to make is that a change must come in the mental attitude of judges. If judges already occupying office can not understand the fundamentals of human liberty and are not willing to study the primer which President Wilson says he is ready to open for them, then they must give way to others of greater understanding. This is an outline of what I had in mind for editorial purposes.

I sincerely hope that you will join in the effort to drive home the necessity of this campaign that must be undertaken by the organized labor movement.

I hope that you will write me from time to time of any special facts of this struggle which you may think it profitable for us to discuss. There is so much information to be digested and we are all so busy that we can best serve our purposes by pooling our thoughts and frequent discussion or correspondence.

With best wishes, I am,

Fraternally yours,   Saml Gompers.
President,   A.F. of L.

TLpS, reel 210, vol. 222, pp. 234–35, SG Letterbooks, DLC.

1. John Frey to SG, July 7, 1916, AFL Microfilm National and International Union File, Molders Records, reel 40, frame 2021, *AFL Records.*

2. On May 19, 1916, the Supreme Judicial Court of Massachusetts overturned the state's 1914 labor law (Massachusetts, Laws of 1914, chap. 778; see "To John Golden," Mar. 31, 1915, n. 4, above). The court ruled the law unconstitutional on the grounds that the right to work was a property right protected by the U.S. Constitution, rather than a personal right, which was the contention of the statute (*John Bogni et al. v. Giovanni Perotti et al.,* 224 Mass. 152 [1916]).

3. SG to Frederick Mansfield, July 7, 1916, reel 210, vol. 222, p. 31, SG Letterbooks, DLC.

4. James A. Donovan and Frederick W. Mansfield served as defense attorneys in the case.

5. SG to Martin Joyce, July 6, 1916, reel 209, vol. 221, pp. 933–34, SG Letterbooks, DLC.

6. Martin T. JOYCE, who served as secretary-treasurer of the Massachusetts State Federation of Labor from 1911 to 1931.

7. Andrew Furuseth, "Americans, Wake Up!" *American Federationist* 23 (Aug. 1916): 653–57.

8. "Massachusetts Court Filches Workers' Rights," *American Federationist* 23 (Aug. 1916): 685–87.

9. "Letter LXVIII: To Lord Chief Justice Mansfield," published in the *London Public Advertiser* on Jan. 21, 1772.

To M. Grant Hamilton

July 21, 1916.

Mr. Grant Hamilton,
3344 Decatur Street, Denver, Colorado.
Dear Sir and Brother:

In reply to your letter of July 9th, in which you make a report upon Federal Labor Union No. 13153[1] of Alamosa, Colorado, I am very glad indeed to learn that you think better conditions can be secured for these workers and that the union can be made stronger and more effective.

The element that you describe as operating to separate Spanish-American workers from United States workers is one of the insidious forces that the trade union movement must try to overthrow. It is to be hoped and anticipated from the better relations that are now being established between the labor movement of Mexico and that of the United States that it will have a reflex effect upon conditions in the United States and help to break down all barriers and unite the workers in support of their common demands and interests. Whatever you can do to contribute to the defeat of this effort in Alamosa will no doubt have a salutary effect throughout the whole of Colorado.

In your letter you state that when the strength of the organization becomes sufficient you will assist the union in formulating its demands and presenting them to the company, and suggest that in the event the company refuses to make concessions, a request be made for sanction to strike.

I think the plan you have suggested a wise one, and will have in mind your request that should a strike become necessary, authority should be given at the earliest moment possible moment as the busy season is rapidly approaching.

I note also what you say relative to the requirement of the law[2] that the Industrial Commission ought to be notified before a strike is declared, and that you state you are willing to incur the liability of a jail sentence. That course of action would, of course, be helpful in securing the repeal of the law and is characteristic of your usual fighting spirit.

From several letters that I have received it is apparent that the campaign to repeal the law providing for compulsory investigation is making headway. Mr. Houston,[3] in a letter to me assures me that he has never been favorable to the principle upon which the law is based, but that he thinks the present commission has given the workers a square deal. He stated that he published information in regard to the activities of the commission and particularly the address of Mr. Williams[4] as news. His position, however, does not recognize the power of an editor and the opportunity that he has to make news and mold public opinion. Perhaps he will come to an understanding of that later.

Let me suggest that you have a conference with Ed Anderson[5] of Pueblo, Colorado. He is awake to the necessary for amending this law.

Let me hear from you frequently, and with best wishes, I am,

Fraternally yours,   Saml Gompers.
President   American Federation of Labor.

TLpS, reel 210, vol. 222, pp. 587–89, SG Letterbooks, DLC.

1. The AFL chartered Federal Labor Union 13,153 of Alamosa, Colo., in 1911.

2. Colorado, *Laws of 1915*, chap. 180, enacted Apr. 10, 1915, established the Industrial Commission of Colorado with authority to supervise the enforcement of labor legislation in the state, investigate labor conditions and relations between employers and employees, and encourage the voluntary arbitration, mediation, and conciliation of labor disputes. Employers and employees in Colorado were required to give the commission thirty days' notice of any changes in hours or wages and were prohibited from engaging in a strike or lockout over a dispute while the commission was investigating the matter.

3. Clinton Craig HOUSTON was editor of the *Labor Bulletin* in Denver from 1913 to 1918.

4. Wayne C. Williams, a Denver attorney, served as a member of the Industrial Commission of Colorado.

5. Edward E. ANDERSON served as vice-president (1911–15) and secretary-treasurer (1916–22) of the Colorado State Federation of Labor.

To Charles Baine[1]

July 31, 1916.

Mr. C. L. Baine,
Secretary, Boot and Shoe Workers' Union,
246 Summer St., Boston, Mass.
Dear Sir and Brother:

Some time ago a matter was brought to the attention of the Executive Council which is of interest to your organization.

An official of one of the internationals who lives in Canada reported that an effort was being made to discredit the international labor movement, to inject partisan politics into labor unions and to promote "religious" labor unions in Canada.[2]

A translation from a report[3] that appeared in the Le Bien Publique of Three Rivers, Canada, states that Archbishop Cloutier, in speaking of trade unions, instructed the workers of his church that they ought to belong to labor organizations that were strictly religious and that they ought not to belong to "neutral" societies. The Archbishop vigorously condemned so-called neutral or international organizations, which are the American organizations. He even asserted that international organizers ought to be prevented from having halls in which to hold meetings. In the sermon an effort was made to identify the work of the American trade union movement with violence and dynamiting and campaigns of organized vengeance. The President of the American Federation of Labor was condemned for the policy that has been pursued in connection with Mexico and for the relations that have been established with the Carranza government. General Carranza was accused of being in collusion with a band of bandits and pursuing the priests and martyrizing the sisters in Mexico.

The Executive Council has no way of estimating just how extensive this campaign to establish religious unions in Canada and to destroy the international organizations has become. It may be that the statement of the Archbishop is not representative of the general church policy, and the facts are presented for your information and guidance.

Since the organization of the American Federation of Labor one of the fundamental principles has been that neither religion, party politics nor any kindred subject was the concern of the trade union movement. Upon these matters trade unionists have the right to their own opinions and their own determinations. As members of trade unions they were concerned with those things upon which there was common agreement and which involved common welfare.

The trade union movement has tried to keep itself free from all religious differences and discussion. It has always held against discussion of these matters within the union and has prevented any effort on the outside to inject these questions into the policies and purposes of the labor movement.

So far as the United States is concerned we have succeeded. Members of trade unions are free to belong to any church they desire, whether Catholic or Protestant, Mohammedan or whatnot. On the other hand, the meetings of local unions, the conventions of the American Federation of Labor have confined their deliberations to the economic needs and demands of the workers. The trade union movement will permit no interference or dictation in the management of economic policies, and it does not attempt to interfere in other spheres which do not properly belong to its jurisdiction. This policy is essential, for the labor movement can succeed only when it holds itself free from all entangling alliances and maintains itself untrammeled in a position to use its full power to secure the demands of the workers.

There is a distinct menace to the workers of this country and Canada in any movement that threatens the international form of organization. The boundary line between the United States and Canada is only an artificial division that constitutes no real barrier to economic and commercial development and unity. Industrial and commercial relations are determined by topographical conditions and by transportation facilities.

Since there is no division between the interests of employers of Canada and those of the United States there can be no division or boundary line to labor organizations if the workers are to be protected and their best interests conserved.

Let me urge that your organization ought to do everything within its power to further the international idea and closer relations between the workers of Canada and those of the United States in your trade. I am sure that when the facts in the case are presented to the Canadian workers they will understand that international organization will in no way interfere with the freedom of their religion or their independence in all other ways.

If you have any information in regard to the subject about which I am writing, I shall be very glad indeed if you will share that information with me.[4]

With best wishes, I am,

Fraternally yours, Saml Gompers.
President American Federation of Labor.

TLpS, reel 211, vol. 223, pp. 123–26, SG Letterbooks, DLC.

1. Charles L. BAINE served as secretary-treasurer of the Boot and Shoe Workers' Union from 1902 to 1931.

2. At a January 1916 meeting of the executive board of the United Brotherhood of Carpenters and Joiners of America, Arthur Martel, a member of the board from Montreal, reported on the activities of religious labor unions in Canada against AFL internationals and submitted a translation from the Quebec newspaper *Le Bien Publique* summarizing Bishop Emile Cloutier's criticisms of American trade unions. The Carpenters referred the matter to the AFL and to the Trades and Labor Congress of Canada (Frank Duffy to SG, Jan. 26, 1916, Files of the Office of the President, General Correspondence, reel 80, frame 105, *AFL Records*).

3. A copy of this translation can be found in the United Brotherhood of Carpenters and Joiners of America Records, reel 2, frame 5, *AFL and the Unions*.

4. Baine replied on Aug. 22, 1916, that his union had encountered opposition from the Catholic Church in Quebec for many years and had been unsuccessful in organizing north of Montreal or in Trois-Rivières. He added, however, that he believed this antagonism was on the decline (Files of the Office of the President, General Correspondence, reel 81, frames 295–96, *AFL Records*).

To Ralph Easley

August 2, 1916.

Mr. Ralph M. Easley,
Chairman, Executive Council, National Civic Federation,
Metropolitan Tower, New York City.
Dear Sir:

The Executive Council at its recent session beginning July 24th,[1] among other matters considered the proposal submitted to them by the National Civic Federation:—that the Executive Council should urge upon Congress that a joint investigation be conducted by the Department of Labor and the Department of Commerce in response to a resolution of Congress calling upon these branches of the government for an investigation of minimum wage legislation.[2] After duly considering this matter, the Executive Council decided that it is not advisable at the present time to ask for this investigation, as the investigation would only serve the interests of that group of individuals who have most to gain from the investigation and from minimum wage legislation—the group of professional workers and students for whom positions would be created by the investigation and the adoption of minimum wage legislation.

The American Federation of Labor expresses the opinions and the demands directly of the organized workers and indirectly of the unorganized. From neither the organized or the unorganized does there come a general demand for minimum wage legislation. In our opinion, therefore, it would be a mistake to call attention to the theories of professionals by the undue prominence that would be inevitably associated with such an investigation. Many times the American Federation of Labor has made plain that it holds this of fundamental importance. The workers will not delegate to any outsiders control over the labor movement or the right to dictate terms and conditions of employment. Our position is clear and the members of the Executive Council did not regard the proposed investigation as expedient at the present time.

With best wishes, I am,

Fraternally yours, Saml Gompers.
President American Federation of Labor.

TLpS, reel 211, vol. 223, pp. 46–47, SG Letterbooks, DLC.

1. The AFL Executive Council met in Atlantic City, N.J., July 24–29, 1916.

2. Ralph Easley had forwarded the National Civic Federation (NCF) proposal to SG on Feb. 21, 1916, and the February meeting of the AFL Executive Council had deferred consideration of the matter until a later time. The proposal embodied a report of the NCF Minimum Wage Commission, which recommended that Congress direct a joint investigation of minimum wage legislation by the Departments of Labor and Commerce.

To William Foster

August 2, 1916.

Mr. William Z. Foster,
Business Agent, Brotherhood of Railway Carmen of A.,
2205 N. Kimball Ave. Chicago, Ill.
Dear Sir and Brother:

In your letter of July 23rd you say that you have in mind writing for the September issue of the *American Federationist* an article showing the gradual encroachment of the Socialist Party upon the trade union movement. I think you are mistaken in your conclusion that the Socialist Party has been growing in power. During the recent past I have had numbers of letters from members of the Socialist Party in which they acknowledge that the economic movement is the hope of the workers in this country and that economic power is that in which the workers must put their trust.

During the past month, particularly in connection with the relations between the United States and Mexico, has been demonstrated the effectiveness of economic organization in dealing with all of the interests of the workers. There is no limitation to the power of economic movement, nor no interest of wage earners which it cannot promote. As you know, the fight of trade unionists for many years has been to prevent the labor movement from being dominated by any theorists, no matter what name they may term themselves, and we have been successful in preventing any outside organization from dominating the labor movement.

If you intend to deal with the fight that the trade union movement has made with the Socialists, I think you ought to present that from the view-point of the victories of the trade union movement. The Socialist Party is now less than ever an organization of wage earners. Its present candidate[1] for president is not a wage earner or a man who understands the labor movement. He belongs to the so-called intellectuals, to that group of people the interests of the labor movement are of only incidental consideration as propaganda for the Socialist Party.

In my opinion the present year marks conclusively the domination of trade unionists' control over the labor movement. Our principles and our policies have demonstrated their value. The Socialist Party has proven itself unequal to dealing with even the political interest of the wage earners, and the American Federation of Labor can show the world its achievements. This is the national view-point of the situation. Of course, in an individual organization the fight for economic policies may be more intense in some than in others. However, in no case can the labor movement afford to take a pessimistic view of the situation.

It is not my purpose to minimize the necessity for opposing socialist principles or theories or the danger contained in them for the trade union movement. I only suggest that you ought not to permit a note of discouragement to dominate your Labor Day article.

With best wishes and anticipating the receipt of your article in time for publication I am,

Fraternally yours,   Saml Gompers.
President   American Federation of Labor.

TLpS, reel 211, vol. 223, pp. 48–49, SG Letterbooks, DLC.

1. Allan Louis Benson (1871–1940), a journalist and socialist writer, was the candidate of the Socialist Party of America for president in 1916. He broke with the party in 1917 when it opposed American participation in World War I.

To Warren Stone

August 2, 1916.

Mr. Warren S. Stone,
President, Brotherhood of Locomotive Engineers,
B. of L.E. Bldg., Cleveland, O.
Dear Sir and Brother:

During our recent meeting which was held the week beginning July 24th the Executive Council directed that fraternal greetings from them should be sent to the officers of the railway brotherhoods and through them to the great rank and file of the railway organizations, and that the American Federation of Labor will protest against and oppose any effort to compel the railway men to submit their demands to compulsory arbitration.

Although we are fully appreciative of the meaning of a general railway strike we hold that the railway companies cannot shift responsibility for such a strike, if it should occur. For months they have persistently refused to do that which would adjust present differences between them and their employes. While a strike involves temporary inconveniences which affect many, free workers cannot be denied the right to quit work—the right to strike in furtherance of demands which concern their manhood and their interests.

It is a fundamental principle of freedom that no one shall be forced into involuntary servitude, that is, to work against his will. This fundamental principle of freedom must be maintained at all hazards. It must not be minimized under any guise whether compulsory arbitration or in the name of public welfare.

The welfare of the whole nation, the maintenance of our republican form of government and our institutions of freedom depend upon this fundamental—the right of a free man to control himself and his labor power.

It is the sincere desire of the American Federation of Labor that the railway brotherhoods shall secure the eight hour workday, an accomplishment which will mean opportunities for better living and for better citizenship.

With best wishes and hoping to hear from you whenever convenient, I am,

Fraternally yours, Saml Gompers.
President, American Federation of Labor.[1]

TLpS, reel 211, vol. 223, pp. 72–73, SG Letterbooks, DLC.

1. SG also sent this letter on Aug. 2, 1916, to William Carter, president of the Brotherhood of Locomotive Firemen and Enginemen, A. E. King, secretary of the Brotherhood of Railroad Trainmen, and C. E. Whitney, secretary of the Order of Railway Conductors of America (reel 211, vol. 223, pp. 74–79, SG Letterbooks, DLC).

Jesse Lewis to Frank Morrison

Hod Carriers, Building and Common Laborers
Local Union No. 224
Cedar Rapids, Iowa Aug 2nd 1916

Mr Frank Morrison
Washington DC.
Dear Sir,

As I am Rec Secy of my Local Union, I am in receipt of a communication from the Committee of Industrial Relation, asking for financial assistance, but the letter does not fully explain itself, in what way or what for is this money to be used.

Please give me some information[1] so I may be able to make this matter plain to my organization.

Thanking you in advance,

I remain, yours Truly   J. L. Lewis

ALS, AFL Microfilm National and International Union File, Hod Carriers, Building and Common Laborers' Union Records, reel 44, frame 2009, *AFL Records*.

1. Frank Morrison replied on Aug. 15, 1916, that the Committee on Industrial Relations was a private organization that developed out of the U.S. Commission on Industrial Relations and depended on contributions from individuals and trade unions because it did not receive government support. He added that the 1915 AFL convention had endorsed the work of the commission and welcomed the support and cooperation of the committee in furthering labor legislation (AFL Microfilm National and International Union File, Hod Carriers, Building and Common Laborers' Union Records, reel 44, frames 2008–9, *AFL Records*).

To Roy Claflin[1]

Aug. 3, 1916.

Mr. Roy C. Claflin,
President, High School Teachers' Union of Washington, D.C.,[2]
304 McLachlen Bldg., Washington, D.C.
Dear Sir and Brother:

In connection with your letter of July 10th, let me call your attention to the editorial in the July issue of the *American Federationist* entitled "Liberty's Hope is in Thy Keeping, Organized Labor,"[3] and the leading article[4] which will appear in the August issue of the magazine. These articles deal with the recent developments which brought about understanding between the labor movements of this country and Mexico, and promise to develop permanent agencies for uniting the workers of these two countries and also the workers of all Pan-American countries. When a Pan-American Federation of Labor[5] shall have been established the next step, of course, will be a world federation of labor.

It seems to me that your particular union can do much for promoting the ideal of internationalism. As teachers you have innumerable opportunities in your daily work which can be utilized for democracy and humanity. In addition to that, you probably know that one of the biggest problems in Mexico is the need for schools. Mexico needs first of all primary and agricultural schools. Since the administration of Carranza a number of Mexican teachers have been sent to this country, particularly to Boston. Your organization might find a chance to be helpful by getting in communication with some of those Mexican teachers.

Let me suggest that you write Colonel Edmundo E. Martinez, 111 West 16th Street, New York City, who is the representative in this country of the Mexican Federation of Labor. He probably can give you information of Mexican teachers or can tell you where you can get necessary data.

There is also another proposal back of which I fear are many enemies of labor. This proposal is to establish a university for Mexico and through that university to invade Mexico with ideals and practices of American commercial and industrial institutions. The achievement of this purpose would be subversive to Mexico's desire to work out her own salvation. It would result in the imposing of American institutions upon the Mexicans.

There is much that can be done for Mexico in creating a willingness on the part of our country to permit Mexico to have opportunities for freedom. You ought by all means to read the recent interview of Hon. Franklin K. Lane,[6] Secretary of the Interior. The interview was published in the New York World of July 16th[7] and has since been published in the Congressional Record.[8]

I am very appreciative of the spirit and the desire manifested in your letter, and hope you will write me later of what you may decide definitely to do.

With best wishes, I am,

Fraternally yours,   Saml Gompers.
President   American Federation of Labor.

TLpS, reel 211, vol. 223, pp. 181–82, SG Letterbooks, DLC.

1. Roy C. Claflin was president of the Columbia School of Drafting in Washington, D.C.

2. The High School Teachers' Union of Washington, D.C., was chartered by the AFL in May 1916 and later became local 8 of the American Federation of Teachers.

3. *American Federationist* 23 (July 1916): 575–77.

4. "United States—Mexico—Labor—Their Relations," *American Federationist* 23 (Aug. 1916): 633–52.

5. The founding meeting of the Pan-American Federation of Labor was held on Nov. 13–16, 1918, in Laredo, Tex., with delegates from the United States, Mexico, Guatemala, El Salvador, Costa Rica, and Colombia.

6. Franklin Knight Lane (1864–1921) served as secretary of the interior from 1913 to 1920.

7. "The President's Mexican Policy. Presented in an Authorized Interview by Secretary of the Interior, Franklin K. Lane," *New York World,* July 16, 1916.

8. *Congressional Record,* 64th Cong., 1st sess., vol. 53, pt. 15, Appendix, pp. 1575–79.

To Thomas French[1]

Aug. 3, 1916.

Mr. Thomas A. French,
Secretary-Treasurer, Arizona State Federation of Labor,[2]
Trades Council Hall, 238 E. Washington St., Phoenix, Ariz.
Dear Sir and Brother:

Your very interesting letter of July 3d was received.

It is evident that you are fully appreciative of the importance of organizing Mexican workers and know how necessary that is for the protection of the workers in this country.

Of course, you are familiar with the tactics of mine operators in trying to use the miners in one country to defeat the miners in the other.

So far as operation is concerned, there is no difference between the copper mines of Sonora and the copper mines of New Mexico and Arizona.

A few days ago Mr. Alfonso A. Rovalo,[3] avowedly representing the organized workers of Sonora, Mexico, was at my office and also had an interview with the members of the Executive Council. Mr. Rovalo said that the workers of Sonora are now fairly well organized and intended, if they had not already done so, to send a representative to Mexico City in order that they might be represented in the national labor organization.

According to Mr. Rovalo's statement, which corroborates information given me by many others, the Governor of Sonora, Adolfo de la Huerta,[4] is very sympathetic to the labor movement and is doing everything within his power to afford opportunities to the workers to organize. I told him of Governor Hunt of your own state and of his splendid humanitarian attitude and understanding of the labor movement. I think that Governor Hunt and Governor Huerta ought to meet in order that they might have a personal understanding and thus be able to better protect the citizens of both states.

According to reports here, it is the intention to reopen the mines in Sonora. I wish you would write me any information in connection with this matter that you think would be helpful.

Of course, there will be many difficulties growing out of efforts to organize the Mexicans, and we shall have to be prepared to meet them. However, organization is necessary for the arbitrary boundary line between the United States and Mexico does not constitute a barrier to economic development and does not separate the necessary economic and commercial relations between people living in the same locality. The fact that so much American capital is invested in Mexico makes the problems of the Mexican workers in a very large degree the problems of the workers of the United States.

Since I wrote you, three other delegates from Mexico have come to the United States, Messrs. Carvallo,[5] Ramos[6] and Alonso,[7] representing the Federacion de Sindicatos Obreros de la Republica Mexicana. They brought greetings from the Mexican workers of their organization and expressed their desire to know about the labor movement of the United States in order that the information might be helpful in shaping policies and methods of the Mexican organization. These representatives left with me a list of over 500 unions that are affiliated to the Federacion, the total membership of which they say is something like 250,000.[8]

Much of the practical work of bringing about better relations between the organized labor movement of Mexico and the United States must necessarily devolve upon those living in the boundary states. It will be very helpful to me and to the accomplishment of that purpose if you will send me from time to time whatever information you may have that throws light upon the situation.

With best wishes, and hoping to hear from you soon, I am,

Fraternally yours,   Saml Gompers.
President   American Federation of Labor.

TLpS, reel 211, vol. 223, pp. 193–95, SG Letterbooks, DLC.

1. Thomas A. FRENCH of Phoenix served as secretary-treasurer of the Arizona State Federation of Labor (FOL; 1916–17, 1920–21).

2. The Arizona State FOL was founded in 1912 and received an AFL charter in 1914.

3. Alfonso A. Ravola (variously Ravallo or Rovallo) was a newspaperman who had been living in Sonora, Mexico, for a year or more.

4. Adolfo de la Huerta (1881–1955) served as interim governor (1916–17) and governor (1919–20, 1921–22) of Sonora and minister of the Secretariat of the Treasury and Public Credit (1920–23).

5. Guillermo Z. Carvallo was a founder and had served as president of the clerks' union (*dependientes del comercio*) in Veracruz.

6. Domingo Ramos was a member of the masons' union (*albañiles*) in Veracruz.

7. José G. Alonso was a member of the cooks' union (*cocineros*) in Veracruz and secretary of the Federación de Sindicatos Obreros de la República Mexicana.

8. See "From Frank Duffy," May 26, 1916, n. 2, above.

To James Sullivan

Aug. 17, 1916.

Mr. J. W. Sullivan,
1937 Stillwell Ave., Bensonhurst, Brooklyn, New York.
My dear Mr. Sullivan:

As I indicated in my memo to a letter[1] to you of a few days ago, I am apprehensive that the American Federation of Labor proposition for the international conference of representatives of National Trade Union Centers[2] may have gone "a ballooning." After carefully reading Secretary Appleton's letter,[3] I am indeed in a quandary as to whether the A.F. of L. proposition will have to be modified or abandoned, for regardless of any personal opinions which may be had, or on which side any sympathies may lie in the present European struggle, it is unthinkable for the American Federation of Labor to participate in a conference supposed to be international when the representatives of the labor movement of any of the countries now engaged in the war would be barred. I am really sorry that you are not going to England first rather than to France,[4] for you could then have a conference with the representatives of the British Trade Union movement and see whether they could not be persuaded to in part at least modify or rescind the action of the Leeds conference.[5] In principle the French labor movement has agreed to the A.F. of L. proposition.

It is due to you to know that I will have a conference here on Friday, August 25th, with Mr. Mahon and Mr. Woll, the fraternal delegates from the A.F. of L. to the British Trades Union Congress,[6] and I am going over this matter with them and I am going to urge them to bring the subject matter before the Parliamentary Committee, as well as before the Congress. I shall give them your Paris address and perhaps they may communicate with you while you are in France.

It will cause me genuine regret should the splendid plan outlined by the American Federation of Labor in its proposal fail because of a want of a broader understanding of the situations which will confront the workers of all the countries now engaged in the strife. The American labor movement has nothing to gain by the proposal as compared to the vast beneficial results which would ensue from a general acceptance of the plan, but if our best understanding and action are misinterpreted or misunderstood and it would be doomed to failure if an attempt is made to hold the conference, it had better be abandoned. I count upon some successful effort being made by yourself, Mr. Mahon and Mr. Woll in an effort to disentangle the entire matter. I shall be very glad to have report[7] as promptly as possible. Perhaps Secretary Jouhaux may go to England in regard to this matter. In any event, I am going to write him[8] by this mail, urging him to do so.

With best wishes, I am,

Fraternally yours,   Saml Gompers.
President,   American Federation of Labor.

TLpS, reel 211, vol. 223, pp. 742–43, SG Letterbooks, DLC.

1. SG to James Sullivan, Aug. 16, 1916, reel 211, vol. 223, p. 174, SG Letterbooks, DLC.

2. The 1914 AFL convention authorized the AFL Executive Council to organize an international labor conference after the war in conjunction with the peace conference, and the 1915 convention reaffirmed that decision. On Mar. 26, 1916, SG sent a circular letter to the "Organized Labor Movement of All Countries" with an invitation to attend such a conference (Executive Council Records, Vote Books, reel 14, frames 543–44, *AFL Records*). Although the original plan was abandoned as a result of British and German opposition, the 1916 AFL convention nevertheless instructed the Council to continue its efforts in behalf of a postwar labor conference.

3. William Appleton wrote SG on July 28, 1916, that the British trade union movement was not averse to a postwar labor conference but opposed the conference as proposed in SG's letter of Mar. 26, that is, between labor representatives from belligerent and neutral nations at the very time that diplomats were negotiating the peace treaty (AFL Microfilm Convention File, reel 27, frame 1383, *AFL Records*).

4. Sullivan went to Europe in the fall of 1916 to discuss AFL plans for a postwar conference with European trade union leaders and to study labor conditions. He returned to the United States in April 1917.

5. The general council of the General Federation of Trades Unions and labor representatives from France, Belgium, and Italy met in Leeds, July 6–7, 1916. The delegates endorsed moving the headquarters of the International Federation of Trade Unions to a neutral country and incorporating international standards on hours of work, protection of women and children, social insurance, hygiene, unionization, and the right to emigrate in the peace treaty ending the war. They did not approve the AFL's proposal for an international labor conference to be held at the same time as the peace negotiations.

6. The TUC met in Birmingham, Sept. 4–9, 1916.

7. Sullivan to SG, Oct. 6, 1916, Files of the Office of the President, General Correspondence, reel 81, frames 479–80, *AFL Records.* For the report of Matthew Woll and W. D. Mahon as delegates to the TUC, see AFL, *Proceedings,* 1916, pp. 235–46.

8. SG to Léon Jouhaux, Aug. 22, 1916, reel 211, vol. 223, pp. 979–82, SG Letterbooks, DLC.

To Thomas Dolan

August 25, 1916.

Mr. Thomas J. Dolan,
President, Local Union No. 11, United Brotherhood of Carpenters
    and Joiners of America,
307 W. Superior Avenue, Cleveland, Ohio.
Dear Sir and Brother:

Your unkind letter of August 12 duly received, in which you enclosed a letter received from Senator Pomerene[1] in response to your request for him to help secure the passage of the Immigration bill during this session of Congress.

I have not time to engage in a controversy with you at this moment, neither will I indulge in any arguments to try to convince you that I am not enjoying any Rip Van Winkle sleep, nor will I accept your challenge to support a political party of "our own," but I will merely restrict myself to saying that I am trying to the best of my ability to carry the mandates of the conventions of the American Federation of Labor on principles espoused by the delegates representing the great masses of organized workers at the annual conventions of the A.F. of L.

If you feel that there should be a Labor Party, I assure you, my dear brother, that there will be no restrictions placed upon you to undertake such a task. The field is open—the world is wide.

I am taking advantage of this opportunity, however, to send you, under separate cover, copy of a small pamphlet containing the legislative achievements of the American Federation of Labor since the Fifty-eighth Congress and up to the close of the Sixty-third Congress.[2] All of the great measures which are summarized in this small pamphlet have been obtained without going to any man, any men or any political parties, with our hats in our hands. We have stood upon our dignity as American citizens. We have made our arguments and we have depended upon the justice of our position. We have neither begged, pleaded, threatened or bullied. We have made progress which I believe you too will be man enough to recognize and acknowledge. I hope you will give this small pamphlet your very careful examination and also review the summarized statement which covers the legislative achievements during this present session of Congress, and which I enclose herewith (the first session of the Sixty-fourth Congress).

I hope that with this information before you, you will see matters in a much clearer light and I trust that you and your associates will never forget the dignity due to a labor representative and to a citizen of the United States when you carry your hat in your hand which is the insignia of civility and not servility. Do not beg for anything which is your guaranteed right and privilege as a citizen of these great United States.

I think it well to also include in this letter the declarations made by the American Federation of Labor on political methods and herewith quote same:

Political Platform Declaration by
the American Federation of Labor.[3]

"The American labor movement is not partisan to a political party; it is partisan to a principle, the principle of equal rights and human freedom.

["We call especial attention to this statement, in order that we may emphasize its soundness and because][4] it has to some extent been disputed. We appeal to public opinion, we do our best to so cultivate it, so that it may become on subjects which we urge sufficiently extensive and strong to be crystallized into law. One political party deals with our policies and rejects them; that is it expresses itself as being in agreement with us on these policies, and if we are to remain true to the principles and policies which we have urged upon the public, we necessarily must work with such party for the accomplishment of our object. If an endorsement of our contentions by a political party is to compel us to abandon those contentions, then it needs but such endorsement of our very existence to compel us to disband. The thought needs but to be stated in order that it may be repudiated. Partisanship is exhibited by adherence to a party which refuses its endorsement, and non-partisanship consists in continued work for our principles regardless of what any political party may do. The President makes the following statement:

["]'Our conventions have frequently declared that our movement has neither the right nor the desire to dictate how a member shall cast his vote. It has been my privilege and honor always so to insist. I have not departed, and can not now depart from that true trade union course. At the Minneapolis convention the following declaration was adopted.

[" ']We must have with us in our economic movement men of all parties as well as of all creeds and the minority rights of the humblest man to vote where he pleases and to worship where his conscience dictates must be sacredly guarded.'

["]Your committee are in full accord with this expression, and desire to reiterate the Minneapolis declaration. . . .[5]

["]We recommend that the policy be continued and that every effort be made to bring the principles for which we contended and for which we shall continue to contend not only to all members of the labor movement, but all friends and adherents of popular government."

I hope that our organizations in your community will be governed by the principles herein announced, and that you will keep me advised as to the progress you make in behalf of remedying the grievances of the workers, and that you will also keep one simple motive in view, and that is, see that a tried and true trade unionist is always on guard in public affairs as well as economic affairs. Let us learn to train and trust our own associates in all the responsible positions of life.

Fraternally yours,   Saml Gompers.
President   American Federation of Labor.

TLpS, reel 212, vol. 224, pp. 390–93, SG Letterbooks, DLC.

1. Atlee Pomerene (1863–1937) served as a Democratic senator from Ohio (1911–23).

2. *Legislative Achievements of the American Federation of Labor* (Washington, D.C., 1916).

3. The 1908 AFL convention adopted this declaration (AFL, *Proceedings*, 1908, pp. 224–25).

4. The text in brackets is supplied from AFL, *Proceedings*, 1908, p. 224.

5. Ellipses in original.

To Robert Woolley[1]

Washington, D.C., August 25, 1916.

Robert W. Woolley,
Democratic National Committee,
30 E. 42d Street, New York City.

In my experience with United States Congresses of two score years I have not seen anything like the fine spirit toward labor, the rights and welfare of all the people, pervading all the branches of the Wilson administration. Labor has been recognized neither in the spirit of deference on the one hand nor patronage on the other. But the spirit of recognition has been the right one that labor should be made part of the national councils; that its patriotism should be conceded, and that its knowledge of its own needs should give it paramount voice in legislation directly and peculiarly affecting its own rights. This fundamental right spirit has guided the Wilson administration to wise and righteous labor legislation. Because of that spirit and its results in definite laws and policies, how can liberty loving Americans loyal to the Republic and its ideals fail to sustain an executive who has done so much for their realization?

Samuel Gompers

TWpSr, reel 212, vol. 224, p. 105, SG Letterbooks, DLC.

1. Robert Wickliffe Woolley was director of publicity for the Democratic National Committee. He served variously as director of the U.S. Mint (1915–16), as director of publicity for the 1917 Liberty Loan drive, and as a member of the Interstate Commerce Commission (1917–21).

From J. Havelock Wilson[1]

The National Sailors' & Firemen's Union
of Great Britain and Ireland.
London, S.W. 13th September, 1916.

My dear Gompers,

Your letter dated August 27th[2] reached me to-day, and I was pleased indeed to hear from you. I have read with much interest your remarks with regard to the proposed International Conference of Labour at the end of the war, and at the time when the representatives of the different countries now at war shall meet to discuss the terms of peace.

It is quite evident to me that a great deal of misunderstanding may and can arise with regard to this subject, and we shall have to be very careful how the matter is approached otherwise very strong feelings may be engendered. Personally I have not taken any part in the discussions that have taken place with regard to this conference up to the present as you will understand the Sailors' & Firemen's Union is not affiliated with the Federation of trades, consequently I was not a delegate at the Leeds Conference, but you can take the assurance from me that Appleton has very broad views on the International side of labour problems, and you may also rest assured that Bowerman is of the same type.

As far as I can ascertain the position to be is that some of the English Trades Unionists resent the American Federation of Labour taking the responsibility of calling an International Labour Conference if one should be held, and I see no reason myself why such a Conference should not take place, but the general opinion as far as I have heard it expressed is that such a Conference should be called by the representatives of labour of the countries who are now involved in the war.

I have no doubt that you and your colleagues take the opposite view, that the proper persons to call such a Conference are the labour men of the countries not involved. I may further say that there is a very bitter feeling prevailing in the Allied countries taking part in any Conference at which the representatives of the German or Austrian labour or socialists would be present. Probably you may not be able to fully understand this position, you may be inclined to the view that once war is finished that all bitterness of feeling should be laid to one side and that the workers of the World should make up their minds to see that in future as far as it is humanely possible that such a calamity as that which has now befallen Europe shall not again take place for a very long time.

Now I should like to explain matters with regard to this feeling from my point of view. First of all right or wrong there is a strong conviction in my mind that Germany alone was responsible for this war. I have seen for over 30 years the preparations that Germany has been making and moreover I have observed amongst the German representative workers the growth of a very domineering attitude to all other workers, but at the same time it was difficult for me to think that Germany would be so mad as to involve Europe in this dreadful war. At the outbreak of hostilities there was no bitterness of feeling against the Germans, but after the sinking of the "Lusitania" and the senseless air raids that have been made on Great Britain when hundreds of innocent men, women and children have been slaughtered a feeling of bitterness has been aroused to a terrible extent, and as far as the seamen are concerned we have very good grounds for complaint. I have knowledge of scores of cases where vessels have been torpedoed by submarines and when the men were endeavouring to escape by the aid of the life-boats the Germans fired on the men in the boats, and a very considerable number of the members of the Seamen's Union were injured and killed in this manner, and furthermore we have the very cowardly murder of Captain Fryatt of the steamer "Brussels."[3]

Now as you know my dear Gompers I have always been a strong internationalist and I hope I am now, but I am bound to tell you I have a very bitter feeling against the Germans at the present time. It may be said and with some truth that the German working men are not responsible for the conduct of the military and naval party in Germany who are conducting the war, but it is very difficult to get me t[o] believe this because just before the war the German Socialist Party boasted very much of the fact that they had over 4,000,000 of voters in the German Socialistic Party; consequently they must have some influence with the German Government.

Now as evidence that there was no bitterness on the part of the British seamen at the outbreak of the war when the British Government commenced to intern persons of German nationality we thought we had a duty to perform in endeavouring to see that German seamen who were members of our Union and were to be interned should have the best conditions possible. We therefore purchased an estate in Northamptonshire, and we obtained permission from the British Government to take over all German seamen under our care, and I myself personally had charge of that Camp. We had 1,000 men there and I did everything I possibly could to see that the conditions of their internment was all that could be desired; they had the very best of food, splendid accommodation, bath rooms, lavatories all fitted up in first class style. They were allowed beer and tobacco and if they did any work they were paid for it. I am sorry to say that whilst there was a large number of the Germans first class men, and their conduct was all that could be desired, yet there was a very large number who were just the opposite; they did not appreciate what had been done for them, and it will always be in my mind their cowardly behaviour when they heard of the sinking of the "Lusitania." A concert had been organised for the evening of that day, and when I got the newspaper informing me of the fact that the "Lusitania" had been torpedoed and some 500 of our members had been done to death without a chance I called the men of the Camp together and explained matters and said that under the circumstances we would suspend the concert. Not a word was uttered at the time, but after I left the hall a large number of the seamen commenced to cheer with delight at the fact that the "Lusitania" had been sunk, and since then, of course, there has been equally as cruel deeds done.

Now you cannot be surprised at my having a feeling of bitterness, and I can assure you it will be a long time before there is a change in that feeling. Our men have resolved that they will not sail with any Germans on British ships for the next 21 years, so you will note that in proposing to call any Conference at which the representatives of Germany or Austria will be present there will be a very bitter feeling created, and I think that is largely responsible for the objection on the part of British Trades Unionists to the American Federation of Labour calling a Conference.

The fraternal delegates who attended the British Trades Union Congress endeavoured to place the position of America before the delegates, and I think they did so with great ability, but the majority of the people in this country do not understand America's attitude; they think that the Americans should have come into this war as well as Great Britain. My own personal opinion is that it would have been a calamity because in the first place I am confident it would have created a state of affairs bordering on civil war, and what assistance could America have rendered to Great Britain—not a great deal I venture to say because whatever men America would have been able to send would have to have been drilled and equipped and we know from experience in this country that cannot be accomplished in a few days. On the other hand it might have prevented the supply of munitions coming to hand which was all important as far as the Allies were concerned.

The people of this country do not realise that there are millions of German born people in the United States, and also millions of descendents of Germans who have close sympathy with their Fatherland. I think myself that President Wilson has done well to keep America out of the war, but it is not everyone who understands that attitude—I do.

If there is anything at all that I can do to keep matters running smoothly as far as the American Federation of Labour is concerned and our own Trades Union Congress you may rest assured that I will be prepared to do all I can. I shall take an early opportunity of allowing both Shackleton and Bowerman to read the letter you have been good enough to send me.

It is our intention to send two delegates from our Union to America this year; they are primarily to attend the Convention[4] of the International Seamen Union of America if it is permissible I should [like?] them also to attend the Convention of the A.F. of L.

With best of greetings, I remain,

Yours fraternally.   J. Havelock Wilson[5]

TLS, Files of the Office of the President, General Correspondence, reel 81, frames 384–89, *AFL Records*.

1. Joseph Havelock WILSON was president of the National Sailors' and Firemen's Union of Great Britain and Ireland.

2. Probably SG to Wilson, Aug. 22, 1916, reel 212, vol. 224, pp. 131–34, SG Letterbooks, DLC.

3. Charles Algernon Fryatt, captain of the merchant steamer *Brussels,* was attacked by German submarines on two occasions in March 1915. He successfully dodged the first attempt and tried to ram the submarine on the second, forcing it to submerge. Captured by the Germans on June 23, 1916, Fryatt was tried and convicted as a *franc-tireur*—a civilian terrorist. He was executed on July 27, 1916.

4. Richard McGhee and James Henson served as fraternal delegates from the National Sailors' and Firemen's Union to the 1916 convention of the International Seamen's Union of America, which met in New York City, Dec. 4–12.

5. For SG's reply see "To J. Havelock Wilson," Sept. 26, 1916, below.

To R. Parmenter Pettipiece[1]

Sept. 16, 1916.

Mr. R. Parm Pettipiece,
Manager, The British Columbia Federationist,
Labor Temple, Vancouver, B.C. Canada.
My dear Mr. Pettipiece:

Your favor of the 8th instant came duly to hand and contents noted with interest. It is, of course, gratifying to learn that there is some movement being made on the part of Chinese workmen in the United States to organize, and as you say that Mr. Ernest Lee, a Chinaman, is interested in the position of the Orientals of your province and desires to know whether it would be possible to secure a charter from the American Federation of Labor as a Federal Labor Union. The subject of the organization of Chinese workmen in the United States has occupied the attention of the active men in our movement for a considerable period of time, and thus far no tangible decision has been evolved. Of course, as you know I cannot act upon my own authority, no matter what my views may be, but in any event you may rely upon the fact that the subject will receive the attention of the Executive Council of the American Federation of Labor before whom I shall endeavor to bring it at the next meeting which convenes in the middle of October.[2]

May I ask you to write me further and more fully upon this subject soon and as often as you can. Perhaps a further lucidation of the matter, together with more detailed information may be helpful. There is no reason why we cannot exchange two or three letters before the meeting of the Executive Council.

With best wishes and hoping to hear from you at your earliest convenience, I am,

Fraternally yours,   Saml Gompers.
President,   American Federation of Labor.

TLpS, reel 212, vol. 224, pp. 1010–11, SG Letterbooks, DLC.

1. Richard Parmenter Pettipiece, president of International Typographical Union 226 of Vancouver and a vice-president of the Vancouver Trades and Labour Council, was a founder in 1910 of the British Columbia Federation of Labor and the organization's first secretary (1910–11). He was the manager of the *British Columbia Federationist* (1911–18), helped organize the Federated Labour party in 1918, and served as a vice-president of the Trades and Labor Congress of Canada in 1923.

2. At its meeting in Washington, D.C., Oct. 16–21, 1916, the AFL Executive Council considered Pettipiece's letter but took no action on it.

To George Perkins

September 18, 1916.

Mr. George W. Perkins,
President, Cigarmakers' International Union of America.
Monon Building, Chicago, Illinois.
Dear Sir and Brother:

On Saturday, September 16th, under the constitutional provisions of the American Federation of Labor, I notified three international union executive officers to each one select an auditor for the accounts of the American Federation of Labor for the year closing September 30, 1916.[1] In two weeks the auditors will come to Washington to the A.F. of L. headquarters to audit the accounts.

In accordance, my attention was called to the fact of the delinquency of the Cigarmakers International Union per capita tax, and I was informed that in July you paid one month's per capita tax and that on September 14th you paid another. In other words, the Cigarmakers International Union is delinquent in per capita tax to the American Federation of Labor for June, July, August and September. It will be a pretty spectacle for the report of the Auditing Committee.

Your attention is called to Article X of the Constitution of the American Federation of Labor.

Section I provides for revenue being derived from a per capita tax to be paid upon the full paid-up membership of all affiliated bodies.

Section II provides that delegates shall not be entitled to a seat in the annual convention unless the tax of their organization has been paid in full to September 30th preceding the convention.

Section III provides that if at the end of three months it (the international union) is still in arrears, it shall become suspended from membership by the Federation, and can be reinstated only by a vote of the convention when such arrearages are paid in full.

You see the situation with which I am confronted. The last act I shall be required to do is to order the suspension of the international union and vacate the office of president of the American Federation of Labor, or upon failure of my so doing have the auditors officially bring the matter to my attention demanding that that course be pursued or a report of the incident to be made by the auditors to the American Federation of Labor convention.

The constitution of the Cigarmakers' International Union provides definitely and absolutely that that organization shall remain in full affiliation with the American Federation of Labor, and the per capita tax is just as much a legitimate obligation to be paid as any other expenditure authorized by the constitution of the international union. By allowing the accumulation of the indebtedness it grows into a considerable sum. Paid in full and then kept up regularly, it is infinitesimal. I should like to know the course you propose to pursue in this matter.[2]

With best wishes, I am,

Fraternally yours,　Saml Gompers.
President　American Federation of Labor.

N.B. Secretary Tracy[3] informs me that the per capita tax due from the Cigarmakers' International Union has remained unpaid from and including January 1916. A pretty state of affairs.

TLpS, reel 212, vol. 224, pp. 984–85, SG Letterbooks, DLC.

1. On Sept. 16, 1916, SG wrote to the presidents of the United Hatters of North America, the International Longshoremen's Association, and the Amalgamated Sheet Metal Workers' International Alliance asking each of them to appoint a delegate to serve on the AFL's auditing committee (reel 212, vol. 224, pp. 928–33, SG Letterbooks, DLC). The auditors appointed were Thomas Harrison, James Moriarty, and M. F. Greene.

2. The Cigar Makers' International Union of America paid its per capita tax for June, July, August, and September 1916—$1,128.72—before the end of September.

3. Thomas F. TRACY was secretary-treasurer of the AFL Union Label Trades Department from 1909 to 1916.

From Achille Person[1]

International Hod Carriers, Building
and Common Laborers Union.
Albany, N.Y. Sept. 18, 1916.

Dear Sir and Brother:

Replying to your favor of Sept. 15th[2] I beg to inform you that this International Union does not make any distinction of race, creed or nationality and therefore does not discriminate against colored laborers. In fact, we have many locals formed of colored laborers exclusively and then we have many more locals of mixed races.

Two Vice-Presidents[3] of this International Union are colored men and are members of two mixed (colored and white) locals.

Therefore Brother Belcher[4] can organize a local union of our craft and we will grant charter for colored laborers, if the local unions will be composed of colored laborers exclusively. If he will form a local union of mixed laborers, we will grant a general charter. Am sending Brother Belcher information concerning this International Union.

Thanking you for your interest and with best wishes and kind regards, I am

Fraternally yours,   (Signed) A. Person.
Gen. Sec. & Treas.

TLtpSr, reel 213, vol. 225, p. 123, SG Letterbooks, DLC. Typed notation: "*Copy.*" Enclosed in SG to George Belcher, Sept. 21, 1916, ibid., p. 122.

1. Achille PERSION, of the International Hod Carriers', Building and Common Laborers' Union of America, served as secretary-treasurer of the international from 1910 to 1950.

2. On Sept. 8, 1916, SG received a letter from George Belcher, vice-president of the Texas State Federation of Labor (FOL), indicating that unions of black barbers, bartenders, carpenters, cooks and waiters, hod carriers, and teamsters could be organized in Beaumont, Tex. On Sept. 15 SG wrote the international unions involved, asking if they could organize these workers or, if not, if they would object to the AFL organizing them (reel 212, vol. 224, pp. 856–60, 862, SG Letterbooks, DLC).

3. William Walter Cordell, a member of Hod Carriers' local 119 of Cincinnati, served as vice-president of the international from 1909 to 1936. James H. Lilly, a member of local 120 of Indianapolis, was vice-president from 1911 to 1918.

4. George W. Belcher was a member of International Typographical Union 339 of Beaumont and a vice-president of the Texas State FOL.

To Arthur Keep[1]

Sept. 19, 1916.

Mr. Arthur Keep,
Editor, The Artisan,
Box 869, Jacksonville, Florida.
Dear Sir and Brother:

In reply to your letter of recent date, in reference to agents coming to your city to engage negroes as laborers in northern states, I find upon inquiry from the Department of Labor, that the Pennsylvania Railroad, the Erie Railroad, the American Tobacco Company and some other employing interests in the northern states have sent agents to several southern localities for the purpose of hiring negro labor.

The officials of the United States Department of Labor have in their possession detailed information which they will gladly impart to you upon application to the Secretary, the Honorable William B. Wilson. The Howard University of Washington has also been active in endeavors to benefit the economic conditions of southern negroes and wherever they could find opportunities for remunerative employment in the north they have endeavored to place people of their race. So far in my inquiries, I have not discovered any grave instance where such efforts were employed to use negroes as strike breakers.

Of course the business elements in the Boards of Trade and Chambers of Commerce and similar organizations of business men in southern towns will do all they possibly can to prevent negroes leaving their localities, working on the basis that they will be able to continue to get negro labor at their own prices if there are two, three or more applicants for every job, and undoubtedly the large employers will not hesitate to get out dodgers purporting to be issued by organized labor, either of your city or other cities, warning negroes not to go north. The community of interest existing among business men in all localities is about the same, and they work unceasingly to protect their own interests.

I am very pleased to observe your statement that you do not propose to allow the Chamber of Commerce to deceive you. Every advantage accruing to the negro as a laborer will ultimately result in being an advantage to the white man as a laborer. Working men, whether white or black who preserve their independence and move from place to place in search of employment, obtain broader experience, are more self-reliant and in time it becomes a valuable asset for men to move from place to place. The economic condition of the workers of the south will show almost immediate improvement if the negroes become migratory.

Please accept my thanks for keeping me informed as to the situation in your city and hoping that you will continue to keep me so informed, I remain,

Fraternally yours,   Saml Gompers.
President   American Federation of Labor.

TLpS, reel 213, vol. 225, pp. 144–45, SG Letterbooks, DLC.

1. Arthur Keep, a member of Journeymen Tailors' Union of America 319 of Jacksonville, Fla., edited the *Artisan* from at least as early as 1914 through 1917.

To Franklin Lane

September 19, 1916.

Hon. Franklin K. Lane,
United States-Mexico Commission,
New London, Connecticut.
My dear Mr. Lane:

The purpose of the United States-Mexico Commission is one that has my deepest interest. As you probably know, it was the workers, the masses of both countries, that first voiced the desire for a commission representing the people of both countries to consider the misunderstandings and the causes of friction that had so nearly precipitated the United States and Mexico into war. The workers felt that there was nothing at issue that justified a war in which the citizens of both countries would be required to make the supreme sacrifice for their country. They felt that war was being created in order to promote the special interests of a few.

It seemed to the representatives of the labor movements of Mexico and the United States as we met in joint conference at the time, that a representative commission of both countries ought to make an inquiry into the methods and purposes of those who were trying to inflict such great wrong upon the people of two nations. We realized that the causes back of the misunderstandings were deep rooted and grew out of the forces that direct the economic, social, and political forces of both nations. As wage earners representing the great majority of the people of both nations, we felt that we had a right to ask that the Commission be authorized to make a very broad inquiry in order to indicate the causes of friction and to enable the Commission to make constructive suggestions that would result in the removal of the forces that made for evil, and to create opportunities for greater freedom and for more complete realization of the possibilities of human life.

There is something very beautiful and wonderful in the vision that has inspired much of the Mexican revolution, and I have felt that the people who could conceive such a vision ought to be assured opportunity to work out their ideals and purposes. It seems to me that the institutions of Mexico are now in a condition of what might be termed fluidity, and that before they harden into definite shape is the great opportunity to give them molds and direction in accord with the highest ideals of freedom, justice and humanity. Whatever is done in this formative period will influence the history of Mexico for years to come.

There has developed in Mexico a very clear appreciation of the distinction between workers and the exploiters. The people there, as you know and have so admirably expressed in your public utterances, are groping after national institutions that shall enable them to put all of the resources of their country, and all of their national institutions to the service of those who perform creative labor.

Although I have, of course, no direct information as to the course which the United States–Mexico Commission proposes to follow, yet even though you may have planned to take up the matters which I have in mind, I cannot feel that my duty has been done without urging that the Commission take into consideration these things that are fundamental, the vital forces of national life, that have their roots in those things which have to do with the maintenance of life itself. While I recognize the necessity of considering the military situation, yet I am sure you will agree with me that this is after all, only a very superficial and temporary aspect of the fundamental vital relations between the people of Mexico and the United States.

Some time ago I presented[1] for the consideration of the commission, a copy of an indictment that had been returned by the Federal Grand Jury in California.[2] The matter with which the indictment dealt, was representative of the international forces for evil which exist in both countries, and which are attempting to use national institutions to further their own purposes, even if the result shall be international war.

By inquiring into this and similar conditions, the Commission of which you are one of the leaders, will be disclosing to the people of both countries, methods by which a few individuals have been able to exploit numbers of their fellow beings, and have perverted products of civilization into agencies for power and self-aggrandizement. There are many who have personal knowledge of the facts connected with the indictment, I could present to you, and who could render valuable assistance to your Commission in connecting up all of the links of evidence which exist, both in this country and in Mexico. Heretofore it has been impossible to get evidence from both sides because much lies in the city of Mexico. Those individuals would be glad to serve your

Commission, because thereby they would be serving the cause of humanity and freedom. That you are sympathetic all know, and it is for that reason and the great service you can render that I take the liberty of urging this matter upon your attention. Of course you know that I shall be glad to render any service possible to the Commission, to the organized labor movements and the people generally of the United States and Mexico.[3]

Sincerely yours,　Saml Gompers.
President,　American Federation of Labor.

TLpS, reel 212, vol. 224, pp. 1023–26, SG Letterbooks, DLC.

1. SG to Franklin Lane, Aug. 26, 1916, reel 213, vol. 225, pp. 241–44, SG Letterbooks, DLC.

2. On Feb. 19, 1915, a federal grand jury indicted Harry Chandler, son-in-law of Harrison Gray Otis, and six others on the charge of conspiring to violate American neutrality laws by seeking to foment revolution in Mexico. Chandler's and Otis's enormous landholdings in Baja California—reportedly some fifteen million acres—were threatened by Venustiano Carranza's proposal to break up the large estates of absentee landlords. The indictment alleged that Chandler had provided money to raise and finance an expedition to seize control of Baja California and install a new governor there. He was tried in May 1917 and acquitted by a directed verdict.

3. Lane wrote SG on Oct. 3, 1916, that he agreed with SG's views on Mexico and would welcome the opportunity to discuss the matter further with him. SG met with Lane in Atlantic City on Oct. 8.

To J. Havelock Wilson

Sept. 26, 1916.

Mr. J. Havelock Wilson,
General Secretary, The National Sailors' and Firemen's Union of
　Great Britain and Ireland,
53, Parliament Street, London, S.W., England.
Dear Sir and Brother:

Your exceedingly interesting letter of the 13th instant[1] came to hand today, and while having the matters which you discuss fresh in mind, I concluded to reply.

Your letter confirms what the cable dispatches published in the newspapers of the United States stated as to the action of the British Trade Union Congress in regard to the proposal of the American Federation of Labor for an international conference of representative labor men from the various countries to be held after the close of the present European war, that is, that the Congress had practically confirmed the action of the Leeds conference refusing participation in such a conference.

Of course with the British labor movement expressing its dissent from the A.F. of L. proposal, and a letter[2] received from Mr. Carl Legien of Berlin, stating that the proposition would be impractical, the American proposal must in itself fall. I have not yet had opportunity to discuss the subject with my associates of the Executive Council of the American Federation of Labor, but I have given them the information by mail[3] and expect at the forthcoming meeting of the Executive Council which begins Monday, October 16, that the A.F. of L. proposition will be formally and officially withdrawn or dropped.

However, in the meantime, that is, under date of Sept. 15,[4] I submitted by mail to my colleagues of the Executive Council a proposal to enter into communication with the representatives of the organized labor movement of the several countries, urging upon them that they insist upon their respective governments selecting at least one representative labor man in their respective delegations to the conference to be held at the close of the war[5] for the purpose of determining the conditions of permanent peace and the treaty and provisions governing the same for the purpose of aiding in the best manner possible to establish the conditions for which the American Federation of Labor declared at the Philadelphia and San Francisco conventions. I take it that you are familiar with those declarations since they have been sent to you,[6] and I assume that you have received them. Otherwise, you might consult them at the office of Secretary Bowerman or Secretary Appleton.

Of course we shall await any official action until after we have definite information directly from the officers of the labor movement of Great Britain and from our fraternal delegates, Messrs. Woll and Mahon, who by the way we expect will return to the United States in the course of a week. When the Executive Council shall have taken action upon the matter and if it be affirmative, I shall of course communicate with the officers of the labor movements in the various countries.

As you know, there are received and published in the United States probably fuller accounts of the progress of the war and the incidents in connection therewith than in the newspapers of possibly any other country. There is no censorship in the United States upon the European affairs, but I confess to you that I am astounded at what you state regarding the interned camp of German seamen in England.

Let me assure you that there was no thought in the minds of our labor men here to assume a function that did not naturally come to us as the proper course to pursue. In European countries the labor movements so far as they were internationally concerned were torn asunder, and any proposition coming from one of the countries engaged in the struggle on one side would in the course of human feeling be resented on the part of the representatives of labor on the other side. There was but one really great country in the first class: one great labor movement of primary importance which could approach all sides without having suspicion aroused as to its motives and purposes, and that was the labor movement of the United States, and the United States as a country. What more natural than without attempting to unwarrantably interfere with the struggle as it was being carried on, at any rate to offer its good offices, to suggest a time and place most opportune where the representatives of the workers of all the countries might meet upon a common level and there and then endeavor to meet the new issues which would confront the people of all the countries, and also to use their power and influence to say to it first that such a terrible holocaust shall not be possible of inauguration within a long period of time, and secondly, to consider the subjects matter that would best protect and promote the rights, interests, welfare and freedom of the workers of all the countries. Is it thinkable that such a conference if held would not have a tremendous influence upon the ambassadors or other representatives of the [various][7] governments meeting to determine the conditions of peace and treaties for the conduct of the affairs of the nations of the world for the future? Speaking as one man, with no more information than is possessed by thousands of others, I cannot bring myself to any other conclusion than that it was a serious mistake to have allowed this opportunity to pass by without taking advantage of it.

I am not unmindful of the bitterness engendered not only by the conflict itself but the manner in which it has been conducted, but that the minds of men have been poisoned on one side of the controversy against the men on the other side goes without question. Nor will I attempt to say that there is not some justification for that feeling. And yet after the curtain has fallen upon this tragedy, the workers of all the countries will be confronted with practically the same problems, and to meet them and endeavor to solve them is not only the course of wisdom but of necessity.

There is no doubt that in the struggles between the men and women of labor and the employers often the bitterest and keenest feelings have been aroused, and yet after the close of such an industrial struggle, conferences between the representatives of these very same workers and employers take place, and an effort made to reach a conclusion upon which the industrial affairs shall be resumed in a manner at least fairly mutual in honor and advantage. To be prompted in any course by bitterness of feeling and resentment is not calculated to bring about the best results.

If the international conference proposed by the A.F. of L. had been approved, I have little doubt that its influence even during the struggle would have been felt and its effect after the war in determining conditions of peace, the treaty, would have included recognition of the fundamental rights of the workers and the interests of the workers which should be considered. However, the American proposal has been thrown in the scrap heap and no amount of lamentations will mend matters in respect to it. I am hopeful that something tangible may yet be accomplished in the subject matter which I have submitted to the Executive Council of the A.F. of L., and to which I have already made brief reference above.

We are in the midst of a Presidential and congressional campaign, the election taking place November 6th, and you can form no idea of how big a factor in the campaign is the European war and situation. I am enclosing to you herein a copy of a letter which I sent under date of August 28, to Mr. H. O. McClurg,[8] which by the way we have had printed and circulated. I am also enclosing to you two little pamphlets which have been issued by Mr. Wilson's campaign managers. I commend them to your consideration. You will observe the pronounced declarations on the questions affecting labor.

Of course we will welcome the delegates which your union will send to the United States to attend the convention of the National Seamen's Union, and of course we shall welcome them to the American Federation of Labor convention which begins November 13, at Baltimore, Maryland. I take it they will be an auxiliary to the elected fraternal delegates from the British Trade Union Congress.[9]

If I get a chance I shall write[10] to both Secretary Bowerman and Secretary Appleton and convey some of the thoughts herein expressed. If in the meantime, however, you can let the gentlemen see this letter, I shall appreciate it.

Won't you do me the kindness of keeping up our correspondence? I shall be very glad to hear from you at any time, and I earnestly hope that you are in the enjoyment of a better state of health than was indicated in your former letter.[11]

With kindest regards and best wishes to you and all our good friends in the great cause, I am,

Sincerely and fraternally yours,   Saml Gompers.
President,   American Federation of Labor.

TLpS, reel 213, vol. 225, pp. 376–81, SG Letterbooks, DLC.

1. See "From J. Havelock Wilson," Sept. 13, 1916, above.

2. See "From Carl Legien," Apr. 2, 1915, above.

3. SG to the AFL Executive Council, Sept. 7, 1916, Executive Council Records, Vote Books, reel 15, frame 140, *AFL Records.*

4. SG to the AFL Executive Council, Sept. 15, 1916, Executive Council Records, Vote Books, reel 15, frames 164–65, *AFL Records.*

5. The AFL Executive Council approved SG's proposal and submitted it to the 1916 AFL convention as part of the Council's report on international labor relations. The convention endorsed it but also authorized the Council to continue its efforts with respect to a postwar labor conference. On Dec. 21 SG wrote the secretaries of the national trade union centers in Europe, Turkey, South Africa, Australia, New Zealand, Japan, Argentina, and Brazil, informing them of the convention's action (AFL Microfilm Convention File, reel 28, frames 2002–3, *AFL Records*).

6. SG is referring to declarations concerning a postwar labor conference adopted by the 1914 and 1915 AFL conventions and sent to representatives of national trade union centers on Dec. 10, 1914, and Mar. 26, 1916, respectively.

7. The text in brackets is supplied from a copy of the letter in the Files of the Office of the President, General Correspondence, reel 81, frame 438, *AFL Records.*

8. SG wrote Harry O. McClurg, a member of Brotherhood of Painters, Decorators, and Paperhangers of America 58 of Birmingham, Ala., on Aug. 19, 1916, in response to an inquiry from McClurg about the records of the presidential candidates in the 1916 election. In his reply, SG favorably compared the record of President Woodrow Wilson, the Democratic candidate, to that of the Republican candidate, Charles Evans Hughes (reel 211, vol. 223, pp. 878–87, SG Letterbooks, DLC). SG's letter was later printed as a circular under the date of Aug. 28 and signed by SG, James O'Connell, and Frank Morrison, the members of the AFL Labor Representation Committee (United Brotherhood of Carpenters and Joiners of America Records, reel 2, frames 741–48, *AFL and the Unions*). The committee issued a second circular on Oct. 14 that emphasized the importance of the election and the accomplishments of the Wilson administration. It was printed in the *AFL Weekly News Letter* on Oct. 21 under the heading "Statement by Labor Representation Committee."

9. The fraternal delegates from the TUC to the 1916 AFL convention were Harry Gosling and William Whitefield.

10. SG to Charles Bowerman, Oct. 30, 1916, reel 214, vol. 226, pp. 757–59, SG Letterbooks, DLC; and SG to William Appleton, Oct. 31, 1916, ibid., pp. 760–62.

11. Wilson to SG, July 17, 1916, AFL Microfilm Convention File, reel 27, frames 1379–80, *AFL Records.*

From Léon Jouhaux

General Confederation of Labor.
Paris, September 28, 1916.

Brother:

I am informed by some Italian labor organizations of the critical situation awaiting Brother Tresca,[1] a militant worker arrested during the miners' strike[2] in the State of Minnesota. This militant Brother, it is said, is to be electrocuted, and it would seem proper that steps be taken to overcome this decision by interesting public opinion and by intervening in his favor.

I trust that in spite of the dreadful calamities the people have had to sustain a campaign by the labor organizations would save this militant member, thereby showing that notwithstanding the excitement a joint interest still remains alive in the hearts of the proletariats.

In the hope to receive from you Brother Gompers,[3] please accept for yourself and the members of your committee, my fraternal salutations,

(Signed) L. Jouhaux.

TLtpSr, reel 214, vol. 226, p. 529, SG Letterbooks, DLC. Typed notation: "*Copy.*" Enclosed in R. Lee Guard to William Green, Oct. 26, 1916, ibid., p. 528.

1. Carlo Tresca (1879–1943) was born in Sulmona, Italy, where he became a member of the railroad workers' union and editor of *Il Germe* (The Seed). Threatened with imprisonment for criticizing the Italian monarchy, he chose banishment as an alternative and emigrated to Switzerland and then to the United States in 1904, settling in Philadelphia. There he edited *Il Proletario* (The Proletarian), the organ of the Italian Socialist Federation, until 1906, and then he published his own paper, *La Plebe* (The Common People), which he moved to Pittsburgh in 1908. He later moved to New York City, where he began publishing *L'Avvenire* (The Future) in 1913 and its successor, *Il Martello* (The Hammer), in 1916.

Tresca was active in the IWW's Lawrence, Mass., textile workers' strike (1912), the New York City hotel workers' strike (1913), and the Paterson, N.J., silk workers' strike (1913). In June 1916 the IWW sent him and other organizers to northern Minnesota, where iron ore miners were on strike. After violence erupted on July 3—mine guards broke into the home of a striker and in the ensuing melee two men, including a guard, were killed—several of these organizers, including Tresca, were arrested as accessories to murder on the grounds that their speeches had been incendiary. The organizers were released in an arranged settlement after the strike ended, and three workers apprehended in connection with the incident pleaded guilty to manslaughter charges and were sentenced to prison terms.

Although not a member of the IWW in 1917, Tresca was indicted in September of that year, along with William Haywood and other IWW members, for conspiracy to interfere with the war effort. Tresca, Elizabeth Gurley Flynn, Joseph Ettor, and Arturo Giovannitti successfully appealed to sever their cases from the others, and the charges against them were dropped in 1919. During the 1920s Tresca emerged as an outspoken critic of the fascist regime of Benito Mussolini, and he continued his antifascist campaign until his death. His stand against fascism led to at least four attempts on his life in the 1930s; he was murdered in New York City in July 1943.

2. On June 3, 1916, iron ore miners in the Mesabi Range struck for an eight-hour day, a wage increase, and an end to the contract system, which based wages on production. By month's end, eight to ten thousand miners, many of whom had joined the IWW Metal Mine Workers' Industrial Union, were out on strike. Local mayors failed in an attempt on July 8 to negotiate a settlement with the companies on behalf of the striking miners, and two federal mediators, Hywel Davies and William Fairley, who arrived on July 27, failed as well. During the week of Sept. 17 the miners voted to return to

work, and the central strike committee officially ended the walkout on Sept. 24.

3. On Oct. 26, 1916, R. Lee Guard sent a copy of Léon Jouhaux's letter, received while SG was absent, to William Green, secretary-treasurer of the United Mine Workers of America (reel 214, vol. 226, p. 528, SG Letterbooks, DLC).

To Hugh Frayne

Sept. 30, 1916.

Mr. Hugh Frayne,
Organizer, American Federation of Labor,
Continental Hotel, New York City.
Dear Sir and Brother:

Your favor of the 29th instant just received and read with the keenest interest, and much of it with deep regret, for I feel with you that the interest of the striking street railwaymen[1] has not been furthered but rather injured by the policy pursued by several of the men in an influential position in the labor movement of New York.

You will recall the fact that there appeared in the newspapers of Sunday morning, September tenth, the declaration not only in favor of a general strike of the working people of the City of New York in "sympathy" with the striking street railwaymen, but that the entire conduct of the railwaymen's strike and the sympathetic strike was to be turned over to "President Gompers" for direction and administration.[2] When in Boston[3] that Sunday morning I bought the newspapers of Boston and New York, and there the whole proposition was "played up" to its fullest extent. They even published the time of my expected arrival in New York that Sunday afternoon, and that I was expected to be at a conference at the Continental Hotel, New York City, for the purpose of taking charge of the railwaymen and the general strike. Even newspaper reporters were waiting for me at the railway station upon my arrival.

I came to the hotel, and as you know, conference was held and I made quite plain not only my position but the position of the American Federation of Labor and its policy in a situation such as was presented, and I expressed my strong dissent from what seemed to be the general trend of thought and action of the men participating in the conference. You will recall also that I prepared a statement[4] which I thought ought to be given out if any statement was given out at all, and if that statement had been accepted by the conference as the expression of its judgment, all efforts could have been concentrated by the working people and the sympathetic public on the street railwaymen's strike and every man and woman of labor doing his and her level best financially, morally, and even politically if necessary, in order to bring about the best results in the interest of the striking street railwaymen. The entire situation would have been different from what it now is.

The question of a general sympathetic strike is a double edged sword and the declaration for such a strike arouses bitterness on the one side and often resentment or indifference on the other. A general strike is so far reaching that its consequences cannot be foreseen, and the making of a declaration without its even superficial execution brings a reaction most injurious to the workers themselves, and places their cause in a position of jeopardy. In any event, the declaration of a general strike right in the initial stages of the street railwaymen's strike was a tactical, monumental blunder. It played the heaviest trump card at the most inopportune time. It was in the character of what is known as an anti-climax. There are other features of mistaken policy to which it is not necessary to refer, but of which you are equally with me aware.

There was a course that I would have suggested, one that might have been effective, but the air of the conference that Sunday afternoon at the Continental Hotel in New York City was so surcharged with ultra, impractical action that I concluded it would have been absolutely useless for me to give expression to it.

We have seen the result of the declaration for the general strike or suspension of work on last Wednesday and now it is proposed that a "convention" is to be held Monday morning, for the purpose of further considering taking action looking toward a general sympathetic strike. You know how deeply concerned I am that the street railwaymen may win outright in all of their demands, for they are justified, but after the close of the street railwaymen's strike whether they win or lose, the labor movement must still go on, for the labor movement represents the cause of justice and freedom and humanity, and though it has had a considerably long life, its greatest work and achievements must be for and in the future. The labor movement has had its defeats and setbacks, but it has survived. It cannot help but survive. It must survive. It will learn by its mistakes and its defeats. It cannot be driven back and it is to these facts to which we must of necessity direct our main thoughts and action.

As I declared in my statement on Sunday, September 10, and have repeated, I will do all that lies in my power to bring into play every power and influence which the American labor movement can wield to aid the striking street railwaymen in their heroic struggle. That declaration stands for all that it implies. You remember my remarks to Mr. Fitzgerald before the meeting at the City Hall over which Mayor Mitchel presided; that inasmuch as Mr. Shonts[5] and Mr. Headley[6] have taken their unwarrantable and unjustifiable position in trying to crush out the organization of the street railwaymen, and to crush out the spirit of the men, that it behooves the Amalgamated Association to do anything and everything within its power and within the law to maintain the rights and interests of the men.

And now recurring to the proposed convention on Monday. Let me prevail upon you to see to it that no mistaken course shall be pursued which is likely to bring injury to the men and women of labor and the movement which is their protector and defender.

There are many matters that press upon my mind for expression in connection with this entire subject, but of which I have now not the time to write herein. This is Saturday afternoon that I am writing this letter to you, and I am desirous of it reaching you tomorrow Sunday and for which purpose I am sending it to you by special delivery.

With assurances that my entire purpose is to be of some practical service to our fellows, I am, with best wishes,

Fraternally yours,　Saml Gompers.
President,　American Federation of Labor.

TLpS, reel 213, vol. 225, pp. 574–77, SG Letterbooks, DLC.

1. On Sept. 6, 1916, drivers and conductors struck the Interborough Rapid Transit Co. (which ran subways and elevated trains in Manhattan and the Bronx) and the New York Railways Co. (which handled streetcars). They demanded a wage increase, a shorter workday, new work rules, and, most importantly, acceptance of their right to organize and to bargain collectively, which they thought they had won in an earlier agreement with New York Railways. Soon over twelve thousand traction workers were on strike, and streetcar service was brought to a standstill; however, traffic on subway and elevated trains, which were not as well organized, was less affected. On Sept. 10 a committee of the city's labor leaders endorsed the calling of a general strike—a step SG opposed—involving as many as eight hundred thousand workers. Local unions were unenthusiastic, and rank-and-file support was weak, and when the general strike finally began on Sept. 27 only a few thousand workers participated. The general strike ended in a few days, and the transit strike came to an end shortly thereafter.

2. The *New York Times*, for example, reported on Sept. 10, 1916, that SG would be asked to "take supreme command of the biggest strike any city has every experienced" in order to "save the day" for the transit strike.

3. Leaving Washington, D.C., on Sept. 2, 1916, SG had traveled to Boston to resolve a controversy involving AFL Cigar Factory Tobacco Strippers' Union 8156 and to meet with James Duncan, organizer Frank McCarthy, and a committee from the Boston Central Labor Union. His trip also included stops in Lewiston, Hallowell, Portland, and Rumford Falls, Maine. After meeting with representatives of the strikers in New York City, SG addressed the convention of the International Union of Steam and Operating Engineers in Newark, N.J., and then returned to AFL headquarters on Sept. 13.

4. A statement by SG, calling on New York City workers to give the strikers moral and financial support and asking the public not to patronize the lines involved in the contest, was published in the *New York Times* on Sept. 11, 1916.

5. Theodore P. Shonts was president of the Interborough Consolidated Corp. of New York and its subordinate companies, Interborough Rapid Transit and New York Railways.

6. Frank Hedley was vice-president and general manager of Interborough Rapid Transit and New York Railways.

To M. Grant Hamilton

October 5, 1916.

Mr. Grant Hamilton,
Organizer, American Federation of Labor,
1019 Karpen Bldg., Chicago, Illinois
Dear Sir and Brother:

Your several letters of recent date have all been read with interest, and I am glad that you are sending me such complete information of the work in Chicago.

In regard to the Adamson Law, you are correct in interpreting my position. The service which the railroads render to the people of this country is necessary to the very life of the people. Society is now so highly organized and specialized that no person or group of persons produces all those things which are necessary, every-day wants, and to supply the needs of physical, social and mental activity. Of course the service rendered by any agency cannot be estimated as a fixed quantity, but the service is of a relative degree of importance dependent upon the particular viewpoint or the particular needs to be considered.

However, it is true that generally speaking the service is vitally important.

It has been necessary in the development of railroads of the country for the government to assist those who had in charge the building and extension of railroads. This was done through grants of territory and through appropriations. The people of the country then have an actual investment interest in many of the railroads. It was necessary in the beginning, when the country was less settled and the difficulties of building trans-continental lines were too great for individual capital, for the people through their government to assist in the work. They, too, participated in the benefits of the results.

When, after the railroads were built, railroad presidents and trustees attempted to utilize railroads as agencies of exploitation and to favor some [private?] interests at the expense of others, through systems of bonuses [and] special privilege, it was necessary for the people of this country to establish government regulation. That regulation has resulted in the elimination of many of the wrongs and in the establishment of better service to all of the people.

Government regulation with private ownership has won the general approval of the people. Of course, not all of the abuses have been remedied, but it has been a general opinion that these wrongs could be greatly decreased through increasing the scope and the vigilance of government regulation.

The American Federation of Labor has taken official action as approving government ownership of railroads and telegraphs. There has been no active effort made to bring about this purpose because we were waiting for a final opinion as to the value of government regulation. However, there can be no doubt that the railroads of the country under government regulation must be regarded as quasi-public institutions. The railroads themselves earn their profits through the service that they render to the people. The people depend upon the service in carrying on the affairs of industry and communication. The time may come when it may be deemed best to substitute government ownership for individual ownership of railroads. The labor movement is not opposed to that purpose when events demonstrate that the change will be for the best interest of the people.

I have already written in response to the inquiry from an officer of the Railroad Telegraphers[1] that according to the wording of the Adamson Law it could be applied to the members of their organization also. If the interpretation is correct that railroads are quasi-public institutions, a discrimination cannot be made as to groups of their employes. An eight hour law applying to one group will naturally be extended to all other groups of workers. However, at the present stage, when the Adamson Law is still on trial and the railroad companies may be seeking eagerly for reasons, particularly reasons of cost, for relief from the eight hour law, there is no reason to try to claim every application to which the law may properly be put.

Our successes in establishing the eight hour principle have been by gradual and insistent demands for its increasingly wider application. It would be very unwise I think to venture any opinion as to the application of the Adamson Law, at the present time. This, I think is the attitude that the railroad brotherhoods are going to take in the matter. One of their presidents has sent me a copy of a letter in which he expresses this viewpoint and suggests that it is better to let the railroads themselves take the initiative. The particular point he was discussing was the constitutionality of the law, but the same principle holds true as to the general attitude that we ought to take, I think, upon questions as to whether or not the law applies to various trades.

The Adamson Law applies to men in the operating service of the railroads. The railroad companies observe a distinction between the operating department and the shops which they have at different points in the country. Railroad shop work has never been under government regulation and is conducted as any other private industry. The Adamson Law would not properly apply to men employed in the shops and constitutes no reason for changing the A.F. of L. policy that industrial relations and private industries should be regulated by agreements between the men organized in unions and representatives of the railroads.

The work done in railroad shops is not directly connected with the transportation work, and therefore does not have the characteristic that makes transportation service a quasi-public institution. The Adamson Law in itself does not constitute any argument for securing the eight hour day by law in railroad shops or in any department of railroad work except the actual transportation service.

As you say, I think you have my position upon compulsion. I regard any movement to replace voluntary institutions by those of a compulsory nature as the greatest menace to the welfare of the workers and an issue which when made becomes of greater importance to the labor movement than anything else.

I am very glad to have the copies of the letters and articles which you are sending out and I hope that you will let me have all others so that our file may be complete showing the activities of the American Federation of Labor to protect the interest of the workers in this political campaign.

With best wishes and hoping to hear from you whenever convenient, I am,

Fraternally yours,   Saml Gompers.
President,   American Federation of Labor.

TLpS, reel 213, vol. 225, pp. 806–9½, SG Letterbooks, DLC.

1. C. H. Meador, general chairman of Order of Railroad Telegraphers Division 126, wrote SG on Sept. 4, 1916, to ask if the members of his union came under the provisions of the Adamson Act (AFL Microfilm National and International Union File, Railroad Telegraphers Records, reel 41, frame 2209, *AFL Records*). In his reply, dated Sept. 20, SG wrote: "Of course, as you know, the enactment of the bill resulted from the demands which the four railroad brotherhoods presented and urged; and the law was for the immediate purpose of averting a strike of the members of these brotherhoods, which seemed imminent. The interpretation and meaning of the law must be determined in the near future; your organization has nothing to lose from presenting claims to the eight-hour day under this law. Of course, the railroad companies will give no more benefits under this law than they are forced to concede, and your organization ought to take up the matter immediately" (reel 213, vol. 225, pp. 93–94, SG Letterbooks, DLC). SG sent a copy of this letter to Henry Perham, president of the Railroad Telegraphers, the same day.

From Frank Duffy

October 6th-1916.

Dear Sir and Brother:—

When your communication under date of September 22nd[1] relative to organizing the West Indian laborers of the Canal Zone was received, I was in Fort Worth, Texas attending the Nineteenth General Convention of the United Brotherhood of Carpenters and Joiners of America. On my return to this office I found your communication referred to awaiting me. In reply thereto I wish to inform you that many complaints have been lodged with me by our Carpenters Union[2] in Panama against the employment of aliens to do United States work. Not only that, but West Indian laborers were hired and used to do Carpenter work at very poor wages. In fact, somewhere about twenty-two cents per hour. They were used exclusively to erect frame buildings while the members of our organization did not get a chance to do this kind of work, for the reason that their rate of wages was very much higher and the authorities believed this class of work should be done much cheaper. You can realize the unpleasantness thus created. Again in putting up shelving, it was said by the authorities that the Carpenters rate of wages was too high and that therefore this work should be done by West Indian laborers or those who would work cheap.

Carpenter work whether in the rough, the smooth or the finish should be done by carpenters and not by laborers or any other class of mechanics. Brother Boyer[3] a member of our Union in Panama was a delegate to the Fort Worth Convention. I had a long conference with him on conditions as they exist on the Canal Zone. He substantiated the complaints that were made to me relative to laborers and others doing Carpenter work. In fact, he informed me it was a shame the way the work was done.

I therefore, as General Secretary of this organization cannot consent to the organization of the West Indian laborers who are working on the Canal Zone and who are now and have been doing work which properly belongs to us. I further protest against aliens doing work for the United States while plenty of our own citizens, even in these good times are out of employment.

With best wishes and kindest regards, I am,

Fraternally yours,
General Secretary.

TLc, United Brotherhood of Carpenters and Joiners of America Records, reel 2, frame 688, *AFL and the Unions*.

1. SG to Frank Duffy, Sept. 22, 1916, reel 213, vol. 225, pp. 265–66, SG Letterbooks, DLC.

2. United Brotherhood of Carpenters and Joiners of America 913 of Balboa, Canal Zone.

3. C. S. Boyer of Ancón, Canal Zone.

From Granville Johnson[1]

Washington, D.C., October 7, 1916.

Dear Sir:

Will you kindly inform me if it is possible for the negro engineers of the District of Columbia to again become benefited under the charter they have. Their number was (94) ninety-four.[2] If that local union, or one similar, for engineers can be revived, please tell us how to proceed.

The time has come now when the colored man feels that he, too, needs the affiliation, cooperation and assistance of that great organization, the American Federation of Labor, which has done, and is doing so much to stamp out the oppression of the laborer by the capitalist.

The colored man is asking only for a chance. We hope that the noble leaders of the Federation will lend aid and that we may be able to look forward to the time when all of the working people of the country will be so unionized that a strike or lock out in any occupation will bring about a universal standstill until capital concedes to us our just deserts.

Thanking you, kind sir, in advance, for an early reply,[3] and with highest esteem, I beg to remain,

Yours in honest endeavor,
(Signed) Granville T. Johnson

TLtpSr, reel 213, vol. 225, p. 919, SG Letterbooks, DLC. Typed notation: "*Copy.*" Enclosed in SG to James Hannahan, Oct. 10, 1916, ibid., p. 918.

1. Granville T. Johnson was a Washington, D.C., stationary fireman.

2. International Union of Steam Engineers 94 of Washington, D.C., was founded in 1902. It was later suspended for nonpayment of dues.

3. SG sent James Hannahan, secretary of the International Union of Steam and Operating Engineers, a copy of Johnson's letter on Oct. 10, 1916, and informed Johnson of this the same day (reel 213, vol. 225, pp. 918, 984, SG Letterbooks, DLC). The local does not appear to have been rechartered.

An Account by Samuel Gompers of a Meeting with the Mexican Commissioners

Washington, D.C., October 12, 1916

Last Sunday, October 8, President Gompers, upon the request of Secretary Lane, Chairman of the American Mexican Commission, now meeting in Atlantic City, went over to Atlantic City for a conference with him. They talked over matters for over two hours. On Monday morning Mr. Gompers left for New York to keep engagements in that city. On Tuesday morning he wired to the Mexican Commission[1] asking for a hearing. He returned to Atlantic City that day, and was heard by the Mexican Commissioners that afternoon and by the American Commissioners the next day, Wednesday. When he returned to the office Thursday morning, he dictated the following to his secretary, Miss Guard:[2]

In my interview with the Mexican commissioners I recalled the fact of the constant sympathy with which the American Federation of labor movement including myself had acted toward the interests of the working people and the masses of the people of Mexico and as a nation itself and this, too, for more than twenty years. I recounted some of the things of the early times in which we had been helpful. Mr. Cabero,[3] Mr. Pania[4] sat all through the conference from the beginning and Mr. Bonillas[5] came in after the conference had been on for more than half an hour. I referred to some of the sympathetic actions toward Mexico in the last five years—the agreement entered into by Mr. Campani[6]—that I had received information from Mexico that the feeling toward Carranza had undergone considerable change by reason of the decree[7] he recently issued in the federal district and the statement that he has now joined the reactionary forces against the effort at freedom [for] which the Mexican workmen were led to believe Chief Carranza stood. I quoted Carlyle's famous observation that despite the fact that people may in the first instance abuse newly found freedom, it was not a proper course to pursue to take freedom from them. The famous Carlyle declaration was that the remedy for the evils resulting from newly acquired freedom is more freedom. The Commissioners gave me an English translation of the decree and it contains all the evil things that have been said about it. It is a resuscitation of the decree under Jaurez[8] promulgated in 1862 and had reference to real political disorders. General Carranza's order had extended it to strikes in munition factories and public service institutions.

After hearing me fully upon the subject the Commissioners showed me the English translation of the decree and a memorandum in connection with it. They then said substantially that Mr. Carranza and his government still are in entire sympathy with the working people and want to keep faith with the labor unions; that he had been accused by the enemies of Mexico both within and without of leaning too much toward the working people; that he and the government were charged with catering to the I.W.W. and the anarchists and encouraging social-ism; that that was one reason why the credit of the country has been somewhat impaired; that Carranza had all his influence, sympathy and power with the workers in every contention they made over the strike[9] inaugurated by them. This strike was not a strike the conditions of which could be conceded. They mentioned the fact that the money of the country now is not coin or specie but is a paper currency; that the demand was not for increased wages but for specie payment which was impossible for the government to carry into effect; that the only notice of a general strike was a small circular declaring that after 48 hours a general strike would be inaugurated; that there was neither the name of an association or a group or an individual so that as a matter of fact the government and its representatives deemed it incred-ible that such a strike would be inaugurated, and sought by every means within its power to find some organization or representative of orga-nization with whom a conference might be had to explain the situa-tion and endeavor to adjust it; that the strike did occur and that for several days there was neither light nor power by which the people might travel through the streets or operate any of the railroads lines or street cars or operate any machinery; that inasmuch as the workers did not give service at the waterworks there was no water supply—peo-ple were unable to perform the ordinary functions of life. People in hospitals, ill, were unable to be kept in any sort of condition by which life might be maintained even in the hospitals, and that under the conditions of which the above is only a part that Mr. Carranza issued the decree and that it was in indefinite form as to labor unions; that no man was shot but one man was sentenced to death.

I called attention to the fact that the philosophy of the workers where they had any at all had been gotten through the Spanish literature from Spanish and Italian speaking countries; that the effort which we were making here was to endeavor to instill the thought into the minds of Mexican workmen to organize upon a constructive, consistent, con-tinuous, voluntary basis; that even with the higher ideals of the Amer-ican workingman yet we are here likely to make mistakes; that it can not be expected that the Mexican workmen would escape errors in course of action when their efforts have been frowned down upon so long, suppressed for centuries, denied the opportunity for self-expres-sion and independence; that the right of assemblage, association, freedom of speech and of press is a necessary element of the education of the people and their assertion of the rights and the maintenance of self-respect.

It was then when I quoted McCauley's statement. In any event, the visitation of the death sentence upon workmen because of their refusal to work was brutal, unjustified, and ought to be reversed.

The commissioners then stated to me that there was no question but the strike was not a real strike for better conditions; it was not intended to accomplish that purpose but that it was a political act to overturn and destroy the government and that it was not intended to be in the interests of the working people.

From various angles I again presented the matter and protested against the decree and against its execution. They then declared that they agreed with me that the severity of the terms of the decree was a mistake. I requested that they make the representation to General Carranza. They said that they would and had no doubt but that as soon as the situation was clarified a bit the decree would be modified or revoked. Incidentally I declared that a government which found it necessary to resort to the extremes as indicated in the decree—the denial of the rights of the working people—did not deserve to be maintained or deserve the sympathy of the American working people.

Later I recounted to them the efforts which were being made for the establishment of a Pan-American labor movement in the hope not only of bettering the conditions of the toilers of each of the countries but also to help in establishing and maintaining the best possible relations between the governments of our respective countries.

TD, Files of the Office of the President, General Correspondence, reel 81, frames 494–97, *AFL Records.* Handwritten notation: "Not complete."

1. Actually SG to Luis Cabrera, Oct. 9, 1916, reel 213, vol. 225, p. 953, SG Letterbooks, DLC.

2. Rosa Lee GUARD was SG's private secretary.

3. Luis Cabrera (1876–1954), an attorney, served as minister of the Mexican Secretariat of Treasury and Public Credit (1914–17, 1919–20).

4. Alberto J. Pani (1878–1955), an engineer, served as director-general of the National Railroads of Mexico (1915), minister of the Secretariats of Industry and Commerce (1917–18), Foreign Relations (1921–23), and Treasury and Public Credit (1923–27, 1932–33), and as ambassador to France (1918–20, 1927–31) and to Spain and Portugal (1931–32).

5. Ignacio Bonillas (1858–1942) served as acting minister of the Secretariat of Communications and Public Works (1914–17) and as ambassador to the United States (1917–20). In 1920 he was an unsuccessful candidate for president of Mexico.

6. The agreement of Feb. 17, 1915, between the Casa del Obrero Mundial and the Mexican government was signed for the government by Rafael Zubarán Capmany.

7. On Aug. 1, 1916, in the face of a general strike in Mexico City, President Venustiano Carranza declared martial law and invoked the Juárez decree of 1862, which stip-

ulated the death penalty for enemies of the state. Under Carranza's order, those discussing, approving, or inciting the suspension of work at factories or other enterprises in the "public service" were subject to arrest and trial before military tribunals.

8. Benito Pablo Juárez (1806–72) served as president of Mexico from 1858 to 1872.

9. In the face of inflation, food shortages, and unemployment, the Casa del Obrero Mundial called a general strike in Mexico City on the morning of July 31, 1916. Carranza responded by closing the offices of the Casa both in Mexico City and in the provinces, declaring martial law, and arresting strike leaders. By Aug. 3 the strike had been broken.

To Ole Lian[1]

October 14, 1916.

Mr. Ole O. Lian,
Youngsgatan 13, Kristiania, Norway.
Dear Sir and Brother:

It is indeed interesting to learn that the organized labor movement of Norway has under consideration the form that ought to be adopted by labor unions, and policies and methods to be used in your trade union struggle. It is a question that has been agitated at intervals here in the United States, but has always been decided in favor of our tried and accepted policy, that is, every organization has been left free to decide upon and adopt the forms of organization that are best suited to the exigencies of the trade, and to the various circumstances and opposing forces with which the workers of the trade have to contend.

With us the labor movement is the natural product of industrial conditions. It is a flexible, adjustable organization that best serves the needs of the trade for which it is adopted. We do not consider that the form of organization is that which is of fundamental importance, but we leave each organization free to adopt whatever form brings the best results under existing conditions. At different times in the history of the labor movement of this country it has been suggested that some particular form has inherent advantages over all other forms and ought, therefore, to become the standard for the whole movement, but the suggestion has never gained favor with the workers.

Industrial organization is a living, growing thing, very sensitive to existing forces and susceptible of many changes to meet improved methods of production or a change in the market demand. The organization of the workers cannot be a hard and fast fixture; it must be something plastic that will change as organization and industry change. The generally prevailing type of organization in this country is based upon local unions of workers belonging to a common trade. These are united into national or international organizations consisting of the workers of that trade in the United States or on the American Continent. These national bodies are federated in the American Federation of Labor.

Following the development of industrial organization upon a large scale, which was accompanied by extreme specialization, wage-earners found that the old trade organizations did not meet all of their new problems; they found that there was a close overlapping of trades and the introduction of machinery into many trades rendered useless much of trade skill. Inventions and discoveries have produced many new materials and developed many new industries with additional trades and new kinds of work. As a result, jurisdictional differences developed between many organizations, but it is a mistake to regard jurisdictional differences as a defect of the organization of the workers; it is no defect at all, but is the inevitable consequence of growth and progress in production. The jurisdictional dispute represents the efforts of organized workers to adjust their organizations to meet new problems. In connection with this matter let me call your attention to an editorial in the January 1916 issue of the *American Federationist,* a copy of which I am sending you. The editorial is entitled "Jurisdictional Claims—Ambitious Hopes."[2]

Industrial unionism as proposed in this country for adoption by the A.F. of L. emanated from a socialist group whose purpose was to defeat the policies of the trade unionists. The labor movement has never objected to industrial unionism, but it has protested repeatedly against attempts to foist that fixed method of organization upon all workers regardless of their desires, or regardless of the peculiar problems existing in their trade. Some of our largest organizations have adopted the principle of industrial unionism; among these are the United Mine Workers of America, and the Brewers' Organization. There are other organizations that have tried the experiment and have reverted to the trade union form. This is what happened in the case of the International Typographical Union.

There is a strong emotional factor in the situation that cannot be ignored. Workers form a very strong attachment for their trade union and for the workers in their own trades or callings. Like all other things about which human sentiment has been surrounded, the workers are not willing to give up their trade organizations. We have devised various methods that afford many of the advantages claimed for industrial unionism, and yet, at the same time retain all of the strength of the trade organization. Trades whose workers are closely associated, form working agreements. Some trades provide for an exchange of working cards. There have been organized five departments directly affiliated to the American Federation of Labor; these are the Building Trades Department, to which belong all building trades; the Metal Trades, the Union Label Trades, the Railroad and the Mining Departments. These departments are able to affect a better adjustment of the claims and interests of the various trades and serve as a clearing house for the problems and the efforts of these various trades.

We have local unions organized upon practically the same basis as the common local unions that have been proposed for the Norway Labor Movement. We call these locals federal unions. They are organized when there are not sufficient workers belonging to any one trade to form a local trade union, and yet there are a number of workers belonging to various trades who wish to become identified with the organized labor movement. Local federal unions are regarded as purely transitory organizations. They are more of a defensive organization than they are an agency adapted to secure increased benefits for the workers affiliated. The problems and the needs of the workers of various trades differ widely; trade conditions and trade exigencies that determine opportune time for presenting new demands differ widely in the various trades. It becomes a serious problem then, how to utilize the economic power of a local federal union to support the demands of the workers belonging to the separate trades. There are elements of human nature and conditions attending the economic problems of the various workers that cannot be ignored. These facts enhance the difficulty of making working agreements with employers. Wage-earners, like all other people, have a greater interest in their own affairs and welfare than in those of their fellow workers in another trade.

The industrial union is a cumbersome agency that has not the effective force and adaptability of the trade union. The proposition to restrict the power and effectiveness of the national organization seems to me deplorable. There is so much work that must be done by a national organization in coordinating the efforts of the various local movements, and in protecting the general movement, that the proposal to devitalize your national movement and to make of it a mere bureaucratic agency, seems nothing less than a colossal blunder. The national organization can accomplish nothing unless it has real power; unless it is the real spokesman and representative for the collective national economic power of the wage-earners. When the wage-earners themselves restrict the power of the national organization, they are restricting its effectiveness along all lines.

The Industrial Workers of the World, which was organized in Chicago in 1905, represent a very small proportion of the wage-earners of this country. It was organized by a group of men connected with the labor movement who had been associated with various discredited plans and visionary theories. In 1908 The Industrial Workers of the World divided into two groups, one having its headquarters at Chicago, and the other at Detroit, fighting each other with the same hostility that they displayed toward employers. The methods and the doctrines of this organization have never found favor and following among workers who had accepted American standards and the American spirit. The I.W.W. can be said to have no real organization in this country; they have organized a local union here and there, but have made no attempt to follow out the pretentious plan which they announce in their constitution and program. Their unions have been formed chiefly where there are colonies of immigrant workers, and where industrial oppression is extreme. These workers, who have not yet learned that industrial welfare must be worked out by following a consistent, definite program, have been incited by the extravagant promises and the wild appeal to violence by the representatives of the I.W.W. to go on strikes. Some of these strikes have involved numbers of workers and have attracted considerable attention. Among them were the strike at Lawrence, Massachusetts; at Paterson, New Jersey; in the hop fields of California;[3] and most recently among the steel workers of Pittsburg,[4] and the iron ore miners of Minnesota.

In conducting these strikes, the I.W.W. leaders have invariably advised workers to use methods that reacted against them, and only resulted in additional victimization. The theory and the purpose of the leaders has invariably been revolution, but they have deceived the strikers by advising them to adopt revolutionary methods instead of methods that would make a strike successful; they have advised against all agreements with employers.

One advantage has almost invariably followed strike movements conducted by the I.W.W. Employers and workers alike have come to have a greater appreciation of the methods and policies of the American trade union movement. In Paterson, New Jersey, a strike of silk workers some years ago was accompanied by violence and suffering on the part of the workers. The strike did not succeed in establishing higher wages or better conditions of work. There were several spectacular methods employed in the strike such as sending the children of the strikers away to neighboring cities to be taken care of by fellow workers, and the production of a play in New York City reproducing strike scenes. However, the strike ended in failure. Since the strike, the silk workers in and around Paterson have been organizing in unions affiliated to the American Federation of Labor, and have been carrying on the constructive work of organization. Through the increasing power of the economic [organiza]tion last year they reduced the hours of work to nine in the textile mills in and about Paterson. What was true in Paterson was true of all I.W.W. strikes.

During the past summer a strike has been in progress among the iron workers in the Mesaba range in Minnesota. The strike was conducted by the I.W.W. and thus far has proved a failure. The organizations affiliated to the A.F. of L. could not interfere in the situation when the I.W.W. were in local control, but they are now seeking an opportunity to enter into that field to organize miners. Experiences in this country have demonstrated again and again that the work of the I.W.W. has brought disaster to the workers involved and has not gained them any agency by which to achieve constructive results. The I.W.W. contains but a relatively small number of the wage earners of this country. It has been given considerable prominence in newspapers and in magazines because of the sensational characteristics of many of their endeavors. As you know that which is sensational secures much wider publicity than normal constructive work. There are in this country a group of social uplifters who filled the magazines with articles describing the I.W.W. and their tactics; however, even these writers now seldom mention that organization.

It is practically impossible to give you any accurate statistics showing the membership of the organization. The officers of the I.W.W. have given out varying and contradictory statements. Two research students have recently published statistics of the organization, but although both students claim to base their figures upon correspondence with the headquarters of both branches of the I.W.W., their figures do not agree.[5] The last figures given show that in 1914 the Detroit national headquarters claimed a membership of two thousand, [and the] Chicago branch [twelve thousand. According to their figures the total][6] membership of the I.W.W. in all America was fourteen thousand.[7] However, I was informed by a professor[8] of political economy in the University of Chicago, who secured his information, not through correspondence but through personal examination of the records in the offices, that both branches of the organization had a membership of not over eight thousand among all American workers. He made this statement to me in 1914.

Those advocates of industrial unionism of your country who are basing their statements upon the achievements of the Industrial Workers of the World have doubtless reached their conclusions from the glowing articles written under the excitement of some I.W.W. strike. The organization has been decreasing in power and importance during the past years.

The constructive labor movement of this country that has been grow-

ing in power and effectiveness is a labor movement that is not bound
or hampered by fixed forms or immutable programs; it is a developing process, a movement toward greater freedom and greater opportunity, restricted only by the ideals and aspirations of the workers.

No one has the right to set himself up in opposition to new thought
and new methods. As a matter of fact, these imply progress, but anyone in advocating new thoughts and new methods which would involve
the destruction of the organizations of the workers which have done
so much to promote and protect their rights and welfare, is not only
obstructing progress but destroying the instrumentality of greater
progress.

We are not lacking in experience in America of the same character
as is proposed in Norway. The Knights of Labor, which had an existence
of about ten years here, was typical. That organization undertook to
do exactly what is proposed in Norway as you describe it. The effort
was ineffective and destructive. We have had several other efforts of a
similar character in addition to the Knights of Labor, and in addition
to the so-called I.W.W. Where are these organizations? What has become of the condition of the workers during their existence? Simply
that the men have either lost courage and confidence in each other
and in themselves too; that some of them have reached the stage or
nearly, of lack of confidence in themselves.

And now just a word in regard to these "common unions" in any one
city. As you know, there are larger numbers in some trades and callings. In others very much smaller numbers. Then in other trades and
callings there are comparatively an infinitesimal number. What consideration would be given to the rights and interests of this small number of workers of a trade in meetings in which the workers would be
in overwhelming numbers. The experience we have had in America
of such form of organization has been that the smaller numbers of men
with equal rights to be heard, have not been heard. Their interests have
been utterly neglected, their voice and judgment suppressed more
flagrantly than even at the hands of the employers. We have seen here,
and no doubt you have the experience in Norway, that there have been
trades and callings composed of small numbers of men which have
been most potential in their power to organize and to secure improved
conditions of life and work, notwithstanding opposition and antagonism to employers. Without regard to number, the right of the workers to organize in their particular trade or calling, or industry, is best
for their own expression, best to protect and promote their rights and
their interests. We ought to instill in the workers in all trades, in their
unions that it is necessary to be helpful to each other in every way
possible, to recommend the principle of fraternity, cooperation, and

solidarity. While it may be true that such a movement as I have endeavored to urge, such a movement as we follow in America, may not meet the fantastic notions of the sensationalists, it yet makes steady, consistent progress, and brings results, and instills courage and hope and common ideals among all the toilers of America. You asked me for my opinion and I have expressed it as fully as it is possible, and considering the time at my command and the many duties devolving upon me. I have answered you frankly, not only as a consequence of my many years of participation, observation, and study of the labor movement of America, and what I could glean and learn from the labor movements of other countries.

Should there be any additional information that you would like in connection with this most important matter that is to come before the special congress of the workers of the country, I should be very glad indeed to be of any possible assistance.

With best wishes and fraternal greetings to you and your associates, I am

Very sincerely yours,   Saml Gompers.
President,   American Federation of Labor.

TLpS, reel 214, vol. 226, pp. 60–69, SG Letterbooks, DLC.

1. Ole Olsen LIAN was chair of the Norwegian Arbeidernes Faglige Landsorganisasjon (National Federation of Labor) from 1907 to 1925.

2. "Jurisdiction Claims—Ambitious Hopes," *American Federationist* 23 (Jan. 1916): 46–47.

3. Inadequate housing, poor sanitation facilities, low wages, and a lack of drinking water led to a strike on Aug. 3, 1913, by hundreds of migrant agricultural workers employed to harvest hops at the Durst brothers' ranch in Wheatland, Calif. The evening the strike began, law enforcement officers attempted to break up a mass meeting of strikers and arrest IWW organizer Richard "Blackie" Ford. Gunshots were fired, a riot broke out, and four persons were killed—two strikers, the district attorney, and a deputy sheriff. The state militia arrived the next day, and Ford and Herman Suhr, another strike leader, were arrested. In January 1914 they were convicted of second-degree murder and sentenced to life imprisonment. In an effort to secure a new trial for the two men and to improve conditions in the hop fields, the IWW initiated a second strike there in August 1914. Although the IWW was unsuccessful in its attempt to free Ford and Suhr (both men remained in prison for a decade), the 1914 strike resulted in an investigation of conditions in the hop fields and the enactment of ameliorative legislation.

4. Probably a reference to a riot that erupted at the J. Edgar Thompson steelworks near Pittsburgh on May 2, 1916. The melee was an outgrowth of an eight-hour strike at the Westinghouse works in Pittsburgh that had begun on Apr. 22 and involved some fifteen thousand workers. When the Westinghouse strikers, a number of whom were organized as the American Industrial Union, marched on the Thompson works in an effort to precipitate a strike there as well, plant guards opened fire, killing three and wounding many others. The national guard was called in to prevent further violence, and the Westinghouse strike was settled by mediation on May 19.

5. Leo Wolman, "The Extent of Labor Organization in the United States in 1910," *Quarterly Journal of Economics* 30 (May 1916): 486–518, 601–24; and George E. Barnett, "Growth of Labor Organization in the United States, 1897–1914," ibid. (Aug. 1916): 780–95, 837–46.

6. The text in brackets is supplied from an extract of the letter in Files of the Office of the President, General Correspondence, reel 81, frame 514, *AFL Records*.

7. Barnett, "Growth of Labor Organization," p. 846.

8. Robert Hoxie.

Excerpts from the Minutes of a Meeting of the Executive Council of the AFL

Monday, October 16, 1916.

MORNING SESSION.

. . .

President Gompers made the following statement to the members of the Executive Council: ["]Gentlemen of the Executive Council:

"It affords me exceeding pleasure and gratification to welcome you at the first meeting of the Executive Council in the new building of the American Federation of Labor. It has been the dream and the hope of the organized labor movement of America for a long, long time at some period of our existence to have a building owned and controlled by the American labor movement itself. Due to the efforts of the Executive Council in recommending to the conventions of our American Federation of Labor, and the ready response of the men in our conventions, the authority was finally given to proceed with the work of selecting a site and of directing the construction of a building.

["]After two years of careful investigation of various sites most appropriate for the structure, finally we selected the site upon which this building now stands at the corner of Ninth Street and Massachusetts Avenue, Northwest, District of Columbia. Later, after the architects were selected to draw the plans and specifications, we selected a firm of architects who were known to occupy the front rank in that profession, Milburn and Heister. Their plans, after considerable discussion and some changes, were approved, and the contract in competition let to the R. P. Whitty Company. It is not necessary now that I should go into the details as to the prices paid and the amount of the contract for the building of the structure, simply to say that having elected Mr. Vice-President O'Connell, Mr. Secretary Morrison, and the President of the American Federation of Labor as a board of trustees, every effort was made to conserve the interests of the American Federation of Labor, and to have a building erected that would do credit and honor, as well as being serviceable to the American Federation of Labor and its great work.

["]The building, as you have seen, is of magnificent and dignified proportions. Its every room and its every facility will make for the best possible work and service. This Executive Council meeting-room in which we are assembled, is large, commodious, generous in proportions, and dignified in its surroundings. It affords the opportunity for a proper place in which to meet and to consider and discuss with such facilities of air and light both by day and by night as to make our sojourn in our meeting-room contribute to a clear and good understanding and opportunity for the cultivation of the best and the expression of the best that is in us.

["]Formerly when representatives of organized labor and others would come to wait upon the Executive Council of the American Federation of Labor, and having business with us, they are required for want of facilities to either sit or stand around in the halls of the old building in which we were renters and tenants. We have provided two ante-rooms and one in which visitors may come, those who have business with us, may come with the opportunity of being seated comfortably and preparing themselves as they may best want to, so that each in turn may come before us and present matters in which they are interested. So that we may escape the adverse comments and criticism made by those who had business with us during our sessions.

["]We have inter-communicating telephones with each room and office in the building. We have four trunk telephone lines connecting us with the outside world.

["]We have arranged some facilities so that in the women's retiring rooms there may be the accommodation for rest rooms and provide not only couches and tables but also such medicines as may be regarded as first aid to those who may be in need of some treatment or rest.

["]We have provided a room in which the girls may have the opportunity of having some hot drink, such as making coffee or tea, or milk. We have provided a roof of promenade tile and whose tensile strength is such as to afford the fullest opportunity for all of the employes in the offices of the American Federation of Labor and its Departments to assemble on the roof to have the opportunity of the air and the sunshine. The roof is partly walled around by brick and at the other part by iron grating. Around the roof we have provided about a dozen settees so that the girls may have the opportunity to be in the sunshine, in the air during their meals, and in order that all may have an opportunity of seeing the wonderful vista that surrounds the entire building. Its elevation of seven stories and basement and roof, gives the opportunity to see on a clear day a distance of more than twenty miles. The Potomac on the one side, Virginia and Maryland, and Mount Vernon, the home and last resting place of the Father of our Country, with all other nearby points of interest. It is said that the Washington Monument affords no better opportunity for a view all around this country than does the roof of the American Federation of Labor building. We have endeavored to make this a building that shall provide all the opportunities for the transaction of our business, and shall be a splendid monument to labor and that in its administration it shall be a model for the employes, for their comfort and their convenience, as well as for the performance of their work.["]

. . .

["]Now I think that this ought to be brought to your attention too, that it is a wonderful transformation from the old mansion which occupied this site to the building of this American Federation of Labor building. The mansion was that of one of America's best known families,[1] rich beyond measure, and slave owners. Right behind the mansion and upon this site was also a slave pen. The trustees did not lose the opportunity of having photographs made, not only of the old mansion, but also of the old slave pen, so that it might be perpetuated in the minds of those who would come after us that upon this site was a building that was finally transformed from slavery and all that typified slavery, to a structure that typifies freedom and liberty and justice.

["]I again welcome you, as I am proud to be with you here this morning on the occasion of our first session, the first session of the Executive Council in this magnificent structure and tribute to labor.["]

. . .

TDc, Executive Council Records, Minutes, reel 5, frames 1249–52, *AFL Records.*

1. The three-story brick residence that occupied the site was erected in 1852. At least as early as 1861 and for many years thereafter, it was the residence of Joseph Ford Thompson (1837–1917), a Washington, D.C., physician. At the time of the 1860 census Thompson owned no slaves; his father, a resident of St. Mary's Co., Md., owned seventeen.

A Circular

Washington, D.C., October 18, 1916.

Dear Sir and Brother:

From various sources as well as from the press reports, information has come to me regarding the migration of negro workingmen from the south, either induced by corporate and other interests or otherwise, to various points in your state, particularly along the Pennsylvania Railroad lines. My information is that the purpose of the corporations is destructive to the best interests of the wage earners and the influence of the organized labor movement both in the state and nation.

I would greatly appreciate if you would investigate this matter as fully as opportunity is afforded and at as early a date as possible and give me all information you can obtain as to why and for what purpose these colored workmen are being brought into the different localities.[1]

Your prompt attention to the above will be greatly helpful to me.

Thanking you in advance, I am,

Fraternally yours, Saml Gompers.
President, American Federation of Labor.

TLcS, reel 214, vol. 226, p. 193, SG Letterbooks, DLC. Typed notation: "This form sent to all District, General and Paid Organizers and to the State Branches: Ohio, Illinois and Indiana."

1. For replies to this circular and other correspondence on this subject, see "From James Forrester," Nov. 15, 1916, below, and AFL Microfilm Convention File, reel 28, frames 1569–73, *AFL Records.*

To Newton Baker[1]

October 31, 1916.

Hon. Newton D. Baker,
Secretary of War,
Washington, D.C.
Sir:

It is with a keen appreciation of the responsibility of the appointment you offer me on behalf of the President that I accept membership on the Advisory Committee to be associated with the Council of National Defense.[2]

It will be my purpose to give service on that Committee mindful of my duty as a citizen of this Republic and of my responsibility to do my part to give a spirit and a purpose to plans for national preparedness that shall make human welfare the paramount consideration.

Please convey to the President my appreciation of the trust expressed by the appointment and my acceptance.

Very truly yours, Saml Gompers.
President, American Federation of Labor.

TLpS, reel 214, vol. 226, p. 741, SG Letterbooks, DLC.

1. Newton Diehl Baker (1871–1937) served as secretary of war from 1916 to 1921.

2. Baker wrote SG on Oct. 30, 1916, to notify him of his appointment to the Advisory Commission of the Council of National Defense (Files of the Office of the President, General Correspondence, reel 81, frame 584, *AFL Records*).

An Excerpt from an Interview

Baltimore, Md. November 12, 1916.

INTERVIEW GIVEN BY PRESIDENT SAMUEL GOMPERS TO MR. ELY[1] OF THE *SAN FRANCISCO BULLETIN*

Mr. Gompers: The manifestations of unrest among the working people of the South American countries, particularly through the activities of what in the European countries and in the United States is regarded as the "intellectuals" that is men of mental attainments and yet who have failed in the professions or in other walks of life, have taken up a movement in which, by reason of the disparity of mentality, are so much superior to the masses of the workers. And as a consequence, the intellectuals regard themselves and are in part accepted as the leaders of whatever there exists of labor movements in these countries. The difficulty in my judgment would be to break through the intellectuals and to reach the real rank and file of the workers, for they may not have a highly developed mentality as to sociology and economics, yet it is safer in their own interests and welfare that they shall have a democratically organized and controlled movement true to themselves and to each other than to be led by the wisdom of any other group.

In America there has been an effort made for years on the part of the so called intellectuals and including the socialist political parties to control and dominate the American labor movement. It has been a great fight covering a period of 30 years to insist and maintain the absolute independence of the American labor movement and to keep its control in the hands of the wage workers. The intellectuals' contributions which some men may make toward the literature and the thought of the labor movement are welcome and gratifying, but when in addition they undertake to control the thought and the activities of the organized labor movement it is then when they must be rapped hard and fought insistently.

If it is to be a labor movement it must be by and for the workers themselves.

I realize of course that in Mexico where peonage and slavery have been in vogue for hundreds of years it is not easy to institute a well organized labor movement. That applies in part to other South American countries and in so far as the American Federation of Labor is concerned, we must work with the instrumentalities at hand and we are working with them sincerely and cordially to accomplish present day needs and having in mind the hope for a thoroughly organized and democratically controlled labor movement in all these countries.

Mr. Ely: What you say regarding South American countries and Mexico, would you apply it equally to Japan?

Mr. Gompers: Yes. About a year or nearly two years ago when Brother Gulick[2] came to me first—or later on the occasion of the second or third visit from him, he asked me whether I had a message to the workers of Japan through him. I thought for a moment, and answered him affirmatively. I then called in a stenographer to my office and speaking to him asked her to take it down.[3] I gave that copy to Brother Gulick and he took it with him to Japan. It was addressed to no one particularly, except that it had its application to the workers of Japan and to the employers, as well as the Government of Japan. I have a few copies of that.

Mr. Ely: I do not know that I have a right to ask you what will happen to the Japanese delegate, Mr. Suzuki, is he going to be seated?[4]

Mr. Gompers: I guess not. I am going to say something to you which is in confidence. In my judgment, the California State Federation of Labor has not done the right thing.[5] My reason for saying this is that if it is the intention of the California labor movement to accept the Japanese upon an absolutely economic, political and social equality, then their action is justified and proper, but if the seating of Mr. Suzuki as a fraternal delegate simply amounts to an outward seeming cordiality and then they try to assume afterwards the same position toward the Japanese as they formerly held, then it is hypocritical.

Mr. Ely: I agree with you there absolutely.

Mr. Gompers: Then the sending of a man to Japan upon the invitation of this Friendly Society of Workmen of Japan, a society instigated and financed by the Government of Japan, and then this representative of the labor movement of California, under the Japanese Friendly Society as it is instituted, goes to Japan and goes there with the mind made up in advance to give Japan a rap—that is hypocritical again.

The American Federation of Labor, the American labor movement is going to be clean cut—either we will take the Japanese by the hands and say "We are with you or you with us," or we will not say anything of the kind and we will not make any pretense. That is what I am telling you confidentially, that is the point.

Mr. Ely: I have watched that thing in California.

Mr. Gompers: You know that what I say is to be treated confidentially. No man has a greater respect for Paul Scharrenberg than I have, both for his mentality [and] his character and caliber. Suppose I would go to Japan with a mind prejudiced, but if I have a mental reservation and accept the courtesy of these people and then come back and deliver additional blows founded upon the defects that any man can discover—look for a thing and you usually find it—

Mr. Ely: Well I have seen these labor leaders there in San Francisco accept the hospitality of the Japanese at dinners galore, not only in hotels, but in their homes, and then I have heard them in private conversation express just as much distrust against the Japanese as they ever did.

Mr. Gompers: Well Brother Ely, I cannot do that sort of thing. I would not be a party to it. Men know where I stand. I have the courage of my convictions. The action of the working people of the United States on the Japanese question was brought from California to the first convention of our Federation in Pittsburg in 1881.[6] They persuaded the American workers and the American workers in turn persuaded the American people so that the regulation of Chinese immigration was first undertaken and Chinese exclusion was finally adopted. It was the California people, the working people of California who brought to the American Federation of Labor, the terrible conditions that they had to meet in regard to the Japanese workers and the American working people brought to the attention of the American people generally the dangers which our California members apprehended and brought it to the attention of the President of the United States, Mr. Roosevelt at the time, who secured what was known as the gentlemen's agreement. We are fully persuaded that the position taken by the California workers in their Chinese exclusion act, and as it was known, asiatic exclusion, was racially sound, nationally sound, industrially sound. Now if the people and the working people particularly of California have changed their attitude actually, they must come to the American Federation of Labor and say so.

Mr. Ely: Sometimes I think they have changed and then again I know they have not. But I think it is time now to have a show-down. If they are on the square, let them say so. If not, let it be known.

Mr. Gompers: So far as the other sections of our country outside of the Pacific coast states are concerned, the Chinese and the Japanese form an insignificant number. We are affected in a way that if California civilization is endangered we have got to stand behind California and if California believes that the danger has passed, that there is no apprehension necessary, then she has got to say it to us. [W]e cannot back up until she has, we cannot change our policy until she has so declared.

Mr. Ely: On the train coming to Chicago, this is what he said to me, that is Mr. Scharrenberg, about Mr. Suzuki being seated.—"I do not believe there will be the slightest objection from any source" and of course you know the State Federation of Labor by unanimous vote instructed the Executive Board to spend the next year in investigating the question of organization of Japanese. Not even the Laundry Workers objected to that, if they did they did not say so to the convention.

Mr. Gompers: California must say so to us in the convention.

Mr. Ely: I would like for them to say it to the convention. If they do not there is only one point I can reach.

Mr. Gompers: You have known me Mr. Ely for quite some years. There may be [ti]mes when it is impractical for me to express an opinion upon any subject and then I cannot be made to talk, but when I do talk I conform my words to my thoughts and acts and my acts to conform to my words. I do not say one thing and act in another way. There are no mental reservations with me.

. . .

TD, AFL Microfilm Convention File, reel 28, frame 1444–45, *AFL Records.*

1. Frederick W. Ely was labor editor of the *San Francisco Bulletin* and represented AFL Stenographers', Typewriters', Bookkeepers', and Assistants' Union 13,188 of San Francisco at the 1916 AFL convention.

2. Sidney Lewis Gulick served as a Congregational missionary in Japan from 1887 to 1913 and taught at Doshisa University, Kyoto (1906–13), and at the Imperial University of Kyoto (1907–13). On his return to the United States he campaigned against Asian exclusion legislation and served as secretary of the Department of International Justice and Good-Will of the Federal Council of Churches of Christ in America (1914–34).

3. "The Rights of the Japanese Working People and the Attitude of the Japanese Government toward Them—A Statement by Samuel Gompers, President of the American Federation of Labor, to Rev. Doctor Sidney L. Gulick," Dec. 17, 1914, reel 191, vol. 203, pp. 375–77, SG Letterbooks, DLC.

4. Bunji Suzuki, president of the Yūaikai (Laborers' Friendly Society), addressed the 1916 AFL convention on Nov. 14 (AFL, *Proceedings,* 1916, pp. 188–91).

5. At its 1915 and 1916 conventions the California State Federation of Labor (FOL) seated Suzuki as a fraternal delegate from the Yūaikai. In addition, the 1916 convention unanimously voted that the executive council of the FOL should investigate the feasibility of organizing Japanese workers in California and accepted an invitation to send a delegate to the anniversary celebration of the Yūaikai in Tokyo in 1917. Paul Scharrenberg was selected to represent the FOL. Nevertheless, the FOL continued to support the exclusion of Asian immigrants.

6. A reference to a resolution calling for the prohibition of Chinese immigration introduced by Charles Burgman and adopted by the 1881 FOTLU convention.

From James Forrester[1]

General Offices
Brotherhood of Railway Clerks
Cincinnati, Ohio November 15, 1916.

Dear Sir and Brother:—

Your letter of October 18th,[2] re the migration of negroes to northern points to work in the railroad service and your request that I investigate it:

Would advise that I have given this matter quite a thorough investigation and find that many negroes have been brought to northern points where they have displaced the white labor. These negroes did not migrate in the true sense of the word, but were imported, the railroads having men in the southern states hiring them and all of them traveling on transportation furnished by the roads.

Those that I find have imported the greatest number are the Penn. Co., the Central New England, the N.Y.[N.]H. & H., the B. & O., the Monon, and the Clover leaf, tho nearly all roads have, to some extent done it. The N.Y.N.H. & H. have imported several car loads of them, in fact have displaced most of the freight handlers and trackmen with them. They use any excuse to get rid of white employes and then fill their places with these imported negroes. This has been going on for some time and now a great majority of this class of railroad help is colored where before it was practically all white. The same is true of the Pennsylvania at most points also the B. & O. Here in Cincinnati, where two months ago all of the freight handlers were white, it is now almost impossible to find a white man employed.

Of course, as soon as the cold weather struck quite some few of them quit and returned to their native heath in the south, but many did not and it has created a surplus of white common labor that would not exist except for this condition, and which is liable to cause us some trouble in future when conditions change and again become normal. There was no real need to import these negroes, there was a sufficiency of white help to handle the business, but the facts are that the white help were awakening to the need and benefits of organization and were demanding more money and better working conditions and the railroads have taken this way of heading it off, winning before they were struck.

The above are the facts. While it is true that an attempt was made to vote some of them in the recent election, that was not the real object of bringing them north. The real object was to displace the white man and prevent organization and thus procure cheaper and more subservient help.

Trusting the above may prove of some benefit and that some plan may be devised to stop this importation, I am, with best wishes,

Fraternally yours,   Jas. J. Forrester
Grand President,   Brotherhood of Railway Clerks.

TLS, AFL Microfilm Convention File, reel 28, frame 1570, *AFL Records.*

1. James Joseph FORRESTER, of the Brotherhood of Railway Clerks, served as grand president of the union from 1915 to 1920.

2. See "A Circular," Oct. 18, 1916, above.

Excerpts from Accounts of the 1916 Convention of the AFL in Baltimore

Baltimore, Nov. 14, 1916.

SECOND DAY—TUESDAY MORNING SESSION

· · ·

Mr. J. E. Morgan,[1] representing organized workers in California and in Kansas City, was introduced by the President. Mr. Morgan spoke at some length of the men in San Francisco who have been arrested charged with responsibility for a bomb explosion in the streets during the preparedness parade some months ago,[2] and asked the assistance of organized labor throughout the country in the effort that is being made to clear these men of the unjust charges against them. He spoke of the interest taken in the case by Mr. Frank P. Walsh and of the fact that Mr. W. Bourke Cochran,[3] the noted New York lawyer and orator, was so impressed by the apparent injustice being done the men that he had volunteered his services to defend them, and was now on his way to San Francisco for that purpose. Mr. Morgan gave a clear and detailed account of all the circumstances connected with the case, the effort of the Chamber of Commerce, the United Railways and other corporations to bring about open-shop conditions in San Francisco, and their efforts to connect labor men with the explosion referred to.[4]

· · ·

AFL, *Proceedings,* 1916, pp. 175, 192.

1. J. Edward Morgan, a San Francisco printer, was a representative of the International Workers' Defense League of San Francisco, an organization formed in 1912 to assist in the legal defense of radicals.

2. On July 22, 1916, a bomb exploded at a military preparedness parade in San Francisco, killing ten marchers and spectators and wounding forty. Thomas Mooney, Warren Billings, Mooney's wife, Rena, Edward Nolan, and Israel Weinberg were arrested

and charged with the crime. Mooney and Billings were tried, convicted, and sent to prison; the others were subsequently released.

3. William Bourke Cockran (1854–1923), a New York City attorney, served as a Democratic member of the U.S. House of Representatives from New York (1887–89, 1891–95, 1904–9, 1921–23).

4. Resolution 137, introduced on Nov. 14, 1916, by delegate Andrew Hill of the Little Rock, Ark., Central Trades and Labor Council, demanded a fair trial for the defendants in the San Francisco bombing case and urged members of affiliated unions to extend financial assistance to help defray the legal expenses involved. The convention did not adopt the resolution but instead referred it to the AFL Executive Council, which directed SG to send letters of inquiry to labor organizations in California. George Sandeman, secretary of the San Francisco Metal Trades Council, responded that few organizations affiliated with the trades council had made donations to the defense fund (to SG, Jan. 16, 1917, Executive Council Records, Vote Books, reel 15, frame 271, *AFL Records*). John O'Connell, secretary of the San Francisco Labor Council, wrote that "the movement in this locality never considered this a case in which labor could afford to interfere" and that the AFL Executive Council "should weigh this matter carefully and see to it that their action will not be used for the propagation of institutions that have for their purpose the destruction of the American Labor Movement" (to SG, Jan. 18, 1917, ibid.). After receiving these replies, the Council voted to take no further action. For Morgan's account of his experience at the convention and other correspondence regarding this resolution, see AFL Microfilm Convention File, reel 28, frames 1597–1631, *AFL Records*.

[November 19, 1916]

WILSON TO LABOR MEN

President Wilson received his first public congratulations upon the result of the recent election at the hands of the delegates to the American Federation of Labor yesterday, and in response to the sentiments of the delegates he expressed the hope that all class distinctions and class feeling in this country would some day be blotted out. The only way to close up every rift among the people, he said, is to establish "justice with a heart in it."

The convention of the Federation, now in session here, recessed for the day in order for the delegates to visit Washington, inspect the new home of the organization there and pay their respects to the President. In presenting the delegates to Mr. Wilson, Samuel Gompers, president of the Federation, warmly felicitated the President upon his re-election, expressed the wish that the new Administration would be as successful as the present one and assured him of the esteem and affection in which he was held by the laboring people of America.

Most of the delegates reached Washington shortly after 1 o'clock. They came over on special cars and went at once to the national headquarters of the organization, where the new building was carefully examined. . . .

MARCHED TO WHITE HOUSE.

A procession of delegates and their wives was formed at the head-quarters. They marched behind a band to the White House, arriving promptly at 5 o'clock. The band was parked in the White House ground and played during the President's reception to the visitors.

The reception took place in the historic East Room. The delegates formed a semicircle in the great hall with Mr. Gompers facing them. Almost as soon as they arrived the swinging doors were thrown open and the President advanced to meet Mr. Gompers, while the whole assemblage burst into applause.

Mr. Gompers, speaking for his organization, stated that the convention several days ago voted unanimously to recess for a day in order to pay a visit of respect and gratitude to the President. The Federation is composed of men of all parties and all races, he said, but they are a unit in their approval of the splendid achievements of the present Administration in behalf of the cause of labor.

"We have come to recognize in you," declared Mr. Gompers, addressing the President, "a man who stands for the principles upon which our voluntary organization rests. We have felt joy in upholding your hands and admiration for the splendid and masterful work you have accomplished. We congratulate you upon the approval of your countrymen and hope that the next four years will be as fruitful as the four years now passing."

THE PRESIDENT'S RESPONSE.

In responding, the President thanked the delegates for calling upon him, but was careful to make no reference to the result of the election. In part, the President said:

"I need not say that, coming to me as you do on such an errand, I am very deeply gratified and very greatly cheered. It should be impossible for me off-hand to say just what thoughts are stirred in me by what Mr. Gompers has said to me as your spokesman, but perhaps the simplest thing I can say is, after all, the meat of the whole matter. What I have tried to do is to get rid of any class division in this country, not only, but of any class consciousness and feeling. The worst thing that could happen to America would be that she should be divided into groups and camps in which there were men and women who thought that they were at odds with one another, that the spirit of America was not expressed except in them, and that possibilities of antagonism were the only things that we had to look forward to. ["]

Would Erase Division Lines.

"As Mr. Gompers said, achievement is a comparatively small matter, but the spirit in which things are done is of the essence of the whole thing, and what I am striving for, and what I hope you are striving for, is to blot out all the lines of division in America and create a unity of spirit and of purpose founded upon this, the consciousness that we are all men and women of the same sort and that if we do not understand each other, we are not true Americans. If we cannot enter into each other's thoughts, if we cannot comprehend each other's interests, if we cannot serve each other's essential welfare, then we have not yet qualified as representatives of the American spirit.

"Nothing alarms America so much as rifts, divisions, the drifting apart of elements among her people, and the thing we ought all to strive for is to close up every rift, and the only way to do it, so far as I can see, is to establish justice not only, but justice with a heart in it, justice with a pulse in it, justice with sympathy in it. Justice can be cold and forbidding or it can be warm and welcome, and the latter is the only kind of justice that Americans ought to desire. I do not believe I am deceiving myself when I say that I think this spirit is growing in America. I pray God it may continue to grow, and all I have to say is to exhort every one whom my voice reaches here or elsewhere to come into this common movement of humanity."

After the speeches all the delegates shook hands with the President.

"Look out for my boys," said "Mother" Jones as she greeted Mr. Wilson.

. . .

Baltimore Sun, Nov. 19, 1916.

[November 21, 1916]

. . .

The Federation enunciated the most revolutionary principle in its history early in the afternoon when it adopted without debate a report of the committee on executive council's report scoring the decision of the Massachusetts Supreme Court for declaring unconstitutional the law protecting organized labor from the "perverted" application of anti-trust legislation and the "abuse" of the writ of injunction.

Would Disregard Court.

The resolution was prepared by Andrew Furuseth,[1] chairman of the committee, and is as follows:

"It seems to be a settled purpose of interests antagonistic to the free-dom of men and women who labor to persuade and then use the judiciary to misconstrue constitutional guarantees and thereby nullify legislative enactments so as to leave but one remedy; and we therefore recommend that any injunction dealing with the relationship of employer and employe and based on the dictum 'labor is property' be wholly and absolutely treated as usurpation and disregarded, let the consequences be what they may.

"Such decisions as the one rendered by the Supreme Court of Massachusetts have their roots in class interests; it is usurpation and tyranny. Freedom came to man because he believed that resistance to tyranny is obedience to God. As it came, so it must remain. Kings could be and were disobeyed and sometimes deposed. In cases of this kind judges must be disobeyed and should be impeached."[2]

Baltimore Sun, Nov. 21, 1916.

1. Andrew Furuseth represented the International Seamen's Union of America at the convention.

2. The convention adopted this report unanimously.

Baltimore, Md., Nov. 21, 1916.

EIGHTH DAY—TUESDAY MORNING SESSION

. . .

President Gompers: A few days ago I announced to you that the Executive Council of the American Federation of Labor had invited the executive officers of the four railroad brotherhoods to visit this convention; also that I was in receipt of a telegram[1] signed by the four executives of the brotherhoods stating that they would be here with us this morning. They are here, and in compliance with the invitation and the spirit of the invitation and the spirit that prompted it I shall present to you the men in the order in which they themselves have expressed a preference to appear before this convention.

. . .[2]

President Gompers' Response.

As President of the American Federation of Labor, I should, before these four brothers leave us, express what I believe is in the minds of the delegates and which I desire to interpret.

You are right welcome with us, Mr. Stone, Mr. Carter, Mr. Lee and Mr. Sheppard,[3] right welcome. We wish you were here absolutely as the delegates to this convention are here. And it is a great comfort to know and to have heard you say that the time is not far distant when four railroad brotherhoods will be a part of the American Federation of Labor.

Let me assure you that self-government is guaranteed to every organization affiliated to the American Federation of Labor, and no species of compulsion is tolerated in our Federation. If we cannot succeed in prevailing upon an organization to do the thing which, in our judgment, it ought to do, if we cannot do that by the expression of our judgment, then we cannot enforce that judgment by any decree or action on our part. It is the essence of voluntary action that has made this Federation the great protestant against wrong, and a powerful influence for the attaintment of right. The jurisdiction question is the one in which we try to be helpful in bringing organizations, each claiming jurisdiction over the same class of workers, to come to a voluntary conclusion to govern themselves. But compulsion—No!

Now, I recall with a great deal of pleasure the occasions when I have had the opportunity to speak to the conventions of some of the railroad brotherhoods; in fact, I think all of them; one of them several times—the Firemen and Enginemen. I was always well received, and my reception I take it was not simply to me personally, but because of the fact that I appeared before the convention as a representative of the American Federation of Labor, and of its spirit as well as its achievements. One of the things that I recall with a great deal of pleasure was my appearance before the convention of the Brotherhood of Locomotive Engineers at Harrisburg about three years ago.[4] It was about that time that the newspapers discovered that this mild-mannered man, Warren S. Stone, did really possess backbone,[5] for several of the Wall street papers just gave him a good rubbing down, and at the convention I congratulated the Brotherhood of Locomotive Engineers upon the fact that the newspapers had at last discovered President Stone. I took occasion to admonish the delegates that sometimes it is necessary for the working people, the organizations of labor particularly, to show that they have both teeth and claws—not all the time, but only when necessary.

Now, without attempting at this time to discuss the Adamson Law— the eight-hour law—it is exceedingly peculiar that those who antagonize the law predicate their action upon the statement that it is not an eight-hour law. Since when have these railroad magnates, or their lawyers, been the advocates of an eight-hour work-day?

Men of the railroad brotherhoods, just this one remark to you: We expect that the railroad brotherhoods will, on the first of January, inaugurate the eight-hour work-day, and I think I can truly say to you that whatever may arise, whatever betide, you have the undivided support of every man and every woman in the organized labor movement as represented in the American Federation of Labor. When the money power of the United States failed in trying to corrupt the electorate of the United States and to mislead them, when their well-laid plans were frustrated by the citizenship of the United States, they showed their colors and a number of them gave to the public the declaration that they were going to resist every effort put forth by organized labor;[6] that they would fight us industrially, politically and legislatively—I need not say that judicially they already have done so—that they represent eight billions of dollars, that there were 15,000 employers, that they employed about seven million working people, and that they were going to use every instrumentality within their power in order to balk, defeat or undo the work of the American labor movement.[7]

Now, that is their right so long as they own the money; so long as they hold that position, they have a right to oppose our movement, notwithstanding the fact that our movement stands for manhood, for womanhood, for childhood, as against their billions of dollars. I say to you it is their lawful right to make the fight against us, and all I can say in answer is: "You men of wealth, be careful how far you go, for there is a limit to human endurance. You throw down the gauntlet and we will accept the challenge!" And when it comes we will quote from the greatest bard the world ever had—"Lay on, Macduff, and damned be he who first cries, 'Hold! Enough!'"[8]

Men, you executives of the railroad brotherhoods, you may count upon the men of labor in this land of ours. You will find that we will ring true and stand true.

. . .

AFL, *Proceedings,* 1916, pp. 283–85, 292–93.

1. William Carter, William Lee, Lucius Sheppard, and Warren Stone to SG, Nov. 20, 1916, AFL, *Proceedings,* 1916, p. 276.

2. Not printed here are the addresses to the convention by Carter, Lee, Sheppard, and Stone (see AFL, *Proceedings,* 1916, pp. 285–92).

3. Lucius Elmer Sheppard served as senior vice-president (1907–19) and then president (1919–28) of the Order of Railway Conductors of America.

4. The 1912 convention of the Brotherhood of Locomotive Engineers met in Harrisburg, Pa., May 8–June 1. SG addressed the convention on May 17. For a copy of SG's address, see Files of the Office of the President, Speeches and Writings, reel 111, frames 258–71, *AFL Records.*

5. A reference to Stone's threat in April 1912 that the Locomotive Engineers would tie up all the railroad lines in the East if railroad managers refused to grant their wage demands.

6. Meeting in New York City on Nov. 16, 1916, the National Founders' Association voted to use its "entire power and influence" to aid the railroads in their attempt to prevent enforcement of the Adamson eight-hour law ("Back Up Railroads in 8-Hour Day Fight," *New York Times,* Nov. 17, 1916).

7. SG is referring to the National Industrial Conference Board (NICB), organized in New York City on Nov. 15, 1916.

8. *Macbeth,* act 5, scene 8.

[November 23, 1916]

AGAINST WAR TRAINING

. . .

One of the hottest fights yet waged by the delegates was started at the forenoon session, and as the outcome the Federation, by an overwhelming vote, reversed its policy[1] adopted at San Francisco a year ago and took a decided stand against "militarism" and military training in the public schools.

The resolution[2] was introduced by a delegate of the Brotherhood of Painters, Decorators and Paperhangers of America. Max Hayes,[3] looked upon as one of the leaders among the Socialists in the convention, took up arms in favor of the resolution as soon as the unfavorable report of the committee to which it had been referred was announced. He declared that Secretary of War Baker had forgotten "what he used to teach in the past" and was "espousing the cause of militarism."[4] He went on to say that "this seems to be a period of militaristic hysteria."

Hits at the Socialists.

Andrew Furuseth, chairman of the committee that had reported the resolution unfavorably, had some criticisms to make against Socialists.

"Children of the master class are being taught to bear arms,"[5] he said, "and I am astounded that you radical Socialists come into this convention asking that the children of the proletariat be prevented from knowing what a weapon looks like or how to use it. You men who will not fight and you women who will not be mothers are an abomination."

President Gompers tried to stem the tide, and issued the warning that the question was a delicate one and that the convention had better not get into a controversy over it, but for once his influence was apparently of little weight.

. . .

Baltimore Sun, Nov. 23, 1916.

1. See "Defense Hotly Discussed by Federation Delegates," Nov. 19, 1915, in "Excerpts from News Accounts of the 1915 Convention of the AFL in San Francisco," Nov. 16–23, 1915, above.

2. Resolution 142, introduced by delegates of the Brotherhood of Painters, Decorators, and Paperhangers of America on Nov. 14, 1916, protested against the introduction of military training in public schools. The committee that considered the resolution recommended nonconcurrence, but after debate the convention both adopted it and set up a special committee "to draw up a resolution dealing with all the phases of militarism" (AFL, *Proceedings*, 1916, p. 310). On Nov. 25 this committee brought in a resolution declaring the AFL "unalterably and emphatically opposed to 'militarism'" or "any form of physical training or . . . mental education, which would tend to inculcate the spirit of 'militarism'" (ibid., p. 383). It went on to recommend that SG appoint

a committee of five to gather evidence and issue a report on the subject. The convention adopted the resolution, but the deteriorating international situation precluded SG's appointment of such a committee. Instead the AFL Executive Council called a conference of labor representatives to meet in Washington, D.C., on Mar. 12, 1917, to issue a statement on American labor's position in peace and in war.

3. Max Hayes represented the International Typographical Union at the convention.

4. At the time of his appointment as secretary of war, Newton Baker was described in press reports as an "ardent pacifist" and an opponent of the preparedness campaign, which he had said was "based on hysteria . . . a manufactured war scare" (*New York Times,* Mar. 7, 1916). Hayes's comment referred to Baker's support of the National Defense Act (U.S. *Statutes at Large,* 39: 166–217), enacted in June 1916, which increased the size of the regular army, established a reserve officer training program, and brought the national guard under more effective federal control.

5. The sections of the National Defense Act pertaining to reserve officer training provided for the military training of males age fourteen or older at colleges, universities, or other established educational institutions upon application from the school. The secretary of war was authorized to issue to such schools whatever "arms, uniforms, equipment, and means of transportation" as he deemed necessary for military training (U.S. *Statutes at Large,* 39: 192).

Baltimore, Md., Nov. 24. [1916]

"FEED AMERICA FIRST" LABOR'S NEW SLOGAN

"Feed America first" was the slogan sounded in the convention of the American Federation of Labor today when it voted unanimously to demand an embargo upon shipments of wheat and other foodstuffs from this country.[1]

Debate brought out the charge that wheat speculators are trying to turn public attention to a prosecution of the bakers, when in fact the cost of all elements in the production of a loaf of bread have advanced to such an extent within the past year that no court would hold the bakers to blame for raising their prices.[2]

A resolution[3] demanding a probe by the Department of Justice, into the "conspiracy" through which the cost of print paper has been doubled and in some cases trebled within the past year was also adopted.

Old-age pensions for the workers were proposed,[4] but this measure was sent to a special committee for study and report a year hence.

Washington Herald, Nov. 25, 1916.

1. The 1916 AFL convention considered a number of resolutions—101, 110, 113, and 116—concerning the high cost of food, fuel, and other necessities of life and calling for export restrictions to alleviate the problem. The Committee on Resolutions combined consideration of all these proposals into an amended version of resolution 110—originally introduced by delegates of the Brotherhood of Painters, Decorators, and Paperhangers of America on Nov. 14—which called for an embargo on the export of wheat and other foodstuffs until the cost of living was reduced to prewar levels. The convention adopted the amended resolution on Nov. 24, together with the committee's recommendation that Congress be urged to investigate market practices that artificially

increased the cost of food, fuel, and other necessities. At its January 1917 meeting the AFL Executive Council referred the matter to SG. The Council reported to the 1917 convention that in accordance with the resolution the AFL had supported passage of both the Food Survey Law, which provided for a survey of the food situation in the country (U.S. *Statutes at Large,* 40: 273–76), and the Lever Food and Fuel Control Act, which authorized the president to issue regulations concerning the production, distribution, and pricing of food and fuel necessary to the war effort (ibid., pp. 276–87).

2. Joseph Cannon of the Western Federation of Miners made this charge during a speech in support of resolution 110. His address is printed in AFL, *Proceedings,* 1916, pp. 242–45.

3. Resolution 105, introduced by delegates from several printing trades unions on Nov. 14, 1916, protested against the rising cost of print paper and urged the Department of Justice to investigate. At its January 1917 meeting the AFL Executive Council referred the matter to SG, who sent a copy of the resolution to the U.S. attorney general, the chairman of the Federal Trade Commission, and members of the House Committee on Interstate and Foreign Commerce and the Senate Committee on Interstate Commerce. For correspondence relating to this resolution see AFL Microfilm Convention File, reel 28, frames 1563–68, *AFL Records.*

4. The 1916 AFL convention considered a number of resolutions concerning the establishment of a pension and retirement system for government employees—44, 80, 133, and 134—as well as a universal pension system for all older employees—25 and 146. The convention referred these resolutions to the AFL Executive Council, which reported to the 1917 convention that no legislation on the subject had been passed by Congress during the course of the year.

[November 27, 1916]

. . .

Ends Convention with Well-Defined Social Reform Program.

Organized labor's efforts in Baltimore during the past two weeks . . . ended Saturday with a well-defined program of industrial and social reform which the wage-earners pledged themselves to bring about by constant appeals to the legislative and administrative branches of the Government. Those efforts were divided before the Federation convened into two sorts—intensive and extensive.

Acting intensively, the Federation tightened the bonds of co-operation among the workers themselves by amicably settling local disputes, refusing to countenance the creation of any more divisions or the issuance of additional charters where the applicants for admission could be brought under the control of an already existing unit, and stamping out or smothering Socialistic insurgency that threatened to destroy old leaders like Gompers and Morrison.

What Extensive Program Includes.

Acting extensively, it raised its voice against military training in the public schools,[1] thereby pitting itself directly against a Government plan for national defense; it called upon Congress to place an embargo upon food;[2] it urged grand jury investigations of the high cost of living and jail sentences for the men responsible;[3] it registered opposition to President Wilson's plan of arbitration in labor disputes, by which the right to strike would be abridged;[4] it suggested the establishment of a commercial union with the South and Central American republics;[5] and favored the creation of an International Federation of Labor to hear and settle all disputes between nations, all with a view to preventing future wars.[6]

Its action upon the eight-hour day principle was an extensive action with an intensive significance. The heads of the four big railway brotherhoods spoke to the convention, exchanged felicitations with it and heard Samuel Gompers say, with every bit of impressiveness he could summon, "we expect" that the Adamson law will go into effect on January 1. Then co-operation between the brotherhoods and the American Federation of Labor was pledged and the eight-hour day was dropped until the day of final adjournment. On that day three resolutions,[7] each calling for a universal eight-hour day by legislative action, were shunted over to next year's convention.

GOMPERS WON OUT.

There was an element in the convention that wanted the universal eight-hour day, wanted it by legislation, and wanted it right away. That element was all ready to beat an unfavorable report upon the resolutions, but it was taken completely by surprise by the recommendation that they be referred to a committee for a report in 1917. The intensive significance of this is that the reputation of Samuel Gompers as a master strategist was preserved, along with his identity as still the biggest outstanding figure in organized labor after two decades of leadership.

Close observation of this convention has helped in an understanding of the spectacle of the biggest labor organization in the world which has passed through and actually created more industrial revolutions and new eras than any other similar body, still governed by and listening attentively to the dictums of the man to whom it listened over 20 years ago. The reasons are simply that Gompers has never lost his ability to stand upon the platform before wageworkers and dream out loud; that he always knows what to say, and when and how to say it; and that he has never lost sight of the value of an unexaggerated ego.

KEPT OUT OF SOCIALISTS' FIGHT.

That is why any attempted review of what organized labor accomplished at its thirty-sixth annual convention must be inextricably interwoven with what Gompers did in the convention. Whatever he had to say about anything usually guided the convention's action, and when he said nothing his silence proved to be just the right stroke of diplomacy at that time.

The element that wanted a universal eight-hour day right away was the Socialist element, and it wanted a lot of other things, too, among them the resolution protesting against militarism. Gompers kept out of this fight entirely, though other leaders with reputations for conservatism fought against the resolution. They were beaten and the Socialists won, which did not tend to make them feel any less kindly toward Gompers. And when the "Grand Old Man," as they call him, got up and hurled forensic thunderbolts at the heads of "the master class," telling the "Pharisees" to beware, and calling upon labor to resist capital—"resist to the utmost"—he made the radicals feel that he was one of them and the conservatives decided that it was time for them to wake up.

ANOTHER SOP TO RADICALS.

Another sop was thrown to the radicals in the resolution declaring that courts which "pervert and abuse" the injunction "must be disobeyed." The defiances of law and order, amounting almost to treason, that were uttered were followed next day by a proposal[8] to establish a legal department through which the "abuses" of the courts could be combated in a law-abiding way. The proposal was voted down, but not because the sentiment of treason prevailed. Insufficient finances and an economical spirit had more to do with it.

Here again Gompers took the floor to denounce all lawyers as "legalized mechanisms," reading at the same time correspondence between himself and a lawyer regarding the method of establishing a legal department, from which it appeared that the expense was prohibitive. His denunciation of the lawyers pleased the radicals, and his apparent concern for economy delighted the conservatives.

The noteworthy fact about the convention, standing out over all others, is that it adjourned without having passed any resolutions that would tend to confirm the suspicions of people who believe organized labor is planning to rip the nation's social fabric to shreds. For that Gompers is to be thanked, because his diplomacy did it—sidestepping when sidestepping was practical, alternately thundering and cooing, and when a safe issue arose, meeting it squarely and settling it.

The net result is a fairly sane plan of action, backed up by the strong organization welded by the convention's intensive legislation, and contemplating certain social and industrial reforms to be brought about through regular safe channels.

There is no doubt that the tendency to Socialism is stronger now in the American Federation of Labor than it has ever been. That is responsible for the organization's change of front on the principle of militarism, but it is not yet too strong to be controlled by the sort of diplomacy of which Gompers is capable. He realizes that organized labor's main strength lies in the respect of the average sane-minded citizen for what it does and says, and that that respect will go just as soon as organized labor loses its head.

Baltimore Sun, Nov. 27, 1916.

1. Resolution 142.

2. Resolution 110.

3. Resolution 30, introduced by delegate William Green of the United Mine Workers of America on Nov. 14, 1916, called for the creation of a federal commission to investigate price increases for the necessities of life and allegations of profiteering by manufacturers, producers, and speculators. It did not, however, recommend jail sentences for profiteers. The resolution was adopted by the convention on Nov. 17, and at its January 1917 meeting the AFL Executive Council referred the matter to SG. The Council reported to the 1917 convention that in accordance with this and other resolutions it had supported the passage of the Food Survey Law and the Lever Food and Fuel Control Act.

4. The AFL Executive Council's report to the convention included a discussion of legislation recommended by President Woodrow Wilson in August 1916 to avert a national railroad strike, including a proposal, modeled on the Lemieux Act, that would have made it unlawful for railroad workers to strike while their demands were under investigation (see "To Warren Stone," July 7, 1916, n. 2, above). Both the railroad brotherhoods and the AFL opposed this proposition, which did not become law. The Council's report recommended that the convention "take an unequivocal position against compulsory institutions and in favor of the maintenance of institutions and opportunities for freedom" (AFL, *Proceedings,* 1916, p. 81). The convention unanimously adopted the Council's report and recommendation.

5. Resolution 92, introduced by delegate Albert Rich of the Texas State Federation of Labor on Nov. 14, 1916, endorsed the establishment of a commercial union between the United States and the republics of Central and South America and called for the use of U.S. credits, loans, and bonds to finance the building of merchant shipping to carry the commerce of these countries. The convention did not adopt the resolution.

6. Actually a reference to the AFL Executive Council's supplemental report on international labor relations calling for "a voluntary union of nations, a league for peace to adjust disputes and difficulties" (AFL, *Proceedings,* 1916, p. 257). The convention endorsed the Council's report as the "basis for an international organization for promoting justice between nations to the end that wars may be averted and human and national rights and freedom maintained" (ibid., p. 389).

7. Resolutions 27, 54 and 85, all introduced on Nov. 14, 1916.

8. Resolution 64, introduced by delegate John Frey of the International Molders' Union of North America on Nov. 14, 1916, called for the creation of an AFL legal department and authorized an assessment not to exceed two cents per capita to meet its expenses. On Nov. 21 the convention referred the resolution to the Committee on Laws with instructions to bring in a report creating the necessary fund to establish the department. The committee reported on Nov. 24, recommending that the per capita tax on national and international unions be increased from three-quarters to one cent per

member per month, with the increase to be set aside as a special fund for the maintenance of the legal department. The report of the committee was defeated by a vote of
11,866 to 8,722, with 558 not voting. At its January 1917 meeting the AFL Executive
Council authorized SG to establish a legal bureau of information. He hired staff to
compile and transcribe court decisions affecting labor, which were then made available to affiliated organizations upon request.

To Sadie Gordon

November 29, 1916.

Miss Sadie L. Gordon,
911 Fox Street, New York City, N.Y.
Dear Madam,

You ask for the attitude of the American Federation of Labor towards
the minimum wage for unskilled labor.

Advocating a policy to secure better industrial conditions for unskilled workers or any class of workers in private industry through legislation is based upon the supposition that the class of workers to be
affected is unorganizable.

The labor movement believes that there is no class of workers that
is not organizable because of disadvantages or peculiar disabilities
under which they may work. Workers in certain trades and industries
may long remain unorganized, but this is due to extraordinary conditions rather than to anything inherent in the workers or in the trade.
In many such trades where the workers have long been unorganized,
when finally there came the opportunity or the great need for organization, those workers have been organized. Take, for instance, the
miners of the country. Thirty years ago, the workers in no trade were
more oppressed than were the miners. Because they were unorganized,
they were helpless to protect themselves and to right their wrongs.
When they finally, with the assistance of the organized labor movement, prepared themselves for the campaign of organization, they
succeeded in building up in many of the states strong, solid organizations, which are the protection of the miners of those states.

There are several states in which the miners are not yet organized.
That is not due to any peculiar condition of circumstance, but to the
fact that the miners there have not yet developed an understanding
of organization and the ability to organize and maintain organization.

Organization is not based upon the fact that in a certain trade or
industry there has developed a skill among the workers that gives them
a strategic advantage upon which they can build up an organization,

but rather upon an understanding of human nature and upon skill in developing the organization itself.

After all, the term of skilled or unskilled labor is purely relative. Modern industrial methods involve the use of machinery and labor saving devices so that the old time skill at a trade rarely exists. However, there is no occupation or trade which does not require a certain degree of ability upon the part of the worker. It is after all, the mental power of the worker that enables him to coordinate his muscles and nerves to the best advantage and hence enables him to be a more skilled workman than some others. There is no trade or occupation that does not develop a certain kind of skill or facility of movement through continually working at that same occupation.

The matter of skill has very little to do with organization or with good conditions of employment. Through skill in organization, the hod carriers of America have secured in many localities better conditions of work and wages than are enjoyed by many in the so-called professions. This explanation discloses why the American Federation of Labor does not advocate a different policy for improving conditions for so-called unskilled workers than the principles which it has maintained for workers in other trades and occupations.

As you know, there are two diametrically opposite methods for promoting the welfare and protecting the interests of the wage-earners. One is for the government to assume responsibility and undertake to establish better conditions and higher standards through legislation. When a law is enacted establishing standards, then the work of making the standard effective is entrusted to some governmental agency. This duty necessarily carries with it a certain degree of compulsion on the part of both employers and employes. Industrial relations, therefore, cease to be matters for voluntary agreement and are subject to the determination of governmental representatives. The other way, which is the one advocated by the American Federation of Labor, is that so far as private industries are concerned, industrial relations ought to be determined by those who are immediately affected by the relations.

Of course, under present conditions it is impossible for the individual employe to enter into a contract with his employer, but through voluntary organizations of workers, wage-earners are able to present and make effective ideas of their own welfare and their concepts of justice. Since the labor organization is a democratic organization and flexible, changing with the needs and the development and the broader concepts of the workers, it is the most effective agency through which they can express their desires and make progress.

Not only is labor organization effective, but it enables the wage-earners to secure better conditions and to make progress without establishing any agency or any precedent that might constitute a delimitation of their power or bestow upon any governmental agency authority that would enable the agency to deprive the workers of rights or privileges that ought to be enjoyed by all free citizens.

Since the labor organizations are voluntary, they constitute no menace to voluntary institutions, which are the basis for all liberty, whether political or industrial.

The American Federation of Labor recognizes the difference between governmental employment and employment in private industries. Since in governmental employment the employer is the state, there is only one way to secure from the state an enunciation of policy and agreement, and that is, through legislation. Therefore, the American Federation of Labor has advocated and has secured legislation to establish the eight-hour day and certain minimum wage standards for government employes. Even when legislation is the method, it is clearly recognized by all that the law secured is a recognition of the economic power of labor organizations.

The principle underlying the establishment of minimum wage by law and the regulation of the hours of work by law is identical. The phase of the problem which has been considered more extensively by the American Federation of Labor is a proposition to establish a general eight-hour day for workers in private industries by law. Proposals for a general eight-hour law were introduced in both the Philadelphia and San Francisco conventions,[1] and the debates upon the subject were published in full in the proceedings of those conventions. If you would be interested in having copies of the proceedings, I should be glad to send them to you; they may be secured for twenty-five cents apiece.

I have discussed in several articles and editorials in the *American Federationist* the principle underlying regulation by law of industrial relations in private industries. I refer you to the following:

January 1915. Economic organization and the Eight-hour day.

February 1915. The Danger of Shifting Duties, and Self-Help Is The Best Help.

March 1915. The Shorter Workday—Its Philosophy.

April 1915. Australasian Labor Regulating Schemes.

May 1915. And They Would "Wish" It On Us. Legislation Hostile to Progress.[2] Fixing Wages By Law Or Unionism.

August 1915. The Workers and the Eight-Hour Workday.[3]

If there is any further information that you desire in your study of this subject, I shall be very glad if I can be helpful to you.

Very truly yours,   Saml Gompers.
President,   American Federation of Labor.

P.S. Copies of the *American Federationist* are ten cents each.

TLpS, reel 215, vol. 227, pp. 308–12, SG Letterbooks, DLC.

1. See "Eleventh Day—Friday Night Session," Nov. 20, 1914, in "Excerpts from Accounts of the 1914 Convention of the AFL in Philadelphia," Nov. 14–22, 1914, above, and "Stormy Talk Ends Labor Convention; Gompers Assailed," Nov. 23, 1915, in "Excerpts from News Accounts of the 1915 Convention of the AFL in San Francisco," Nov. 16–23, 1915, above.

2. *American Federationist* 22 (May 1915): 353–54.

3. *American Federationist* 22 (Aug. 1915): 565–93.

To W. D. Mahon

Dec. 19, 1916.

Mr. W. D. Mahon,
President, Amalgamated Association of Street and Electric Railway
   Employes of America,
104 East High St., Detroit, Michigan.

Dear Sir and Brother:

Mr. Santiago Iglesias, representative of the American Federation of Labor in Porto Rico, has brought to my attention and has placed in my hands the application of the street railway employes of San Juan for charter of affiliation to the Amalgamated Association. He has also handed me your letter of November 28th addressed to Mr. Rafael Alonso,[1] in which you return the charter fee and inform him that your Executive Board has decided not to attempt to organize the Street Railway men of Porto Rico.

I am sure you will appreciate the fact that it is the furthest from my desire or intention to interfere in the least particular with the internal affairs of any organization affiliated to the American Federation of Labor, but yet in view of the work which the American Federation of Labor has for years conducted in Porto Rico and the constant effort which has been made to organize the workers of every trade and calling in the Island, and have them affiliated to their respective National or International Unions or directly to the A.F. of L., it seems to me that I [would be remiss][2] in my duty did I not urge upon you and your colleagues of the Executive Board to reconsider the action taken in this matter.

Porto Rico is a component part of the United States; it is anticipated that before the close of the present Congress a law will be enacted giving full citizenship to the people of Porto Rico. Many of the National and International Unions have issued charters to local unions of their trades and callings in Porto Rico. I am firmly of the opinion that it would be a mistake on the part of the Amalgamated Association to decline to issue a charter to the Street Railway Employes of San Juan.

Mr. Iglesias informs me that the street railway men are all white men. I again urge that the matter be reconsidered and ask that you let me hear from you at your early convenience as I am holding the charter application together with the charter fee of $15.00.

Trusting that I may hear from you at an early date[3] and with kind regards, I am,

Fraternally yours,   Saml Gompers.
President,   American Federation of Labor.

P.S. In addition to the above it is not amiss to call your attention to the fact that a movement has been inaugurated for the organizing of the workers of Pan American countries; also to establish a Pan American Federation of Labor. No doubt you have seen in the newspapers of this morning[4] copies of cablegrams exchanged between Mr. Carlos Loveira in Havana regarding the strike[5] of the motormen, engineers and firemen in Havana. Indeed, yesterday I sent you a telegram[6] upon that subject. Surely if in the first stages of the effort to be of mutual assistance and to bring about a larger, broader and more comprehensive labor movement in all American countries, if, I say, the first stages are met by refusal on the part of the international union to issue a charter to the workmen in Porto Rico, I am afraid it will be regarded as quite a set-back to the project, and in this instance Porto Rico is a possession of the United States.

S. G.

TLpS, reel 216, vol. 228, pp. 154–56, SG Letterbooks, DLC.

1. W. D. Mahon to Rafael Alonso, Nov. 28, 1916, AFL Microfilm National and International Union File, Street and Electric Railway Employees Records, reel 41, frame 1658, *AFL Records.*

2. The text in brackets is supplied from a copy of this letter in AFL Microfilm National and International Union File, Street and Electric Railway Employees Records, reel 41, frame 1657, *AFL Records.*

3. Mahon replied on Dec. 26, 1916, that he would place the matter before the next meeting of the union's executive board (AFL Microfilm National and International Union File, Street and Electric Railway Employees Records, reel 41, frame 1656, *AFL Records*). On Mar. 7, 1917, he wrote that the board would issue a charter to the San Juan street railway employees if they would agree to pay the dues and other costs involved, and SG sent a copy of Mahon's letter to Santiago Iglesias on Mar. 9 (ibid.).

4. "Call Gompers' Aid in Cuba," *Washington Post,* Dec. 19, 1916.

5. In December 1916 Cuban railroad workers, including street railway carmen, struck after organizers were fired for trying to form a union. By late December workers had come to an agreement with the Cuban Railroad Co., but those employed by the Havana Central remained on strike for at least a few weeks more.

6. SG to Mahon, Dec. 18, 1916, reel 216, vol. 228, p. 12, SG Letterbooks, DLC.

An Address by Samuel Gompers at a Celebration of His Sixty-seventh Birthday and Fiftieth Wedding Anniversary

January 28, 1917

Mr. Samuel Gompers: Mr. Toastmaster,[1] Friends:

To sit here this evening and to listen to what has been said in regard to me and to be unmoved would write me down as one devoid of feeling, devoid of the character of manhood.

Believe me, when I say that I have suffered more than I can undertake to express to you. It is hard to speak in response to what has been said. It is as if a mirror has been set before me, which reflected upon my mind and in my heart that which has been uttered tonight. My inclination would be to jest, to participate with you in happiness and conviviality rather than pathos. I intend to tell you an anecdote, and I am going to try to get away, if I can, from the very serious thoughts which have been pressing upon me.

In the long ago, a member of the United States Senate found it necessary to return to his home state in the South, to seek the good will of his fellow citizens, so that he might be re-elected. He was traveling across the country not in the fast-going railroads of today, but in the old, time-honored buggy, with its horse and with a colored driver. There were two men walking in the opposite direction in which the Senator and his colored man were going, when one said to the other, "Do you see that man there in the buggy? Why, he is a great man. He is a wonderful man." And the darkey had heard the observation, just as well as the United States Senator, and he leaned over a bit, nudged the Senator, and said, "Say, boss, I wonder who he means, you or me?" (Laughter)

I felt somewhat in the position of the old darkey, when all these splendid tributes were paid to me tonight. I sometimes take an introspective view of myself, and ask myself this question: Am I really deserving of all these tributes? For I am conscious of but this one fact: I hold it to be a self-evident duty of every man, of every woman, to be of service to their fellows. (Applause) The opportunity of like service isn't given to all of us. If each man does the day's work, as opportunity is given him, he has done his level best and measures up to the man who has wider and broader opportunities. (Applause)

There cannot and must not be any step backward in the great march of the human family for justice and right. (Applause) I, together with you, may be compelled to endure injustice and wrong, but it must not be endured without protest. (Applause)

I have tried my level best to serve, to express the hopes and the aspirations of the intelligent and the enlightened, and have dared to voice the inarticulate yearnings of those who do not know. (Applause) And perhaps at times, if this were questioned, they might have repudiated the assumed authority to speak for them.

I shall not, at this time, enter into a consideration of either my life or my work, nor shall I enter into a discussion of the economic problems with which the toiling masses must deal and help to solve. I can make only slight reference to the fact that I have seen great changes, wonderful improvements come into the work and into the lives of the toilers of my time.

This great movement of ours is for a better life, for a better day; it does not simply believe in cataclysms or revolutionary methods for achievements, but in the constant, persistent, never ending work to make today a better day than yesterday, to make tomorrow a better day than today, and to make tomorrow and tomorrow's tomorrow, each a better day than the one that has gone before it. (Applause) Through this evolutionary work, we endeavor to see to it that there shall come more light into the lives of the wealth producers of the world, to persist day in and day out, year in and year out, decade after decade, in this wonderful struggle of the ages, for justice. We are only emerging from that great, black, dark time so splendidly described by our friend, Judge Parker, from the time of slavery and serfdom, from the time when the worker was typified by the man with the hoe, with a bent back and receding forehead. The great labor movement has accomplished this fact: That the men of labor now stand erect, not defiant, but determined and looking the whole world in the face, demanding and insisting that justice and freedom and humanity shall be the first consideration in our public, private, industrial, political and social life. (Applause)

To build character is of the first importance to our movement; to know what we aim to accomplish and then proceed, unswerved by any other consideration, to go on and carry on that work. We protest against that movement's being diverted even for a moment from the straight path of its progress and success.

I appreciate the very many things that have been so kindly said of me; one of them particularly, that I have not had money possession as one of the ideas and ideals of my life. And I might as well say here, or repeat here an expression of that grandfather[2] of mine, now passed away, an expression I repeated at the Philadelphia Convention of American Federation of Labor, something like this: "If God Almighty will only save me from poverty, I will save myself from riches." The American Federation of Labor has provided a salary for my services in the Federation, which just enables a fellow to live decently, not luxuriously, and believe me, I am carrying my grandfather's maxim into actual operation. (Applause)

Of what use is money to anyone, beyond using it for the real needs of life? I have four grown children now,[3] three boys and one girl, and the three boys have been taught a trade, and they work at the trade. They are union men too. One is a printer, one a granite cutter, and one is a cigar maker. (Applause) And my three boys are married and are now raising families. Our girl, (turning to Miss Gompers) well, she is our pet and boss. (Laughter) Perhaps my reference to this family is in line with carrying out the thought that I had in mind. They will not be left a fortune, they will not be left as the heirs to large means; there is one thing that I did try to leave them, and that is a realization of the duty to do their share in the effort to establish a better labor movement that it can protect and promote their interests as workers, (Applause) that they may find the struggle for life not quite so hard as I found it when I entered the industrial field. That is the legacy that will be left to my children! If, incidentally, there may come some tribute of respect for what I have tried to do, that I am sure they will appreciate. (Laughter)

All that has been said of my wife's assistance and encouragement and sacrifice is all within the limit of truth, and I will not take up your time and your attention to speak of the very many instances in which that has been demonstrated. She has been willing to share what I had, and if there wasn't anything to share, we both went without it. (Applause)

My father, bordering on his ninetieth year, whom you have seen and heard this evening, was a working man, and my mother[4] an honored woman, the mother of eight children, all of them workingmen; my four living brothers,[5] who are here, are workingmen, and my two sisters[6] are both wives of workingmen. All through my entire family, even to first, second and third cousins, nephews and nieces, there is not any one of them who is not a workingman, or a working woman. And, as far as I can trace back, that great work of Victor Hugo applies to me and mine, the "History of a Proletariat Family."

It may be interesting to relate this fact. There are four living generations, of good standing membership in the Unions of their respective trades now, my father, myself, my son, Sam, and his daughter.[7] That doesn't occur very often, by reason of the fact that death, business opportunity, etc. sometimes prevents this. But my father is a member in good standing of the Cigar Makers' International Union of America; I, a member of that same organization; my Sam, a member of the International Typographical Union, and his daughter, a member of the Stenographers, Typewriters and Bookkeepers' Union.[8] (Applause)

Perhaps I ought to confess, for Mrs. Gompers and myself, that there are two of the links that are not here tonight; but we have five living generations in the Gompers' family, (Applause) my father, myself, my son Henry, his daughter and her little boy.[9] (Applause) So, judging from what I have said to you on that score, and seeing that young dad of mine, it is likely that I may be with you for some time yet. (Applause)

Perhaps I ought to relate a little incident that may be of some interest this evening. There is a man in this hall, Jack Davis, who, fifty years ago tonight with his affianced,[10] and my affianced, Sophia, and myself (four of us) simply got married; he and his fiancee standing up for us, and we, in turn, standing up for them. When I entered the building this evening and he and I saw each other for the first time in a few years, we both made the same exclamation, he pronouncing my name, Sam, and I pronouncing his name, Jack, and we both embraced each other, and he said, "It was fifty years ago tonight." It did seem almost as though this meeting had been arranged.

I was very happy on my birthday anniversary, yesterday, to be at the silver wedding of my son, Sam, and his good wife.[11]

There are many more things that I would like to say to you tonight, but I doubt the wisdom of saying them, for it is far beyond the reasonable time when men and women should be asked to remain any longer for the purpose of hearing an address.

For all that you have said and done, for all that you have not expressed in word or action, but as I can draw the inferences of what is in your hearts and in your minds, on behalf of my good wife and myself, I thank you more than I can find words to express, and my only hope is that as long as I live, I may have the opportunity of giving service, if not as President of the American Federation of Labor, if not in an official capacity, that I may at least be of service in the ranks for the great democracy of labor, for the great movement for the democratization of the world's affairs; and that will be the means of obliterating from men's hearts and minds the bitterness of strife, the struggle and destruction that we witness, or which we hear of or see, which is now going on; that you and I and those who shall follow us may do our share in promoting the thought in the minds of the people, that they wish peace rather than war and struggle. (Applause)

There comes back to me again this one thought of building character. You can't stop wars by simply entertaining the thought that war shall cease. It is the character building which is the duty of our time. Force and compulsion always bring in their wake a reaction of tremendous importance to the welfare of the people, to wish for peace, to work for peace, to pray for peace, and to make the breaking of the peace an offense against the conscience of the world.

Ladies and gentlemen, and friends, if it were not so late, I should like to continue with my talk, but as it is, I must ask you to excuse me from further remarks, and I want to again thank you from the very bottom of my heart. (Applause)

TD, AFL Microfilm Convention File, reel 28, frames 1643–44, *AFL Records.* Handwritten notation: "Address by President Samuel Gompers at his birthday and 50th Wedding Anniversary New York. January 28, 1917."

1. James Duncan served as toastmaster.
2. Samuel Moses GOMPERS.
3. Alexander Julian, Henry Julian, Sadie Julian, and Samuel Julian GOMPERS.
4. Sarah Rood GOMPERS.
5. Alexander, Henry, Louis, and Simon GOMPERS.
6. Bella and Henrietta GOMPERS Isaacs.
7. Florence Gompers.
8. AFL Stenographers', Typewriters', Bookkeepers', and Assistants' Union 11,773.
9. Sophia Gompers Knight and Charles Knight.
10. Mary Ancona.
11. Sophia Dampf Gompers.

GLOSSARY

ALPINE, John R. (1863–1947), was born in Maine and worked as a gas fitter in Everett, Mass., and then Boston, where he was president of United Association of Journeymen Plumbers, Gas Fitters, Steam Fitters, and Steam Fitters' Helpers of the United States and Canada 175 (1904–5) and of the Boston Building Trades Council (1905). Alpine served as special organizer, vice-president (1904–6), and president (1906–19) of the international union (from 1913, the United Association of Plumbers and Steam Fitters of the United States and Canada) and as an AFL vice-president (1909–19). During World War I he was appointed to the Cantonment Adjustment Commission that supervised labor relations on military construction jobs. He lived in Chicago from 1906 until 1920, when he moved to New York City, where he was employed by the Grinnell Co. as assistant to the president for labor relations. In 1931 President Herbert Hoover appointed him assistant secretary of labor in charge of the Federal Unemployment Service.

AMMON, Charles George (1873–1960), a postal worker, was born in London. He served as chairman of the Fawcett Association, a mail sorters' union (1911–19), was editor of its journal (1904–11, 1918–19), and was later organizing secretary of the Union of Post Office Workers (1921–28). A member of the Labour party, Ammon served on the London County Council (1919–25, 1934–46) and as a Member of Parliament from North Camberwell (1922–31, 1935–44). In 1944 he was elevated to the House of Lords.

ANDERSON, Edward E. (1869?–1937?), was born in Michigan and by 1903 was working as a barber in Pueblo, Colo. He served as secretary of Journeymen Barbers' International Union of America 219 of Pueblo (1904–15) and as vice-president (1911–15) and secretary-treasurer (1916–22) of the Colorado State Federation of Labor. He also served for a time as president of the Pueblo Trades and Labor Assembly and the Pueblo Union Label League and was editor and publisher of the

541

Pueblo Labor Press. Anderson moved to Denver during 1916 and from 1929 to 1932 was secretary-treasurer of Barbers' local 205 of that city.

APPLETON, William Archibald (1859–1940), was born in Nottingham, England, where he worked as a lacemaker, and later moved to London. He served as secretary of the Amalgamated Society of Operative Lacemakers (1896–1907), secretary of the General Federation of Trade Unions (1907–38), and president of the International Federation of Trade Unions (1919–20).

BAINE, Charles L. (b. 1870), was born in Canada and immigrated to the United States with his family in 1880. He settled in Chicago where he worked as a shoe cutter and served as business agent of Boot and Shoe Workers' Union 133. He was elected to the executive board of the Boot and Shoe Workers in 1899 and served as the union's secretary-treasurer from 1902 to 1931.

BARNES, John Mahlon (1866–1934), was born in Lancaster, Pa., and became a member of the KOL in the 1880s. He joined the Cigar Makers' International Union of America in 1887, serving as secretary of local 100 of Philadelphia (1891–93, 1897–1900) and local 165 of Philadelphia (1903–4), and was elected a vice-president of the Pennsylvania Federation of Labor in 1902. He joined the Socialist Labor party in 1891 and was corresponding secretary of the Philadelphia Central Committee and an organizer for the party's Philadelphia American Branch in the 1890s. A founder of the Socialist Party of America in 1901, he was secretary of its Philadelphia branch and the Pennsylvania representative on its national executive committee in the early years of the decade. He served as the party's national secretary from 1905 until 1911 and as its campaign manager in 1912 and 1924.

BAUMEISTER, Albert (1882–1953), a resident of Berlin and a waiter by trade, served as secretary (1908–13) of the Internationale Union der gastwirtschaftlichen Angestellten (the International Union of Restaurant Employees) and was later the editor of the *Internationale Rundschau der Arbeit* (*International Review of Labor*).

BERGER, Victor Luitpold (1860–1929), was born in Nieder-Rehbach, Austria, and attended the universities of Vienna and Budapest before immigrating to the United States in 1878. He lived in Bridgeport, Conn., for two years, working as a boiler mender, metal polisher, and salesman, and then moved to Milwaukee, where he taught German in the public school system. In 1892 he resigned and bought the *Milwaukee Volkszeitung.* He changed its name to *Wisconsin Vorwärts* in 1893 and edited the paper (later the *Vorwärts*) until 1911. He was a founder of the Social Democracy of America in 1897, the Social Democratic Party of the United States in 1898, and the Socialist Party of America in 1901. He served on the Socialist party's national executive committee from 1901 until 1923. He edited the weekly *Social Democratic Herald* from 1901 to 1913 and the daily *Milwaukee Leader* from 1911 until his death. In 1910 he was elected alderman-at-large for Milwaukee and later that year was elected a congressman, serving from 1911 to 1913. After his reelection to Congress in 1918, he was found guilty of conspiracy to violate the Espionage Act and sentenced to twenty years' imprisonment in early 1919. He was released on bail pending review of the case, but Congress refused to seat him. Reelected in 1919, he was again denied his congressional seat. The U.S. Supreme Court overturned Berger's conviction in 1921, and he was elected to Congress again the following year, serving from 1923 to 1929.

BERRES, Albert Julius (1873–1940), a long-time resident of Washington, D.C., served as chairman of the executive council of the District of Columbia branch of the Pattern Makers' League of North America (1906–10) and as a member of the union's executive board (1909–14). Berres also served as secretary-treasurer of the AFL Metal Trades Department (1908–27), resigning that position to become secretary in charge of industrial affairs for the Motion Picture Producers' Association in Hollywood, Calif.

BERRY, George Leonard (1882–1948), was born in Tennessee. After serving in the Spanish-American War, he took a job as a press feeder for the *St. Louis Globe-Democrat* and joined the International Printing Pressmen's and Assistants' Union of North America in 1899. About 1902 he earned his pressman's card and moved to San Francisco, where he was an active member of Printing Pressmen's local 24, serving as its president (1906) and then as business agent. Berry was president of the international union from 1907 until his death, moving to union headquarters in Cincinnati in 1907 and then to Rogersville, Tenn., in 1911. He served in the army during World War I, taking a leave of absence from his union responsibilities, and in 1921 helped organize the American Legion. He founded the International Playing Card Co. in 1926 and was the owner and publisher of the *Rogersville Review,* a weekly paper. He later served as an AFL vice-president (1935) and as a Democratic U.S. senator from Tennessee (1937–38).

BEVIN, Ernest (1881–1951), was born in Winsford, Somerset. He left school at the age of eleven and about 1894 moved to Bristol, where he worked as a mineral water delivery man. He formed a Bristol carters' branch of the Dock, Wharf, Riverside, and General Labourers'

Union in 1910 and from 1914 to 1920 served as an organizer for the Dockers' union. Bevin was secretary of the Transport and General Workers' Union (1922–40), a leader of the 1926 general strike, and a member (1925–40) and chairman (1936–37) of the general council of the TUC. In 1940 he became part of Winston Churchill's wartime coalition government, serving as minister of labour and national service (1940–45), and after the war he served as foreign minister in the Labour government (1945–51).

BOHM, Ernest (1860–1936), was born in New York, worked as a compositor, clerk, and manager of a cloak operators' union early in his career, and became secretary of the Excelsior Labor Club of the KOL in 1881 and corresponding secretary of the New York City Central Labor Union in 1882. During the 1880s and 1890s he was active in the organization of the brewery workers, serving briefly in 1888 as an editor of the *Brauer Zeitung,* the official journal of the National Union of the United Brewery Workmen of the United States. He was later secretary of Brewery Workmen's local 31 (Ale and Porter Brewers) and of the New York City Brewery Workmen's local executive board. He supported Henry George's 1886 mayoral campaign and in 1887 participated in founding the United Labor party and served as secretary of the Progressive Labor party. Bohm was a member of the Socialist Labor party and, from 1896 to 1898, secretary of the executive board of the Socialist Trade and Labor Alliance. He served as secretary of the Central Labor Federation of New York City (1889–99) and of the Central Federated Union (CFU) of New York City (by 1913, the CFU of Greater New York and Vicinity) from 1899 to 1921. From 1919 to 1921 he was secretary of the New York City National Labor party (from 1920, the Farmer-Labor party), and from 1921 until his death he was a leader of AFL Bookkeepers', Stenographers', and Accountants' Union 12,646, holding several positions, including the presidency.

BOWERMAN, Charles William (1851–1947), a London typographer, was secretary of the London Society of Compositors (1892–1906), served as president (1901) and secretary (1911–23) of the TUC, and was a member of the Parliamentary Committee of the TUC (1898–1923). He served as a Labour Member of Parliament from 1906 to 1931.

BRAIS, Eugene J. (b. 1881?), was born in Canada and immigrated to the United States in 1891. He joined Journeymen Tailors' Union of America 162 of Cleveland when it was organized in 1900 and later served as its business agent (1907–9). He was elected secretary of the Tailors (from 1914 to 1915, the Tailors' Industrial Union) in 1909 and moved to Bloomington, Ill., in 1910 when his term began. He was reelected in 1914 but resigned in January 1915 to become secretary of the newly organized Amalgamated Clothing Workers of America, moving to New York City. He resigned that office as well when the Tailors voted to rescind their amalgamation with the Clothing Workers, and by 1916 he had returned to Illinois.

BROCK, James F. (b. 1879), born in California, served as an organizer and later as president (1912?–32) of the Laundry Workers' International Union.

BROWN, J. G., served as president (1907–9, 1912–18) of the shingle weavers' union (to 1913, the International Shingle Weavers' Union of America; 1913–14, the International Union of Shingle Weavers, Sawmill Workers, and Woodsmen; 1914–16, the International Union of Timberworkers; and from 1916, the International Shingle Weavers' Union of America). He was an AFL salaried organizer in 1907 and again from 1915 to 1918.

CAROTHERS, Francis K. (1868–1952), worked in Chicago and Kansas City, Mo., before serving as president of the American Federation of Musicians for a single term (1914–15). He later moved to California, where he became active in Musicians' local 47 of Los Angeles.

CARRICK, Michael Patrick (1857–1904), was born in Ireland, immigrated to the United States in 1872, and as a young man was a member of Pittsburgh KOL Local Assembly 1397. He helped organize the Brotherhood of Painters and Decorators of America in 1887 and was secretary of Painters and Decorators' local 15 of Allegheny, Pa., between 1887 and 1894. He also served as secretary (1895) and agent (1897) of the United Labor League of Western Pennsylvania and vice-president (1897) of the National Building Trades Council. When factional struggles split the Painters and Decorators in 1894, Carrick supported the western faction and served the union as organizer and president (1896–97). In 1901 he was elected secretary-treasurer of the reunited Brotherhood of Painters, Decorators, and Paperhangers of America, an office he held until his death.

CARTER, William Samuel (1859–1923), a native of Austin, Tex., worked as a railroad baggageman, fireman, and engineer from 1879 to 1894. He edited the official journal of the Brotherhood of Locomotive Firemen (1894–1904) and later served the union (from 1906, the Brotherhood of Locomotive Firemen and Enginemen) as secretary and treasurer (1904–9) and president (1909–22). From 1918 to 1920 he was director of the Division of Labor of the U.S. Railroad Administration, during which time he took a leave of absence from the presidency of the union.

Coffey, Frank M. (1870–1948), was born in Iowa and in 1893 moved to Lincoln, Neb., where he became a member of International Typographical Union 209. He served as president (1910) and secretary-treasurer (1913–22?) of the Nebraska State Federation of Labor and was chief deputy commissioner (1915–16) of the Nebraska Bureau of Labor and Industrial Statistics. Coffey later took up the practice of law and from 1935 to 1943 was presiding judge of the Nebraska Workmen's Compensation Court.

Conway, Henry J. (1858?–1926), was born in Chicago. By 1891 he was working as a clerk in a shoe store in St. Louis; around 1902 he returned to Chicago, where he was active for a time in Retail Clerks' International Protective Association 195 and was business agent for the Chicago Clerks' Council. He served as president (1896–98, 1906–9), vice-president (1898–1906), and secretary-treasurer (1909–26) of the Retail Clerks, moving to the union's headquarters in Denver in 1909 and to Lafayette, Ind., in 1912.

D'Alessandro, Domenico (1869–1926), was born in Italy and immigrated to the United States in 1895. A day laborer in Boston, he was president of AFL Laborers' and Excavators' (Italian) Union 11,679 from 1904 until it joined the International Hod Carriers' and Building Laborers' Union of America in 1906 as local 209. D'Alessandro served the international union (from 1912, the International Hod Carriers', Building and Common Laborers' Union of America) as organizer (1907), vice-president (1907), and president (1908–26). He lived in Albany from 1910 until his move to Quincy, Mass., around 1918.

Daly, Timothy M. (1863–1949), immigrated to the United States from Ireland in 1867. A member of Metal Polishers', Buffers', Platers', Brass Molders', and Brass and Silver Workers' Union of North America 34 of New York City, he served as president of the international union in 1892–93, 1895–96, and 1909–15.

Debs, Eugene Victor (1855–1926), born in Terre Haute, Ind., entered railroad work as an engine-house laborer and became a locomotive fireman. Elected secretary of Brotherhood of Locomotive Firemen 16 of Terre Haute in 1875, he became grand secretary and treasurer of the Locomotive Firemen and editor of the union's official journal in 1880. Debs resigned as an officer of the brotherhood in 1892 to begin building a single union for all railway workers and resigned the editorship of the journal in 1894. He founded the American Railway

Union in 1893 and led it in the successful 1894 Great Northern Railroad strike. Imprisoned for six months in 1895 for his role as president of the union during the Pullman strike, he turned his energies to political activity after his release. In 1896 he supported the People's party campaign, in 1897 he was a founder of the Social Democracy of America, a socialist communitarian movement, and in 1898 he participated in founding the Social Democratic Party of the United States, an organization committed to socialist electoral activity. Debs served on the party's executive committee and in 1900 polled a hundred thousand votes as the presidential candidate of the Social Democratic party and a wing of the Socialist Labor party led by Morris Hillquit. In 1901 he was a founder of the Socialist Party of America, and he ran for president as its candidate in 1904, 1908, 1912, and 1920. In 1905 Debs participated in founding the IWW, a revolutionary syndicalist industrial union that he hoped would function as the economic arm of the Socialist party; he left the IWW three years later. During World War I, he was prosecuted under the Espionage Act and sentenced to ten years in prison. SG supported the campaign for clemency that culminated in a presidential pardon for Debs in 1921.

DONOGHUE, Mortimer M. (1867–1939), born in Connecticut, joined United Association of Journeymen Plumbers, Gas Fitters, Steam Fitters, and Steam Fitters' Helpers of the United States and Canada 3 of Denver in 1900. After moving to Butte, Mont., he joined Plumbers' local 41, which he later served as president (1906–7). He also served as vice-president (1907–9) and president (1909–19) of the Montana State Federation of Labor.

DRAPER, Patrick Martin (1867?–1943), was born in Aylmer, Que. At the age of fifteen he began working at the Government Printing Bureau in Ottawa, where he joined International Typographical Union 102 in 1887; when he retired in 1933 he was superintendent of the bureau. He served his local as president (intermittently between 1893 and 1942) and was an organizer for the international union in 1900–1901. Draper also served as secretary-treasurer (1900–1935) and president (1935–39) of the Trades and Labor Congress of Canada.

DUFFY, Frank (1861–1955), was born in County Monaghan, Ireland. At the age of two he immigrated with his family to England and in 1881 came to the United States, settling in New York City. There he joined United Order of American Carpenters and Joiners 2 and served as the first president of the order's executive council for Greater New York. In 1888, when the order merged with the Brotherhood of Carpenters and Joiners of America to form the United Brotherhood of Carpenters and Joiners of America, Duffy became a member of Carpenters' local 478. He served as president of the local's executive council (1888–1901) and as its business agent (1896–98), and for four terms he was financial secretary of the brotherhood's New York district council. He was an organizer for the Carpenters in 1896 and four years later was elected to the union's executive board. Duffy served the brotherhood as secretary-treasurer (1901–2), secretary (1903–48), and editor of the union's official journal (1901–41). He moved to Philadelphia in 1901 and then to Indianapolis in 1902 when the union changed the location of its headquarters. Duffy served as an AFL vice-president from 1914 to 1939. He was also a board member of the National Society for the Promotion of Industrial Education (1912–20), served on the Indiana State Board of Education (1915–19), and was a member of the American labor mission to the 1919 Paris peace conference.

DUNCAN, James (1857–1928), was born in Scotland and immigrated to the United States in 1880. He joined the Granite Cutters' National Union of the United States of America in 1881 and during the early 1880s served as an officer of the union's locals in New York, Philadelphia, Richmond, and, finally, Baltimore, where he settled in 1884. He was Maryland state organizer for the Granite Cutters, organizer for the AFL, and president of the Baltimore Federation of Labor (1890–92, 1897). Duncan served the Granite Cutters (from 1905, the Granite Cutters' International Association of America) as secretary (1895–1905), secretary-treasurer (1905–12), and president (1912–23) and edited the union's official journal from 1895 to 1928. He was an AFL vice-president (1895–1928) and acting president of the Federation during President John McBride's illness in 1895. He was also a member of the National Civic Federation Industrial Department (1901–2) and executive committee (1903 to at least 1923). President Woodrow Wilson appointed him a member of the Root mission to Russia in 1917, and he also served as a member of the American labor mission to the 1919 Paris peace conference.

EASLEY, Ralph Montgomery (1856–1939), was born in Browning, Pa., founded a daily newspaper in Hutchinson, Kans., and then moved to Chicago to work as a reporter and columnist for the *Chicago Inter Ocean*. In 1893 he helped organize the Chicago Civic Federation, leaving the *Inter Ocean* to serve as the federation's secretary. He resigned from that position in 1900 and moved to New York City to organize the National Civic Federation, bringing together prominent representatives of business, labor, and the public in cooperative reform efforts and in the settlement of labor disputes. Easley served as secretary of the National Civic Federation (1900–1903) and as chairman of its executive council (1904–39). In his later years he increasingly devoted himself to opposing radical labor organizations and social movements.

FITZPATRICK, John J. (1871?–1946), was born in Athlone, Ireland, and, after the death of his parents, was brought to Chicago by his uncle. He worked in the Chicago stockyards and in a brass foundry and then took up horseshoeing and blacksmithing, joining Journeymen Horseshoers' National Union of the United States (from 1892, International Union of Journeymen Horseshoers of the United States and Canada) 4 of Chicago in 1886. Over the years he served variously as the local's vice-president, treasurer, business agent, and president, and he was its longtime representative to the Chicago Federation of Labor (FOL). Fitzpatrick was an executive committee member (1899–1900), organizer (1902–4?), and president (1900–1901, 1906–46) of the Chicago FOL and an AFL salaried organizer (1903–23). He ran unsuccessfully for mayor of Chicago on the Labor party ticket in 1919, helped lead the 1919 steel strike, and served on the National Recovery Administration Regional Labor Board (1933–35).

FLETT, John Alexander (1860–1941), was born in Hamilton, Ont., where he became a carpenter. A member first of KOL Local Assembly 2225, he joined Brotherhood of Carpenters and Joiners of America 18 in 1884 and also played an active role in Hamilton's Trade and Labor Assembly. He was vice-president (1898–1902) and president (1902–4) of the Trades and Labor Congress of Canada and served as an AFL salaried organizer in Canada from 1900 until 1925.

FLOOD, Emmet T. (1874–1942), was born in Illinois and worked as a teamster in Chicago, where he joined International Brotherhood of Teamsters 715 (Department Store Drivers). He served as an AFL salaried organizer from 1904 to 1925, organizing, among others, a nurses' and attendants' union in Illinois state hospitals. Flood retired from the labor movement after SG's death and worked in the trucking business.

FORD, Charles P. (1879–1932), was born in Mount Vernon, Iowa. By 1902 he had moved to Schenectady, N.Y., where he began working for General Electric and joined International Brotherhood of Electrical Workers 247, serving as its president (1904–5) and later as chair of the grievance committee for the Schenectady district council. In 1912 Ford became secretary of the international union, serving until 1925, when illness forced his resignation, and he was chair of its executive council from 1926 until his death. He was a founder of the Electrical Workers' Benefit Association in 1922 and of the Union Cooperative Insurance Association in 1924, serving the latter variously as vice-president, general manager, and president. From 1923 until his death he was a member of the board of directors of the Mount Vernon Savings Bank.

FORRESTER, James Joseph (1867–1939), was born in Ohio. The son of a farmer, he taught school to put himself through college and was admitted to the bar in 1888. He was employed as a letter carrier in the 1890s and then took a job as a railway clerk. Forrester served the Brotherhood of Railway Clerks (from 1919, the Brotherhood of Railway and Steamship Clerks, Freight Handlers, Express and Station Employes) as organizer (1907–8), deputy grand president (1908–10), vice grand president (1910–15), and grand president (1915–20). He was later a member of the U.S. Railroad Labor Board (1920–21), the brotherhood's vice grand president for legislative matters (1921), and its national legislative counsel (1922–25). Following the union's 1925 convention, he participated in the organization of the rival American Federation of Express Workers, which he served as president until 1928. A resident of Washington, D.C., he later worked as a special investigator for the immigration bureau of the U.S. Department of Labor (1931–33) and, until he retired in 1937, as a researcher and statistical expert for various government agencies.

FOSTER, William Z. (1881–1961), born in Taunton, Mass., was a member of the Socialist Party of America from 1901 to 1909, joined the United Wage Workers' Party of Washington in 1909, and became a member of the IWW in 1910, participating in the Spokane free-speech campaign. He then traveled to Europe, where he became a convert to the strategy of "boring from within" existing trade unions. After unsuccessfully contesting the AFL's right to represent the American labor movement at the 1911 meeting of the International Secretariat in Budapest, he returned to the United States and settled in Chicago. He left the IWW in 1912, joined the Brotherhood of Railway Carmen of America, and organized and was a member of the Syndicalist League of North America (1912–14) and the International Trade Union Educational League (1915–17). Between 1917 and 1919 he led AFL organizing campaigns in the packinghouse and steel industries, and in 1920 he founded the Trade Union Educational League. The following year he went to Moscow and, upon his return, joined the American Communist party. He was the party's candidate for president in 1924, 1928, and 1932 and served as the party's long-time chairman (1930?–44, 1945–57) and chairman emeritus (1957–61). He died in Moscow, where he had gone for medical care.

FRANKLIN, Joseph Anthony (1868–1948), was born in Sedalia, Mo., and took up the boilermaking trade in 1892. A charter member of

Brotherhood of Boiler Makers and Iron Ship Builders of America 221 of Pittsburg, Kans., he served the Boiler Makers (from 1906, the International Brotherhood of Boiler Makers, Iron Ship Builders, and Helpers of America) as vice-president (1906–8) and president (1908–44).

FRAYNE, Hugh (1869–1934), was a member of Amalgamated Sheet Metal Workers' International Association (from 1903, Alliance) 86 of Scranton, Pa., and a vice-president of the international union (1901–2, 1904–5). He was an AFL salaried organizer from 1902 until his death and beginning in 1910 was in charge of the AFL's New York City office. During World War I, Frayne chaired the labor division of the War Industries Board.

FRENCH, Thomas A. (b. 1880?), was born in California and later moved to Phoenix, Ariz., where he served as secretary-treasurer of the Arizona State Federation of Labor (1916–17, 1920–21).

FREY, John Philip (1871–1957), was born in Mankato, Minn., and moved to Montreal in 1878, where he lived until the age of fourteen. He worked in a Montreal printing shop and on a farm and lumber camp in Upper Ontario before moving with his family to Worcester, Mass., in 1887. After finding work first as an errand boy and then in a grocery, he apprenticed at the age of sixteen as a molder. In 1896 he helped organize Iron Molders' Union of North America 5, serving as the local's president until 1900 and as vice-president of the Molders from 1900 to 1903. Frey moved to Bellevue, Ky., in 1903 after he was appointed editor of the union's official journal, which was published in Cincinnati, and about 1909 moved to Norwood, Ohio. He served as editor of the journal until 1927 and was president of the Ohio State Federation of Labor from 1924 to 1928. Frey moved to Washington, D.C., to serve as secretary-treasurer (1927–34) and president (1934–50) of the AFL Metal Trades Department.

FURUSETH, Andrew (1854–1938), was born in Furuseth, Norway, and went to sea in 1873. He immigrated to California in 1880, making his home in San Francisco, and in 1885 joined the Coast Seamen's Union, serving as secretary from 1887 to 1889. He later served as secretary of the Sailors' Union of the Pacific (1891–92, 1892–1936) and president of the International Seamen's Union of America (1897–99, 1908–38) and was a legislative representative in Washington, D.C., for the AFL (1895–1902) and for the Seamen.

GARRETSON, Austin Bruce (1856–1931), was born in Winterset, Iowa, and in 1884 joined Order of Railway Conductors of America 53 of Denison, Tex. He served the order as grand senior conductor (1887–

88, 1891–99), assistant grand chief conductor (1888–89, 1899–1906), grand chief conductor (1906–7), and president (1907–19). From 1913 through 1915 he served on the U.S. Commission on Industrial Relations.

GERMER, Adolph F. (1881–1966), was born in Germany, immigrated to the United States in 1888, and began working as a miner in Illinois at the age of eleven. He served as vice-president (1907) and secretary-treasurer (1908–12) of the Belleville subdistrict of United Mine Workers of America District 12 (Illinois) and then as an organizer for the international union (1913–14). Germer was national secretary (1916–19) and national organizer of the Socialist Party of America, and in 1919 he was convicted under the Espionage Act for obstructing the draft during World War I. He was sentenced to twenty years in prison, but in 1921 the U.S. Supreme Court overturned his conviction. Germer later worked in the California oil fields as an organizer for the Oil Field, Gas Well, and Refinery Workers' Union (1923–25), edited the Rockford (Ill.) *Labor News* (1931–35?), and was active in the Committee for Industrial Organization and the CIO (1935–55).

GOLDEN, John (1863–1921), was born in Lancashire, England, where he worked in the cotton mills and was a member of the Mule Spinners' Union. Blacklisted for union activities, he immigrated to Fall River, Mass., in 1884, where he was employed as a spinner and served as treasurer (1898–1904) of the Fall River Mule Spinners' Association. Golden was president (1904–21) of the United Textile Workers of America and editor (1915–21) of the union's official journal, moving to Brooklyn to oversee its production. He was also a member of the National Civic Federation executive committee from 1913 to 1921.

GOMPERS, Alexander (1857–1926), SG's brother, was born in London and immigrated with the family to the United States in 1863. He was a cigarmaker and an early member of Cigar Makers' International Union of America 144. He married Rachel Bickstein, and they had six children.

GOMPERS, Alexander Julian (1878–1947), a son of SG and Sophia Julian Gompers, was a cigarmaker and cigar manufacturer in New York City and Washington, D.C. From 1914 to 1947 he served as an official of the New York State Department of Labor. He and his wife, Ella Appelbaum Gompers, had three children: Esther, Sophia, and May.

GOMPERS, Bella (b. 1867), SG's sister, was born in New York. About 1886 she married Samuel Isaacs, a Boston cigarmaker.

GOMPERS, Henrietta (1869–1954), SG's sister, was born in New York. About 1887 she married Harry Isaacs, a tailor. They settled in Boston.

GOMPERS, Henry (b. 1853), SG's brother, was born in London and immigrated with the family to America in 1863. A cigarmaker and member of the Cigar Makers' International Union of America, he married Sarah Wennick, a Dutch immigrant, and they had two sons.

GOMPERS, Henry Julian (1874–1938), a son of SG and Sophia Julian Gompers, was the AFL's first office boy (1887) and later became a granite cutter. About 1914 he moved from New York City to Washington, D.C., where he ran Gompers' Monumental Works. He and his wife, Bessie Phillips Gompers, had four children: Sophia, Samuel, Alexander, and Louis.

GOMPERS, Louis (1859–1920), SG's brother, was born in London and immigrated with the family to the United States in 1863. He became a Brooklyn cigar manufacturer and president of the Brooklyn Retail Tobacco Dealers' Association. He married Sophia Bickstein, and they had seven children.

GOMPERS, Sadie Julian (1883–1918), the younger daughter of SG and Sophia Julian Gompers, was born in New York City. After the family's move to Washington, D.C., she studied voice and then for a time sang in vaudeville and on the concert stage. She died of pneumonia during the World War I influenza epidemic.

GOMPERS, Samuel Julian (1868–1946), a son of SG and Sophia Julian Gompers, was born in New York City. He left school at the age of fourteen to work in a New York City print shop and moved to Washington, D.C., about 1887 to work first as a printer in the Government Printing Office, then as a compositor in the U.S. Department of Commerce and Labor, and later as a clerk in the U.S. Census Office. He was a member of the Association of Union Printers and the Columbia Typographical Union (International Typographical Union 101). In 1913 he became chief of the Division of Publications and Supplies of the U.S. Department of Labor, and in 1918 he became chief clerk of the Department of Labor, a position he held until 1941. Gompers and his wife, Sophia Dampf Gompers, had one child, Florence.

GOMPERS, Samuel Moses (Salomon Mozes; 1803?–81), SG's paternal grandfather, was born in Amsterdam. Originally a calico printer, he later became an import-export merchant. He married Henrietta Haring, and they had six children: Solomon, Fannie, Clara, Kate, Sarah, and Simon. In 1845 he immigrated to London and about 1869 came to the United States, returning to London in 1876.

GOMPERS, Sarah Rood (1827–98), SG's mother, was born in Amsterdam. About 1847 she moved to London to live in the Gompers household and in 1849 married Solomon Gompers. She immigrated to the

United States with her family in 1863 and in 1872 gave birth to her fourteenth and last child.

GOMPERS, Simon (1865–1953), SG's brother, was born in New York City and was employed there as a sheet metal worker. He married Leah Lopez, and they had five children. The family moved to Norwalk, Conn., in 1924.

GOMPERS, Solomon (1827–1919), SG's father, was a cigarmaker who was born in Amsterdam and immigrated to England with his family in 1845. He became a member of the cigarmakers' union there in 1848. In 1863 he immigrated to the United States with his wife, Sarah, and their six children.

GOMPERS, Sophia Julian (1850–1920), SG's first wife, was born in London and immigrated to the United States about 1858. She was living with her father and stepmother in Brooklyn and working as a tobacco stripper in a cigar factory when she married SG in 1867. Between 1868 and 1885 she and SG had at least nine children, six of whom lived past infancy: Samuel, Rose, Henry, Abraham, Alexander, and Sadie.

GREEN, William (1870–1952), was born in Coshocton, Ohio. He left school after the eighth grade and, at the age of fourteen, became a water boy for track layers on the Wheeling Railroad. At sixteen he joined his father in the coal mines. In 1888 he joined the local chapter of the National Progressive Union of Miners and Mine Laborers, which later became local 379 of the United Mine Workers of America. Green held various offices in his local—secretary, business agent, vice-president, and president—and served as president of subdistrict 6 of United Mine Workers' District 6 (Ohio; 1900–1906), as president of District 6 (1906–10), and as statistician (1911–13) and secretary-treasurer (1913–24) of the international union. In 1910 and again in 1912 Green was elected to the Ohio senate, where he introduced a workers' compensation law and supported such measures as the limitation of hours for women workers, the income tax, and the direct election of U.S. senators. In 1914 he became a member of the AFL Executive Council and, after SG's death in December 1924, became AFL president, an office he held until his death.

GUARD, Rosa Lee (1882?–1937), was born in Charlottesville, Va., and educated in local public schools. She moved to Washington, D.C., about 1897 and the next year began working as a typist at AFL headquarters, where she became chief clerk and then SG's private secretary. After SG's death, she served as chief clerk to his successor, William Green.

HAMILTON, M. Grant (1864–1920), was born in Michigan and moved to Denver in the 1880s, where he joined International Typographical Union 49 and worked as a linotype operator. He later served as an AFL salaried organizer (1903–12, 1914–15, 1918–19) and as a member of the AFL Legislative Committee (1908, 1912–13, 1915–18). In 1919 Hamilton was director general of the Working Conditions Service of the U.S. Department of Labor.

HANDLEY, John J. (1876–1941), was born in Horicon, Wis. In 1899 he joined International Association of Machinists 440 of Rockford, Ill., and about a year later moved to Milwaukee, joining Machinists' local 66. He served as business agent for Machinists' District 10 from 1903 to 1910 and was secretary-treasurer of the Wisconsin State Federation of Labor from 1912 until his death.

HAYES, Denis A. (1860–1917), a native of Ireland, came to the United States in 1866, settling in the glass-blowing center of Zanesville, Ohio, where he entered the industry. He later moved to Newark, Ohio, joining United Green Glass Workers' Association of the United States and Canada 24. He served as vice-president (1894–96) and president (1896–1917) of the international union (from 1895, the Glass Bottle Blowers Association of the United States and Canada), moving to Philadelphia about 1896. Hayes was an AFL vice-president from 1901 to 1917. He served on the National Civic Federation executive committee in 1901 and from 1903 to 1917.

HAYES, Frank (1882–1948), was born in What Cheer, Iowa, and after moving with his family to Illinois began working in the mines part time at the age of thirteen and full time after completing high school. In 1904 he was elected secretary-treasurer of the Belleville subdistrict of United Mine Workers of America District 12 (Illinois) and in 1908 was appointed secretary-treasurer of District 12. Hayes served as vice-president (1910–17) and president (1917–20) of the United Mine Workers and in 1912 ran unsuccessfully for governor of Illinois as a candidate of the Socialist Party of America. In 1920 he resigned his office due to ill health and moved to Denver, where he started a mining company. Hayes was a special representative for the United Mine Workers in Colorado from 1920 until his death and in 1937–38 served as Democratic lieutenant-governor of the state.

HAYES, Max Sebastian (1866–1945), was born near Havana, Ohio, and apprenticed as a printer at the age of thirteen. Moving to Cleveland in 1883, he joined International Typographical Union 53 in 1884 and served as an organizer for the international union for the next fifteen years. A founder of the *Cleveland Citizen* in 1891, Hayes worked as the paper's associate editor (1892–94) and editor (1894–1939). He was active in the Cleveland labor movement as corresponding secretary (1896–97) and recording secretary (1898–1901) of the Cleveland Central Labor Union, recording secretary (1902–3) of the United Trades and Labor Council, and recording secretary (1910) of the Cleveland Federation of Labor. Politically, Hayes worked in the People's party campaign in 1896, was active in the Socialist Labor party from 1896 to 1899, and was a founder of the Socialist Party of America in 1901. In 1919 he chaired the executive committee of the National Labor party (from 1920, the Farmer-Labor party), and in 1920 he was the party's vice-presidential candidate. Hayes was a charter member of the Cleveland Metropolitan Housing Authority in 1933, and from 1933 to 1935 he served on the Ohio State Adjustment Board of the National Recovery Administration.

HAYS, John W. (1860–1931), was born in Canada and immigrated to the United States in 1863. He entered the printers' trade in 1878 and joined International Typographical Union 186 of Fargo, N.Dak., in 1882. By 1884 he was living in Minneapolis, where he joined Typographical local 42, serving as its president intermittently between 1897 and 1904. He was district organizer (1898–1904), vice-president (1904–9), and secretary-treasurer (1909–28) of the international union and president of the AFL Union Label Trades Department (1916–28). After his retirement, Hays moved to the state of Washington but soon returned to Minneapolis, where he remained active in the trade union movement.

HEBERLING, Samuel E. (1866–1943), was born in DuBois, Pa., and went to work as a switchtender for the Pennsylvania Railroad at the age of eighteen. He later moved to Denver, where in 1902 he joined Switchmen's Union of North America 35. In 1904 he was appointed to the vacant post of third vice grand master of the Switchmen, and he served the union as third vice grand master (1904–5), first vice grand master (1905–7), first vice-president (1907–11), and president (1911–21). Declining renomination, Heberling became involved in mining in Colorado. He retired in 1937.

HILFERS, Henry F. (1862–1932?), was born in Germany and immigrated to the United States in 1865. He became a cigarmaker in Newark, N.J., during the late 1880s and served as secretary of Cigar Makers' International Union of America 138 of Newark (1903?–22). Hilfers also served as secretary of the Essex Trades Council (1907–29) and the New Jersey State Federation of Labor (1909–26) and was an AFL salaried organizer (1912, 1917 to at least 1924). He was president of the

Newark Union Cooperative Cigar Co. (1922), the Labor National Bank of Newark (1927–29), and the Union National Bank of Newark (1930–31).

HILLMAN, Sidney (1887–1946), was born in Zagare, Russian Lithuania. Twice arrested and imprisoned for his revolutionary activities, he left Russia for England in 1906 and came to the United States in 1907, settling in Chicago. He became an apprentice cutter in 1909, joined United Garment Workers of America 39, and emerged as a leader of the Chicago garment workers' strike against Hart, Schaffner, and Marx in 1910–11. In early 1914 he became chief clerk of the New York cloakmakers' joint board of the International Ladies' Garment Workers' Union, but he resigned the post later that year to become president of the newly formed Amalgamated Clothing Workers of America, an office he held until his death. Hillman participated in founding the Committee for Industrial Organization in 1935, chaired the Textile Workers' Organizing Committee and the Department Store Workers' Organizing Committee, and served as a vice-president of the CIO (1938–40) and chair of its Political Action Committee (1943–46).

He was a founder of the Amalgamated Trust and Savings Bank of Chicago in 1922, serving as its director, and the Amalgamated Bank of New York in 1923, serving as chairman of the board. During the 1930s he served on the labor advisory board of the National Recovery Administration, the National Industrial Recovery Board, and the Council for Industrial Progress. In 1936 he was a founder and treasurer of Labor's Non-Partisan League, which supported President Franklin Roosevelt's reelection effort. He later served as a member of the National Defense Advisory Commission, associate director of the Office of Production Management, and head of the labor division of the War Production Board.

HILLQUIT, Morris (1869–1933), was born in Riga, Latvia, and immigrated to the United States with his family in 1886, settling in New York City. He joined the Socialist Labor party in 1887 or 1888 and was part of a faction that broke with Daniel DeLeon's leadership in 1899. Two years later he participated in the formation of the Socialist Party of America. Hillquit emerged as a leading figure in the Socialist party and served as a member of its national executive committee (1907–12, 1916–19, 1922–33) and as party chairman (1929–33).

In 1888 Hillquit helped found the United Hebrew Trades and was its first corresponding secretary. He graduated from the law school of the University of the City of New York (now New York University) in 1893 and subsequently developed a successful law practice that included serving for many years as counsel to the International Ladies' Garment Workers' Union (1914–33). He was also a director, trustee, and lecturer at the Rand School and the author of a number of works on socialism. Hillquit twice ran unsuccessfully on the Socialist party ticket for mayor of New York City (1917, 1932) and was five times a candidate for the U.S. House of Representatives (1906, 1908, 1916, 1918, 1920).

HOLDER, Arthur E. (1860–1937), was born in Wales and apprenticed as a machinist in England, where he joined the Amalgamated Society of Engineers in 1875. After immigrating to the United States, he settled in Sioux City, Iowa, where he joined KOL Local Assembly 212 in 1883 and International Association of Machinists 178 in 1894. Employed in the railroad shops and as an organizer, Holder moved to Des Moines in 1900 after he was appointed deputy commissioner of the Iowa Bureau of Labor Statistics, serving from 1900 to 1903. He was elected president of the Iowa State Federation of Labor in 1901 and served until 1903. In 1904 Holder moved to Washington, D.C., where he was associate editor of the *Machinists' Monthly Journal* until 1906. He served on the AFL Legislative Committee from 1906 to 1917, helping to draft key pieces of progressive labor legislation. He was a member of the U.S. Vocational Education Board (1918–21) and served as secretary of the Conference for Progressive Political Action, which supported Robert M. LaFollette for president in 1924. After working for the U.S. Department of Labor, he retired to Florida about 1931.

HOUSTON, Clinton Craig (1865–1930), was a peripatetic labor editor and a long-time member of the International Typographical Union. He worked as a printer for the *Norfolk Daily Pilot* and served as recording and corresponding secretary of Typographical local 32 of Norfolk, Va. (1895–96), before moving to Atlanta by the late 1890s. There he was employed by the *Atlanta Constitution* and served as financial and corresponding secretary (1898–99), secretary-treasurer (1900–1901), and president (1902) of Typographical local 48, organizer for District 5 (southeast) of the international union (1899–1904), and editor of the *Journal of Labor* (1898–1900). Houston represented Fulton County in the Georgia state legislature from 1900 to 1903 and was a founder and the first secretary-treasurer of the Georgia State Federation of Labor (FOL; 1899–1903). He subsequently moved to Birmingham, Ala., and then, around 1907, to Colorado. He worked in Pueblo as a linotype operator, joining Typographical local 175, and served as editor of the *Colorado Industrial Review,* secretary of the Pueblo Trades and Labor Assembly (TLA; 1909–11), and vice-president of the Colorado State FOL (1909–10). Moving to Denver, Houston joined Typographical local 49 and served as editor of the *Labor Bulletin* (1913–18) and president of the Denver TLA (1915). In 1919 he moved to New York City and then to Washington, D.C., where he joined Typographical local 101 and served until his death as an editor of *Labor,* the journal of the railroad brotherhoods.

HUBER, William D. (1852–1925), was born in Waterloo, N.Y., where he attended public school and served a four-year apprenticeship as a carpenter. He worked as a foreman for six years in Canisteo, N.Y., later moving to New York City and in 1892 to Yonkers, N.Y. He was a founder of United Brotherhood of Carpenters and Joiners of America 726 in 1894, serving as its president for six terms as well as holding all of the local's other offices at various times. Huber served as vice-president (1898–99) and president (1899–1913) of the Carpenters and as an AFL vice-president (1906–13). As the brotherhood's president, he moved to Philadelphia and, following the union's change of head-quarters in 1902, to Indianapolis, where he was a member of local 75. He was also a member of the National Civic Federation executive committee (1903–4, 1906–12). On retiring from the presidency of the Carpenters, he was appointed a traveling representative for the union.

IFFLAND, Charles (1859–1922), was born in the region of Hesse in southwest Germany. He immigrated to the United States in the 1870s, left for England to work as a baker, and then returned to the United States around 1878, settling in New York City. He was a founder of the Journeymen Bakers' National Union of the United States in 1886, and he later served the union (from 1903, the Bakery and Confectionery Workers' International Union of America) as an organizer and, from 1912 until his death, as corresponding secretary.

IGLESIAS Pantín, Santiago (1872–1939), was born in La Coruña, Spain, where he attended local schools and in 1884 apprenticed as a cabinetmaker. After working briefly in Cuba he returned to Spain in 1886. In 1888 he moved to Havana, where he took part in the independence movement led by José Martí, served as secretary of the Circolo de Trabajadores (Workmen's Circle) from 1888 to 1895, and edited the newspaper *La Alarma* in 1895. He fled to Puerto Rico in 1896 following the suppression of the Cuban labor movement and Gen. Valeriano Weyler's order for his arrest. In Puerto Rico he was a founder and editor of several labor journals: *Ensayo Obrero* (1897–98), *Porvenir Social* (1898–1900), *Union Obrera* (1902–6), and *Justicia* (1914–25). In 1899 he helped organize the Federación Libre de los Trabajadores de Puerto Rico (Free Federation of the Workers of Puerto Rico), serving as its president from 1900 to 1933. He was also a founder in 1899 of the Partido Obrero Socialista de Puerto Rico (Socialist Labor Party of

Puerto Rico), reorganized in 1915 as the Partido Socialista de Puerto Rico (Socialist Party of Puerto Rico). Moving to Brooklyn in 1900, he worked at his trade and joined United Brotherhood of Carpenters and Joiners of America 309. He returned to Puerto Rico the next year as an AFL salaried organizer for Puerto Rico and Cuba, a post he held until 1933. He also served as a Partido Socialista member of the Puerto Rican senate (1917–33), secretary of the Pan-American Federation of Labor (1925–33), and Coalitionist resident commissioner from Puerto Rico in the U.S. House of Representatives (1933–39).

JOHNSTON, William Hugh (1874–1937), was born in Nova Scotia and immigrated to the United States in 1885. He settled in Rhode Island, where he apprenticed at a locomotive works, joined the KOL, and, in 1895, helped organize International Association of Machinists 379 in Pawtucket. He later moved to Providence, where he served as president (1901) and business agent (1906–8) of Machinists' local 147. He was also president of Machinists' District 19 (New England; 1905) and president and general organizer of Machinists' District 44 (Navy Yards and Arsenals; 1909–11). Moving to Washington, D.C., around 1910, Johnston joined Machinists' local 174. Well known as a socialist, he was president of the international union (1912–26) and a member of the National War Labor Board (1917–19), and in 1922 he helped organize the Conference for Progressive Political Action. He resigned his union office following a stroke but later served as vice-president of the Mount Vernon Savings Bank and then returned to work at Machinists' headquarters in Washington, D.C.

JONES, Mary Harris "Mother" (1830–1930), was born in County Cork, Ireland, and grew up in Toronto, where her father worked as a railroad construction laborer. She was employed as a teacher in Monroe, Mich., as a dressmaker in Chicago, and then again as a teacher in Memphis, where she was married in 1861. Jones lost her husband and four children to a yellow fever epidemic in 1867 and soon after moved back to Chicago, where she took up dressmaking again. Losing her business in the Great Chicago Fire of 1871, she became active in the KOL and, during the railroad strike of 1877, went to Pittsburgh to assist the strikers. From that time on she labored as an organizer, working particularly with miners but also on behalf of child laborers and a wide range of others, including textile, streetcar, and steel workers. She remained active in labor affairs into her nineties.

JOUHAUX, Léon (1879–1954), was born in Paris and went to work in a match factory at the age of sixteen. He became secretary of the Fédération Nationale des Ouvriers Allumettiers, the French match-workers' union, and in 1906 was elected its delegate to the Confédération Générale du Travail (General Confederation of Labor; CGT). In 1909 he served briefly as the CGT's treasurer before becoming secretary of the organization, holding that position until 1940, and again from 1945 to 1947. Jouhaux served on the Labor Committee of the Ministry of Munitions and on the Commission on Foreign Labor during World War I, and he was a French delegate to the League of Nations from 1925 to 1928. Arrested by the Vichy government and interned in 1941, he was turned over to the Nazis in 1943 and held in Germany until 1945. After the war ended, the CGT was reorganized and Jouhaux resumed his post as secretary; he resigned in late 1947 and left the CGT. In 1948 he was elected president of the CGT-Force Ouvrière (Workers' Force), serving in that office until his death. He also served as vice-president of the International Federation of Trade Unions (1919–45), the World Federation of Trade Unions (1945–48), the Administrative Council of the International Labor Organization (1945–54), and the International Confederation of Free Trade Unions (1949–54), and he was vice-president (1946–47) and president (1947–54) of the National Economic Council of France. Jouhaux received the Nobel Peace Prize in 1951.

JOYCE, Martin T. (1876–1931), was born in Massachusetts and left school at an early age to train as a tailor. He soon left that trade to take up electrical work, and on the completion of his apprenticeship in 1902, he joined International Brotherhood of Electrical Workers 103 of Boston, remaining a member of that local until his death. Joyce served briefly as president of the Boston Central Labor Union (1905?) and as secretary-treasurer (1911–31) and legislative agent (1925–31) of the Massachusetts State Federation of Labor.

KIRBY, James (1865–1915), was born in Kankakee, Ill., and worked as a millwright in Chicago. He joined United Brotherhood of Carpenters and Joiners of America 199 in 1898 and was later president of the Chicago Carpenters' district council (1904–6). He served as president of the Structural Building Trades Alliance (1905–8), the AFL Building Trades Department (1908–10), and the Carpenters (1913–15). He was a resident of Indianapolis at the time of his death.

KLINE, James Waller (1860–1937), was born in Luzerne Co., Pa., and subsequently moved to Kansas City, Kans. A railroad and machine smith, he joined KOL Local Assembly 3694 of Kansas City and, later, International Brotherhood of Blacksmiths 66. He served the Blacksmiths (from 1903, the International Brotherhood of Blacksmiths and Helpers; and from 1919, the International Brotherhood of Blacksmiths, Drop Forgers, and Helpers) as a trustee (1901–3), vice-president (1904–5), and president (1905–26).

LARGER, Bernard A. (1861?–1928), a Cincinnati clothing cutter, was a member of United Garment Workers of America 100 of Cincinnati. He served as president (1897–98, 1900–1904) and secretary (1904–28) of the international union.

LAURRELL, Carl Ferdinand (1844–1921), a cigarmaker, was born in Sweden, where he served as secretary of the Scandinavian section of the International Workingmen's Association until forced into exile. After working in Hamburg, Germany, for several years, he immigrated to the United States in 1871 and became active in the New York City labor movement. He became SG's mentor during the 1870s and subsequently remained close to him as a member of the United Cigarmakers and the Cigar Makers' International Union of America.

LAWLOR, Martin (1868–1959), was born in Ireland and immigrated to the United States in 1885 or 1886. After working briefly in New York City, he moved to Bethel, Conn., where he became an apprentice hatmaker and, in 1890, secretary of the Bethel Hat Makers' Union (from 1896, United Hatters of North America 1). In 1892 Lawlor was named to the board of directors of the National Hat Makers' Association of the United States. When that organization merged with the International Trade Association of Hat Finishers of America in 1896 to form the United Hatters of North America, Lawlor continued as a board member. He served the United Hatters as vice-president (1898–1904), secretary (1904–11), and secretary-treasurer (1911–34). After 1934, when the United Hatters merged with the Cloth Hat, Cap, and Millinery Workers' International Union, forming the United Hatters', Cap, and Millinery Workers' International Union, Lawlor served as the new union's vice-president (1934–36), secretary-treasurer of its Men's Hat Department (1934–36), and label secretary (1936–59).

LEE, William Granville (1859–1929), was born in La Prairie, Ill. In 1879 he became a brakeman on the Atchison, Topeka, and Santa Fe Railroad and in 1880 was promoted to conductor. He subsequently worked on the Wabash Railroad, the Missouri Pacific, and, from 1891 to 1895, the Union Pacific. He joined Brotherhood of Railroad Trainmen lodge 18 of Sedalia, Mo., in 1890, and in 1891 he helped organize lodge 385 of Kansas City, Mo., which he served as lodge master and financial secretary. Lee served the Brotherhood of Railroad Trainmen as first vice grand master (1895–1905), assistant grand master (1905–9), grand master (1909), president (1909–28), and secretary-treasurer (1928–29).

LEGIEN, Carl (1861–1920), was born in Marienburg, Prussia, and raised at an orphanage in nearby Thorn. He apprenticed to a wood-carver at the age of fourteen. After three years of compulsory military service and two years as a traveling journeyman, Legien settled in Hamburg and joined the local union of woodcarvers in 1886. He was elected president of the Vereinigung der Drechsler Deutschlands (Union of German Woodcarvers) at its founding in 1887. In 1890 he stepped down from this office to become secretary of the newly founded Generalkommission der Gewerkschaften Deutschlands (General Commission of German Trade Unions). He led this organization (from 1919, the Allgemeiner Deutscher Gewerkschaftsbund [General German Federation of Trade Unions]) until his death and edited its official journal, the *Correspondenzblatt,* from 1891 to 1900. A member of the Sozialdemokratische Partei Deutschlands (Social Democratic Party of Germany), Legien served as a Socialist deputy in the Reichstag from 1893 to 1898 and from 1903 until his death. He was instrumental in integrating the concerns of the German union movement into the political program of the Sozialdemokratische Partei. Legien helped inaugurate the meetings of the International Secretariat of the National Centers of Trade Unions in 1901 and served as secretary of this organization (from 1913, the International Federation of Trade Unions) from 1903 to 1919.

LENNON, John Brown (1850–1923), was born in Wisconsin, raised in Hannibal, Mo., and in 1869 moved to Denver, where he helped organize a local tailors' union and the Denver Trades Assembly. He later moved to New York City and then to Bloomington, Ill. He served the Journeymen Tailors' National Union of the United States (from 1889, the Journeymen Tailors' Union of America) as president (1884–85), as a member of the executive board (1885–87), and as secretary and editor of the union's official journal (1887–1910). He was treasurer of the AFL from 1891 to 1917, served on the U.S. Commission on Industrial Relations (1913–15), and was a commissioner of conciliation for the U.S. Department of Labor from 1918 through at least 1920.

LIAN, Ole Olsen (1868–1925), was born in Tønsberg, Norway, and later moved to Christiania (Oslo), where he joined the local printers' union. In 1901 he became a member of the executive committee of the Norwegian printers' union and in 1903 became its chair; he later served as chair (1907–25) of the Arbeidernes Faglige Landsorganisasjon (National Federation of Labor). Lian was a member of the central committee of the Norwegian Labor party from 1906 until his death, serving as vice-chair from 1912 to 1918, and a Labor Member of Parliament from 1916 to 1921.

Lord, James (b. 1879), was born in England, immigrated to the United States in 1890, and became a member of United Mine Workers of America 1213 of Farmington, Ill. He served as vice-president (1912–14) of United Mine Workers District 12 (Illinois), president of the AFL Mining Department (1914–22), treasurer of the Pan-American Federation of Labor (1918–24), and, briefly, as an AFL salaried organizer in California (1922).

Lowe, Archibald Brown (1845–1918), was born in Scotland. His family immigrated to Ireland when he was an infant and to Ontario, Canada, when he was twelve. In 1862 Brown went to work as a section-man on the Brockville and Ottawa Railway (subsequently a division of the Canadian Pacific Railway) and later became a section foreman. In 1892 he joined the newly formed United Brotherhood of Railway Trackmen, a Canadian union, and served as an organizer. In 1898 he joined the Brotherhood of Railway Trackmen of America, serving that union (from 1902, the International Brotherhood of Maintenance of Way Employes) as organizer (1898–1900), vice-president (1900–1908), and president (1908–14).

McBryde, Patrick (1848–1902?), was born in Ireland and raised in Scotland, where he became active in local miners' organizations. He came to the United States in the late 1870s and remained for several years before returning to Scotland. About 1884 he again immigrated to the United States, settling in the Pittsburgh area, where he joined KOL Local Assembly 151. McBryde served as secretary-treasurer of the National Progressive Union of Miners and Mine Laborers (1888–90), was elected to the executive board of the newly founded United Mine Workers of America in 1890, and then served that union as secretary-treasurer (1891–96). After retiring from the United Mine Workers in 1896, he served as commissioner for mine operators in Ohio.

McDonald, Duncan (b. 1873), was born in Ohio and later moved to Illinois. He began working at the age of eleven and in 1898 joined the United Mine Workers of America. McDonald served on the executive board (1904–8) of United Mine Workers District 12 (Illinois), on the executive board (1908–9) of the United Mine Workers, as president (1909–10) and secretary-treasurer (1910–17) of District 12, and as president (1919–20) of the Illinois State Federation of Labor. He was active for many years as a socialist in Illinois and, from 1914 to 1920, in the cooperative movement. He served on the executive committee of the National Labor party (from 1920, the Farmer-Labor party), and from 1925 until at least 1935 he ran an art and book store in Springfield, Ill.

McGuire, Peter James (1852–1906), was born in New York City, became a member of a carpenters' union there in 1872, and joined the International Workingmen's Association. In 1874 he helped organize the Social Democratic Workingmen's Party of North America and was elected to its executive board; that year he also joined the KOL. During the late 1870s McGuire traveled widely, organizing and campaigning on behalf of the Workingmen's Party of the United States and the Socialist Labor party (SLP). After living for a time in New Haven, Conn., he moved to St. Louis in 1878 and the following year was instrumental in establishing the Missouri Bureau of Labor Statistics, to which he was appointed deputy commissioner. He resigned in 1880 to campaign for the SLP and for the Greenback-Labor party. In 1881 he was elected secretary of the St. Louis Trades Assembly and participated in founding the Brotherhood of Carpenters and Joiners of America. He served the Carpenters (from 1888, the United Brotherhood of Carpenters and Joiners of America) as secretary (1881–95) and secretary-treasurer (1895–1901). McGuire moved to New York City in 1882, was a founder of the New York City Central Labor Union, and became a member of KOL Local Assembly 1562—the Brooklyn "Spread the Light" Club. He later moved to Philadelphia. He served as secretary of the AFL from 1886 to 1889 and as an AFL vice-president from 1890 to 1900.

McNulty, Frank Joseph (1872–1926), was born in Londonderry, Ireland, and immigrated with his family to New York City in 1876. He began working as a wireman in 1888, helped organize International Brotherhood of Electrical Workers 52 of Newark, N.J., in 1899, and then served as vice-president (1901–3) and president (1903–19) of the international union. During World War I he was vice-chairman of a railway board of adjustment and traveled to Italy and France on behalf of the government. He was later deputy director of public safety in Newark (1919–22), Democratic congressman from New Jersey (1923–25), and chairman of the Electrical Workers' executive board (1919–26).

Mahon, William D. (1861–1949), was born in Athens, Ohio, and worked as a coal miner in the Hocking Valley district. In the late 1880s he moved to Columbus, Ohio, where he worked as a mule car driver and helped to organize street railway workers in the early 1890s. In 1893 he was elected president of the Amalgamated Association of Street Railway Employes of America and shortly thereafter moved to Detroit. He served as president of the union (from 1903, the Amalgamated Association of Street and Electric Railway Employes of America) until retiring in 1946. Mahon was presiding judge of the Michigan State

Court of Mediation and Arbitration (1898–1900), a member of the executive committee of the National Civic Federation (1903 to at least 1923), and an AFL vice-president (1917–23, 1936–49).

MILLS, Ernest (b. 1868?), was born in England and immigrated to the United States in 1887. He settled in British Columbia, where he became secretary of Western Federation of Miners 22 of Greenwood (1904–5) and a member of the Western Federation of Miner's executive board (1905–7). Mills served as secretary-treasurer of the international union (from 1916, the International Union of Mine, Mill, and Smelter Workers) from 1907 until 1926, moving to the union's headquarters in Denver.

MITCHELL, John (1870–1919), was born in Braidwood, Ill. He became a miner in 1882 and worked in the Illinois coalfields except for two brief sojourns in the mines of Colorado, New Mexico, and Wyoming. He also read law for a year during the 1880s. In 1885 he joined KOL National Trade Assembly 135. A member of the Spring Valley, Ill., local of the United Mine Workers of America in the early 1890s, he was elected secretary-treasurer of the northern Illinois subdistrict of United Mine Workers' District 12 (Illinois) in 1895, became the lobbyist for District 12 in 1896, and was elected a member of the union's Illinois state executive board and appointed a national organizer in 1897. Mitchell was elected vice-president of the United Mine Workers in 1898, became acting president later that year, and served as the union's president until 1908. He was also an AFL vice-president (1899–1913). A founder of the National Civic Federation in 1900, he served as a member of its executive committee (1901, 1903–10), Industrial Department (1901–2), and executive council (1904–10). He was later a member of the New York State Workmen's Compensation Commission (1914–15) and chair of the New York State Industrial Commission (1915–19).

MOONEY, Thomas Joseph (1882–1942), was born in Chicago and lived in Washington, Ind., until the age of ten, when his father died; his mother then moved the family to Holyoke, Mass. Mooney went to work at the age of fourteen and soon apprenticed as a foundryman. He moved to East Cambridge, Mass., and around 1902 joined the Core Makers' International Union of America; from 1903 he was a member of the Iron Molders' Union of North America. In 1908 Mooney moved to California, living first in Stockton and then in San Francisco. He became a socialist, participated in the 1908 presidential campaign of Eugene Debs, attended the 1910 International Socialist Congress in Copenhagen, and briefly joined the IWW. In 1911 he was a founder of the *Revolt,* a weekly socialist newspaper in San Francisco. Mooney was arrested in December 1913 after the electrical workers' strike against the Pacific Gas and Electric Co. and tried three times for illegal possession of explosives. The first two trials ended with hung juries; the third resulted in an acquittal. He was arrested again after a bomb exploded during a San Francisco Preparedness Day parade on July 22, 1916, killing ten and injuring forty. He was convicted of first-degree murder in 1917—on what was later shown to have been perjured testimony by a key prosecution witness—and sentenced to death. After widespread protests and the personal intervention of President Woodrow Wilson, his sentence was commuted in 1918 to life imprisonment. He was pardoned by the governor of California in 1938.

MORONES Negrete, Luis N. (1890–1964), was born in San Fernando de Tlalpan near Mexico City, began working as an electrician around the age of sixteen, and joined the Casa del Obrero (House of the Worker) in 1912. He organized an electricians' union in Mexico City around 1915 and was a founder of the short-lived Confederación del Trabajo de la Región Mexicana (Confederation of Labor of the Mexican Region) in 1916. In 1918 he participated in organizing the Confederación Regional Obrera Mexicana (Mexican Confederation of Labor), serving as its secretary and head of its policy-making board, Grupo Acción, and in 1919 he was a founder of the Partido Laborista Mexicano (the Mexican Labor party). He later served as director of factories in the Secretariat of War and Navy (1920–23) and as minister of the Secretariat of Industry and Commerce (1924–28).

MORRISON, Frank (1859–1949), was born in Frankton, Ont. In 1865, his family moved to Walkerton, Ont., where he became a printer. Beginning about 1883, he worked at his trade in Madison, Wis. In 1886 he moved to Chicago, where he joined International Typographical Union 16. From 1893 to 1694 he studied law at Lake Forest University, becoming a member of the Illinois bar in 1895. The following year he was elected secretary of the AFL, serving in that post from 1897 to 1935 and as AFL secretary-treasurer from 1936 until his retirement in 1939. During World War I Morrison chaired the wages and hours subcommittee of the Committee on Labor of the Advisory Commission of the Council of National Defense.

MOYER, Charles H. (1866–1929), was born in Iowa and moved to Montana in 1882. In the 1890s he worked as a miner in the Black Hills, living in Deadwood, S.Dak., and serving as president of Western Federation of Miners 2 of Deadwood from 1894 to 1896. He was a mem-

ber of the Western Federation of Miners' executive board from 1899
to 1902, was appointed general agent and organizer in 1901, and
served the union (from 1916, the International Union of Mine, Mill,
and Smelter Workers) as president from 1902 to 1926. Moyer was a
founder of the IWW in 1905 and served briefly as a member of its executive board. In 1906 he was kidnapped by Colorado and Idaho authorities and extradited to Idaho, where he was jailed on charges of
conspiracy in the murder of former Idaho governor Frank Steunen-
berg. After his codefendants William Haywood and George Pettibone
were tried and acquitted in 1907 and 1908, charges against him were
dropped. Moyer lived in Denver from around the turn of the century
until at least 1926 and spent his final years in Pomona, Calif.

O'CONNELL, James (1858–1936), born in Minersville, Pa., learned
his trade as a machinist's apprentice and worked as a railroad machinist. He served as a lobbyist for the KOL in Harrisburg, Pa., in 1889 and
1891. Joining National (from 1891, International) Association of Machinists 113 of Oil City, Pa., around 1890, he became a member of the
Machinists' executive board in 1891 and later served the international union as grand master machinist (1893–99) and president (1899–
1911). He moved to Chicago in 1896. O'Connell served as an AFL vice-
president (1896–1918) and president of the AFL Metal Trades
Department (1911–34). He was also a member of the National Civic
Federation executive committee (1901, 1903–10) and Industrial Department (1901–2), the U.S. Commission on Industrial Relations
(1913–15), and the Committee on Labor of the Advisory Commission
of the Council of National Defense.

OLANDER, Victor A. (1873–1949), was born in Chicago. After leaving school, he worked for a time in a factory and then, at the age of
fourteen, became a sailor on the Great Lakes. He served as business
agent (1901–3), assistant secretary (1903–9), and secretary (1909–20)
of the Lake Seamen's Union (from 1919, the Sailors' Union of the
Great Lakes) and as vice-president (1902–25), secretary-treasurer
(1925–36), and member of the legislative committee of the International Seamen's Union of America. Olander was also active in the
Chicago Federation of Labor (FOL) and the Illinois State FOL, serving as secretary-treasurer of the latter body from 1914 until his death.
During World War I he was a member of the National War Labor Board
and the Illinois State Council of Defense, and he later served on the
National Recovery Administration district board for Illinois and Wisconsin, the Illinois Department of Labor Unemployment Compensation Advisory Board, and the board of directors of WCFL, the radio
station of the Chicago FOL. He was a lifelong resident of Chicago.

OUDEGEEST, Jan (1870–1951), was born in Utrecht, Netherlands. A railroad worker, he was a founder in 1898 and the first president of the Nederlandsche Vereeniging van Spoor- en Tramwegpersoneel (Netherlands Association of Railway and Tramway Employees); he continued as an officer of that organization until 1942. He was elected secretary of the Nederlandsch Verbond van Vakvereenigingen (Netherlands League of Trade Unions) in 1905 and served as its president from 1908 to 1918. During World War I Oudegeest was head of the auxiliary office of the International Federation of Trade Unions in Amsterdam, and from 1919 to 1927 he was secretary of the organization. Also active in local and national politics, he served as a member of the lower (1918–22) and upper (1928–36) chambers of the Dutch parliament and from 1927 to 1934 was chairman of the Sociaal-Democratische Arbeiderspartij (Social Democratic Workers' party).

PEARCE, William Charles (b. 1859), was born in England, began working in coal mines at the age of eight, and was orphaned when he was thirteen. In 1880 he immigrated to the United States, settling in Corning, Ohio, in 1882. He became a member of the local miners' union and served as secretary-treasurer (1891–96) of United Mine Workers of America District 6 (Ohio). From 1896 to 1900 he was secretary-treasurer of the international union, moving to Columbus, Ohio, and then Indianapolis. Resigning his office in 1900 after an audit revealed discrepancies in the accounts, Pearce went into business in Indianapolis.

PERHAM, Henry Burdon (1856–1949), was born in England, immigrated to Canada in 1871, and became a telegrapher and ticket clerk in Ontario in 1872. Moving to the United States in 1876, he was blacklisted for his participation in the railroad strike of 1877 and became a prospector. In 1889 he took a telegrapher's job with the Denver and Rio Grande Railroad in Gunnison, Colo., and joined the Order of Railway Telegraphers of North America. He served the union (from 1891, the Order of Railroad Telegraphers of North America) as chairman of the Denver and Rio Grande system (1891–97), secretary and treasurer (1897–1901), and president (1901–19), moving to the union's headquarters in Peoria, Ill., in 1897 and to St. Louis in 1901. He was also an AFL vice-president (1909–19).

PERKINS, Edgar A. (1866–1945?), was born in Indiana and worked as a proofreader in Indianapolis. A member of International Typographical Union 1, he served the State Federation of Trades and Labor Unions of the State of Indiana (from 1897, the Indiana Federation of Labor; and from 1907, the Indiana State Federation of Labor) as chairman of the legislative committee (1892–95) and as president (1895–1909, 1910–13). Perkins resigned to become chief inspector of the Indiana State Board of Inspection (1913–15) and was chairman (1916–17) and board member (1918–20, 1926–29, 1933–41) of the State Industrial Board of Indiana.

PERKINS, George William (1856–1934), born in Massachusetts, began his career in the Cigar Makers' International Union of America by joining Albany, N.Y., local 68 in 1880. He served as a vice-president of the Cigar Makers from 1885 to 1891 and as acting president for six months in 1888 and 1889. In 1891 he was elected president, an office that he held for the next thirty-five years. In 1918 he was appointed to the AFL's Commission on Reconstruction and represented the American labor movement at the International Federation of Trade Unions conference in Zurich. He became president of the AFL Union Label Trades Department in 1928, serving until his death.

PERSION, Achille (1882–1950), was born in Italy, immigrated to the United States in 1904, and became a member of International Hod Carriers' and Building Laborers' Union of America 190 of Albany, N.Y. He served the international union (from 1912, the International Hod Carriers', Building and Common Laborers' Union of America) as vice-president (1909) and secretary-treasurer (1910–50). Persion moved to Quincy, Mass., in 1918, when the international headquarters relocated there from Albany, and then moved to Washington, D.C., in 1940, where he lived for the rest of his life.

PROEBSTLE, Joseph (b. 1870), was born in Germany and immigrated to the United States in the late 1880s or early 1890s. By the late 1890s he was working as a brewer in Houston, Tex., where he was a member of local 111 of the National Union of the United Brewery Workmen of the United States. He later moved to Cincinnati and from 1904 to 1922 served as financial secretary of the Brewery Workmen (from 1902, the International Union of the United Brewery Workmen of America; from 1917, the International Union of United Brewery and Soft Drink Workers of America; and from 1918, the International Union of United Brewery, Flour, Cereal, and Soft Drink Workers of America). From 1915 to 1922 he also headed the union's Anti-Prohibition Department. In 1926 Proebstle served as a lobbyist for the U.S. Brewers' Association.

RATCHFORD, Michael D. (1860–1927), was born in Ireland and in 1872 came to the United States and began work as a miner in Ohio. He served as president (1890–92) of the United Mine Workers of America local at Massillon, Ohio, president of United Mine Workers'

District 6 (Ohio; 1895–96), and an organizer (1893–94) and president (1897–98) of the international union. He resigned the union's presidency to serve on the U.S. Industrial Commission (1898–1900) and later served as Ohio commissioner of labor statistics (1900–1908). Ratchford left public office to work for the mining industry as commissioner for the Ohio Coal Operators (1909–12), secretary of the Pitts Vein Operators (1911–12), and from 1913 as commissioner for the Illinois Coal Operators' Association.

REID, James J. (1873–1914), was born in Scotland and immigrated to the United States in 1889. By 1901 he was working as an electrical lineman in Erie, Pa. He was elected vice-president of the International Brotherhood of Electrical Workers in 1905 and continued in that position until 1908, when a special convention of the brotherhood— later ruled illegal—elected him president. After an unsuccessful struggle for recognition by the AFL, Reid resigned his position in 1913.

RICKERT, Thomas Alfred (1876–1941), was born in Chicago and attended business college before becoming a garment cutter and joining United Garment Workers of America 21 of Chicago at the age of nineteen. He served as president (1904–41) and acting secretary-treasurer (1934–41) of the international union and was an AFL vice-president (1918–41). During World War I he served on the National War Labor Board.

ROWE, Thomas William (1868–1946?), was born in England and immigrated to the United States in 1871. By 1893 he was working as a glassblower in Toledo, where he was secretary of American Flint Glass Workers' Union 81 in the mid-1890s and again about 1900. He served the Flint Glass Workers as elected agent or organizer (1898–1901), vice-president (1901–3), and president (1903–16). In 1916 he joined the Owens Bottling Co. of Toledo as chief statistician. Rowe managed factories for the American Bottle Co. between 1922 and 1928 and then worked in various supervisory positions for the Owens-Illinois Glass Co.

RYAN, Martin Francis (1874–1935), was born in West Virginia and moved to Texas at the age of eighteen. In 1899 he joined the Brotherhood of Railway Carmen of America as a charter member of Fort Worth lodge 23, and he was a member of Pine Tree lodge 81 of Beaumont, Tex., when he was elected to the executive board of the Railway Carmen in 1903. He subsequently served as vice grand chief carman (1905–9) and president (1909–35) of the brotherhood. Ryan also served as an AFL vice-president (1923–28) and treasurer (1929–35), and he was a founder and treasurer (1927–35) of the Union Labor Life Insurance Co. At the time of his death, he was living in Washington, D.C.

SASSENBACH, Johann (1866–1940), was president (1891–1901) and secretary (1909–21) of the German saddlers' union and a member (1902–23) of the Generalkommission der Gewerkschaften Deutschlands (General Commission of German Trade Unions; from 1919, the Allgemeiner Deutscher Gewerkschaftsbund [General German Federation of Trade Unions]). He was later the secretary of the International Federation of Trade Unions (1927–30). A member of the Sozialdemokratische Partei Deutschlands (Social Democratic Party of Germany), Sassenbach served on the municipal assembly of the city of Berlin (1905–15) and on the city's municipal council (1915–19).

SCHARRENBERG, Paul (1877–1969), was born in Hamburg, Germany. After immigrating to the United States, he moved in 1898 to San Francisco, where he joined the Sailors' Union of the Pacific, a regional branch of the International Seamen's Union of America. He served as business manager (1902–13) and editor (1913–21, 1922–37) of the *Coast Seamen's Journal* (from 1918, the *Seamen's Journal*) and as a member of the Seamen's executive board. Scharrenberg was also secretary-treasurer of the California State Federation of Labor (1909–36), secretary of the California Commission of Immigration and Housing (1913–22), and secretary of the California Joint Immigration Commission (1921–36). Expelled from the Sailors' Union of the Pacific in 1935 in a political dispute, he moved to Washington, D.C., and became the legislative representative of the Seamen (1936–37) and, later, a lobbyist for the AFL (1937–43). He subsequently served as director of the California Department of Industrial Relations (1943–55) and as a member of the U.S. Advisory Committee on Public Health (1947–53).

SCHLOSSBERG, Joseph (1875–1971), was born in Russia and immigrated to the United States in 1888. He settled in New York City, where he joined the Cloakmakers' and Operators' Union, participated in the 1890 cloakmakers' strike, and after 1900 served as editor of several New York City Yiddish-language labor publications. A member of United Garment Workers of America 156, Schlossberg supported an unauthorized strike of New York City tailors in 1913 and then served as secretary-treasurer of the secessionist United Brotherhood of Tailors. In October 1914 a dissenting faction of the Garment Workers elected him secretary of their newly formed union, which was reorganized in December of that year as the Amalgamated Clothing Workers of America. He served the Clothing Workers as secretary (1914–15, 1915–20), vice-president (1915), secretary-treasurer (1920–40), and editor of the *Advance*, the union's official journal (1917–25).

SHEPPARD, Lucius Elmer (1863–1934), was born in Bridgeton, N.J., and worked variously as a railroad brakeman, conductor, baggage master, and yardmaster. He joined Order of Railway Conductors of America division 170 of Camden, N.J., in 1885 and later moved to Cedar Rapids, Iowa. He served the Order as grand junior conductor (1901–6), assistant grand chief conductor (1906–7), senior vice-president (1907–19), and president (1919–28).

STILLMAN, Charles B. (1885–1948), was born in Michigan. He moved to Chicago as a young man and worked there as a high school teacher, becoming a member and later president of AFL 14,221, the Chicago Federation of Men Teachers. In June 1915 he issued a call to organize a national teachers' union, which led to the founding of the American Federation of Teachers in Chicago in April 1916. Stillman served as president (1916–23) and vice-president (1923–24, 1925–26) of the union and as an AFL salaried organizer (1919–23).

STONE, Warren Sanford (1860–1925), was born in Ainsworth, Iowa, and became a locomotive fireman on the Chicago, Rock Island, and Pacific Railroad in 1879. He was promoted to engineer in 1884 and subsequently joined Brotherhood of Locomotive Engineers' lodge 181 of Eldon, Iowa, which he served as first assistant engineer (1896–97) and grand chief engineer (1897–1903). Stone served as grand chief engineer of the Locomotive Engineers from 1903 to 1924 and as president of the union from 1924 until his death.

SULLIVAN, James William (1848–1938), a printer from Carlisle, Pa., served his apprenticeship in Philadelphia and moved in 1882 to New York City, where he worked for the *New York Times* and the *New York World* and joined International Typographical Union 6. A strong supporter of land reform, he edited the *Standard* with Henry George from 1887 to 1889 and was managing editor of the *Twentieth Century* from 1889 to 1892. He later participated with SG in the Social Reform Club and the People's Institute of the Ethical Culture Society. He became a leading advocate of the initiative and referendum, traveling to Switzerland in 1888 to gather information for his *Direct Legislation by the Citizenship through the Initiative and Referendum* (New York, 1892). Sullivan served with SG in the National Civic Federation, accompanied him to Europe in 1909, helped to edit the *American Federationist,* and served with SG on the Advisory Commission of the Council of National Defense during World War I. He opposed labor movement involvement in socialist political activities, publishing *Socialism as an Incubus on the American Labor Movement* (New York, 1909) and a report critical of English socialism (in Commission on Foreign Inquiry, National Civic Federation, *The Labor Situation in Great Britain and France* [New York, 1919]).

SULLIVAN, Jere L. (1863–1928), born in Willimansett, Mass., worked as a waiter in New England, Chicago, and St. Louis, and founded St. Louis KOL Local Assembly 9124 (Waiters), which later became local 20 of the Hotel and Restaurant Employees' National Alliance (from 1898, the Hotel and Restaurant Employees' International Alliance and Bartenders' International League of America). He was active in Hotel and Restaurant Employees' local 6 of Salt Lake City in the 1890s, returned briefly to St. Louis in 1899, and then moved to Cincinnati, where he joined local 161. Sullivan served as vice-president (1899) and secretary-treasurer (1899–1928) of the Hotel and Restaurant Employees and edited the union's official journal, *Mixer and Server,* from 1900 until his death.

SUZUKI, Bunji (1885–1946), was born in the Miyagi Prefecture on the Japanese island of Honshū. He graduated from the law school of the University of Tokyo in 1909 and then worked as a journalist before founding Yūaikai (Laborers' Friendly Society) in 1912. From 1912 to 1930 Suzuki served as president of Yūaikai and its successor organizations (Dai Nihon Rōdō Kumiai Sōdōmei Yūaikai [Japanese Federation of Labor Unions], founded in 1919; Rōdō Kumiai Dōmeikai [League of Labor Unions], founded in 1920; and Nihon Rōdō Sōdōmei [Japanese Federation of Labor], founded in 1921). He attended the 1915 and 1916 AFL conventions, was an adviser to the Japanese delegation at the Paris peace conference in 1919, and served as a member of the workers' group of the governing body of the International Labor Organization from 1928 to 1934. He was elected three times to the Japanese Diet, serving from 1928 to 1930 and from 1936 to 1942.

TAYLOR, Claude O. (b. 1875?), was born in Michigan. By 1907 he had moved to Grand Rapids, where he worked as a barber and served as president (1907–9) and secretary (1910) of Journeymen Barbers' International Union of America 8. Taylor also served as secretary (1910) and president (1911–12, 1917–18) of the Grand Rapids Trades and Labor Council and was president (1912–17) of the Michigan State Federation of Labor. About 1912 he opened the Taylor Printing and Publishing Co. and a short time later began publication of the *Observer,* a weekly labor paper that ceased publication around 1931. By 1918 Taylor was a member of American Federation of Musicians 56 (the Grand Rapids Musicians' Protective Association), and he served as the local's secretary from 1924 to 1926. From 1939 to 1942 he was secretary and then secretary-treasurer of International Brotherhood of Teamsters, Chauffeurs, Stablemen, and Helpers of America (from 1940, the International Brotherhood of Teamsters, Chauffeurs, Warehousemen, and Helpers of America) 406 of Grand Rapids.

TAYLOR, James A. (1875–1947), was born in Indiana and moved to Seattle in 1903. He was a member of International Association of Machinists 79 of Seattle and was the business agent for his union and for Machinists' District 26. Taylor served as an organizer (1914–21) and vice-president (1921–25) for the international union, as president of the Seattle Metal Trades Council (1917–20), and as president of the Washington State Federation of Labor (1928–45).

THORNE, Florence Calvert (1877–1973), was born in Hannibal, Mo., and was educated at Oberlin College and the University of Chicago. Between 1912 and 1918 she worked as a research assistant to SG and as an editor of the *American Federationist;* she left the AFL in 1918 to take a position with the U.S. Department of Labor and also served as a member of the Committee on Women in Industry of the Committee on Labor of the Advisory Commission of the Council of National Defense. Beginning in 1919 Thorne assisted SG in preparing his memoirs, *Seventy Years of Life and Labor,* completing the book in the year after his death. From 1925 she was an administrative assistant to William Green and Matthew Woll. Between 1933 and 1953 Thorne served as director of the AFL Research Department.

TILLETT, Benjamin (1860–1943), a British seaman and dock worker, was a founder of the Tea Operatives' and General Labourers' Association in 1887 and a leader of the 1889 London dock strike. He served as secretary of his union, reorganized in 1889 as the Dock, Wharf, Riverside, and General Labourers' Union of Great Britain and Ireland, until 1922. Tillett was a member of the Parliamentary Committee of the TUC (1892–95) and a founder of the Independent Labour party in 1893, serving on its executive council during its first year. In 1900 he helped establish the Labour Representation Committee, the predecessor of the Labour party, and in 1910 he helped organize the National Transport Workers' Federation. He served as a Member of Parliament from 1917 to 1924 and from 1929 to 1931.

TOBIN, Daniel Joseph (1875?–1955), was born in Ireland and immigrated to the United States about 1889, settling in Cambridge, Mass., in 1890. He worked in a sheet metal factory and then as a motorman for a Boston street railway company, joining a local assembly of the KOL. By the end of the decade he was working as a teamster and had joined Boston local 25 of the Team Drivers' International Union, later serving as its business agent. Tobin was elected president of the Teamsters (from 1903, the International Brotherhood of Teamsters; and from 1910, the International Brotherhood of Teamsters, Chauffeurs, Stablemen, and Helpers of America) in 1907 and moved to Indianapolis; he served in that office until 1952. He was also a member of the National Civic Federation executive committee (1911–14), AFL treasurer (1918–28), and an AFL vice-president (1935–55).

TRACY, Thomas F. (1861–1916), was born in Massachusetts and worked as a cigarmaker in Boston. He served as president of Cigar Makers' International Union of America 97 (1894) and of the Boston Central Labor Union (1893–94, 1897), as a member of the Massachusetts State Federation of Labor's legislative committee, and as a vice-president of the Cigar Makers from 1896 until his death. Tracy was also a member of the AFL Legislative Committee (1900–1903, 1906–9) and secretary-treasurer of the AFL Union Label Trades Department (1909–16). He moved to Washington, D.C., in 1910.

VALENTINE, Joseph F. (1857–1930), was born in Baltimore, where he apprenticed as an iron molder. After moving to San Francisco, he joined Iron Molders' Union of North America 164 and served as the local's president from 1880 to 1890. He was elected vice-president of the Molders in 1890 and moved to Cincinnati. He held that office until 1903 and then served as president of the union (from 1907, the International Molders' Union of North America) until he retired in 1924. He was also a member of the National Civic Federation executive committee (1904 to at least 1923), a vice-president of the AFL (1906–24), and a vice-president of the AFL Metal Trades Department (1908–24). In 1927 he returned to San Francisco.

WALKER, John Hunter (1872–1955), was born in Scotland, immigrated to the United States in 1882, and began working in the mines in Coal City, Ill. He returned briefly to Scotland and then settled permanently in the United States in the 1890s. Walker served the United Mine Workers of America as an organizer for West Virginia, president of the Danville, Ill., subdistrict of District 12 (Illinois), and then as executive board member (1905–6) and president (1906–9, 1910–13, 1931–33) of District 12. He was president of the Illinois State Federation of Labor (1913–19, 1920–30) and in 1915 helped organize the Illinois State Cooperative Society, serving as its first president (1915–21). Walker ran on the Socialist Party of America ticket for a seat in the Illinois General Assembly in 1904 and for the House of Representatives in 1906. Expelled from the party in 1916, he was active in the American Alliance for Labor and Democracy and was appointed by President Woodrow Wilson in 1917 to the President's Mediation Commission. Disillusioned with Wilson and the Democrats by 1919, he joined the National Labor party (from 1920, the Farmer-Labor party) and was its unsuccessful candidate for governor of Illinois in 1920. In 1930 he and other opponents of United Mine Workers' President John L. Lewis launched the Reorganized United Mine Workers of America in Springfield, Ill., and he served as secretary-treasurer of this short-lived union. Around 1952 he moved to Denver.

WATERMAN, Homer F. (b. 1876), was born in Michigan and around 1906 moved to Kalamazoo, Mich., where he worked as a clerk and a bartender. He served as secretary (1908–10) of Hotel and Restaurant Employees' International Alliance and Bartenders' International League of America 368 of Kalamazoo and as vice-president (1908–11) and secretary-treasurer (1911–15) of the Michigan State Federation of Labor. He resigned the secretary-treasurership after complaints about financial improprieties led to an investigation of his accounts and later worked as a papermaker.

WEEKS, Edwin William (b. 1873), was born in England, lived for a time in Canada, where he was a member of the Brotherhood of Railway Carmen of America Jubilee Lodge 6 of Winnipeg, and then settled in the United States in 1907, joining Railway Carmen's Kaw Valley Lodge 44 of Kansas City, Kans. He served as secretary-treasurer of the Railway Carmen from 1907 to 1926, when he retired from office due to failing health and returned to England.

WHITE, John Phillip (1870–1934), was born in Illinois and later moved with his family to Iowa, where he entered the mines at age fourteen. He served as secretary-treasurer (1899–1904) and president (1904–7, 1909–10) of United Mine Workers of America District 13 (Iowa) and as vice-president (1908) and president (1911–17) of the international union. White was later adviser to the U.S. Fuel Administration (1917–19). He died in Des Moines, Iowa.

WILSON, James Adair (1876–1945), was born in Erie, Pa., where he joined a local of the Pattern Makers' League of North America in 1898. He served as president of the Pattern Makers (1902–34), moving to New York City and then, in 1906, to Cincinnati. Wilson also served as an AFL vice-president (1924–34) and, later, as a labor counselor for the International Labor Organization in Geneva.

WILSON, Joseph Havelock (1858–1929), was born in Sunderland, England, and briefly apprenticed as a printer before running away to sea at the age of thirteen. Making his living on land after 1882, he joined the North of England Sailors' and Seagoing Firemen's Friendly Society in 1883 and served briefly as its president (1885–87) before founding the National Amalgamated Sailors' and Firemen's Union of Great Britain and Ireland in 1887. He served that union as secretary

(1887–93) and president (1893–94). When it was dissolved he organized the National Sailors' and Firemen's Union of Great Britain and Ireland (from 1926, the National Union of Seamen), which he also served as president (1894–1929). In 1896 he helped organize the International Transport Workers' Federation. Wilson served as a Member of Parliament (1892–1900, 1906–10, 1918–22) and as a member of the Parliamentary Committee of the TUC (1889–98, 1918–19).

WILSON, William Bauchop (1862–1934), was born in Blantyre, Scotland, and immigrated to Arnot, Pa., in 1870. The son of a coal miner, he began working in the mines at the age of nine, became a member of a local miners' union, and was later elected its secretary. Blacklisted in 1880, he worked briefly in sawmills and lumber yards in the West and then as a fireman on the Illinois Central Railroad before returning to Pennsylvania. He settled in Blossburg, where he worked in the 1880s and 1890s as a miner and check weighman in the Tioga County mines and, for a time, as a typesetter for the *Blossburg Advertiser.* Wilson was master workman of District 3 of KOL National Trade Assembly 135 from 1888 to 1894 and headed the Independent Order of the KOL, organized by the United Mine Workers of America, from 1894 to 1897. In 1890 he was a founder of the United Mine Workers, serving on its executive board and, during the 1890s, as president of District 2 (Central Pennsylvania). He was secretary-treasurer of the United Mine Workers from 1900 to 1908. Wilson was elected to Congress as a Democrat from Pennsylvania in 1906, serving from 1907 to 1913 and chairing the House Committee on Labor between 1911 and 1913. He was the first U.S. secretary of labor, serving from 1913 to 1921, and a member of the Council of National Defense.

WOLL, Matthew (1880–1956), was born in Luxembourg and immigrated to the United States in 1891. He grew up in Chicago, where he apprenticed as a photo engraver in 1895, and around 1900 he joined International Photo-Engravers' Union of North America 5 of that city. Woll served as president of the Photo-Engravers (1906–29) and as a vice-president of the AFL (1919–55) and AFL-CIO (1955–56). He was also a founder and president (1929–56) of the Union Labor Life Insurance Co.

ZUCKERMAN, Max (1868–1932), was born in the Russian Ukraine and immigrated to the United States about 1891. He settled in New York City, where, after working for a short time in a pearl button factory, he became a cap cutter and joined the local cap makers' union. He served as secretary (1904–13) and secretary-treasurer (1913–27) of the

United Cloth Hat and Cap Makers of North America (from 1924, the Cloth Hat, Cap, and Millinery Workers' International Union).

ORGANIZATIONS

The Journeymen Bakers' National Union of the United States was organized in 1886, participated in the formation of the AFL that year, and was chartered by the AFL in 1887. In 1890 it adopted the name Journeymen Bakers' and Confectioners' International Union of America; in 1903 it became the BAKERY and Confectionery Workers' International Union of America.

The Boot and Shoe Workers' International Union of America was organized in 1889 by seceding locals of shoemakers' National Trade Assembly 216 of the KOL; it affiliated that year with the AFL. In 1895 the Boot and Shoe Workers merged with another AFL affiliate, the Lasters' Protective Union of America, and with the remnant of National Trade Assembly 216 to form the BOOT and Shoe Workers' Union.

The National Union of Brewers of the United States was organized in 1886 and affiliated with the AFL as the Brewers' National Union in March 1887. Later that year it changed its name to the National Union of the United Brewery Workmen of the United States; it became the International Union of the United BREWERY Workmen of America in 1902. After a prolonged series of jurisdictional disputes the AFL revoked the union's charter in 1907 but reinstated the Brewery Workmen in 1908. In 1917 the union became the International Union of United Brewery and Soft Drink Workers of America and, in 1918, the International Union of United Brewery, Flour, Cereal, and Soft Drink Workers of America.

A group of AFL federal labor unions organized the National Brickmakers' Alliance in 1896 and affiliated with the AFL the same year. In 1901 the union absorbed several local unions and changed its name to the International BRICK, Tile, and Terra Cotta Workers' Alliance. In 1913 seceding members formed the United Brick and Clay Workers of America, and the two groups merged under that name in 1917.

The Bricklayers' and Masons' International Union of America was organized in 1865 and changed its name to the BRICKLAYERS', Masons', and Plasterers' International Union of America in 1910. It did not affiliate with the AFL until 1916.

The International Association of Bridge and Structural Iron Workers (from 1915, the International Association of BRIDGE, Structural, and Ornamental Iron Workers and Pile Drivers; and from 1917, the International Association of Bridge, Structural, and Ornamental Iron Workers) was organized in 1896 and affiliated with the AFL in 1901. It soon became involved in jurisdictional conflicts with several metal trades unions and was suspended from the AFL in 1902 for nonpayment of dues. After the conflict was resolved in 1903, it rejoined the Federation. It was briefly suspended again in 1917 during a conflict with the United Brotherhood of Carpenters and Joiners of America.

The Brotherhood of Carpenters and Joiners of America was organized in 1881 and was chartered by the AFL in 1887. In 1888 the Brotherhood and the United Order of American Carpenters and Joiners merged, forming the United Brotherhood of CARPENTERS and Joiners of America.

The Cigar Makers' National Union of America was organized in 1864 and changed its name to the CIGAR Makers' International Union of America in 1867. It participated in the formation of the FOTLU in 1881. The following year, seceding New York City locals formed the Cigarmakers' Progressive Union of America, which rejoined the International in 1886. The AFL chartered the Cigar Makers in 1887.

The Retail Clerks' National Protective Association of America was organized in 1890 as an AFL affiliate. It changed its name to the Retail CLERKS' International Protective Association in 1899.

The Amalgamated CLOTHING Workers of America was organized in New York City in December 1914 by a seceding faction of the United Garment Workers of America.

The National Brotherhood of Electrical Workers of America was organized in 1891 and affiliated with the AFL the same year. In 1899 it became the International Brotherhood of ELECTRICAL Workers.

The American FLINT Glass Workers' Union, organized in 1878 by locals formerly affiliated with the KOL, affiliated with the AFL in 1887. It withdrew from the Federation in 1903 over a jurisdictional dispute but reaffiliated in 1912.

The Tailors' National Protective Union joined with members of KOL Garment Cutters' National Trade Assembly 231 in 1891 to form the United GARMENT Workers of America. The new union affiliated with the AFL the same year.

The Amalgamated Window Glass Workers of America, organized in 1904 with the merger of the Window Glass Workers' Association of America and the United Window Glass Workers' Association of America, affiliated with the AFL in 1906. When the union was dissolved by court order in 1908, it reorganized as the National Window GLASS Workers. It affiliated with the AFL in 1918 and disbanded in 1928.

The Granite Cutters' International Union of the United States and the British Provinces of America was formed in 1877. In 1880 it changed its name to the Granite Cutters' National Union of the United States of America and in the following year participated in the formation of the FOTLU. It joined the AFL in 1888, left the Federation in 1890, and then rejoined it in 1895. In 1905 it adopted the name GRANITE Cutters' International Association of America.

The United Cloth HAT and Cap Makers of North America was organized in 1901 and received an AFL charter in 1902. As a result of a jurisdictional dispute with the United Hatters of North America over the noncloth hat trade, the union was suspended in 1918. In 1924 the Hat and Cap Makers reached an agreement with the Hatters and re-affiliated with the AFL; the AFL convention that year approved the union's change of name to the Cloth Hat, Cap, and Millinery Workers' International Union.

The United HATTERS of North America was created in 1896 by the merger of the International Trade Association of Hat Finishers of America and the National Hat Makers' Association of the United States. It received an AFL charter the same year.

The International Hod Carriers' and Building Laborers' Union of America was organized and affiliated with the AFL in 1903. It became the International Hod Carriers' and Common Laborers' Union of America in September 1912 and the International HOD Carriers', Building and Common Laborers' Union of America in December of that year.

The Journeymen Horseshoers' National Union of the United States was organized in 1874. It changed its name to the International Union of Journeymen HORSESHOERS of the United States and Canada in 1892 and affiliated with the AFL in 1893.

The Waiters' and Bartenders' National Union was organized and affiliated with the AFL in 1891. The following year it changed its name to the Hotel and Restaurant Employees' National Alliance and, in 1898, to the HOTEL and Restaurant Employees' International Alliance and Bartenders' International League of America.

The International LADIES' Garment Workers' Union was organized and affiliated with the AFL in 1900.

The Shirt, Waist, and Laundry Workers' International Union was organized and chartered by the AFL in 1900. It changed its name to the LAUNDRY Workers' International Union in 1909, when the AFL awarded jurisdiction over shirt workers to the United Garment Workers of America.

The locomotive engineers organized the Brotherhood of the Footboard in 1863. In 1864 the organization became the Brotherhood of LOCOMOTIVE Engineers.

The Brotherhood of Locomotive Firemen was organized in 1873 and in 1878 merged under its name with the International Firemen's Union. In 1906 it adopted the name Brotherhood of LOCOMOTIVE Firemen and Enginemen.

The Lumber Handlers of the Great Lakes was founded in 1892 and received its AFL charter in 1893 as the National Longshoremen's Association of the United States. In 1895 it was renamed the International Longshoremen's Association. It became the International Longshoremen, Marine, and Transport Workers' Association in 1901 but changed its name back to the International LONGSHOREMEN's Association in 1908.

The Order of United Machinists and Mechanical Engineers of America was organized in 1888 and the following year changed its name to the National Association of Machinists. It changed its name again, in 1891, to the International Association of MACHINISTS, affiliating with the AFL in 1895.

The Brotherhood of Railway Track Foremen of America was founded in 1891. In 1896 it reorganized to include white track laborers as well as foremen and changed its name to the Brotherhood of Railway Trackmen of America. Granted an AFL charter in 1900, the union was renamed the International Brotherhood of MAINTENANCE of Way Employes in 1902 and the United Brotherhood of Maintenance of Way Employes and Railway Shop Laborers in 1918. The union was suspended from the AFL in 1919 and reinstated in 1922.

The Metal Polishers', Buffers', and Platers' International Union of North America was organized in 1892 and chartered by the AFL the same year. In 1896 it merged with the United Brotherhood of Brass and Composition Metal Workers, Polishers, and Buffers to form the Metal Polishers', Buffers', Platers', and Brass Workers' Union of North

America. It added "International" to its name in 1899, "Brass Molders" in 1901, and "Silver Workers" in 1903. The constitution adopted in 1907 dropped "International," and the constitution effective on Jan. 1, 1912, dropped "Brass Molders," making the union's new name the METAL Polishers', Buffers', Platers', and Brass and Silver Workers' Union of North America. In 1917 the union became the Metal Polishers' International Union.

The United MINE Workers of America was established in 1890 with the merger of the National Progressive Union of Miners and Mine Laborers and KOL National Trade Assembly 135. The new union affiliated with the AFL the same year.

The Western Federation of MINERS, a regional industrial union that claimed jurisdiction over mine, mill, and smelter workers in the hard rock mining industry, was founded in 1893 and affiliated with the AFL in July 1896. It paid no dues to the AFL after December 1896, however, and in 1898 it disaffiliated; it subsequently helped organize the Western Labor Union (renamed the American Labor Union in 1902). In 1905 it participated in the formation of the IWW, but it withdrew three years later and reaffiliated with the AFL in 1911. In 1916 it changed its name to the International Union of Mine, Mill, and Smelter Workers.

The National Union of Iron Molders was organized in 1859. In 1874 it became the Iron Molders' Union of North America, and in 1881 it participated in the formation of the FOTLU. It was chartered by the AFL in 1887. In 1907 it changed its name to the International MOLDERS' Union of North America.

The American Federation of MUSICIANS was founded in 1896 and affiliated with the AFL the same year.

The Brotherhood of Painters and Decorators of America was organized in 1887, affiliating with the AFL the same year. The union withdrew from the Federation in 1891 but reaffiliated the following year. In 1894 it split between western and eastern factions headquartered, respectively, in Lafayette, Ind., and Baltimore. The eastern faction adopted the name Brotherhood of PAINTERS, Decorators, and Paperhangers of America in 1899, and the two factions merged under that name in 1900.

In 1887 members of nine KOL local assemblies organized the Pattern Makers' National League of North America. It received an AFL charter in 1894 and in 1898 changed its name to the PATTERN Makers' League of North America.

The International PHOTO-ENGRAVERS' Union of North America was organized in 1900 by seceding locals of the International Typographical Union, which recognized its jurisdiction by a referendum vote in 1903, effective Jan. 1, 1904. The AFL chartered the union in 1904.

The International Printing Pressmen's Union of North America was founded in 1889 and affiliated with the AFL in 1895. In 1897 it changed its name to the International Printing PRESSMEN's and Assistants' Union of North America.

The Order of Railway Telegraphers of North America was founded in 1886, reorganized as the Order of RAILROAD Telegraphers of North America in 1891, and chartered by the AFL in 1900.

The Brotherhood of RAILWAY Carmen of America was organized in 1890 through the merger of the Brotherhood of Railway Car Repairers of North America, the Carmen's Mutual Aid Association, the Car Inspectors', Repairers', and Oilers' Protective Association, and the Brotherhood of Railway Carmen of Canada. It received an AFL charter in 1910.

The Order of Railway Clerks of America was organized in 1899 and affiliated with the AFL in 1900; it withdrew from the Federation in 1901. The organization adopted the name Brotherhood of RAILWAY Clerks in 1904 and reaffiliated with the AFL in 1908. It adopted the name Brotherhood of Railway and Steamship Clerks, Freight Handlers, Express and Station Employes in 1919.

The National Seamen's Union of America was organized in 1892 as a federation of several regional sailors' unions, including the Sailors' Union of the Pacific, the Lake Seamen's Union, the Gulf Coast Seamen's and Firemen's Union, and the Atlantic Coast Seamen's Union. It affiliated with the AFL the following year and in 1895 changed its name to the International SEAMEN's Union of America.

The Tin, Sheet Iron, and Cornice Workers' International Association was organized in 1888 and affiliated with the AFL the following year. Its charter was recalled in 1896. The union reorganized in 1897 as the Amalgamated Sheet Metal Workers' International Association, which was chartered by the AFL in 1899. In 1903 it merged with the Sheet Metal Workers' National Alliance, a secessionist group that had broken away from the union in 1902, to form the Amalgamated SHEET Metal Workers' International Alliance. In 1907 the international amalgamated with the Coppersmiths' International Union and, in 1924, absorbed the chandelier, brass, and metal workers, adopting the name Sheet Metal Workers' International Association.

The Journeymen Stone Cutters' Association of North America was organized in 1887 and was chartered by the AFL in 1907.

The Amalgamated Association of Street Railway Employes of America was established in 1892 and affiliated with the AFL in 1893. It absorbed the Brotherhood of Surface Car Employes in 1894 and in 1903 changed its name to the Amalgamated Association of Street and Electric Railway Employes of America.

The Switchmen's Union of North America was organized in 1894 and affiliated with the AFL in 1906.

The Journeymen Tailors' National Union of the United States, composed of custom tailors, was organized in 1883 and chartered by the AFL in 1887. It changed its name in 1889 to the Journeymen Tailors' Union of America and in January 1914 to the Tailors' Industrial Union. It merged that year with the Amalgamated Clothing Workers of America but seceded from the Clothing Workers in 1915 and reassumed the name Journeymen Tailors' Union of America.

The American Federation of Teachers was organized in Chicago in April 1916 and chartered by the AFL in May of the same year.

In 1898 several team drivers' locals combined to form the Team Drivers' International Union, which received an AFL charter in 1899. Seceding Chicago locals organized the Teamsters' National Union in 1901, and in 1903 the two unions merged to form the International Brotherhood of Teamsters. In 1910 it changed its name to the International Brotherhood of Teamsters, Chauffeurs, Stablemen, and Helpers of America.

The National Union of Textile Workers of America was organized in 1891 and affiliated with the AFL in 1896. It changed its name to the International Union of Textile Workers in 1900 and the following year merged with the American Federation of Textile Operatives and several AFL federal labor unions to form the United Textile Workers of America.

The International Shingle Weavers' Union of America was organized and affiliated with the AFL in 1903. In 1913 the union changed its name to the International Union of Shingle Weavers, Sawmill Workers, and Woodsmen and in 1914 to the International Union of Timberworkers. In 1916 the shingle weavers reorganized under the union's original name.

The National Typographical Union was organized in 1852 by a group of locals that had held national conventions in 1850 and 1851 under the name Journeymen Printers of the United States. In 1869 the union adopted the name International TYPOGRAPHICAL Union. Although its members participated in forming the FOTLU in 1881 and in organizing the AFL in 1886, the Typographical Union did not affiliate with the Federation until 1888.

INDEX

Names of persons or organizations for whom there are glossary entries are followed by an asterisk.

An italicized page number indicates the location of a substantive annotation in the notes following a document. While this index is not cumulative, it includes references to substantive annotations or glossary entries in earlier volumes that are relevant to this one but that are not repeated here; these appear first in the index entry. For example, reference to the American Anti-Boycott Association in volume 7 appears in this index as *7:246n;* and the glossary entry for Henry Broadhurst in volume 3 appears in this index as *3:**.

Actors' Union, White Rats, 292n

Adamski, Albert, 406, *406n*

Adamson, William, 450n

Addams, Jane, *231–32n,* 274n; letter to, 231

AFL. *See* American Federation of Labor

Aguilar Vargas, Cándido, 306, *307n*

Aishton, Richard, 312n

Albuquerque, N.Mex., peace conference (1916), 433n

Alexander, DeAlva, 200n

Alonso, José G., 429n, 467, *468n*

Alonso, Rafael, *7:53n,* 533

Alpert, Nathan, *405n;* letter to, 403–5

Alpine, John R.,* *14n,* 74n, 270–71, 274n, 436; elected AFL vice-president, 38n, 226n, 348n

Amalgamated Copper Co., 270–71, 275n

American Alliance for Labor and Democracy, 383n

American Anti-Boycott Association, *7:246n,* 285n

American Association for Labor Legislation, 276–77, *277n*

American Association of University Professors, 429, *430n*

American Federation of Labor (AFL): audit of accounts of, 478–79, 479n; board of mediation and conciliation, 224–25, 225n; and central bodies, political discussions in, 164–66; Defense Fund, *6:128n,* 29–33, 33n, 268; legal bureau of information, 530n; legal department, 528, *529–30n;* office boy, 308; officers, election of, 38n, 225–26, 226n, 348, 348–49n; officers, salaries of, 213, 214n; organizing, assessments for, 38, 38n; per capita tax, 30; war and peace, convention resolutions on, 231, 232n, 265, 291, 292n, 485

—Building Trades Department, *6:175n,* 261n, 503; and Carpenters and Joiners of America, United Brotherhood of, 70, 73n; convention, 1913, 347n; convention, 1915 (San Francisco), 355n; and Sheet Metal Workers' International Alliance, Amalgamated, 70, 73n

—conventions: 1897 (Nashville), *7:64n,* 103n; 1904 (San Francisco), *7:36n,* 9n; 1906 (Minneapolis), 424, *424n,* 472; 1908 (Denver), *8:79n,* 276n, 423–24, 471–72, 472n; 1910 (St. Louis), *8:108n,* 145n; 1911 (Atlanta), *8:146n,* 145n; 1912 (Rochester, N.Y.), 19, *21n;* 1913 (Seattle), *21n;* 1913 (Seattle), accounts of, 19–21, 23–38; 1914 (Philadelphia), 25, *28n;* 1914 (Philadelphia), accounts of, 210–26; 1915 (San Francisco), 106n, *107n,* 340, 355n, 363; 1915 (San Francisco), accounts

587

Bolander, Carl N., 260, *261n*
Bolivia, and civil war in Mexico, 363n
Bonillas, Ignacio, 498–500, *500n*
Boot and Shoe Workers' Union,* 452,
    452n; convention, 1899 (Rochester,
    N.Y.), *5:111–12n;* local 94 (Chicago),
    302, *303n*
Boston building trades conference
    (1914), 66, 68n, 70, 73n
Boston Building Trades Council, 68n
Boston Central Labor Union, *1:166n,*
    492n
Boston Elevated Railway Co., 390n
Bowerman, Charles W.,* *105n,* 385n,
    474, 485, 487; letters to, 105, 162–63,
    384–85
Boyer, C. S., 496, *497n*
Brady, Peter J., *153n;* letter to, 152–53
Brais, Eugene J.,* 71, *74n,* 236, 236n
Brandeis, Louis D., *6:83n,* 409–10, 410n
Brazil, and civil war in Mexico, 363n
Brewery Workmen of America, Interna-
    tional Union of the United,* *34n,*
    181; and industrial unionism, 502; ju-
    risdiction of, 143–44, 146n, 148
Brick and Clay Workers of America,
    United, 203, 205n
Bricklayers', Masons', and Plasterers' In-
    ternational Union of America,* 70,
    73n; convention, 1914 (Houston), 70,
    73n; jurisdiction of, 73n
Brick, Tile, and Terra Cotta Workers' Al-
    liance, International,* 74n, *205n*
Bridge, Structural, and Ornamental
    Iron Workers and Pile Drivers, Inter-
    national Association of,* 191n, 300,
    302n; jurisdiction of, 305n; strike,
    1915 (Bridgeport, Conn.), 304, *305n*
Brindell, Robert P., 290, *292n,* 311n
Broadhurst, Henry, *3:*,* 337
Brock, James F.,* 148, *149n*
Brooklyn Central Labor Union, *2:68n,*
    62, *63n*
Brown, George W., *50n*
Brown, J. G.,* 221, 223–*24n*
Brown, Morris, *3:143n, 6:364n,* 23, 24–
    25n
Brown, Rome G., 316, *318n*
Brunet, G. R., 15, *15–16n*
Brussels, German occupation of, 195,
    197n

Brussels (steamship), 475, 477n
Bryan, William J., *4:234n,* 3, 287n, 292n,
    354, 430–31, 433n
Buchanan, Frank J., *8:*,* 153n, 292n
Buck's Stove and Range Co. cases: con-
    tempt case, *7:249–50n,* 105, 106n; in-
    junction case, *7:249–50n,* 106n;
    Mitchell and, 105, 106n; Morrison
    and, 105, 106n; SG and, 105, 106n
Budd, Britton I., 388, *390n*
Buffalo Central Labor Council, 406n
Buffalo Copper and Brass Rolling Mill,
    strike against (1916), *406n*
Burgman, Charles F., *3:*,* 515n
Burnett, John L., *8:346n,* 103n, 405n
Burnett immigration bill. *See* Legisla-
    tion, U.S.: immigration act (1917)
Burns, John E., *4:*,* 337; letter from, 326
Burns, William J., *8:214n,* 23
Burton, Harry P., 232–33, *233n*
Butte, Mont., labor situation in, 154,
    155n, 177, 179–82, 190, 270–72, 274–
    75n
Butte (Mont.) Miners' Union. *See* Min-
    ers, Western Federation of: local 1
    (Butte)
Butte (Mont.) Mine Workers' Union,
    155n, 181, 183n, 270–72

Cabrera, Luis, 498–500, *500n*
Cabs, union, SG and, 266–67, 267n
California: Japanese in, 206n; landhold-
    ing by Asian immigrants in, 206, 206n
California State Federation of Labor,
    6:244n, 206n, 513, 515; convention,
    1914, 206n; convention, 1915, 515n;
    convention, 1916, 515n
Call, Homer D., *7:*,* 280n
Calumet and Hecla Mining Co., strike
    against (1913–14), *8:512–13n,* 11–13,
    13–14n, 25–28, 43–44, 44n, 46–47,
    47–48n, 51–52, 52n, 64–67, 68n, 177,
    181–83, 210, 211n, 301
Calumet (Mich.) *News,* 28n
Camomile, David A., 343, *344n*
Campaigns, political
—1884, 86–87
—1906: AFL and, 3; AFL financial re-
    port, 3, 8n
—1908: AFL and, 3–4; AFL financial re-
    port, 3, 8n

University of Illinois Press
1325 South Oak Street
Champaign, IL 61820-6903
www.press.uillinois.edu